The Sustainable Fashion Handbook

Thames & Hudson

The Sustainable Fashion Handbook

Sandy Black

Desire and fashion

Design and innovation

Self and beauty

1

Culture and consumption

Craft and industry

3

Transparency and livelihood

Techno eco

5

New fashion paradigms

Speed and distance

Ecology and waste

Sustainable fashion?

Sustainable fashion? An oxymoron if ever there was one, given the passionate global fixation on having the hottest, the latest, the Must-Have or the It-item.

Working at the coal-face of fashion, as I have for more than thirty years, I freely admit my guilt as a fashion-obsessive. My crime is a wardrobe stuffed with clothes I never wear and never will wear: handbags and shoes still in their boxes and wrappings; accessories purchased on a fleeting whim and forgotten just as quickly. At the same time I treasure certain items: high-street dresses I have owned for twenty years or more and still wear regularly; fading, threadbare Chinese and Rajasthani jackets maybe a hundred years old; tribal jewelry once worn by a bridegroom at a wedding in the High Atlas mountains; accessories handcrafted in the Rift Valley from bits of an old carburettor.

My wardrobe – like those of many fashionistas – is full of contradictions, much like sustainable fashion itself.

The concept of 'sustainable fashion' – and its close relative 'eco-chic' – is something that increasingly troubles and perplexes us in the 21st century. We can take encouragement from the efforts increasingly being made around the world on both a corporate and an individual scale. But it is surely not enough. What more could we, and should we, be doing?

Sandy Black's book offers detailed, fascinating and well-researched answers to this question, setting out, in word and image, the complex, inter-dependent, economic, ecological, cultural and social factors that make up the monstrous global behemoth that we know as modern fashion. Professor Black does not advocate the end of fashion – it is, after all, an intrinsic part of the human experience that goes back as far as the Neolithic era, and many modern livelihoods depend on it. Rather, her book is a wake-up call for awareness, an informed and informative investigation into best practice, and a detailed investigation into strategies and methods that can lessen the harm fashion inflicts in its constant search for the new.

Hilary Alexander
Fashion correspondent, *Daily Telegraph*

Opposite: Zulu from the Shared Talent South Africa series, 2007.

Interrogating fashion

The Fashion Paradox

The business of fashion is full of contradictions: the craftsmanship of couture and bespoke set against fast and cheap fashion; the luxury of Bond Street or Fifth Avenue versus the poverty of many producer communities; inherently wasteful cycles of seasonal change that nonetheless sustain livelihoods; an obsession with the new alongside the valorization of vintage; and the transience of current fashion, which itself involves regular revivals of styles from previous eras. I developed the concept of the 'fashion paradox' to encapsulate this complex web of contradictory perceptions and practices – comprising economics and employment, trade, design and manufacturing, buying and marketing, and cultural identity that collectively make up the global fashion industry.[1] Whether involved in the creation, production, communication or representation of fashion, or simply as its consumers, everyone is implicated in the destructive aspects of this endemically unsustainable system, where obsolescence is inbuilt. As public awareness of issues and demand for product transparency have grown, there is now an urgent imperative for change, but the question remains: can fashion ever really be sustainable, or is the very term 'sustainable fashion' an oxymoron?

The Power of Fashion

Nevertheless, it is important to respect the power of fashion and adornment, and understand its significance in cultures throughout the world, from the earliest peoples to the present day. As humans we seem to be hard-wired to take an interest in our dress. Fashion performs many roles: it is a social catalyst, a communication medium that functions in both personal and public spheres, as it is simultaneously both inward- and outward-looking. It enables us to enhance our self-esteem and express our identity, displaying our status and sexuality via coded messages, both subtle and overt. Through our clothing we can show we belong to the crowd or make radical statements that proclaim our differences. In many professional contexts, appropriate clothing can make a real difference to success, whereas the 'wrong' clothing can cause one to be stigmatized. Of course, we may simply want to be seen to be 'cool' by wearing the latest fashions. Fashion provides livelihoods, and sustainable fashion must continue to meet our personal and symbolic needs, while addressing the intrinsic problems of the fashion system. Sustainable fashion does not mean the end of fashion.

The Fashion Industry

The fashion industry (comprising designer and basic clothing, footwear and accessories) is highly complex and characterized by short runs, fast turnover and a diverse range of products channelled through a fragmented and frequently changing supply chain distributed over many global locations. The clothing, footwear and textile sector is a significant global economic force, the fifth largest sector, employing up to 40 million worldwide, of which up to 19 million are employed in China, 2.7 million in the EU and 400,000 in the UK (excluding retail) – around the same as the aerospace and automotive sectors combined.[2] Fashion consumption in the UK, for instance, has grown significantly in recent years: there was a 37% increase in the amount of clothes purchased per capita between 2001 and 2005.[3] Since the mid-1990s and the abolition of the Multi Fibre Arrangement and trading quotas, increasing globalization of manufacturing has taken place, and faster fashion cycles have pushed the prices of products down, while simultaneously increasing the level of production and the consequent environmental impact. The fashion system operates across a broad range of market levels: individuals and small designer businesses working in bespoke or small-batch production for niche luxury markets; mass-market commodity clothing, such as T-shirts, sold in supermarkets and 'value' stores; the 'fast fashion' of high-street brands that aim to be exactly on trend and on time; and higher priced designer-branded fashions that lead the trends. Offshore manufacturing is now the norm in fashion and textiles across Europe and the US, for example, with only a fraction of the former domestic manufacturing capacity remaining. However, new technologies and processes that are less labour intensive are beginning to encourage the return of manufacturing to countries with high labour costs, enabling new business models to be developed. These innovations include seam-free clothing production, fashion garments made on demand (rather than shipped from stock), personalization of fashion items to customers' individual preferences and engineered individual garment fitting supported by online measuring systems and virtual fitting rooms. All of these concepts aim to increase customer satisfaction, streamline production and eliminate overstock. The case studies and commentaries throughout the book, particularly in Chapter 5, illustrate some of these potential developments.

Taken holistically, the textile and clothing life cycles consume more energy and water than do the product life cycles of any other industry other than construction or agriculture. Cleaning, drying and ironing of clothes by the consumer is especially costly in this respect. Currently, garments and their component parts are well-travelled commodities with brief lives, often discarded long before they are worn out. For fashion designers, decisions about materials, styling and construction must be balanced with timeliness, cost, speed of delivery required, manufacturing skills and location. The ability to address sustainability issues such as waste, traceability and transport miles, in addition to these design factors and constraints, adds a burden that many fashion designers and design teams, already working under strong time pressures, are currently unwilling or unable to take on. A fragmented supply chain contributes to a lack of clear ownership of these problems between consumers, designers, manufacturers, suppliers, retailers and legislative bodies.

The fashion industry is one of the few remaining craft-based industries: the manually operated sewing machine is still the principal means by which garments are made. This fact enables 'mass customization' and personalization in fashion (in which mass-production processes are reconciled with personalized choices in apparel or footwear) to become technologically feasible. Online retail systems have emerged that have the ability to facilitate individual consumer choice while maintaining the benefits of mass production.[4] In 2004 Nike pioneered the NIKEiD online system of customization for trainers, enabling colours, fabrics and lettering to be chosen, and most significantly, for measurements for each foot to be specified differently. Others, such as MiAdidas, followed suit. British retailer Marks & Spencer introduced its customized 'Design your own Shirt' online service in 2007; the resulting shirts were found in a Which? consumer-guide study to be better fitting than their Savile Row equivalents.[5] Bodyscanning technology is starting to impact made-to-measure clothing in product categories such as jeans (Bodymetrics.com, for instance) and shirts (Brooks Brothers, for example).[6] By better satisfying customer needs through personalized preferences, it may be possible to reduce the rate at which fashion products are consumed and replaced.

In comparison with other creative industries, such as architecture and product design, the fashion and textile industries have been slow to tackle the thorny problems of sustainability. In the past few decades awareness and action with regard to sustainability has increased enormously across every industry sector, with progress especially visible in the areas of transport and food. Earlier initiatives and actions by individual designers and campaign groups began to coincide with a wider political response to climate change and environmental action in developed countries. In the UK the Stern Review (2006)[7] was published, the think-tank Forum for the Future was set up and the government established action plans for sustainable production and consumption in several key product areas including clothing.[8] In the US the Nobel Prize-winning film *An Inconvenient Truth* (2006), featuring former US Vice President Al Gore, brought climate-change issues to a global audience. EU legislation on landfill, waste electrical equipment and registration of chemicals came into force, and ethical and environmental issues rose to a prominent position in the public spotlight. Campaigning NGOs such as War on Want and the Pesticide Action Network produced hard-hitting reports on clothing- and cotton-workers' conditions. The media played a key part, with magazines and newspapers issuing 'green' supplements and a new wave of publications, films and television exposés focused in this area.[9]

Literature on 'eco' design, sustainable design or 'green' design began to appear in the 1960s and 70s and has continued to expand, albeit mainly focused on architecture and product design.[10] More recently, authors such as Jonathan Chapman and Stuart Walker have presented creative and emotionally engaging design strategies and solutions to the issues of sustainable product design.[11] However, publications specifically addressing sustainable design strategies in fashion and textiles have emerged only recently.[12] A growing emphasis on sustainability is now strongly evident throughout the fashion industry. In addition to the early British initiative, academic and industry networks and projects have been set up in Scandinavia,[13] and, importantly for volume fashion, in the US. The Sustainable Apparel Coalition, launched in 2011, involves some of the largest global brands and retailers, including Nike, Gap Inc., H&M, Levi Strauss, Marks & Spencer, Patagonia and Walmart, together with government agencies, NGOs and academic institutions.[14]

The Sustainable Fashion Handbook is intended as a comprehensive guide to this new landscape, signposting important issues, setting out different perspectives and elucidating current and future developments. It reflects the interdisciplinary nature of fashion and its complex ethical and ecological dimensions – as manifested in the production, consumption, marketing and representation of fashion – which often involve conflicting priorities that must be reconciled. This volume therefore incorporates first-hand perspectives from a number of different sources: essays and expert commentaries from academics and industry practitioners; interviews with designers and company representatives, and case studies involving large and small businesses; together with fashion industry images and specially commissioned visual narratives that highlight particular thematic strands of enquiry. Chapter 1 focuses on the operation of the contemporary fashion system, emphasizing the scale of the industry and the practices of everyday fashion at the mass-market level. Chapter 2 concentrates on designer fashion, including innovations in design and the education of future designers within the sustainability paradigm. Chapter 3 examines the global nature of production and the issues affecting the workers who are involved in manufacturing everything from textiles to finished garments. Chapter 4 offers insight into the ecological impact of 'fast' versus 'slow' fashion, especially the waste generated. Chapter 5 describes the impact of new technologies on the craft-based fashion industry and highlights exciting possibilities for creating sustainable products in the future. The comprehensive resources listing provides many further sources of information.

The title of this introduction is taken from that of a multidisciplinary network that I convened in 2005 with the aim of bringing industry professionals and academics with disparate areas of expertise together to share knowledge and create an agenda for future research in sustainable fashion design.[15] It is hoped that *The Sustainable Fashion Handbook* will continue this work in the same interdisciplinary spirit, making it accessible not only to seasoned players in the industry, but also to students and fashion lovers who are just embarking on the journey towards sustainability awareness. Throughout its many strands of enquiry, the ultimate aim of this volume is to elaborate possible strategies for the future, seeking answers to some of the key questions surrounding sustainable fashion:

> How can fashion become more environmentally and ecologically sound?
> How can designers make a difference?
> How can we slow down fashion?
> How can we reconcile conflicting priorities in a fast-moving industry?
> How can ethics and aesthetics be integrated?
> And – finally – can fashion ever really be sustainable?

Sandy Black

Self and beauty

Culture and consumption

Preceding pages: Adam & Eve, 2009, styling and photography by Gavin Fernandes.

The business of fashion is a complex mix of personal, cultural, economic and social factors. The three key themes of this chapter are identifying fashion cultures, understanding the everyday business of fashion and matching ethics with aesthetics. Three essays by Pamela Church Gibson, Otto von Busch and Emma Neuberg examine some of the cultural influences and consumption practices in contemporary fashion that are filtered through a range of media including billboard advertising, films, fashion and celebrity magazines and, more recently, by interactive online websites.

The words 'fashion' and 'clothing' (and, in the US, 'apparel') denote different aspects of our relationship with what we wear. 'Clothing' and 'apparel' can be understood as our everyday basic garments, commodities purchased out of necessity; 'fashion', on the other hand, represents consumers' discretionary choices, which can be driven by all manner of personal and symbolic motivations: desire, aesthetics, novelty, conformity – both internally and externally stimulated. However, these are not fixed definitions: 'fashion' and 'clothing' morph fluidly into one another. Jeans, for instance, are now basic clothing but can also have high fashion content. Even the proportions of the humble T-shirt are restyled over the seasons, influencing fashionability and presenting new choices for the wearer. Edward Barber's photographs of everyday fashion sum up the personal eclecticism and daily choices of a range of people of different ages.

It is estimated that global consumption of clothing is worth between US $550 billion and US $570 billion (£340 billion–£355 billion) annually, with approximately a third consumed in Europe, a third in the US and a third in Asia.[1] The sheer size and scope of these mass markets, from T-shirts to fast-moving trend-led fashion, is highlighted in the profiles of companies such as Continental Clothing, Muji, Uniqlo, H&M and Topshop. The interviews and commentaries show how large and small businesses approach the complexities of reconciling environmental and social sustainability with fashion, exemplified by the work of Katharine Hamnett, Edun, Stella McCartney and Eileen Fisher. Importantly, more information has become available over recent years, and we all, as consumers, are increasingly aware that once the purchase has been made, how we use our basic clothes – how often we wash them, and how we dry them, for instance – has an enormous impact on the environment in terms of energy, water and detergents. These impacts are visually demonstrated by the denim trousers life-cycle analysis.

Ultimately this chapter asks 'can fashion ever be sustainable?' It is clear that corporate actions for change are spreading throughout the global fashion industry. With new thinking and actions on the part of individuals, this has the potential to generate significant sustainability gains.

The game of fashion and LOOKBOOK.nu

OTTO VON BUSCH, *a haute couture heretic and DIY-demagogue, is also a researcher at Parsons the New School for Design.*

Fashion is full of paradoxes. Certainly one of the most profound of these is how we try to express individuality using ready-made objects whose meanings are primarily created outside of ourselves. We assemble an outfit to express our modest uniqueness: individual but at the same time not too individual. We try to say something personal through fashion, yet it can never be totally autonomous. Similarly we cannot have our own personal language; it has somehow to be shared to work as communication. Fashionable expression is thus stuck in between the heteronomous process of creation as a communication tool and the autonomous will of the wearer to express something personal.

Traditionally fashion has been a totally ready-made phenomenon, usually dictated from above according to linear logic or imitation and repetition. Subcultures and styles that bubbled up to the top have been defined by leading personalities within their genres. This type of system functions much like a radio antenna, broadcasting fashion to everyone; each consumer can tune in to a brand, style frequency or subculture pirate station. Some have better reception than others, but every consumer is a passive receiver. Only the active designer, stylist or magazine is a transmitter. Although this image of fashion has worked well over the last centuries, something else seems to be happening today. Fashion seems to be acting in less linear, more self-organized ways, and with the advent of the internet new ecological niches have emerged. Fashion is not primarily diffused and repeated in a cause-and-effect manner, as when we directly imitate something we see in an image in a magazine. But it still follows basic rules that give it an organic quality and dynamic characteristics. Fashion follows a sort of logic in the way it spreads between people. It acts like a meme, a gene-like unit of information or 'virus of the mind', to use Richard Dawkins's term,[1] or like an epidemic, to use contemporary advertising jargon.

If we want to study this type of viral fashion, a useful model is the editor-less style community of the website LOOKBOOK.nu, where everyday fashionistas upload images of their latest outfits and comment on each other's ways of dressing and modelling. Here the roles of designer, stylist, model, producer and consumer are blurred, and all community members have many ways to participate in the creation of new looks, which spread on the forum. Images and outfits are tagged with information such as brand and colour, and this information becomes a searchable code for each look. If we were to construct a taxonomy of LOOKBOOK as a living being, this tagged information would be the genotype of the look, its genetic constitution. Its photograph would the phenotype, or the look's observable characteristics.

What grows at LOOKBOOK.nu is organic fashion, a special life form of cultural production and style transmission that acts as a living system. There is no central control, but rather a constant drift of new turbulence and flow. It is something like a swarm

of fashionistas creating their own user-generated magazine made out of interactions and exchanges rather than styles being funnelled through editors and other gatekeepers. Yet the inner mechanisms

Right: Screenshot from LOOKBOOK.nu. Users can hype each other's looks and tag them with metadata. The looks can be indexed according to brand, type of garment or colour.

Left and far left: Two images from users Andy T (Andre Torres Rodriguez) (*left*) and Leopard Z (Zhang Jing) (*far left*). One could analyse the LOOKBOOK phenomenon via the way that phenotypes and genotypes are tagged in the LOOKBOOK interface: palettes (phenotypes) and brands (genotypes).

Fashion follows a sort of logic in the way it spreads between people. It acts like a meme, a gene-like unit of information or 'virus of the mind'...or like an epidemic, to use contemporary advertising jargon.

of fashion remain the same, as it seems that fashion spreads between us following basic protocols as well as unwritten inter-subjective social commands. Greatly simplified, these commands can be formulated as basic rules or laws. There are only two modes: in or out. The basic rules of fashion could be described as follows:

1. If the fashion expression is too unique, it is not fashion (it is too original).
2. If the fashion expression is too popular, it is out of fashion (it is too popular).
3. If an accessible status group wears the fashion, it is in fashion (it functions by imitating the ones we like and differing from the ones we dislike).
4. Fashion expressions are somehow contagious, but at the same time fashion cannot be too original or too popular (as in rules 1 and 2).

As I was thinking about these basic rules of fashion, I was surprised by how much they came to reflect a game simulation I have been fascinated with for a long time, a simple game but with consequences so vast that they are challenging to comprehend. This is John Horton Conway's 'Game of Life'.

The 'Game of Life' generates complexity by means of very simple rules. From simple combinations of binary data, starting from an elementary configuration, unexpected results emerge. Since its publication in 1970 the game, as a generator of so-called 'cellular automata', has fascinated mathematicians and biologists.[2] It is a game of computer-generated artificial biology, resembling an evolution of life through uncomplicated protocols, visually playing with emergence and self-organization. Even with simple rules complex patterns arise, including rudimentary organisms or life forms. By following the patterned behaviours of cells and neurons, theorists such as John Holland and Daniel Dennett have argued that the simple rules of these cellular automata can explain how complex organisms like ourselves, and even free will, can evolve over vast oceans of time.[3] The most intricate system can evolve from extremely simple micro-repetitions of protocols; there is no need for an overarching mind for order to emerge out of what seems to be chaos.

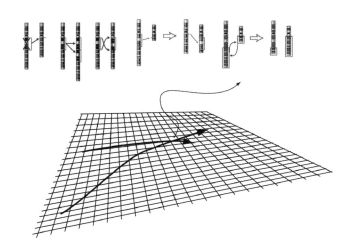

Right: The flat grid of the viral 'Game of Fashion', where looks meet, mutate, and generate new intensities, lives and patterns. At LOOKBOOK it is done without a hierarchical, centralized and elevated editor or designer–god. All squares have the prospect of being equally active, as all have the same potential for agency and spread of intensity.

Right: The Gosper Glider Gun, a seemingly random starting pattern that repeats endlessly, moving between the two stable dots. During its journey it also gives birth to a constant stream of new gliders, which come to crawl away across the grid. Is this the pattern of a fashion house, a micro-culture or perhaps a miniature scheme of fashion itself?

The game board consists of a two-dimensional square grid, each cell of which is considered to be either 'live' or 'dead'. The game-play is very simple. You only play in solitaire mode, as it is actually a zero-player game; you merely set up the initial configuration and then let the rules determine the fate of your life form. The game is in this sense the initial seed; the simulation follows its evolution, with every iteration or generation re-applying the rules to the new form. Thus Conway's game is a simple starting point for life simulation, and with every initial configuration new patterns arise over time. The rules are as follows:

1. A cell dies of loneliness if it has one or zero neighbours ('death by isolation').
2. A cell dies of overcrowding if it has four or more neighbours ('death by overcrowding').
3. A live cell with either two or three neighbours survives to the next generation (the cell is 'stable').

Right: One evolutionary path towards the birth of a 'blinker': an emergent dissipative structure that repeats itself endlessly after eight generations. Is this the life-pattern of a classic suit jacket, little black dress or pleated pants?

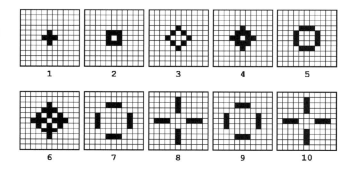

4. A new cell is born if it has exactly three neighbours ('birth').

These simple rules applied to various starting configurations evolve into unexpected forms over generations, and although they show certain traits and characteristics, the simple rules continue to apply. Some evolve to become stable but oscillating 'blinkers', while others move around or crawl over the grid and are known as 'gliders'.

The evolution of such patterns is interesting to watch, but yet more complex patterns also emerge. Some formations move in repetitive patterns while giving birth to independent life forms. These patterns produce offspring! Simple patterns of black and white create 'life', almost like cells. New life forms shoot out of their bodies and are called 'guns'. One example is the Gosper Glider Gun, which produces a new living glider every fifteen generations. Such a pattern literally illustrates the viral diffusion of ideas or intensities, new memes that emerge via interactions involving simple protocols.

To understand the connection between the rules of fashion and Conway's 'Game of Life', we can turn to the French sociologist Gabriel Tarde, who wrote extensively on social and economic psychology and the laws of imitation. According to Tarde, social relations emerge through interactions between people, through close social imitations and their metamorphosis, which in turn become innovations. He used an analytic resource that he called 'idea

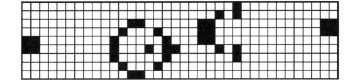

germs', which at their full potential, at the moment of innovation, create 'vibrations'.[4] The Tardian social imitations are just like cell multiplications or the firing of neurons between nerves, transmitting information via synapses. Tarde calls such transmissions 'rays of imitation'.[5] These vibrations are pure difference, pure intensity. To put it bluntly, we can say that they are either on or off, black or white. As such they resonate well with Pierre Bourdieu's notion that '[f]ashion is the latest fashion, the latest difference.'[6]

We could say that this is what fashion is: the latest intensity, the latest firing of social life and social micro-imitation. It does not require much imagination to see an analogy between this viral approach and fashion, itself signifying a social vibration of status and desire that dies over time, usually in a season or two. We come to be immune to last season's fashion, just like the risen fatigue threshold of a recently fired nerve. Indeed most of us have some 'dead' garments buried in the back of the wardrobe that once were highly vivid, but somehow died a quick death as the wave of vibration passed by.

Thus we can see the game of fashion, or the LOOKBOOK fashion system, as a viral ecology of living parts. This is not a mechanical system of simplified cause-and-effect relationships, of designer dictations and passive, blind followers. In the living system of LOOKBOOK, every actor is both sender and receiver, and as the virus mutates fashion bends and is constantly reinterpreted. It is a flat field of two-way agency and pure viral intensity, yet it follows the playful rules of cellular diffusion and emergence.

If we shift our focus from the top-down linear diffusion model and regard fashion as a phenomenon of small micro-repetitions, imitations of the latest looks firing throughout social networks, we can adopt a new approach to sustainability in fashion. As before, the overall system of fashion, the infrastructure of producers, retailers and media, has a vital role to play. After all, they stand behind the main production mechanism of clothes and thus have the biggest environmental impact.

However, with the help of a viral perspective, we can also see how to intercept the micro-repetitions and social milieus where imitation happens and engage change there. This means that we should try to spread the actions of sustainability where the act of imitation happens: between people at ground level, between local neighbours in the imitative grid, among friends and fans on social-media platforms such as LOOKBOOK. With small tactical interventions at a personal micro-level, we can build self-esteem and introduce more skills and knowledge by engaging users in participatory co-creation and by empowering 'prosumers' – producing consumers – through co-design and open workshops. Skills and knowledge can make rays of imitation oscillate differently between people. Such tactics might not reach the top-down system of fashion, but spread change and empowerment virally. Even at this scale we are not outside the realm of fashion – we tap into the energy it produces for new needs and send new signals through its rays of imitation. Fashionistas can never be totally independent; that would not be fashion (remember fashion rule 1). However, we can make them realize how they are interdependent, and how new communities and sustainable practices can be built by means of the Game of Fashion.

So, following the ideas of Gabriel Tarde, fashion has no autonomous innovators; it has no overall system through which to master us. All fashion is a contagion, a pestilence, a viral transmission, a firing of interconnected neurons in constant mutation. Fashion is a germ capital, rays of imitation spreading like wildfire between our resonating minds, actions and bodies. It is as if fashion has a life of its own, parallel to ours as humans, in which the latest memes make us temporarily dizzy with trend fever. We are the vectors of fashion. But this also means that we have the power to affect how it flows through us to others. We can tune it towards more sustainable agendas every time the imitation replicates between us.

Let us, then, re-examine the application of the rules. A fashionista does not need to be autonomous to feel alive. On the contrary; a fashionista feels alive by abiding by the rules, and by being engulfed in the firing intensity of the social game, by being highly connected rather than disconnected. This is the unpredictable game that is fashion, this vibrant celebration of life. The game is indeed played on a 'field', as Bourdieu suggested. And it only refers to the last season or, to use the terms of the 'Game of Life', the last 'generation'. If it was skinny jeans last season, now it is flares. If it was white last season, now it is black. It might not always be that simple, but at least we all know the rules: it should neither be too original nor too popular. Fire up the neurons, here we go! What a lovely game to play.

We should try to spread the actions of sustainability where the act of imitation happens: between people at ground level, between local neighbours in the imitative grid and among friends and fans on social media platforms such as LOOKBOOK.

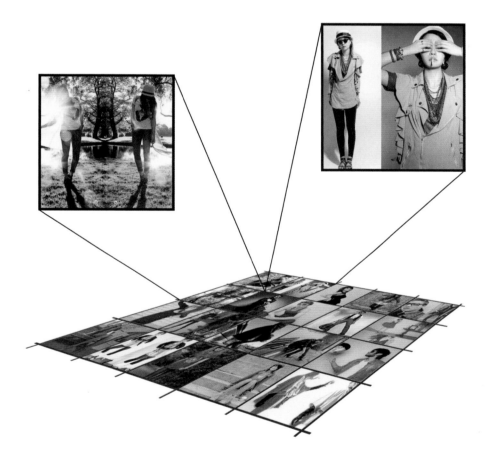

Above: The smooth plateaux of LOOKBOOK facilitate viral lines of imitation and innovation, and encourage new patterns of fashion to emerge. Users receive a stream of new looks within the online community.

Sustainable fashion in the age of celebrity culture

PAMELA CHURCH GIBSON, *reader in cultural and historical studies at London College of Fashion, has published extensively on film, fashion, fandom, history and heritage.*

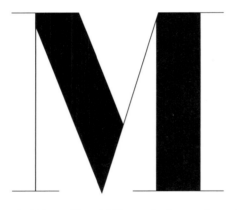

More than a hundred years ago Thorstein Veblen first articulated and named the concept of conspicuous consumption in his critique of American society, *The Theory of the Leisure Class.*[1] His study focused on American nouveaux riches, millionaires who had made massive fortunes in industry; now they were anxious to flaunt their new status and so disclaim the grimy origins of their wealth. These men chose two arenas in which to display their money and taste. First, they built themselves new homes: huge mansions, often modelled on English country houses, which boasted carefully tended lawns and tastefully designed and planted gardens. Inside were sumptuous draperies, imported antique furniture and – where their owners had both the revenue and the necessary advice – important paintings, which they hung in prominent positions. Secondly, the bodies of their wives were significant as sites of display. At night expensive jewels could be arranged around their necks, in their earlobes, on their arms and fingers, and across their impressively cantilevered bosoms. By day they could show off Parisian couture, furs and huge ornate hats laden with fruit, flowers, feathers and sometimes even an entire stuffed bird. Some of these women were, to use the old-fashioned term, 'fashion leaders', and so they might be sketched and photographed in illustrated papers and the latest women's magazines. However, their influence was limited to a small sphere: the upper middle classes. Mass-market women's magazines did not make their appearance for another twenty years; there was as yet no 'fashion for all'. That too would follow in the second and third decades of the 20th century, with new developments in garment technology, retailing and mass culture.

Today the concept of conspicuous consumption has a new and terrible relevance, particularly for those of us concerned with sustainability in fashion. Fashion leaders are the celebrities who dominate our culture; their frequent changes of outfit and accessories are on show not only in the tabloids, on the internet and in the new raft of celebrity magazines that have dominated publishing over the past decade, but also in the respectable broadsheets and fashion glossies. Print journalism has caved in and changed in response to the rapacious demand for celebrity images. Unlike the milieu described by Veblen, our celebrity world is a seemingly democratic one and, it seems, global as well. Our celebrities themselves are often from humble origins, and their images are available for mass consumption and emulation.

The luxury brands, which seem so far largely untouched by recession and which have continued their relentless global expansion, particularly in China, now routinely employ celebrities – usually young actresses – rather than fashion models for their advertising campaigns. (The exception, of course, is Kate Moss, who is now a celebrity as well as a supermodel.) More significantly, these brands routinely offer their latest products to celebrities – often via stylists – to be showcased in paparazzi shots: the latest It-bag to be displayed on the arm by day, vertiginously heeled shoes to be shown off on the red carpet by night. Leading fashion designers, of course, routinely provide the opulent gowns for the annual Oscar ceremonies in Hollywood, which are now far more important than runway shows for generating maximum publicity. So designers no longer pack the front row at their shows with fashion editors, as was once traditional, but with celebrities. Jess Cartner-Morley, writing in *The Guardian*, suggested that pictures of those in the front row were of greater interest to the public than the clothes on the catwalk.[2] At the Chanel show in Spring 2009, this point was underlined when the photographers left their pens and swarmed across the catwalk to photograph Kate Moss, seated next to her rock-star boyfriend. It took some time to clear the space so that the show proper might begin.

Obviously most of those who seek to emulate celebrities cannot afford the luxury goods they see; they could, however, approximate the look of Kate Moss through her extremely lucrative collaboration with the high-street store Topshop, also launched in the US. They may pore over pictures of Victoria Beckham's thirty Hermès 'Birkin' bags, named of course after yet another celebrity, or they might seek out a counterfeit. There is a recent and disturbing rise in unsecured debt among young women on both sides of the Atlantic, something that has been well documented in the press in both the US and the UK. Most young women seem to spend their money – or run up their debts – on the swift high-street translations of celebrity looks, from bags and shoes to evening wear, for a truly convincing counterfeit is actually rather expensive. Cheap copies of celebrity party-going outfits top every table of throwaway fashion so far produced, and, according to one anonymous industry source, the average party top is worn only 1.7 times before being thrown away. For these cheap high-street copies cannot even be recycled; made of synthetic fabrics, with poor finishing, they are destined for landfill.

The celebrities of course personify this century-old concept of conspicuous consumption, right down to their palatial homes, splashed across the pages of the magazines. But now, as I have suggested, this parading of new wealth is spread more evenly across different levels of society. Since the emergence of American rap music in the 1980s, its stars have been famous for their love of bling, from the ubiquitous gold chains to the occasional diamond-studded tooth. Some have been dressed by designers for their tours, others have produced their own clothing ranges; all have long fed the

Cheap copies of celebrity party going outfits top every table of throwaway fashion so far produced, and, according to one anonymous industry source, the average party top is worn only 1.7 times before being thrown away.

desire for the newest pair of expensive trainers. Professional footballers also sport designer labels, as well as subsidising the endless, heavily photographed shopping sprees of their wives or girlfriends, the so-called 'WAGS', who are now arguably role models for young girls. Some, such as Alex Curran and Coleen Rooney, actually write fashion advice columns for celebrity magazines, while others grace chat shows, appear on reality television programmes and – in the case of Victoria Beckham and Cheryl Cole – are invited to be photographed for the cover of *Vogue*. Some of their footballing partners, for example David Beckham and Cristiano Ronaldo, wear diamonds in their own ears and on their fingers, which sparkle brightly on the pitch and for the cameras. No mention has been made of ethical sourcing for these stones despite the extensive press coverage of both their purchase and display – there is even a YouTube video of Ronaldo entitled *Diamonds Are Forever* (2009). The question was dramatically brought to the fore when supermodel Naomi Campbell became involved in the widely publicized 'blood diamonds' scandal in 2010.[3] The former dictator of Liberia, then on trial for war crimes, had allegedly made her a gift of some stones when she met him at a charity dinner in South Africa. She subsequently found herself giving evidence in court at The Hague. The media followed the trial with great interest; Campbell's court appearance was televised in its entirety. It might be hoped that this publicity could eventually help those workers involved in the highly dangerous and poorly paid work of diamond mining.

So it seems that Veblen's analysis is more pertinent than ever – in 2004, the *Boston Globe* devoted its front page to a conference convened at the New School for Social Research in New York to study the contemporary resonance of his work. His analysis of style concluded that 'in order to be reputable, it must be wasteful'[4] – something that horrified him even then, long before the full implications of our wasteful global lifestyle were revealed. The 2004 conference was comprised in the main of academics, but among the invitees was

Left: Kate Moss attends the launch party for the opening of Topshop's Knightsbridge store on 19 May 2010 in London.

Above: Footballer Wayne Rooney and his then-girlfriend Coleen McLoughlin arrive at David and Victoria Beckham's pre-World Cup party on 21 May 2006 in Sawbridgeworth, England.

Harper's American editor Lewis Lapham, who declared in his presentation that 'conspicuous consumption is practically the American way of life.'[5] The conference had no new practical solutions to offer, apart from suggesting that a responsible approach to the spending of money might require leadership and encouragement. Veblen himself turned to primitive societies to provide examples of a more acceptable way of living and of different value systems. Ironically, of course, some of the idyllic island communities he described are today vulnerable to the encroachment of mass tourism, while television and the internet can create desires in the most 'primitive' of societies for the trappings of the American way of life.

One of the problems that those concerned with fashion must address is the way in which celebrity culture has so fuelled the desire for novelty that the traditional fashion cycle has speeded up beyond recognition. New garments are delivered to the lower-end high-street stores every four weeks or so. And, like the luxury brands, these lower-end shops – cited by too many irresponsible fashion journalists as the clever 'cheap as chips' way of obtaining the latest looks – are thriving as never before. One company director of a leading discount chain reported anonymously that the recession had seen his company's profits increase by 30%.

What leadership might be provided in this dispiriting climate to encourage sustainable fashion and to make it successful? The 'affluent elite', according to a 2007 report by the World Wildlife Fund UK, have channelled their aspirational desires into the wish to create a better world; they are looking for brands that acknowledge social and environmental issues.[6] This is obviously true of some high earners and certainly of traditionally eco-conscious middle-class liberals. The problem is surely to find a way of disseminating this desire, and the priorities that accompany it, across and through acquisitive societies, now thoroughly used to the instant gratification of the cheap fashion fix. Some celebrities have, of course, become involved with environmental issues, with global poverty and with sustainable fashion. Angelina Jolie has been given official status by the UN in her

crusade against poverty, Madonna has opened a school in Malawi, and Leonardo DiCaprio has joined American politician Al Gore to crusade against global warming, while Bono's wife, Ali Hewson, has ventured into the world of eco-friendly design.

But sustainable fashion is invariably far from cheap – though Kate Moss has certainly done good work by making second-hand items newly desirable as 'vintage', and in championing charity shops. Nevertheless, brand-new sustainable fashion is not available on every high street, nor is it ridiculously inexpensive. Sadly many high-street shoppers are still unmoved by accounts of exploited workers, let alone bothered about despoiled rivers and climate change. I stood outside a well-known emporium selling cheap clothes while recording a demonstration that had been organized to draw attention to a televised account, that very night, of the appalling conditions in which the clothes on offer had been made. The shoppers not only ignored the demonstration but considerably outnumbered the participants.

A further problem concerns the designs provided by those who create sustainable fashion. Many potential customers see them as not answering their needs – they are insufficiently innovative, not quite fashionable enough. I was present at a meeting where a well-known, extremely influential fashion blogger was asked what she thought about sustainable fashion. A charming girl, she blushed, looked rather guilty and answered with considerable honesty, 'I'm afraid I don't find sustainable fashions very interesting.' A study of her own outfits in her lavishly illustrated blog shows them to be an extraordinarily creative mixture of designer labels, high-street pieces and the occasional exotic vintage discovery; one can understand why she might find some eco-conscious garments rather dull.

This is a real problem to be addressed by those of us who champion sustainability – and it will involve a rebranding exercise as well. For too many people, everything sustainable is likened to visual stereotypes that must be challenged and replaced, shaking off the taint of middle-class Puritanism. Younger celebrities, those most popular with the readers of the magazines specifically devoted to the relationship between celebrities and high-street retail, must first be convinced of the importance of sustainability and then recruited to the cause. Of course, any campaign has to be considered within the context of wider debates around fashion, which has historically been vilified as frivolous and lightweight, yoked to problematic notions of 'the feminine', as incompatible with feminism and as dependent upon continual, needless change. Work over the last twenty years within the field of cultural studies has led to a proper understanding of fashion's place within a wider socio-historical context and its importance in the formation of identity. Elizabeth Wilson, in her book *Adorned in Dreams* (1984), showed exactly how misguided was the prevalent belief that feminism must denounce and renounce fashion.

The only argument that has yet to be convincingly refuted is that regarding the link between fashion and constant unnecessary change. As I have argued here, developments within late capitalism and the

One of the problems that those concerned with fashion must address is the way in which celebrity culture has so fuelled the desire for novelty that the traditional fashion cycle has speeded up beyond recognition.

impact of celebrity culture have worked together to accelerate change and promote the current desire for cheap, disposable fashion items. But this is itself a fashion that may change. A reaction against celebrity extravagance in the current worldwide recession has already begun, albeit only in certain sectors of the press. There is, too, the recurrent mantra within the media that we are entering a new age of austerity and must adapt our behaviour accordingly. India Knight, self-proclaimed child of the 1980s, that greed-is-good decade, published a book called *The Shops: How, why, and where to shop* (2003) that listed the best, most expensive places to find designer clothes, beauty treatments, flattering haircuts and *objets* with which to adorn the home. Five years later, her introduction to *The Thrift Book: Live well and spend less* (2008) explained why she became interested in sustainability on every front – and that is just what the later book set out to encourage. The challenge for those of us anxious to promote sustainable fashion is how to create similar Damascene conversions across society as a whole; there is little evidence on the high street at the time of writing that the public have eschewed their weekly outings to 'the shops'.

A universal interest in the famous is as old as journalism itself and was encouraged by the film industry almost from its inception; it does not automatically lead to the spending of money on throwaway fashion. The heyday of Hollywood was the zenith of star influence on style – a star, it should be noted, is not to be confused with a modern celebrity. Stars were of interest because of the way they looked on screen rather than in paparazzi shots en route to nightclubs. Women who followed the female stars of the 1920s and 30s would try to emulate their heroines through the simple purchase of a lipstick or the adoption of a hairstyle. Though they might purchase the odd garment inspired by a film, they were just as likely to make their own, aided by the paper patterns provided in magazines, as well as the now long-closed haberdashery sections to be found in department stores, and the once-ubiquitous drapers' shops. The work of film scholars such as Jackie Stacey and Rachel Moseley proves, through the extensive

Above: Police try to control the unexpectedly large crowds at the opening of the Primark store on Oxford Street in central London, 5 April 2007.

interviews they conducted, that this practice of DIY emulation continued into the 1950s and even the 60s.[7] Nowadays, sewing skills are no longer handed down from one generation to the next, nor is the ability to knit or a knowledge of how to make jam. However, in the new age of austerity there are clear signs of a revival of interest in knitting, sewing and baking. This may be the signal for a new media jamboree, but it can only be beneficial.

In March 2009 the *International Herald Tribune* hosted a conference on 'sustainable luxury' in Delhi, India. *IHT* fashion editor Suzy Menkes, writing in the *New York Times*, reflected on the event, suggesting that there could and should be a separation of luxury from fashion, which would mean that 'the essence of the luxurious would be a private joy in something that was crafted to last.'[8] This may be completely appropriate for those with high disposable incomes. But in order to create *truly* sustainable fashion, it must not be – like the fashions of Veblen's day – the sole prerogative of the elite. High-street shoppers must be acknowledged, addressed and involved.

The hidden persuaders and their dark screens of meaning

EMMA NEUBERG, *who founded the not-for-profit Slow Textiles Group, is a researcher and lecturer at Chelsea College of Art, University of the Arts London.*

In societies that promote sustainability, it is surprising that billboard advertising is on the up. Public advertising, particularly illuminated billboards, signs and video displays, not only uses vast amounts of energy, but also promotes the message that everyone should consume more, regardless of whether they can afford to do so. Along any escalator and on any subway platform in New York, Hong Kong or Kuala Lumpur, the proliferation of such publicity, especially liquid-crystal display banners, has marked a significant change in our everyday urban landscape. Pedestrians, passengers or passers-by have no choice in the matter. Even as they read their newspapers or talk to friends, there is the continuous background movement, glow and flicker. Not to mention the message.

Below: Still from a video advert at Euston Underground station, London, 2009.

The great irony in the advertiser's message is that it tells us what *they* want. The dynamic is not dissimilar to that of bullies in the playground or office who are forever forcing their drama on others. Most people walk away or avert their gaze; others, feeling more susceptible, become involved. Unfortunately, in an increasingly technology-oriented society with growing divorce statistics, rising population figures, and ethno-cultural differences, pollution, financial commitments, divergent belief systems, job insecurities and the resultant stress, bullies – much like billboard advertising – will be on the rise.

Advertising represents a top-down system. Negotiation with the viewer does not come into it. There is the message and the receiver. There is also the transmitter, which asserts itself on a scale of anything from 0.05 to 50 m², 24/7. The wattage of a large billboard amounts to approximately 387,485 kWh per year.[1] Rather like an über-bully, its persistence, command and distribution suggest an interminable monologue.

An ad represents the vision of a brand. It is an exposé of a corporation's projected direction and self-image. If we take an everyday perfume ad, such as that for Dior's Addict (2007), as an example, we gather instantly that Dior is selling the frisson and glamour of addiction. In the Web version (2008), a woman is trapped in a dark padded cell, clawing the walls. Intermittent flashes of light and sound convey her inner torment. In a moment of respite she touches a cabinet containing a perfume bottle and the word 'Addict' fades in, an acrid shade of yellow.[2] In another of Dior's perfume ads, this time on television for Pure Poison (2007), we see a woman possessed by a beast within, dark, raging and fanged. Both woman and beast crawl and slide, reptile-like, through a shiny corridor, appearing full of compulsion and fury until they reach a perfume bottle and a voice whispers 'The new seduction by Dior'.[3]

All three commercial artefacts can be construed as literal expressions of the Dior company. Gripped by fervour, without thought or reflection, robed in the house's clothes and jewelry, models enact the feelings apparently aroused by addiction or poison. One might

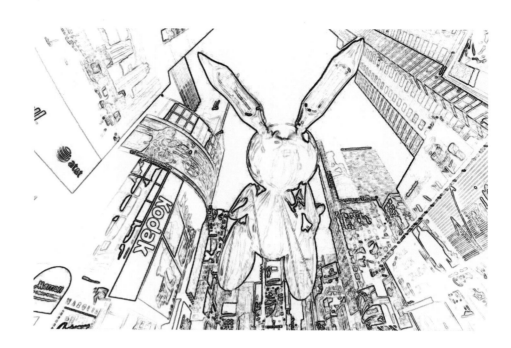

say, interpreting these ads from a psychoanalytic viewpoint, that they are cries for help. After all, Dior is showing the participants' sweat, their sense of being overwhelmed and conflicted.

Given the omnipresence of the screen in our daily lives, we are touched by a continuous stream of ads. Moving from one location to another, there they are, throbbing and bouncing on an electronic display near you. These illuminated parables of modern life become the wallpaper of our public and private spaces, rather like scenes from Ridley Scott's futuristic *Blade Runner* (1982). With so much media space to fill and competition *sans frontières* for our attention, advertisers' content becomes ever more sensational, extreme and, as we shall see, dark. If a company as traditional and hierarchical as Dior uses the language of addiction and poison to sell its story, what shall we find elsewhere?

In one of Dolce & Gabbana's womenswear images from its Autumn/Winter 2007–8 print campaign, we see a group of women wearing red aluminized dresses with corset-like metal belts. A naked man is being forced to his knees by one of the women. They are in a windowless room reminiscent of a padded cell with quilted walls. None of the characters are looking at the others, and their hair is tied back in an efficient, ready-for-business fashion. The women appear complicit in an act of 'amusing' abuse; their relational abilities seem limited to those of abuser and clown. A group of people who monkey about during an assault is dysfunctional: like a gang of bullies, it represents an assembling without power. In terms of British psychologist Wilfred Bion's Basic Assumption Group theory, it indicates an anxious, ill-equipped collection of individuals caught in a social space that does not know negotiation, whether actual or internal.[4] This is a place of impending takeovers from which the ability to think, articulate and differentiate is absent. On one level, the image describes a landscape of psychosis and violence experienced inwardly, then acted outwardly. Here these devices are being used to sell clothes.

British psychoanalyst, author and specialist in women's body issues Susie Orbach spoke in 2008 of

'internalized corsetry', of fashion having become a 'site of terror'.[5] Perhaps that is what we are being presented with in these advertisements: a vista on some unspeakable, terrifying place. It is significant that the women are shown in corsets – metal, inflexible, restrictive and painful to wear, not to mention medieval in their retro-futuristic symbolism. Orbach's internalized corsetry, which alludes to a constrained ability to think, voice and negotiate, is rendered tangible before our very eyes. On closer inspection, the woman approaching the viewer and victim in the Dolce & Gabbana ad is brandishing a whip: the lead persecutor's 'terrific' fashion accessory.

In another Dolce & Gabbana advertisement, this time from the company's Spring/Summer 2007 print campaign, a naked man is apparently about to be penetrated by one of several fully clothed male onlookers. The looming figure unzipping himself is faceless. (Violation as undertone is reinforced by the fact that another image from the same campaign, showing a woman being held to the ground by a man while several other males look on, was banned

Above: Author's drawing of Shibuya billboards at night, Tokyo, 2007.

Top: Author's drawing of daytime illuminated and video advertising in Times Square, New York City, 2007.

in a number of countries.) The naked man lies on the floor, eyes closed, one leg splayed and face half visible. A seated figure is doing up his tie as if getting dressed. As in the banned ad, the clothed dominant figures wear outfits from Dolce & Gabbana's menswear collection; the naked man, without Dolce & Gabbana clothes, is the 'victim'.

As with the banned womenswear ad, several readings of this image are possible. In one the consumer identifies with the victim awaiting penetration by a faceless figure, as if in fantasy. In another, the consumer identifies with the faceless undresser soon to release himself. From a psychological perspective, the former suggests a desire for abuse. Psychologically speaking, the presence of an internalized abuser is created by experience of actual abuse in some form. The latter indicates the drive to abuse, which also stems from exposure to it. The two are part of the same paradigm, which describes the power dynamic between two states or psychic positions. Placed in a mainstream garment advertisement, the drama suggests that the role of the abuser, which comes with having the upper hand, tallies with the wearing of the brand. The victim is the one without the clothes. This echoes the 2007–8 ad: he who does not wear the brand gets abused. A leading ideological group thus enjoys abusive pathology as a relational device with its viewers, customers and potential customers.

Taken literally, as if analysing a portrait, this picture depicts a kind of corporate self-image. 'He', the bullish corporate persona, has the clothes, whereas the unconscious, floored 'outsider' does not. 'He' and his similarly clad clones (all in white or, in the 2007–8 example, red) take advantage of the 'unconscious' nude one after the other. The older man, marked by his black clothes – symbolizing the original abuser or dark 'other'[6] perhaps – points to the victim as if directing the scene. Concurrently, abuser and victim reveal an internal dynamic that suggests an unconscious dialogue, within the corporate image, relating to abuse. The ambiguity and complexity of meaning arise in the content of the image itself, its relationship with its creators and its, and their, relationship with the viewer.

There are many interpretations of such fashion images. Aspects that the viewer evidently enjoys also exist: the ambiguity, the drama, the gloss, the taboo, the frisson. For the purposes of this discussion, however, we are reading these advertisements as symbolic and literal stories that punctuate our cultural, commercial, professional, private and social space. Ads are largely construed and constructed as fantasy and dream. One of the 20th century's most influential books, Sigmund Freud's *The Interpretation of Dreams* (1900), emphasized the literalness and significance of symbolism in dreams: '[T]here is a psychological technique which makes it possible to interpret dreams, and that on the application of this technique, every dream will reveal itself as a psychological structure, full of significance, and one which may be assigned to a specific place in the psychic activities of the waking state.'[7] With this is in mind, let us look at some other everyday images.

In a billboard and magazine ad by Italian label Diesel (Spring/Summer 2008) we see three figures running in different directions across a sunny city street, blinded by dollar bills. They are related insofar as each one runs with arms outstretched, wears black and white, embodies the same vertiginous, out-of-control feeling and anticipates collision.

If we interpret the scene, this time as a moment from a dream, the atmosphere is one of precariousness, chaos and vulnerability. The dreamer appears caught in something that incites danger and fear and, simultaneously, arouses questions about value, purpose, coherence and direction. The configuration of the runners may allude to an internalized triangular relationship, suggesting that a regressive state is somehow being enacted – blindly – and leading the protagonist to a giddying place where role, identity and position are questioned. Overall, this 'dream image' suggests that individuation, differentiation and separation from regressive behavioural patterns have yet to take place.

In another ad from the same campaign, a man and a little girl run along a suburban pavement holding hands. It is after dark and the man appears to be reading a storybook. The child wears slippers

The fictional individuals depicted in all of these ads appear to be non relational: characters that a psychologist might diagnose as showing signs of disturbed pathologies, borderline personality disorders and failed or failing relationships.

and holds a cuddly toy as if ready for bed. A woman in the background runs from her front door, dressed in a towelling robe and evidently under duress. The relationship between the individuals is ambiguous. Dream or reality, their shared language is one of stress, haste, confusion and urgency. The inclusion of a child in this scene of difficulty seems to convey the passing of tension, disparity and non-containment to the next generation, not to mention the man's inner feminine child and other psychic structures.

Both images embody the vertiginous, out-of-control feeling denoted by the tag line 'Live Fast'. The images show us what Fast Living, Fast Fashion and Fast Feelings look and feel like. They illustrate cultural affect. We may laugh because of the sense of familiarity, but 'behind' the screen is a societal ocean of confusion and lack, not to mention an impending sense of collision.

In October 2008, Diesel released one of its first online advertisements, 'XXX' – an indicator of the nascent era in Web 2.0 marketing, a stage in online advertising that was more sophisticated, entertaining and strategic than what had come before.[8] Setting a new benchmark in terms of fashion advertising, this 76-second ad consists of a montage of dated porn films edited together with drawn cartoons overlaid to cover the multiple shots of genitalia. No clothes or products available from Diesel stores are displayed. The short celebrates the company's thirtieth year in business and as an international brand phenomenon; parties were held in twenty-seven countries on the same day. The ad simply communicates the label's association with youth and hedonism via images of sexual performance.

In Spring/Summer 2009, in a similar viral seeding exercise, the German online fashion brand Jungstil released a short showing two young women fighting over a garment in one of their elegant store interiors.[9] The short becomes abusive when one girl floors another with a punch across the face. We see the victim fall to the floor with force, then bounce back to life in computer-game style. She then hurls herself onto the jubilant girl carrying the prized top to the changing room. Moments later, an ear has

been bitten off, then an arm ripped off. Within seconds, young women all around the shop floor are attacking each other. The final shot is of a blood-stained hand sliding down a changing-room door. Text is typed across the final frame: 'better shop online'.

The fictional individuals depicted in all of these ads appear to be non-relational; characters that a psychologist might diagnose as showing signs of disturbed pathologies, borderline personality disorders and failed or failing relationships. A dark humour runs underneath, and that darkness has a double-edged relationship with the viewer – not least as the viewer, passenger or passer-by is rendered complicit in the viewing space. The ideological message permeates the social and cultural skin. Yet a paradox lies in the fact that these promotional enactments are openings onto the underlying dynamics of the brands. They relay corporate messages, the projection of what the labels' groups of consulted individuals want to communicate.

In view of potential insights into the psychic activities of the corporation, the collection of dream-like symbols that we have identified so far – the addict, the padded cell, the inner beast, the takeovers, the red dress, the abuser, the non-relational 'others', the persecutor's accessory, the precarious environments, the blindness, the lack of control, the acts of frenetic sex and group violence – tell a story of anguish, disturbance, distress and fragmentation. If these were attributed to an individual or group of individuals in a clinical setting, they would signal mental and behavioural difficulty and dysfunction to say the least. If we borrow from psychology and group analytic theory for a moment, we gain new insight into what these symbolic scenarios may contain. British analyst S. H. Foulkes states that 'both health and disturbance are things that belong to...groups as a whole, the network, and not just the individual...the disturbance which we see in front of us, embodied in a particular patient, is in fact the expression of a disturbed balance in a total field of interaction which involves a number of different people as participants.'[10]

Traditional forms of social and cultural containment are on the way out. The anchors of the eternal, the dependable, the timeless and the spiritual are manifested less and less within the global scenario.

If this seems far-fetched, extending the darkness expressed in a commercial artefact to include the self-promoting group or network, one has only to recall the pervasive influence of psychology in advertising during the 20th century. Freud's nephew, psychologist Edward Bernays, not only created complex manipulation systems on behalf of private corporations and the American government in order to sway public opinion and international politics but his cousin Anna Freud's work as a child psychoanalyst inspired an ongoing dialogue among manufacturers, advertising agencies, motivation researchers and psychologists.[11] There is a long history of commercial interest in the relationship between psychology and message manipulation, albeit with a focus on the commercial effectiveness of the content, not the psychic activities of the company – to which we shall return.

Generic evidence today suggests that advertisements are frequently consumed and interpreted as art by creative and risqué maestros of art and direction. This is particularly evident in the growing number of personal blogs that celebrate and invite comment on favourite ads and viral seeding campaigns.[12] It marks a deceptive premise that needs unscrambling before we delve further: ads sell stuff; they are created by collective groups and are 'read' by millions of individuals, all of whom recognize the messages and their 'harmless' promotional language. Denial of more complex meaning or implication, in this age of unconsciousness, appears to be the norm.

If, on the other hand, we elect to (a) challenge unconsciousness and (b) concentrate the psychological focus on perpetrators rather than recipients – if, in other words, we consider ads as the unconscious projected fantasies of the corporation – new insights may be gleaned. Ad campaigns take on new meaning as portals onto the collective identity of the company, expressions of the network and its psychic activities. This allows passers-by and pedestrians to at least have a framework for unpicking and mapping out the discomfort, anguish, disturbance, bullying, distress and fragmentation that

is broadcast so freely and publicly by the perpetrators, their signs and signifiers.

It is not hard to conceive that an ad's content intimates the internal workings, desires and perspectives of a corporation at a given time. It is not hard to apprehend that the bestial takeover, the addict, the abuser, the blinded runners and the dismembered shoppers are projections of the people who participate in the imagineering process. (Just ask yourself whether you would bite the ear of a woman buying a top that you liked or gang-rape an unconscious man together with peers from your style tribe.) The corporation presents itself in the singular but is made up of many voices, employees and consultants who believe in the same story. In their myth-building and desire to sell, the group vision becomes inflected with distortion, tautology and parody. Destructive forces in groups are a natural phenomenon.[13] Internal forces are known to be particularly active in working groups; hence the envy, anxiety, adulation, projection, lust, back-stabbing and competition that go on. These darker forces have been condensed by British analyst Morris Nitsun into a phenomenon called the 'anti-group'.[14] For the sake of stimulating debate and making hitherto unspoken phenomena conscious, are not the unconscious or naked viewers, innocently passing by one flickering site to another, being presented with the destructive manifestations of the anti-group, its veiled messages, repressed pathologies and adolescent projective cycles?

By 2007 the average American was destined to see 1,095,000 advertisements per year.[15] This was certainly a burdensome weight, if not an unsustainable one. Today mental health-related illness is on the rise. In October 2008 the director general of the World Health Organization (WHO), Margaret Chan, made the following announcement: 'The global financial crisis is likely to cause increased mental health problems and even suicides as people struggle to cope with poverty and unemployment.'[16] According to the WHO, it is feared that as financial downturn 'hits the real economy and more people fall into debt', the impact on mental health will increase. Chan told a meeting of mental health experts that '[p]overty and its associated stresses including violence, social exclusion and "constant insecurity" are linked to the onset of mental disorders…It should not come as a surprise that we continue to see more [of them]'.[17]

Traditional forms of social and cultural containment are on the way out. The anchors of the eternal, the dependable, the timeless and the spiritual are manifested less and less within the global scenario. A small community may, psychologically speaking, 'contain' the words of its faith, but what about a global industry with a commercial precept? Fashion, retail and luxury-brand campaigns (Dior's 'Addict – Admit It' and 'Pure Poison – The New Seduction', Gucci's 'Rush' and 'Envy Me', Diesel's 'Live Fast' and 'XXX' and Twist's 'Play with Yourself', to name but a few) reveal contemporary society's dark tales of containment. Like all commercial stories, they signal American commentator Vance Packard's hidden persuaders' cover stories of conscious and unconscious construction.[18] Dressed in post-production gloss and effective styling, these ads represent modern-day veils of seduction, deflection and denial.

The advertiser's story is a projection. When the projection describes a dark scenario, it has the capacity to promote and exacerbate that scenario. If viewers are open to radicalization by the darkness, it resonates with them.[19] If viewers' internal others are susceptible to the drama, the message is received and invested in.[20] Perhaps a sale is made. The overriding social implication, however, is one of illness or disturbance, as Foulkes has called it.[21] The proliferation of destructive messages that we laugh at, look forward to, celebrate, buy into, find amusing, become immune to and ignore becomes our normalized cultural backdrop, our literal and symbolic wallpaper.

On 1 January 2007 the population of São Paulo said 'No' to this disturbing trend, asking, 'Why should citizens endure this visual pollution?' Ever since then, most of the city's billboard space has remained blank. Across France, too, individuals have said 'Stop'. Since 2007 a national group called Les Déboulonneurs has been defacing billboards with sprayed messages such as 'Pollution Mentale'.

If we refer back to the group analysts:

'Ill health is thought of as a disturbance in communication, a blockage that gets located in a…configuration of individuals; effectively, the disturbance is located in a particular place. "The neurotic [and psychotic] disturbance is bound up with deficient communicability and is therefore blocked…The language of the symptom, although already a form of communication, is autistic…" When autistic meaning is converted into social meaning, the communication flows again and health is restored. "[The therapeutic process is] directed towards increasing transformation from autistic neurotic symptom formation to articulate formation of problems which can be shared and faced by all."'[22]

The dark content of the advertising campaigns at which we have been looking represents an 'autistic', neurotic site on a celebritized world stage. All those electronic transmitters with their pulsating light and disturbed dynamics expound what Foulkes termed 'autistic neurotic symptom formation'.[23] Even if they merely mirror the darker aspects of human nature and contemporary culture, by using the image, the idol, to push more product, they perpetuate the systems and symptoms inscribed therein. The relief of laughter and purchase may temporarily appease and disguise the myth, but a sense of post-purchase guilt or redundancy frequently leaves the consumer with a hint of the underlying deception. The conversion into ameliorating social meaning, as Foulkes describes it, is not achieved through this model.[24]

Social meaning arises through communication and debate. Action is required to bring debate into focus. This has happened legally in São Paulo and illegally in France. Where to next? If no debate occurs, the ads filling public and private space will continue to promote their 'autistic' perspectives. And the oppression that individuals feel beneath their artificial luminescence when they see them on escalators, platforms, bus stands, building façades, motorways, seat backs, roundabouts and curbsides will grow. The top-down systems, the messaging, the myths, the *pollution mentale*, the veiled pathologies and the projected neurotic and psychotic blocks will be felt and forwarded.

Sustainability is related to the wellbeing of people as well as the environment. To date, the wellbeing of people within the fashion industry has been largely directed at workers' rights and working conditions. This important issue is in many ways entirely separate from the health of the privileged citizen living in the glittering metropolis. Or is it? The proliferation of branded messages that incorporate a unilateral message to combat competitors, as in Al Ries and Jack Trout's book *Marketing Warfare* (2002), coupled with the destructive content unpacked in these pages, pass on a language, a dynamic, a system intended to wear us down and win us over. Addiction and mania; brutality, cruelty and violence; and blindness, speed and chaos are all communicated. Despite the advertisers' proclaimed innocence – Dolce & Gabbana was quoted as saying 'Spain must be a little backwards' when the Spanish authorities banned the aforementioned Spring/Summer 2007 ad[25] – all of these 'entertaining' unconscious power enactments are publicly displayed, assimilated, imitated, normalized and contained by us, the passers-by – thus affecting our civic conditions and rights.

For young people, the advertiser's creation is particularly potent. It has a mesmerizing, dumbing affect that insists upon belief and subscription. This is the case because young people tend towards structuralist modes of thinking, more oppositional, black-and-white, either/or forms than those of adults. All the nuances, the grey areas, of life have yet to be experienced, described, understood and named. As soon as the message says, 'All change' (for the next big thing), young people usually follow. This has two key effects on the susceptible individual.

The first is social: the assimilation in young minds of top-down aggressive power systems – such as the mock 'rape' scene in Dolce & Gabbana's Spring/Summer 2007 ad, which appeared on billboards, or Jungstil's short film, transmitted via social media such as Twitter and Facebook, featuring young women dismembering each other – as accepted grown-up relational models, rather than as playful fictions. At best these models may encourage competition in the playground over what style product a teenager wears; at worst they may reinforce dysfunctional emotional skills, such as those that lead to envious attack. Indeed, envious attack in Britain is a growing youth problem. British psychologist Herbert Rosenfeld wrote extensively on the 'internal mafia gang', a very real collection of internalized persecutors among young people who have difficult emotional histories. Through 'fear of annihilation' they have an active 'addiction to death' and inclination towards 'magical thinking' whereby, if an assault is committed, they believe that the victim will spring back to life, just as in the Jungstil ad.[26]

The second effect is cultural: the 'all change, follow the leader' cycle exerts pressure on every level, not just on the speed and quality of production and the subsequent implications for working conditions, of which the fashion industry is fully aware, but on the promotion of material abundance, excess, instant gratification, disposability, invincibility, aspiration, expectation, presumption, material desire, material rights, material ambition, ownership, individualism, selfishness, narcissism, aggression, confusion, strain, psychosis, blame, attack, debt, stress, destructive behaviour, homogeneity and the dissolution of the immaterial – all of which, if not properly contained, promote adolescent thinking in young and older people alike, not to mention landfill.

In 2009, British psychologist Mike Tait presented a paper at the Dark Forces – Destructive and Self-Destructive Feelings in Adolescence conference at the Institute of Group Analysis in London. In this paper he spoke of the adolescent projective cycles of today's broadcast media.[27] Adolescent thinking, he said, is marked by regressive antics, displacement, blame and denial. Sound-bite culture and 76-second online ads depend on similar structures. Like billboard advertising and bullies, the sensationalist format relies on people's susceptibility to divisiveness and unilateralism.

What is it about the clothing and apparel industry that needs to promote a cultural identity of blind behaviour and envious attack?

Today a visible shift is taking place in online advertising. Fashion and footwear companies are edging ever closer in their courtship of computer-game storytelling. Japanese shoe company Onitsuka Tiger created a virtual trainer for their Spring/Summer 2009 print campaign. The virtual shoe housed a virtual city that housed a terrorizing green monster – all of which could be uploaded with the USB memory stick that came with the analogue purchase, presumably for the customer's avatar to inhabit and battle with.[28] In Japan in 2008, PlayStation 3 joined with Dress to help customers clothe their avatars as well as their physical selves.[29] Puma's 2009 online campaign featured a blend of real and virtual time, showing shoes and apparel that appeared to melt and burn while being worn.[30] In 2008 Prada dressed manga heroine Deunan Knute in the computer game-like warring environment of the film *Appleseed Ex Machina* (2007). A Nike viral advertisement in 2009 showed a female celebrity escaping paparazzi with parkour moves, shifting seamlessly from an ordinary paparazzi film clip into what could be footage from a video game.[31] Tokidoki (Italy) advertised cartoon bullets and skeletons (whose 'Hello Kitty' styling appeals to children) on footwear and clothing set up for future analogue–virtual–analogue transitions (such as 3-D printouts).[32] Diesel showed a girl dismembered by a laser in its 'Human After All' viral campaign in 2007.[33]

By way of psychological explication of this trend, Tait offers further insights into the drives behind destructive anti-social behaviour: '[T]he environment must be tested and retested in its capacity to stand the aggression, to prevent or repair the destruction, to tolerate the nuisance, to recognize the positive element in the anti-social tendency (as an expression of hope by the adolescent), to provide and preserve the object that is to be sought and found.'[34] If aggressive advertising is like an anti-social adolescent, then these ads are expressions of hope that society will contain their darkness, and accept them unconditionally.

Yet why should society do so? The public space is the people's space. Why should people tolerate adolescent, destructive advertising that promotes dysfunctional behaviour and consumerism? What if cars were sold through images of dismemberment? What if white goods were sold through murderous associations? What if food products were promoted through scenes of sexual assault? What is it about the clothing and apparel industry that needs to promote a cultural identity of blind behaviour and envious attack?

Fashion's growing proximity to displays of dysfunctional enactment is a cause for concern. The psychosis, killing, mutilation and chaos described here bring apparel and aspirational appearance closer to manifestations of communication blockage and societal ill-health. By association, fashion, beauty and appearance come to represent a dystopian site full of anguish, confusion, mixed messages and compulsion.

Questions about the link between advertising, adolescent thinking and social dysfunction became more than simply theoretical in August 2011, when when clothing, footwear and apparel stores were the focus of four days of looting as thousands of young Britons rioted in the streets of London, Birmingham and Manchester after a young man from north London was shot dead by police. There was no spokesperson or political agenda for the action, only copy-catting and blind enactment as thousands of people openly stole fashion goods in the full glare of CCTV and broadcast media. Following the riots, self-professed anarchist Boff Whalley commented in *The Independent*, 'These are kids brought up in an age of buy and sell. Labels, logos, status, advertising. This is the world we've given them; a world they're throwing back at us.'[35]

In a sustainable society, the fashion industry will need to consider the relationship that is promoted between people and their clothing, bearing in mind the kind of communication strategies we have seen here and the consumer behaviours they may have encouraged. This is the fashion industry's social and cultural legacy at the turn of the millennium and, as this book indicates, it is a legacy that is now being addressed.

'The seeds were sown in my personal life, then they came into my business life.'

STELLA McCARTNEY *is not perfect – she is happy to acknowledge that there are bound to be contradictions in trying to live and work ethically, aesthetically and sustainably, especially when you are working in fashion.*
By Sandy Black

Above: Portrait of Stella McCartney taken by her older sister, the photographer Mary McCartney.

Opposite: Shorts and shoes by Stella McCartney, Spring/Summer 2011, featured in *Nylon*, December/January 2010/11. (Top by Jill Stuart, Spring/Summer 2011.)

'I'm not going to stand here and claim to be 100% green or 100% perfect all the time,' McCartney told the *Evening Standard* as she was launching her Care by Stella McCartney range of organic cosmetics in May 2007.[1] Well known for being a fashion designer with a conscience – refusing to use fur or leather when designing first for Chloë and later for her own-name label – McCartney does, however, admit to having worn vintage leather shoes. Daughter of Beatle Paul McCartney, she has followed the family tradition of advocating vegetarianism and animal rights and supporting PETA's anti-fur campaign. Despite initially resisting offers to work for the Gucci Group conglomerate (now PPR Luxury), reportedly due to their widespread use of fur and leather, McCartney finally signed with them in 2001, vowing to keep her own eco-principles intact. She has continued to develop her signature luxurious but easy-to-wear clothes, creating a global luxury brand that reported a first-time profit in 2007.

'About 50 million animals die for the sake of fashion ever year, which is extremely wasteful, and significantly contributes to climate change,' McCartney has observed. 'There are a lot of alternatives to using leather in accessories. We use PU made in Italy, and not PVC, but also velvets, cottons, linens, raffias, sustainable wood, recycled nylons…at the end of the day, it's more creative.'[2] Highly successful collaborations have marked this phase of McCartney's career, especially her collection designed for H&M in November 2005, which sold out in an hour. The designer style items in this range, available at a fraction of the luxury price, were made in China, with a wider range of available sizes than is usual in luxury brands. McCartney also designed a range of non-leather bags for Le SportSac, and since 2004 has been involved in an ongoing collaboration with Adidas, designing sportswear that included her designs for the 2012 British Olympic team uniforms.

In recent seasons McCartney has produced a small 'eco' collection, originally championed by Barneys in New York in Autumn 2007. The success of this collection helped to turn the tide in designer fashion. 'More and more people like to talk about this [ethical] side of our brand,' McCartney has said. 'There are definitely other aspects to consider. There are organic fabrics, low-impact dyes. My fashions are mainly made in Italy, so child labour is not an issue for us. We do work a lot on fair trade. The first question that comes up when we open a store is: can we use wind power? Sometimes we can, sometimes we can't. We use organic cotton and conventional cotton; I'd rather use organic cotton but I can't always afford to or get enough of it…I don't think you can ask a consumer to compromise. I don't think you can say "Here is this jacket that looks terrible but it's organic, and here is a really beautiful jacket that's cheaper but don't buy it because it's not organic." My job is to create beautiful luxurious things. I love that people come into the store and don't even know that something is organic or in faux leather. That's the biggest challenge, having people not notice.'[3] As far as designing the eco collection is concerned, she adds, 'the most challenging thing was trying to play by the rules…you have less colours and less fabrics available to you, they're a different quality than the type that you are used to. I wouldn't say there are restrictions but there are challenges…If I have 200 metres of fabric in storage that we didn't use up in previous collections, I will always turn to use that again before ordering more fabric.'[4]

'I am a fashion designer,' McCartney emphasizes. 'I am not an environmentalist.'[5]

'Edun is a fashion brand that was created to make beautiful clothes in a way that was fair to everyone and would benefit Africa.'

EDUN *is the fashion label initiated by Ali Hewson and her husband, rock star and campaigner Bono, in 2005 to promote ethical principles and fair trade.*
By Sandy Black

Ali Hewson and Bono first visited Africa in 1985, following his involvement in the groundbreaking Live Aid concert fund-raiser. They began to work with small factories in Lesotho to manufacture clothes.

A successful mix of altruism and fashion may not be easy to achieve, but Edun's mission is to encourage others in the fashion community to do business in Africa and to help bring the continent out of extreme poverty. The company works on a micro level to build skill sets and create volume work for factories that produce the clothes, and on a macro level to explore partnerships for sustainable communities. According to Hewson, during the 1980s Africa had a 6% share of world trade; by 2002 this had dropped to 2%. If the country regained just 1%, this would be equivalent to US $70 billion in exports – five times the amount of international aid the continent currently receives. In 2007 the T-shirt sub-brand Edun Live was launched: a 100% African product 'grown to sewn' on the continent from cotton seed to manufactured garment. Edun Live sells bulk blank T-shirts for merchandising, creating volume orders for production. In 2008 Edun started the Conservation Cotton Initiative (CCI), together with the Wildlife Conservation Society (WCS), working with small-scale cotton farmers to rebuild communities.

Edun's fashion collection was developed with creative direction from the respected New York-based designer Rogan Gregory, who also founded the Loomstate organic cotton jeans company. By autumn 2008 garments were being produced in India, Peru, Tunisia, Kenya, Uganda, Lesotho, Mauritius and Madagascar, with 21% coming from Africa. As Gregory told *Wallpaper** magazine in 2008: 'It's not easy making a collection that's organic or making it in Africa. There's a lot of bureaucracy...[but] we're making a larger percentage in Africa than we were before and have sourced many factories that actually have amazing capabilities.'[1] However, meeting manufacturing quality criteria and delivery dates proved to be a challenge, and in response to the global recession American stores such as Saks Fifth Avenue and Barneys reduced or cut their orders. Edun needed massive investment from its celebrity owners to stay afloat, and Gregory left the company.

In May 2009 the LVMH group of luxury brands (Louis Vuitton Moet Hennessy) bought a 49% stake in Edun. This partnership has two significant benefits: it supports Edun to become a truly viable business in the future; and it gives LVMH an instant buy-in to an ethical fashion brand at a time when consumers are demanding greater social and environmental responsibility. Following lengthy

Every journey began in Africa. Ali and Bono wear Edun; Ali carries the Louis Vuitton/Edun collaborative bag.
Profits from the bag, as well as Ali and Bono's fee benefit Conservation Cotton Initiative Uganda.

Follow Ali and Bono on louisvuittonjourneys.com

LOUIS VUITTON

Opposite: Conservation Cotton workers in Uganda, June 2011.

Left: Ali Hewson and Bono in Africa, wearing Edun and Louis Vuitton, from the Louis Vuitton Core Values advertising campaign, October 2010, photographed by Annie Leibovitz.

Below: Conservation Cotton in Uganda, June 2011.

negotiations, including establishing supplier codes of conduct, a new management structure was put in place and a new designer, Sharon Wauchob, was appointed. Wauchob, a former designer for Louis Vuitton who has had her own fashion label since 1999, showed her first collection for Edun in September 2010.

One compromise following the partnership with LVMH has been to move some of Edun's fashion manufacturing to China and Peru, although 100% of its T-shirts are still produced in Africa, and, despite the fact that some of the original factories Edun worked with in Africa have now closed, the company hopes to have 40% of its total production in Africa by 2013, furthering its philosophy of for-profit business rather than charity and trade rather than aid.[2]

In Edun's Autumn/Winter 2008 collection, African poetry was printed inside the pockets of jeans, adding authenticity and interest to the garments, which bore swing labels that read 'We carry the story of the people who make our clothes around with us.'[3] Edun's commitment to its mission statement, which proclaims 'respect for the people who make our product; the community where we make it; the materials we use; and the consumer', appears to have been maintained. In 2010 CCI Uganda provided business and enterprise support to 3,500 cotton farmers in Northern Uganda, and expects this number to grow as farmers displaced by civil war return. In 2010 Edun began a collaboration with Made, a jewelry producer that uses local artisans based in Nairobi, Kenya,

to produce Edun jewelry and to provide beading and metalwork for garments in the Spring/Summer 2011 collection.

Together with Made's non-profit arm Made Africa, Edun also supports the Bidii School located in Kibera, Kenya, one of the poorest urban communities in Africa. Even while its own corporate restructuring was in progress in 2010, Edun launched a series of T-shirts designed by the students, with all sale profits going to the school.

Edun's view on trade regulation in Africa

'No African person or government wants to rely on foreign aid for the provision of basic needs. Africans want a fair system, which lets them trade with rich nations and earn more money, so they can grow their economies and pay for their own education and healthcare. As it stands now, the global economy is not equitable – wealthier countries are able to dictate unfair trading terms to developing countries by using protectionist policies to support their own producers artificially and limit market access to poor countries. In order to help Africa invest in health, water, roads and education systems for its people, and grow sufficiently to reduce its dependency on development assistance and debt relief, trade opportunities must increase. An expanded and fairer trade system would allow African countries to earn the resources they need and not only achieve the Millennium Development Goals, but also reach a more important goal for Africa: self-sufficiency. But instead of earning more money to invest in improving the lives of its people, Africa has been earning less and less.

The African Growth and Opportunity Act (AGOA) is a US Trade Act that significantly enhances US market access for (currently) 38 Sub-Saharan African (SSA) countries. The Act originally covered an 8-year period from October 2000 to September 2008, but amendments signed into law by US President George Bush in July 2004 further extend AGOA to 2015. However, after September 2012 African nations will need to ship garments made from either local or American-made fabric in order to obtain duty-free status. For now, garment manufacturers can have duty-free access to the US regardless of where the fabric comes from. This is referred to as the Third Party Fabric Provision. This provision was due to end in September 2007 but was extended until 2012, which gives the African continent some more time to develop its industry. Although 5–6 years might seem like a long time, in the context of what needs to be accomplished during this period, it is not. It is really a race against time.

Behind the scenes, Edun along with other brands and organizations (for example, The Whitaker Group, MAFAF, the ComMark Trust and ACTIF) are helping get a further much-needed extension. This means that if the ability of sub-Saharan African regions to make fabric is not developed before the expiration of the Third Party Fabric Provision in 2012, then the apparel industry in these regions could suffer dramatically, leading to the loss of thousands of African jobs.'[1]

'It's not easy making a collection that's organic, or making it in Africa...'

Below and opposite:
Sharon Wauchob for Edun, Autumn/Winter 2011.

'Buy less. choose well.'

DAME VIVIENNE WESTWOOD, *always the iconoclast, three times named British Designer of the Year, has in recent years turned her passionate attention to the urgent issues of climate change and rainforest depletion, inspired by James Lovelock's Gaia theories.*
By Sandy Black

'If we do survive,' Vivienne Westwood has said, 'we will have to change our thinking. Quickly or slowly, we are going to have to change our whole outlook on life, and learn not to want the things that we think we want.'[1] Promoting her ideas on British television in July 2009, she advocated a new people's politics: 'We can only be saved by public opinion…we're at war with something that's never happened before, we have to make politicians do what we want.'[2]

Without irony, Westwood encourages people to buy and consume less, but when they do buy fashion, to choose well (and perhaps buy hers): 'Invest in one lovely pair of trousers. There's a lot to be said for people that wear the same thing over and over – its cool. And you just can't get that with cheap clothes. That, I think, is where I have something to offer above the majority of retailers. That's something I can say in my defence as a fashion designer.'[3]

These ideas inform Westwood's designs in unexpected and intriguing ways. Her Autumn/Winter 2008 collection, called 'Chaos Point', reflected a fusion of references including awareness of climate change and concerns about the future of the population. This collection was quite child-like in its proportions, featuring, for instance, a ball gown that was shown on the catwalk by a model on stilts to emphasize its long asymmetric swathes of trailing fabric (which are wrapped around the tree in the image on pp. 40–41). The prints for this collection were based on drawings done by Nottingham school

children who were first briefed by Westwood about global warming and then asked to imagine that they were eco-warriors or freedom fighters in the forest. (She used to be a teacher.) It also is a precursor to the DIY ethos she later introduced into her work. Her Spring/Summer 2010 collection was based on the notion of DIY fashion made from re-purposed furnishing fabric and tablecloths, or – as she herself wears it – from several metres of luxurious duchesse satin draped and pinned around the body. Westwood admits to not washing her clothes very often, presenting her fashion philosophy for recession this way: 'Buy less, choose well, if it's dirty don't bother to wash it, don't keep buying things for the sake of it.'[4]

Writing in *Dazed and Confused* magazine, Rod Stanley named Westwood's 'three inspirational imperatives of the role of culture, a consciousness of the plight of the planet, and of always dressing the part'.[5]

Interviewed by Hilary Alexander after her Spring/Summer 2011 Paris show (pictured on p. 42), Westwood says, 'I spend my time trying to understand the world I live in. You have to understand the past to know anything about where we are now, and you do that through culture. You only get out what you put in.'[6]

Her messages are strong and to the point. She speaks her mind in public and politicizes the platform of fashion to train a spotlight on the immense problems facing humanity. In this way she hopes to engage a new, untapped audience.

Opposite: Vivienne Westwood at a live reading of her manifesto 'Active Resistance to Propaganda' at the Design Museum, London, 2008, photographed by Mary McCartney.

Overleaf: Ballgown from Westwood's Autumn/Winter 2008 'Chaos Point' Gold Label collection.

Above: Vivienne Westwood
with her models in the finale of
her Spring/Summer 2011 Gold
Label show, Paris.

Opposite: Press release for
Westwood's 'DIY' collection,
Spring/Summer 2010.

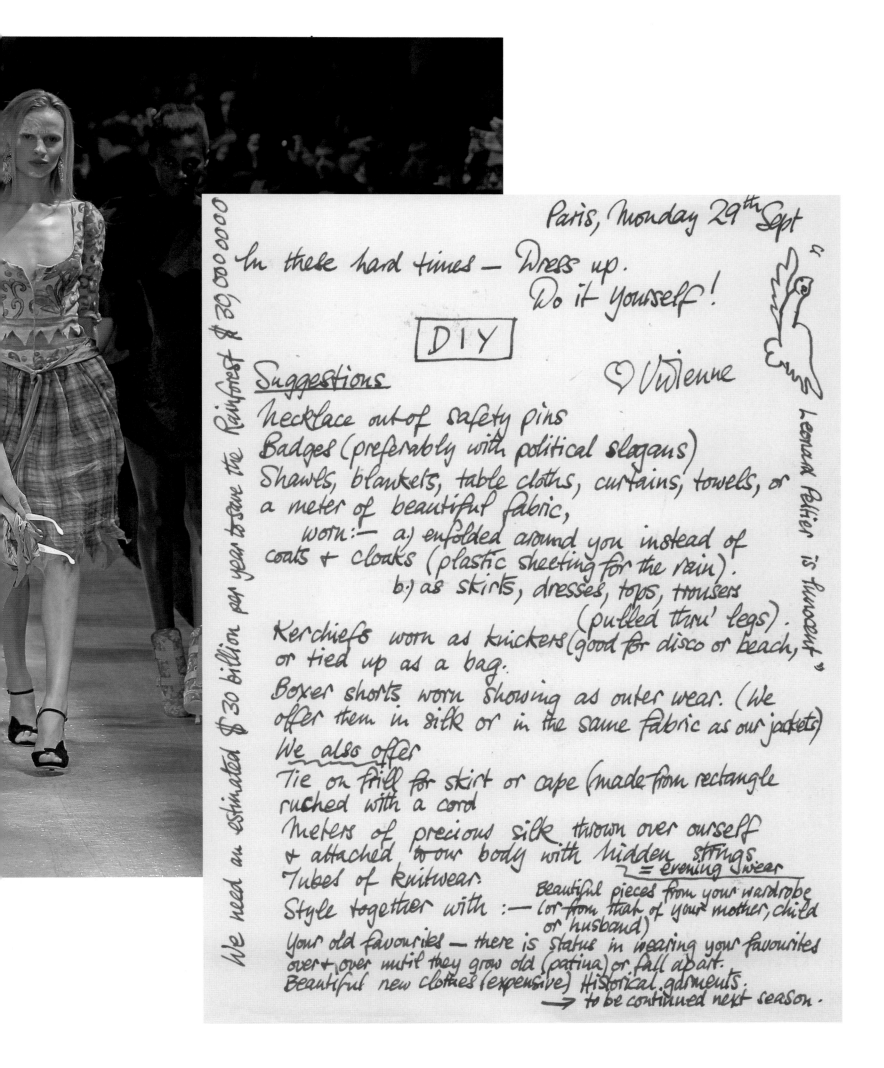

Paris, Monday 29th Sept

In these hard times — Dress up.
Do it Yourself!

DIY

♡ Vivienne

"Leonard Peltier is innocent"

Suggestions
Necklace out of safety pins
Badges (preferably with political slogans)
Shawls, blankets, table cloths, curtains, towels, or
a meter of beautiful fabric,
    worn:— a.) enfolded around you instead of
coats & cloaks (plastic sheeting for the rain).
        b.) as skirts, dresses, tops, trousers
                    (pulled thru' legs).
Kerchiefs worn as knickers (good for disco or beach,
or tied up as a bag.
Boxer shorts worn showing as outer wear. (We
offer them in silk or in the same fabric as our jackets)
We also offer
Tie on frill for skirt or cape (made from rectangle
ruched with a cord
Meters of precious silk thrown over ourself
+ attached to our body with hidden strings.
Tubes of knitwear.   = evening swear
Style together with :— Beautiful pieces from your wardrobe
                        (or from that of your mother, child
                            or husband)
Your old favourites — there is status in wearing your favourites
over + over until they grow old (patina) or fall apart.
Beautiful new clothes (expensive) Historical garments.
            → to be continued next season.

We need an estimated $30 billion per year to save the Rainforest $30 000 000

'Clean up or die'

Unofficially crowned 'queen of sustainable fashion', designer and campaigner **KATHARINE HAMNETT**
*was made a CBE in January 2011. Hamnett's collections span four decades, and have been sold in over
700 stores in forty countries. Her influence – from slogan T-shirts to new stonewashing – is widespread.
By Sandy Black*

In 1989 Hamnett launched her campaign for
environmentally and ethically sound practices
in the fashion industry supply chain,
championing the use of organic cotton to
reduce pesticide use and provide better lives for
small-scale cotton farmers and their families.
Her slogan T-shirts, with messages such as
'CLEAN UP OR DIE', found new resonance in
the early years of the 21st century as awareness
of climate change and energy and resource
depletion increased. As Hamnett's pioneering
stance has begun to bear dividends in the
wider fashion community, she has revisited her
archive, relaunching her womenswear fashion
collection for Summer 2011, featuring iconic
signature styles, traceable supply chains and
sustainable materials. These include organic
cotton denim, silk, recycled cotton buttons and
zips made from recycled polyester, processed in
compliance with recent European legislation on
chemicals. The collection, named 'Here Comes
the Sun', aimed to be 'glamorous, elegant,
sexy and responsible, made as ethically and
environmentally as possible'.[1]

Hamnett remains committed to the benefits
of using organic cotton: 'Growing organic cotton
acts as a carbon sink, and the returns are worth
much more to farmers. In addition, they have
greater food security as organic cotton crops are
rotated with food crops.'[2]

Her fabrics come from India, Madagascar
and Turkey. The T-shirts are produced in India
in one of the most advanced socially certified
factories, which has the highest standards
of environmental processing, and state of
the art dyeing and water treatment facilities.
The factory also has social programmes in all
aspects of the community, including women's
empowerment, and has supported 140 schools
across the country, as well as a teachers'
training college and a university.

Hamnett explained her inspiration for
'Here Comes the Sun' in this way: 'We receive
enormous amounts of free energy in the form of

This page and opposite: 'Here Comes the Sun', Spring/Summer 2011 collection featuring updated signature styles from the Hamnett archive.

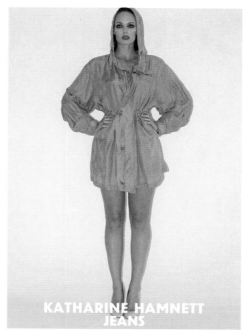

solar radiation, enough to fuel the planet. We should exploit this and stop our dependence on crude oil and unsafe technologies like nuclear. It is important as consumers and voters that we all know the facts, and realize the immense power that we have so that we can do what is needed to save the world. Take action. You can make the difference.'[3]

Reflecting on the progress made in the last five years towards a more sustainable fashion industry, she has said: 'Consumer awareness has soared in the last five years, and industry is going to have to change the way things are done. Consumers are driving change; they are enfranchised – the power to change the world is in their wallets and it is life-affirming. Once people have the information (about cotton growing and pesticides, for instance) and realize the negative environmental impact, their conscience is awakened, and they see it threatens all of us (and particularly their children's futures) – it's not a fashion issue. I can be optimistic because young people are more aware and far more responsible than their parents, and will steer the world in a more responsible manner. The sustainable clothing movement is more open to sharing information and problem solving jointly. Companies such as Tesco are important because it has to happen in the mainstream. These are the pioneers of the next chapter in fashion.'[4]

Nonetheless, Hamnett acknowledges that there is still progress to be made. 'It has to be possible to produce normal exciting fashion sustainably, but price is the big issue. The true environmental cost of clothing manufacture and labour is not being reflected in the price borne by the consumer. Transparency has generally improved, and a new standard ISO 26000 has just been implemented by the US Fair Labor Association Workplace Code of Conduct. It is great if people are buying more fashion – it provides livelihoods – as long as you make it responsibly.'[5]

'Sustainability needs the whole company, a whole supply chain and engaged customers.'

EILEEN FISHER *is a womenswear brand based in New York, with stores in London, selling a range of understated, minimally styled casual clothes that aim to 'give women what they need to relax into themselves'.*[1]
By Sandy Black

Eileen Fisher produces an 'Eco Collection' using organic cotton, linen and denim fabrics, with both cotton and knitwear produced in Peru. Throughout the whole of its range, however, the brand's underlying design principles of simplicity, beauty, comfort, ease, function and versatility prevail. 'We build timelessness into our design process, with shapes and fabrics that connect from season to season,' says Shona Quinn, sustainability leader at Eileen Fisher.[2]

'We recognize that one of the best environmental gifts we can give you is clothes you'll love for years and years. Life cycle is about wear – and care. The greatest environmental impact comes from dry-cleaning shops and home laundry rooms. Most contemporary detergents work perfectly well in cold water, saving on energy. Most of our line is either hand- or machine-washable; our care instructions call for cold water.' Women are the focus of Eileen Fisher's business, and also of the company's philanthropic and charitable work, which supports budding female entrepreneurs and awards grants to non-profit organizations across the US that empower women and build self-esteem.

Quinn speaks about the company's approach to sustainable fashion with enthusiasm. 'To make fashion sustainable means we have our work cut out for us. A first step may be to get to a place when all of our fibres, trims and packaging can safely return to the earth or be melted down to be used again. A second step – create a sustainable production process that does no harm to the environment. This can be challenging when it comes to the dyehouse. A third step would be delving deeper into the wants and needs of consumers and finding ways to shift the "wants" from high-eco-impact products to sustainable products – not an easy task when designers don't have all the tools and materials they need to make these products.'

Quinn sees the work of engineering this shift as a collective task for the whole fashion industry. 'All of the industry players have a

This page and opposite: Eileen Fisher Spring/Summer 2011 collection. Building on core fabrics and yarns each season, Eileen Fisher customers can adapt their wardrobes, combining new with old.

responsibility to create a sustainable fashion industry. Their work can be supported by government incentives – but it shouldn't be the only motivator. Additionally, customers need to educate themselves about the environmental aspects of clothing and purchase products that they feel good about. We need to find innovative ways to express what sustainable fashion is – it can mean many different things and impacts different aspects of fashion design such as materials, style, quality, reusability.... Company leaders can support design teams by understanding and engaging in the challenges that sustainability brings to the designer. But in the end it's not just about a designer – sustainability needs the whole company, a whole supply chain and engaged customers.'

Eileen Fisher herself sees the company's LAB store as an example of how organizations can be creative in furthering their philanthropic mission, even if the economy is tough. 'In September 2009, we quietly launched a unique retail business model called EF LAB. The LAB store is different from our other fifty-two stores nationwide due to its product assortment. It stocks four categories of clothing: our newest delivery of clothing; clothing from past season's collections; samples – designs not available elsewhere (and many not yet in production!); and recycled clothes, starting at $5 (£3) per item.'

The recycled component is what most excites Fisher. 'By mixing pieces from past seasons with clothes in our current collection, it really speaks to the timelessness of the clothing and how many ways you can work these pieces across time, creating more value in each item. To ensure the EF LAB store has inventory in the recycled section, the EF Foundation launched Recycling Rewards, which rewards customers for recycling their gently used Eileen Fisher clothing. Money raised from the recycled garments is distributed to non-profit organizations.'

The design of a new prosperity

SIMONETTA CARBONARO *is an independent consultant and a professor at the Swedish School of Textiles, Borås, lecturing in design management and humanistic marketing.*

When we ponder whether fashion can ever be sustainable, we must first consider that there is no absolute certainty about the complex issue of sustainability, whether in fashion or in other areas. In fact we have not yet even agreed on what we mean when we talk about it. There are many theoretical models and many definitions. One interpretation suggests that true sustainability could be achieved through balancing three pillars: economic sustainability, social sustainability and environmental sustainability. Yet most of the time this tripartite structure is actually in a kind of imbalance because it usually lacks the main driving force of social change: culture – that is, beauty, meaning and the arts. If we do not embed culture into sustainability, and, vice versa, embed sustainability into culture, we are unlikely ever to be able to create a new model of real prosperity.

With regard to the business dimension of fashion, we can at present look to pioneering companies, which by their profit-making nature are part of the economic dimension of sustainability. These companies understand sustainability not as a fixed model, but as a never-ending process of mitigating their ecological footprint and improving their social impact. They are doing their best to find the point of intersection between business needs and environmental and social interests, but balancing these interests with the fact of a growing global population and its attendant challenges to cultural diversity is yet another extremely difficult task! I agree with the great entrepreneur Yvon Chouinard – founder of the outdoor clothing company Patagonia and a pioneer of what we currently understand to be best practices for a sustainable apparel industry – that no company in the world that is based on an industrial model of mass-market production can pretend to be sustainable. To conceive of sustainability as an ordinary corporate goal, rather than as a new state of being, is therefore a problematic aspect of our already problematic industrial mass-market system. The old industrial system is based on the consumption of energy and resources, with the aim of constantly increasing output. Since we know that resources and energy are presently finite, and with no silver-bullet technology on the horizon that would make them infinite – not to mention the absolute parameters of our time and space – we know that the system is not going to work in perpetuity. We have to create a new paradigm. We must understand that any new systems or models that we create and develop cannot be based on a similarly hubristic attitude and single-minded outlook. We must humbly discover what is contained within the message of nature, which has always been able to perpetuate itself, thanks in large part to its diversity. Consequently, we have to begin to consider diversity as one of the primary ways to achieve prosperity.

Yet these businesses alone cannot force us to adopt a new way of living – the responsibility for that lies with all of us. At the moment I believe that there are two main drivers that can effect the 'evolutionary' change necessary for the human race to conceive of prosperity from a holistic standpoint. Firstly, people are starting to understand and acknowledge that seemingly trivial behaviours such as shopping in fact link them with something bigger – the fashion system as we know it – that is endangering their everyday lives, their futures and the futures of their children. This new awareness is gathering momentum all over the planet. It is these 'everyday' people, who want to revive hope in the future, who drive companies, direct governments, and from whom the push will come to make change. Secondly, there are the people I call 'entrepreneurial artist-citizens', who work not just within their presumed cultural territory, but also take social, ecological and economic responsibility for fueling the engine of a postindustrial economy. This new kind of hybrid creative person, whether she or he is working in the so-called fine arts, design or other cultural spheres, is writing the code for a new economy of culture – not a culture of economy. Such individuals also embed in the material and immaterial products they are bringing to the marketplace ideas that go beyond the materialism of consumerism to function as symbols of a better way of life.

The role of design in sustainable fashion is similar to what we now call 'design thinking' in other areas of design. It is a holistic approach to product development that not only is based on life-cycle analysis but also focused on wider anthropological shifts, promoting new meanings and new styles of thought, not just new sustainable lifestyles. In that sense, the real work is that of redesigning design. We have come from a model of modern design that was mainly driven by the 'form follows function' diktat, to postmodern design that seemed to be oriented around the slogan 'form follows fiction', and are now moving towards a new intellectually engaged 'form follows sense' approach.

This is why I think that over the last five or ten years design has been slowly becoming an art again. In the field of fashion, for example, this trend is exemplified by the work of Lucy Orta in France, Sandra Backlund in Sweden, Antonio Marras in Italy, Helen Storey in the UK, and Andrea Zittel in the US. Like artists, the designers of this new generation do not simply respond to or anticipate people's wishes and wants: they actually create new visions of the future, visualizing and giving material form to creations that are not merely things to possess, but embody striving, hope, and meaning in objects that we can see, touch and feel.

What we are talking about here is not simply change but a complete cultural transformation, and in order to navigate it we need to have our minds and spirits activated. This is not just an issue for designers to tackle. We need to embed a new humanism in all the arts, that same creative gesture that artists have given us in the past. There are signs that today's art – art in the broad sense of expressive cultural practices that bring meaning into our lives – is returning to its pre-Enlightenment, pre-industrial humanistic roots, with a new blossoming of artists who are committed to social and cultural transformation. This is what we desperately need.

Yet the acknowledgment that we live in deeply distressed times does not mean that we should allow ourselves to become pessimistic. I have seen many big companies make strides towards sustainability in the last few years that I had never believed would happen. People are pushing even the big corporations to change, and they are changing. This is happening in fashion, in food production and in the construction of our built environment, and we see this increasingly reflected in the way that these and other fields are being taught. Local communities are reinvestigating traditional artisanal modes of production, and small-scale solutions are popping up everywhere. Researchers see these as signs of a wider trend, even if it has not yet become uniformly visible in the mainstream. Some of the more prominent monoliths of consumer culture – such as Walmart – that originally trained us to become hyper-consumers are starting to change their business policies in response to this shift in public opinion. In the case of these very large corporations, even small changes in their production and routing have positive repercussions for our planet that are very significant.

All the companies I have worked with over the last ten years have started to focus on rethinking their value-chain creation, the step-by-step process of designing, developing and marketing products. The most advanced among them have stopped thinking of sustainability as a trend for developing special premium price 'eco' or fairly traded collections; rather, they are embedding sustainability in every level of their business operations and in each activity of their value chains. They aim not to continue the anachronistic process of tweaking products with so-called added-value, but build into their production and products the real values that align with real prosperity.

This is all very good news, but ultimately I think that the breakthrough innovations will not emerge from inside the industrial mass-market production and retail system. The real transformation of the fashion industry will be wrought by the 'majority minority', and will arise out of the vast, diffuse creativity of the many individuals who are courageous enough to attempt to construct the future we thought we had lost.

Everyday fashion

EDWARD BARBER *is a photographer specializing in portraiture. His work is concerned with light, space and environment. His subject matter is often hidden, overlooked, personal or difficult to access. By Sandy Black*

Some say everyday clothing is not fashion – but the choices we make when we get up in the morning and decide what to wear construct our image both for ourselves and for the outside world. Our look is likely to comprise a mix of old and new, high street and high-end brands, dependent of course on available budget. In Western societies we have far more clothes than are physically required simply to keep ourselves warm and protected, so our choice of clothes reflects how we might be feeling, or how we might wish to feel. Is today the day to make a bold statement, wear a carapace, embrace practicality,

or provide a comfort blanket? Do we wish to stand out as an individual or blend into the group? The specific outfits we put together represent an eclectic mix of favourite items, new buys and classic pieces, according to the formality of the context, whether work, travel or leisure.

In this specially commissioned series Edward Barber takes the 'straight-up' portrait as his starting point, a genre that was an innovation in the new fashion style magazines of the 1980s and continues today with publications such as *FRUiTS*. He selected thirteen individuals of different ages,

and photographed them in London locations chosen as appropriate to their daily life, work or leisure activities. Each list of clothes demonstrates a very personal eclecticism and style, a hybrid far removed from the dictates of one fashion designer's 'look'. Occasionally the accessories speak louder than the clothes. Many pieces are timeless, hard to date for the untrained eye, which misses the nuances of cut and proportion that mark the subtle evolution of everyday fashion. These images, although documenting the seemingly quotidian, present new juxtapositions, readings and possibilities.

Left:

Adham
Jacket: Beyond Retro
Trousers: Wrangler
T-shirt: Sunn O)))
Gloves: Gift
Boots: Beyond Retro

Opposite, clockwise from top left:

Bevan
Hat: Jean-Charles de Castlebajac
T-shirt: Tesco
Cardigan: Duffer of St George
Jeans: J. Lindenberg
Socks: John Smedley
Trainers: Vans

Paolo
Shirt: La Renasciente, Rome
Jumper: Cashmere Company
Trousers: M&S
Sandals: Bally

Ashleigh
Jacket: Marks & Spencer
T-shirt: V&A shop
Skirt: Marks & Spencer
Shoes: Hobbs

Nina
Jacket: H&M
T-shirt: TK Maxx
Jeans: Gap Organic
Trainers: Gola

Page 52, clockwise from top left:

Yulia
Vest: Rock & Republic, Bicester Village Outlet
Jeans: Rock & Republic, Bicester Village Outlet
Trainers: Nike

Stef
Hat: H&M
Vest: Stella McCartney for Adidas
Trousers: Adidas
Socks: Sweaty Betty
Trainers: Nike

Sonya
Coat: Top Shop via Leeds Market
Dress: Swedish vintage
Shoes: Paris vintage
Tights: Marks & Spencer

Neil W
T shirt: Kauai Surf Shop, Hawaii
Shorts: Crew Clothing, Padstow
Shoes: Birkenstock
Watch: Omega Titanium Chronograph

Page 53, clockwise from top left:

Neil S
Jacket: Barbour International 1950s
Shirt: American vintage
Jeans: Nudie
Boots: LL Bean
Belt: 1940s vintage

Kieran
Jacket: Burton
T-shirt: Camden market
Trousers: Barnet market
Shoes: Karrimor

Neil B
Jacket: Ralph Lauren
Shirt: Ralph Lauren
Trousers: MacGregor
Trainers: Converse

Nancy
Coat: Marni
Skirt: Marni
Jumper: Lanvin
Boots: Tods
Necklace: Made by a friend in Italy

Continental Clothing

CONTINENTAL CLOTHING *is one of the largest stock suppliers of plain T-shirts and casual clothing, selling 6 million T-shirts per year worldwide.*
By Sandy Black

Below: A typical Continental T-shirt.

Earth Positive Apparel®-Life Cycle Analysis
The total carbon footprint of the Ascension T-shirt over its life cycle (kg/CO$_2$e)

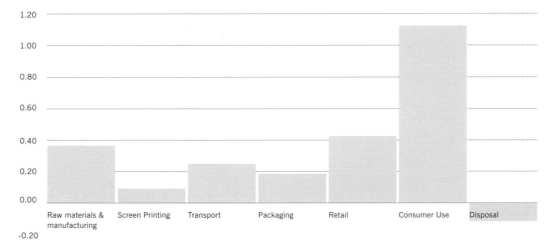

Since 2007 Continental Clothing has pioneered a programme to deliver the 'perfect T-shirt' – cotton T-shirts that are not only sustainably and ethically produced, but also commercially viable at a mass-market level. This range, which currently forms about 20% of the company's production, is branded Earth Positive. As a key stakeholder in the UK government's Sustainable Clothing Action Plan development from 2007 to 2010,[1] the company committed itself to working with the Carbon Trust and the Fair Wear Foundation to achieve Global Organic Textile Standard (GOTS) in producing an organic, ethical, ecologically sound, low-water and low-carbon range of shirts and sweatshirts. Detailed life-cycle analyses were conducted for all stages of production and a completely new supply chain was then set up, which achieved a 90% reduction in carbon footprint. This included the use of renewable energy sources and allowed the company to proclaim Earth Positive apparel as 'the most progressive ethical clothing on earth' – a claim

at least in part endorsed by its industry award for the best organic textile product, received in 2009. However, in line with other studies, the analysis of Earth Positive's environmental impact showed that the consumer-use phase of the average T-shirt (based on twenty-five washes, and including tumble-drying and ironing) almost equalled the carbon footprint of its entire production process, particularly as 46% of wearers used tumble-dryers.

The organic cotton for Earth Positive products is grown and manufactured in India, whereas the cotton used for the rest of Continental Clothing's T-shirts – both conventionally farmed cotton and cotton-in-conversion (to organic) varieties – comes mostly from Egypt and the Aegean. This organic cotton is often blended with other fibres such as bamboo or tencel viscoses for garments manufactured in Turkey in smaller runs and for other fashion lines. Approximately 1 kg of lint cotton is required for each T-shirt, and around 6,000 bales of organic cotton are ordered at the beginning of the harvest.

ASOS

CAREN DOWNIE, *fashion director at ASOS, and formerly of Topshop, explains how a sustainability ethos is being developed at this fast-moving retail environment.*
By Sandy Black

Having started life in 2001 as an aspirational shopping website providing celebrity looks at high-street prices, the online fashion retailer ASOS (As Seen On Screen) has since evolved into a powerhouse of accessible fashions for younger women and men (under 35). One of a new generation of online-only retailers, Asos is now a highly successful destination shopping portal for constantly changing fashions, receiving around 15 million hits per month, offering 600 womenswear brands, as well as menswear and children's clothing. Top-selling items are dresses, shoes and accessories, including jewelry and bags, with some items selling out in a single day. The most visited part of the site is its 'New In' section. The market for transactional fashion websites has continued to open up in recent years, with rival Net-A-Porter vying with ASOS for market share and position, and bricks-and-mortar retailers such as New Look and River Island entering the field. Caren Downie, who joined ASOS in 2008 after

more than nine years as buying director at Topshop, buys in 50% of its brand names from around the world, including Australia, Scandinavia, South America, Spain and the UK. The other half of the ASOS range is developed with an in-house team of twenty-two designers, enabling a speedy four-week sketch-to-product turnaround for items such as sweaters, or three months for a coat. The offerings are still very much celebrity driven – for example, a £50 ring based on a design worn by Victoria Beckham sold 400 pieces in a matter of days. Although ASOS manufactures inexpensive pieces in China, Vietnam, India, Morocco, Romania, Mauritius and Bali, higher-priced British-made goods still sell well, if they are right in fashion terms. Despite having built its reputation on on-trend 'fast fashion', ASOS's product range is far less seasonal than it was a decade ago, as both the recent economic downturn and growing customer concerns about waste have had the effect of increasing interest in 'classic' pieces. This comes as a relief to Downie, who has expressed concern that 'the fashion industry is beginning to eat itself up'[1] with excessively fast turnaround.

As far as ethics of production are concerned, ASOS started from a low factory base, but now audits almost 100% of its factories and joined the Ethical Trading Initiative in 2009. The company aims for continuity of production – with denim from Turkey or China, soft wovens and shoes from China and India, and jersey from all over the world. ASOS stocks ethical brands such as People Tree and Made under its new Green Room umbrella platform, and has its own organic jersey range. However, Downie believes there is still a lot to achieve in educating the customer, in, for example, the difference between 'sustainable' and 'ethical' products. 'The customer is more interested in

fashion and design than in sustainability. It has to be fashion first, but backed up by ethical credibility and sustainable effort.' A special range, ASOS Africa, launched in 2010, is made in collaboration with Kenyan business SOKO, incorporating beadwork and handweaving, providing local people with jobs and training, and education and crèche facilities for their children. However, ASOS customers may not yet appreciate that the range is handcrafted.

Downie feels that the fashion industry is not always given enough credit for its efforts to improve sustainability. ASOS aims to show its customers what they are doing, but recognizes that adequately educating the consumer about ethical issues and sustainability will take perhaps ten to fifteen years. Buyers are now more knowledgeable, but the pressures of maintaining the margins ultimately determine many actions. Despite these obstacles, ASOS ultimately wants to provide a guilt-free shopping experience for its customers.

Left and above: ASOS, Autumn/Winter 2011.

Muji and Uniqlo

NICK CAMBRIDGE *highlights the largely unpublicized sustainable practices of two innovative Japanese clothing companies.*

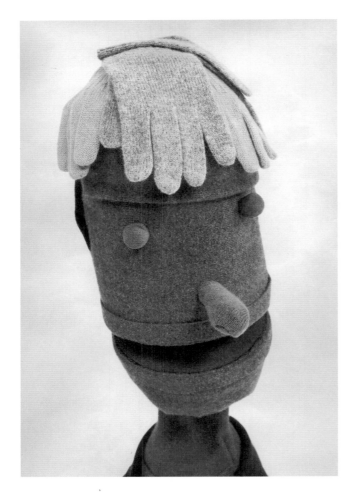

Above: One of the playful marketing images that helped to re-establish Uniqlo in the West, 2009.

Below: Detail of Muji recycled cotton jersey T-shirts, part of its core clothing range.

Opposite: Uniqlo promotional leaflet for its take-back scheme, 2011.

Ask any passer-by in central London where it is possible to purchase Japanese-designed clothes and it is likely that you will be directed to Muji or Uniqlo. In some aspects the two companies appear quite similar. Both draw attention to their Japanese origins while offering the consumer perfectly executed versions of garments derived from the sartorial heritage of the West. Both companies have used sound as a metaphor to describe their design ethos – an executive director of Muji's parent company has spoken of 'reducing the noise'[1] of everyday life through the development of shared values, while the philosophy of Uniqlo's founder is articulated in the slogan 'if the clothes shout louder than the person, then the person cannot be heard'. Somewhat surprisingly, neither has sought to emphasize its 'green' credentials outside of Japan, where their advertising campaigns highlight their use of sustainable technologies, natural fabrics and recycled packaging.

In other respects, the two companies are rather different. Most purchasers of Muji clothing are relatively high earners (generally in their thirties, working in the media-related industries) with a preference for minimalist design,[2] whereas Uniqlo's core customer is the teenage student looking for stylish, affordable casualwear. Muji garments are available in a limited, restrained palette; Uniqlo prides itself on offering an unsurpassed range of colour options. The two companies might almost be said to operate at opposite ends of the binary that typifies Western expectations regarding Japanese creativity, characterized by the melding of traditional values with contemporary technology.

Muji began as an in-house operation at Japan's Seiyu Corporation, developed in response to worsening global economic conditions. Commercial opportunities that lay in the use of simple materials, minimal packaging and efficient production processes were realized in a range of unbranded, quality goods. In 1989 Ryohin Keikaku was set up as an independent company to market a comprehensive range of lifestyle products built around a design ethos of value for money, simple, functional design and understated colour.

Clothing was to be produced without dyeing or bleaching the fabric: colour ranges were limited to natural tones. Two years later, in partnership with Liberty of London, Muji opened in London's Carnaby Street, in a premises incorporating materials salvaged from demolition sites and scrap-yards, reflecting the company's commitment to protecting the environment.[3] (A second London store in Covent Garden retained its original brick wall and sash windows, with a recovered wooden beam serving as a clothing rail.) Muji now offers casualwear in fabrics derived from sustainable and organic sources. Removable linings allow jackets to be used year-round, extending their useful life. A cut-to-size raincoat from the 2006/07 collection appeared to take inspiration from Issey Miyake's A-POC range. The company recycles leftover and discarded yarns from its factories to create a randomly striped jersey fabric, and short fibres collected during spinning and combing processes become a 'rescued' cotton cloth; both are used to make socks and T-shirts. A reduction in storage and transportation costs has been achieved by vacuum-packing some versions of the Muji T-shirt into 2-inch cubes.

In 1984 Oguri Shoji, a menswear wholesaler in operation since 1949, opened an outlet in Hiroshima selling casual clothing intended to be worn by 'anybody, anywhere, everyday'.[4] The Japanese penchant for abbreviations led to the store being named Uniqlo – derived from the English description 'unique clothing warehouse'. Seven years later the parent company changed its name to Fast Retailing, reflecting the commercial approach that underpinned its rapid expansion into one of the largest apparel-makers in the country. Uniqlo now enjoys a reputation in Japan as an 'ethical' company, thanks to policies that include donating clothes to disaster-relief funds, recycling returned garments, supporting the Special Olympics, formulating a code of conduct for its production partners and campaigning against environmental damage caused by the dumping of toxic waste.

In 2001 Uniqlo opened in the UK, targeting customers who might otherwise shop at Gap

In their understated approaches to marketing, both Muji and Uniqlo have been able to suppress the 'noise' associated with fashion by encouraging purchasers of their clothing to express their individuality.

or Marks & Spencer. The company focused on the use of high-quality fabrics in a wide range of colours, which extended to more than thirty options for some basic items. In the UK the company published a free house-magazine called the *Uniqlo Paper*. The first issue featured a piece on the Kaihara denim used in jeans, highlighting the peculiarly Japanese attention to detail displayed by the company's production team of master craftsmen. In 2006 Uniqlo made further attempts to change the perception of the company as a discount retailer, developing a business plan that included publicity campaigns, joint ventures with fashion magazines, designers and celebrities and an overhaul of its retail environments.[5] While Uniqlo exploits the benefits of textile technology – thin micro-fibre tops that are as warming as chunky knitwear, and innovative HeatTech fabric (made from milk protein) that turns moisture into heat – the company's most radical move has been to bring in designer Jil Sander. Despite a vigorous, if prosaic, advertising campaign conducted in newspapers, on billboards and public transport, the company's in-store information did not actually reveal the identity of the 'world-renowned designer' of the Uniqlo +J line. However, the quality fabrics, sharp tailoring and sophisticated shades on offer at selected outlets promised to move the brand into a more fashionable league.

The paucity of coverage that these two environmentally friendly Japanese apparel companies have received in the media may be explained by the lack of sartorial purchase that their clothes are seen as possessing by the fashion establishment. In producing collections consisting of basic items of casualwear, the connotative associations that would attach to more designed garments are largely absent. In this regard, and in their understated approaches to marketing, both Muji and Uniqlo have been able to suppress the 'noise' associated with fashion by encouraging purchasers of their clothing to express their individuality – an aspiration achieved in part through the application of sustainable design principles to their creative outputs.

ALL–PRODUCT RECYCLING INITIATIVE

UNIQLO RECYCLE

IF YOU HAVE UNIQLO APPAREL THAT YOU WISH TO RECYCLE, PLEASE DONATE THEM AT YOUR LOCAL UNIQLO STORE

– Only products sold by UNIQLO are acceptable for recycling.
– Please bring the clothing item(s) you wish to recycle directly to the UNIQLO store nearest you.
– Please be sure to bring both pieces for paired items such as socks.
– Please refrain from bringing in items that are wet or significantly soiled
– Please bring in clothing item(s) that has been washed.

H&M

AMELIA WILLIAMS *explores the efforts of the low-priced global apparel chain to improve its ethical and environmental performance.*

Established in 1947 by Erling Persson, fast-fashion giant H&M (Hennes & Mauritz) has grown into a profitable force in the global apparel market. The Swedish-based company's success is largely a result of its business model of 'fashion and quality at the best price'. In order to achieve significantly lower prices than its competitors, H&M orders huge quantities from its suppliers. To demonstrate that H&M's low costs are not a result of exploiting Third World countries, the company instituted a code of conduct in 1997, which all its suppliers must follow, and maintains inspectors in the countries in which its products are made.

COS (Collection of Style), launched in 2007, is part of the H&M group. It features classic wardrobe pieces for the mid-market consumer who wants 'designer quality at High Street prices'.[1] The collections range from essential basics to stylish cocktail dresses and smart men's suits. It is founded on the same concept as H&M, although its prices are approximately twice as expensive. COS adopted H&M's strong ethical values and the company's suppliers follow H&M's code of conduct.

H&M was ranked the world's 21st most valuable brand in 2010, worth US $16.1 billion.[2] According to a statement from branding consultancy Interbrand: 'The Swedish retailer H&M irreverently mixes high fashion inspiration with bold-print low prices, and demonstrates that it knows the quality of its brand promise is about more than product and price points...H&M takes responsibility for the integrity of its operation chain, from employees to materials.'[3] H&M prides itself on its ethical principles and in 2007 was nominated for *Ethical Corporation*'s top ten most innovative internal sustainability initiatives. Today the company maintains that consideration for people and the environment is key in every aspect of its business.

H&M has taken many steps towards improving its environmental performance. Its 2009 Sustainability Report states that H&M 'aims to minimize impacts at every stage of our products life cycle, from how cotton is grown to the way our customers use our garments'.[4] This is evidenced by the company's use of sustainable materials in its 'Garden Collection' (Spring 2010), which was made entirely of 'environmentally adapted' materials including Tencel, as was its 'Conscious Collection' (Spring 2011). H&M has also expanded its organic cotton range, with the aim of increasing use of organic cotton by at least 50% per year until 2013. So far H&M has exceeded this target, using 3,000 tons of organic cotton in 2008 and 8,500 tons in 2009, but also attracted controversy when lab analysis in January 2010 revealed that some garments labelled certified-organic cotton were contaminated with genetically modified (GM) cotton from India, which also supplies more than half the world's organic cotton. H&M's other environmentally friendly initiatives include recycling hangers, reducing packaging and signing up to the UN Global Compact's CEO Water Mandate.

In 2004 H&M began releasing collections developed in collaboration with leading fashion designers. Designers had a variety of different strategic motivations for collaborating with H&M. For Stella McCartney the collaboration provided an opportunity to communicate her ethical views to a wide consumer audience. This resulted in H&M substantially exceeding its commitment to using organic cotton. McCartney's one-off collection was a huge success in 2005. The high-profile collaborations have continued with Karl Lagerfeld, Comme des Garçons, Lanvin and Versace.

As a global brand, H&M has come to have huge impact on everyday clothing and fashion, and its persistently strong ethical values have aided its popularity. It is incredibly difficult to create reasonably priced, ethically produced fashion but H&M continues to pursue this essential goal through new projects such as Future Fashion, which is funded by the Mistra Foundation, Sweden.

Left: H&M's first 'Conscious Collection', Spring 2011, featuring sustainable fabrics such as organic cotton, Tencel® and recycled polyester.

EJ Foundation T-shirt

THE ENVIRONMENTAL JUSTICE FOUNDATION *works to end child labour and pesticide use in the cotton industry.*
By Sandy Black

The T-shirt is now one of our most familiar clothing items, worn all over the world. Since Katharine Hamnett created her iconic slogan T-shirts in the 1980s, featuring messages such as 'Clean up or Die', the campaigning T-shirt has been used by charities and NGOs to give people a sense of belonging to a cause, proclaiming solidarity, and raising funds and awareness at the same time. The Environmental Justice Foundation's campaign, which works to end child labour and pesticide use in the cotton industry, has since 2007 teamed up with fashion designers, including Katharine Hamnett, Alice Temperley, Ciel, John Rocha, Giles Deacon and Betty Jackson, to create attractive designs on the theme of childhood and lost innocence.

Right: Alice Temperley's T-shirt design for EJF's 'Pick your Cotton Carefully' campaign, modelled by Devon Aoki.

Energy and environmental impact of washing and drying clothing

CHRIS JARDINE *is senior researcher in solar voltaics, microgeneration and energy policy at the Environmental Change Institute, University of Oxford.*

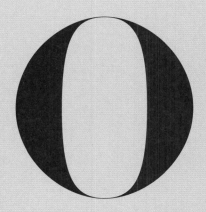nce it has been manufactured and sold, clothing's main environmental impact arises from washing and drying by the consumer. This requires the utilization of energy – which, if fossil fuel derived, will result in the emission of climate-altering greenhouse gases into the atmosphere. It is estimated that the average washing machine uses 270 kWh of electricity per year, and the average tumble-dryer 365 kWh. This compares to an average household electricity consumption of 3300 kWh per year – so each washer or dryer uses roughly 10% of an average household's electricity consumption. Of course, not every house has both – in the UK, for instance 77% of homes own washing machines, but only 35% own tumble-dryers. Nonetheless, the washing and drying of clothes makes up a substantial proportion of a household's electricity use.

In terms of addressing the in-use environmental impacts of clothing, there are a range of options that householders can undertake. First, a washing cycle will use the same amount of energy regardless of whether the machine is full or empty, so there is an environmental and economic incentive always to wash with full loads. Second, a washing machine uses by far the majority of its electricity heating the water (as opposed to operating spin cycles), so energy can be conserved by washing at as low a temperature as possible.

As far as drying is concerned, the most environmentally responsible actions are to dry garments outside on a washing line, or inside on a well-spaced clothes rack. This is reflected in the technological trends in appliance design. Detergent technology has improved dramatically in recent years, enabling lower-temperature washes. Indeed, some new detergents claim to be as effective at 15°C, and hot-fill machines are now rare. It is estimated that reaching the technical limit of washing machines would result in an annual consumption of just 72 kWh per year. We are also seeing higher spin speeds, which although resulting in a marginal increase in energy use in the washing machine, results in drier clothes and much lower consumption in tumble-dryers, should they be used. Tumble-dryers can run off gas, which is a cleaner fuel than electricity, although this technology has not taken off in the UK to the extent that as it has in Europe and the US. In future, tumble-dryers are likely to utilize the more efficient heat-pump technology, with a technical potential of 128 kWh per year.

However, these technological improvements are being offset by social changes – ownership levels of washing machines and tumble-dryers are increasing, and people are washing clothes more often. The latter is a particularly interesting social phenomenon, where people's motivation for washing clothes is now less to remove dirt than to remove smells. This practice results in both higher energy use and a shorter garment lifetime. It may be that a device capable of freshening clothes (the mechanical equivalent of a can of Febreze) could provide the 'garment quality' we require with much lower energy expenditure, allowing washing machines in future to be used more sparingly, solely for removing dirt.

What if the washing machine became a service and not a product?

CLARE BRASS *is the founder of SEED (Social and Environmental Enterprise + Design) Foundation.*

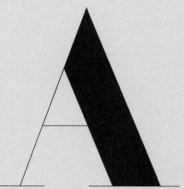

n interesting service initiative has recently been trialled by washing machine manufacturer Electrolux, which, like most companies, normally measures its success in number of units sold. In 1999–2000 the company trialled a project in Gotland, Sweden, to see if it was possible to make money without selling machines. Instead they supplied householders with washing machines at no cost, and then charged them for the individual washes, using 'smart meters' to measure usage, for which customers were charged through their electricity bills. Although a full-scale pay-per-wash system was not implemented by Electrolux following the trial, due to concerns at the time about consumer acceptance of such systems, potential exists for the future.

Here, then, we are approaching a viable solution to the disposal problems of used machines. Because the manufacturer retains ownership of the machine under such a scheme,

A 'pay per wash' system could have a real impact on consumer behaviour, encouraging more responsible usage, prompting the customer to ask basic questions such as: 'Is the machine full?' and 'Do my clothes really need washing at all?'

it has an incentive to design for maximum longevity and ease of repair or upgrade, using materials that can be remanufactured or recycled at the end of the machine's life. At the same time, a 'pay-per-wash' system could have a real impact on consumer behaviour, encouraging more responsible usage by prompting the customer to ask basic questions such as: 'Is the machine full?' and 'Do my clothes really need washing at all?' The initiative puts people face-to-face not only with the washing machine, but also with the electrical system, encouraging changes in behaviour while effectively delivering an identical result. Without nagging advertising campaigns or other forms of hopeful pleading, the likely outcome is a more rational resource use.

The life cycle of denim trousers and its related environmental impact

This life-cycle analysis compiled by Bio Intelligence Service for the French Environment and Energy Agency ADEME in 2006 shows that the greatest environmental impact of denim trousers is in the consumer use and laundry phase.

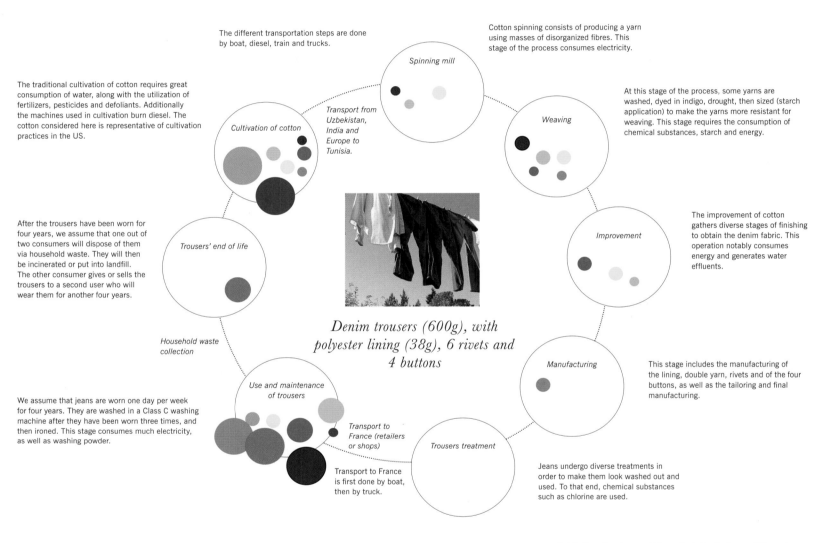

The different transportation steps are done by boat, diesel, train and trucks.

Cotton spinning consists of producing a yarn using masses of disorganized fibres. This stage of the process consumes electricity.

Spinning mill

The traditional cultivation of cotton requires great consumption of water, along with the utilization of fertilizers, pesticides and defoliants. Additionally the machines used in cultivation burn diesel. The cotton considered here is representative of cultivation practices in the US.

Cultivation of cotton

Transport from Uzbekistan, India and Europe to Tunisia.

At this stage of the process, some yarns are washed, dyed in indigo, drought, then sized (starch application) to make the yarns more resistant for weaving. This stage requires the consumption of chemical substances, starch and energy.

Weaving

After the trousers have been worn for four years, we assume that one out of two consumers will dispose of them via household waste. They will then be incinerated or put into landfill. The other consumer gives or sells the trousers to a second user who will wear them for another four years.

Trousers' end of life

Improvement

The improvement of cotton gathers diverse stages of finishing to obtain the denim fabric. This operation notably consumes energy and generates water effluents.

Denim trousers (600g), with polyester lining (38g), 6 rivets and 4 buttons

Household waste collection

Use and maintenance of trousers

Manufacturing

This stage includes the manufacturing of the lining, double yarn, rivets and of the four buttons, as well as the tailoring and final manufacturing.

We assume that jeans are worn one day per week for four years. They are washed in a Class C washing machine after they have been worn three times, and then ironed. This stage consumes much electricity, as well as washing powder.

Transport to France (retailers or shops)

Transport to France is first done by boat, then by truck.

Trousers treatment

Jeans undergo diverse treatments in order to make them look washed out and used. To that end, chemical substances such as chlorine are used.

Environmental indicators:

Climate change
This indicator reflects the emissions of greenhouse gases that are responsible for climate change.

Primary energy consumption
This indicator expresses the consumption of natural energy resources.

Ozone layer depletion
This indicator reflects the damage done to the ozone layer.

Human toxicity
This indicator reflects emissions into the air, water and soil of toxic substances that present a potential risk for human beings.

Aquatic eco-toxicity
This indicator reflects emissions of toxic substances into the water that present a potential risk for fish and other animals.

Water eutrophication
This indicator reflects the potential decrease in aquatic fauna and flora due to excessive growth of algae that consume oxygen; the growth of such algae is facilitated by an excessive concentration of nutrients in the water (especially nitrates and phosphates).

Water consumption
This indicator reflects the water consumption that is directly linked to the trousers' life cycle (irrigation of cotton fields, water consumption during the manufacturing and utilization of trousers).

Production of household waste
This indicator reflects the quantity of waste that is produced as a direct result of the trousers' life cycle (loss of cotton, washing-powder packaging, waste trousers).

Distribution of environmental impacts during the trousers' life cycle:

Contributes between 5 and 9% to the total life cycle

Contributes between 10 and 34% to the total life cycle

Contributes between 35 and 59% to the total life cycle

Contributes more than 60% to the total life cycle

Can fashion ever be sustainable?

SANDY BLACK *Experts from academia, private industry, NGOs and the media offer answers to some of the core questions surrounding sustainability in fashion:*

1 *Can fashion ever be sustainable – or is it a contradiction in terms?*
2 *What are the biggest barriers?*
3 *How should responsibility for sustainable fashion be distributed between consumers, manufacturers, retailers and government?*
4 *What is the role for design towards a sustainable fashion industry?*
5 *Are you optimistic for positive change in industry towards sustainable fashion?*
6 *Can you give good examples of actions taken by companies, small or large?*

Tony Ryan

Pro Vice Chancellor of the Faculty of Science at Sheffield University

1

No, not as it's currently constructed, as something that's disposable. So fashion has to change itself in order to become sustainable.

2

Things being thrown away. Useful things being turned into waste. But the biggest barrier I see is the basic tenet of consumption for the sake of consumption. We should allow things to get old, and we should allow things to be unfashionable without attracting prejudice.

3

It's hard to see where government should come in, because fashion is essentially about choice, so you can really only involve government if you want to limit choice. But government can help in posing the question about how we deal with resources, in a way that then puts the onus on consumers, manufacturers and retailers. If we mandate that we can use only one kind of fabric, buttons or zips to facilitate recycling, then fashion would disappear entirely. But we could say that if we make an article of clothing from polyester, everything in the garment must be polyester so that the whole thing can be recycled, with a similar rule for clothing made of cotton or wool, because the problem for recycling fashion is that everything is made from mixed [fibres] and the labour cost of un-mixing it is much higher than the intrinsic value of the material. The onus needs to be on the consumers, the manufacturers and the retailers, and they should share the burden.

4

Design and marketing are the two gripes of this design- and fashion-challenged scientist. The designer and the marketer create the desire for a product, so there's a lot of responsibility on them to decide for which objects they create that desire. So the question becomes 'How can we create a desire for things that are intrinsically more sustainable?' and 'How can we create value systems that encourage fashion and design to become intrinsically more sustainable?' I want my daughters to ask 'Why are you wearing that? It can't be recycled,' in the same way that they will say 'We're not eating those beans because they've been air-freighted from Kenya.' When we reach that point, then the whole value system will have changed.

5

I'm optimistic because people have come together to talk about these issues – not only activists and academics, but also manufacturers. The role that fashion plays in self-actualization is key. That's never going to go away – people are always going to need fashion – so it's a question of 'How can we challenge that?' How can we make people pride themselves in the fact that the clothes they wear are intrinsically sustainable? I'm very optimistic that the more we talk about these things the greater the positive change we can bring.

6

A good example of positive action taken by clothing companies is converting PET bottles into fleece. I have a suit from Marks & Spencer that I wear every day to work, which is made from recycled drinks bottles. It's not a particularly comfortable suit to wear but it's great that Marks & Spencer sells a suit made from recycled material. There are lots of positive examples like that. I'd much rather have a suit where everything was made from cellulose or PET so that the whole suit could be recycled again into another suit. We've yet to reach that stage but I'm sure we will eventually.

Peter Waeber

CEO of Bluesign Technologies, Switzerland

1

No, because everything we are doing has an impact on the environment. But fashion can definitely be more or less sustainable. The design step is very important; it is this stage that is responsible for good or bad fashion. From a sustainability point of view fast fashion is not such a good thing, and slow fashion is being discussed as a solution for the future; for instance, we create a particular style that is so good that we like it for one or two years. An example of this sort of enduring design is the work of Le Corbusier: he created chairs in 1928 that are still fashionable. We should motivate young designers to create good design. Some designs are just for fun, but if you really like the design you should still have it in your house after four or five years.

2

There are many barriers to sustainability, but what comes to mind is that we do not have enough good data to say definitively 'this is sustainable' or 'that is not sustainable'. We have to develop our instruments, but we also need better data to help designers make the right decisions. You cannot simply tell designers to work only with organic cotton or Tencel or polyester – a designer needs some freedom. However, we also have to give the designer guidance from a scientific viewpoint.

3

That's probably the most complex question. I deal every day with the problem of how to explain the complexity we encounter in the supply chain regarding chemicals. For example, are you talking about risk assessment, water emission or workplace conditions, or using resources in a safe manner? If we are talking not about simple cotton products, but about laminates, or about the shoe business, then all these issues are more complex. It's hard to communicate all this as a simple message at a consumer or governmental level. It's not done with simple marketing. We have to find new ways of communicating, new ways of marketing and new ways of telling the story – and that story must be true and transparent. The younger generation must be willing to work to promote sustainability so that people can make the right decision in future.

4

Design is more than just creating a nice product, a fashionable product. Design involves responsibility: you can no longer just use a nice colour, spot the right trend and make a new collection. A designer today has to deal with much more complex issues – it's a cybernetic system. It's like a spider's web and if you choose a wrong direction, the whole web moves. We can talk about optimizing resources, reducing toxins or whatever, but everything is interconnected. Designers today cannot only be designers; they have to be something of a philosopher. The consumer will be more educated in the future, so a designer has to convey a message that is true and authentic.

There are some designers today who already bring that message to their work and I believe that they will make the changes we need.

5

When I see you the younger generation I have to be optimistic; if I look at the older generation I cannot be. We have to engineer a paradigm shift and therefore we need people with power, people who can think outside the box; we need new energy and new faces and authentic stories.

6

There are a lot of companies that make me happy and that's what drives me to work on this topic. Following the example of Patagonia, there are a lot of clothing companies in the outerwear industry that do a fantastic job. There are also large mainstream companies, such as Nike, who are often given bad press by NGOs and newspapers, but are doing good work in improving their performance on sustainability issues.

LUCY SIEGLE, *ethical living correspondent, The Observer*

Sustainable fashion can exist but I don't think it is summed up necessarily in one handbag or shoe. It will always mean different things for different consumers. Partly it depends on how radical you're prepared to be with your fashion spend and your sourcing. Is your goal to attain maximum wears per piece or do you want to (and can you afford to) buy into real innovation, through cutting-edge fibres? Or you could buy no new clothes at all, just refashion your existing pieces or develop or join a lending library for clothes. I detect some frustration, especially in the media, that 'sustainable' or 'ethical' fashion isn't a simple, homogenized concept, but I find all the variables exciting. The important point is that the producer, consumer and designer all draw a line in the sand and say 'I will no longer accommodate or create clothes that are socially or environmentally exploitative.' After that, it's about using intelligence to avoid the pitfalls. My ideal vision of a sustainable wardrobe is a collection of pieces by designers who each contribute to sustainability with a slightly different emphasis but have the common goal of preserving the health of this brilliantly creative industry.

Per Stoltz

IKEA Green Living project
leader, Sweden

1

Today there are very few products, if any,
that are truly sustainable, but I think
there are clear possibilities to move
incrementally in that direction and
hopefully we will be able to achieve
sustainable products in the near future.

2

The biggest barriers could be our
knowledge of how to make more
sustainable products with existing
technology. Another barrier is the
speed with which we need to transition
to a more sustainable society.

3

Speaking from a corporate perspective we
should be more responsible for creating an
entirely green range and not leave it to
the consumer. I don't believe in having
both a green and a non-green range.

4

Design has a big role in the industry
because it's the stage where you have all
the choices – in specifying materials and
shape, for instance. That's where to bring
in sustainability aspects, at the beginning.

5

I am optimistic because I can see a lot
of things have changed in the last five
years, with many more companies
taking responsibility, many of them
large firms as well, setting examples for
other companies to follow.

6

One good example is the Better Cotton
Initiative: a lot of companies working
together to facilitate a more
sustainable cotton. All these companies
are drivers of change in that industry.

Dilys Williams

Director for sustainable fashion
at London College of Fashion

1

I don't think sustainability has an
end-point. I think it will forever be
evolving, and I think fashion is well
placed to respond to the environment it
is in. It is an expression of ourselves, our
culture and context. So yes, we can be
much more in tune than we currently
are, but we will still always need to
evolve and change our practices.

2

Having been a designer working in the
fashion industry for a long time, the first
big barrier is the definition of fashion itself.
It has been hijacked by a commodity-
based, fast-fashion, low-priced product,
lacking in emotional durability. So I think
that one of the biggest barriers is the
need for a redefinition of what fashion
really is about. If that can be achieved,
fashion is well placed to communicate
and encourage changes in lifestyle and
behaviour. Fashion is a way of exploring
beautiful things so that we can live the way
we want to live.

3

Design has a huge role and when I
think about design I don't just think
about the sketch artist, the pattern
cutter or the production machinist.
Design is every decision that's made
along the whole process, from the
original concept right through
to the way we redesign clothes ourselves
when we are wearing them. The
designers who create the original concepts
play an important role because they
impact on everybody else further along
the line. If you think about any product
design the initial decisions are the ones
that dictate all of the other decisions. So
it's an incredible opportunity, but it's
also a huge responsibility.

4

Fashion involves everybody, so you
can't assign responsibility in one place
or another. There's definitely a role for
designers. I think there's also a role for
each of us to be active as citizens and to
think more seriously about what we
want to say about ourselves through the
things that we wear, and to ask more
questions. Manufacturers in the current
system are very much at the whim of
buyers and designers and they can get
squeezed in the middle. There has to be
shared responsibility along the supply
chain: designers, manufacturers, buyers
and distributors need to come together
and find out where those roles and
responsibilities overlap.

5

I'm optimistic that there's a lot we can
do and the opportunities are out there.
Only ten years ago I could walk into
Première Vision [fabric show] or a
showroom and ask for organic cotton
and people would say that all cotton
is organic. We've come a long way in
the last decade, but we are only just
beginning to scratch the surface and it
will take a lot of stamina, a lot of energy
and some great leadership to continue
the process.

6

There are now many very different
good examples and that is what is
encouraging. There isn't only one
way to do it. At one end of the
spectrum, some great sportswear
companies, from Patagonia to Nike,
are doing certain things that are
appropriate to their business. At the
other end of the spectrum are conceptual
designers such as Hussein Chalayan, or the
company From Somewhere, who are
recycling. There are lots of different
examples and you can't pitch one against
another and say this is the leader to follow.
That's an exciting thing for fashion
designers because each of them wants
to find his or her own way; each wants
to contribute in some way that's better
than current industry practice.

Argentina denim: culture, politics, fashion

GAVIN FERNANDES *is a fashion photographer and art director specializing in portraiture. His work explores the complex socio-political issues surrounding the themes of cultural identity, religion and gender.*

Denim occupies a unique and ubiquitous place in global culture. It is said that at any one time half the world's population is wearing denim. Denim is a textile that both bonds with and expresses the individual through long periods of wearing. Here the iconic Lee denim jacket has been deconstructed, customized and reconstructed by Argentinian student designers (modelling their own designs) in a project conceived by textile designer Kate Lewis and commissioned by the British Council. Photographed by Gavin Fernandes in 2003 in Buenos Aires, using locations specially chosen for their symbolic resonance, these images record individual designers' explorations of national identity, culture, diversity and politics. During a time of economic crisis, when the signs of unrest were evident, with banks protected by metal doors and walls covered with torn political posters, these young designers used denim as a visual language, communicating a narrative through clothing.

This page and opposite: Graffiti and battered metal doors reveal political tensions; a denim jacket becomes a form of armour.

During a time of economic crisis, when the signs of unrest were evident…these young designers used denim as a visual language, communicating a narrative through clothing.

This page and opposite:
Denim jackets that reflect both the nineteenth-century formality of the Recoleta Cemetery (*right*) and the present-day unrest represented by a wall of torn-down election posters (*left*).

Consumer understanding of sustainability in clothing

Excerpts from Public Understanding of Sustainable Clothing,[1] *a report prepared by Nottingham Trent University and Sheffield Hallam University for the UK Department for Environment, Food and Rural Affairs (DEFRA) in 2008. The report explored consumers' attitudes and habits towards purchasing, washing, maintenance and disposal of clothing, and their understanding of sustainability impacts in the clothing life cycle, which was found to be low.*

Recommendations

Improve the public's knowledge of sustainable clothing practices, using the appropriate media.

Integrate information into the retail environment on the sustainability implications of clothing acquisitions, use and disposal.

Build on the 'Wash at 30°C' campaign and consumers' desire for economy to promote good habits in tumble-dryer use.

Encourage clothing skills and awareness for children and adults, including repair, through government departments.

Work with retailers and local councils to increase people's understanding of the reuse of clothing and recycling of fibre in order to divert textiles from the waste steam.

Develop greater understanding of informal second-hand markets and their potential to promote reuse.

Explore opportunities to build people's trust, especially between government, industry and NGOs, develop agreed standards and remove clothing with the most significant impact from the market.

Provide better labelling on the source of products, such as the origin of cotton, and explore options to increase recovery of clothing through 'take back' schemes.

Develop understanding of the motivational characteristics of each environmental behaviour segment and target strategies at these motivations.

Explore options to use fiscal measures and trade policies to promote sustainable clothing.

'I don't get too emotional about clothes after six months.'

Male participant, 62, p. 32

Many people give used clothes to charity, but only those which are deemed to be fit to be sold for reuse; there is little awareness of recycling fabrics. Charity shops and doorstep collections are often seen as the most convenient ways to dispose of unwanted clothes, rather than selling them; when such reuse is inconvenient, clothes are more liable to be thrown away. p. 20

Clothing that is well made and intended to last tends to be associated with quality rather than sustainability. p. 19

Many are aware of the cost of tumble drying, in economic terms more than energy terms, and many use line drying whenever possible. p. 8

Even amongst the most pro-environmental, clothing choices most often derive from considerations of identity and economy rather than of sustainability impact. p. 8

Repair work to clothing is no longer undertaken as a normal, regular activity due to a perceived lack of personal skill and the relative cheapness of new clothes. p. 19

People's rationale for their washing routines often drew from standards of cleanliness, relating to sweat and skin contact, rather than environmental considerations. Some participants were able to make judgments about appropriate washing temperatures from the information provided on labels, for example, by treating the temperature indications as a maximum. Several participants said that the temperature they used to wash clothes was linked to the reason for cleaning them. Clothes with visible dirt or an odour were washed at a higher temperature than those that had been worn but were not visibly dirty. p. 26

'Throw it, if it's ready for the bin, the proper bin, not recycling. It's good riddance, you know? You sort of feel yourself physically throwing it.'

Female participant, 20, p. 37

Many people, particularly in younger age groups, purchase cheap, fashionable clothing from low-budget retailers, fully aware that it will not last long in a reasonable condition. p. 8

Fashion and cheap clothing influence clothing choices, but have different impacts on consumers depending on their life stage. Participants from all segments reported buying cheap clothes and being influenced by fashion to varying degrees at different stages of their lives. There was little evidence of environmental concern moderating this behaviour, though there was a sense of weary resignation to fashion trends ('all that nonsense'). It would be wrong to assume that all consumers are 'dupes' of the fashion system. People appear tactical in their clothing acquisition in ways that give them some creative ownership of the process of shopping for cheaper fashion items. p. 63

Even among consumers with a positive general orientation to pro-environmental behaviours and some understanding of sustainability impacts, clothing choices most often derive from considerations of identity and economy rather than sustainability impacts. p. 8

'I personally think it's a bit like going down the road to being vegetarian. I think if you had to go this way, you would have to stop buying everything to be guilt free.' Female participant, p. 42

'You need to learn about these things, be educated about what is happening and how you can change things. If you choose not to do that, that's fair enough. But I can guarantee you that if more of that is in the media and we learn more about fair trade and what's happening to these people and pesticides and stuff like that... even if one person changes their opinion, that's one person more.' Male participant, p. 47

While individuals might know which clothing habits are 'good' from a sustainability point of view, they do not necessarily act on this knowledge. People may behave in a pro-environmental manner, such as line-drying and using charity shops, but this may merely be an advantageous side effect of their 'normal' routines. p. 63

Desire
and fashion

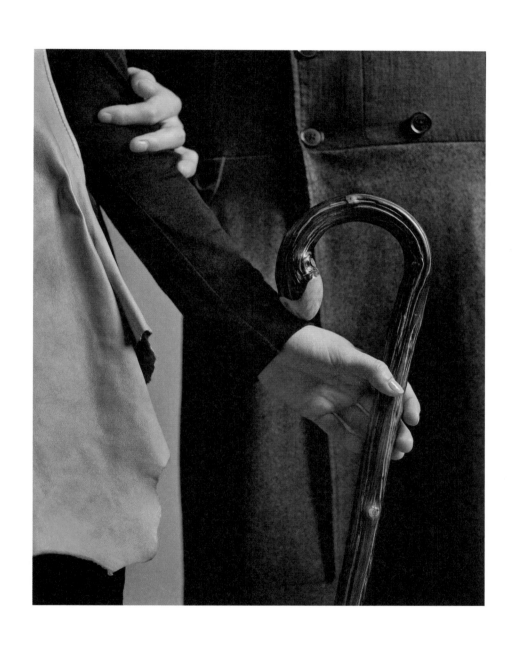

Design and
innovation

Fashion design innovators

Fashion design processes

Preceding pages: Yohji Yamamoto womenswear and menswear, Autumn/Winter 2008, styling and photography by Gavin Fernandes.

Fashion creativity and education

Innovative designers are the life-blood of the entire fashion industry. Such designers lead trends, shift paradigms, shatter preconceptions and create new aesthetics of beauty. The ripples of innovation are often felt over years or even decades. At the same time, novelty for its own sake is a criticism often levelled at both the fashion and product-design industries. Although the pursuit of novelty is vital in keeping industry wheels turning, as consumption rates and production volumes have increased exponentially, the rate of turnover has clearly become unsustainable.

It is essential to embed sustainability into all the stages of the design process at macro and micro level, and we need new design thinking to formulate innovative ways of making and consuming fashion. Education plays a key role in raising awareness: by building sustainability into the curriculum at all levels, we can train the emerging generation of designers and industry players to question the status quo and contribute towards the radical change for sustainability required across the developed world. In this chapter, essays by Dilys Williams and Frances Corner examine the new contexts and approaches necessary for fashion education to support such radical change. The essays, and interviews with design innovators such as Hussein Chalayan and Dai Fujiwara, also examine the role of the designer and the realities of design processes within small and large companies, including Bless, Timberland and NAU. Tools to support designers to consider sustainable life-cycle issues within fashion are beginning to be developed, both in academia and in the industry. Recent initiatives such as the Sustainable Apparel Coalition in the US, and Nike's Considered Materials Index have potential for significant impact in the sector.

The spread of branded designer fashion has become a significant part of the global economy, branching out to include accessories and perfumes. The ethos of the designer-brand and luxury-goods industry, and the relationships between the various companies, are further discussed in Chapter 4.

'Understanding nature, how we relate to it, and understanding our bodies better is key in making progress in terms of sustainability.'

Part-artist, part-sculptor, part-showman, part-fashion designer, **HUSSEIN CHALAYAN**
discusses the importance of innovation for the future of sustainable fashion.
By Sandy Black

Above and opposite: Hussein Chalayan
'Inertia' collection, Spring/Summer 2009.
Inspired by the dynamics of air flow, the
collection uses moulded latex to give the
appearance of dresses freezing in motion.

Since launching his own label in 1994, Chalayan has twice been named British Designer of the Year and retrospective exhibitions of his work have been staged at the Gröningen Museum in the Netherlands (2004), the Design Museum in London (2009) and the Musée des Arts Décoratifs in Paris (2011). Chalayan's pioneering approach to fashion draws on fields as diverse as anthropology, science and technology, as well as his personal philosophy. His fashion shows, installations and film collaborations are memorable spectacles that often comment on the human situation and political issues, expressing concepts such as displacement, trans-migration and transformation, through precise, visionary choreography of effects provided by an impressive range of collaborators and technical experts. Funding such conceptual performances and exhibits is a struggle for any independent fashion designer to sustain while maintaining a viable business. For this reason Chalayan has periodically undertaken consultancy for external brands and designed theatre costumes. In 2009 he entered a new partnership phase to become creative director of sports brand Puma, part of the PPR Group.

Q Does the concept of sustainability have a place in your development process?

A Sustainability is a big subject. The kind of fabrics we use don't really exist in a sustainable form. You can find basics, like cotton poplins, and jerseys. But anything beyond that just doesn't exist and is so expensive. We are still not part of a system where we can benefit from more elaborate but sustainable fabrics. So the only way I can contribute is if I start a new project myself, working with developers to create my own fabrics, as one-offs. But of course it is still not realistic to think of doing the whole collection this way; it is not cost-effective. You need more people in the industry to get together for sustainability to happen on a bigger scale. Right now it is all happening on a boutique scale. At the moment I am working on a project with Puma that will involve sustainable fabrics and hopefully create jobs in Africa.

It would be good to see the day when we don't have to think separately about these issues. The influence of designers should not be underestimated, do you agree?
Yes, we are role models. And we are scrutinized. I eat organic food; why shouldn't I wear organic cloth? But even organic food is not always convenient or possible to consume. It has probably taken fifteen years for food but I hope we can move faster in fashion.

Are there tensions between the innovative and commercial aspects of your work?
'Commercial' is a nullifying word. Anything you can use I find worthwhile. If you are confident enough to wear a chain around your neck, that is your choice. What I propose as a designer is to connect gaps in the world. You can always carve a niche in the market by doing what has been done, but I always wanted to do something different. My graduation collection ['The Tangent Flows', 1993] was based on a story I wrote and each piece represented a part of the story or re-enacted parts of it. The clothes become the components of the story or its residue.

There is a strong narrative and thematic conception in your work. Do you ever get inspired by stories related to ecology and sustainability?
I have all-encompassing projects that people read in different ways. I had a project that was about climates, but it wasn't about sustainability. It was about how the body is like a climate; about life- and death-cycles.

I think people are more careful about what they put in their bodies than about what they wear. There is a lot more going on in organic food than in textiles. What you put inside your body is much more intimate and immediate and it affects your health. When you wear something your ultimate goal is to look good to yourself and to others, to feel good and confident, to feel cool or warm. How you feel is reflected in how you look, just like you feel about your food – you are what you eat. So can you say that you are what you wear? When I think of this, I always think of Japan, where there is a real affinity with nature, [and] the way they shape nature is so high-tech. One of the best ways of becoming more in touch with nature is to abandon our urban lifestyle every now and again.

Far left: Hussein Chalayan for Puma Black Label, Urban Swift Shoe (inspired by Chalayan's 'Inertia' collection), Autumn/Winter 2011.

Left and opposite: Hussein Chalayan for Puma, 'Urban Mobility' collection menswear, womenswear and footwear, Autumn/Winter 2011, featuring angular lines inspired by camera shutters and overlaid X-ray photographic imagery.

A lot of the time people cannot see how our realities are connected. I think that we need to be re educated to understand those connections and then. maybe. we would be able to rebuild what we have around us.

If you think about Japan, they have limited resources and because of this they had to become more inventive. One way to become more inventive is to reduce the number of ingredients you use. Japan has been successful because they always had to use this technique. Good technique is not just about being high-tech and digital; It is more about being creative, and how you use the resources you have at your disposal.

A lot of my work becomes a prototype or an art project. Some of the digital things I do take a very long time to develop. I would love to take my digital dress idea further. In the past I have tried to work with magnetic fabrics, and it would be great to become affiliated with a lab so that I could achieve this. A lot of the time I am using technologies that do not have much to do with fashion, and the people who know about these technologies tend to be scared of fashion. I find that Scandinavia is much more open-minded in this respect than the UK, Germany, the Netherlands or even the USA, where the willingness for risk-taking is no longer present.

My digital dresses would need a lot more time to be developed beyond art projects into wearable objects. I would love to do this, but I have no resources to pursue it. A big company could come along and take the idea as their own and develop it much further. This is not about my ego, but about

making a dream come true. My goal is to make a real-life contribution, such as somebody being able to open their jacket and see a video message from their child, or creating a garment in which the lining or outer colour can change. Or a garment that can interact with the environment. But an LED specialist is not a fabric specialist, and it takes large teams to accomplish something like this.

You have generated more experimental fashion concepts than anybody else I can think of. Your shows have always been spectacles – is this something you feel you now have to do every time?
I am a very curious person. I like to discover new things, constantly move on. But I don't want my ideas to remain just as prototypes. At the moment I am the person who comes up with ideas while other people make them happen, but why shouldn't I be the one who can make them real, in practical terms?… I can do that with my ideas for clothes but it is different when it is technology-based because the timescale is much greater, and you need people and investment.

If you have to choose only one way you would like to move forward, what would it be?
Motion dresses and video dresses. The video dresses were about climates – one was about the undersea

world, with fishes swirling around; one was about summer and another about spring, so you had repeat cycles of opening and closing [see p. 315].

It all started with remote-control dresses, which were at the time very innovative ideas.
Yes, that's where it all started. They were ideas I knew would not be real. Before them was the airplane dress, which led to the motion dress.

The next step is actually to have fabrics in which everything is inbuilt. We had a complex corset structure that controlled everything. It was a lot of work and it was really expensive.

Isolation, as in Japan for example, is a key state for creativity and invention to take place. It is very important to spend time on our own, to think on our own, and be detached observers of behaviour. For me they are very much related to creativity. And finally you need to communicate because you need to interact. But ultimately I think that understanding nature and how we relate to it, and understanding our bodies better are key to making progress in sustainability. I think we are detached from our bodies. It starts with food, because if you don't love food you don't love life. I don't know anyone who is interested in design and beauty who is not interested in food. It all goes together.

Fashion should go with that because it is a way of living. It is about love for life. In order to understand your body, you need to spend time in water; you need to swim. You need to take walks in mountains; you need to eat fruits and vegetables; you need to smell the plants; you need to have sensory experiences. This is something that is more often present in the Mediterranean culture. I go a lot to Istanbul; I like going there because it still has a sensuality that feeds you. You can eat stuffed vine-leaves or artichokes. When artichokes grow, they make noise, a crackling noise, that you can hear. Or you can climb up a fig tree.

So is this where you draw your creative ideas from?
Yes, I am an emotive designer but I am also a rational designer. I think emotive has to come first.

Then I try to make rational sense of it. So I would like to relate to clothes more in the way I relate to food, for example. I don't always want natural-looking fabrics; sometimes I don't want a linen shirt because I think it's too rustic. In Japan you can look at a fabric and think it's synthetic but it's actually natural, and that is interesting to me.

How can technology come into this and make things happen?
Technology can allow you to maintain a certain level of isolation while also communicating your ideas. Also, the only way I can make some of my dresses real is to involve experts in different technologies: a mechanical engineer, an electrical engineer, a programmer, someone from the automotive industry and maybe someone who works with conductive fibres.

How do you feel about the fashion industry?
I work in fashion but I am not really in it. Does that make sense? I wouldn't say that I am in the fashion industry. I am a kind of outsider, not out of my own choice.

Is this because you don't think of your brand as a profit-led business?
Of course I do. When I was younger, I was very naïve – I had an idea I wanted to pursue and that was all. Even today I hate the idea of depending on someone. But the only way to move forward is through partnership. We need a great deal of investment. Hardly any designer of my generation doesn't have a partner. The idea of the partnership is to move on but not necessarily to do it in expected ways.

Your shows are spectacles; they get a lot of press attention.
This can sometimes be a hindrance as well. We don't make huge profits but people do buy and wear our clothes and they keep them for a long time. There is a sense of timelessness to them.

So your designs are 'slow fashion'?
That's a very good way of putting it. I am interested in processes because processes inspire what we do. You can think of fabrics in a more creative way. Working with electrical wire is as important as working with seaweed. Or working with the two together. The choice that you make in using something in place of a natural substance could lead to a very innovative result. It could be creatively sustainable. So we should think of creative sustainability, not just logistical sustainability.

One of the most interesting angles in your [sustainability] concern is the idea of designers understanding how things work. Designers should look into physics, geometry, maths and drawing, then think about how and what we could be doing with basic ingredients in their raw form. Some things may seem irrelevant, but they are not. A lot of the time, people cannot see how our realities are connected. I think that we need to be re-educated to understand those connections and then, maybe, we would be able to rebuild what we have around us.

'I have endeavoured to experiment to make fundamental changes to the system of making clothes.' Issey Miyake[1]

*A highly skilled textile designer, **DAI FUJIWARA** joined the Miyake Design Studio in 1995, working closely with Issey Miyake to develop the revolutionary A-POC manufacturing process. Between 2006 and 2011 he was creative director of Issey Miyake Inc. By Sandy Black*

From 1997 Dai Fujiwara was instrumental in the development of the groundbreaking A-POC ('A Piece of Cloth') concept, first launched in 1998 and shown at La Fondation Cartier in Paris. The radical innovation was to conceive and programme the outlines of garment pieces within a tubular warp-knitted fabric structure, lines which joined back and front together to form a three-dimensional shape when opened out. This process completely eliminated the need for cutting out and sewing garment pieces, creating a single-step process of manufacture. Garments, and sometimes even entire wardrobes, were made from the cloth, which did not unravel and could be customized, eliminating waste and minimizing labour and processes. As the success of this concept developed, a new paradigm for clothing was created, which was then applied to double-cloth woven fabrics. Innovative and experimental designs were continually produced, in knitted and woven form, including denim jackets and jeans. In 2006 Fujiwara was appointed creative director of all the Issey Miyake brands. He set about integrating the A-POC concept into the main production processes, under the label A-POC INSIDE.

Q With A-POC INSIDE, is A-POC still a work-in-progress or has it now matured?

A Since Autumn/Winter 2007 A-POC has been integrated into the Issey Miyake brand. It is not just a clothing line; it is a specialized philosophy

Left: Issey Miyake, A-POC woven double-cloth denim skirt and trousers, Autumn/Winter 2007.

Opposite: Issey Miyake, 'Queen', featuring innovative tubular warp-knitted clothes cut straight from the roll of fabric, from his A-POC 'King and Queen' collection, Spring/Summer 1999.

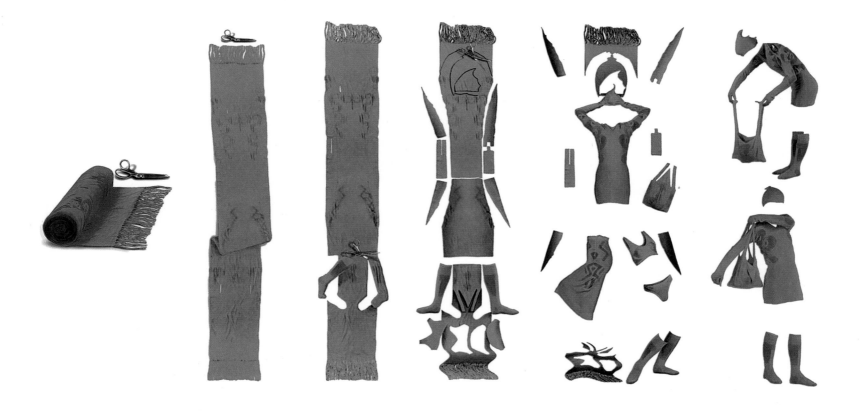

and a design solution. The application of the A-POC system to the mechanics and clothing production of the Issey Miyake women's and men's lines will revitalize each, adding a burst of energy and sparkle. A-POC is paradoxical: it is both an industrial product produced in a high-tech environment and a sensuous craft product made by human hands.

How do you help your customers understand the A-POC INSIDE concept?
Clothes produced by the A-POC INSIDE technique have its logotype stitched onto the label, so you can easily identify them. But we don't make a sales promotion tool to let our customers know how A-POC INSIDE clothes are produced, as we did with the former A-POC brand. At present our customers know what the technique is and our shop staff explain the concept to our new customers.

Some time ago you said that eventually knit and weave might merge closer together. Is this coming true through the latest technology?
New materials and improved spinning techniques have made an impact. However, knit and weave still seem to be holding onto their own territories.

What are your creative goals for the different Issey Miyake ranges?
Issey Miyake is a brand that encompasses both goals and beginnings. I think it's very powerful to continue to make modern clothes that express the concept of value built up in the past.

You have collaborated with some unusual partners, such as James Dyson. How have you benefited from this type of collaboration?
I was satisfied with the result of the collaboration with Mr Dyson in terms of both business and creation, since we received a great response and sold more than expected at the stores. I'm sure that Dyson has had a profitable result as well. If you respect each other, there are no boundaries among scientists, politicians and teachers.

Our natural resources are limited. Do environmental concerns play a role in your creative direction? How much do you think the fashion industry should respond to these concerns?
Consumption of fashion changes as time goes by. The problem is not the amount of change in fashion but whether or not the quality of fashion needs to change. Fashion has a power to spread information among people. If we put environmental issues at the centre of the capitalist structure, I think there might be a chance of bringing about a good result. Environmental issues are very important to me. The Issey Miyake brand has always had its own philosophy of cherishing nature.

How would you like to see fashion/clothing twenty or thirty years from now?
Each person has preferences. That means that there are millions of different inclinations. While fashion tries to meet the expectations of consumers, they get tired of fashions very quickly. In the new framework of trading, cheap places of

production are preserved by private companies rather than by governments. They are producing goods for the trend market. Under industrial capitalism, enterprises will be pushed to the edge. Since fashion has a long history, the know-how of people buying clothes and the industrial structure that supports it will all be sorted out via revolutionary distribution network all over the world. The various problems of copying designs and design rights will be forgotten in the wake of the World Wide Web. The new global rules that were created to protect the environment and conserve energy will have the effect of creating important new legal restrictions and personal values. Fashion clothing that makes people happy will be the most important thing.

'What keeps me awake at night is being forced to make the compromises we have to make.'

GALAHAD CLARK, *a seventh-generation son of the British shoe-manufacturing dynasty Clarks, has pioneered new approaches to footwear through product innovation and sustainable design.*
By Sandy Black

All images these pages: Shoes from the United Nude range, photographed by Maria Downarowicz.

Above: 'Mono Jane' shoe, moulded in one piece, and 'Möbius' boot.
Opposite above: 'Eamz' pump with cantilevered heel.
Opposite below: 'Fold' shoes made from a single piece of nylon elastic fabric.

Galahad Clark is managing director of VivoBarefoot, launched in 2004, one of several footwear brands he has been involved with. In 2002 he redeveloped Terra Plana, the artisan-made sustainable footwear brand. Although VivoBarefoot, which was born out of Terra Plana, has been trading for less than ten years, it already has an influential presence in the international footwear market, with five retail shops in London and Brighton, one in New York, worldwide franchises and a significant online presence. Clark and VivoBarefoot take a holistic view of the entire life cycle of footwear production and seek to minimize the environmental impact and enhance the social benefit of their products. The majority of the firm's production is based in China, under the careful scrutiny of Clark, who is a Chinese speaker. Sustainable product development is key to Clark's ethos, and a practice he develops for external companies as an independent design consultant.

VivoBarefoot also includes several other affiliated companies and associations, and its reach is therefore significant for a relatively small business with an annual turnover of only £10 million (but growing fast). The brand Worn Again, originally developed by Terra Plana in collaboration with the Anti-Apathy campaign, is now managed by Cyndi Rhoades of Anti-Apathy, and focuses on the upcycling and reuse of waste materials such as denims and corporate wear, including Eurostar train employees' uniforms (see p. 259). Another affiliated brand is Soul of Africa, which has been developed to provide employment and practical aid to impoverished African communities that are also grappling with the effects of AIDS. Its shoes are produced from local materials with hand-stitching and only minimal glue. The brand is sold primarily by Clarks but has also been taken up by other large British retailers, such as Next, so far raising £1.2 million (US $2 million) for charitable causes in Africa. New designs are currently being developed to enhance the brand's appeal and move its products further into the mainstream market.

Perhaps the most interesting brand with which Galahad Clark is involved is the United Nude (UN) label – a design-led range of innovative high fashion women's footwear. United Nude has six stores and six further franchises worldwide. Creative direction for United Nude comes from Clark's architect partner Rem Koolhaas, who brings analytical design to fashion-product development, transforming shoe design and production. United Nude is consequently known for radical designs that do not respond to seasonal changes in fashion; rather, they offer perfectly developed solutions to major issues in shoe production, and are design classics in their own right. The brand's well-known 'Möbius' shoe, for example, is crafted from a one-piece sole, heel and upper inspired by the mathematical phenomenon of the twisted Möbius strip. First launched in 2003, its sales have continued to increase steadily.

Shoes can have over a hundred components, and attempting to ensure that the entire product is ethically produced and environmentally friendly is a difficult problem to address, as is the very premise of an eco-friendly shoe company in the first place, as Clark admits, 'You have to get used to horrendous contradictions in fashion – how can we run an eco-business and keep pumping more shoes into the world?'[1] The United Nude approach shows a way forward. When comparing the sustainability of a United Nude shoe with a Terra Plana shoe, it is perhaps surprising to find that the United Nude shoe invariably creates a lower environmental footprint, scoring better on VivoBarefoot's in-house eco-matrix. For example, a Terra Plana shoe made from hemp, using minimal glue and stitched construction, featuring a PET mesh lining and a healthy (flat) heel design, scores worse than the United Nude high-heeled, fully moulded 'Mono Jane', which is made entirely from synthetic

materials. The United Nude shoe is much more energy efficient, especially as it is lighter and easier to ship around. It is also created from only one material, which facilitates possible recycling; it lasts longer than a hemp shoe and, as it is assembled from only four components, it requires less effort and energy to manufacture, compared to the typical shoe that can require nearly 140 separate operations to produce. This runs contrary to what many people automatically assume is 'environmentally friendly' manufacturing – the mantra that 'natural is best' is not always correct. Despite its excellent 'green' credentials, however, no environmental claims are made publicly for United Nude products, as its shoes are intended to appeal to the consumer solely on design and aesthetic grounds.

The Terra Plana eco-matrix scores each shoe product on five different aspects, which are based on a typical life-cycle analysis: 1) how difficult it is to make; 2) efficiency of production and number of components; 3) the materials used in the upper; 4) good design and appearance; and, most importantly 5) comfort. These aspects are all highlighted on the company's packaging.

End-of-life is a major problem for shoes and one of the fashion industry's major sources of waste. At present 20 million pairs of shoes are sent to landfill annually in the UK alone. Research is underway to create efficient and non-toxic incineration and gasification processes to reclaim energy from trainers, but fashion shoes, which typically incorporate internal metal shanks, still pose obstacles to recycling. VivoBarefoot's current projects therefore include designing for better reparability and producing an easily recyclable shoe made of cardboard.

Ultimately, however, Clark aims to create new footwear icons. His favourite classic shoes include the original 1947 Clarks desert boot (a comfortable shoe with only three components, which now include a recycled sole), and the iconic Dr Martens boots (which are fully stitched, durable, abrasion resistant and comfortable). As Clark often says, 'good design is sustainable design'.

'As climate change becomes ever more obvious and pressing, consumer tastes will trend more strongly towards sustainable choices'

PETE LANKFORD *is creative director of Timberland, which several years ago decided to launch an ecological line of footwear.*
By Sharn Sandor

Q Could you tell us a bit about your role in Timberland's efforts to improve sustainability?

A Several years ago Timberland decided to launch an ecological line of footwear. Like most companies engaged in creating greener products we began quite naturally by focusing hard on the variables we could reduce or remove: boosting recycled content in base materials, sourcing regionally, and choosing reduced-energy manufacturing processes. In short, we pursued a strategy of reducing our carbon footprint; making incremental improvements by creating less waste and making more efficient use of materials. But a strategy of incremental improvement is not necessarily a powerful message that resonates with consumers. If I don't persuade you to pick my shoe over the competition's less-green offering, then all my company's green efforts don't mean a thing. Effective design communicates to users clearly and powerfully in a simple – and therefore understandable – manner.

Above: A typical Timberland Earthkeepers™ men's boot.

I work as both a creative director and a practising designer at Timberland and head up our green design efforts, which are showcased via the Earthkeepers™ collection. Effective design has never been more challenging. We live in a world that is interlinked, complex, and dynamic…This is especially true of green or sustainable design where each choice (alone and as part of a whole) affects the outcome. Having trained as a product designer I am biased, but I believe that good designers and their designs not only mirror users' desires (as fashion often does) but can also lead in establishing new directions.

The nature of choice, and the desire for individuality, guarantee that no single direction will meet everyone's expectations. A certain percentage of fashion can be sustainable but this will depend heavily on shifts in cultural taste. Fur, for example, used to be very popular and was a sign of luxury. Times have changed – with some nudging by PETA (People for Ethical Treatment of Animals), as well as cultural drift, fur has become a self-consciously antagonistic fashion choice. As climate change becomes ever more obvious and pressing, consumer tastes will trend more strongly towards sustainable choices. At some point, unsustainable products will quite suddenly seem wrong – this is exactly what occurred with the Hummer.

At Timberland, at least for the present, I work under the premise that 'green' is a free gift with purchase – that is, you cannot ask the consumer to compromise on style, price or quality when offering a green alternative. We have adopted a product strategy called Design for Disassembly (DFD). This means the shoe has been constructed in a way that allows it to be taken apart after it's useful life as a shoe is over.

How should responsibility for sustainable design be distributed between consumers, manufacturers, retailers and government?

'Responsibility' suggests a certain degree of sacrifice in the service of collective good. Only government is able to set a level playing field via rules that everyone is obliged to abide by: lead-free toys are an example of this in action. So I think governments can and should set the tone around sustainable goods much more deliberately than they have already. The inconclusive outcomes of the Copenhagen climate summit in 2010 suggest that government representatives are not yet ready to act boldly and decisively around climate change.

Dropping down a notch on the hierarchy of responsibility and influence is the business community. Businesses come together around expert collective action. If they are headed up by the right person, businesses can direct their expertise towards sustainable ends. The trick, of course, is to do so while not compromising the bottom line. The Toyota Prius is probably the best-known example of a company managing to 'thread the needle', so to speak. Beyond selling a good car that addresses environmental issues, the Prius has become a powerful symbol for the Toyota brand and thus has a positive effect far beyond its direct contribution to the company's bottom line.

What is the role for design in creating a sustainable fashion industry?

It begins with the personal. I think defining the role of design starts with yourself and what you believe is important. Then you extend your convictions to action, whether it be in the designs you create or the larger ripple effect you may have by raising the standard of what is considered acceptably green. I consider myself a pragmatic idealist. By this I mean that I don't hold much faith in the will, good-heartedness and sustained effort of large organizations to solve this problem (or any problem) that extends beyond their own defined self-interests. Too often organizations such as BP, Monsanto or Union Carbide are caught by a catastrophe that exposes their real motivations, but the same criticism can be applied to governments and special-interest groups as well. What I do have faith in are individuals – and by extension, small groups of committed people – to effect change from the bottom up. Ideally I envision an ongoing

Above: Timberland promotional image, 2011.

Designers are T-shaped

esigners are basically problem-solvers whose skills have, up until now, been nurtured to solve industrial and commercial problems. We now face some of the biggest and most wicked problems we have ever encountered. Economic growth is all well and good so long as there are enough material and human resources available to sustain it. Our wellbeing is not only about material goods, but also about happiness. What we can do as educators is to enhance the valuable skills that designers have and get them using those skills to redesign not only the products that we buy but also the lifestyles that we live and the systems that organize our lives. Designers can do this if we brief them to do it: they are 'T-shaped', as Tim Brown of [global design firm] IDEO says. 'They [designers] have a deep knowledge in one field, but every project they do forces them to branch out… They are able to explore insights from many different perspectives and recognize patterns of behaviour that point to a universal human need.'[1]

CLARE BRASS, *'Sustainable Design Is Just an Educator's Fantasy', symposium address, London, July 2010*

conversation between design professionals who care about sustainable fashion and consumers who seek out sustainable designs – this 'conversation' would happen via the designs themselves.

Do you have any examples of effective actions?
Probably the most effective and powerful actions are those that change the conversation. Sometimes that is accomplished by abruptly raising consumer expectations (Google comes to mind) and other times by completely restating the problem. A couple of examples: the Prius is not a powerful product because it is going to save us from ourselves singlehandedly, but because it subtly suggests you can have a 'normal' car and still go green. It also slyly begs the question 'Why wouldn't you buy a hybrid?' The result? All the other major auto companies are now frantically releasing hybrids and competing in a 'who's greener' game that didn't exist a decade ago. That's powerful. Timberland is doing a good job with its Earthkeepers™ 2.0 programme. Designing for a shoe's 'next life' has meant simplifying the design on the front end because every part that is put together during manufacturing must be able to come apart later for recycling.

The discipline of simplicity has had an unexpected benefit: helping the supply chain reduce its own carbon footprint. By keeping designs simple in concept and expression, the DFD collection makes a clear impact on the consumer; it is durable and attractive in design and, most importantly, it raises the bar on what it means to be truly green. This is not to say that the work has been easy – it hasn't – but when we get them right, simple solutions have the potential to change the game.

Sustainable fashion and textile design

REBECCA EARLEY *is reader in textiles at Chelsea College of Art, University of the Arts London, and coordinator of the Textiles Environment Design (TED) project.*
By Sandy Black

Below: Emma Rigby, 'EnergyWaterFashion', MA graduate collection featuring designs to encourage reduced energy and water use, London College of Fashion, 2010.

It takes a huge shift in the way we live our lives to be sustainable. But I am optimistic. As academics we have to inspire students and drive new projects. We need to create ways in which to measure the impact of projects and ideas that we are developing for the future. A few years ago, Chris Sherwin, who studied furniture at Loughborough University, said that if you're going to subscribe to sustainability you've got to ask yourself where the biggest change will be made and where the biggest impact will occur. For him that meant stopping being a furniture designer and working for Forum for the Future, a nonprofit organization advising business and government on sustainability. That has always stayed with me. Now I myself have changed from being solely a designer.

The biggest barriers to sustainability are consumers, cost and, interestingly, the traditional structures of companies. In order to embed sustainable design thinking and practice in companies, there needs to be a shift in how departments work and relate to each other. Cross-departmental projects are important for big companies as the innovation doesn't stop in design departments. I did a workshop in Sweden with people from a company's marketing department. Working directly with designers made them terribly excited as they could see how to link a marketing campaign to the idea of sustainability right from the outset.

As far as cost is concerned, the driving question now is not 'Where can I get sustainable organic cotton?' but 'How much is it going to cost me?' I'm involved in workshops with companies that are trying to cost sustainable textiles and fashion. It is not easy to show a costing model for sustainability. Companies are moving closer to adopting sustainable ideas and approaches, but they want to make sure that there will be a return on the investment.

Since 2006 TED has developed ten strategic design approaches (see opposite). For each of the

TED's ten sustainable design strategies

1

Design to minimise waste

How can we reduce the waste that is created in the textile industry, both pre and post consumer? This strategy includes zero-waste cutting and recycling, but it also introduces the idea that we need to examine what makes stuff desirable and why people might value it.

2

Design for recycling/upcycling

This strategy explains how when you design for future recycling/upcycling, the thought process anticipates the practice of recycling and re-purposing textiles. It includes design for closed-loop systems and disassembly.

3

Design to reduce chemical impacts

This strategy is about using appropriate process and material selection: we can consider using organically produced materials; employ mechanical technology to create non-chemical decorative surface pattern; seek convincing alternatives to harmful chemical processes such as devore, chemical dyes and mordants.

4

Design to reduce energy and water use

Here we consider, in the production phase: exhaust printing and dyeing, dry patterning systems, air-dying, projected patterns and distributed manufacture. In the use phase: design for no/low launder, 'short life' textiles, technical coatings to reduce washing, innovative and informative labeling, localization and natural energy systems.

5

Design that explores clean and better technologies

How can we use technology to make more sustainable textiles? Can we use new technologies to save energy and materials in the production or 're-surface' of pre-consumer polyester, laser/water-jet/sonic cutting, laser/sonic welding, and digital printing.

6

Design that looks at models from nature and history

How can the practices of the past and models from the natural world inform textile design and production in the future? This strategy shows how textile designers can find inspiration and information for future sustainable design in studying the textiles, habits and societies of the past as well as exploring biomimicry.

7

Design for ethical production

This strategy is about design that utilizes and invests in traditional craft skills, both locally and globally. It promotes ethical production that supports and values workers' rights, and the sourcing of fair-trade materials. It questions what ethical production means at home, and how it differs according to the scale of production and manufacture. It also includes designers acting as facilitators for sustainable and social enterprises in traditional craft communities.

8

Design to replace the need to consume

This strategy is about making stuff that lasts: things that we want to keep and look after. It is about Emotionally Durable Design; Slow Design; the design and production of textiles and products that adapt and improve with age. This strategy encourages the value of experience, the customization of clothing and textiles, and the culture of DIY. It includes recycling and reuse. It is also about consumer participation in co-design, collaborative consumption, crowd-sourcing and social networks.

9

Design to dematerialize and develop systems and services

This strategy introduces the concepts of designing services – such as lease, share, repair – that support existing products, and of employing user-centred methods to design public services. It promotes multi-functional products and conservation of materials via temporary or non-invasive installations. It is about the development of on-line and local communities of producers and consumers.

10

Design activism

In this final strategy we encourage designers to leave behind their focus on 'the product' and work creatively with consumers and society at large. It is about designing events and communication strategies that go beyond product design to increase consumer and designer knowledge about the environmental and social impacts of textile products. In doing so, textile designers become 'Social Innovators', using their design skills to meet social needs.

Right: Shuan Samson, MA graduate collection featuring needle-punching techniques used to combine and utilize end-of-roll wool fabrics, Central Saint Martins, 2011.

ten we've tried to show how our thinking developed. I've always liked design activism, the idea of moving beyond the product and into the realm of education and dissemination, even politics. It's so good for us to open up our collaborations a little bit. The buzz about sustainability is now about social activism and engagement. It's about what happens at the level of basic research.

The question of where responsibility lies among consumers, retailers, manufacturers and governments is an interesting one. If I replace the word 'responsibility' with 'opportunity', I can see projects and ideas that would link all these parties together. In terms of responsibility it's always going to come down to politics and economics being the drivers. Designers are quite poor at understanding politics and economics (myself included). I'm becoming more interested in political activism and the effects our economic situations have in other areas. Ironically there has been a growth both in interest and in activity in sustainable fashion because people are increasingly wondering what else they need to do to survive, grow and innovate. Sustainability seems quite a good idea now, having almost been forced upon us through crises. There is less money around and it's being spent more carefully. So now if people want smart textiles, they want smart and *sustainable* textiles. That the sustainability movement still has a sense of growth is apparent from the increase in the number of small companies and initiatives and the continued burgeoning of relevant publications.

When I was curating the exhibition 'Eco Fashion in the UK' (Craft Council, 2006), I thought we could change a lot, but now I have seen a little of what companies are prepared to take on and how far they're prepared to go. In a way it's a less optimistic picture, but a more realistic one. I'm interested to know if those same companies would consider using academics as intermediaries to work more closely with consumers. Websites and digital platforms are the way to reach Generation Y. We're going to see a lot more people working in this area, but an impact study is needed to test the realities of engagement with online platforms.

Small companies are always going to be important to showcase sustainable ideas; they are the testing grounds. Small designers need to maintain their hands-on approaches to materials, but perhaps they could also be part of the upscaling and handing on of these ideas to the higher-volume level of fashion. This would entail training designers to work with companies. Many burn out after two or three years because there is a massive gap in infrastructure and support after a certain point.

A successful example of action taken by a large organization is the PPR Group – owners of Gucci, Puma and many other brands. They have reinvented their corporate social responsibility programme and created a chief executive officer for sustainability for the whole group, under the name PPR Unite. This total rethink includes training of designers in the sourcing of materials. At Marks & Spencer, meanwhile, Plan A has changed the way designers think about their process. The luxury companies, though, have a long-term battle ahead of them to achieve materials sustainability and they find that they cannot say anything about what they are doing for fear of being criticised in this area. So change is on the way.

Rebecca Earley was in conversation with Sandy Black.

Above: Emma Rigby, 'EnergyWaterFashion', MA graduate collection, London College of Fashion, 2010.

Yohji Yamamoto

Born in the ruins of post-war Tokyo, Yohji Yamamoto is one of the most respected and influential designers of his time. These extracts from his biography reveal his insights into sustainable fashion.

'When fabric is left to age for a year or two, it naturally contracts, and at this point it reveals its charm. The threads have a life of their own, they pass through the seasons and mature. It is only through this process that the true appeal of the fabric is revealed. In releasing one collection after the next on a six-month cycle, it is impossible to design clothing from fabric that has been allowed to age. The intense jealousy I occasionally feel towards used clothing comes from this fact. It was in just such a moment that I thought, "I would like to design time itself."'[1]

'Human beings, whether young or old, have an innate desire to be understood; they build things and they speak in order to make their presence known. In this sense my work might be considered the epitome of some gaudy attempt to attract attention… [In] terms of a reaction to the growing environmental crisis, I felt that screaming out for ecological solutions and volunteer work would not be nearly as effective as the complete disposal of all man-made edifices, all cobbled-together explanations, and all the mountains of garbage. Or, to take it one step further, it seemed the best thing one could do for the sake of the earth would be to die on the spot. Though they pour toxic waste into the rivers, humans will only pay attention to it on the day the dead fish rise to the surface.'[2]

From Ai Mitsuda, *Yohji Yamamoto – My Dear Bomb: A Biography* (2010).

Right and opposite: Yohji Yamamoto, Autumn/Winter 2009.

Considerate design: supporting sustainable fashion design

SANDY BLACK AND CLAUDIA ECKERT *Sandy Black developed the project Considerate Design for Personalized Fashion in collaboration with Claudia Eckert, a senior lecturer at the Open University, with researchers from London College of Fashion, to develop tools to support fashion designers in thinking about sustainability. The project was funded by the UK Arts and Humanities Research Council and the UK Engineering and Physical Sciences Research Council under the Designing for the 21st Century initiative (2007–9).*

 ompared with other sectors, such as architecture, product design or food, action on behalf of sustainability in fashion has been slow to develop in both the industry and among consumers because the nature of fashion appears contrary to the spirit of sustainability. However, in the wider context of climate change and improved global communications, momentum has gathered strongly over the last decade. Pioneer sustainable-fashion designers such as Katharine Hamnett have raised the profile of organic and ethically produced clothing through meticulously sourced collections that have been widely publicized. As an independent designer, Hamnett could invest the necessary commitment and resources to ensure that every element of her collection is fully sustainable and produced as locally as possible under fair wage conditions.[1] However, this is not possible for most designers, who work under great commercial pressure, including timeliness and strict cost parameters, and who are subject to corporate management decisions.

The complexity of the fashion supply chain has made the concept of environmentally and economically sustainable, ethically responsible clothing extremely difficult for the mainstream industry to address. There is a contradiction at the heart of the fashion business, which Sandy Black has termed the 'fashion paradox'.[2] Fashion's built-in obsolescence may be intrinsically unsustainable, but the desire for fashionable renewal is an inherent cultural construct. Fashion is also a powerful economic driver, sustaining global industry and keeping millions in employment. It is only during the past decade that growing awareness of environmental and ethical issues in this fast-moving industry has begun to translate into concerted, visible action on the part of both designers and retailers.

The Industry Context

The consumption of fashion in the UK has grown significantly in recent years; there was a 37% increase in the amount of clothes purchased per capita between 2001 and 2005.[3] Globalization of production, along with the development of faster fashion cycles, has pushed the price of products down while increasing their environmental impact across the globe. Garments and raw materials travel around the world, often using unsustainable air freight for fast delivery. At the same time, the *rate* of production and consumption has also gone up. Fashion companies are struggling to respond quickly to changing trends or negative customer feedback. Previously, locally situated production runs were flexible and tailored to customer demand. Now, when products offered are not what customers want, more goods end up marked down in sales, feeding the waste stream and landfill.

Fashion products have in many cases become cheap, disposable items that customers buy without thinking where they have come from or how they were made. Purchases are optional – people rarely need a particular item at any one time; rather they purchase for pleasure. Styles, colours and materials change rapidly. Many purchases are made on impulse and a great deal of clothing is never worn before being thrown away. With the aim of assisting designers to create more sustainably designed fashion products that will engage consumers for longer periods of time, a concept and process called 'Considerate Design' is being developed at the London College of Fashion and the Open University.

Supply-chain Issues

The clothing supply chain is highly complex and time-sensitive, involving many components and subcontractors in different locations. With the exception of a small number of staple clothing products, such as basic T-shirts or underwear, fashion garments are produced by ever-changing suppliers in relatively small production runs (typically in the order of a few thousand, often much less) compared to engineered products, for example. The time invested in designing a product is therefore a significant

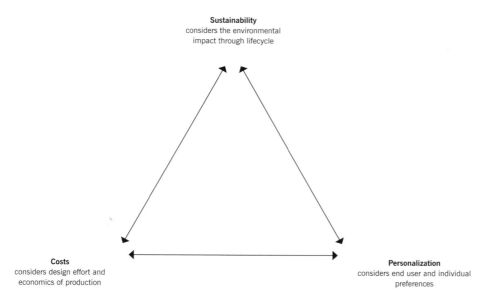

Sustainability
considers the environmental
impact through lifecycle

Costs
considers design effort and
economics of production

Personalization
considers end user and individual
preferences

Above: Figure 1, showing the triangle of relationships in Considerate Design.

part of its costs. Owing to the large number of pieces in a collection, tracing garments' ethical and environmental supply chain adds to this cost, increasing designers' and company management's reluctance to do so. Standard logistics systems used in large companies are not able to monitor provenance of materials and standards of certification.

The range of variables in the production of both basic clothing and seasonal fashion is therefore high compared to mass production in many other industries. Through relatively small batch sizes, purchasing power (and therefore influence over much of the fashion and textile supply chain) is limited, as small quantities are typically sourced from numerous suppliers. Volume is broadly related to price and market level. Supermarkets and high-street brands manufacture perhaps a thousand per style variation, a designer label hundreds or even dozens. A start-up design company works in very small-batch production, whereas couture and bespoke clothing services a market of one.

The fashion supply chain has traditionally been based on trust, with few suppliers being certified to guarantee ecological or ethical production. Small companies have had little knowledge of the environmental credentials of their fabrics. However, since 2007 European government REACH legislation (Registration, Evaluation, Authorization and Restriction of Chemicals) has begun to address the environmental impact of chemicals, and certification has increased.[4] However, designers' ability to check their suppliers' claims remains limited by the tight time schedules of seasonal fashion production.

Fashion Customers

The ethical dimension of garment production has an increasing public profile, although cost is still of paramount importance. A survey by consultants GfK found that 54% of consumers would rather buy clothing that is ethically made as long as they do not have to pay more.[5] Consumers now expect retailers and manufacturers to demonstrate greater responsibility and transparency regarding their

suppliers at all levels of the value chain, from fibre to garment. In the absence of established legislation, accountability for the sustainability of clothing and fashion is thus distributed among consumers, retailers, designers and suppliers.

Direct product comparison has not been a driver of ecological or sustainable fashions as it has been, for example, in the automotive industry, where production processes are similar across companies and heavily legislated. In fashion, however, there is an enormous variability in the impact of both resources and production processes: two similar-looking garments, such as T-shirts, jeans or sweaters, can have vastly different production processes and global life histories, from fibre to finished garment manufacture.

The Fashion Life Cycle

Although a widely accepted theory in product design is that 80% of an item's environmental impact is determined by the materials choice,[6] this notion breaks down when it comes to staple items such as T-shirts, underwear and jeans, which are frequently laundered, or outerwear, which is often dry-cleaned. Consumer use and aftercare are major parts of the life cycle and environmental impact of clothing prior to its end-of-life disposal stage. Behaviour patterns regarding washing, ironing, tumble-drying and dry-cleaning vary dramatically, depending on individual decisions, contexts and preferences. Studies have shown that for some types of clothing the use phase can cause most of the impact. A frequently cited study, the life-cycle analysis of a polyester blouse by Franklin Associates, found that more than 82% of energy requirements, 66% of solid waste and 83% of carbon-dioxide emissions derive from the consumer-use phase.[7] Similarly, the report *Well Dressed?* analysed the energy profile of a T-shirt when washed, ironed and tumble-dried twenty-five times and found that 65% of the total energy used was due to laundry compared with 7% from transport.[8] Kate Fletcher and Mathilda Tham's Lifetimes project, carried out in 2004, examined variations in consumer behaviour and use across different items, including jeans, underwear, outerwear and party clothes.[9] Considerate Design

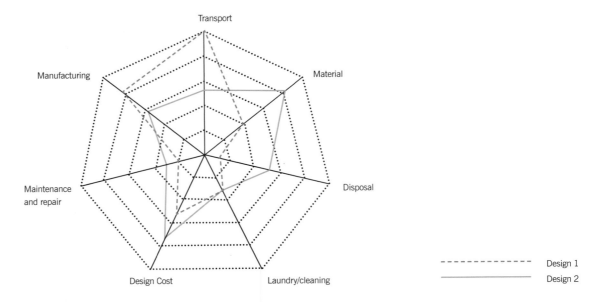

Transport

Material

Manufacturing

Disposal

Maintenance
and repair

Laundry/cleaning

Design Cost

- - - - - - - - - - Design 1
_____ Design 2

assists in considering life-cycle issues at the design stage, where informed trade-offs are possible to balance impact between different scenarios and help the decision-making process.

User-centred Fashion: Bespoke and Customized Products

Mass customization in fashion is becoming technologically feasible and can enable production to return closer to the place of consumption. Online and physical retail systems are used in a growing number of product areas such as footwear, jeans and shirts, with the ability to respond to individual consumer choice while maintaining the benefits of mass production. For example, in 2004 Nike introduced the NIKEiD online system of customization for trainers, enabling colours and fabrics to be chosen, lettering to be added, and, most significantly, each foot to be specified differently. By better satisfying customer needs it may be possible to reduce the rate at which products are consumed and replaced. By developing methods to assess the cost of the design effort, it can be determined whether customization is economically viable for new and existing business models.

The Considerate Design Concept

The Considerate Design concept creates new links between sustainability, personalization and cost within the fashion design and production process (see Figure 1). Its aim is to reduce the environmental impact of fashion consumption in two ways: (a) by giving customers what they want through customized products, and (b) by helping designers to assess the environmental impact of the items they are producing. Few fashion designers realize the environmental impact of their decisions. 'Sustainability' is a vast concept to contemplate, which can paralyse rather than motivate designers. Considerate Design aims to break down design for sustainability into elements relevant to fashion. It considers the environmental impact of the supply chain, the end user and the life cycle of the product, using methods applicable to the economic framework and the constraints within which designers work, whether in bespoke, small-batch production or mass manufacturing.

The concept has been tested within three different scenarios: industrial production of personalized knitwear, bespoke handmade bags and experimental pseudo-textiles using rapid manufacturing technology. A two-fold approach is adopted to assist at different scales within the industry. For large-scale manufacturing, to compare costs and tasks, process modelling (using P3 software tools developed by the Engineering Design Centre at the University of Cambridge[10]) is adapted for the fashion industry. Environmental-impact analysis using a simple accessible footprinting tool to identify and assist decision-making is aimed at designers in small or larger companies (Figure 2). Existing literature on eco-design or green product design outlines both theoretical models and, more recently, practical tools designers need to develop more sustainable approaches in response to previous critiques.[11]

Fashion designers make choices primarily on aesthetic or financial criteria. In trying to assess environmental impact, they have to trade off diverse factors such as the costs of transporting garments and their raw materials versus the impact that the garments' disposal will have (see Figure 2). Here we use a concept similar to the eco-strategy wheel originally developed in 1997 by Hans Brezet and Caroline van Hemel and adapted by others.[12] The Considerate Design project works on identifying a set of factors that contribute to the environmental impact of fashion products. As many of these factors are themselves far from simple, they can be broken down further in a hierarchical manner so that designers can visualize and assess individual ones.

The spider diagram shown in Figure 2 represents the impact of individual factors on a scale of low to high, thereby drawing impact profiles of design alternatives. Designers can thus assess and compare the footprints of alternative scenarios and target their efforts to reduce the impact of certain factors, comparing production routes or materials depending on costs. In the first instance designers can provide their own estimates so that the diagram provides a visualization of the connectivity between many complex factors. However, the assessments of

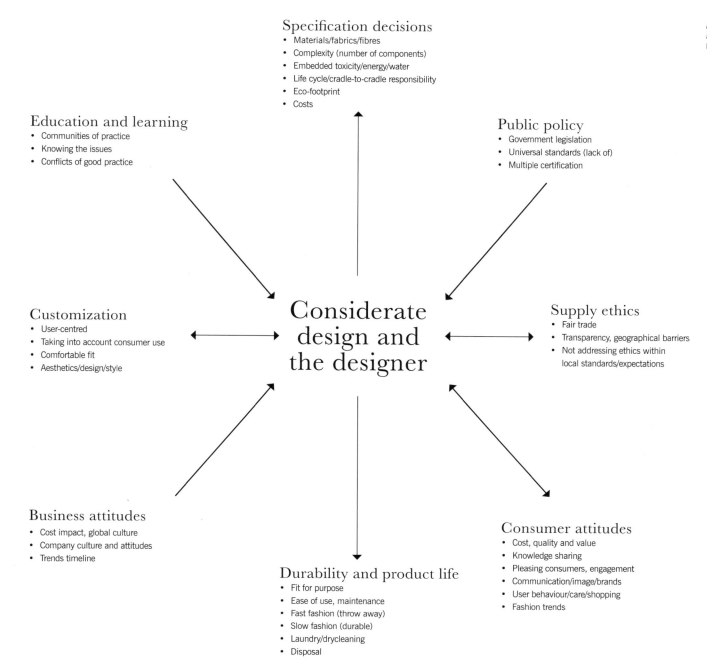

Specification decisions
- Materials/fabrics/fibres
- Complexity (number of components)
- Embedded toxicity/energy/water
- Life cycle/cradle-to-cradle responsibility
- Eco-footprint
- Costs

Education and learning
- Communities of practice
- Knowing the issues
- Conflicts of good practice

Public policy
- Government legislation
- Universal standards (lack of)
- Multiple certification

Customization
- User-centred
- Taking into account consumer use
- Comfortable fit
- Aesthetics/design/style

Considerate design and the designer

Supply ethics
- Fair trade
- Transparency, geographical barriers
- Not addressing ethics within local standards/expectations

Business attitudes
- Cost impact, global culture
- Company culture and attitudes
- Trends timeline

Consumer attitudes
- Cost, quality and value
- Knowledge sharing
- Pleasing consumers, engagement
- Communication/image/brands
- User behaviour/care/shopping
- Fashion trends

Durability and product life
- Fit for purpose
- Ease of use, maintenance
- Fast fashion (throw away)
- Slow fashion (durable)
- Laundry/drycleaning
- Disposal

Left: Figure 3, showing factors affecting fashion designers and lines of influence.

individual factors will in future be automated in order to reach a comparative overall measure. Considerate Design spider diagrams can be accessed at different levels of complexity and for different aspects of the supply chain. They are particularly useful in identifying additional costs of personalization against other factors, such costs often being hidden.

Figure 3 illustrates the context in which a fashion designer works and the multiple factors that influence decision-making within and external to companies whether they are large or small. Some factors are within the direct remit of designers whereas they may be powerless to affect others. However, with increased knowledge, their sphere of influence can grow. Although detailed environmental impacts are beyond the feasible responsibility of many designers, the enhanced traceability information emerging from the textile industry, together with the increased availability of more sustainable materials, will enable them to make better material choices.

Design decision-making in the fashion-clothing sector operates under a number of key constraints, notably high time pressures, remote manufacturing, saturated markets and increasing competition.

Dynamic supply chains create severe difficulties in achieving sustainable design, and responsibility is dissipated throughout the chain, with players at different points completely unconnected. Key decision makers are retail buyers, whose focus is on the right product at the right time and price, and designers, whose focus is on the balance of style, aesthetics and cost. Communication between the two determines economic success. As communication throughout the entire supply chain becomes more transparent, the influence of informed design decisions can grow accordingly. In a saturated market the desire for greater individuality has increased, and Considerate Design can assist in harnessing sustainable benefits for personalized products, countering fast and throwaway fashion by meeting consumer needs more accurately and perhaps disrupting established wasteful systems. Considerate Design helps assess the viability of these personalized products and the costs of the design effort, ensuring that the concept of 'sustainable fashion' becomes a reality, and not an oxymoron.

Designers fashioning the future industry

DILYS WILLIAMS *is director of the Centre for Sustainable Fashion at London College of Fashion, University of the Arts London. She previously worked as a designer in the fashion industry with well-known brands.*

Below and opposite: Accessories created by Shared Talent students from London College of Fashion, LISOF and the Boitumelo Project, Johannesburg, 2007.

ASPIRATIONS OF FASHION DESIGNERS

We all ask ourselves the question at one time or another: What is it that I am really doing with my time, thoughts and energy – and why? This is shortly followed by a 'what if?' moment of wonder and dreaming.

As a trained and experienced hands-on design practitioner in the fashion business, I have always enjoyed taking the tactile properties of cloth and other materials and, using the body as the starting point, sculpting, shaping, cutting and constructing. Engaging a technique, creating a link to a place, time or person, and considering how somebody stands, moves and reacts to the wearing of a piece, all inspire the creative process of plotting a collection. Later I see pieces I have designed turn up on market stalls and in charity shops or pass me in the street, witnessing further stages in their form and function. In conversing with many practising and aspiring designers, I am reminded that fashion, as a discipline, is a way of satisfying the designer's yearning to create, to communicate through making, bringing energy and excitement to a given situation. It heralds a desire to both challenge and reflect contemporary social needs. We seek a connection to others and to ourselves through what we make and do.

How can the aspirations of designers inform a forward-looking fashion industry in which social justice, ecological balance, culture and identity are all part of the definition of fashion? According to the Norwegian philosopher Lars Svendsen, 'An understanding of fashion is necessary in order to gain an adequate understanding of the modern world.'[1] Similarly, an awareness of the modern world is necessary for fashion designers. The context in which we live and work has changed dramatically within my lifetime through the realization that the types and scale of our activities are completely out

Miriam Rhida's award-winning design for the second Fashioning the Future competition, on the theme of 'Water', 2009.

of what we did was a third aim. How, we wondered, does what we do affect others, and how does what happens to others affect us?

One of the greatest opportunities for me as a sustainability-led fashion designer is to learn about hitherto disconnected processes in the fashion system and to create links with design for sustainability activities outside of the industry. This process of exploration offers new creative approaches, encouraging a designer to think beyond the catwalk, salesroom or online display to consider the whole life of a piece: its wear and maintenance, and what happens to it after it has lost the affection of its wearer. This is an entirely new challenge, one that can at times seem overwhelming, but – if approached with a balance of insight, sound knowledge and focused creative expression – signals a new era in the definition of the designer's role. Fashion has the ability to focus on an object that is a manifestation of a collective mindset at a particular time. A garment is therefore both an expression of an ideology and a tangible piece that you can hold and wear. 'Clothes,' observed French theorist Roland Barthes, 'are the material basis of fashion, whereas fashion itself is a cultural system of meanings.'[3] At a time when a shift in mindset is exactly what we need, fashion has the ability to move us by means of both its system of social beliefs and its materiality.

Fashion is an important way of connecting with each other. We use the visual signals of our attire and personal style to relate to others and express ourselves. But, as we move forward, we are also creating ways to be less connected. The current priorities of fashion – price, speed and quantity – have propagated an industry in which, within a single generation, we have severed many of the traditional links between designer and maker, creating short-lived, homogenized products. These products reduce fashion to disconnected visions that communicate little about who we really are and do not display the resources and skills employed in their making.

This was the impetus behind three innovative programmes at the Centre for Sustainable Fashion. The first, Shared Talent, is a gradually evolving forum for gathering individual experiences that offers an alternative to the hierarchical approach usually associated with fashion development. The Fashioning the Future Awards recognizes experimental responses to specific themes related to sustainability. Finally, the business support programme at the Centre for Sustainable Fashion, which helps designers in growing and developing their businesses in London, encounters many examples of sustainable design-thinking in action, indicating the growing understanding of sustainability in the industry.

of sync with the balance of nature, which we defy at our peril. The fashion business has specific issues to address regarding the ecological, social, cultural and economic implications of its activities, from the seed of a design idea through the life (or lives) of a piece, and the ever-evolving changes in definitions of fashion. In order to achieve our aspirations as designers, we need to revolutionize the parameters within which we work.

These parameters presented a key challenge for us at the Centre for Sustainable Fashion when we started out in 2008. Through dialogue with a diverse range of people who had a shared interest in looking beyond the usual confines of our activities to form a vision of design for the future, we developed our own criteria to work by, areas to benchmark and terms within which to question decisions.[2] Living within the limitations of nature was one of these criteria. How would nature do a particular thing? Building a transformed fashion industry was another goal. We asked ourselves what we were really here to achieve. Putting human wellbeing at the centre

Shared Talent is a people centred learning process inspired by sustainability thinking and values. The focus is on how participants come to understand and consider the impact of their work.

SHARED TALENT

Shared Talent is a people-centred learning process inspired by sustainability thinking and values. The focus is on how participants come to understand and consider the impact of their work. The first Shared Talent project was designed to bring diverse disciplines together to give participants first-hand knowledge of the sorts of items that can be made and to exchange knowledge between designers and producer communities.[4] This knowledge included the preferences and interests of potential markets with a view to future product development and export sales. The focus was on the relationships and understanding generated through the process of design and development of specific pieces.

Shared Talent 2[5] evolved from its predecessor, through collaboration with Tabeisa, a charity that supports poor communities in Africa.[6] The emphasis was on longer-term learning, based on the sharing of perspectives and skills, to offer benefits that would endure beyond the project timeline. Tangible outcomes included ranges of products offered for sale through the Exclusive Roots online store.[7]

Shared Talent 3 (convened in India) adapted the model by bringing together different elements of the design and development process, and by including designers at different points in their career development.[8] The aim was to facilitate understanding of sustainability issues among designers, makers and buyers, between individual designers and between people in different geographical locations and cultural contexts, each with their own perspectives.

The Shared Talent process provided a forum to explore design practice in which sustainability values such as cooperation, participation and resourcefulness were strongly expressed. As part of the process, we recorded the responses of participants before, during and after the formal project activities. These wide-ranging responses were often intuitive and emotional rather than analytical in nature, yet distinct themes did emerge, which offer possible responses to the questions posed at the start of this essay.

Awareness of cause and effect

For many participating designers, Shared Talent offered their first opportunity since graduating from college to question their motivations and professional identities and to explore the values that informed their practice. For some this also triggered deeper questioning of other aspects of design and development, raising the possibility that sharing could be seen as a novel type of aspirational behaviour that might offer an alternative code of practice. Offering a way of working that encourages exchange of knowledge as a part of the product development

process represents a shift from the current fiercely protective system, in which secrecy and hierarchy are seen to confer creative and financial advantage.

For some, this opportunity for enhanced reflection led to exhilaration and excitement at newfound knowledge and strength gained from each other's support. For others, however, the enormous complexity of the issues generated inertia. To a certain extent the project framework, which required participants to produce tangible products, mitigated these feelings of being overwhelmed, giving participants the opportunity to respond to new information by focusing on the physical process of fashioning garments.

The participants' self-questioning reflected a number of key social, cultural and developmental perspectives. There was a clear delineation of priorities between those living in India and in Europe. For the Indian participants, sustainability was thought of first and foremost in terms of human wellbeing. For the European participants, ecological integrity was the primary concern. These differing perspectives offered an additional opportunity for learning. In the case of Shared Talent 3 this learning manifested itself in the tendency for participants from industrialized countries to begin looking to less industrialized countries for examples of good practice.

Thinking and learning through making

Shared Talent is practice-based, and the intense pleasure associated with making was expressed by many of the participants, and regarded by some as a need. Participants viewed the act of making as heightening the vitality of conversations, providing a material, tangible texture to the discourse that linked active experimentation in design practice to the intangible values of sustainability. Sustainability, when manifested in object form, can be experienced, touched and responded to emotionally, and vital and original ideas can be generated through material experimentation, problem manipulation and resolution. As one participant recorded, 'We discussed what sustainability means to us collectively and individually every night and worked on our ideas during the day in the workshop.'[9] Another participant wrote, 'I finally feel as though I know what I am doing, now that I am actually "doing" something – making garments.'[10]

Seeing time pressures differently

Shared Talent is an immersive experience that requires participants to agree to commit their time. Indeed, time pressures dominate most fashion professionals' day-to-day work. Participants spoke of the 'indulgence' of taking time out of their normal

'We discussed what sustainability means to us collectively and individually every night and worked on our ideas during the day in the workshop.'

All photos from the Shared Talent India project, Delhi, 2009.

Above: Dye pots at Alps Industries near Delhi.

Right: Shared Talent group workshop.

Top right: Hand-painting fabric at Jharcraft workshop near Delhi.

Centre right: Shared Talent embroidery group.

Bottom right: Participants create a design by draping on the stand.

Opposite: Batik dresses in modal fabric designed by Nitin Bal Chauhan, a participant in Shared Talent India, 2009.

Prior to their Shared Talent experience. a significant number of participants struggled to feel confident with the sustainability aspects of their own work.

Dress and shoes by Lu Flux,
'Dame and Knight' collection,
Autumn/Winter 2010

Left: Scarf from Borders and Frontiers Collective designed by Nina Børke of Werksemd, 2010.

practice, but recognized that once relationships, honesty and trust had been established, working together enabled them to do more better and faster and to enjoy the process as well as the outcome.

Most fashion, from luxury down to supermarket level, operates on a short-term development cycle. Vision, reference points, production, showcasing, acceptance and success are all realized within a restrictive timescale and the limited frame of reference of the existing fashion system. Shared Talent, while also taking place within a limited timescale, gives designers a bigger, bolder long-term vision to realize, rather than simply thinking ahead to the next season. Prior to their Shared Talent experience, a significant number of participants struggled to feel confident with the sustainability aspects of their own work. Following their involvement in the project, participants reported enhanced practical capabilities, including increased confidence: 'Now I know how it can apply to me and what I can offer. I am sure that I will always keep sustainability in my head.'[11]

FASHIONING THE FUTURE

The Fashioning the Future Awards is another of the Centre for Sustainable Fashion's initiatives to encourage designers to think creatively about sustainability. Since its launch in 2008, the competition has attracted responses from fashion courses and institutions in India, South Africa, Australia, all corners of Europe and the USA. Briefs have been developed to nurture questioning and experimental responses to themes including consumption (2008), water (2009) and uniqueness (2010/11). It is important that Fashioning the Future celebrates global and local perspectives and encourages interdisciplinary reflection, while not forgetting the importance of beauty and aesthetics. The awards were developed with the intention of engaging with fashion-related organizations internationally, offering a platform for enquiry, experimentation and the acknowledgment of excellence. The finalists and winners recognized through Fashioning the Future have all demonstrated creativity, ingenuity and resourcefulness.

Here are descriptions of past winning entries, in the designers' own words.

Miriam Rhida – Winner of Fashioning the Future Award for Design 2009[12]

My work for this brief presented the opportunity to explore, visualize and create products, which are stylish and innovative but also have a strong economically friendly and sustainable element. After researching and trying to understand the flexible nature of the term 'sustainable', looking closely at a variety of materials that are now available to use in fashion and all the finishing possibilities, my work came down simply to questioning the source of everything used. It began my journey of being aware, understanding the necessary and unnecessary, and just how simplicity with craft can be way more than I expected.

The material used lends itself perfectly to the brief. The hemp plant is a natural, renewable and eco-friendly resource, which can be used to not only create fibres and fabrics, but also provide food and fuel. Hemp satin was the fabric of choice as it is a lightweight, elegant and fairly fluid fabric that was quite easily frayed to create the desired effect.

The idea behind the products was to create garments with minimal waste through a handmade craft technique. By using only a 1 m x 150 cm fabric piece, slicing it in half and meticulously fraying the fabric at the edges, I created the shape of the front and back of a pattern piece for a simple shift dress. This left a fringe effect all the way around the edge of fabric pattern piece. Using these fringes, the back and front were joined by knotting the side and shoulder seams together.

This fraying technique can also be used to create shapes on the garment such as curves, linear patterns and varied hems and necklines. This adds an interesting and aesthetically pleasing element to the design, making it look more feminine, elegant and, most importantly, wearable. In addition, the technique allows for minimal fabric waste leaving a pile of long threads, which can be later re-used for stitching or weaving.

'After researching and trying to understand the flexible nature of the term "sustainable"…my work came down simply to questioning the source of everything used.'

Opposite: Christopher Raeburn upcycled military parachute dress, 'Digital Rainbow' collection, Spring/Summer 2010.

Natural dye extracts were used to colour the fabrics and to ensure that the eco-friendly element would still be strongly present. These dyes are very concentrated, water-soluble and inter-mixable powders, which are made mainly from plants. The result created beautiful harmonious shades of pinks, oranges and golden-browns. These pieces have elicited in me a strong direction that I will take beyond the here-and-now: I'll keep questioning constantly and hopefully retain a core ecological element in my future textile-driven designs.

Kerrie Luft, finalist Fashioning the Future 2009
My concept is based on embracing the technological advances in the field of rapid prototyping and applying them to elements of shoemaking, changing the traditional method bywhich shoes are manufactured. I have recently explored the technology by rapid prototyping titanium to create innovative heels for a collection of high-end ladies' shoes (see pp. 318–19).

Applying the technology to footwear allowed me to replace the traditional methods of casting and model-making to create contemporary heel designs that challenge convention and utilize unconventional materials in an innovative way.

Creating the design in a digital world allows both the designer and the consumer to visualize the product before it is manufactured. This could also offer the consumer an alternative way to shop. From a designer's perspective it allows a digital library to be maintained and minor adjustments to be made without the cost of casting and re-making moulds.

The technology is currently most commonly used in the fields of dentistry and aerospace; however, I believe it has huge potential in offering a new initiative in footwear design. Fashion is so disposable at present and I believe that using rapid prototyping as a tool within the footwear industry will allow the consumer the opportunity to invest in more sustainable products that are original and offer longevity.

Karina Michel, highly commended for Role of Materials Award 2009
India has now become the world's largest producer of organic cotton; however, the impacts of a garment do not stop at the farm…It is estimated that of the 26 million tons of cotton fibre consumed in India, 0.21 million tons are wasted during yarn manufacturing and 30% of waste is generated during bulk garment-cutting. My concept is to live and work in India in collaboration with Pratibha Syntex, India's first fully vertically integrated garment manufacturers and its second-largest producer of organic cotton, in a collaborative effort to reduce textile waste in the fashion industry by providing an alternative low-impact material.

The scope of the project plays into a focused strategy of tackling garment-cutting and spinning waste generated on the industrial floor by creating a reclamation system that recycles all waste back into fabric form and reintroduces it into the loop of design. I've named the initiative the Reinstated Fibre Project. It is an effort to reduce consumption of fibre, energy, and water by sourcing from self-generated factory waste. My role as designer is to lead a team of fabric developers, patternmakers, printers and operators to create a garment collection of reinstated fabrics that not only showcases recycled fibre, but also implements the concept of zero-waste design in a number of pieces. The collection, called 'Loop', aptly derived from 'closed-loop recycling', is a practice-led strategy aimed at not only reducing waste, but also completely eliminating fibre/fabric waste and serving as an exemplary model for India's textile industry.

LONDON STYLE
An important and inspiring barometer with which to gauge change in relation to issues around sustainability is to take a snapshot of designers growing and developing their businesses. As I am based in London, I have been able to work closely with a number of designers involved in the business-support programme at the Centre for Sustainable Fashion.[13] Here are a few notable examples of sustainability design thinking in action.

Borders and Frontiers
Collaboration: the act of working with others on a joint project – is the founding principle behind Borders and Frontiers. Surprising and delightful prints for T-shirts, dresses and scarves are created in collaboration with bloggers, artists, photographers, architects, scientists and other designers. Borders and Frontiers also has a strong interest in the integration of sustainability thinking with product development, as one of a new generation of pioneers who comfortably allow ethics and aesthetics to inform each other. The brand has been sold through Colette, Urban Outfitters and ASOS and is expanding into the Asian market.

Lu Flux
Patchwork: something made up of a variety of incongruous pieces or parts. Lu Flux creates beautiful, intricate and, most importantly, high-quality menswear and womenswear using a patchwork of reclaimed fabrics. The freshness, authenticity and quirky flamboyance of the Lu Flux aesthetic have been well received, particularly in the Japanese

market. Its celebration of the incongruity inherent in patchwork stands against mass homogenization and flies the flag for unique fashion.

Michelle Lowe-Holder

Timeless: without beginning or end, eternal, everlasting. These are not words often associated with fashion accessories, but in the case of Michelle Lowe-Holder they hold true. Lowe-Holder's accessories are created from offcuts and waste materials from previous ready-to-wear collections. Intricate hand-folded, crocheted and woven collars, cuffs and bibs utilize everything from plastic and leather to floral prints and African wax fabrics. This approach, grounded in thrift, provides an interesting model for closed-loop product development, diverting waste from one product group to facilitate the creation of another.

Christopher Raeburn

Authenticity: of undisputed origin or authorship; genuine. These are all claims that Christopher Raeburn can rightfully make for his luxury men's and women's outerwear. His commitment to creating a brand with true authenticity and British heritage is coupled with his keen interest in utilizing the most efficient and effective materials and techniques. Decommissioned military textiles, with their inherent strength and durability, form the mainstay of Raeburn's collections, which nonetheless avoid combat shapes and styles. The brand has been sold in Liberty and Browns in London, Isetan in Tokyo and Barney's in New York.

White Tent

Beauty: the quality present in a thing or person that gives intense pleasure or deep satisfaction to the mind. White Tent values intelligent pattern cutting, carefully considered fabric selection and an eye for unusual and arresting detail. In its new role as an ethical entrepreneur working with a Portuguese high-end manufacturer, White Tent secured an EU grant to develop its collections while nurturing the skills of workers in a region that suffers from high unemployment and economic deprivation. The label has a strong commitment to addressing ecological issues via its choice of materials. As is the case with many emerging designers, White Tent's commitment to sustainability is an inherent part of its values, but is rarely used as a marketing tool. Craftsmanship and quality are the mainstays of the brand's identity, backed up by a responsible approach to production.

CONCLUSIONS

Fashion affects us all. Having taken part in a number of judging panels of competitions looking at various aspects of sustainable design, it has always been the fashion category that raises the tempo, volume and interest of everyone in the room. We are all involved. What could be better than to engage this medium of expression as a route to innovation, and for designers to harness their ability to evolve and amplify a visual, material language that communicates the urgency of the global ecological, social, economic and cultural challenges of our times?

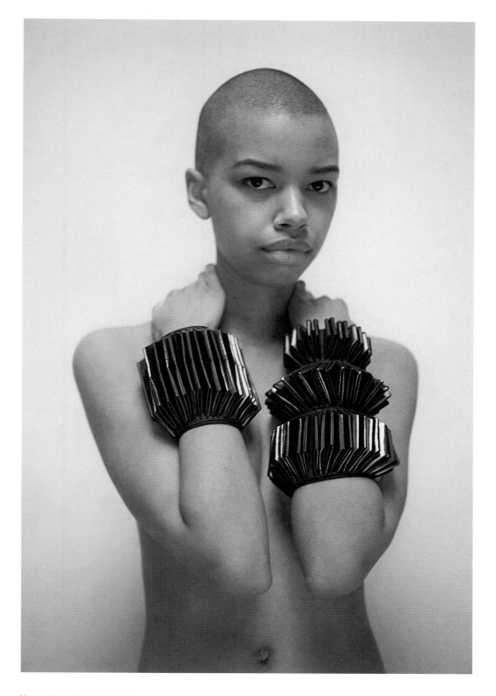

Above and opposite: Accessories by Michelle Lowe-Holder, using upcycled fabric scraps, 2010.

Fashion affects us all…it has always been the fashion category that raises the tempo, volume and interest of everyone in the room. We are all involved.

Joining the dots: connecting design to a sustainable future

CLARE BRASS AND FLORA BOWDEN *Brass set up the SEED Foundation, an organization that explores new avenues of collaborative entrepreneurship for designers.*

Is it possible to square the circle between product design and sustainability? In an atmosphere in which consumerism is routinely equated with environmental damage, the answer can all too easily appear to be no. Attempts to bring a green agenda to products can look like token gestures within a system of production and consumption that is in itself unsustainable.

Certainly product design is intimately associated with the last century's consumer revolution. In Britain the connection was made explicit after the Second World War. The Design Council came into existence to help get Britain back on its feet economically at the end of the war; the 'Britain Can Make It' exhibition in 1946 was intended to show how the design of the nation's industrial products was being improved. These innovations played an important part in driving post-war economic recovery and set the scene for the way in which the design profession would evolve.

It remains true that almost all designers today are involved in the creation, promotion or selling of goods. The design industry's success and contribution to the economy boils down to a process of consumers buying things, using them up (or just becoming bored with them) and then buying new ones. While to some this model seems almost a law of nature, it is beginning to look susceptible to change. Even apart from the environmental argument, it is becoming clear that consumption, as it is currently practised, can be unfulfilling for consumers themselves. The New Economics Foundation, among others, has shown that while the UK's economic output has doubled in the past thirty years its population is no happier.

To assume that design cannot be part of the necessary change is to assume that the discipline has never been about anything but the creation of luxuries. In fact, at its core, design is about solving material problems and facilitating connections. There is no reason to assume that, as material circumstances change, product design cannot change with them. I believe that designers can not only play a role in developing these alternatives but also that this role is central to the process.

The product problem

Changing circumstances are already, of course, encouraging the development of new kinds of products. A plethora of green designs has already appeared on the market, made from materials that are responsibly sourced, less toxic or carbon-intensive and more recyclable. As this trend begins to be visible in mass consumer products, one might reasonably assume that it could represent potential for a significant reduction in environmental impact.

Unfortunately the situation isn't as straightforward as it might seem. As recent well-publicized debates over food production have demonstrated (the benefits of imported fair-trade fruits and vegetables versus locally grown produce, to give one thorny example), a product's ethical credentials are a matter of more than just its material properties. Virtually everything we consume is supported, from production through disposal, by wider systems devised without a sustainability agenda in mind. It is because of this that the risk of tokenism is so great.

To address this problem, many designers have begun to use Life Cycle Analysis (LCA), a powerful tool that allows them to factor in the less visible aspects of an object's ethical footprint, from sourcing of materials through production processes, supply chains and shipping, as well as the longevity of the object and the ease with which it can be disassembled and recycled.

The often surprising findings of this process indicate the need to weight options carefully. Under LCA scrutiny a cotton T-shirt, for example, which might initially seem to be more sustainable than a polyester shirt as it is made from natural fibres, could in fact lose by a substantial margin. Conventional cotton is a thirsty crop, yet one often grown in parts of the world where water is scarce, and it is typically cultivated using huge amounts of pesticide and fertilizer. It is also difficult to recycle. Polyester, on the other hand, requires no pesticides and little water to produce; it can be washed at a lower temperature and, if the right systems are in place, it can also be recycled repeatedly into new polyester.

Nonetheless there are still a number of pitfalls that LCA cannot address on its own. These include the inadequacy of wider systems that are not under direct control of the product designer. Many Nokia mobile phones, for example, are meticulously designed to be recycled. Yet, of the 128 million phones disposed of every year in the USA, only 1% is actually diverted from landfill because *there is no infrastructure to deal with this relatively new waste stream.* The effort going into the sustainable design of objects is often being squandered in practice. Furthermore, LCA does not account for social factors. If our polyester T-shirt is made by an under-age worker in a sweatshop, it surely does not warrant the implied merit of being labelled a 'sustainable' product, even if it technically meets the mark.

Another insight beyond the scope of LCA is that the way we currently consume products is frequently unsustainable even if the products themselves are 'green'. The benefits of low-voltage light bulbs, for instance, will be partially nullified if users think their energy savings make it acceptable to leave the lights on for longer. Our current ideas around sustainability in design frequently fail to account for the actual behaviour of the people who use the products.

The list goes on. A real 'elephant in the room' for product designers is the widespread overproduction and overconsumption of objects, green or otherwise. As a society we now own so much that we no longer have space to store everything. One testament to this is mushrooming of self-store warehouses in the dark corners of our cities, as well as the steady stream of useable objects being sent to landfill.

Finally, and perhaps most damningly, many existing methods of sustainable material production effectively remain the preserve of the luxury consumer market. Unworkable on grounds of cost for large-scale production, such techniques have little hope of influencing mass consumer products. Here the charge of tokenism has most force. It is quite possible for an object to be wholly green in its materials but for its net environmental benefit to be effectively nil because of this issue of scale.

All of this might seem to add up to a lot of problems, but in fact they all boil down to the same basic issue: an object cannot be truly sustainable if the behaviour it generates is not. In sum, then, LCA's real message must be that product designers (this includes fashion and clothing designers) need to look beyond the products themselves and work towards changing behaviour. Is this too much to ask? No – it's already happening.

Designing systems

How can a product designer affect a system? To put it simply, by designing a product that changes the way that system works.

The iPod provides a useful study of how this can be accomplished. Despite consumers' deep sentimental attachments to CDs, vinyl records and bricks-and-mortar music shops, the convenience of MP3s quickly won the day. The music industry now predicts the total disappearance of CDs within five years, bringing with it huge savings in materials, haulage and packaging waste.

The role of the iPod in all this depends upon, but also exceeds, its status as a design icon. Key to its success has been the fact that it was designed as a combination of product and *service* – iTunes, the infrastructure designed to support the iPod. In an incredibly short period of time more than 100 million iPods have swamped the market, and iTunes has become a familiar tool throughout the developed world. Apple software is now on 30% of the world's computers, and the iTunes store has 70% of the digital music market. The lesson is that if a product is designed to make systemic change simpler and more enticing, that change can happen seamlessly and painlessly.

Of course the iPod itself can hardly be held up as a shining example of sustainable design. It has been much criticized for its built-in battery, which cannot be changed by the customer and encourages otherwise functional units to be replaced unneccessarily. Worse, its manufacturers have continued the old-fashioned marketing ploy of perpetually encouraging upgrades to new models, with the concomitant abandonment of old ones that are still functional.

Both of these issues converge in the question of the object's disposal. It is all too easy to envisage millions of iPods going to landfill, some with still useable batteries lodged in their casings, inaccessible even to owners who would have liked to salvage them as backup batteries for their new iPods. Why did Apple design the product this way? One can only speculate that if the company thought it was going to be responsible for the iPod's disposal, it might have done things differently.

Redesigning ownership

Objects are often just tools for getting a job done and, in the case of tools that are used only infrequently, private ownership might not always be the best solution. Many private cars, for example, spend a great deal of time parked, but still need to be taxed, maintained and insured at substantial cost. Many of us own DIY tools such as electric drills, which on average spend an estimated 98% of their lives idle. As mentioned already, it is beginning to be clear that happiness is not rooted in owning more stuff. Perhaps, then, if it could be made sufficiently convenient, many of us might be content to get from place to place, put up shelves and so on without actually owning the tools we use to do so.

Zipcar is a flexible and ultra-localized urban car-hire service that provides the convenience of a private car without the burdens of ownership. It also sidesteps the usual inconveniences of traditional car rental – such as the need to reserve the car well in advance, travel to and from the rental lot and pay for a full-day minimum hire – providing an easy-to-use service with a simple and attractive interface. Cars are parked all over town, ready to be unlocked with a swipe card by subscribers renting the vehicles on an hourly or daily basis. The nearest available car can be found by using a simple online tool. The process is cheaper and easier than car ownership and, since it is effectively mass car-sharing, has real potential to reduce the number of vehicles on the road. Furthermore, the pay-per-use model encourages rational decisions about when a drive is necessary.

Since the challenge of Zipcar was to create a well-designed service, its founders turned to service designers to ensure good useability and mass customer appeal. Service design is a relatively new discipline whose engagement with an increasingly complex network of connections can seem to involve a move away from traditional design objects and materiality in general. In discussions about service design, the term 'dematerialization' is frequently bandied about. In fact there are always vital material elements holding the network together: the touch-points via which individuals use the service. In the case of Zipcar the service could not exist without specially adapted cars and the swipe cards that access them.

All of this has obvious implications for product design. If an object is designed to act as the delivery point of a service, key aspects of the designer's brief

How does one square a company's new desire for product longevity with a consumer populace habituated to desire newness? Will that desire dissipate as consumers become used to the reliability of products built and serviced to last?

immediately alter. The most obvious change, as we have indicated already, is the object must be easy to repair and upgrade and easy to disassemble and recycle, so that the material costs of the company providing the service (and continuing to own the object) will be as low as possible.

Beyond that, there is the somewhat more ambiguous problem of the object's desirability. How does one square a company's new desire for product longevity with a consumer populace habituated to desire newness? Will that desire dissipate as consumers become used to the reliability of products built and serviced to last? Or do designers need to think about providing ways of refreshing not only the workings of such products but also their appearance? Finally, designers will need to think of these products not as isolated units but as dependent on a wider infrastructure. Zipcar users, for instance, depend on the internet for booking and locating cars. These are examples of infrastructure facilitating new kinds of product and user behaviour. However, products can also be designed to address infrastructural problems more directly.

Rethinking infrastructure

The infrastructure that supports our lives is largely invisible to us. Even the more complex aspects of infrastructure within our own homes – wiring or boilers, for instance – are usually kept out of sight. Our waste is managed almost entirely behind the scenes, without the disposal processes interfering with daily life. While we are used to selecting precise quantities of consumer goods upfront and within budgets, we buy public utilities largely blind. We use as much water, gas and electricity as we like and are rarely cognizant of the bills we receive. This invisibility makes it harder for us to understand and thereby change the way we use these systems. We are never made palpably aware of the consequences of our own actions.

To the extent that we perceive infrastructure at all, it is largely through the objects that connect us to it: light switches, electrical goods, water taps, plug sockets and rubbish bins. It seems reasonable to imagine, then, that such objects could also be designed to heighten our awareness of infrastructure. The smart meter does just this. It takes the electricity meter out of the cellar and puts it in a prominent place in the house so people can see how much electricity they are using in real time. Studies show that this markedly reduces energy consumption.

The effectiveness of this device is only limited by the difficulty of visualizing quantities of energy. In other words most people have little idea of how much energy a 'watt' actually represents. In response to this problem design company DIY Kyoto created the Wattson, a smart meter that tots up cost rather than simply measuring wattage and displays the information in an elegant, desirable, contemporary designed object. To further aid comprehension at a glance, its green numeric readout becomes redder as more power is used. The company has also developed Holmes, a piece of supporting software that displays the past twenty-eight days' worth of energy usage, and tells the user which appliances were responsible, and when; it also calculates how much energy has been saved in relation to the previous month. This data can be shared and compared, enabling savings and encouraging collaboration within groups or communities. If this software were to be installed on the desktops of town mayors or facilities officers in large corporations it could have an enormous cumulative impact. Similar devices to tot up usage of other utilities would be equally powerful.

In the same vein the a smartphone application Carbon Diem™ tells people about their carbon emissions. Its designer, Andreas Zacchariah, has created a small piece of software that, added to a mobile phone, can identify the user's different forms of transport by virtue of their relative location, velocity and the pattern of their activity, and calculate the individual's travel carbon footprint. It can then tell the user how many carbon credits need to be purchased in order to offset their carbon footprint.

Energy is now at a premium and the environmental cost of electricity production is becoming clear. However, even as awareness improves, the increasing numbers of electrical goods in our homes mean that energy consumption is going up. Many standard everyday products – cordless phones, for example – are left on all the time, while numerous others have a built-in standby function that causes a constant low-level drain on the power system that is huge in aggregate. We are inundated by products that need recharging – laptops, mobile phones, cameras and so on – and these are responsible for around 18% of domestic energy consumption. Furthermore, upgrades to newer models are frequent and many of these products contain scarce materials such as copper and platinum that are not easily salvageable at end of the object's life.

In short, a great deal of recent product design has been conducted as if the issue of sustainability did not exist. How might things look if the opposite were true? The beginning of an answer may lie in the networks service designers are already exploring. Our homes are increasingly networked. Phones, televisions, computers and music players are increasingly connected, allowing unprecedented ease in the sharing of informational resources. Similarly, the power of the network for sharing material resources is also being explored via initiatives such as the London Reuse Network. The rise of online communities such as Freecycle and Ecomodo and clothes-swapping 'swishing' events is testament to the ever-growing appetite for reuse of objects, on the part of both those disposing of them and those acquiring them.

Could a similarly networked approach allow sharing of natural resources? Whirlpool's recent Green Kitchen project suggests at least one instance in which it could. In this fascinating experiment, one appliance's waste becomes another's resource. Water that goes down the sink is filtered and stored, warmed by waste heat from the fridge and used (ready heated) in the dishwasher. Heat from the oven and humidity from the dishwasher are channelled to a glass-fronted unit to create an ideal microclimate for growing herbs. The beauty of such a system is that it has responsibility built in. Rather than guilt-tripping consumers for over-using infrastructure and appliances that were never designed for sustainability anyway, it compensates for the wastefulness of the existing system, delivering cost and energy savings *with no loss of convenience*.

But why stop at compensating for outdated infrastructure? Why shouldn't designers think about changing the infrastructure itself? At present there are two types of electricity in use: AC (alternating current) and DC (direct current). Despite its high voltage and consequent danger, AC was used when the first power grids were established in the nineteenth century because it loses less power over distance. Unfortunately, all rechargeable equipment – anything that runs on a battery – requires DC energy. That's why battery-powered appliances such as mobile phones need a transformer to allow their batteries to be charged from a domestic plug. This carries several downsides. First, there is a 10–16% loss of energy in the transformer's conversion from AC to DC. Second, transformers are habitually left plugged in, causing a constant drain of electricity even when not in use. Finally, when products break or are upgraded, their transformers are frequently sent to landfill, still operational, because they are not compatible with the replacement products. It is precisely here, in the gaps between different industries and disciplines, that product designers can step in to make change. In a sense this is not so different from what they do already.

Design is protean. Rather than being confined to one particular set of parameters, it perpetually engages with any area where a material problem needs solving. From one context to another, it brings methodologies such as simple visualization and prototyping that are almost universally applicable for testing new approaches and communicating them to varying interest groups. Advanced design thinking increasingly recognizes the need to address relationships rather than deal with isolated objects. It examines the connections between things, the infrastructure that supports them and the people who use both. What if some of this design thinking were to be applied to the fashion industry, rethinking systems, infrastructure and connections?

Designing a product or a piece of clothing to be less unsustainable is obviously good practice. But how can we exploit our creative skills and our capacity to delight in order to create sustainability in the first place? Designers are good problem-solvers, but we need to resist simply solving problems and start creating visions for a different future, designing new ways of doing things. Drawing on our power and resources as design thinkers and educators, it is possible to make things happen. Perhaps in future everyday clothes can become part of a new service system in which they are hired or shared, or designed for disassembly and reconfiguration.

Ultimately design always affects behaviour and is always about facilitating connections. As we have shown, products never exist in isolation. The point is to be profoundly aware of their connectedness and, rather than seeing this as a threat, put it to work strategically to shape new, sustainable approaches for the 21st century.

'The business case for corporate responsibility is a source for innovation'

NIKE has long supported a research and development programme to improve athletes' performance. Technological innovation in materials and construction reveals corresponding sustainability benefits. By Amelia Williams

In 1964 Phil Knight and Bill Bowerman created Blue Ribbon Sports (BRS) in order to provide athletes with better shoes. It wasn't until 1972 that the company we know today as Nike was launched. Nike is now one of the world's leading designers, marketers and distributors of footwear, apparel, equipment and accessories for a wide range of fitness activities.

Innovation has always been key to the evolution of Nike apparel, through research into fabrication and construction for technical performance, and in products that engage consumers via personalization. For example, the Swift Suit used at the Beijing Olympics (2008) was made from recycled polyester. Significant innovations in Nike footwear include the Pegasus 25 (2008), which had a significantly reduced materials content, the Flywire (2009), which utilized tensile fibres of Kevlar for support, and the Flyknit (2012), which had a one-piece upper, precision engineered for an ultra-lightweight,

virtually seamless shoe. Even Nike shoe boxes are now made of recycled card.

In order to reduce costs and improve productivity, the company outsources its manufacturing to independent contractors outside the US, with footwear products in particular manufactured in developing countries. This has resulted in anti-globalization protestors and human rights activists criticizing Nike for taking advantage of cheap overseas labour.[1] In the late 1990s the Nike Sweatshop Labour case, in which children as young as ten were discovered to have been making shoes, clothing and footballs in Pakistan and Cambodia, generated mass controversy over the ethics of the company's business practices. According to Hannah Jones, vice president for corporate responsibility at Nike, 'we became the poster child for all things having to do with poor working conditions.'[2] Nike responded to these negative allegations by putting in place a code of conduct for all of its suppliers and, working

with Global Alliance, reviewed its factories.[3] In an attempt to prevent further damage to its reputation, Nike also created its first corporate social responsibility report.

Over a decade on, Nike has transformed itself from a perceived pariah of child-labour violations to a model for corporate responsibility. Jones sees her role as making sustainability an overt business goal for the company: 'the link between sustainability and Nike as a growth company has never been clearer. There are serious potential impacts of social, environmental and economic shifts on labour forces, youth support, supply chains and products.'[4] Furthermore, says Jones, 'we're really beginning to see what the business case for corporate responsibility is when we see it as a source for innovation and growth.'[5]

A recent Nike corporate responsibility report outlines some important initiatives for the company, demonstrating that it is actively pursuing a sustainable agenda and social justice.[6] The first important point is Considered Design. This combines sustainability principles and innovative performance products for athletes by reducing or eliminating toxics and waste and increasing the use of environmentally preferred materials. Nike has begun to incorporate Considered Design in all of its key categories (see pp. 114–15). The company's long-term vision is to produce products using the fewest possible materials, designed for easy disassembly, allowing them to be recycled into new products or safely returned to nature at the end of their life.[7] The firm recognizes the need for technology that facilitates recycling. Nike's Air Jordan XX3 was the first basketball shoe designed using the Considered ethos and in 2011 the company set the target that all footwear should meet baseline Considered Design standards. Other initiatives include the GreenXchange (see pp. 114–15), an online marketplace where Nike encourages the sharing of intellectual property and ideas relevant to sustainability; Lean and Human Resource Management, which marries lean manufacturing principles with green business

Opposite: World Cup footballers from nine countries wearing national kit by Nike, made from recycled polyester.

Right: Nike Pegasus lightweight running shoe with recycled rubber soles, designed using the Considered process.

'The link between sustainability and Nike as a growth company has never been clearer. There are serious potential impacts of social, environmental and economic shifts on labour forces, youth support, supply chains and products.'

practices; Sport for Social Change, such as the Grassroot Soccer project in Africa, which is a community programme that combines HIV/AIDS awareness with sports; and the formation of a group called Business for Innovative Climate and Energy Policy (BICEP) – which is lobbying for strong climate and energy legislation in the US.[8]

NikeiD, originally developed in 1999 and relaunched in 2004, is an innovative online platform designed to facilitate interaction between the brand and consumer. Business through the site has continued to grow. The NikeiD studio allows the customer to create his or her own expression of the Nike brand. According to Trevor Edwards, Nike's vice president for brand and category management, 'The world has changed and consumers interact with brands on their own terms.'[9] The NikeiD business has more than tripled since 2004, with more than 3 million visitors to the NikeiD website.

Interactive products such as the Nike+ iPod sports kit, launched in 2006, which measures

and records the distance and pace of a run, have changed the way more than a million people think about exercise. Nike was no longer relevant to just one aspect of a runner's exercise regime, such as footwear, but became the very centre of it. Moreover, the device allowed users to communicate with other runners around the globe. In 2008 nearly a million users logged on to the Nike+ service and signed up to run a 10 km race sponsored by the company.[10] Sales of related products have hit US $56 million but Nike+ has done more than just drive sales; it has helped Nike fundamentally reshape the relationship between brand and consumer by creating a platform for connectivity and interactivity.

- Nike's mission statement is 'To bring inspiration and innovation to every athlete in the world'.
- Nike is named for the Greek winged goddess of victory.
- Nike employs more than 33,000 people globally.
- Nike's corporate headquarters is in Beaverton, Oregon.
- The first NikeTown store opened in Portland in 1990.
- Wholly owned Nike subsidiaries include Cole Haan, Converse Inc., Hambro and Hurley International.
- Nike operates in more than 160 countries around the globe.
- Nike sells to approximately 19,000 retail accounts in the US.
- The company has 700 contract factories.

"Considered" is about creating performance products for our athletes, but with a smaller environmental footprint'

LORRIE VOGEL, *Considered Design general manager for Nike, spoke to Sharn Sandor about the company's sustainability initiatives.*

Q For a large-scale business such as Nike, it must have been difficult to establish and understand your environmental footprint. Could you tell us about this process and how long it took you to come to conclusions?'

A Nike has been working towards sustainability since the early 1990s when we introduced our shoe-recycling programme – Reuse a Shoe – and we began measuring our environmental footprint in 1998. We wanted to focus on our largest environmental impacts – waste, water, toxics and energy – and target reductions for each of these areas.

How do you look at these things from a product level?
With regard to materials used in our products, we have an assessment where we weigh all of our materials. We look at how sustainable they are and give them a rating. If we look at waste in our products, we are talking about pattern-cutting efficiency. Then we score the processes we use on how environmentally friendly they are.

How does it work? Do you give each product a score and then try to improve that score if it's not a good one?
We have our Considered Design index and have set targets for all of our products. For fiscal year 2011, we wanted 100% of our footwear to achieve our 'considered baseline' standards; for our apparel, we wanted 100% to meet our baseline standards by

2015. So we score each product based upon less waste, less toxics and using more environmentally friendly materials and we set up target goals. It looks as though our Spring 2011 footwear is going to hit the target of 100% meeting baseline standards. We're excited about that.

How do you overcome the challenges of 'eco' materials costing more than their conventional counterparts?
We wanted to make sure that our Considered Design index was a balanced index, so that when you reduce waste, you save money. When you use environmentally friendly materials they tend to be more expensive, so what we try to do is balance out our waste reduction with the cost of environmentally preferred materials so that it becomes cost neutral.

Is that difficult to measure on such a large scale?
It's not that difficult to measure. When we measure pattern efficiency, we can see the materials we don't have to purchase and that's where we can see the savings.

How do you handle the process of integrating sustainability across the company and the supply chain in practical terms?
Our long-term strategy is focused on innovation, collaboration, transparency and advocacy. We develop targets against our largest environmental impacts and we drive these goals throughout our company and supply chain in order to prepare for a future sustainable economy. Challenges still remain, and transparency and collaboration are the keys to moving forward.

Would you say sustainability can be profitable?
Our goal is to create a more sustainable approach aimed at providing greater returns for our business, community, factory partners, consumers and the planet. We must use this opportunity as a source of growth and innovation. We don't look at this shift as a choice; we believe that these decisions move us towards a more sustainable economy.

When fashion-led companies say that they can't be more sustainable because it is more expensive, how would you suggest they could start incorporating more sustainable practices?
I would say they have to look at all of their environmental impacts and probably the first thing they should focus on is reducing waste. I do think there will be a point when we will have gotten to all of the low-hanging fruit around waste and then we will really need to see more legislation – it's already starting to happen.

Would you say that the changes Nike makes in its policies are responsive to customers' demands or do you lead the way and educate the customer?
We recognize that we must develop processes to prepare us for a more sustainable economy and that our consumers are becoming more aware of these issues. With today's social and environmental realities, this larger commitment is critical to Nike's growth.

There are still a lot of people who aren't familiar with your sustainable practices; they just remember Nike's child-labour issues in the past. How would you educate those consumers about what you are doing now?
Nike has focused on transparency and so people can look at our corporate social responsibility report and understand the continuing improvements we have made around labour.

How and why did you develop the Considered Design ethos and how would you define it?
When we talk about the Considered Design ethos it's about embedding it in everything we do in the company. It is not just a product line – it is an ethos that affects the future of the company. Considered is about every choice the designer makes and about developing more sustainable choices – not only reducing our overall environmental impact but also creating a vision of where we want the future to be. We have a 'closed-loop' vision, in which we take materials from

Opposite: The Air Jordan XX3 basketball shoe issued in 2008 was the first to utilize the Considered ethos to reduce environmental impact during its manufacture.

Right: Disassembled soles of Nike trainers made from Green Rubber, which has greatly reduced environment impact. Worn-out soles are ground up and used to make surfacing materials for playgrounds and sports pitches.

'Nike believes in the importance of transparency to spur further industry collaboration and fast track sustainable innovation.'

an old shoe and an old shirt and then grind them up and turn them into a new shoe and a new shirt so that we can keep materials in play and not have to continue to tap into the earth's resources.

Is it correct that if your designers come up with a more sustainable way to do something they receive rewards?

We set company targets for all of our products to hit Considered baseline standards, so each season we rate our categories, such as soccer, running and basketball. Through our index we also encourage innovation, so if they come up with a new design that is more sustainable, we will put that onto the index and give them additional bonus points. We also give our designers early adopting points – so if you adopt a more sustainable innovation within a year you get additional points, because we want sustainable innovation being adopted at a much faster pace.

You are applying the Considered index to your subsidiaries such as Umbro, Cole Haan and Converse. Do they use the same materials as Nike? Do you share mills and even fabric itself?

Now that we've learned so much about the index and the Nike brand, we can share this information and the implementation of the index…every group is different but we do a lot of sharing. They explore different material options in the same way as the Nike brands, and we rate those materials in the same way.

What plans do you have to apply the index more widely?

We recently opened up our apparel environmental-design tool on the web. It is based on the Considered index; we've made it easy for other brands to look at the way Nike measures products. With the materials-assessment tool they can see how we assess materials and how we look at waste. It's all about sharing within the industry in the hope there will be more collaboration towards achieving higher global standards.

Do you find there is enough collaboration between industry, government and non-profit organizations, or is there a need for more?

Nike believes in the importance of transparency to spur further industry collaboration and fast-track sustainable innovation. We need to start creating global standards to encourage the adoption and development of sustainable product-design standards to create a level playing field. Early in 2009 we launched the GreenXchange, an online marketplace for sharing intellectual property, to share our commitment to the power of open innovation and collaborative networks and to fuel sustainable innovation by making our patented technologies available for research and licensing. There are a lot of existing resources, so this is about sharing the great work and best practices that are out there.

Have you been able to share some of your patented technology with other brands?

Nike opened up over 400 patents on the GreenXchange and a good example is our environmentally preferred rubber. We put it into the GreenXchange and we're starting to see that companies are interested in using the material. When our chemistry team came up with the environmentally preferred rubber, it removed 96% of toxins by weight, so it was a significant improvement…Within the GreenXchange we have interest from companies outside our industry, such as bicycle and car-tyre companies: they

are learning about the work we are doing and we are learning some of the work they have done.

Who knows what sorts of things will be shared in the future?

That's what is so fun about this. The GreenXchange is all about open innovation and you really never know where it's going to go. It's like when the internet first started and no one could predict where it would finally end up.

This reminds me of a researcher at University of the Arts London, Kate Goldsworthy, whose specialization is in recycled polyester fabrics and laser cutting: she partnered with a company in the north of England making bags for potato chips using recycled materials, and was able to do something completely new for textiles using the innovation of this potato-chip bag maker.

That's what is so great. When we talk about sustainability it's not a competitive space so it's a great opportunity to break down barriers around collaboration in industry.

The Considered Index programme is one of the foundations of the Apparel Index, which is being developed by the Sustainable Apparel Coalition, together with the Eco Index developed by the Outdoor Industry Association in the US.

With thanks to Erin Patterson, global corporate communications manager, Nike

Left and opposite above: Two installations with wallscapes, Bless ten-year retrospective exhibition at Museum Boijmans van Beuningen, Rotterdam, 2005.

Opposite below: Bless No. 26 Cable Jewellery, 2005, 'designed to decorate our messy cables'.

'Fashion is often very old-fashioned, very conservative as it is taught in schools.'

BLESS *is the design and clothing company formed by Desirée Heiss and Ines Kaag in 1996, three years after they met at a fashion students' competition in Paris.*
By Sandy Black

Heiss is based in Paris and Kaag in Berlin, and the company maintains offices and shops in both locations. Their unique collaboration has produced a distinctive, experimental and unconventional series of objects, installations, collections and presentations, which are each denoted by a number and title. The series has evolved over time to comprise clothes, accessories and interior and lifestyle products. It includes re-appropriated found objects (such as leather socks and printed bedsheets for Bless No. 8) and new objects,

such as hanging shelves (Bless No. 22 Perpetual Home Motion Machines), a knitted fur hammock (Bless No. 28 Climate Confusion Assistant) and a punchbag computer (Bless No. 40 Whatwasitagain), which subvert expectations with their pragmatism and sharp sense of the absurd. When asked about their guiding philosophy, Heiss and Kaag answer only that 'There is no philosophy of style. We don't come up every season with a theme, or inspiration – it's always just a mix of things we need.'[1]

The title of 'Bless No. 00 Fits Every Style' was adopted as the company slogan, together with the concept of 'themelessness'. Throughout the years, Heiss and Kaag have built up a vocabulary of elements that form a language of their own, such as mismatched or incongruous fabrics, unusual forms, extreme plays on scale, everyday objects, and extraordinary accessories and jewelry. 'We work with things that already exist, trying to collect them or put them in a different background to make them unusual.'

In 2005 Bless was offered a retrospective show in Rotterdam's prestigious Museum Boijmans van Beuningen to mark ten years of the company. 'We said to the curator that we didn't feel at all like showing our products in a museum. On the other hand, of course, we didn't want to lose the opportunity. So we came up with the idea of life-sized pictures, which we later called 'wallscapes'. Our idea was to picture our products in atmospheres or surroundings – private places – the way we could imagine people would have been collecting and using them. We wanted a more natural setting for our pieces.'

Over the years more people have begun to understand the Bless ethos. 'We really had a hard time in the beginning. We started – not as a joke – but just to try something out. When we did the fur wigs for Bless No. 00 [which were later commissioned by Martin Margiela for his Autumn/Winter 1997 show], it was important to try something else straight afterwards [because] we were afraid of being categorized, labelled as hat designers…' Heiss and Kaag's refusal to limit their work to predictable fashion or design categories initially presented serious obstacles to their commercial prospects. 'From the very beginning we switched fields all the time, but this became difficult. Some Japanese buyers, for example, who had discovered that Bless pieces perfectly matched their shops and their programmes, were so disappointed when we did something different the next season, such as covers for furniture.'

Although Heiss and Kaag still resist Bless being labelled as a fashion line, clothing accounts for a significant amount of its offering. 'Of our forty-three collections to date, about one-third are objects, and two-thirds clothes.' However, the clothes are only part of these thematic 'collections', which have a scope and variety that transcends the boundaries of a conventional fashion collection: 'we create a special display for the collection; for example, the hanging furniture pieces [Bless No. 22]…Our work is not only fashion, but not only design either.' Each

of their collections is grounded in a statement, often published as an extended illustrated manifesto in new arts or lifestyle magazines: 'Nowadays we always make a collaboration and publish our "look book" within a magazine.' These collaborations with magazines have been ongoing since collection No. 23. Bless No. 37 was featured in the third issue of *apartamento*, 'an everyday life interiors magazine' based in Barcelona and Milan; Bless No. 42 was published with the second issue of *Condiment*, an Australian magazine of 'adventures in food and

form'. In the latter collaboration images of the Bless clothes collection take up the centre pages, but also subversively infiltrate every other page and feature in the magazine.

Much of the Bless clothing collection is unisex, and No. 37, entitled New Sheheit (a tongue-in-cheek amalgamation of 'she, he, it') made this its central theme. Heiss and Kaag maintain that 'the difference between the masculine and feminine clothes is not so relevant any more'. Handcraft, especially in the form of knitting, has been another key element of the Bless design vocabulary since the beginning. Both Heiss and Kaag created the original handmade samples and early production pieces of accessories such as knitted shoes (the only part of their collection that is now produced in China), at a time when handmade and knitted items did not have their present cachet. 'When we started Bless at the end of the 1990s, we felt a bit embarrassed about the craft part,' they recall.

The two founders of Bless have evolved a strong and powerful working relationship that has grown over time. They discuss it somewhat reluctantly. 'It's a very German mentality – it's strange to talk about ourselves – other people say what is special with Bless is that we are so persistent and insistent. Of course sometimes we have to give up or just wait for the right project'. The patience to wait for the right opportunity to realize their creative ideas, without compromise, and make them work on a larger scale is an important value. 'Sometimes it's just not the right moment, the network is not supporting our needs in that way. It may be a strength or also a handicap. We try to establish a company that is really stable and also remain independent, which is hard – nobody is putting in money. Five or six years ago we tried to produce the clothes collection in Italy, but it's only possible to do this with a backer. Bless is so special that people have not been interested in taking the risk, for fear of failure.' They therefore remain independent both by desire and circumstance.

Although Bless situates itself outside the mainstream fashion system, for several years now it has produced a collection of clothes each season. 'In terms of the commercial aspects, we understand that for the shops it is difficult for them to maintain their customers if you miss a season. We started a while ago to abandon the idea of a collection in the classic sense – a few trousers, a few skirts, and so on – but to work on our own classic pieces, which people like and which we continue to develop.' feel strongly about the concept that long-lasting fashion is more sustainable. 'What we hate about fashion is the unsustainability – we hated throwing away pieces – and this is why we didn't do a [fashion] collection for a very long time.' Local – in this case, European – production is important to ensure both sustainability and good craftsmanship. 'We realized it's impossible to offer really good quality if you are going between producers, doing one T-shirt in Italy, other pieces in Germany or France. "Made in Italy" means a higher price but good quality, although some of the clothes are still sewn in China. The fur pieces were the first we produced in Italy...In Italy there is the knowledge, experience and tradition

– they understand the process. Sustainability for us means classic references and classic details, therefore Italy is the right place for production.'

Although Bless is a small company, it makes between 1,500 and 2,500 pieces of clothing per season, a level of production that is not trivial, and that Heiss and Kaag are reluctant to increase. 'It's not our aim to become big, with all that pressure to be efficient and earn more money. Of course we do want to become more efficient, but the company was never meant to be a cash cow. We want the luxury of having maximum freedom, both style-wise and in our ability to do unreasonable things. We wanted to create the perfect men's jacket, for example: we knew we couldn't really sell it [due to high price] to other shops, but we could take private orders from individual people who appreciated it.'

Heiss and Kaag are emphatic about the manner in which they want to be responsible in business. 'For us it is more interesting to maintain our focus on getting better – becoming more efficient, and making the people we work with feel secure. It's not just about where the clothes are produced – it's much more important to care for the people sitting next to you. You can't call it sustainability, but this is what interests us.'

Bless classics include items such as knitted shoes, necklaces made from other jewelry, and the hood coat, which has been part of the collection for more than six years, selling better every season. Does that take Bless outside the fashion cycle? 'Classic pieces do not ever go out of fashion, but if

'It's not just about where the clothes are produced it's much more important to care for the people sitting next to you. You can't call it sustainability, but this is what interests us.'

they are classic then maybe they have never been part of fashion. In our own shops we offer a service where people can come and order an older piece, because this is also part of what we believe in. You can say that this is also no longer fashion – it's an archive. It might be like the Slow Food movement: slow fashion.'

Heiss and Kaag remain ambivalent about fashion, even as they encourage its evolution through their conceptual yet pragmatic approach. 'In fashion a designer creates something without any real need. When you look at new designs it's hard to identify whether the clothes are from this year or ten years ago, or whether the designer is young or old. Fashion is important for young people because it's about belonging or not belonging.' This ambivalence is also the pair's strength, allowing them to remain true independents in eschewing some parts of the fashion system and embracing others, working with ideas that evolve and demand active participation, developing continuity yet retaining excitement, and perpetuating the strongest, most successful designs in an evolutionary manner. In doing so, Bless offers important insights into our relationship to everyday clothing and objects, creating a renewed perspective, active purpose and functionality in long-lasting products developed to 'fit every style'. This is the ultimate goal of Heiss and Kaag, who dream of one day inventing a useful product with such universal appeal that it will simply bear the name 'Bless'.

Above: Hanging storage shelves, Bless No. 22 Perpetual Home Motion Machines, 2004.

Opposite: Fashion outfits combining heavy knits, fringing and draped wovens from Bless No. 43 Knowhowhow, Autumn/Winter 2011.

'We are independent and haven't got any commercial restrictions on what we produce, only the restrictions we put on ourselves.'

ELEY KISHIMOTO *comprises the husband-and-wife duo Mark Eley and Wakako Kishimoto, whose distinctive boldly printed fabrics are produced sustainably in the UK. By Sandy Black*

Mark Eley and Wakako Kishimoto set up their printed fabric business in 1992, initially producing designs for other fashion companies, including Alexander McQueen, Marc Jacobs, Louis Vuitton and Jil Sander. They soon developed their own fashion line, selling in the UK, US and Japan. In 2003 their first ten years were celebrated with a Fashion in Motion presentation at the Victoria & Albert Museum in London.

Eley and Kishimoto are noted for applying their print design skills across a wide range of products, including their signature 'Flash' print used on the G-Wiz electric car, as well as other designs found on accessories, wallpaper, chairs, shoes and mobile phones. Maintaining their unique handwriting and eschewing passing trends, Eley Kishimoto style themselves on their website as 'shapeshifters of the print world'. Operating as designers in a broad range of media, including magazine publishing, has become their forte and the duo are currently engaged as artistic directors for Laura Ashley.

The couple like to set an example of sustainable practice to inspire others. For the Autumn/Winter 2009/10 season Eley Kishimoto collaborated with ethical clothing company People Tree (see pp. 170–71) and its founder Safia Minney to produce a capsule collection in fair trade printed organic cotton, with garments made in India. This collaboration helped increase the pair's understanding of sustainability issues in fashion, including the negative impact mass produced clothing can have on producers and manufacturers, and informed their own creative development. In

Above: Eley Kishimoto collection, Autumn/Winter 2009, unusually staged on a patterned catwalk.

the wake of this experience, Eley discussed the company's attitudes, actions and values with regard to sustainability, focusing on fabrics and the printing production process, which can be notoriously problematic in environmental terms.

'We have been taking steps to improve our printing over the past few years, looking for sustainable printers in England. We now have our own print factory and we have always used water-soluble inks. Our binders now have no white spirit. Our water waste does still hold some chemicals, which we need to sort out. We don't dye our cloth; we only print it, mainly using pigment dyes that are closest to meeting Soil Association standards. For us to use organic cotton suppliers, it has to be appropriate for the cost as well. There are limitations on the available colours and quality of organic cotton fabrics, but fabric suppliers are becoming more aware of the issues and requirements. Designers working on a relatively small scale, as we do, need the [environmental] certificates attached to new cloth; otherwise they have to rely on the factories that make the fabric for this information.

'Our strategies [for sustainability] include using British chemicals, products and base cloths, which can be road-shipped within this country, although we also have to sell and ship internationally. We're employing local communities. We do our own printing and our own distribution. We currently have 70 or 80 stockists of the main collection, down from 130, but it's 260 including all the licensees for watches, sunglasses and

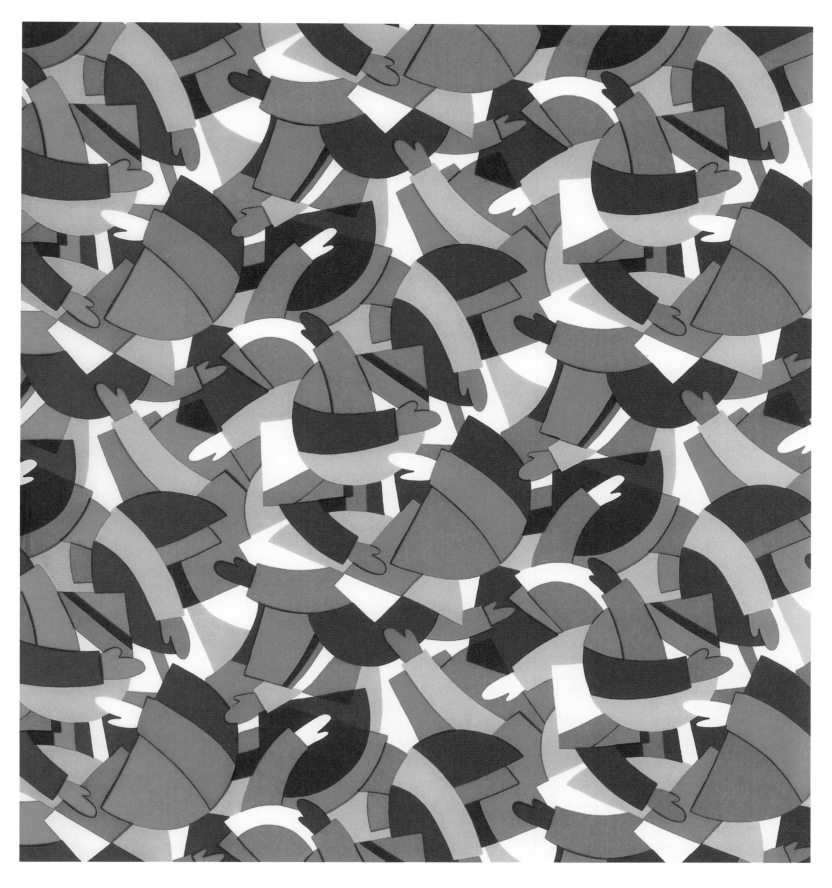

Above: 'Tricky sleeves' print design by Eley Kishimoto, 2007.

'We now have our own print factory and we have always used water soluble inks. Our binders now have no white spirit. Our water waste does still hold some chemicals. which we need to sort out.'

Below, left: Poster for Eley
Kishimoto Spring/Summer 2001
collection featuring the trademark
'Flash' print.

Below, right: Knitwear from
Eley Kishimoto Autumn/Winter
2011/12 collection.

Opposite: Total printed look from
Eley Kishimoto Autumn/Winter
2011/12 collection.

shoes. People in our position in the middle market producing say 6,000–7,000 units a season don't make enough money to afford the facility as well as paying for the manpower plus creativity and marketing. It's not possible unless you get to a volume of about 15,000 units per season with thirty or forty styles: then you start to make a profit that pays for the investment in the marketing. Every designer working on the scale that we do has to have a supplementary occupation. Recognizing this, we are starting two new branches of Eley Kishimoto so that we can do what we want at the time we want to do it, stepping outside of the fashion system.

'We are open because we are independent and haven't got any commercial restrictions on what we produce, only the restrictions we put on ourselves... We might compromise to ease productivity and to get things out on time, but not to fulfil commercial desires. We don't do the black jumper or the black dress, which are perceived as commercial. We've made money but it's not enough to sustain what we do over a year. We've invested in our company every year with income generated from consultancies and collaborations.

'I've always imitated corporations. We got income from consultancies; we got enough press about what we do; we then created this one brand – Eley Kishimoto – which then diversified into sunglasses and other products, but this was confusing. Now I've created another company in Japan, Eley Kishimoto Holdings, and teamed up with investors for a percentage of sales of kimono, sunglasses, jewelry etc., based on the intrinsic value and integrity of the brand.

'There are now a group of brands, as well as the main Eley Kishimoto line. Each has its own ethos. The EK Jam Factory label made its first delivery to Anthropologie in 2009 in the US and

ELEY KISHIMOTO
CORDIALLY INVITE YOU TO VIEW OUR NEW SPRING/SUMMER 2001
COLLECTION AT THE FOLLOWING SITES:

LONDON	PARIS	TOKYO	NEW YORK
METROPOLITAN HOTEL	GALERIE PATRICIA DORFMAN	MACH 55 5-45-12 TOTOEI SHIBUYA-KU	THE NEWS INC. 495 BROADWAY, 5F.
OLD PARK LANE, LONDON, W1Y 4LQ.	61 RUE DE LA VERRERIE, 75004 PARIS	TOKYO 151-0053 JAPAN.	NEW YORK, NY 10012.
ARRIVE 23/09/00 DEPART 27/09/00	ARRIVE 09/10/00 DEPART 15/10/00	ARRIVE 09/09/00 DEPART 15/10/00	ARRIVE 15/09/00 DEPART 15/10/00
9.00AM-8.00PM	9.00AM-8.00PM	TEL. (0) 3 5465 1405.	TEL. 212 925 9700.
R.S.V.P.	PRIVATE VIEW PARTY 09/10/00	FAX. (0) 3 8046 9561.	FAX. 212 925 1550
	6.00PM-9.00PM R.S.V.P.		

ENQUIRIES
FOR ALL ENQUIRIES OR TO MAKE AN APPOINTMENT. TEL. +44 (0) 208 674 748 FAX. +44 (0) 208 674 3516

the UK, delivering four signature styles four times a year. The Dai Jobu label is a menswear concept that produces things associated with motorbikes and perfect workwear that never changes – the perfect workshirt, the one-shape T-shirt – and also incorporates a group membership. There are also the Wakako Kishimoto and ESP lines.

'We built a tower in Covent Garden in 2008, and created funny printed street furniture around London. All of this other stuff is happy playfulness – it enables us to communicate with a different audience and create a wider identity. We are not just fashion designers – even though it all started with textiles – and we see ourselves as designers, not artists. Now are confident enough to move away from the fashion calendar, although it is very difficult to get off that demanding and all-encompassing conveyor belt of fashion…I am most proud of being able to make new creative decisions every day and come up with new formulas and ideas, keeping my independence.

'A few years ago, in a collaboration with Going Green we decorated the G-Wiz electric car, using our 'Flash' print. One hundred decorated cars were produced and sold around England. I had taken part in the Gumball Rally for a few years, but this time I wanted my car to generate as few emissions as possible to raise awareness of alternative energy supplies. It's about using alternative systems – and not just one system.

'There's still a need for pioneers in sustainable fashion, as the system that exists at the moment does not support the availability of new resources. There needs to be a public demand, a desire for the concept of sustainable fabrics to grow. It's still very early days; it may take fifteen or twenty years for sustainability to become the norm in the fashion and textile industries. High-end and high-volume fashion are very different worlds, with different responsibilities. It's a lot easier for design companies like us to make our own choices.'

Key lessons for sustainable innovation

MARTIN CHARTER, *director of the Centre for Sustainable Design at the University of the Creative Arts UK, summarizes the findings of his department's long-running series of Sustainable Innovation conferences on sustainable product development.*

1
Managing the transition to low-carbon and resource-efficient economies and societies will involve significant challenges.

2
Our ability to measure sustainable/eco-innovation at a macro level is at an early stage.

3
We need to identify market opportunities for sustainable products, services and technologies more clearly.

4
Much of sustainable/eco-innovation has been dominated by the supply side (a 'technology push' rather than a 'demand-side' pull).

5
We need to find ways to stimulate more demand-side pull.

6
We need to think more holistically about where the opportunities for sustainable/eco-innovation are in the value chain.

7
We need to build networks among stakeholders to enable sustainable/eco-innovation.

8
Niche players can create change but the realities of the market can be quite bloody.

9
Visionary leadership is key.

10
We need to encourage customers to drive sustainable/eco-innovation.

11
There are organizational challenges associated with driving sustainable/eco-innovation – some may not be comfortable with it!

12
It is about managing change and breaking through middle management's 'layer of granite'.

13
We need to provide incentives to enable sustainable/eco-innovation within the organization and throughout the value or supply chain.

14
Embedding appropriate and customized processes and tools within the organization is key to implementation of sustainable/eco-innovation.

15
There is a need for demonstrable examples of bottom-up sustainable/eco-innovation, such as case studies and personal stories.

'The most sustainable product is the one that is not made but is recycled from what already exists.'

PETER KALLEN *is design director of NAU, a design-led company based in Oregon in the US that produces sportswear and outdoor lifestyle clothing from ethically sourced materials.*
By Sandy Black

NAU's unconventional approach to business is one expression of the company's philosophy of seeking new solutions for the fashion system. The brand built up a strong following between 2005 and 2007 but could not sustain its growth plan in a recession and closed in early 2008. Later the same year it relaunched with new backing and enhanced online presence, but with the same underlying ethos, as described by NAU's marketing spokesman Ian Yolles. 'What we did and how we did it was bold and audacious. We set out to design an entire company from the ground up with sustainability at the centre of our thinking. We challenged conventional paradigms when it came to our approach to philanthropy, the notion of "business unusual" and the way we engaged with our community. In some ways it was the right set of ideas at the right time. It seems to have struck a chord.'[1] One of the inevitable casualties of the relaunch was a reduction in the percentage of profit, from 5% to 2%, that the company could give to philanthropic causes via their Partners for Change programme.

Design director Peter Kallen explains the corporate ethos this way: 'Sustainable fashion (or any product) is a challenge – the most sustainable product is the one that is not made but is recycled from what already exists, either as raw materials or as a pre-existing finished object. At NAU we have chosen two paths towards sustainability: materials and design.[2]

Presently we use recycled PET, traceable organic cottons and wools, as well as recycled cottons and wools. We strive to craft timeless pieces that integrate into the customer's wardrobe and have multiple uses. The clothes are built to move seamlessly through the wearer's day in a variety of conditions and settings, allowing them to have fewer items that do more things. The idea is to make a product that is more sustainable, considered and useful.

Our biggest obstacles in acheiving this are:

1. Raw materials: the availability of [sustainable] raw materials to create the fabrics and trims continues to be a challenge.

2. Perception: there is a perceived aesthetic that is associated with a product that is 'sustainable' – the idea that it is something to wear for a trip to the ashram, and that you must be shrouded in hemp that feels like a burlap bag.

3. Commitment: when you are pioneering a new direction it takes commitment from all levels to make sure the supply chain will work, and that all of the partners are willing to make this commitment to being sustainable. It costs money and time to create something new.

4. Acceptance: our products need to be accepted and valued by customers for what is put into them.

Aside from all of this, people need to realize the value of sustainability and understand the positive change it can effect for all of us. Part of this realization includes the fact that a sustainable product will cost more to create, but the value and impact it can have is priceless. In time I believe the cost equation can be equalized, but to start with,

Right and opposite:
Womenswear and menswear,
NAU, Autumn/Winter 2011.

the raw materials alone can often cost up to 20% more than their conventional equivalents.

Design is the driving force behind sustainability. Designers can provide leadership, guidance, exploration and influence. It is our responsibility to integrate sustainability into all our products and business models from this day onward. We need to take this initiative ourselves because the fashion wheel is BROKEN! It needs a big kick in the backside to change its bad habits. I am encouraged and inspired by the change that is possible, starting with sustainability and expanding from there…I love fashion and design and am optimistic that collectively we can be agents of change who will steer the ship towards a new destination.

This is our philosophy on design and sustainability: sustainable fashion means timeless colours, smart design, eco-friendly materials and simple care. For you, it means style: you'll want to wear our clothes for more than just one season. Our principles of design are rooted in a blend of beauty, performance and sustainability.

1. Beauty: a passion for the aesthetic in all things. We design for lasting beauty with product colors, details and shapes that are minimalist, modern, and timeless.

2. Performance: meeting or exceeding an intended use. We design products that protect from the elements, and establish a visual tone that allows for multifaceted use – styles look as good on city streets as they perform well in the wild.

3. Sustainability: balancing the 'triple bottom line' of people, planet and profits. We design for social, material, and aesthetic sustainability. 2% of profits on every sale goes to our humanitarian and environmental Partners for Change. Our cut and-sew factories must adhere to our code of conduct. The materials we use include natural and renewable fibres produced in a sustainable manner and synthetic fabrics that contain a high recycled content. We minimize toxics in all product finishes and dyes and use salvaged and recycled materials for our retail fixtures.

These core design principles of beauty, performance and sustainability are our core business principles, too.

'There is a perceived aesthetic that is associated with a product that is 'sustainable' the idea that it is something to wear for a trip to the ashram. and that you must be shrouded in hemp that feels like a burlap bag.'

Catalysts for change: a political future for fashion education

FRANCES CORNER *is head of college at London College of Fashion. Her research has examined issues such as lifelong learning and employability, as well as teaching and learning methods.*

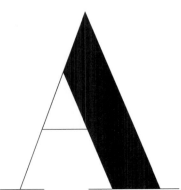t the outset of the 21st century we are all becoming increasingly aware that we need a new global economic model. The pressures of climate change, limited resources, a global recession that has highlighted the downside of consumerism and greater understanding that our desire for cheap goods is paid for by the workers who produce them are all coalescing to bring about a realization that perhaps we need a change in thinking. This is particularly important if we are to meet the challenge of creating a global economic infrastructure that is both environmentally and ethically sustainable. All industries, businesses and individuals are going to need to reassess the parts they have played in creating the current situation and the roles they might play in developing a new, greener, more ethically viable model. The fashion industry, because of its preoccupations with the body, identity and our physical requirements, enables great insight into ourselves, our cultural values and our place in the environment. It also gives us the opportunity to rethink our approach to consumption. Fashion educators have a critical role to pay in this.

The global challenge is to develop a 21st-century economic infrastructure based on low carbon and low energy, and aiming for zero waste. To achieve this, a simple reliance on the markets or on governments to find the solution is not going to succeed. An opportunity for institutions of higher education to bring together a range of specialists and disciplines to co-create a variety of solutions is beginning to emerge. Fashion educators are already working with retailers, manufacturers and aspects of science, engineering and technology in the development of new products that are more intelligent, multifunctional and fit for purpose, yet well designed, aesthetically satisfying and commercial. What has been missing to date has been a sustained approach enabling such institutions to seize the implications of the politics of fashion, placing it centre stage with their students, graduates and researchers. It is becoming clear that fashion educators have a responsibility to address the political context of fashion through their teaching, research and relationships with industry and to thereby act as catalysts in the creation of a new greener, ethically aware fashion industry.

'Clothes,' observed James Laver, 'are inevitable. They are nothing less than the furniture of the mind made visible, the very mirror of an epoch's soul.'[1] In any reassessment of fashion's political context and the potential impact that it can have in developing a greener economic infrastructure, it is useful to consider how everything begins with the garment. Our garments interact with us, protecting us from the environment and allowing us to live fulfilling lives – being naked in the wrong context is still a great taboo. They give us, as individuals and as a broader society, what we need to operate on a physical level. Clothing conventions allow us to attend a party or go for a job interview. They also enable us to express and communicate ideas about our personalities and values. As Joanne Entwistle has put it, 'Dress in everyday life cannot be separated from the living, breathing, moving body it adorns.'[2] Thus dress conventions are central to our lives.

Around clothing and fashion – both essentially comprised of three-dimensional objects that mould to and fit our body shapes – a whole other world has emerged: the designer, the fashion show, the multimedia disseminators, the flagship shops. All of these help to persuade us to purchase what is ultimately a simple piece of fabric. The infrastructure that has grown up around the garment has been created to help us buy the lifestyle that the clothes have come to embody. Clothes and fashion have become symbiotically entwined with culture, thereby expressing not only our personal identities but also aspects of society. As Herbert Blumer stated in 1969, fashion 'always seems to keep abreast of the times. It is sensitive to the movement of current developments as they take place in its own field, in adjacent fields, and in the larger social world'.[3]

Over the generations this has become more apparent. A real turning point for fashion's relationship with identity and society came in the 1960s. This period saw a tangible desire manifest itself for greater freedom of expression, as demonstrated in the student protests, the riots of 1968, and the rise of feminism and black power. At this point, as Richard Martin has explained, a 'fundamental schism' occurred as fashion separated itself from wealth and power, expressed previously in its relationship with the elite, and instead developed an alliance with art and culture. The consequence of this schism has been wide-ranging and significant. Fashion became 'avant-garde in sensibility, it came under and drew from the thrall of popular culture and it became the nexus of democratic social values and the clarifying aesthetic order of art'.[4] It was intrinsically linked with how we as individuals express ourselves. In the 1960s short skirts became a symbol for how clothes could express and reinforce a social revolution that brought freedom from previous social constraints. The 60s demonstrated the power of fashion to reach out and embrace new sections of society in order to express a social revolution because the clothes that allowed them to demonstrate their ideas were affordable and easily purchased. By offering modern democracy a means of expression, fashion became embedded within consumption and capitalism. The democratization of fashion, which builds upon its inherently aspirational nature, was made possible because of ready access to cheap but better-designed clothes. We all want to be able to buy this dream. Such democratization demonstrates how fashion can express both the individual and society's ideas, but what hasn't been sufficiently recognized is that this is made possible through the physical resources of both people and planet. It is this lack of recognition that begins to underline the political implications of fashion and the importance of the role that fashion education can play. Whether by helping us as individuals to understand the implications of fashion, or by helping society to recognize the price of the freedoms and desires it has come to judge as significant, it is at this juncture that the political power of fashion and the responsibility of fashion education become evident.

Fashion has responded to the demand for goods, and its means of production and distribution make fast delivery and the meeting of consumption needs possible. So the democratization of fashion has signalled a hugely significant upward shift in our consumption levels.

Fashion's Impact

There is no underestimating the global significance of fashion and its means of production, which links world economies. As Western consumption levels have increased, so production and manufacturing in the developing world have expanded. Fashion has become inherently bound up with our global economic infrastructure.

As individuals we consume in a personal style that makes our individuality clear, but this style is nevertheless linked to the group or section of society we aspire to be a part of. These groups or 'tribes', supported by the internet, don't just express themselves through clothing but also through books, restaurants, accommodation, household goods and holidays. They are global in nature, and they feed and are fed by retailers, advertisers, designers, manufacturers and the media – being fashionable is no longer just about clothes but about all aspects of our lifestyle. Thus in 21st-century consumption, the creative and cultural industries are significant contributors to our global economies. Fashion has responded to the demand for goods, and its means of production and distribution make fast delivery and the meeting of consumption needs possible. So the democratization of fashion has signalled a hugely significant upward shift in our consumption levels.[5]

Fashion has grown into a vast global industry playing a key role in many world economies. Internationally the global apparel, accessories and luxury-goods market generated total revenues of US $1334 billion in 2008.[6] The clothing industry itself is worth over $1 trillion and is ranked the second biggest global economic activity for intensity of trade.[7] In 2004 the total British spend on clothing was £37.4 billion.[8] This does not take into consideration, for example, the symbiotic relationship fashion has with the cosmetic, beauty and homeware industries. If we also include those sectors, which underpin the selling and communication of fashion, notably through retail,

Our developing knowledge of the effects of the production and consumption of fashion on our environment and the people who create it is becoming increasingly hard to ignore. Fashion educators are becoming aware of the need to incorporate clear examples into the curriculum...

media, public relations, internet sales, advertising and magazines, what emerges is a complex, interrelated, global business. Such a powerful economic driver has meant that fashion is now at the heart of most world economies,, whether they be emerging economies producing garments and products or more developed economies in which, for example, fashion weeks are seen as a key component of a nation's cultural development.

Although parts of this vast industry are beginning to confront the effect fashion is having on the world's

resources both human and physical, nevertheless the global fashion industry wastes many of our most precious ones in its production. Our developing knowledge of the effects of the production and consumption of fashion on our environment and the people who create it is becoming increasingly hard to ignore. Fashion educators are becoming aware of the need to incorporate clear examples into the curriculum and research activities, and to challenge students and researchers to create solutions. A precious resource such as water is a key example. A T-shirt uses 5,000 pints of water in its production from crop to shop,[9] yet once we have purchased it we will wash it without considering whether it is really necessary; globally Unilever estimates that there are 7 million washes every half hour using their laundry products.[10] Economists recognize that shortage of water is going to be one of the key flash points for future conflicts. Finding ways to reduce our dependence on water in the production of garments is a real and urgent challenge.

Similarly, many resources are exploited in the production of fashionable clothes. Gold has been integrated into clothing and fashion for generations as its properties have captured our individual and collective imaginations. However, obsession with its properties has meant that it has developed a destructive aspect. Gold mining displaces local communities, arsenic used in the process contaminates drinking water and rivers, and natural areas, even those officially protected, are destroyed. According to the recent World Wildlife Fund Deeper Luxury Report, 'mining is a major threat to biodiversity and to frontier forests.'[11] The 'Golden Rules' campaign, with support from Oxfam and others, has been started to turn gold from a curse into a blessing. Using the power of the consumer and retailer, this campaign encourages brands and retailers alike to follow these Rules to ensure, for example, that human rights are protected and safe working conditions are provided; that operations are not in conflict zones and that communities are not displaced; that dumping in lakes and rivers no longer takes place; that mines are opened and closed appropriately and are not located in areas of ecological value; and that independent verification takes place to see that the Rules are being followed.

There are other significant ethical implications around the production of clothes that fashion educators need to address. The manufacturing of garments provides an opportunity for developing countries to create sustainable livelihoods. In Kenya, for example, 30,000 people work in the clothing industry, and each job has been proven to generate five other jobs.[12] Employment has also allowed women in countries such as Bangladesh to become more independent. Local governments are capable of suppressing independent union organizing efforts in order to maintain lucrative contracts at the cost of deteriorating conditions for workers. The aggressive buying practices of the retail industry, with its short lead times and irregular demand for quantity, have increased the number of workers on casual or temporary contracts who do not have the same benefits as full-time workers. They have no job security, a factor underlined by the fact that retailers switch suppliers quickly when a new low-cost factory enters the market. There is forced overtime (often not optional and frequently unpaid), poor wages due to low-cost competition and the use of subcontractors to cope with the fluctuating demands of fast fashion. Many of the subcontractors rely on home workers, which can encourage child labour, or migrant workers who have had their passports taken away, resulting in pressurized working conditions. Poorly enforced and inadequate local laws often prevent legal action being taken against factories, and garment workers frequently earn such a low wage that they cannot afford to feed their children three meals a day.

There are further political implications in educating people about fashion's effect on developing countries, notably our wasteful approach to our clothes. The second-hand clothes market is worth $1billion globally, a consequence of the growth of the fast-fashion market and the subsequent increase in poor-quality second-hand clothes that Western consumers don't want. This has led to an increase in the number of second-hand clothes bales being sold to Africa. Julius Nyerere, the first president of Tanzania, called these bales 'Dead white man's clothing' and banned the import of this type of 'Cultural Colonialism' in the 1960s. Today, however, the US's largest export to Tanzania is second-hand clothing.[13] While it does create jobs, it also suppresses the local production of clothes, which is ironic, given that Africa produces the largest amount of cotton in the world.

If we are to have a balanced economy that respects the world's resources and aims, then as consumers we should be addressing the results of our consumption patterns, taking responsibility for the political, economic and social consequences of our desires. Fashion education has a pivotal role to play here. In the UK we buy a third more clothes now than four years ago.[14] Yet we are careless with these purchases, dumping 1.2 million tons of clothing into landfill in 2005 in the UK alone.[15] Often we don't even wear our purchases, consigning them to the back of the wardrobe, thus showing a disregard

...as consumers we should be addressing the results of our consumption patterns, taking responsibility for the political, economic and social consequences of our desires. Fashion education has a pivotal role to play here.

for the resources, both human and physical, that made them. However, this vast industry is having a significant effect not only on the environment but also on society, which feels increasingly dislocated. If you can't buy the dream, alienation and dissatisfaction are your only outlets. In their book *The Spirit Level* (2009), researchers Richard Wilkinson and Kate Pickett examine the correlation between unequal societies and individuals' health and well-being, pointing to the contrast between material success and social failure. Their argument is that 'if we are to gain further improvements in the real quality of life, we need to shift attention from material standards and economic growth to ways of improving the psychological and social well being of whole societies.'[16] They go on to demonstrate that the more unequal the income distribution, the greater the social problems.

The opportunity is for fashion to embrace its political dimensions, not just taking on the global challenges we face and finding ways of creating a more sustainable and environmental production system, but also using the power of the individual garment to express the need for a more sustainable industry, one that values inclusiveness and supports communities. As we begin to understand the pressure that we, as both individuals and broader communities, exert on the world's finite resources, so we must respond and adjust our lifestyles. The difficulty facing many of us is the lack of clear guidelines as to how we can change, with no obvious choices and no sense of direction from either governments or the industry. Institutions of higher education can help make the link between personal behaviour and the global implications of satisfying our desire for garments.

Catalysts for Change: The Politics of Fashion Education
As governments debate strategies for our economic futures, green industries and technologies could be set at the heart of financial strategies to help tackle unemployment and financial regeneration. As *The Great Transition*, the New Economics Foundation's 2009 report, put it, 'By sharing our resources more equally, by building better communities and a better society and by safeguarding the natural environment, we can focus on the things that really matter and achieve genuine and lasting progress with higher levels of well-being.'[17] There is a significant opportunity for fashion education institutions to play a key role in realizing this approach; such institutions are ideal catalysts as they are in the position of being able to bring together key stakeholders and cutting-edge thinkers. Indeed, education as such has become more important as the skills and abilities we need to analyse and process information are in greater demand. Educational institutions can set the bar for innovative design that exploits the possibilities of technological developments to create a wide range of beautifully designed, sustainable, ethical garments that express our values and identities.

Internationally a number of institutions have already established centres for sustainable design to help coordinate and drive the changes that are needed. For example, Pennsylvania State University has a Center for Sustainability, and the University of Texas at Austin has established a Center for Sustainable Development whose mission is to 'lead the study and practice of sustainable development in Texas, the nation and the world through complementary programmes of research, education and community outreach'.[18] Washington State University has an Institute of Sustainable Design, while in Denmark the TEKO and KEA design schools have established the Centre for Responsible Design with financial support from the Ministry of Education. The Swedish School of Textiles at the University of Borås has created an annual conference and project, Design of Prosperity: The Sustainability of Our Present Future, that brings educators together with industry and creative thinkers to address the issues around ethics and the environment.

Similar thinking was behind the move by the London College of Fashion when it established the Centre for Sustainable Fashion

and the Centre for Fashion Science. The centres' interdisciplinary nature encourages dynamic interaction among cultural theorists, scientists, architects, management and marketing theorists, fashion designers, and a host of industries and organizations. The result is continual cross-fertilization of ideas that bring about innovative solutions, which in turn are brought to a wide audience. Part of the purpose of these and other such centres is to provide consumers with a range of options, some of which will be clothes made from sustainable materials. Technology will also be central to changing how we think and feel about our clothes. Wearable technology, interactive garments and clothing that primes the body for different psychological roles will all play a central part in changing our relationship and attitude to what we wear. As garments become more personalized and interact with the world around us, so we will come to value them again. Less may become more. Fashion should become about eclectic personal style as we wear organic, vintage, refashioned items, clothes we have swapped or even clothes with technology that will change their colour. Such wardrobes will encourage an emotional engagement with what we wear, supporting us in looking after garments and making us value their total life cycle.

Governments are beginning to explore related ideas already. For example, the Japanese Ministry of the Environment began, with its Cool Biz project in 2005, to focus on reducing the country's carbon emissions by turning down air conditioning. A 'no necktie, no jacket' policy for summer wear, relaxing strict dress codes, has been adopted by the public and businesses alike. Working with fashion designers to make more casual styles acceptable in the work environment, the government has even held a fashion show, and everyone from the prime minister down has had a part to play. The project has revealed how the cultural and behavioural practices around clothes play a key role in addressing climate change.

As a major global business, the fashion industry demands a serious system of fashion education. Educators are in the privileged position of training the next generation of designers, who will play a pivotal role through research, consultancy and enterprise activities. As the dual agendas of climate change and quality of life move centre stage, so 21st-century fashion courses are preparing their students for an industry that will have to transform itself to meet these challenges – challenges that both bring a political dimension to fashion education and make education a potent catalyst for change.

Seven luxury myths

THE WORLD WILDLIFE FUND (WWF) *published an influential report in 2007 that evaluated the environmental and social performance of leading luxury brands and suggested ways to redefine the concept of 'luxury' to include sustainability. Here the report tackles seven of the luxury industry's commonly held misconceptions about the value of adopting environmentally and ethically sound practices.*

1

'Luxury is about conspicuous personal indulgence, so it can never be moral.'
Wrong! Luxury is about being and having the very best. Products that cause misery or environmental damage, now or in the future, are not longer considered by affluent consumers to be best in class. Such products do not feel luxurious to the more ethically and environmentally concerned consumers of today.

2

'Luxury consumers in new markets do not care about ethics or the environment.'
Wrong! As new markets mature, their more affluent citizens increasingly follow international trends, including awareness and concern over social and environmental issues, and a desire for their purchases to provide meaningful experiences. In certain regions, this arises not only from international influences, but also from local values, such as lien in China.

3

'Brands cannot tell consumers what to care about.'
Wrong! Brands tell consumers what to care about all the time, both directly and by implication or demonstration. Examples include models selected for their body shape, fashion and personal care tips in the media, and advertising.

4

'Luxury brands can only build in value through materials, design and marketing.'
Wrong! Value can be provided via benefits to people, communities and environment affected by production, marketing and distribution. These benefits help to build the intangible value of the brand. This implies and requires a high level of collaboration between marketing, design and other business functions.

5

'Heritage will maintain luxury brand value.'
Wrong! Fifty years hence, what a luxury firm does today will be part of its heritage, and another company that is created today will also have a heritage. A company's heritage from the 19th or 20th centuries will not stay the same, but will be interpreted on the basis of contemporary values and the company's activities during the 21st century. Luxury brands need to see heritage as an evolving phenomenon, and work at contemporary heritage creation by shaping the future proactively.

6

'Legal action is the only way to address counterfeiting.'
Wrong! Changes in technology and communications, combined with the promotion of labels by luxury brands, mean that counterfeiting will continue, even in the face of legal challenges. Therefore luxury brands must reconsider their emphasis on logos and seek to connect with deeper values.

7

'Luxury brands have less impact on society than other companies, so need to offer nothing more than philanthropy and compliance.'
Wrong! Luxury goods involve diverse supply chains that have impacts on communities and nature throughout the world. Various stakeholders, including investors, increasingly expect verifiable and comparable information on social and environmental performance, resulting from a systematic approach. In many cases, non-luxury consumer goods companies outperform luxury brands in aspects of corporate sustainability.

Extract from the World Wildlife Fund (WWF) 'Deeper Luxury' report, 2007[1]

'What I don't like about fashion is all the fakeness.'

LAURA QUEENING *creates a range of stylish, contemporary accessories under the name Aura Que, manufactured by the Fair Trade Group Nepal to increase ethical production in the developing country.*
By Dilys Williams

Laura Queening graduated in 2007 from the Cordwainers Accessories BA Honours course at London College of Fashion, winning several awards. She was involved in the CSF Shared Talent for Trade project in South Africa (see pp. 98–99) and the LCF@Oxfam Designer Showcase before establishing her fair trade accessories brand Aura Que for Autumn/Winter 2008, producing leather and knitted products in Kathmandu, Nepal. Each product is individually handcrafted in a factory that employs local people, some of whom are affected by disabilities, providing an income for themselves and their families. Wherever possible Queening incorporates local materials such as allo fabric produced from a Himalayan plant, handmade brass fittings, lokta paper and traditional woven cloth. The accessories use high-quality cowhide leather that is a by-product of the food industry.

Queening spends about five months of the year in Kathmandu, working directly with the producers, sourcing materials and developing skills with the leather producers. Aura Que is a thriving business, supporting Laura's design aspirations and allowing her to pay her workers 30% more than the average Nepali wage via the Fair Trade Group Nepal. Additional benefits for the workers include sponsoring children's education and paying for families' healthcare. Laura is also currently exploring ways in which she can assist an organization working to support women who are susceptible to human trafficking by offering them employment in Nepal.

Q **What is at the centre of your design thinking and the crux of your business?**

A It's ethical fashion accessories. My interest in ethical fashion evolved from my desire to combine my career in design with my love of adventure, people, travel and culture.

What is allo material and where do you find it?
It's similar to a hemp fabric; it's made from a composted plant stem that the Nepalese spin into yarn. It comes from the plant *Girardinia diversifolia*, the Himalayan giant nettle, which grows at the altitude of 1,200–3,000 metres, but what is even more interesting is the story of the people involved in making the fabric – it's not just about sourcing exotic materials.

What was it that made you decide to take the route you've taken?
I made my first decisions during my degree course. What I don't like about fashion is all the fakeness – the stylists, the photography – and I really wanted to get away from all that stuff. I didn't like the idea of working for a corporate brand, designing something and sending it off to China and never meeting the person who was making it. It seemed too clinical. I wanted to do something that was just a bit more personal, where you knew the people you were working with, and knew that you were helping them out.

What would you say are the greatest opportunities and the greatest challenges that you face?
One can also be the other. Working in Nepal is an adventure: trying to encourage small businesses, family businesses and established charities when at the same time you've got a European design business to run and markets to satisfy. It is challenging because you have to design within the technical capabilities of the workers. I can have a hundred ideas of crazy

things that I want to do but when it comes to business I also have to find something that sells, fits a price point, works for the producers and also fits with my design aesthetic. So that's been one of my biggest challenges so far: finding something that will sell but that feels good for me to be endorsing.

Do you see the social aspect of your work as a hindrance or an opportunity?
It's probably a bit of both. It's difficult being one person trying to set up something so far away. There's a lot of research and groundwork, the building of relationships and getting used to timeframes, lead times and how people work. It's a huge learning curve. It probably creates more work, but it's really exciting. It's risky but I quite like that.

Do buyers interrogate you more because of the nature of your work?
Yes, they want everything to be right first time. I've got two types of buyers: the ones for whom the ethical concerns are key; and the ones who are in it for the aesthetics and just like the style. I've been to meetings where I've shown my work and never been asked about the process behind it and I don't think they've even read the product labels. I like that – I don't want my label to be the selling point; I don't want it to be a sympathy buy. But sometimes I do need a bit of leeway with lead times and quality control. Some of my leather manufacturers have had leprosy, or have had family members affected by it, and that can slow down the rate at which they can work.

Do you think that fashion needs a new aesthetic?
I have to say to customers that every piece is unique. There are going to be variations. But that adds to the quirkiness and the story behind the brand and I don't think people should see that as a fault.

Above: Each design is brought to life in a Nepalese factory that employs local people, according to fair trade principles.

Opposite: Aura Que products such as this hand-knitted scarf are made in Nepal using local materials that include buffalo leather, banana yarn and hand-woven cotton.

Do you think that certification and labelling is important?
People ask me about certification all the time, but isn't it enough that I'm physically there all the time? I'm always at the leather factory, trying to work out their layout, improve efficiency, find out what new tools I need to buy for them back in the UK. This has given me a better idea of what's right: for instance, when they need breaks. Some of the paperwork attached to certification is ridiculous and the people involved cannot understand it, or even receive it if they haven't got access to email.

Where do you see the fashion industry going in terms of social and ecological issues?
I hope it's going to become more socially aware. A lot of new designers are graduating who are more informed and better equipped for change. So maybe a new generation is going to come through with a new perspective on fashion.

What would be your ultimate vision for your company?
I'd like to scale it up and get the department stores interested and ordering. I want to put profits back into the Leprosy Trust and women's anti-trafficking charities. But I want to know exactly where it's going. Obviously that doesn't pay the bills, so I also have to spend the time getting the products out.

What would be the best help you could get now?
Orders. Make Nepal closer. I do think about the miles that my pieces travel.

The carbon footprint of shipping is significant but you also have to think about the big picture and decide where your strengths can best be employed.
It's definitely the lesser of two evils. You can't do everything at once. Becoming ethical is huge; it's just like learning to walk. Take the steps that you can.

'Classics' and sustainability

DAVID WOLFE *is an American trend forecaster championing classic design.*

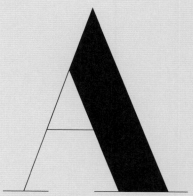

Although the current underlying concept of fashion is one of constant change and built-in (or 'designed-in') obsolescence, this is not entirely accurate. Fashion does not have to be ever-changing and disposable in order to be fashion. The time-honoured and true definition is that 'Fashion is a reflection of the society that wears it.' If society is aware of sustainability and, indeed, if sustainability becomes a 'chic' pursuit, then society can override the quick turnover of fast fashion. This methodology seems more likely to be acceptable to European consumers who are not as addicted to disposability as are American shoppers.

There are several methods of incorporating the concept of sustainability into the flow of fashion. Most obvious of these is a longer closet-life for garments, an easy expression of style longevity. This requires sensitive, subtle design that is not predicated on gimmicks and faddish interpretations. So-called 'classics' always find a market, but the increasing interest in sustainability gives them even more appeal. Higher-quality textiles and superior craftsmanship are key to making this approach into a viable commercial concept. Some creative designers have already attempted to recycle manufactured items by deconstructing them and using the material for newly fashioned garments. This method recalls the 'Make Do and Mend' campaigns instituted during the Second World War to combat textile shortages and, as such, I believe that it can only be considered a novelty rather than a realistic long-term solution.

'Well-designed, well-made clothing is in itself sustainable.'

SHELLEY FOX *is a London-based designer and researcher who, since the mid-1990s, has gained a reputation for innovative fashion concepts and experimental textile techniques. In 2009 she became the Donna Karan Professor of Fashion at Parsons The New School of Design in New York City and established their masters' programme in fashion.*

Below and opposite: Shelley Fox, Collection No. 6, Spring/Summer 1999. Inspired by Victorian medical images of bandaging, this collection featured shredded and blowtorched surfaces.

There is a big gap between large companies and small independent designers. Large companies are in a much better position to make a big difference. They have a big impact on policy-making, on the manufacturing process and on the way the waste is disposed of. For somebody like me [an independent designer] it is always a struggle.

Good design is sustainable. Using high-end fabrics to make well-designed, well-made clothing is in itself sustainable. The ideas of recycling [clothing] have good intentions, but do not actually make a wider impact.

The key may be in thinking bigger on one hand and educating the consumer on the other. Perhaps the economic crises will have a beneficial impact on consumers because people will start asking themselves 'Do I really need this? Should I invest in something that may last longer?'

The big issue, of course, is the lack of sustainable fabrics. But the process also has to be design-led. When bigger companies start producing fabrics that are sustainable and also look good, then we can move on.

If I could choose between organic and non-organic or sustainable and non-sustainable materials I would of course choose organic and sustainable. But this is not always possible. As a smaller designer I always have to deal with issues of minimum quantities of fabric, which immediately limits my options…[But] there is something satisfying about this idea. It narrows your choices. It can form part of the integrity of a garment.

Well-made, well-designed clothes are inherently sustainable when you compare them to the cheapest high-street fashion. Maybe, as in the organic food movement, eco-fashion is just a beginning and eventually everyone will integrate sustainability into normal, everyday practice.

Craft
and industry

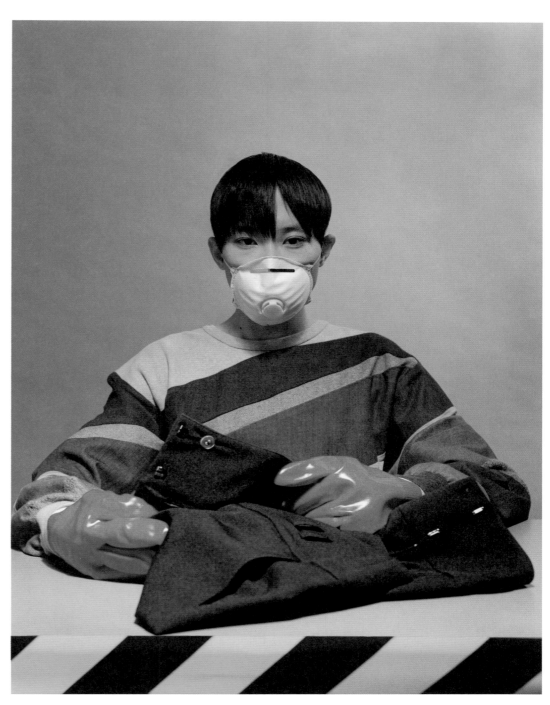

Transparency
and livelihood

Ethical issues and transparency in the supply chain

Fashion craft

Preceding pages:

Page 136 above: 'Three Monkeys, See', photography and styling Gavin Fernandes, model's clothes and visor by Bless.

Page 136 below: 'Three Monkeys, Hear', photography and styling Gavin Fernandes, model's clothes by Bless.

Page 137: 'Three Monkeys, Speak', photography and styling Gavin Fernandes, model's clothes by Bless; industrial accessories C. W. Tyzak.

The greening of the fashion industry

Certification and labelling

The fashion supply chain is long and complex, spanning the globe from raw materials to finished product and sale. Up to 40 million people worldwide are involved in the manufacture of clothing and textiles, many in developing countries that depend largely on garment exports for income. The fashion industry represents one of the few remaining craft-based industries in which, despite some automation, individual manual skills still play a significant part, from hand embroidery to machining garment pieces. In recent years frequent media exposés by investigative journalists and campaign groups such as Greenpeace and the Clean Clothes Campaign and have brought the formerly invisible lowest extremes of the supply chain into sharp focus. As a consequence, consumers are demanding greater transparency and responsive actions have been instigated. However, small-scale producers of textile raw materials such as cotton or cashmere and craft workers and garment workers sub-contracted to larger factories often experience working conditions that fall short of international standards. Liz Parker and Sam Maher's essay sets out important issues and the ethical case for change, while Parker's case study of the British retailer New Look presents an example of positive action.

Inspired by pioneering companies, the greening of the fashion industry is taking place as businesses develop their sense of corporate social responsibility and strive to address environmental, ethical and social-justice issues. Profiles of large companies such as Marks & Spencer, Gap and Walmart illustrate this trend. Industry organizations such as the Ethical Trading Initiative in the UK and the Sustainable Apparel Coalition in the US are supporting companies to take action, but Tim Jackson questions whether the underlying model of growth that is still being followed can be sustainable. The support infrastructure to assist retailers, brands and manufacturers in developing traceability and championing good practice is exemplified by companies and organizations such as Historic Futures, Made-By and the World Fair Trade Foundation.

At the producer end of the spectrum, both textile artisans and garment workers are celebrated in an essay by Eiluned Edwards, and in case studies of small and large businesses working in Africa, India and South Asia, including Choolips, People Tree and Monsoon. The approach of designer and luxury brands is discussed, including insights from Dries Van Noten, who is known for working with textile artisans. Finally, the debates surrounding different types of cotton are identified, and the complex issues pertaining to certification and labelling are discussed by experts in the field.

Hidden people: workers in the garment supply chain

LIZ PARKER *is a freelance researcher, project manager and educator, focusing on ethical and sustainable fashion.*
SAM MAHER *has worked for the UK-based garment workers' rights campaign group Labour Behind the Label since 2002.*

n the surface the garment industry has made a positive contribution to the economic development of many countries across Asia, Africa, Latin America, Europe and North America. The industry generates direct employment for over 25 million people around the world. Infrastructure such as roads and utilities is developed to support it, and its existence stimulates business in other sectors such as transportation. It is a crucial source of foreign exchange for many countries: garment manufacturing accounted for around 14% of Cambodia's gross domestic product and for 82% of exports in 2008, employing 45% of its manufacturing workforce.[1] In Sri Lanka the garment industry has been the largest net foreign exchange earner since 1992, accounting for 45% of the country's export revenue.[2] Bangladesh's economy relies on the ready-made garment industry. Having grown from US$6.4 billion in 2005 to US$12.5 billion in 2010, it accounts for 80% of the country's export earnings. It is estimated that 3.5 million Bangladeshis work in the sector.[3]

Although the economic value of the global garment industry is estimated at US $1.3 trillion,[4] its potential to alleviate poverty and contribute to social development is hindered by its failure to provide decent wages and conditions for its workers. Important improvements have been made, but the millions of pounds that have been spent on corporate social responsibility (CSR) programmes have so far failed to end the abuse of labour rights that has become synonymous with garment and textile production. The poor working conditions and poverty-level wages that continue to plague the industry are in part due to a failure to address some of the root causes of workers' rights abuses, including the power structure of an industry based on long subcontracting chains and intense competition. The invisibility of workers and the exclusion of their voices from the ethical trade debate (which in itself represents a continuing workers' rights violation) is another key factor in the industry's failure to make genuine and sustained improvements to working conditions.

Overview of Conditions

It has been well documented over the last twenty years that few garment workers have had their basic labour rights respected, as enshrined in the UN Universal Declaration of Human Rights[5] and the International Labour Organization Declaration of the Fundamental Principles and Rights at Work.[6] Although some abuses are particularly acute in certain countries – for example low wages in Bangladesh, contract labour in India and lack of freedom of association in China – workers in every country where garments are produced, including the UK,[7] Europe and the US, may be subject to low wages and poor working conditions. Violations of workers' rights are linked to all types of fashion brands and retailers, not only to brands that sell low-priced clothes.

It would be wrong to suggest that no improvements have been made as a result of consumer campaigns and CSR. While cramped, overheated workplaces still exist at the bottom of export supply chains, there have been improvements in first-tier suppliers, particularly in relation to visible issues relating to health and safety, ventilation and lighting.[8]

However, even in relation to health and safety, where the greatest improvements have been made, concerns remain over the number of preventable deaths and injuries. In 2010 in Bangladesh alone, two factory fires killed a total of forty-nine workers. The Clean Clothes Campaign report on the fire at the Garib & Garib Sweater Factory in February 2010 states, 'It appears, from witness statements and press reports, that emergency exits were blocked, the front gate was locked and fire extinguishing equipment was either missing or inappropriate. According to one survivor, rescue efforts were further hampered by the fact that firemen had to cut the window grills to access the building and rescue the trapped workers'.[9]

Where improvements have been made to the built environment, many factories, particularly the biggest ones, appear modern, clean and safe, and contradict the traditional image of a sweatshop. But scratch the surface and low wages, long working hours, irregular employment, child labour, forced labour, union-busting, sexual harassment, non-payment of severance pay and abusive conditions come to light. Garment production is often subcontracted out to smaller production units and home-based workers, and it is in this hidden part of the supply chain that the worst abuses tend to happen. However, even in apparently modern first-tier factories, workers are regularly subject to harassment, discrimination, forced overtime, insecurity and poverty wages.

Strong claims are made about the positive impact the industry has had on women across the world.

This has largely been through the empowerment opportunities provided by the ability to work and earn an independent income. We don't deny that the industry has this potential, and that to an extent the claims made for it in terms of the potential for supporting women's empowerment are valid. However, this empowerment function is undermined by the increased pressure to work harder and faster, the need to combine often excessive working hours with family duties and the insecurity of the work, which is often provided on a temporary or piece-rate basis.

It is also important to recognize the great extent to which gender inequalities existing in society at large are often reinforced in the workplace. Women are disproportionately employed lower down the supply chain in less skilled positions in factories, in small workshops and as homeworkers. These represent the lowest-paid and least powerful positions in the industry, and their work is often under-recognized and undervalued by their employers, their families and even other workers. They rarely hold positions of power within trade-union structures and find that their voices are excluded from discussions and demands around working conditions.

Sexual harassment against women workers by male supervisors is common. Indonesian women workers report that 'pretty girls in the factory are harassed by male managers. They come on to the girls, call them into their offices, whisper into their ears, touch them…bribe them with money and threaten them with losing their jobs if they don't have sex with them.'[10] Compulsory pregnancy tests when women workers are being recruited are not uncommon – women who are pregnant or refuse the tests are not hired. Those who become pregnant during employment often try to hide the fact to avoid dismissal and may be unable to claim maternity pay or access childcare facilities. The long and unpredictable hours are often incompatible with caring for children.

Poverty Wages and Insecure Work

Low wages remain a particular issue for many workers since they are rarely able to earn enough to maintain even a basic standard of living for themselves and their families. Trade unions, labour-rights groups and workers are increasingly demanding that wages be increased from beyond the legal minimum to the level of a living wage. For example, in July 2010 workers in Bangladesh took to the streets in protest at their low wages. On 26 July 2010 the Bangladeshi wage board – made up of government officials, garment manufacturers and union leaders – took heed of these calls and announced that the minimum wage for entry-level garment workers would be raised to 3,000 taka a month, or about £28, constituting an 80% rise from 1,662.50 taka. In September 2010 thousands of Cambodian workers participated in a nationwide strike to demand an increase to the minimum wage that more closely reflected a rise in the cost of living. A number of brands and retailers have now committed themselves to paying a living wage, but for many workers this remains a promise rather than a reality.[11] A number of barriers need to be broken down if the levels of wages across the industry are to come anywhere close to providing a living wage.

The lack of clarity over how to define a living wage is cited by many brands as an impediment to implementation of their paper commitments. Although Article 25.1 of the UN Universal Declaration of Human Rights states that '[e]veryone has the right to a standard of living adequate for the health and well-being of himself and of his family, including food, clothing, housing, medical care, necessary social services, and the right to security', what this means in terms of a living wage in each country remains a matter of debate. Although the ability to define a specific minimum wage is not straightforward, there are calculations being done by different groups that could be called on. Trade unions often have a figure they are demanding in each country; the Asia Floor Wage (AFW, see p. 202) has developed figures for Asia; and many local NGOs have been making cost-of-living calculations. Although the methods used and amounts cited may be controversial, the fact is that all are well above minimum wage. Any attempts to implement wages

Left: The cutting section of a garment factory in Dhaka, Bangladesh, 2010.

based on any of these figures could and would represent a significant improvement in workers' lives. The easiest way to ensure a living wage for all workers would be for governments to set statutory minimum wages at levels closer to a living wage. This is far from reality in any garment-producing country in the world, although the gap between minimum and living wage levels is more stark in some countries.

Brands and retailers regularly shift production between countries and regions in search of lower prices – a so-called 'race to the bottom' on wages and conditions. Governments are therefore under pressure to keep production costs in general, and wages in particular, low to ensure the survival of their industries, resulting in minimum wage levels being kept artificially depressed. In Bangladesh the new minimum wage of 3,000 taka still equals less than £1 per day and is far below the 5,000 taka called for to permanent workers, such as social security, maternity leave, healthcare and pensions, and are often exempt from other labour legislation on hours and wages. This represents a decrease in wages in real terms.

Putting Workers at the Centre

Many workers are treated as little more than machines who have to keep quiet, not visit the toilet when they need to and face being put onto even more menial tasks, sacked or blacklisted should they dare to complain. They are rarely involved in coming up with solutions to address the violations of their rights. This is not because workers don't know they are being exploited, don't understand how or why it's happening, or don't have ideas about how the industry should change. In fact most of the workers we have met over the last ten years know exactly why they face the problems they do and who is responsible.

Until the women and men involved in producing clothes are recognized as real people, as human beings, we will never create an industry that makes all those working in it proud, an industry that does not involve the suffering of one person to make another look beautiful. The people who sit behind the sewing machines, who operate the cutting tools or who pack clothes into boxes have hopes, dreams and aspirations. They love; they are part of families; they have feelings; they have their own stories.

Yet the fact is that many of the industry's decision-makers have never met a garment worker or considered how their decisions can directly affect the lives of the people who will put that decision into action. If they do think about workers at all, it is usually as poor, uneducated victims and not as intelligent human beings. By developing empathy with workers and involving them directly in decisions about their work and workplaces, factory owners, agents, buyers, designers and merchandisers can contribute to transforming the industry. This does not mean treating people with pity or as victims, but creating a space in which they can flourish, make their own decisions and be co-creators of a more just world. Such an industry could then genuinely claim to be empowering its workers.

The Role of Trade Unions

Workers form trade unions to defend their rights and improve their working conditions. Through a trade union, workers have a collective voice and the vulnerability that individual workers are exposed to by making a stand on their own is removed. The right to join a trade union, known as freedom of association, is enshrined in the UN Declaration of Human Rights and International Labour Organization Conventions. Though a fundamental right, it is repeatedly violated across the world.

The right to freedom of association is often combined with a second right, that of collective bargaining. This is where the trade union negotiates improvements that will apply to all workers employed in a particular workplace. It allows workers to share the risk of making demands and to increase their power within employee–employer relationships. In a proper system of industrial relations, union representatives will negotiate with factory owners to establish a range of rules and regulations on

Right: The sewing section of a factory in Dhaka, Bangladesh 2010.

by garment workers' trade unions. It is further still from the 10,000-taka living wage the AFW campaign has calculated as the minimum needed to provide Bangladeshi workers with a decent livelihood.

Putting a brake on this race to the bottom is one reason why the AFW,[12] an alliance of workers' organizations from across Asia, proposes a different approach. The principle behind the AFW is that there should be an equivalent minimum wage for all Asian garment workers, based on a simple calculation according to actual costs of living in each country. The AFW is different in each national currency, but would provide workers with sufficient income to buy the equivalent set of goods and services in all countries. Setting such a 'floor wage' would ensure that wages were not reduced beyond that level and prevent the relocation of production to other regions or countries because of low wages. The implementation of the AFW would also require brands and retailers to address their pricing policies so that a living wage could actually be paid.

Wages should not be seen in isolation from the whole remuneration package including benefits, or from the number of hours worked and stability of employment. One of the trends most responsible for the deterioration of working conditions over recent years has been the drive for more 'flexible' workforces. This has led to a large percentage of the workforce being removed from permanent employment and placed on short-term or temporary contracts. Some workers in Indonesia, Cambodia and India are even employed on daily or weekly contracts. It has also massively increased the role of labour agents and agencies, allowing labour supply chains to develop and pushing the responsibilities for employment conditions even further away from the brands and from factory owners themselves.

All of this leads to increasing insecurity for workers. It means that they are no longer able to earn regular wages and that they are unable to plan for the future and even less able to resist other changes in conditions, including working hours, wages and health and safety. They often have no entitlements to the benefits provided wages, hours, benefits and conditions, which will be enshrined in a collective bargaining agreement (CBA).

Within the garment industry these trade-union rights are systematically denied to workers. Because is more difficult for casual and temporary staff to organize, a combination of the use of casual labour and short-term contracts by suppliers, and the tighter lead times, lower cost and flexible production demanded by fashion brands and retailers, undermine the right to freedom of association. An organized workforce would protest against the long working hours and low pay necessary to meet these orders. So, in order to keep business, factories are likely to crack down on workers who try to organize.

Those workers who do try to form unions often face discrimination, harassment, dismissal and even violence, while the perpetrators are rarely brought to justice. The failure to remedy such incidents underlines the dangers inherent in attempting to organize and acts as a disincentive to others.

Cambodian workers we met in 2007 told us of their dilemma regarding which of the three trade unions operating in their factory they should join. Their options were to join a government-backed union, a management-backed union or the independent union that they acknowledged would be the most effective at defending their rights. The workers told us that they were unlikely to join the independent union, however, because the fear of being attacked was simply too great: three leaders of that union had been assassinated in recent years.

The right to join a union and the repression of activists are largely ignored by the media reporting on working conditions in the garment industry. Few brands and retailers are taking steps to support the right of workers to organize, and many turn a blind eye to the repression of this right by their suppliers. Most consumer activists do not cite freedom of association as one of their key concerns. However, it is through trade unions that workers can collectively and safely raise their demands and play a central role in addressing the abuses they face in the workplace. So-called ethical solutions that exclude trade unions – and, by extension, workers – contribute to the marginalization of workers themselves and perpetuate the idea of them as victims and a focus for pity, not as human beings fighting for justice. Despite the long hours and squalid conditions faced by many employed in the garment industry, the workers we have had the privilege to meet have been proud women who were prepared to fight to improve their conditions and the lives of their families. These women have been able to bring about some improvements through their organizing efforts. It is clear that international support for their struggle, which has shamed brands and retailers into taking action, can help enable workers' voices to be heard.

The Corporate Response

Many fashion brands and retailers start to address labour issues in their supply chains only after workers' rights violations are exposed by workers, campaigners, trade unions or the media. The companies' initial reaction is often denial of responsibility: we don't own the factories, therefore it's not our problem.

Once brands and retailers have acknowledged their responsibility, they tdevelop an internal set of rules, known as a code of conduct, with which factories are expected to comply. Ethical trading staff may be employed, and audits (inspections) of factories are demanded. One benefit to brands or retailers is that when evidence of low wages, union-busting or other violations of workers' rights are presented to them, they can respond by arguing that they have a code of conduct and that they carry out audits: we've taken action, the audit shows everything is in order at the factory, therefore it's not our problem.

The flaws in this voluntary, private approach are now widely recognized.[13] Problems of audit fraud and audit fatigue are well documented, and audits are acknowledged as being little more than evidence-gathering activities that do not address the root causes of poor working conditions. Auditors may be poorly trained and may have little or no background in the issues they are being asked to assess. By interviewing workers inside a factory or even in front of managers, they fail to provide a safe environment in which

Left: Women working in a garment factory in Dhaka, Bangladesh, 2010.

workers can talk openly about their concerns. This policing or compliance approach encourages violations of workers' rights to be hidden. Suppliers themselves now know how to pass such audits and coach workers on what to say, subcontract out work to clandestine factories not covered by audits, and present fake records of wages and hours of work. Audits therefore fail to pick up those issues that are not immediately visible to the auditor, but that constitute some of the worst violations, including union-busting, sexual harassment, discrimination and forced labour.

Some brands and retailers publish corporate reports in which they own up to violations and collect data to show where they can make and are making improvements. They may also publish lists of their supplier factories. However, most brands and retailers still fail to develop a full understanding of their supply chain. When presented with evidence of labour-rights abuses involving a factory producing their clothes, a common response is therefore to declare that the factory is not one of their suppliers. This requires workers, often at great risk, to gather evidence such as labels or shipping notes to prove that the factory is indeed a supplier to the brand in question so that it or the retailer can intervene and be held accountable.

The impact of pricing and purchasing practices on workers only really came to the fore in 2004, when Oxfam published its landmark report 'Trading Away Our Rights'.[14] Since then other publications have supported its conclusions, including the joint report 'Material Concerns' (2008),[15] produced by Impactt and Traidcraft, which gives a clear account of how purchasing practices can have significant consequences for workers. As a Hong Kong-based agent interviewed for the report stated, 'A bag they maybe bought for £3.50 they now want for £3.20. Or if they wanted it for £6.20, they now want it for £5.20. That is happening a lot. In general they want more on the bag for less money.'

Although low wages and poor conditions are in large part down to the unwillingness of factory owners to pay decent salaries to their workers, the prices that buyers are prepared to pay to suppliers and that consumers are willing to pay on the high street have a significant part to play. As one shop sells extraordinarily cheap clothes, other brands and retailers come under pressure to reduce prices themselves. This pressure is pushed down the supply chain and ultimately affects the workers, who are forced to bear the brunt through lower wages, longer hours and increasingly unpredictable working patterns. The impact is felt even outside the factory making the cheapest clothes: prices are driven down across the industry, creating a spiral in which wages are falling in relation to inflation, effectively reducing their real value year on year.

The Impactt/Traidcraft report shows how the impact of purchasing practices on workers' rights extends beyond price to other aspects of critical-path management. Delays caused by the slow signoff of sampling can mean lead times are squeezed and workers consequently forced to work excessive, often unpaid overtime. Similarly, costs associated with last-minute changes to styles may have to be absorbed by the supplier factory. Consequently, workers may again need to work unpaid overtime.

Another trend in purchasing linked to the emergence of fast fashion is last-minute ordering. Orders are placed close to the expected delivery date depending on popular trends at that time, or small initial orders are placed with larger last-minute follow-on orders depending on the popularity of the line once it is in the shops. This shifts the risk of an increasingly unpredictable consumer market from the buyer to the supplier factory. Since orders are being placed much closer to the delivery date, suppliers have less stability and are unable to plan production in advance. This increases the risk of forced overtime, temporary employment and unauthorized subcontracting to meet orders, as suppliers are reluctant to turn down orders even if they are already working at full capacity. For workers this may mean precarious employment without contracts, periods of too much or too little work, or being forced to work overtime or risk losing their jobs. For women workers in particular, this adds to their 'triple burden' as they are still obliged to carry out household duties once they return home, leaving little or no time for rest.

Some brands and retailers have begun to train staff including buying and design teams about the

Right: Workers at the inspection section of a garment factory in Dhaka, Bangladesh, 2010.

Another common approach is for brands and retailers to join a multi-stakeholder initiative (MSI). The main initiatives for fashion brands and retailers at the moment are the Ethical Trading Initiative (ETI), Fair Wear Foundation (FWF) and Fair Labor Association (FLA). These organizations support a collaborative approach among their members, who include brands and retailers, NGOs and, in the case of the ETI and FWF, trade unions. All aim to provide an opportunity to share learning and work together to address specific issues in their supply chains. The FWF and FLA are also verification initiatives, which means that they make attempts to verify companies' claims about workers' rights issues.

Purchasing Practices

Those companies that are taking more serious steps in the direction of corporate responsibility now acknowledge that their behaviour directly affects workers and are starting to develop programmes of work focusing on their purchasing practices.

impact their decisions can have on workers, and have introduced scorecards that reward buyers for buying from 'cleaner' factories. A handful of companies are initiating projects with factories to pilot new approaches to buyer–supplier relationships and to addressing working conditions. If the results are positive, the projects are rolled out to other factories in the supply chain, but the examples of this are few.

In general the issue of pricing policy still remains largely off the table. Despite the increasing consensus regarding the impact of purchasing practices on working conditions, brands and retailers have, on the whole, failed to address the problem adequately and buyers remain under pressure to deliver cheaper, better-quality products more quickly than ever before.

Power Imbalance

The unequal power relationship between buyer and supplier is not the industry's only unbalanced power relationship. The industry's very structure underpins the widespread violation of workers' rights. This is rooted in fundamentally unequal power relationships and resource distribution, a situation in which women workers at the very bottom of the chain are the least powerful and most poorly recompensed, and the brands and retailers are the most powerful and profitable.

The constant search for growth and profit by brands and retailers plays a role in perpetuating the drive for ever lower production costs and lies behind the stark inequality between those at the bottom and those at the top of the supply chain. In 2007 we met a group of Cambodian garment workers producing clothes for Tesco. During the meeting we tried to explain to these women, who earned around £50 a month, that Tesco made an annual profit across all sectors of its business of over £1 billion. This colossal profit was an inconceivable sum to these young women, who had gathered late at night after work to strategize how they could improve their working conditions.

Governments have an important role in addressing the power imbalance in the industry, but widespread failures to enforce national laws regulating working conditions – and in some countries, a lack of such laws at all – mean that workers are denied the protection to which they should be entitled. In some countries where the garment industry accounts for a significant part of the economy, the government is closely linked to the manufacturers. This enables the industry to exert significant and unequal influence over labour policy at the national level. Even where this isn't the case, laws are ignored or weakened by governments keen to attract or retain foreign investment in order to keep their economies strong and employment levels high.

Consumers can also exercise their power more responsibly. There is a need for greater consumer awareness and action to challenge the dominant model of fashion consumption. For consumers this will require more than simply buying from one retailer rather than another; it will necessitate a different attitude and approach to fashion

Left: A row of workers in a garment factory in Bangladesh, 2010.

consumption. Current moves in this direction include the increasing interest in better quality, buying less, fair trade, slow fashion, vintage and second-hand clothing, and upcycling of clothing.

Conclusions

Over the last twenty years, the mainstream garment industry has made progress in addressing poor working conditions, but the impact of this is often limited to larger suppliers, where the buyer has greater influence, and to issues that are immediately visible. Nevertheless, even the leading brands and retailers in the field of CSR have yet to find ways to eradicate low wages, long working hours, violations of the right to freedom of association, forced labour, child labour, sexual harassment or dangerous working environments from their supply chains. Many of their suppliers are also failing to provide regular employment to all their workers.

To bring about more significant and sustainable change, buyer–supplier–worker relationships need to be built on trust and partnership, thus breaking down the inequitable power relationships that underpin the current way international trade in garments works. Governments need to provide a framework for this to happen, suppliers need to address root causes of workers' rights violations in their supply chain, and consumers need to be able and willing to pay the true cost of garment production.

In reality few people think about the women and men who have made the clothes they buy. As fashions have become cheaper and more expendable, the value placed on clothing and, in turn, the skills, time and effort needed to make them has been reduced. This needs to be addressed if a fundamental rethink of the garment industry is to happen. Workers need to be recognized as people with lives and aspirations, whose skills, talent and intelligence are vital to a vibrant, successful industry. Their struggles, stories and demands need to be brought into full view, listened to and acted on. Only then will we have a chance of creating a just and sustainable industry that can meet its potential for transforming lives around the world.

Erin O'Connor visits embroidery workers in India

From 'Weaving a Fairer Future', Behind the Seams, [TRAID's newspaper] Issue 2, 2009, with photographs by Rufus Exton

I was…on my way to Rajiv Nagar, a resettlement slum in East Delhi, to visit an embroidery centre for local women home workers, one of three funded by UK-based charity TRAID (Textile Recycling for Aid and International Development). The centre is run by the Self Employed Women's Association (SEWA), the biggest women's trade union in India, working to empower some of the poorest women workers in the world. The centre brings women workers and buyers together to increase their incomes and make them visible in the textile supply chain. It's also a central and communal space for work, chat and gossip…As I saw my trainer's fingers fly over the fabric with ease, for the first time I understood how much work and talent goes into completing a single garment…[1] It is impossible not to be awed by the resilience and and creative force of women that merely ask for their skill in the global supply chain to be acknowledged and fairly paid.'[2]

Opposite below left: O'Connor shows off her henna-decorated arms.

Left: O'Connor is shown the intricacies of sequin and appliqué beadwork in the SEWA workshop, Delhi, 2009.

Above and below: SEWA members sewing garments and embroidering fabric.

Can sustainability be cool?

CARYN FRANKLIN *is a fashion commentator and founder (with Debra Bourne and Erin O'Connor) of the campaign All Walks Beyond the Catwalk. www.allwalks.org*

an sustainability be cool? Sustainability is an inclusive word. I like it. I like it because it refers to so many things...exploring and making responsible choices around materials, environmental impact and labourer welfare is just one application I can see. I have been investigating others.

When we formed All Walks Beyond the Catwalk back in May 2009, it was against a backdrop of growing unease around the unsustainable body and beauty ideals we were constantly seeing. The look iconified by our industry is unrealistic, unkind (albeit unintentionally) and potentially damaging. As we developed All Walks, we began to feel very strongly that there should be an insider voice challenging our industry's accepted norms and calling for more inclusivity.

The prolific broadcasting of only one body and beauty ideal (pale, rail-thin and very young) via new media channels has meant that young women now see more unachievable images of beauty in a single day than I saw throughout my entire adolescence. So in creating campaigns with top image-makers and high-end designers, using professional models aged eighteen to eighty, with a variety of different skin tones and dress sizes ranging from 8 to 16, we purposely set out to celebrate a much needed broader vision of bodies and personal appearances. Just as importantly, in an environment in which creativity and identity are increasingly corporatized...we set out to celebrate the individual. This is the foundation upon which British fashion is built. We lecture up and down the country in colleges and universities, and we are slowly changing the curriculum to incorporate an understanding of 'emotionally considerate design and practice'. We see ourselves as empowering students to channel their own uniqueness in pursuit of creativity. To this end we have recently launched the Centre of Diversity at Edinburgh College of Art.

Things have to change...the cut, the fit, the ethical production and manufacture of the garments are only part of the picture – the all-important bodies that are routinely chosen to wear these products are ill-considered. Because of this, many young women have internalized an image of femininity that is sold to them by the fashion industry as a set of seasonal rules and become dissatisfied – even unhappy – with their perfect, wonderfully shapely silhouettes… Young women need to see curvy women, and vital-looking women in their sixties, seventies and eighties, in order to understand that beauty isn't just one thing; it is many things. In a global marketplace whose consumer base is more diverse than ever before, we need to see lots of racial differentiation too...surely it's a lucrative business proposition, if nothing else.

At All Walks we think corporate thinking is exploitative. It's not cool to undermine young women's confidence; it's not cool to create clothes that only work on an undernourished body, and it's not cool to operate with so little awareness of these issues. If fashion could wake up to the power it has to communicate positive messages to women – and, of course, men as well – about their bodies, it could be a huge force for positivity...and that would be very cool indeed.

We lecture up and down the country in colleges and universities, and we are slowly changing the curriculum to take in an understanding of 'emotionally considerate design and practice'.

'Perhaps the key issue for fashion is the short product life cycle'

TIM WILSON *is co-founder of Historic Futures, which has developed String, a platform that supports clothing retailers in managing supply-chain traceability.*

Historic Futures is a company that has developed String, an online platform to allow business networks to manage and share batch-level product information throughout the supply-chain. String provides brands and retailers with visibility into their extended supply chains, with applications including raw-material origin-management and reporting key performance indicators such as 'product miles', water used and energy consumed.

Q **Historic Futures was one of the pioneers in this field. How you would position yourself now?**

A Understanding of the importance of complete supply-chain visibility to the development of eco-fashion is progressing, but there remains much to be done. For many it is still not seen as relevant; for others it is considered a lofty, futuristic goal. So the pioneering continues...

Can you tell us a bit about String?
String is an effective online traceability platform that allows companies within a supply chain to receive and send complete and accurate traceability information, file attachments and custom datasets (including certificates, specifications, images, video etc.) relating to their products and business processes. We have recently launched Textiles Solutions, an application of String with data-entry and reporting tools focused specifically on the needs of the textiles industry. I started working in the traceability field more than twelve years ago and founded Historic Futures with Simon Warrick in 2003, specifically to develop technologies and commercial strategies to improve transparency in global supply-chains.

You work across industries. What are the key issues the fashion industry faces in terms of traceability?
Perhaps the key issue for fashion is the short product life cycle; from design to production to

store to waste product. In an environment in which velocity through that life cycle is considered essential, it can be difficult to embrace concepts related to product history, such as the question of where the product came from and how it got here. It is considered either impossible ('We're going too fast for that') or unnecessary ('The next thing will be along in a minute anyway, so who cares?').

As consultants, where do you start when working with a company?
We work with organizations throughout the supply-chain, so the approach varies. At the brand level, the challenges tend to be more cultural and organizational, whereas in production environments the issues are of a more practical and process-oriented nature. We worked with Walmart on its Love, Earth® range, which is the world's first collection of fully traceable jewelry. According to Leslie Dach (Walmart executive vice president, corporate affairs and government affairs) 'Not only does the [String] technology work great, but the sales are great too'.[1]

Could you tell us about your collaboration with Marks & Spencer?
We are working with Marks & Spencer to provide full traceability from raw material to store across all of its clothing and home product ranges. It's an important part of the company's Plan A commitment, with Mike Barry (head of sustainability at Marks & Spencer; see pp. 190–91) recently describing traceability as being 'at the very heart of everything we're trying to change for the future'.[2]

Do your clients tend to be large companies or do you also work with smaller businesses? From your point of view what are the key differences when it comes to the size of the business?
Our clients tend to be large, international brands and retailers, although many smaller brands are also using

String through our partnerships with Made-By (see pp. 152–53). Large brands are able to influence their suppliers' behaviour more effectively than small ones, but their internal decision processes take longer. We work internationally, and, generally speaking, Europe (including the UK) tends to be a leader in understanding supply-chain transparency as a driver of trust and loyalty, as well as improving sales and sustainability performance.

Can companies make changes in isolation, or are there bigger changes that need to take place in order for full traceability to be possible?
Any individual business can make its product 'traceability enabled' by recording data in String from goods received to goods despatched. This will not in and of itself deliver full traceability to source, but it is an essential step along the way and is increasingly recognized by buyers as adding value to the product.

What is the effect of improved traceability on suppliers in developing countries? What are the key problem areas? Can you comment on technology (or lack thereof) and how this can be addressed?
Improved traceability improves business: efficiency, trust, sales and sustainability performance have all been seen to increase. The key issues are fear of change (and fear of transparency), as well as the time and energy required to effect the change. We have worked hard to ensure minimal technology requirements to use String, so thus far we have not found technology to be a determining factor.

What are your views on international laws in terms of traceability and where do you see room for improvement?
Supply-chains are global and there are few examples of well-drafted, meaningful international laws to regulate them.

Prosperity without growth

TIM JACKSON *is professor of sustainable development at the University of Surrey and director of the Research group on Lifestyles, Values and Environment (RESOLVE). The following are extracts from his book* Prosperity without Growth: Economics for a finite planet *(Earthscan, 2009).*

It's notable that the UK, one of the most fiercely liberal market economies, has also been a vociferous champion of sustainability, social justice and climate change policy. The UK's 2005 Sustainable Development Strategy received widespread international praise. Its 2008 Climate Change Act is a world-leading piece of legislation.

There is a real sense here of policy-makers struggling with competing goals. On the one hand government is bound to the pursuit of economic growth. On the other, it finds itself having to intervene to protect the common good from the incursions of the market. The state itself is deeply conflicted, striving on the one hand to encourage consumer freedoms that lead to growth and on the other to protect social goods and defend ecological limits.[1]

On the role of government

The role of government is to provide the capabilities for its citizens to flourish – within ecological limits … at this time, responsibility entails shifting the balance of existing institutions and structures away from materialistic individualism and providing instead real opportunities for people to pursue intrinsic goals of family, friendship and community.[2]

On the role of structural change

Subtle but damaging signals [are] sent by our government, regulatory frameworks, financial institutions, the media and our education systems: …success is counted in terms of material status (salary, house size and so on); children are brought up as a 'shopping generation' – hooked on brand, celebrity and status.

Little wonder that people trying to live more sustainably find themselves in conflict with the social world around them. These kinds of asymmetry represent a culture of consumption that sends all the wrong signals, penalizing pro-environmental behaviour, and making it all but impossible even for highly motivated people to act sustainably without personal sacrifice…Simple exhortations for people to resist consumerism are doomed to failure.

Structural changes of two kinds must lie at the heart of any strategy to address the social logic of consumerism. The first will be to dismantle or correct the perverse incentives for unsustainable (and unproductive) status competition. The second must be to establish new structures that provide capabilities for people to flourish, and particularly to participate fully in the life of society, in less materialistic ways.[3]

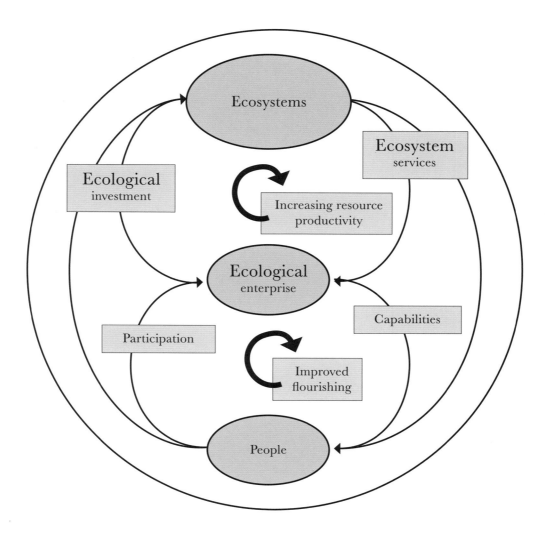

Above: Diagram showing a bounded economy of capabilities for flourishing.

On a different economy

A different kind of economy is essential for a different kind of prosperity. Let's forget for a moment about growth. Let's concentrate instead on summarizing what we want the economy to deliver. Surprisingly, it boils down to a few obvious things. Capabilities for flourishing. The means to a livelihood, perhaps through paid employment. Participation in the life of society. A degree of security. A sense of belonging. The ability to share in a common endeavour and yet to pursue our potential as individual human beings. It sounds simple enough! But of course, delivering these goals is a huge challenge.

Productive activities in such an economy… have to satisfy three clear principles:

• positive contribution to flourishing
• provision of decent livelihoods
• low material and energy throughput

Note that it isn't just the outputs from these activities that must make a positive contribution to flourishing. It's the form and organization of our systems of provision as well. Economic organization needs to work with the grain of community and the long-term social good, rather than against it.[4]

'This is like a "traffic light" system, but it's only as good as how you implement it.'

ALLANNA McASPURN, *former director of the UK Ethical Fashion Forum, is CEO of MADE-BY, a European multi-stakeholder, non-profit organization with the stated mission to 'make sustainable fashion common practice'. By Sandy Black*

MADE-BY is a non-profit organization founded in 2004 by Dutch NGO Solidaridad, with financial support from the EU and others. Solidaridad works in fair trade with tea, coffee and fruit growers in the field. MADE-BY focuses on the textile and fashion supply chain, working in Peru, China and Bangladesh. Its goals include 'matchmaking' between brands, impoverished farmers in the developing world (growing cotton and other fibres) and garment manufacturers, as well as raising social standards within CMT (cut, make and trim) operations in these countries. By joining the MADE-BY programme fashion brands receive guidance and support to improve sustainability in their supply chains and can communicate their progress via an annual 'score card' that records the changes and step-by-step improvements that have been made.

MADE-BY also supports communication with the consumer via an online checking system with corresponding coding on the garment label, and a signature blue-button logo, helping to raise customers' awareness of the hidden people at the bottom of the supply chain.

Allanna McAspurn, CEO of MADE-BY explains the evolution of the company's process and how it works: 'MADE-BY and its scorecard system have grown along with the development of sustainability within the fashion industry. We began with a social score card that benchmarked standards for social conditions within factories. We then created a fibre benchmark to help brands to understand the environmental impact of the fibres they were using, and we recently created an online wet-processing tool that is accessible for all.[1]

'When I looked at the MADE-BY model and what we offered to the brands, there was a distinct target market, with a different chain of command. There are big brands with CSR departments; we already have good relationships with them, and we raise awareness among that group because their practices influence the small- and medium-sized brands. Then there are really small brands that are very holistic, doing things the right way, but they tend to have a very small supply chain. They're really great

to have on board to show best practice, but for me it's about wanting to have an impact in the wider fashion industry. It's important to work with brands that have a reasonable number of links in their supply chains where you can do the work.

'So I've focused on the medium-sized brands with turnovers of around 300 million euros or pounds. They are beginning to think about sustainability, but they don't necessarily have CSR people within their brands. They want to work with a few fair-trade lines; they've tested a few things but they don't have an integrated sustainable strategy embedded in their organization. They may have one person looking into it, alongside his or her main job. So these brands are looking for a partner to help deliver their sustainability strategy. We can be that partner; we can deliver that goal successfully within that size of supply chain. The size of these companies and number of employees varies according to whether or not they do their own retailing. If they are multiple independents with all their own staff, they can have anything from 17 to 1,700 employees. If they are in concessions where they are using their own staff, it depends on the retail level. But there are brands that have a turnover of 160–70 million euros that don't have a large number of employees.

'We look at each brand individually and we offer different services. As well as the basic membership, we also do consultancy projects. We've found that that's a good way for larger brands to test the relationship. They may have a sustainable strategy in place already and want only 'add-ons' such as specific training or a specific research project; or they may want to start a relationship with us and see how our tools work. Track and Trace (T&T) (as done by Historic Futures, for example; see p. 149) is only a small part of what we do. T&T will only give people details on a particular chain or series of chains, but our score card brings all the production data together. We then verify that data – we check the suppliers against certification standards, for instance, and then create the score card.

'MADE-BY is also a communication tool to help consumers understand where their clothes have come from. It's a way of getting customers engaged and interested in the issues, so it's obviously a good way for brands to demonstrate what they've been doing as well. After a twelve-month period working with us, the brands have a score card published, and that's an important thing to ensure transparency. If people say that they're working with MADE-BY, it's important that we demonstrate how they are working with us. If they are using our label, the label simply says that they're working with MADE-BY on a strategy for social and environmental improvement. The score card then gives the details. We want MADE-BY to be very much a brand label rather than a product label. We feel strongly that you should address the entire spectrum of the brand's collection.

'It's not always easy to look across the whole collection to see what you can do both socially and environmentally, in a step-by-step way, to make improvements. It can of course be good to have organic and fair trade lines, and that's what we promote, but these have to be integrated into the entire collection as a long-term goal, not kept in separate supply chains. The point is for companies to look at their normal supply chains.

'Organic cotton is a key issue, because organic farms are paid a fair-trade premium. It's important for us to nurture those farms and for us to match-make between them and clothing companies. In creating a bespoke toolkit for the fashion industry that addresses the sustainability issues that are relevant to fashion, information about cotton is important, because cotton is a big component of fashion collections – but it's not the only one. We've created a fibre benchmark, which provides guidance on the environmental impact across the whole collection, incorporating all the key fibres that are used.

'We are also working a lot with recycled fibres, if they look as if they will have a very strong environmental impact. With one Danish brand, Jackpot, we have done quite a lot with recycled polyesters, and started to blend some fibres as well, as a first step. And the collection looks great – it looks just as it did before, only more sustainable!

'We're looking at both social and environmental improvements. Ours is an initiative that is set up to address the challenges within fashion. So it's not something that came out of the farming movement. The tools are specific to fashion, even in the case of our environmental benchmark. This is like a "traffic light" system, but it's only as good as how you implement it. Fibres are classified by environmental impact of the raw material into groups rated A (highest) to E (lowest). The overall scorecard is made up of both the social standards and the fibre benchmarks. So we create workshops around the tool and ask questions such as "How practical is it to change from a class D fibre to a class B?" and "What impact does going from one grade of fibre to another have on the company: where will it source that material; what impact is that material going to have on feel, fit and washing ability?" We always try to create bespoke solutions for the brand; it's very much a tailor-made approach. I would say that is the approach of a consultancy, using a toolkit that's right for fashion.

'We're not certified ourselves, so we don't say this is "certified by MADE-BY". Instead we work to harmonize existing certifications into a single benchmark so that people can understand quite simply how much of the supply chain is classified as A, B, C, D or uncertified. On the website there's a pie chart; you can click on it and it tells you what these different classifications represent, and which certifications sit behind each one, and then you can click on the certifications themselves to see what criteria they judge. Finally there's a full document that shows how we have constructed the matrix for benchmarking all of it. There is not so much information on the fibre benchmark due to commercial sensitivities, but we try to be as transparent as we can about our methodology. You cannot simply apply the same range of certification to factories in all countries, so we found that a bespoke solution works best.

'Brands have to sign up with us for three years to show their a commitment. They begin with an internal score card and put an action plan in progress. Then they get the MADE-BY label, and swing tags to use across the collection. The garments have the MADE-BY button sewn in to indicate that they are part of a traceable or sustainable line.

'It would be good to see more small and medium-sized fashion brands begin to address the sustainability issues in their supply chains. Right now most are not engaging beyond rudimentary compliance.

'We are really happy to see that larger fashion brands are turning their attention up the supply chain, moving beyond social issues at factory level to begin tackling effluent waste in their wet-processing units, assessing the environmental impact of the fabrics they are using in their collections, and generally starting to become both socially and environmentally aware.'

Above: Spring/Summer 2012 menswear from MADE-BY partner brand Ted Baker.

Blueprint for sustainability: the evolution of traditional Indian textiles from local consumption to the global market

EILUNED EDWARDS WITH ISMAIL KHATRI *Eiluned Edwards has researched extensively in South Asia, in particular the crafts, textiles and dress of India. Ismail Khatri is a manager at Khatri Mohammad Siddik and Co.*

In the past three decades the handmade textiles of Kachchh district, Gujarat, western India, have made the transition from products serving a discrete, local market to global commodities. In the first instance this transformation was brought about by the collaboration of leading craftspeople, the Gujarat State Handicrafts Development Corporation (GSHDC) and the National Institute of Design (NID) in the 1970s. This was followed by interventions by NGOs and bold entrepreneurship on the part of some of the craftspeople themselves. One of the leading figures to have emerged at this time was Khatri Mohammad Siddik, a block-printer and dyer from the village of Dhamadka in the east of the district. His fascination with natural dyes, and his recognition that new markets were needed in order to sustain crafts as culturally and economically viable, contributed to a revival of both natural dyes and block prints in Kachchh and, more widely, in India. Following his demise in 1999, his sons Razzak, Ismail and Jabbar inherited the family business. While nurturing the legacy of a traditional craft, they have extended the company's design repertoire by manipulating traditional patterns, diversified its range of products to include printed wool and silk goods and, in the past decade, adopted eco-friendly production methods and begun to use organic fabrics extensively. Thus was a one-man enterprise based on supplying the sartorial

Right: Sameja cattle herder wearing an *ajrakh* hip-wrap and shoulder cloth, Kachchh, 2007.

needs of local pastoralists and farmers transformed into a growing business serving a niche fashion market in Europe, North America, Australasia and Japan.[1]

Cultural Heritage

In Kachchh the hereditary occupation of the Khatris is dyeing and printing fabric using engraved wooden blocks (in other parts of India they are known as merchants). The Khatris lay claim to a craft tradition that is believed to go back at least 4,000 years in western India. Statuary excavated at the site of Mohenjodaro (in present-day Pakistan), a significant city at the time of the Indus Valley or Harappan civilization (1700–2500 BCE), shows that the Harappans wore clothing decorated with patterns that are still printed today. While it is impossible to say whether or not these were printed designs, it is noteworthy that the motifs have been in continuous use over millennia. The discovery of strands of cotton believed to have been dyed with madder at the same site confirms that the Harappans had the technology to process cotton and produce dye-fast fabrics. Later fragments of resist-printed cotton textiles from Gujarat dyed with indigo, madder and iron were excavated at Fustat in Egypt; these date to the medieval period (9th–15th century CE) and offer material evidence of the skill of Indian artisans.

The ability of Indian dyers to produce richly coloured textiles using natural dyes such as indigo, madder, turmeric, pomegranate and iron, rendered colour-fast by the use of mordants, was unmatched in the rest of the world until the late 19th century. In 1864 the English chemist William Henry Perkin's distillation of aniline led to the development of synthetic dyes. In 1899 the German company Badische Anil Soda Fabrik (BASF) started to market synthetic indigo. The global textile industry embraced synthetic dyes with enthusiasm; they were fast-acting, easy to use and permanent, and initially little consideration was given to their impact on the environment. By contrast, natural dyes take time to produce and require careful handling on the part of the dyer. Their production is seasonal, labour-intensive and sensitive to the vagaries of the climate. For example, indigo (*Indigofera tinctoria*), historically India's most important dye, requires abundant rain and heat during the growing season, without which the plant fails to produce a sufficient concentration of indigotin (the chemical that produces the characteristic blue) in its leaves. Harvesting, which takes place at dawn while the dew still sits on the leaves, is still carried out by hand. The process of extracting indigo from the leaves takes a further three days, and the resulting 'cakes' require at least three weeks to dry. Indigo is an expensive dyestuff and can be temperamental when used – factors that account for Indian dyers' preference for synthetic indigo (known as 'German indigo' in India).

Craft Development

By the 1950s the use of natural dyes had all but died out in India, and the state of crafts generally was moribund, overshadowed by the belief of Prime Minister Jawaharlal Nehru that the future of independent India lay in the wholesale industrialization of manufacture and production.

The formation of the modern state of Gujarat in 1960 was to play a key role in the process of industrial growth; it is now one of the most heavily industrialized states in the republic, and a globally significant site of production for textiles and pharmaceuticals. But craft production and a village-based economy had been at the heart of Mahatma Gandhi's vision of an independent India, and his philosophical legacy is evident in the craft-development policies introduced from the 1950s onwards under the auspices of the Ministry of Handlooms and the Ministry of Handicrafts. In Gujarat two key institutions were established in the 1970s: the GSHDC and the NID. Craft was seen as 'an important plank in the integrated rural development programme',[2] but at the time, textiles made by hand from natural fibres were losing ground to synthetics as the Gujarati 'polyester boom' flourished. The number of artisans working full-time at their craft, already in steep decline by the early 20th century, dwindled even further, and children no longer followed their parents into the family business. It was the remit of the GSHDC to integrate rural development with craft regeneration. The NID was, in tandem, intended to produce designers who would shape the material life of the newly independent nation; they were meant to bridge the gap between traditional craft products and the needs and taste of first the urban market in India, and then those of overseas markets. From 1973 onwards the

Left: Detail of *ajrakh* border designs, block-printed by Ismail Khatri, Kachchh, 2003.

GSHDC sent its officers to all parts of the state to map craft activity and establish a network of artisans. The corporation hired professional designers to collaborate with individual artisans and craft clusters, and to harness their expertise while developing new ranges of goods that would be viable on the national market. Laila Tyabji recalls going to Kachchh as a young designer in 1978: 'Indian crafts seemed to have got stuck in such a rut, as far as any development went…I think when the market changed, it wasn't able to respond to the shift in the kind of consumer'.[3] Many artisans were wary of these interventions and stuck to what they knew, despite ever-diminishing returns; others took a leap of faith. For some, including Khatri Mohammad Siddik, there was no looking back.

Mohammad Siddik and Company

Prior to contact with the GSHDC, Mohammad Siddik's clients were Rabaris (transhumant pastoralists who herd camels, sheep and goats) and Muslim cattle herders in Banni, north Kachchh. He printed turban cloths for the Rabaris and dyed plain red cloth for the women's blouses; for the Muslim clans, such as Jat, Mutwa, Node and Sameja, he made a variety of printed cloths for wearing, including the highly prized *ajrakh*,[4] which remains a signature item of the herders' apparel. At that time all of Mohammad Siddik's work was done with synthetic dyes. However, he had an abiding fascination with natural dyes and was aware that knowledge of them, of the process of resist-printing and of the use of mordants, was ebbing away as most Khatris had switched to using synthetic dyes. He took it upon himself to teach his three young sons Razzak, Ismail and Jabbar how to dye and print with indigo, madder, pomegranate, turmeric, onion skins and iron, in order to sustain the legacy of his ancestors. With input from professional designers such as Laila Tyabji and faculty and students from the NID, Mohammad Siddik developed a new range of goods featuring natural dyes; these were marketed by the GSHDC and sold through Gurjari, the retail outlet established by the GSHDC in Ahmedabad, Gujarat's commercial centre. The dimensions of block-printed textiles such as *ajrakh*, *lunghi* (hip wrap or shoulder cloth) and *jimardhi* (used as a skirt by older women in Kachchh) were adjusted, and the pattern repeats were adapted to suit the sizes of bedspreads, cushion covers, tablecloths, saris and *dupattas* (scarves). These designs were also produced as fashion fabrics and sold by the yard. The new products were popular with customers in urban India and eventually penetrated the international market.

Alongside its product development activities, the GSHDC launched a programme of exhibition-cum-sales and practical workshops in the main metropolitan centres of India, which brought the artisans into direct contact with customers. This face-to-face contact allowed Mohammad Siddik to consolidate his business

with clients in Delhi, Mumbai and Chennai, and also introduced him to foreign customers, several of whom not only placed regular orders but also invited him to exhibit his work and demonstrate his craft overseas. He became an able spokesman for his craft and for the role of craft broadly in India, and Dhamadka became internationally famous as a centre for block-printing with natural dyes. Mohammad Siddik's contribution was recognized by the government of India in 1981, when he was honoured with a National Craft Award. His advocacy for a revival of natural dyes and the burgeoning business he passed on to his sons, allied to the company's ongoing collaboration with Kutch Nav Nirman Abhiyan (the umbrella organization of NGOs working locally in the craft sector), has persuaded a new generation of artisans that there is a viable market for high-quality goods made with natural colours. 'Some people…were doing this for generations, they were working with vegetable dyes,' M. B. Khatri, a naturalist and local historian in Kachchh, has observed. 'Mohammad Siddik was one of them. He, I think, revived these vegetable dyes … Now the future is bright for natural dyes because more and more people are coming into this field.'[5]

Since Mohammad Siddik's demise in 1999, the company has been run by Razzak, Ismail and Jabbar. The issues that influenced their father's thinking – the sustainability of the cultural and material heritage of Kachchh (and India generally), and the development of traditional craft as a viable, commercial proposition – continue to underpin the family business. In the past decade, however, environmental sustainability has become a serious concern to all three men, leading them to adopt eco-friendly methods of dyeing and printing using mainly organic fabrics.

Environmental Sustainability

Block-printing and dyeing require a large volume of running water. Historically Khatris established their workshops near rivers and simply washed and rinsed the fabrics in the flowing water, spreading the cloths on the surrounding land to dry and bleach in the sun. 'My ancestor, Jindha Jiva, chose the site of Dhamadka because the River Saran ran through it,' Ismail Khratri has said. 'A good supply of running water is necessary for the different stages of dyeing and washing the cloth.'[6] Effluent was either washed away or thrown on the midden; little thought was given to either water treatment or waste management. Kachchh is an area of acute water shortage, a geologically unique region of salt desert (*rann*) whose fragile environment has been degraded by irrigation schemes introduced to support the industrialization of agriculture, the so-called 'Green Revolution' launched in the 1960s. The uncontrolled sinking of tube wells by local farmers and others in the ensuing years has over-exploited the natural aquifer, resulting in creeping desertification and a recurring cycle of drought. The absence of a coordinated water-management policy in the district, and dam projects in the higher course of the Indus in Pakistan (the Indus feeds the groundwater table in Kachchh), caused the River Saran to dry up permanently in 1989. Mohammad Siddik and his sons, confronted by the loss of their livelihood, sank a well, installed an electric pump to circulate the water and constructed

Right: Sufiyan Khatri dyeing *ajrakh* in 'German' indigo, Kachchh, 2005.

Left: Workers processing indigo at a production unit in Tamil Nadu, 2006.

a series of large concrete tanks in which to wash and rinse their cloth. Other Khatri families did likewise.

Sustaining the craft of block-printing and dyeing in Kachchh now has as much to do with managing the environment as with finding viable markets. In addition to coping with the environmental challenges, Mohammad Siddik's sons' regular foreign customers have specified that their orders be fulfilled using eco-friendly fabrics and dye materials. Apart from prompting them to source organic cotton (another niche market in India) and to investigate *ahimsa* silk (so-called 'non-violent silk' because the silkworm is not killed during processing), it has also compelled them to address a commonly held assumption that natural dyes must be eco-friendly. While the dyestuffs they regularly use – which include indigo (natural and synthetic), madder, alizarin (synthetic madder), onion skins, turmeric, pomegranate husks, henna, rhubarb and *sappan* wood (Brazilwood) – are harmless, and meet the specifications of the International Organization for Standardization (ISO 14001),[7] a number of the mordants, or 'metallic salts',[8] traditionally used to bond colour to fabric are highly toxic. Previously copper (copper sulphate), chrome (potassium dichromate/dichromate) and tin (stannous chloride) were widely used; nowadays the Khatris' staple mordants are alum (potassium aluminium sulphate) and iron (iron acetate), which is used to achieve the colour black and to sadden other colours. Both of these mordants comply with ISO 14001 (2004). Although their work does not carry official ISO certification yet, the brothers have assiduously revised their working practices with guidance from the office of the UN Development Programme (UNDP) in Mumbai.

Craft Futures

In January 2001 the Gujarat earthquake razed Dhamadka and took the lives of many Khatris. Although the village has been restored with help from the UNDP, the facts of its ongoing water problems, its remoteness from Bhuj (the administrative and commercial centre of Kachchh) and its position on a major fault line persuaded the Khatri community as a whole that a site for a new village should be sought. By March 2001 a suitable location had been found just 13 km from Bhuj with sufficient space for at least seventy-five workshops. The foundations of the new village, known as Ajrakhpur in honour of the signature cloth of the Khatris, were laid in 2002. The project has been led by Ismail Khatri and a team of

his fellow caste members from Dhamadka, working in conjunction with Abhiyan and the Jamiat-Ulama-i-Hind (a Muslim NGO based in Delhi), with input from the Ahmedabad Textile Industries Research Association (ATIRA) and the Vivekanda Research and Training Institute, Mandvi (VRTI).

The idea of Ajrakhpur as a model village and a hub for dyeing and printing was proposed by Abhiyan in 2001. The village is part of an ambitious district-wide scheme to create clusters of craft specialists in an orbit around a central office in Bhuj that provides information, design input and liaison with potential clients, and handles all aspects of PR. An integrated development plan has been drawn up for the village itself that includes earthquake-resistant accommodation, much of which has now been built by the Jamiat, and purpose-designed workshops, which have been constructed by the VRTI. At the heart of the development will be an effluent treatment plant designed to serve the whole community. Devised by ATIRA, the plant is intended to provide a model of water management, complying with the norms specified by the Gujarat Pollution Control Board. It will reduce the overall volume of water used by the Khatris (currently about 72,000 litres a day) by reusing it up to five times, treating it so that it is suitable for different activities before finally releasing it from the system to be used for irrigation. The whole project was stalled for over a decade while the district authorities deliberated on a change of land use from agricultural production to industrial usage. Without this clearance, Ismail Khatri and his colleagues were unable to apply to charitable organizations and development agencies for support to construct the plant. Clearance has recently been granted and an expression of interest in securing support for the project was made by the Charities Advisory Trust in the UK in March 2012. A small-scale prototype plant will be constructed and tested later this year (2012), financed by the Khatri community of Ajrakhpur, after which it is hoped funding for the full-scale plant – estimated to be several million rupees – will be secured. Confronted by ongoing environmental challenges, bureaucratic obstacles and financial difficulties, these guardians of a unique tradition remained resolute, sustained by faith: 'Inshallah, we will be successful this time.'[9]

The company of Khatri Mohammad Siddik and Sons offers an example of a successful craft enterprise in rural India. A review of the strategies adopted by Mohammad Siddik in order to sustain his craft heritage (and family business) in the face of a declining local market and disappearing expertise reveals that part of his success lay in his willingness to collaborate and innovate, seizing opportunities as they were presented. A generation later, the challenges confronting his sons have as much to do with the environment as with sustaining craft. They are addressing these in collaboration with their regular customers, government agencies and NGOs. Despite natural disasters, a hostile environment and the ministrations of a sluggish bureaucracy, the company is a successful and inspirational enterprise; nonetheless, the precarious position of craft in rural India is apparent. Let faith prevail.

Perspectives on fashion and textile manufacturing

SANDY BLACK *discusses how manufacturing in the textile and clothing industry across Europe and the US has in recent decades migrated eastwards to lower-wage locations around the world. This visual essay gives insights into very different working scenarios in Eastern Europe, Turkey and China.*

Borås East

As part of the annual 'Dignity' series at The Swedish School of Textiles in Borås, in 2007, the project 'Borås East' was designed by two universities to investigate and document working lives in factories producing textiles and clothing for Sweden, and to explore what this collaboration means for the people in each country.[1] The complex relationships between global trade and livelihoods became apparent, as explained by project organizers Jan Carlsson and Pelle Kronestedt. 'Companies in Borås were pioneers in moving production to former Soviet republics and other Eastern European countries. At least 10,000 employees are working in those countries for companies that have some relationship to Borås. More than 30,000 people are directly or indirectly dependent on orders from Borås, and companies here depend on the very skilled and competent workforce.'[2] However, employment in the Eastern European garment industry was under threat as more production moved to new countries developing their clothing manufacturing

Right: Sewing jeans at Forteks factory, Istanbul, 2007, photographed by Sandra Henningsson.

Opposite top left: Washing machine after the stonewashing process, Yilteks factory, Istanbul, photographed by Malin Palm.

Opposite top right: Forteks denim jeans factory, Istanbul, 2007, photographed by Sandra Henningsson.

Opposite centre left: Products and producers at the Tirotex factory, Transnistria, Moldova, 2007, photographed by Pelle Kronestedt.

Opposite centre right: Tending the weaving machines at Tirotex, Transnistria, Moldova, 2007, photographed by Pelle Kronestedt.

Opposite below: Dyeing fabric at Yilteks, Istanbul, 2007, photographed by Malin Palm.

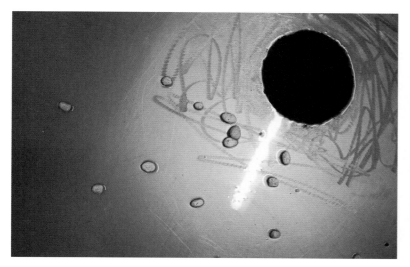

Right above: A young boy working with his parents at a small jeans workshop, Xintang, Zengcheng. He earns 0.15 yuan per garment for snipping loose thread ends off finished jeans; in one day he can do about 200.

Right below: Workers sew jeans in a makeshift shed that serves as a workshop in Xintang, Zengcheng, 2010.

Opposite above: Every morning, workers at a denim-washing factory must search through wastewater to scoop out stones that are washed with the fabric in industrial washing machines to make stonewashed denim for jeans, Xintang, Zengcheng, 2010.

Opposite below: A shop at the International Jeans Wholesale City in Xintang, Zengcheng, 2010.

industries, such as Uzbekistan, and many workers migrated with their skills. Kronestedt saw this shift in action during a visit to a factory in Tiraspol in the Republic of Transnistria, Moldova, reporting that 'Workers in the Tirotex factory work with everything from cotton fibre from Uzbekistan to finished products in plastic bags for the shops.'[3]

Project participant Malin Palm recalls his visit to the Yilteks textile factory in Istanbul, Turkey. 'The factory was highly regarded for its professional workers and their knowledgeable washing engineer. But the production cost is relatively high in Istanbul and when we visited the factory, production was already cut down to half speed. In a couple of years the employees dropped from over 100 to 28.' One factory worker, Ulcun Özarslan, told Palm that foreign companies appreciate their knowledge and help at first. 'But when we have taught them everything we know, what then? In a few years we will be unemployed again.'[4] Sandra Henningsson, another participant, visited a jeans factory near Istanbul. 'Due to the competition from China with its noticably lower prices, the workers in the Forteks factory are forced to keep a high tempo and perform at a high quality in making the jeans, giving long working days. Men do most of the sewing. Women cut the remaining threads, cut out the patterns, do ironing, sew on small parts, tags and details on the jeans, and [use] small stones to make them look worn and "modern". Few of the workers are registered workers, and if you're not registered you don't have the same right to a minimum salary.'[5]

The Jeans Capital of the World

Denim jeans have become an iconic global product, produced in the millions annually. They require a considerable amount of manufacturing resources and labour, and in parts of the industry human exploitation and lack of environmental protection have taken a heavy toll. Exposure in the media has helped to create awareness of abuses, and both voluntary and legislative actions

are gradually being taken to improve such situations.[6] However, much remains to be done. In a study based in Guandong, a major textile and clothing producing area of China, Greenpeace highlighted a number of issues, outlined in its *Dirty Laundry* series of reports and called for action by the major brands involved.[7] The manufacture of jeans illustrates some of the most visible and gross pollution caused by China's textile and clothing industry. The textile industry is an important sector of China's economy, with more than 50,000 textile mills in the country.[8] In 1995 China became the largest exporter of textiles in the world and it has maintained that position ever since.[9] Across China there are 164 textile industry clusters where companies specialize in manufacturing certain products, for

example Xintang, known as the jeans capital of the world.[10] The economy of Xintang revolves around the complete production process for jeans: from spinning, dyeing and weaving to cutting, printing, washing, sewing and bleaching. Xintang's jeans and clothing business began in the 1980s, and since then its output has skyrocketed.'[11] More than 60% of China's jeans are produced in Xintang, which also accounts for 40% of all of China's exported jeans.[12]

As a result of the Greenpeace toxics campaign, in November 2011 several global brands including Nike, Adidas, Puma and Li-Ning, and retailers H&M and C&A committed to 'Detox' – to eliminate all releases of hazardous chemicals from their production processes and products throughout their supply chains by 2020.

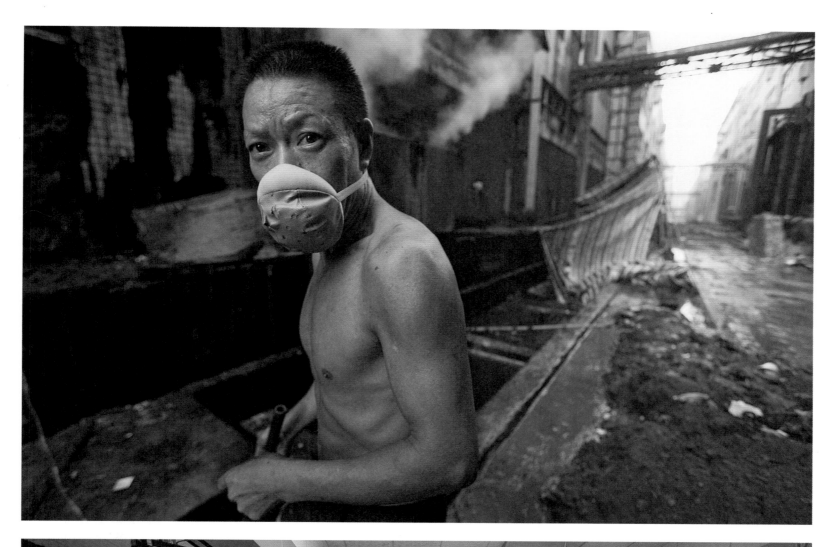

'I want to make clothes for real people who will wear them for a long time.'

DRIES VAN NOTEN, *descended from a long line of tailors, is one of the original 'Antwerp Six' who emerged from the now-famed Fashion Academy in Belgium, and started a new-wave design aesthetic when the group showed in London in 1986. Here he discusses ethical production, the fashion industry and life as an independent designer.*
By Sandy Black

In the twenty-five years since his debut, Van Noten has built and maintained an independent business, gaining a loyal following for his sophisticated designs for both womenswear and menswear, which incorporate a distinctive melange of fabrics, many sourced personally by the designer. Despite his esteem for traditional textile craft skills, he also embraces modern technologies such as digital printing. His designs are currently sold in over 400 outlets worldwide and he was awarded International Designer of the Year by the Fashion Council of America in 2008. Asked by *Dazed Digital* magazine in October 2009 for one word that sums up his collections, he answered, 'It's authenticity, I think. The clothes come straight from the heart and I want to make clothes for real people who will wear them for a long time and not just for one season.'

Q It's been a difficult time for fashion. Is the recession easing for your business?

A I'm a designer as well as a businessman. I own my own business; the situation may be different for other designers. But I don't think that the political, ecological and financial situation we find ourselves in is a problematic one. It also creates opportunities. People have to give answers to what is happening to the world at the moment and the fact that you give answers…that's quite interesting: at least somebody understands that something is going wrong. It would be a pity if people, especially the big groups, which have the financial ability to do so, just say 'OK we are going to wait until it's over and continue the way we are'. Things have to change in a way that is appropriate and right.

What things have to change?
Fashion became too complicated. Marketing became more important than creation. I don't know who is interested in buying summer clothes in November. When you go to all the big cities all

'I think nearly everyone in the Western world has enough clothes in their wardrobe to wear for the rest of their life.'

Durability – or rather longevity – is this innate to your design philosophy?

It's part of my personality. I have the freedom to do the things the way that I want to do them. I also have financial freedom.

You are one of the few independent companies around.

When you have big financial groups, you have a kind of financial structure that involves people who do not come out of the fashion business. It's all the same to them whether they sell cars, chocolate, computers or fashion. They apply the same rules to all products. Fashion is quite specific. Of course cars have to be created and fashion has to be created but they just think of the turnover – how can we turn two seasons into four? Where we once had four delivery seasons, they now have eight. People see new things every month. For me the act of buying involves expectation: you see a fashion show and then you have to wait a few months before those pieces are in the store. I like that sense of expectation – I always compare it to children who see little wrapped presents under the Christmas tree and know that they have to wait five days before opening them. Often the longing or the wanting of the item is better than actually having it.

I think since 1986 you have had some challenges?

We went through some rough times, financially, organizationally and also creatively. What's nice is having been in the business for such a long time that you know you will have your high and low moments. Sometimes your moments of low appreciation are not the same as your moments of low creativity. Sometimes you think your collections are not the strongest; at other times you fear doing really strong collections. And sometimes the time is not so good for you. Two years ago everything was going well, with the opening of new stores, but then the [global financial] crisis struck. Of course it shakes you. Fashion never gives you the possibility of getting – lazy is not the right word – maybe a bit more relaxed.

What makes us want something new?

Employment and industry. The skills needed for making fabrics, printing weaving, knitting embroidering. It would be a pity to say it is 'only' fashion, because fashion covers so many things, everything to do with culture and art. I want to use these in my work. The collection I made for next summer: authentic fabrics. It's not really a cry for attention, but a wish to focus again on these things, on what we still can make. Where we normally put a lot of effort into making our own fabrics, this time we have searched all over the world for authentic fabrics. This included looking in museums like the ethnographical museum here in Antwerp, where we found beautiful documents of ikats from Uzbekistan, and some batiks, Indonesian materials. We took the documents to Italy, where we photographed them and printed them digitally. In the case of the ikats we found some small-scale weavers in India who could make ikats by hand, which is not the most easy thing to do. We also worked with a small atelier in Uzbekistan – the fabric had to travel two days by donkey to get there.

the streets look the same. All over the world the shops look identical…There are too many clothes in the world. When people ask me 'Is your fashion ecological?' I say the only truly ecological thing I can do is to stop making fashion. I think nearly everyone in the Western world has enough clothes in their wardrobe to wear for the rest of their life.

How do you see fashion?

I have quite a personal way of looking at it. I don't want to dictate fashion. I just want to make clothes that people can wear in a way that they want. That is the important thing. That's why when I do a fashion show, the outfits that I put together are only one way to wear the clothes; afterwards, if you want, you can shorten them, cut the sleeves out, you can over-dye them, you can embroider them, wear them however – I don't care.

Do you actually know any customers who have done that?

What I appreciate is when people wear my pieces from a few years ago mixed with new pieces. Several years ago when I visited a store in Boston the owner invited clients to assemble their own little museum. Everybody brought in the pieces they had bought from the first collection and put them in the old presentation boxes from the store. Some of them had also brought pictures showing the memories that they associated with those clothes. Everybody was doing something different with them. That was really nice.

Above and above left: Dries Van Noten, Autumn/Winter 2010/11. Silver metallic decorations were hand-embroidered to embellish this collection.

Opposite: Dries Van Noten Autumn/Winter 2008/09. Rich layered prints revived a forgotten technique, also replicated digitally.

Sustainability is a part of our business. But as a design brief it would limit us, and we already have enough limitations on our creativity.

Left and opposite below: Subtle ombré shaded effects achieved by skilful garment dyeing techniques, Dries Van Noten, Spring/Summer 2011.

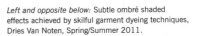

Do you ever reuse fabrics from a collection?
Never. I want to keep things fresh for me and for my team. I don't want to get bored. I don't want to make it easy. When a collection is finished I clear the tables and throw everything away and start again. Sometimes after the research period we end up close to where we started…[but] sometimes we arrive somewhere we hadn't predicted. This is what keeps me awake and stimulates my team.

How long do you allow for research?
We continue with research until we are happy. For instance, this season we took a month longer than we expected, so there was a lot of delay for the collection. I only have the two lines, menswear and womenswear. I refuse to do pre-collections. I refuse to do diffusions.

The longevity of your pieces – does this tie in with the emerging 'slow fashion' movement?
I have to do business. I have the responsibility to produce. I have responsibility for all the people working for me. We work with two manufacturers in Italy and India. In the busy months we have 3,000 people working for us. If you don't have the embroideries to make every season, then those people are going to have a problem. Sometimes even when I am not feeling so much like embroidery I still order some, so it can still be made by hand.

Do you refer back to previous work?
My team looks back at my archive, where we have examples of every shoe we have made. [Right now] we're using a shoe design from 1993 but we will change the heel this time.

What about ethical issues in the supply chain?
With my producers, of course you never know. Sometimes you don't know because of the sub-contracting. In India we work directly with the villages. We have two agents in Calcutta. We have ateliers who take the embroidery down to the villages. People can still earn their money in the villages and not have to live in cities, which is a problem today. That way young people and even younger people – children – can work, because often people are against child labour. But children [there] have to work in the garden. Every girl is taught how to knit by her mother. Is this bad? I don't know. It's the same with embroidery: it's a culture – so long as the children can still go to school – after school they can work. There is a pride in the work, and that is a most important thing: the pride of making something beautiful, finding the joy, the richness in the fact that they can do beautiful

Left: Digitally printed top, Dries Van Noten, Spring/Summer 2011.

things. If you can give work to good healthy villages, it's different from people having to work in the horrible factory and live away from home. In India our work always goes to the same village, though it's not always the same amount of work. The same is the case for our factories in Italy. I design with this in mind.

We still try to make as much as possible in Belgium, but it is not easy with a production time of three weeks. More refined pieces are still made mostly in Italy and France in traditional ateliers. Price-linked pieces such as men's shirts we make in Romania and Hungary, which are the only [European] countries that can produce shirts at a price at which you can sell them. One strange thing is that the cost of producing a woman's cotton blouse can be three times that of a man's shirt.

What about the use of fur?

I have nothing against fur, if the animal hasn't suffered. I appreciate the skill of the people who work in such materials. Plastics are doing more damage to the environment.

Do you think the craftsmanship behind the product is more important?

No. I think the idea behind the craftsmanship is more important. Good craftsmen can still produce ugly things that are well made.

Is yours a luxury brand?

It is a mistake to confuse luxury with status. It used to be that luxury meant staying at a 5-star hotel, but now luxury means living in a little cottage in the country.

Does luxury have responsibility?

Everyone has to take responsibilities for themselves. Topshop has different solution. They produce fifty-two ranges a year. I don't want to be the old wise man handing down advice. We get appreciation for the way we do fashion. When we opened our store in Paris, people were shocked in a good way. It's not like a store. You have to ring the doorbell to get

in and it's hidden away, not on a high street. It's more like an apartment…We don't advertise. In the beginning I didn't have the money or the time. We had two pages of adverts, but why make all that money and spend it on marketing? After a few years when we could afford it we didn't need it any more – and it would harm our image now!

Are you a brand or a label?

We are a brand but not a label. A brand stands more for a principle. Every garment incorporates all we stand for, our heritage; our respect for the past while looking to the future. I am not nostalgic, but I do respect our heritage.

Where did your love of textiles come from?

My mother taught me about things. Looking at a tablecloth that was hand embroidered, for instance.

Does the word 'sustainability' come into your discussions?

Sustainability is a part of our business. But as a design brief it would limit us, and we already have enough limitations on our creativity. I dream of making bias-cut dresses but we do not have the manufacturing ability to do so. I feel that the skills are disappearing. The family businesses are struggling. I keep a lot of these businesses open in Belgium. We don't only use old skills, however: I like Japanese polyesters and digital printing. You can do amazing things with new technologies.

'This is never just about business but also about believing in a dream and supporting each other.'

Knitwear and fashion designer **RISTO BIMBILOSKI** *does not like to overcomplicate the sustainability issue.*
By Duska Zagorac

The Macedonian-born designer's signature label is fast becoming the 'green' label to watch but he does not see himself as a pioneer of sustainable fashion. 'I just never lost sight of my roots. They are as important to me as my involvement in luxury fashion. I just combined the two'.[1] Bimbiloski studied fashion in Paris until 1993, and then worked as assistant designer for Jean Colonna and Thierry Mugler, followed by a stint in graphic design. After four successful years as head designer of men's knitwear at Louis Vuitton, Bimbiloski is now exclusively dedicated to his own brand, Bimbiloski. 'The label grew consistently and now requires my full attention. The woven part of the collection needed to evolve and become as strong as the knits; the print developments became an intrinsic part of my signature and I decided to show at New York Fashion Week.' Even the way Bimbiloski expands his business is a matter of simple logic. 'The US was always the market that reacted well to my collections. So we decided to base my sales and PR there, and today we have fifteen sales points in the States'.

Bimbiloski's early collections of handmade Balkan-inspired knitwear pieces quickly attracted a prestigious clientele. Bergdorf Goodman and Neiman Marcus were among the first to embrace his industrial take on ethnic design. At that time, sustainability was not an issue: his pieces were selling purely on the basis of their interesting design and high-quality finish. Although his collections were always produced ethically, this was never at the forefront of his marketing strategy.

Bimbiloski started producing his label in 1999 with four local knitters in his native Ohrid. 'We built a small shed in my mother's garden. The ladies would come in the morning with their knitting needles and they would just do what they normally do – chat, drink coffee and knit. Their work was very well executed and they were very fast – this is because these women come from a very long tradition of knitting and for them handcraft is something completely natural.' But as the label grew from a small knitwear range to

a full ready-to-wear collection, so did the demands on the production line. In the summer of 2007 Bimbiloski opened a factory that produces not only knitwear, but also the cut-and-sew collection. Bimbiloski now employs 120 workers but the core philosophy remains the same. There is still a homely welcoming atmosphere and a sense of it being a business that gathers a local community. Bimbiloski recollects that 'word spread fast across the neighbouring villages that there was an opportunity here for any woman who is good at knitting. They would just knock on our door with a plastic bag full of jumpers they made for their family. We would look at their work and would give them a trial. If they were good, we offered them work. These women would never have imagined that they would have an opportunity to earn money by using their skills or even be employed, as most of them don't have any formal qualifications. Yet today they are able to support their families.'

The company itself is family run. Bimbiloski's mother Ristana runs the factory on a daily basis while Bimbiloski does most of his designing in Paris, where he is based. He makes regular trips to Ohrid to give direction and oversee the production. Bimbiloski's brother Alek runs the business side and the showroom in New York. 'Working with the family is not always easy but it is immensely satisfying. Family business is based on different principles because this is never just about business but also about believing in a dream and supporting each other. Everybody who works with us is also part of our extended family, so this naturally translates into every garment we make.'

If there is one ethical concept that moves Bimbiloski, it is the idea of connecting the end user to the origin of the garment. 'Today most people don't care where their clothes come from or even give a thought to who it was made by. I would like our clients to be aware and to value the way their garment was made because I think it is special. This is not to say that I would like someone to buy a piece from our collection only because it was produced with love and care. A garment has to

work in its own right, but I think that knowing something about its origin can also provide a different kind of pleasure. Perhaps it's similar to knowing that you can eat food that not only tastes good but was grown organically on a family farm.'

Bimbiloski's thinking cannot be separated from his own roots. Born and bred in the former Yugoslavia, he was shaped by its socialist society of the 1980s, which at the time was more liberal than that of the rest of the Eastern bloc. Western culture and influences were present, although the economy and society were closer to the socialist model, in contrast to the hyper-capitalism that was then sweeping the West. 'This was a very interesting time. While I had access to Italian *Vogue*, to me it was more fiction than reality. Luxury fashion simply did not exist in socialism – it was considered elitist and represented the overindulgence of the West. But, equally, throwaway fashion did not exist either. People would just buy a few clothes that would have to last for a very long time and mending them was part of the culture.'

Bimbiloski was particularly inspired by traditional dressmaking when developing his label. 'During socialism, every respectable middle-class woman would have her own dressmaker. Women would look at foreign magazines for inspiration, source quality fabrics and have their clothes made by a local tailor. This was done partly out of necessity, because what was available in the shops at the time was certainly not inspiring, and the desire to have beautiful clothes did not evaporate with the new political system.' It was the notion of these dressmakers that inspired Bimbiloski when dreaming up his own label. 'I wanted the clothes to have that tailor-made feeling that also implied quality in both fabrics and craft. I wanted to make clothes that have longevity, that are modern yet classic – for instance, a black cocktail dress made of high-quality wool that will remain in a woman's wardrobe for a very long time.'

Bimbiloski's designs are influenced by Balkan tradition but this is not his only source of inspiration. 'I am not interested in clichéd views

Right: Dramatic digital print for Bimbiloski's
Spring/Summer 2010 collection.

of what "ethnic" should look like. It is a kind
of a prejudice to start with. We live in a global
community today. I am influenced by my work
and life in Paris as much as by the socialist
aesthetics of my youth, traditional Macedonian
patterns or a holiday in Bali.'

A few years ago Bimbiloski started
experimenting with digital printing, and his own
signature prints now dominate his collection.
'The prints are a kind of second skin or a body
paint on which I then build the clothes. The prints
also convey the main idea of the collection in
a very direct, photographic way.' The prints are
developed exclusively in Italy, where he also
sources most of his materials.

Bimbiloski finds that quality sustainable
materials are still difficult to source. 'I just wish
there were more interesting options available,
especially in terms of sustainable yarns. At the
moment it is really difficult because the colours
are still very basic and the prices limiting. But
everybody is aware of the necessity to address
this issue so I hope that we will see a change soon.'
One ingenious solution that Bimbiloski has found
to address the problem of obtaining sustainable
materials is his recent experiment with knitted jeans
made from recycled fabric. 'We knit thin stripes
cut out from old second-hand jeans. It gives me
a new and sustainable way to produce jeans that
also fits with my knit profile.'

Being small and self-reliant has proved to
be a great advantage to Bimbiloski in turbulent
economic times. 'In the past two seasons we
actually had the strongest increase. Part of it is
due to developing a complete collection while
accentuating the niche knits and exclusive prints.
The other part is due to having our own production
unit, which gives us more control over deliveries
and quality in such delicate garments. I am happy
that our atelier increased almost 100% in capacity,
and in the next season we are also producing two
other interesting American labels. I guess this is
another successful long-term project that evolved
in a natural way.'

Monsoon

SANDY BLACK *examines the clothing and accessories company's ethos.*

Monsoon started life in 1973 as a single boutique in London's bohemian Kensington. Together with its sister store Accessorize, founded in 1984, it is now a global brand with 400 stores in the UK and more than 600 in 70 countries worldwide, including the US. Originally inspired by its founder Peter Simon's travels to India, the company, which is still run by Simon, remains true to its roots. Its product ranges utilize handcrafted embroidered and block-printed fabrics, which are made in India using natural and organic fabrics.[1] The company is proud of its ethical stance, signing up to the Ethical Trading Initiative in 1999 as a founding member and continuing to proclaim its mission as 'Living Our Values and Ethics since 1973'. In Spring 2011, the LOVE collection (an acronym of the company motto) was launched, 'celebrating a fusion of modern design with Indian crafts and organic fabrics' and featuring techniques such as tie-dye, bandhani and crochet alongside recycled saris.

Monsoon sets aside funds for the ethical side of its business, which includes the Monsoon Accessorize Trust, established in 1994 to work with disadvantaged communities in Asia and sponsor of the Estethica ethical fashion section at London Fashion Week since 2007. Monsoon's 'Boutique' collection of homeware and gifts was developed in collaboration with several fair trade NGOs such as SEWA (a women's support group and trade union for home workers in India; see pp. 146–47) to sustain traditional crafts. One SEWA centre in Delhi has been funded by the Trust. The 'Boutique' range works with a lower profit margin (with profits channeled into the Trust) and longer lead times than do the company's mainline collections. Monsoon also instituted its 'Clothes for Life' charity take-back scheme in 2009 to give customers an opportunity to repurpose their unwanted clothing.

Working with around 250 main suppliers, Monsoon manufactures unstructured clothing in India, knitwear, denim and structured outerwear in China, and, more recently, in Turkey, which is able to provide a faster six-week production cycle to enable Monsoon to compete in the high street. Crucially, however, the company has committed to a 'Right First Time' design and buying programme to minimize the last-minute changes that pressurize its supply chain. Monsoon still uses a substantial quantity of natural fabrics alongside polyester and other synthetics, but for mainstream fashion items the £1/metre premium it must pay for organic fabrics is not cost-effective at the price points acceptable to its customers. To maintain the balance of signature fabrics and costs, embroidery for the mainline range must be done in factories by machine.

'Fashion can be beautiful and desirable and still be sustainable. Everyone has a conscience and consumers will... appreciate knowing what their clothes stand for.'

Already recognized in the industry as a leader in corporate transparency,[2] Monsoon has committed to becoming even more transparent, and to reaching out and educating the consumer who only appreciates throwaway fashion and instant gratification. Its revamped website shows both its factory and village production sites. Monsoon has a long-standing presence in India, with an office in Delhi where a locally recruited design team is based.

Shailina Parti, design director at Monsoon since 2010, who introduced the LOVE collection to a new audience at Estethica, believes that 'fashion can be beautiful and desirable and still be sustainable. Everyone has a conscience and consumers will increasingly appreciate knowing what their clothes stand for. Monsoon remains affordable to the British consumer but is still committed to working with natural fabrics and hand craft skills, and manages [its] valuable supplier partnerships and trade in an ethical way.'[3]

This page and opposite: Designs from the Monsoon mainline collection, Autumn/Winter 2011.

People Tree

Well known as a pioneer of ethical trading, People Tree was founded in 1997 by Safia Minney in Japan and now has 600 shops worldwide.
By Sandy Black

People Tree began life as the clothing line of the Fair Trade Company, a 'green' retailer operated by the campaigning environmental NGO Global Village. People Tree now has 600 shops in Europe and Japan, with concessions in Topshop and John Lewis, and also selling to ASOS. It eschews factory production, preferring instead to create close partnerships with 4,000 organic farmers and artisans who work in small-scale village operations in India, Bangladesh, Peru and Kenya, producing handmade textiles, clothing and jewelry. Some villages have as many as 600 people engaged in embroidery, knitting or handweaving. The company works in partnership with more than fifty fair trade groups to provide technical assistance and supports local social projects such as schools.

In its early days People Tree sold T-shirts and casual wear to a primarily older and environmentally aware customer base, but as the market for fair trade fashion has broadened, its designs have become more sophisticated. Since 2007 People Tree has collaborated with designers Bora Aksu and Richard Nicoll (promoted by *Vogue Japan*) and Eley Kishimoto, Thakoon and Orla Kiely have provided exclusive collections. Actor Emma Watson, who has long championed the brand, created a collection for its Fair Trade Youth range. Tracy Mulligan, head of design since 2009, explains People Tree's new approach: 'We select from fashion forecasters the trends that most suit the hand skills of our partners, which is the other way round from the norm.'[1] Founder Safia Minney expresses the brand's evolution another way: 'The People Tree collection…shows [that] Fair Trade fashion can sit at the high end and look fabulous.'[2]

Right: 'Alpine Grove' dress in Fair Trade organic cotton, Orla Kiely for People Tree, Spring/Summer 2012.

Opposite above left: Hand-weavers at Swallows Workshop in Bangladesh prepare to wind yarn onto bobbins.

Opposite above right: This weaver at Swallows Workshop can produce up to 7 m of cloth in a day.

Opposite below: Workers at Eastern Screen Printers in Bangladesh screen-printing cotton by hand to produce fabric for Orla Kiely bags.

'Fashion is political. If you buy a dress from People Tree, you do so in the knowledge that you are helping to distribute wealth more widely around the world.'[3]

'It's a beautiful relationship, the batikers and the garment manufacturers'

ANNEGRET AFFOLDERBACH *of British ethical fashion brand Choolips defines herself as an entrepreneur who puts ethics first, but always with a keen eye for commercial viability, as she explains to Sandy Black.*

Q **Tell us about the breakthrough that set you on your ethical fashion journey.**

A I set up Choolips in 2003 and the first collection that I designed used organic and sustainable materials. At that time there wasn't anybody else at London Fashion Week showing that kind of thing. I was able to have my own off-schedule catwalk show thanks to funding from the Prince's Trust that allowed me to make my first collection and set up my business. The show was well received, but people were saying 'this [ethical fashion] is suicide – what are you doing? It's very entrepreneurial, but it's never going to work.' I still had to do it because that's what I believed in. The collection didn't sell in the UK, but it did in the US and in Japan.

What was your design philosophy at the time?
The idea was to have unique garments that were handcrafted. As well as the handcrafted element, they also had elements of textiles and traditions that could easily be replicated in conventional production. I was looking at 'rusting' cottons; I was looking at dip-dyeing and hand embroidery – things that could be done in production here in the UK, rather than going out into the big world the way that I do it now. I wanted to make a ready-to-wear collection for women who wanted special garments to wear to work, and not necessarily for doing the washing up; women who wanted to look nice in their everyday lives. I designed primarily for petite women. Because I felt that the idea of using sustainable materials and organic materials was already difficult enough, I thought that if I put my clothes in a niche market it would probably give me a good selling point. Luckily it did, and that's why the Japanese were interested in the collection and I was able to sell it to specialist boutiques in New York. But I found that I didn't enjoy it. I can't say that I didn't enjoy being in the fashion industry, but I didn't enjoy the process of fashion week. It was my inexperience as well. It was overwhelming.

Above: Choolips's third collection, made in Ghana, Spring/Summer 2009.

Opposite: Choolips's signature batik-printed bold designs, made in Ghana, Spring/Summer 2011.

Did you come through college?
I didn't. I'm learning as I go along. It was a massive experience for me, the attention that you get – it's very invasive. I'm not that kind of person. I'm quite happy to be in the background doing my thing. There was something missing for me. I wanted to be able to say 'this is me' and stand up in the public eye to say 'this is what I believe in'. So I took a year off and worked as a stylist and art director in the film and music industry, which gave me a heap of different experiences and let me think about how I would build a more structured business. I also looked at my values as a person and the things I grew up with. I have always had a huge love for textiles and colour, and I wanted my work to reflect that. I grew up in a Christian family in East Germany, so there was a contrast between my home upbringing and the schooling that I had: humanitarian values within a socialist ideal. So I needed to do something with people.

I left Germany in 1994 when I was nineteen and lived in Whitechapel [East London]. One of the things that's always fascinated me is local history so I decided to look at what went out of the ports in the Docklands, which were all part of textile trade. Where did the slave trade take people? That was my starting point. I went to the Gambia in 2005 and did my first bit of research with batik makers there. I spent a few weeks testing how long it would take people to replicate designs if they were open-minded enough to do more Western-style production, or whether I could make their ideas of production work for us. So I did a lot of work on the ground.

Why the name?
It's always been the name I wanted to use. Tulips, my favourite flowers, became 'Choolips'. The brand is fun, playful, on-trend, and some pieces are timeless. They're comfortable and always include an entire collection of dresses, with one playsuit as a teaser for the buyers. A couple of buyers asked me to do other pieces so that they would be able to buy them in as a collection, but now they've gone for the whole range of dresses. Let people see it and then they can decide.

Left: An outfit from Choolips third collection, Spring/Summer 2009, made in Ghana.

Below right and opposite: Dresses from Choolips, Spring/Summer 2011 collection, made in Ghana.

had both good minds for business and artistic flair in the skill of batik. I began to look at Ghana, which had a stronger economic infrastructure and good connections to the UK. I found that Ghanaian craftspeople did stamp batik-making, which suited my designs and is a much simpler process. I decided that before I made another trip to Africa, while I was saving up the money, to design a collection of prints so that I could get samples made there and then come back and work step-by-step. I had just finished that collection on paper when the Ethical Fashion Forum advertised its Design for Life Ghana competition, which was set up in collaboration with [the nonprofit organization] Tabeisa.[1] It was an amazing coincidence to find an organization that was also looking at the infrastructure of West Africa. So I submitted the designs, and Julia Smith[2] and I won the competition and I got the opportunity to test-drive the business.

The dresses from the project were bought by Topshop. Claire Hamer (buyer) and Melanie Frame (head of the technical department) asked Julia and me to set up the quality control for this production for Topshop – a big responsibility. So much of what I do now I set up during those first six months of that collection being developed. That was in 2006 and the collection went into Topshop stores in April 2007.

Julia and I each had very different designs and we were allocated different people to work with in the same co-op. It was a great process for both of us. Now we've gone quite separate ways. We did our two collections with Topshop and then I did my first independent one. I told Topshop 'you can buy the collection but you can't have exclusivity'. They've learned a lot about fair trade through my work. I spent so much time on the ground in Ghana and knew what their challenges were: I understood how the Ghanaians work culturally and how they work as individuals, and built a good understanding between us.

I wanted to be confident that my Ghanaian partners could manage a bigger business on their own, without me needing to be there all the time.

How did you start making dresses?

I just did it! I made my first pattern when I was about sixteen. I wanted to have something a bit different so I took apart a pair of Thai pants [wide trousers]…I painted my own silk and cut silk panels and made a pair of those trousers for myself. Once I had decided to set up my label, I went to an organization called Fashion Works, which helps designers who are coming from different routes to acquire the skills they might be lacking. So I was placed with a tailor who helped me with my pattern cutting…Doreen Adusai of Fashion Works is still helping me as a mentor; she is a fantastic lady who was given an OBE for her efforts in fashion. She helped me to make my collection happen. I also did work placements with two designers I love, Michiko Koshino and Hukka Lyall, who is a New Zealander doing corsetry and embroidery. In approaching Michiko I just found out where the studio was, walked in and said 'I don't care if I [just] make you tea – you're not turning me away'. I wasn't scared. I'm not afraid of being turned down. The British Council said I was fearless. I'm not afraid to go in there and ask for something; you get when you ask. People find it refreshing. This mentoring happened during 2002 and 2003; then I went looking for people who could do my sampling for me, and I found an Afro-Caribbean lady. The tailor I worked with was also Afro-Caribbean. They worked hard but there was always music and laughter. The spirit did something for me. I discovered that this was where I needed to be in the world: somewhere with with sunshine and personality. I was drawn to batik traditions, but I needed something that would

work as a commercial idea. That's why I was drawn to the Gambia, where there was already a good infrastructure in place.

You are an entrepreneur rather than a fashion designer?

I'm a fashion entrepreneur. I look at fashion and particularly textiles from an aesthetic point of view, but it also needs to be a venture that's commercially viable. It has to have a profitable ethical supply chain, not just create beautiful things. I also think ethical fashion has to be accessible. It shouldn't just be a range of mid-level or high-end fashion, because the majority of people can't afford that. It's something that could be sitting on the high street in the most aesthetically pleasing way. That's where the entrepreneurial bit comes in: figuring out how to make the clothes work commercially without destroying the traditions that go into producing them, and doing this without making the clothes so cheap that they become clobber that sells for £20. I also want to develop a business model that I can take to various places throughout the world and replicate. It's almost like developing a franchise business model. It isn't quite there yet, but it's on the way.

What has been problematic so far? How have you produced and promoted your collections?

This is where my world changed completely. I came back to the UK, but I wasn't completely convinced about working in the Gambia. The people there were proper artisans, but they weren't business-minded, and for what I wanted to do I needed people who

[Juliana's workshop] used to have four posts and a bit of corrugated iron on top. Now it's a proper house. She's been able to train four workers and she's laid a water pipe.

It's a beautiful relationship with the two companies: the batikers and the garment manufacturers. It's a supplier and client relationship and I want to keep it that way. Even though the orders come through me, they are in charge, they say when it can be done. I didn't know how well it could work between supplier and client. It has a level of fairness I never thought could be present in business.

What have been the challenges in production?
I have had very few problems with delivery. The only difficulty has been during the rainy season when the fabrics can't dry in time. Or the challenge of certain colours not being right. Some colours are difficult and I have to say to Topshop they can't have that colour. I tell Topshop that they can expect delivery within a certain time window rather than giving them a single fixed delivery date.

My delivery timeframe is usually 800 units in about eight weeks. They bought 1,500 units the first time. Then I put my price points up and they bought less, and increased their prices at retail.

What impact would you say you have had in Ghana?
Juliana (my batik producer) has expanded her workshop. She's improved her workshop – she used to have four posts with a bit of corrugated iron on top. Now it's a proper house. She's been able to train four workers and she's laid a water pipe. I've been teaching her to think about business in a different way and look at freelancing. So she's becoming an entrepreneur herself.

What responsibility do you have to keep the orders coming in?
Juliana knows the work is seasonal. I'm trying to put products in place that will level it out. I'm also trying to sell the textiles in their own right to bring in money during those quiet periods. But Juliana has lots of other clients.

You have to make sure you get your orders out on time, of course. I'm looking at managing that in a new way, because I'm looking at expansion. I'd like to have Choolips quality controllers who go into the businesses, rather than the businesses themselves doing their own quality control without knowing what they are doing, which is too much of a risk. That's something I'm putting in place with the help of someone who has a lot of experience in textile production in Ghana. The other big challenge is to make sure my things always have a freshness to them. Looking at traditions and my love for colour and seeing if Julianna can be pushed to take her techniques beyond the limitations of tradition. Part of that is introducing new colours that have commercial appeal.

Is it fair trade?
I'm not certified as a fair trader but my wages are higher than the Fairtrade benchmark. I pay eleven to thirteen times the average Ghanaian wage. This part of the story is a main selling point. I am looking to provide ethical fashion at an accessible price point. I want young people to realize they can wear a different beautiful garment every day if they choose to, so long as it has all the right elements and is ethical. Eventually I want to produce ethical collections not only in Ghana, but also in India and China.

'The soul of the parish is making.'

GOODS OF CONSCIENCE *is a sustainably produced clothing line started in 2005 by a Catholic priest, Father Andrew More O'Connor, in the Bronx, the poorest borough of New York City.*
By Sandy Black

A system of benefices is being built in the US to develop local workshops, which employ locally and act globally, producing clothes that look good, feel good, and do good, based around a unique hand-woven cloth called Social Fabric™.

Father Andrew More O'Connor, who founded the project following a retreat in Guatemala during which he learned of the death of a priest who had worked among the country's Mayan communities, explains its underlying philosophy: 'The soul of the parish is making. I propose that we put our parishes

to work making something: bicycles, plates, shoes, beer, miracles, something tangible, anything local. The parish does not need to worry about competing with China, but can offer something of real quality with the added value of local origin – "the work of human hands." Built to serve the working classes, inner-city parishes can become home to small-scale workshops that manufacture for local markets.

Consumer savvy and the growing demand for sustainably produced goods and fair trade dovetail with a burgeoning taste for the local: locally grown

food and locally produced goods. Particularly in the inner city, parishes have the space and the human resources for manufacturing. The parish as manufacturer could – and would – support its community in both body and soul.'

Putting his ideas into action, Father O'Connor has developed a special high-quality cotton fabric that is hand woven by Mayan communities in Guatemala using simple backstrap looms. Social Fabric™ is made from a combination of local Guatemalan colour-grown cotton and modern light-reflective yarns. O'Connor, who originally trained in the visual arts, initially developed this unique cloth for use in ecclesiastical art projects, and has now adopted it produce stylish and original clothing that he designs himself with the assistance of a pattern maker. O'Connor sees these designs as part of his wider vocation. 'My own tastes govern the design of the clothing, which is a happy distillation of the parameters of the cloth I am using and the life of the missionary. I like the clothing to be functional and transitional, from the informal to the formal. I want to convince the consumer to dress symbolically, participating in a reality that the clothing visibly signifies.' High-quality material is important not only to the quality of the clothes themselves, but also as source of pride and opportunity for the communities that produce it: 'Rather than use cheaper materials, the reflective yarn we use mediates a psychological inferiority the weavers feel about the worth of their labor that is often reflected in the use of inferior materials to

undersell local competition. Social Fabric™ enables the them to live in such a way that their livelihood does not kill off their living.' The cotton is distributed through the Textiles Proteje based in the Museo Ixchel in Guatemala City, and is sold by weight to the weavers; finished cloth is then sold by weight back to the museum, which quality-checks it before it is shipped to Goods of Conscience in New York City. The museum also invites the weavers to showcase their art, encouraging them to feel proud of their work.

The fabric is then dyed (where required) and garments are made up in New York City by a small number of local contract workers. The business's ecological and ethical credentials are becoming increasingly well known in association with the brand and the unique aesthetic of Social Fabric™. Sales are made primarily over the internet and at trunk shows, but interest from eco-design retailers is increasing. O'Connor explains how the profits from these sales directly benefit the weavers in Guatemala: 'Chicacao is the main city and it is divided into sixteen *aldeas* – little villages of a few thousand inhabitants each. San Pedro Cutzan is the *aldea* where our team of twenty weavers live. In February 2010, I distributed the first fifty uniforms and satchels to 200 children in San Pedro Cutzan as part of our school uniform project. I also wrote a check to the local parish for US $1,250, which paid for food and medical aid. The uniforms are highly symbolic to the community because their cloth and their cotton is made in a North American

Above: A suit from the Goods of Conscience range, using Social Fabric™ cloth woven with reflective yarn detailing, photographed in Guatemala.

Opposite: A workshop in the Bronx, New York City, that manufactures clothing for Goods of Conscience.

style. The food and medicine aid is significant too, since it fortifies the elderly who care for the children and helps the children learn. Fair trade allows the community to earn badly needed cash.'

Father O'Connor believes that the project has the potential to improve not only practical conditions in producer communities, but also the values of modern American society. 'The four principles of Goods of Conscience are Individuality, Common Good, Subsidiarity and Preferential Option for the Poor. A local parish as a place to live, work and pray offers, potentially, a holistic environment in which to develop new communal structures that can modify consumer appetites and habits. Some American parishes dabble in T-shirts and cause-related goods, but this is more of a reflection of affluence and leisure than necessity. These ventures are not brave enough. We need to begin living in a new way, tapping into our ancient beliefs and practices: making something out of little or nothing, building sacred dependency on one another, imbuing the ordinary desiderata of life with intelligence and the savour of love.'

Colour-grown cotton cultivation

Colour-grown cotton comes from ancient cotton varieties that grow naturally in shades of cream, brown and green. The vibrant natural colours of this native 'heritage' cotton owe their richness to the moist soil, humid climate and good drainage on Guatemala's Pacific coast. Restricting the direct application of fungicides and insecticides builds the health of the soil, which has been continually planted with cotton in polycultural conditions since the 1940s. The seed collection amassed by Horatio Villavincencio, now deceased, is a critical legacy, especially in light of the dominance of Monsanto Corporation's annual acquisition of wild seed in the villages of Nuahalá and Santa Ana, north of Atitlán, which limits access to the seed both locally and globally. One advantage of handwoven colour-grown cotton is its resistance to wrinkling. The Maya use a natural mercerization method that utilizes a byproduct of tortilla production: calcium and cornstarch create an alkaline polish for the cotton shaft as well as giving the warp a silky slip.

Manish Arora: Indian craft and high fashion

PHYLLIDA JAY *profiles the successful Indian fashion designer, famed for championing traditional Indian handcrafts. Photographs by Matjaz Tancic.*

Manish Arora is an Indian fashion designer noted for his commercial success and vibrant use of traditional Indian crafts. Western silhouettes form the canvases to which Arora applies traditional embroidery, appliqué and beading techniques, reinventing them with his distinct style.

Arora graduated in 1994 from the National Institute of Fashion Technology in Delhi, launching his own label, Manish Arora, in 1997 and his diffusion line Fishfry in 2001. Collaborations followed with brands such as Reebok, Nescafé, Swarovski and Swatch, giving him global exposure and providing capital for expansion. He first showed at London Fashion Week in 2005 and Paris Fashion Week in 2007, where he continues to showcase his collection. In 2011 he was appointed creative director at French design house Paco Rabanne, an appropriate match for Arora's exuberant, often theatrical, design sensibility. As the first Indian designer to head a European fashion house, this appointment is important to India's emerging fashion identity on the global stage. His debut show for the label in Spring/Summer 2012 received critical acclaim as a 'futuristic light display'[1] Arora is aware of his role as an ambassador of Indian design. 'I am the only Indian fashion designer to consecutively show fourteen shows in Paris, yet I'm from a country of 1.3 billion people. For me it's very important to take India and show it to the world. The world doesn't need another Western designer, what it needs is a modern Indian designer.'[2]

Crafts are central to Arora's efforts to modernize Indian design. His work with Indian craftspeople has been compared to the model of the French couture atelier. In this way tradition crafts receive high value-added design development, which opens up new markets for traditional skills.

Arora's bold and inventive use of Indian handcrafts has been influential to younger Indian designers as an example of how traditional crafts can work in high-level fashion design.

Above and opposite: Manish Arora, Spring/Summer 2009, photographed in London's Brick Lane by Matjaz Tancic.

Design for Development: a creative tool for bottom-up development

JUDITH CONDOR-VIDAL *is director of Trading for Development, an organization that aims to show how ethical business practices and high-quality fashion products can bring development to poor communities by encouraging traditional crafts, forging links with fashion houses and universities, and marketing fair trade products worldwide.*

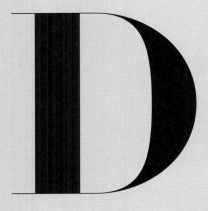

esign for Development is a creative tool that we generated during a Trade for Development (TFD) experience with textile and fashion tutors Toni Hicks from the University of Brighton and Maria Skoyles from Cherwell Oxford Valley College, and members of the World Fair Trade Organization (WFTO) who work in countries such as Bolivia and Brazil. TFD uses 'Design for Development' as a practical framework that aims to connect fashion schools with members of the WFTO and the market, namely, buyers interested in acquiring ethically sourced products. TFD Design for Development aims to alleviate poverty through trade, meeting the needs of the producer and end-user consumer (market), using appropriate technologies for the communities we're working with, and providing learning opportunities for project participants.

In the Design for Development process we work directly with the people we want to help, starting wherever they are, aiming to 'walk together out of poverty'. For example, a member of a cooperative of weavers earning less than a dollar a day in Bangladesh who is an expert on embroidering and weaving will study techniques and visual inspiration and develop new designs and products using their skills. The learning is a two-way process; for example, undergraduate students from Brighton learned about ethical trading and the artisans' skills base and production capabilities. In turn, the students offered information about contemporary visual inspiration, colours and themes to assist new product development by the producer groups. This ensures the new products such as tops and bags are relevant to the European market, for retailers such as Topshop.

These are the notes that came out of our workshop discussions.

STARTING POINTS:
1. Understanding the relationship between poverty and the fashion industry and opting to do something about it.

2. To use the design process as a problem-solving tool.

3. To ask ourselves what 'sustainability' actually means.

4. Understanding how the definition of sustainability can differ between the global south and north.

Key issue:
Each context and community is a special case that requires an individual approach, but part of this process is also to highlight the norm.

The method:
1. Local context: when working with a community we need to have an appreciation of economic, political, social and cultural factors; we need to know about the labour markets, organizational skills and structure.

2. The international context: importance of natural fibres and their distribution globally; understanding of inequality and poverty and the link between these and trade regimes.

DESIGN FOR DEVELOPMENT IN ACTION
The Project:

1. Develop a saleable piece that is sustainable: it uses the skills of the people we are working with and the resources available.

2. Developing community-based monitoring and evaluation tools such as a form of quality control.

3. Our project seeks to utilize locally available and sustainable materials in their manufacture.

4. The project needs to be based on in-depth research in the use of sustainable local materials.

5. The project will also seek to provide skills training and sustainable employment opportunities for women.

6. We aim to identify through this process which organizations are the most likely to be the final manufacturers of the project.

Exploring community capacity:

Designing affordable and sustainable pieces also requires a good sense of the market and the capacity of producer communities. This will be achieved through the next steps:

1. Research of the materials that exist in the community, including buttons, zips, wool, material.

2. Produce two swatches (samples): a complex sample and a simple sample that demonstrates the variety of available skills.

3. Design a prototype piece that is responsive to local resources and skills.

4. Establish or support a small manufacturing facility for the production of the piece.

5. Learn how local residents manufacture the products, understand their production logic and then analyse how this could be improved through the provision of technical and management training and skill building.

6. Manufacture and distribute an initial run of a sample.

7. Provide community-based training in management and maintenance relevant to the piece we are making.

8. Establish a system of community-based project monitoring and evaluation.

When working with a community we need to have an appreciation of economic, political, social and cultural factors.

CONCLUSIONS:

The project is an open-source, ongoing process combining ethical design practices and social responsibility to support members of the WFTO network. It will look at issues on climate change, use of sustainable materials, loss of biodiversity, and transport. These will be discussed with producer groups, buyers and students. During project implementation TFD provides training to local people in the manufacture of resulting designs as well as in basic designs. TFD will then market the final piece.

Desired outcomes

1. Our aim is for these projects to provide part of a solution to alleviating poverty through trade, using Design for Development techniques.

2. We hope to increase problem-solving skills so that participants are able to address future issues with skill and confidence.

3. Design for Development aims to connect communities with designers and buyers, and to make use of the design process as a problem-solving tool.

4. Design for Development supports designers and design students as a valuable resource in addressing and relieving poverty. Through involving students of design and designers in related research and dialogue at all levels of the project we aim to make these links sustainable at both ends of the supply chain.

5. This approach requires new knowledge, skills and collaborative partnerships. We are interested in organizing tutors and students to forge links with fair-trade producers and members of the WFTO.

6. Design for Development will encourage sustainable innovation, leadership, communication and campaigning. It will explore the idea of designers as facilitators, and the role of design as a tool for developing sustainable solutions.

'The main challenge that we face is finding factories that can manufacture at both the right quality level and within an acceptable timeframe.'

JANE SHEPHERDSON *is CEO of Whistles and former brand director at Topshop.*
By Sandy Black

Left and opposite: Knitwear and sheepskin aviator jacket, Whistles, Autumn/Winter 2011.

Q **After leaving Topshop you worked at Oxfam and People Tree before taking on Whistles. Were your choices part of a reaction to your Topshop experience?**

A Working with People Tree was more of a continuation of the work I had started [via People Tree's in-store concession] at Topshop, and an opportunity for me to get more involved and to learn more. Oxfam was very different. They approached me, and I was delighted to discover that my skills were transferable to the charity sector. It is something that I would have gladly done while still at Topshop, but I was never asked! I have always felt that a business should try to give something back to the community, and that it should treat its workforce with integrity and fairness, so this gave me an opportunity to become more involved.

What is the legacy of Topshop and how do you see your contribution to the fashion climate at the time?
I have been labelled as 'the woman who invented fast fashion' which is completely untrue, as fast fashion has been around for years. What I set out to do was to raise the standard of high-street shopping, to inject excitement, great design, amazing customer service and a sense of theatre into stores, and I think we achieved that in Topshop. I am delighted that many of Topshop's competitors have also upped their game and are now doing exciting things themselves.

How would you define the Whistles customer, and how is it different from the Topshop customer?
The Whistles customer is probably a little older than the average Topshop teenager, and wants well-designed fashionable clothes that will last for more than just the current season. She wants quality fabrics and a pleasant environment in which to buy them. She buys fewer clothes, and each purchase is much more considered.

As more brands are coming into the 'high fashion at an affordable price' market, where do you see Whistles's position?
Whistles has to be fashionable, but not slavishly so. It has to have its own identity: we have to interpret the macro trends in our own way, and in a way that our customers can relate to. It takes time to fully develop a house style, and this autumn is only our third season, so we are not there yet. Our first season was probably not edgy enough, and this season is slightly too edgy in some categories. It is a case of trial and error: we are constantly learning what our customers want from us, and what we feel the brand should be.

From the viewpoint of sustainable design, how do you balance seasonal fashion and timeless style?
This is the hardest thing to get right! Every day we have internal battles over the fashionability of the

something to the collection, and the pieces would have to stand up in their own right, and not just as a PR story.

What are the main challenges of producing quality at reasonable price? What are the key compromises you have to make?

The main challenge that we face is finding factories that can manufacture at both the right quality level and within an acceptable timeframe. We produce a lot in Europe for that reason, and also because there tends to be less time wasted in the interpretation of a style. We do, however still produce some more labour-intensive garments in China, but cannot use any factories [that usually manufacture products for high street retailers], as they are not able to produce the small quantities that we require, or achieve the better-quality make. We tend therefore to seek out smaller, often family-owned units who have specialized in producing a premium product. The drawback is that they also tend to be expensive, and when you add in a more expensive cloth, it can get prohibitive.

collection versus the timelessness of it. We are so bombarded by seasonal fashion, and what is 'hot' that it can be hard to create a collection that cuts its own groove. Customers, too, are so aware of the season's looks and trends that something can easily be seen as unfashionable, and therefore unwanted, if it doesn't fit in with what the magazines are selling. We have seven designers, who all have their own areas of expertise, be it prints, soft wovens, knitwear or bags, and they all collaborate so that we achieve a cohesive handwriting. I have a design director and a brand director, who manages a small team of buyers, or product developers; they are really the two people who are the keepers of the Whistles design direction. My role is to help them to define that direction in the first place, and then to be objective, and to question whether we are still doing what is right for the brand. I then make sure that our store creative and marketing [teams] fully reflect that same direction.

You recently collaborated with Roksanda Ilincic. How do you choose designers for special collections and where do you see these collaborations going in the future?

We collaborated with Roksanda because we had known each other for some time, and had always wanted to work together. When I took over Whistles, it seemed the perfect opportunity. I was nervous, as there are so many collaborations these days and I didn't want this to be just one more, but I felt this was something a bit different. Our manufacturing is of such a high standard that I knew we could produce a collection that would be special, and would reflect Roksanda's aesthetic. The days of just doing a collaboration for the sake of it, or for the PR exposure, are drawing to an end. Customers are more and more savvy, and less and less inclined to be taken in by something that doesn't actually live up to expectations. We might well collaborate with more designers, but again, it would have to be someone we know would add

You set out to make Whistles a transparent, ethical business. What are your goals for the future?

We are still working on making Whistles a transparent, ethical business. Since we started last year, we have changed almost 90% of the supply base for various reasons, and are now working with all of our factories to get them to a standard that we can be happy with. The next step is to try to work with fair-trade producers, both for them to start producing small collections for us, and also for us to learn from them, and see how much cross-fertilization we can achieve with our existing manufacturers. This is very much an ongoing project.

Do you think it is possible to balance the needs of a retail business to expand its customer base and increase sales with a desire to encourage sustainable consumption?

It is a dilemma for all retailers, but one that is not going away, so we need to find a balance. Perhaps the answer is to ensure that we are seeking out the latest technologies in order to produce more materials out of waste products, save our resources as much as possible and encourage our customers to recycle their clothes – i.e., when they buy something new, to give their old clothes to a charity such as Oxfam who will either sell them or turn them into something that is needed.

Would you say it is easier for a smaller company to manage a transparent business?

Having worked in both large and small companies, I think it's much easier in a small company. So much of the task is delving down through the supply chain to find out who is doing the work, and then ensuring that they are doing everything to the standard you require. The more suppliers you have, the longer it takes. The downside of being a small business is that you have less power to make them change. If you represent only a small percentage of their business, you cannot make as many demands – and those who aren't committed to change probably won't ever

really embrace it anyway. Approximately 40% of the clothes are made in Portugal, 10% in Greece, 10% Romania, 30% in China and the remainder in Turkey, India and the UK. The retailer has to take responsibility for production, and make a reasonable effort to find out exactly where and how a garment is being produced. As a customer I want to know where my money is going.

How much responsibility is it reasonable to expect on the part of the fashion retailer?

My typical customer demands more than a regular high street customer, as I think she is more discriminating. There is a perception that if something is more expensive, then the people making it have been paid more, which of course isn't always the case. I don't think we are leading the way at all; we are just doing what we feel is responsible and what our customers would demand of us. To expect most retailers to encourage their customers to consume responsibly (i.e., buy less) is unrealistic, as their focus will always be to make a profit, and that will always be through selling more clothes. I have made a choice to move into a segment of the market that depends less on gratuitous consumption and more on considered purchasing, but few have that luxury, or, indeed, would make that choice! The most a retailer can do is to encourage their customers to give their old clothes to a charity shop, so that they do some good instead of ending up in landfill.

What policies are required to meet the demands of ethical businesses on both a national and an international level?

There is a need for legislation to force retailers to be more transparent and to provide information on how and where an item is manufactured. Then, at least, the customer can make an informed decision as to whether or not she wants to buy it. We expect this when buying food, so perhaps it is inevitable that it will happen with clothing. Internationally, retailers should be working with local trade unions and NGOs to ensure that the minimum wage is in fact a living wage, and that all of their manufacturers are adhering to it.

Gap

AMELIA WILLIAMS *investigates the environmental and social values of Gap Inc., which was established in San Francisco in 1969, and now has over 3,000 stores worldwide, employing more than 130,000 people.*

Gap is one of the world's largest speciality retailers and operates five of the most recognized apparel brands in the world: Gap, Banana Republic, Old Navy, Piperlime and Athleta. Gap sells moderately priced quality casual apparel. Its products range from wardrobe basics such as denim, khakis and T-shirts to fashion items and accessories for men and women.

Social responsibility is now fundamental to how the company does business. Gap has been nominated for many ethical awards, including the Human Rights Campaign's Corporate Equality Index (2005–2010) and Canadian magazine *Maclean's* Top 50 Socially Responsible Corporations in 2010. The company was also nominated by *Ethical Corporation* as having one of the top ten most innovative internal sustainability initiatives in 2007, and was chosen by *Ethisphere* magazine as one of its World's Most Ethical Companies in 2007–2010, in recognition of the company's commitment to ethical leadership and corporate social responsibility.

In recent years Gap has made efforts to assert itself as a leader in ethical and socially responsible manufacturing after previously being criticized

for the use of child labour in its supply chain. In 2007 Gap's ethical image was threatened when an illegal sweatshop using child labour was discovered in India. A spokesman admitted that children appeared to have been caught up in the production process, affirming that 'at Gap, we firmly believe that under no circumstances is it acceptable for children to produce or work on garments. All of our suppliers and their sub-contractors are required to guarantee that they will not use child labour to produce garments.'[1]

Environmental responsibility is also important to Gap. In April 2010 the company's 'Recycle Your Blues' campaign collected more than 270,000 pairs of jeans. The denim was then recycled into housing insulation for 500 homes in underprivileged communities. Ivy Ross, executive vice president of marketing, said that the success of the recycling programme 'demonstrated our strong commitment to doing what's right for the environment and our communities.'[2]

Gap has taken many steps towards improving its environmental performance, outlined in the company's new social responsibility website, which stresses that Gap is focused on reducing energy use, supporting sustainable design innovation and limiting output and waste. Since 2003 Gap has participated in the US Environmental Protection Agency's Climate Leaders programme to reduce energy and greenhouse gas emissions. Between 2003 and 2008 the company reportedly reduced greenhouse gas emissions by 20%. Gap encourages clean-water practices at denim laundries and is working to improve product packaging, use more alternative fibres in its products and design more sustainable stores.

Designers at Gap are constantly creating 'greener' clothing. Alessandra Brunialti, vice-president for design and product development at Banana Republic launched its Heritage Collection for women last summer. The collection featured silk made from soy and also incorporated hemp and organic cotton. She and the team are currently exploring designs that incorporate recycled paper and hemp fibre.[3]

Inspired by the success of H&M's designer collections, the first of of Gap's many collaborations with designers was in 2006 with Roland Mouret. Mouret's collection featured ten dresses that had details recognizable as Mouret's work, such as the folded cap-sleeves of the 'Galaxy' dress. Three red designs by Mouret were sold as part of the charitable RED initiative, with 50% of profits going to organizations fighting Aids in Africa.[4] Mouret stated, 'I was interested in the opportunity to make my designs available to a broader audience and

was particularly excited about the Gap (PRODUCT) RED involvement.'[5] Other designer collaborations followed, including Valentino, Stella McCartney and Diane von Furstenburg for Gap Kids.

Following its recovery from controversy over its manufacturing practices, Gap's overarching strategy of corporate social responsibility and its ethos regarding environmental and ethical issues have strengthened the company's brand significantly.

Walmart and Asda

AMELIA WILLIAMS *reports on the efforts of the world's largest retailer to improve performance on sustainability issues.*

Founded in Arkansas in 1962 by entrepreneur Sam Walton, Walmart operates a chain of large discount department stores and a chain of warehouse stores in the US. It is currently the world's largest retailer by revenue, operating 8,500 stores under fifty-five different names in fifteen countries.[1]

In 1999 Asda became one of many European supermarkets to be wholly owned by Walmart. Asda is the second largest supermarket chain in the UK with 17% of the grocery market.[2] The original company was formed in 1965 by farmers in Yorkshire and expanded southward throughout the 1980s. In 1991 Archie Norman became chief executive. He was inspired by Walmart's 'everyday low price' strategy, which focused on consistently low prices rather than a series of promotions backed by expensive advertising, and the company soon became known for being significantly cheaper than its rivals.

Walmart sells everything from pharmaceuticals to apparel and 60% of its sales are non-grocery items. Like Walmart, Asda sells a wide range of non-grocery items, and in 1990 developed its own clothing line, the George at Asda range. The George range was created by George Davis, who since the 1980s had been design director of British high street retailer, Next, which he founded. Davis left Asda in 2000 following its takeover by Walmart, but the George range continued to be successful.

As the first major supermarket to have its own fashion range, Asda started the trend for supermarket fast fashion that was soon copied by its rivals, such as Tesco. Before Asda's clothing range, the notion of buying clothes from a supermarket was considered to be very down-market. One possible reason for the shift in attitude was that many people found it less stressful to shop in a supermarket than in a high-street store.[3] Today George is stocked by 3,000 stores in seven different countries.

The George line has continued to evolve and expand. In 2006 Asda became the first supermarket to stock wedding dresses, which were priced at £60. In 2010 the teenage pop star Miley Ray Cyrus launched her new Miley and Max clothes range at Asda for teenage girls.

As a member of the UK Ethical Trading Initiative since 1998, and the UK government's Sustainable Clothing Action Plan (SCAP) since 2009, George at Asda is also making efforts to improve the ethical image of its clothes. Following exposés of workers' conditions in reports by War on Want, the Clean Clothes Campaign and others,[4] in 2009 Asda, together with Marks & Spencer, launched an innovative twelve-month pilot project in Bangladesh, where the George range is made, to improve management and worker skills, wages and factory productivity through lean manufacturing efficiencies, thus decreasing working hours and increasing the quality of clothing. The company also installed webcams in some factories in Bangladesh as part of its effort to increase transparency and monitor conditions in its supply chain. Due to the success of this pilot with four factories, Asda announced in 2011 that it would work with seventeen additional factories in Bangladesh and plans to roll out the scheme to factories in India and China.[5] Given that George works with over 700 factories worldwide, and 60 in Bangladesh, this is a small but significant step towards improving garment workers' conditions in a country where wages are among the lowest in the world.

Criticism from the charity Action Aid that 'these improvements still fall woefully short of a living wage',[6] has stimulated action by Asda to set targets for its clothing factories to use transparent labour costings per garment using a method called 'Standard Minute Value' by 2013.[7] Through SCAP, George at Asda has 'committed to further develop their ethical and audit process to cover more elements of the supply chain including fabric mills.'[8]

Asda claims that it is 'committed to sustainable development and reducing the impact our stores have on the environment.' According to the supermarket's 2010 sustainability report, Asda has reduced its direct carbon emissions output by 83,000 tonnes over the previous two years. The company has reduced its own-brand packaging by 27% and launched a 'bag for life' campaign in 2009. According to Walmart's 2012 global responsibility report, in its 2011 US operations the company diverted 80% of waste generated from landfill.[9] Since 2005, Walmart has set three goals to guide its efforts to become a more responsible company: 'to be supplied 100% by renewable energy; create zero waste; and sell products that sustain our resources and the environment'.[10]

Although such ambitious corporate sustainability goals may be difficult to achieve in full, a global company as large as Walmart has the ability to achieve positive change on a massive scale by making relatively small changes to its operating practices through its supply chains, simply due to its size and buying power. Equally valuable is the example that the George brand, as a pioneering supermarket clothing range and still one of the largest such labels in the market, can set for the rest of the 'value' fashion sector worldwide.

New Look and Echotex

LIZ PARKER *describes a British high street retailer's initiative to improve working conditions with its supplier in Bangladesh.*

This case-study is an example of how a mainstream high-street retailer is acknowledging its responsibility for working conditions in its supply chains and is taking concrete steps with companies to address them. In this project, New Look models a two-way relationship between retailer and supplier by changing its buying practices as well as looking to the factory to make improvements to its management systems. The activities implemented in the project are not the only way a company can improve working conditions, nor has the project necessarily created a model factory, but it is a good illustration of a collaborative approach that has opened dialogue about what needs to done to bring about lasting change.

Acknowledging, like other leading fashion brands in the UK, that there is room for improvement of working conditions in its supply chain, New Look is running projects to find ways to address the root causes of workers' rights infringements in its supply chain. The British high street clothing retailer developed a new working plan with Echotex, one of its suppliers, which has received national awards for its environmental work. Echotex is based in Bangladesh, a country where industry wages are amongst the very lowest in the world. The New Look/Echotex project aims to reduce excessive overtime while increasing pay for the people involved in manufacturing their products. The strategy includes New Look addressing its own buying practices to ensure that the benefits of the project are felt into the future.

New Look was founded over forty years ago by Tom Singh, OBE as a ladies' fashion retailer based in the south-west of England. Its brand identity is about delivering fashion excitement, newness and value. It now sells clothing, lingerie, shoes and accessories in over 1,000 stores worldwide. The company is a market leader in fashion (womenswear, footwear, accessories and teen ranges) and has a growing market share in other areas (menswear and children's clothing). New Look is currently the third-largest womenswear and accessories retailer by value in the UK, with 6.0% market share.[1] The company directly employs over 20,000 people globally and in 2009 worked with

331 suppliers covering 1,016 factories across thirty-two countries. New Look publicly voices a commitment to ethical trading and animal welfare, as well as a pledge to limit its impact on the planet by reducing the waste to landfill and cutting energy consumption. Its main production is in Bangladesh, Cambodia, China, India, Turkey, Vietnam and Moldova. This sourcing network is managed by New Look's British head office, working through distribution hubs in the UK and Singapore.

Echo Sourcing, the parent company of Echotex, was established in the 1990s by Shafiq Hassan and his design partner Para Hamilton as a 'design to delivery' organization. Together with their Bangladeshi friends they envisioned building a garment manufacturing plant in Dhaka that would create employment for 500 people. They now collectively own three factories that employ 11,000 people and produce upwards of two million garments per month, supplying New Look and other fashion outlets. Echotex is the largest of these three factories and was established three years ago. It employs over 5,000 people in its vertical production

operation manufacturing knitted jerseywear fashion items. Echotex has its own on-site knitting, dyeing and production plants as well as an effluent treatment plant (ETP) that has already won a national environmental award. Committed, forward-thinking and people-centred managers are employed to help bring to fruition the vision of the company's directors in creating commercially viable production sites with excellent systems of people management, industrial engineering, modern equipment and technical expertise to deliver better lives for workers and their children.

New Look's 'Leaving a Legacy' report outlines its approach to ethical trade.[2] It is a member of the Ethical Trading Initiative (ETI) – a British alliance of companies, trade unions and voluntary organizations, working in partnership to improve the working lives of people across the globe who manufacture or grow consumer goods. New Look's code of conduct is based on the ETI's Base Code and covers trade-union rights, health and safety, child labour, living wages, working hours, discrimination, regular employment and harsh and inhumane treatment.[3] The ETI code also includes environmental considerations. In 2009 the company carried out 200 social audits (factory inspections) to diagnose problems in their supply chain. The audits highlighted health, safety and hygiene, wages and working hours as the key issues needing to be addressed. In common with other leading companies in ethical trade, New Look publicly accepts that working conditions in their supply chain may not always meet the standards they require and that infringements of workers' rights sometimes occur in factories supplying them.

New Look ask all their suppliers to take ownership of any such issues, to work with New Look to tackle problems and to be open and honest in their communication. 'Our work with our suppliers has shown us that the way we buy can sometimes make it more difficult for factories to meet our ethical standards. If we confirm our orders late, make late changes in design, change the size of orders or are slow in completing paperwork, product turnaround times are increased, reducing a suppliers' ability to provide decent jobs for workers.'[4] To address this, New Look trains its designers, buyers and merchandising staff to consider the implications of their decisions for workers. The company's main ethical thrust is in piloting projects in different countries to tackle the root causes of poor working conditions both with other retailers and with their own suppliers. The company acknowledges this as a work in progress, but hopes that 'by sharing our programme, incomplete as it is, we will encourage our customers, stakeholders and others to respond and make further suggestions'.[5]

One example of a New Look collaborative project to promote sustainable and ethical change in its supply chain was carried out in Dhaka, Bangladesh, in 2006–9. The project was facilitated by Impactt Ltd, a specialist ethical supply-chain consultancy, and sought to address long working hours and low pay in the Echotex factory and its smaller predecessor. New Look and Echo Sourcing shared the project costs 50/50. At the start of the project, working hours were often high (sometimes more than 70 hours per week) and pay far from a living wage, with the lowest 'helper' grade workers earning only an average of £20 per month. Workers therefore needed to work extra hours to top up their basic pay. 'On top of that, management systems were under-developed, efficiency and productivity were low and management was unsure of how to value its workers.'[6] Within Echotex, the project had a number of elements:

1. Worker consultation to listen to the concerns of the workers.
2. Human resources management, including the introduction of a procedure for workers to discuss their concerns with management.
3. Production-incentive scheme under which workers receive a bonus linked to productivity.
4. Improved industrial engineering and production planning.
5. A provident fund to provide workers with a means to save money in order to reduce their vulnerability in case of hardship.
6. Free lunch for all workers aimed at improving nutrition.
7. Enthusiastic backing for the project from senior management.

There were regular meetings between supplier representatives and buying teams to discuss the project. In addition, New Look addressed its own practices. It identified ethical champions among its buyers, improved forecasting of order flow and volume to enable the factory to plan its production schedule and guaranteed a minimum-volume contract for the supplier, giving Echotex's owners confidence to invest in improvements. The project returned a 45% reduction in overtime working within six months and a 25% increase in take-home pay for workers. This helped to improve employee retention and reduce absenteeism as well as improving product quality. Freedom of association for workers to choose whether or not to join a trade union was not fully addressed within the project, although an active workers' committee was established. The project has identified a framework within which New Look can work with its suppliers as they move towards meeting the standards outlined in New Look's code of conduct, while also acknowledging the need for further collaboration over the long term.

Adapted from: E. Parker, *Steps towards Sustainability in Fashion: Snapshot Bangladesh*, edited by L. Hammond, H. Higginson and D. Williams, London College of Fashion and Fashioning an Ethical Industry (2011), pp. 12–15.

Below and opposite above: Clothes from New Look's summer 2011 range.

Opposite below: New Look store in Liverpool, UK.

Sustainability in the luxury industry

BURAK CAKMAK, *former Gucci Group director of corporate sustainability, examines the new conception of luxury.*

Today the luxury industry is under increasing pressure to evolve in order to adapt to the new concerns of our times. Traditionally the ways in which luxury items have been produced – using natural, high quality and often locally sourced materials that are then transformed by the precise craftsmanship of skilled artisans – have had a relatively low impact on the environment in comparison to that of the mass market. As high fashion expands into new territories, the importance of using innovation to create new and dynamic ways of consuming is becoming clearer for an industry that is bigger than ever before.

A result of the economic downturn has been a marked change in consumer habits, and non-essential items have been hit hardest. In order to compensate, the industry has to offer deeper value to satisfy the demands of would-be customers who increasingly expect their luxury purchases to be manufactured in an environmentally responsible manner. The future of design has to move beyond the traditional characteristics of luxury: beauty, desire and exclusivity. A first step that has been taken by many environmentally aware luxury brands is to use recycled materials. A good example is Hermès, who introduced a new line of decorative accessories called 'Petit h', created from upcycled scraps, including defective inventory and factory-floor leftovers. Biomimicry – an ancient design and engineering principle that takes its

Opposite left: Signature accessories combined
with lavish embellishment, Marc Jacobs
for Louis Vuitton, Spring/Summer 2012.

Opposite right: Art Deco-inspired cocktail dress,
Frida Giannini for Gucci, Spring/Summer 2012.

Below left: Marc Jacobs for Louis Vuitton,
Autumn/Winter 2011.

Below left: Colourful fur and satin at Gucci's
90th anniversary show, Frida Giannini for
Gucci, Autumn/Winter 2011.

inspiration from the forms of nature – is also a
relevant area of exploration. New breakthroughs
of relevance for luxury fashion designers include
fibres manufactured in the same manner as
spiderwebs, self-cleaning surfaces inspired by
the lotus plant and a fabric that emulates shark
skin. The results will be designs that both that
transcend the sustainability conundrum and
inspire wonder in the consumer. Luxury houses
are increasingly supporting the development of
these technologies through new partnerships. For
example, acknowledging the value of investing in
the future of luxury, the Gucci Group sponsored
a new PhD scholarship at Central Saint Martin's
College in London, aimed at promoting creativity
and innovation in sustainable textiles.

As consumers increasingly push for
sustainably sourced products, the luxury fashion
industry finds itself pulled towards supporting
innovation. This is creating the conditions for a
widespread paradigm shift in which sustainability
is regarded as central to good design rather than
merely an afterthought, and thus a core element
of what the luxury industry has to offer. We are
moving towards a scenario in which luxury brands
can only be desirable to the consumer if their
creations are supported by positive values. These
values include not only beauty, creativity and
exclusivity, but also a love of innovation and a
sense of respect for the environment throughout
every stage of luxury product creation.

Marks & Spencer's commitment to sustainability

MIKE BARRY, *head of corporate social responsibility, has been in charge of Marks & Spencer's high-profile Plan A sustainability strategy since its inception in 2004.*
By Sandy Black

British retailer Marks & Spencer's (M&S) business has been progressing towards sustainability since the 1970s. The pace of growth has accelerated dramatically since 2004, when Plan A was first developed. Launched three years later, the Plan comprised a list of a hundred targets to be achieved by 2012 across five key areas: climate change, waste, sustainable raw materials, fair partnerships and health. One of the main commitments was for M&S to become carbon neutral, and to be sending nothing to landfill by 2012. After three years of operation, the Plan was judged to have been successful, having achieved 45% of its targets, and was therefore extended by adding eighty further goals for 2015. By mid-2011, ninety-five of the hundred and eighty targets (53%) were reported to have been achieved.

The embedding of sustainability in the M&S business model is a story of pioneering change in a notoriously difficult-to-change industry. According to Mike Barry, the company's head of corporate social responsibility (CSR), in the 1970s the M&S business was simply philanthropic, making donations to charity. In the 1980s, with social unrest on Britain's streets, the company, which had a store on every high street, invested to connect with communities. During the 1990s a CSR policy was developed based on risk-management strategies; it focused on preventing bad things from happening within the supply chain, including the use of child labour, poor factory standards or the mixing of toxins into dyes. Establishing a basic level of corporate responsibility by 2000 gained the company a good reputation, including two British awards for most responsible company in 2004 and 2006.

Although this approach resulted in incremental improvements (around 2% per year) in sustainability targets, in 2004 the company's new chief executive officer Stuart Rose instigated the more ambitious programme Plan A 'because there is no Plan B'. The aim was to tackle all the issues within sustainability from carbon reduction, zero waste and energy efficiency to recycling and ethical sourcing. Barry has stressed that the company was not cherry-picking a few areas (developing a separate eco-friendly range or using some organic cotton, for example), but was aiming to build sustainability into every product sold. The business case for doing this systemically for all of the 2.4 billion items of food and 350 million garments made available under Plan A was to make money through efficiencies. Barry has also stated that the company has reaped £70 million per year in cost benefits to date throughout the value chain, with the true impact with regard to clothing being not in the stores but in customer use – stemming, for example, from the 'wash at 30°C' campaign.

For Barry, Plan A is a 'change programme' that has also created new revenue streams. 'The aim is that within M&S, sustainability becomes the norm for everyone (all 78,000 within the business) – not just policed by a few hundred managers. It aims to integrate sustainability, becoming embedded as an ethos of "how we do business". Therefore every director has Plan A built into their bonus potential, and by 2020 all clothing products must have at least one Plan A action built in. This aim is enabled by governance and reporting structures that have driven the adoption of initiatives such as Better Cotton (BCI), improved dye houses, and recycling of polyester and clothing.' This activity amounts, he observes, to only 'roughly 10%' of what needs to be achieved. Although M&S is, relatively speaking, a leader in sustainable business, the remaining 90% is targeted for 2030: 'zero carbon emissions, zero waste, closed loop processes, 100% sustainably resourced materials, and to improve human life whenever the business touches people – throughout the supply chain, as customers or employees'.

As Barry describe it, CSR amounts to being 'less bad', and he acknowledges that continuous development to improve on the current situation is difficult. With some qualifications he cites forty big businesses that have similar sustainability goals, including Nike, Walmart (to a degree), Coca-Cola, Pepsi, IBM, GlaxoSmithKline, Vodafone (to a degree), DuPont (to a degree) and McDonald's (to a degree). Up to 4,000 other companies have started the journey, including supermarkets Sainsbury's and Tesco. The recession has caused some businesses to put their plans on hold, but, perhaps surprisingly, not to reverse them, despite the market contracting and costs rising, with inputs such as cocoa, cotton and polyester all at record prices and remaining volatile for up to two years.

Commenting specifically on the future of the fashion sector, Barry observes that 'when the impact of China's and India's growing markets is felt, there will not be enough raw materials for everyone. If 2–3 billion people within India and China start consuming as the West does in the next 20–30 years, this will create an estimated 100 billion items of clothing being sold across the world, equivalent to the demand from buying, say, a new dress every month (not a week or a year). Although this is a great business opportunity, where will the resources come from – the cotton, polyester, or factories? In the West, we are witnessing a crisis of confidence in capitalism, a latent disquiet about "the system" – big business, governments, media and politics. The encampments of protesters at St Paul's Cathedral in London and on Wall Street in New York are just the beginning. Disquiet will be accelerated by new technology and social-media campaigns, which can be damaging to business and ill-informed, but still make their impact. We are entering a new phase of a disruptive and unpredictable world, fuelled by a combination of factors: cost inflation, a febrile customer, new technology and new competitors for the ethical high ground.'

He predicts that in the next ten years someone will invent a new business model for fashion (in a similar manner to Google) that is entirely about sustainability, and that the new paradigm will disrupt the market. 'For example, eBay is a sustainability player even though it was not conceived in that way. Therefore M&S needs to be flexible and able to respond, to be in touch and on its toes. For the first time businesses are starting to think the unthinkable. Something existential will happen that will radically change the status quo – such as astronomical cost inflation, or a massive oil price hike. We now need to be looking outside the business to survive – in the 1990s M&S was too insular. American companies and consumers may not be so advanced [in sustainability] as the EU, but the US is better at innovation, so the US will be the game changers. For today's clothing we must focus on a supply chain that is not just buyer-led or based on copycat production, fastest to market, or having the best dye houses and colour designs. In the new paradigm, productivity, sustainability and efficiency will be key drivers of how and where products are sourced within the supply chain for a more balanced outcome – more than just the right

product at the right price. This means intervening further back in the supply chain. Here M&S has a head start due to having 100% of its own production. Raw-material knowledge and traceability are key, requiring mass intervention in the materials supply chain. Sustainability is not just about fair trade and organic – if we use 60,000 tons of cotton it all has to come under one of the categories of BCI: fair trade, organic or recycled.'

The vexed question of fast fashion versus long-life classic designs is squarely within Barry's sights. 'There is,' he observes, 'a dichotomy in fashion retail. Fast fashion will continue at one extreme (knock out product in a week, throw it away in a week). The other extreme is longevity, but the middle will get squeezed. The M&S clothing take-back scheme in partnership with Oxfam started in January 2008 and has handled half a million garments – Oxfam has raised £1 million and the clothes have had a good secondary use. It's a win-win situation: on Big Give days 150,000 extra people have come into M&S stores. M&S has always traded on its high-quality clothing proposition and traditions; the clothes last longer, and so are worth a second life with Oxfam.'

Plan A, which started out as what Barry calls 'a classic social and environmental plan with targets for materials usage in energy reduction, and also factory targets', has moved on to a second incarnation, 'still with social and environmental targets but feeding into sustainability through customers, stores, product, employees, infrastructure of stores, and investors'. M&S, he says, 'is looking at sustainability through those five lenses, rather than a bottom-up NGO-driven agenda. Overall, the customer is responsible for just 5% of the impact of the product, the remainder being the operation of M&S factories and supplier infrastructure'. When asked whether M&S would ever advocate selling fewer goods to meet sustainability goals rather than continual growth, he replies, 'We can create more value for investors and shareholders but not necessarily based on volume of sales. If we redefine the value system this may equate to the same financial result. Retail models will be redefined, possibly becoming more service than product oriented.'

Fashion, Barry firmly believes, can be made to be sustainable: 'We will always need clothing and therefore an industry. The fittest and nimblest will be in the final (sustainable business) segment.'

For today's clothing we must focus on a supply chain that is not just buyer-led or based on copycat production, fastest to market, or having the best dye houses and colour designs.

The GM cotton debate: science or ideology?

DAMIEN SANFILIPPO *is former cotton programme coordinator for the Pesticide Action Network UK.*

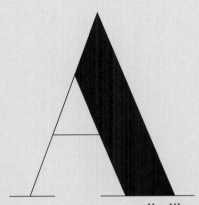ccording to an article published in the *Daily Mail* in late 2008,[1] genetically modified (GM) cotton was responsible for the tragic deaths of thousands of Indian cotton farmers who committed suicide after their harvest failed. Organizations such as the International Food Policy Research Institute were prompt to counter these claims, arguing that GM cotton had benefited farmers' livelihoods in India. Rarely has a technology provoked such polarized and passionate debate.

Monsanto, the company that dominates the world market for GM cotton technology, argues that not only does GM benefit the environment by reducing pesticide use, it is also needed to feed the world's growing population. But are these claims too good to be true? Global pesticide use reduction is the primary objective of the international Pesticide Action Network (PAN). Yet the consensus among the 600 independent organizations and experts that constitute the network is that GM is not the appropriate solution to deliver on these promises.

Although this debate may appear to some to be ideological in nature, it is not. The issue at stake is crucial: world agriculture is not sustainable. 'Business as usual is no longer an option,' said Robert Watson, lead scientist at the UK Department for Environment, Food and Rural Affairs (DEFRA) who led a recent international assessment of agricultural technology for development.[2] Under the auspices of the UN and the World Bank, this project brought together four hundred scientists from around the world. In a landmark report approved by fifty-seven governments in spring 2008, the scientists agreed that a radical paradigm shift in agriculture is urgently needed.

Can GM cotton contribute to this change? This is no time for an ideological debate. It is time we started looking at the facts, not only through the narrow lens of agronomic and genetic research, but by means of a broad multidisciplinary assessment encompassing the fields of agronomy, ecology and development. Ultimately, the 50 million farmers who grow cotton, most of them in developing countries, deserve the chance to be able to make their own informed decisions, free from commercial pressures and other external ideological or business interests.

The GM technology

GM cotton includes both herbicide-tolerant and insect-resistant technologies. Herbicide-tolerant cotton, which is genetically modified to survive blanket spraying of herbicides while competing plants are eradicated, does not contribute to pesticide reduction. Despite its wide adoption by American farmers, it is irrelevant for most of the world's cotton farmers, who are smallholders and use virtually no herbicides. We will therefore concentrate here on Bt cotton, an insect-resistant variety that has been engineered to contain the toxin from the bacterium *Bacillus thuringiensis* (Bt), which kills some insect pests. Its ability to kill one of cotton's major pests, the cotton bollworm, cannot be disputed. As a result Bt cotton has often led to reduced insecticide spraying in short-term trials. Promoters of GM cotton claim that this property will also lead to increased yield as a consequence of lower pest pressure, thus improving the overall performance of cotton production.

The most optimistic studies reveal that, in the case of American intensive and GM-dominated cotton agriculture, yields have clearly improved in the past ten years, and insecticide usage has decreased. In the developing world, although studies are mixed, some suggest significant overall improvement in the Indian cotton sector since the introduction of Bt cotton, and up to a 60% reduction in insecticide usage in Chinese Bt cotton production. However, PAN UK has identified just as many well-documented failures as success stories. Despite the indisputable effectiveness of the technology, many doubts persist about the true benefits of GM seeds for cotton's performance and farmers' livelihoods, especially whether these benefits can be replicated globally (especially in the context of smallholder farming) and sustained in the long term. These doubts are in no way ideological, but arise from the data currently available and from our knowledge of the dynamics of pest pressure and the economic, social and ecological implications of pest-management practices.

Above: Organic cotton fibres being processed.

Short-term benefits?

The short-term benefits of Bt cotton are not as clear-cut as has been suggested. In the US yield increase has only been significant since 2003, but had remained stagnant between 1996 and 2002, the period during which GM cotton became ubiquitous there. Other factors have also contributed to American cotton's recent improved performance, including an increased proportion of the crop under irrigation and favourable weather conditions (both of which have a great impact on cotton's performance), as well as other parameters such as a successful boll weevil-eradication programme. Therefore, although Bt cotton probably contributed to a reduction in insecticide usage, it played only a partial role whose exact extent is difficult to pin down.

In India studies showing improved performance generally documented the introduction of Bt cotton within well-supported Integrated Pest Management (IPM) farming projects. In such projects farmers are trained in crop management and supported throughout the season. This is very atypical, and therefore unrepresentative of the current situation in most of Africa and South Asia. It is also unclear to what extent the improved performance is due to GM seeds, optimal rain distribution or overall farming practices. Furthermore any positive results would be difficult to replicate on a global scale, as most farmers – tens of millions of them – do not currently have the capacity to implement best practices. Simply introducing GM seeds within current conventional farming systems in developing countries would likely not yield the same results.

Basic ecological processes will challenge the short-term benefits derived from Bt cotton. The technology, however effective, relies on a single intervention targeting one group of pests. But in the real world Bt cotton operates in an incredibly complex ecological matrix, comprising a wide range of pests and beneficial insects. While Bt cotton controls the primary pests, secondary ones will invariably move in to replace them, requiring more pesticide usage. Evidence from China suggests that this is already happening, with a significant increase recently in the use of endosulfans. Evolutionary pressures will invariably build resistance to the Bt toxin, following the exact same phenomenon observed with indiscriminate use of pesticides. As insects become immune, more chemicals, or chemicals of ever increasing toxicity, need to be used, resulting in the so-called 'pesticide treadmill' and trapping farmers in an endless cycle of escalating input costs. The constant presence and high level of the Bt toxin over extensive areas, which arises from widespread adoption of Bt cotton, will increase the likelihood of insects building resistance to the toxin. PAN UK has evidence from the US and other regions that this, unsurprisingly, is already happening. New GM traits will need to be developed ad infinitum, suggesting that farmers may eventually step off the pesticide treadmill only to step on the genetic treadmill.

The inappropriate technology

The debate over Bt cotton's effectiveness may still be unresolved and is certainly interesting from a scientific perspective. But it is ultimately irrelevant for one simple reason: the strategy behind GM technology does not actually respond to the major problems facing cotton farmers.

It is easy for those who are not intimately involved in cotton production to be seduced by GM studies showing such apparently promising results as 30% less pesticide and 20% higher yields. But these figures leave those working on sustainable cotton development totally indifferent. The reality is that most cotton farmers operate at productivity far below optimum and use far more insecticide than is really needed in the context of conventional farming. The problem here is lack of training and support. For the past fifteen years countless projects from around the world have shown that through participatory training in IPM, farmers are easily able to halve their pesticide usage while increasing their yields. It is not unreasonable to think that dissemination of best practices, combined with key investments such as organic fertilization capacities and water harvesting, could eventually double the productivity of key regions such as India or Sub-Saharan Africa. Even within organic farming in these regions, the most experienced farmers sometimes obtain double the yields of their conventional neighbours.

Agro-ecological farming practices, which are adopted in their most radical form by organic farmers and can easily be adopted by conventional farmers too, imply investing in skills and knowledge, and a holistic combination of a wide range of both traditional and innovative technologies. These practices bring higher productivity gains than GM technology because they favour investment in local knowledge and inputs, as opposed to expensive technologies from abroad. This approach can also contribute to solving the second most serious problems facing cotton communities: financial precariousness caused by increasing input costs and associated indebtedness.

This brings us back to the heartbreaking distress of Indian communities depicted in the *Daily Mail*. It is clear that, despite what the article suggests, Bt cotton is not the primary cause of the thousands of suicides. This tragic situation has been going on for years, and is mainly due to the effect of the pesticide treadmill described above (where farmers are trapped in a cycle of reliance on expensive inputs), linked to the unfavourable lending terms they are asked to sign up to. What is evident is that Bt cotton has been presented to these farmers as a complete technological package offering them a way out of their misery. Of course Bt cotton is only a tool. Cotton's most prominent body, the International Cotton Advisory Council, which is generally pro-GM, recognizes that Bt cotton should only be used as part of a broader integrated approach to pest management – including resistance management strategies – which requires helping farmers to build their ecological knowledge and expertise in agro-ecological practices. These prerequisites, as well as the obvious need for equitable access to finance, have been grossly overlooked, and when Bt cotton failed to deliver on its misleading promises, Indian farmers' disillusionment reached a new high; the rate of farmers' suicides shows no sign of going down.

The debate over the potential benefits of Bt cotton will continue as more research is carried out. However, it is crucial that within this debate the risks and limitations of GM technology are properly assessed in a multidisciplinary context. More importantly, the debate should not distract from the fact that proven solutions to cotton production's many problems already exist. Research into Bt cotton's effectiveness should not divert resources from the crucial work being carried out to disseminate best practices and alternatives to increasing pesticide use.

The GM cotton debate: why it is important to differentiate between science and the use of science

SIMON FERRIGNO *is a consultant in sustainable agriculture policy and organic and sustainable cotton.*

I am an advocate of organic cotton, and of increasing sustainability in cotton through other initiatives such as Fairtrade, Better Cotton and Cotton Made in Africa. All of these attempt to a greater or lesser degree to address sustainability challenges in cotton production. Nevertheless, I am about to argue against blanket opposition to genetic engineering, or biotechnology as it is also known.[1]

Organic cotton is an ideal solution for many small farmers, while the benefits of genetic modification (GM) are often overstated. However, the approach adopted by anti-GM campaign groups is lazy, a simple message designed to separate people from their membership subscriptions, just as the simple arguments by the GM industry are designed to separate policy makers from their funds.

I do not subscribe to anti-GM rhetoric because it is anti-science. Science is the reason we are able to debate sustainability. Serious organic farming uses science. The debate has become polarized between two extremes: the Dr Frankenstein camp, which thinks GM will solve everything, and the Luddites, who think it offers nothing. The reality is more complex, even if I am not convinced that we should expend as much time or effort on GM crops as we do at present. The reality for small farmers is that their urgent and primary needs are secure land tenure and access to tools, equipment and finance.

What is genetic engineering?

Genetic engineering (n): *gene-splicing, recombinant DNA technology (the technology of preparing recombinant DNA in vitro by cutting up DNA molecules and splicing together fragments from more than one organism)*[2]

Biotechnology is 'a broad term encompassing utilization of living organisms for the improvement of living organisms'.[3] Genetic engineering refers specifically to gene splicing or recombinant DNA, which allows the introduction of new DNA to organisms, which can then produce new proteins. New traits can thus be incorporated or existing traits strengthened.[4] It is this area that causes controversy and has led to the highly emotive and misleading term 'Frankenfoods'.

In 2009 genetically engineered (or modified) cotton was planted in eleven countries on 16 million hectares (49% of total cotton area). Most GM cotton is grown in the US, India and China, as well as in Australia, Brazil, Argentina, South Africa, Mexico, Colombia, Burkina Faso and Costa Rica.[5] You are more than likely already wearing GM cotton and have been for a few years (the anti-GM NGOs having made surprisingly little noise about this).

Why science and technology need to be considered separately from introducing technology

It is of course right to be concerned about the private domination of biotechnology allowing increasing corporate control over seed supply, but this has nothing to do with the science. Science and technology are a matter of the advancement of knowledge; the introduction of technology calls for society's value judgement regarding what is good or bad, right or wrong. It is in this second arena that proper assessment has been drowned out by rigid positions from different stakeholders seeking a competitive advantage. We might term this the 'Monsanto versus Greenpeace problem', both sides being unwilling to give ground because of self-interest in the area of market share.

We moved from being hunter-gatherers to a people capable of defeating major diseases by creating surplus funds that allowed bright people to innovate, experiment and generate new technology. We need science; we also need a code of ethics that tells us whether or not we use it, and within what parameters. Once we start rejecting science, we reject the possibility of discovering better ways of doing things.

The anti-science rhetoric of some campaigners is sometimes ill-informed. It tries to reduce debate. At the heart of the problem is, on the one hand, an inability to comprehend the difference between science and the application of science and, on the other, the grasping hands of agribusiness, which may also not grasp the difference but which has a remarkable talent for squeezing money out of agriculture. Neither side shows much hard understanding of development, poverty and hunger, yet both are quite happy to hijack the arguments that suit them.

The current range of applications of GM technology in the field are narrowly governed by the private interests of the technology and patent owners. This has led opponents to equate these specific applications with the science as a whole; thus the debate on potential public goods is lost. This is not to say that GM is a major or even a minor solution to the world's problems, but that research and development should still look at what contributions the technology might make to sustainability. An obvious angle to explore would be increasing the drought resistance of cotton. There are strong arguments for better public control of science and technology, of course, but these require more public interest in, and better understanding of, science. Neither Frankenstein nor Ludd had the answer – one ignored the possibilities of unintended consequences while the other failed to see what freeing humans from the burden of labour could accomplish.

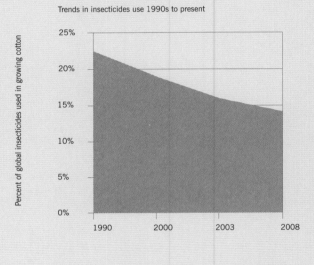

Trends in insecticides use 1990s to present

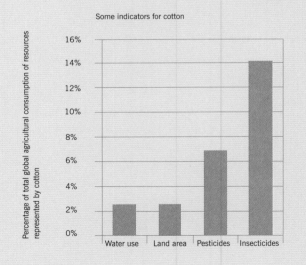

Some indicators for cotton

Has GM cotton contributed to greater sustainability?

Insecticide use in cotton farming has dropped from representing 22.5% of total global use to 14.1% in recent years. It now accounts for 6.2% of global pesticide use as against 11% in 1988.[6] The use of so-called 'crop-protection chemicals' reached its highest level in the 1990s.[7] There are many factors behind the downward trend, including the promotion of Integrated Pest Management (IPM) in some countries. Biotechnology has been reported as a factor for others, including some achieving high yields and relatively low input use without GM.[8]

A recent report by the Social, Economic and Environmental Panel (SEEP) of the International Cotton Advisory Committee[9] reported many of these trends (although it did not cover herbicides, the use of which is reported by some sources to have risen with biotech crops).[10] The report acknowledges gaps and uncertainties in the data. There are significant differences in pesticide use (active ingredient per hectare) in different countries, from 4.9 km ai/ha in Brazil to 0.6 kg ai/ha in Turkey. Turkey's cotton yield is double the world average and its yields have doubled since the 1980s.[11] It has a GM-free policy to take advantage of trends in sustainability and organic cotton. Australia reduced pesticide use and increased yields after introducing GM cotton but also implemented Best Management Practices (BMP).

The importance of regulatory and management systems in reducing input use and improving the sustainability of cotton cannot be overstated. The SEEP report claims it is 'plausible' that biotech cotton has helped the reduction in pesticide use, but acknowledges that many other factors may have played a part, including 'BMPs, weather, policies [and] pest pressures'.[12] Alongside GM cotton, India put a strong focus on IPM, eliminated some pesticides and removed pesticide subsidies. India is also a large producer of organic and fair trade cotton. Productivity has increased substantially.

Integrated pest and crop management programmes and Farmer Field School training (the latter involves farmers learning about the ecology of their own fields and how to better manage production and pests and diseases by working alongside scientists and trainers) suggest how to address many issues of sustainability. The problem? Not enough funding, and these programmes don't have the lobbying capacity of agribusiness to promote their case and seduce policy makers.[13]

Some argue that 'production conditions override genetic factors in determining higher yields', looking at average yields in different countries.[14] Others argue that technology such as GM is the key, but clearly GM is not always a factor. Poor systems in seed supply and land use, loss of soil fertility and misuse of inputs will negatively affect productivity; therefore sustainability and productivity improvements demand a range of approaches. There is no magic bullet.[15] Investment is needed in many areas.

The case against GM cotton is not proven. Neither is the case for it. What is important is to remember that genetic engineering is just science, and that science is intrinsically neither harmful nor beneficial. Harm or benefit is determined by how scientific knowledge is used. The point is not to be afraid of science. Be afraid of (and remain vigilant for) its misapplication for private gain rather than public good. These are not the same thing. Concerned citizens should know as much science as possible, call regulators and private enterprise to account with facts, and demand strong codes of ethics to govern the application of scientific advances. At the same time, concerned citizens should also call to account those who claim to represent them, such as campaigning NGOs.

Genetically Modified Organism (GMO)[16]

The term 'genetically modified organism' (GMO) is legally defined by the EU. An organism is 'genetically modified' if its genetic material has been changed in a way that does not occur under natural conditions through cross-breeding or natural recombination (Article 2 of the EU Directive on the Deliberate Release into the Environment of Genetically Modified Organisms; 2001/18/EG).

Individual cases can be very controversial if the organism in question has been genetically modified in a way that does not occur 'naturally'. The fact that cultivated plants scarcely resemble their wild relatives is an example of dramatic, human-induced genetic modification that would not be defined as 'genetically modified'.

Paradigm-shifting in transparency and traceability

JOHN MOWBRAY *is editor of EcoTextile News, a trade journal for sustainable textiles and related products*

upply-chain transparency and the traceability of products – from fibre through to the shop floor – will be the major focus of clothing brands and retailers in the next five years as they look to map their supply chains and produce real-time metrics to support their sustainability credentials. The word 'greenwash' has now become a verb in the national and international press as a negative way to describe the behaviour of companies who market themselves on the basis of green claims with little evidence of sustainable sourcing, or sometimes even a complete lack of certification. In time, as 'greenwash' becomes an everyday accepted term at the consumer level, the move by retailers to improve their genuine green credentials and avoid reputational brand damage will only increase. This shift is already taking place. The announcement of a new Sustainable Apparel Coalition of leading brands and retailers in March 2011 may prove a game changer for the global textile and clothing sector. Sustainability has now gone mainstream. The participating brands (including Walmart, J. C. Penney, H&M, Hanes and Timberland) which together make up over 50% of world apparel sales by value, are committed to using a new eco-index to measure the environmental impact of the products they source.

In around five years, expect to see a new generic eco-consumer swing-ticket developed by this coalition that will be found on millions of garments, and perhaps even on interior textiles, across the globe and across many different brands.

These anticipated new developments will have massive ramifications across the global textile supply chain and a large positive impact on the environment. Forward-thinking suppliers are already starting to act; for instance, some leading polyester yarn producers are already making commitments to turn their entire product ranges into recycled offerings.

Other early signs of this quantum shift are moves to produce a more sustainable cotton sector in which using fewer pesticides and less water and ensuring greater profitability for farmers in the developed world become common practices. The ultimate aim is to produce 1 million tonnes of this 'Better Cotton' so that it can be traded as a commodity to improve the forward planning of buyers and farmers alike.

In another unexpected move, polluting textile dyehouses in India have been closed by local authorities after they breached new environmental legislation. This has disrupted supply chains and these types of sourcing problems – caused by tougher environmental legislation that aims to protect water supplies – will become more common. Western buyers may then start to look closer to home for some of their more urgent requirements.

Bluesign standard

PETER WAEBER *is CEO of Bluesign Technologies, a Swiss company that offers bluesign® standard, an independent textile certification programme*

Can fashion ever be sustainable? Yes, of course it can, but it is easier for small-scale production runs in a cottage industry. The bigger question is whether mainstream fashion can ever be sustainable. With a growing global population, high-volume production runs for mainstream fashion seem likely only to increase. While the answer to this final question also depends on the definition of the word 'sustainable', given that every product we make has some ethical and environmental impact, I do believe that sustainable fashion in this sense is currently impossible to achieve completely, unless some unseen technological advance comes along or perhaps an environmental catastrophe occurs that rapidly changes the purchasing mindset of today's consumers.

For now it is all about Reducing our Impact on The Environment. The RITE group is a British nonprofit organization that was set up in 2007 to advance this goal. It is organizations such as this one – working closely with retailers and legislators – that will eventually change the industry's way of thinking. It's down to the retailers and brands to create the market pull for sustainable products. The development of a new eco-label for consumers is a good start but it remains to be seen if this really is enough.

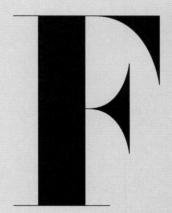

Full transparency is the goal of many stakeholders in the supply chain attempting to optimize the process of reducing their ecological footprint (not only their carbon footprint) and the amount of toxic chemicals released into the environment. Therefore we need instruments to manage these complex supply chains – easily implemented instruments that are customized for the textiles and related industries. Brands and retailers have to show responsibility: they are going to play an increasingly dominant role in their supply chains with regard to achieving environmental standards and honest and transparent communication with the consumer about their efforts. An important instrument is the rating of products (based on Life Cycle Analysis) to provide consumers with information about environmental footprints that is consistent between all brands and retailers, avoiding confusion due to the presence of different rating scales. Third parties need to be involved to ensure that the information available to consumers is accurate.

Organic textiles: standards and certification

LEE HOLDSTOCK *is trade relations manager for certification for the Soil Association, a British charity that campaigns for sustainable food, farming and land use.*

Organic textiles have been around for a long time in one form or another, but textiles that meet the current established definitions of 'organic' are very recent. Looking at the timeline, Soil Association standards for organic food in the UK have been around since 1973, but organic textile standards arrived only as recently as 2002. Standards are vitally important in agreeing a common definition for 'organic'; without them it is hard to define what really is organic, what has been considered so in the past, and what has been the size of the market for such products.

'Organic' denotes a primarily ecological method of agriculture. Consumer understanding of organic textiles is bound to be less sophisticated than that of organic food because the relationship of farming to textile products is less immediate. How many consumers realize that cotton garments start their journey on a farm?

The whole organic market has changed in recent years. Consumers are increasingly motivated by factors other than their own immediate health, with factors such as carbon emissions and animal welfare becoming increasingly important considerations. This shift has aided the popularity of organic non-food products, for which benefits to personal health have never really figured in the customer's purchasing decision. However, there are other obstacles to widespread consumer preference for organic textiles. Consumers have a number of considerations that out-rank 'organicness': cost is common to both food and clothing sectors, but with clothing, factors such as look, feel and fit take priority over ethics.

Organic Standards

The Soil Association has always developed its own private standards, ensuring they embody the core principles of the organic movement globally, while also considering the expectations of British consumers. Its standards for food and farming pre-date the present EU regulations by eighteen years and still exceed them in many areas. The Soil Association symbol and certification has become the most recognized and trusted organic mark in the UK.

When it came to setting textile manufacturing standards, we realized that we were dealing with a sector that was totally unregulated, without common baseline standards and covering an extensive geographic area. This is the reason we quickly became involved in an initiative to create a single common international standard: GOTS (Global Organic Textile Standard). It covers all of the essentials that we think consumers would demand of an organic textile product. As a result we now have a single global standard, with the option to apply either a new 'lower-recognition' global symbol, or the appropriate established national certifier symbol (such as ours) to the product. We hope that British brands, retailers and manufacturers will continue to use our symbol, making things simple for the consumer, who already has some familiarity with our mark.

When the Soil Association symbol is on a textile product, it means that the production of the fibre on the farm, its processing into textiles and the manufacturing of the final product have met organic standards, and have been checked at every step of the processing supply chain for social and environmental responsibility. Soil Association Certification inspects its licensees upon application and then on an annual basis. GOTS includes the fibres and accessories permitted (some synthetics are allowed), labelling requirements, social criteria (to International Labour Organization [ILO] Basics), traceability and separation, chemicals allowed in processing, waste-water treatment, environmental policy and quality requirements. With more than 3,000 businesses registered globally, GOTS is fast becoming the only viable global organic textile mark, perhaps with the exception of the Organic Exchange blend mark, which indicates only that the textile incorporates a certain percentage of organic fibre, rather than the final product itself being organic. Although GOTS currently includes basic social criteria, I would like to see it develop more detailed ethical criteria that better encourage cooperative relationships in supply chains, rather than relying on an external audit approach.

All certifiers accredited to GOTS will have to be ISO 65 accredited (ISO is the International Organization for Standardization, which specifies accepted norms for bodies operating product-certification systems), so they will be well versed in operating certification systems that revolve around strong material and product traceability. Provided all links in the supply chain are fully GOTS-audited, I don't see any significant issues with organic integrity being compromised. Indeed GOTS has already developed an operating manual for certifiers aiming to harmonize operational approaches where different interpretations of ISO 65 requirements exist. Social auditing will be more challenging, which is why GOTS wants to develop more detailed criteria in this area.

Organic has a lot to offer, environmentally and socially, and we need to ensure that this is communicated. Education of consumers is of key importance here.

Regulation of Organic Textiles in the EU and the US

If there were regulation relating to use of the term 'organic' for textile goods, this would clearly create a market advantage for truly organic textiles. We support the idea of regulation in principle to recognize those who make the effort to go beyond greenwashing (a form of spin in which green marketing is used deceptively). The current EU directorate has shown little interest in extending existing organic standards to include organic non-food goods/sectors such as textiles. The European Committee for Standardization has started the process of attempting to define and harmonize green and organic terms used by the textile industry across the EU. Currently the national standards organizations of individual member states (for example the Business Standards Institute in the UK) are being consulted. Even if no actual

regulation appears, the processes may result in either EU policy, voluntary ISOs or guides that signpost existing EU regulations.

Regulation across a wide community such as the EU brings its own problems. Often the lowest common dominator is the result. The Soil Association has continued to set higher standards than EU organic food and farming regulations and is unimpressed by the development of a mandatory EU organic food logo, which means nothing to British consumers and is seen as a threat to our symbol. Federalization of organic standards in the US is potentially even worse for consumer empowerment and ongoing development of independent standards. The US Department of Agriculture's National Organic Program (NOP) standard not only has a mandatory mark or seal but also insists that no individual state certifier sets any higher or additional standards. As far as textiles are concerned, NOP currently only insists that the fibre is grown in line with USDA/NOP requirements, with the Organic Trade Association having abandoned the drafting of American organic-fibre standards to embrace GOTS. GOTS may well be global, but the rest of the world outside the EU and the US will still have to ensure that their fibres are grown to organic farming standards equivalent to those operated by the EU or USDA.

Outlook for the Future

Standards development will always come in bursts, and we are probably in a lull following the recent publication of GOTS Version 3. The Soil Association is continuing to see a steady stream of requests for certification of textiles, up around 2% in 2011, despite recessionary forces, but growth has undoubtedly slowed as the market starts to mature. Now that much of the development work in this area is complete, we are finally entering a period of stability in the regulatory arena. Future challenges will relate to implementation, maintaining integrity and communicating clearly to consumers what 'organic' offers.

The Asia Floor Wage campaign

THE ASIA FLOOR WAGE (AFW) *is a proposal for a standard international minimum living wage for garment workers, promoted by the Clean Clothes Campaign.*

The Asia Floor Wage (AFW) is a demand for a minimum living wage that can be standardized and compared between countries.

The AFW Alliance brings together a wide range of labour organizations from India, Bangladesh, Cambodia, Indonesia, Sri Lanka, Thailand, China and Hong Kong. Also involved are trade unions, labour NGOs, anti-sweatshop movements, solidarity groups, and scholars from Europe and the US. Together we have come up with a way of establishing a floor on the 'race to the bottom' and preventing wage competition between Asian garment-exporting countries: the Asia Floor Wage Campaign. By uniting together and adopting a common Asia-wide bargaining strategy, garment workers and their representatives and supporters in Asia and elsewhere can campaign for improved pay and conditions without the fear of causing job losses.

The Asia Floor Wage is based on the income required for a single earner to support a family of four (two adults and two children) by working a legal maximum working week (but no longer than 48 hours), excluding any payment for overtime or other bonuses/allowances. It accounts for the cost of a fair amount of food per day, plus other essential living costs such as healthcare, housing, clothing, childcare, transportation, fuel and education. By expressing it in a single convertible sum – what we are calling 'purchasing power parity in US$' or 'PPP$' for short – we can achieve a wage demand that is applicable in each country and across borders.

The AFW Alliance has agreed to a figure of 3,000 calories for the level of basic food required on a daily basis. Adopting such a nutritional threshold means that local groups can then define how their own basket is filled. It is a variable food basket that takes into account differences in local food habits.

In 2011 the target AFW was calculated at 540PPP$ per week. In local currency this would translate into monthly wages of:
- Bangladesh 12,248 BDT
- Cambodia 692,903 Riel
- India 7,967 Rupees
- Indonesia 2,132,202 Rupiah
- Sri Lanka 19,077 Rupees
- China 1,842 RMB

A Few Statistics Relating to the International Garment Industry

- According to the 2006 statistics of the UNIDO (UN Industrial Development Organization) Industrial Statistics Database (INDSTAT) around 26.5 million people work within the clothing and textiles sector worldwide…These figures are only people employed in manufacturing – not retail or other supporting sectors.[1]

- Around 70% of clothing workers worldwide are women. In Bangladesh, Haiti and Cambodia clothing and textiles account for more than 80% of total exports.[2]

- The economy of Bangladesh relies on the garment industry – having grown from US $6.4 billion in 2005 to US $12.5 billion in 2010 – and accounts for 80% of the country's exports. It is estimated that 3.5 million Bangladeshis work in the sector, the majority of whom are women. Bangladesh is one of the few countries that has gained market share in Europe during the recent global recession.[3]

- Wages are rising quickly in many countries typically associated with low cost labour. For example, in Bangladesh in 2010, worker unrest and trade union pressure led to an 80% rise in the minimum monthly wage for the lowest grade worker, from US $24 in 2006 to US $43.[4]

- In 2005 more than 12 million people were employed in China and nearly 1.2 million in Brazil in clothing, textile and footwear sectors.[5]

- The global number of child labourers declined from 222 million to 215 million, or 3 per cent, over the period 2004 to 2008, but there are still 115 million children in hazardous work. Only one in five is in paid employment. The overwhelming majority are unpaid family workers.[6]

What is Fair Trade?

THE WORLD FAIR TRADE ORGANIZATION (WFTO) *has formulated ten principles that organizations must follow to be considered Fair Trade. (This is a separate initiative from the Fairtrade Foundation certification that is applied to commodities such as coffee.)*

rinciple One: Creating Opportunities for Economically Disadvantaged Producers
Poverty reduction through trade forms a key part of the organization's aims. The organization supports marginalized small producers, whether these are independent family businesses, or grouped in associations or cooperatives. It seeks to enable them to move from income insecurity and poverty to economic self-sufficiency and ownership.

Principle Two: Transparency and Accountability
The organization is transparent in its management and commercial relations. It is accountable to all its stakeholders and respects the sensitivity and confidentiality of commercial information supplied. The organization finds appropriate, participatory ways to involve employees, members and producers in its decision-making processes. The communication channels are good and open at all levels of the supply chain.

Principle Three: Fair Trading Practices
The organization trades with concern for the social, economic and environmental well-being of marginalized small producers and does not maximize profit at their expense. Suppliers respect contracts and deliver products on time and to the desired quality and specifications. Fair Trade buyers, recognizing the financial disadvantages producers and suppliers face, ensure orders are paid on receipt of documents. An interest free pre-payment of at least 50% is made if requested.

Principle Four: Payment of a Fair Price
A fair price is one that has been mutually agreed by all through dialogue and participation, which provides fair pay to the producers and can also be sustained by the market.

Principle Five: Ensuring No Child Labour and Forced Labour
The organization adheres to the UN Convention on the Rights of the Child, and national/local law on the employment of children. The organization ensures that there is no forced labor in its workforce and / or members or homeworkers.

Principle Six: Commitment to Non-Discrimination, Gender Equity and Freedom of Association
The organization does not discriminate in hiring, remuneration, access to training, promotion, termination or retirement based on race, caste, national origin, religion, disability, gender, sexual orientation, union membership, political affiliation, HIV/AIDS status or age.

International Labour Organization Declaration[1]

The International Labour Organization (ILO), an agency of the United Nations, is the international organization responsible for drawing up and overseeing international labour standards. It brings together representatives of governments, employers and workers to shape its policies and programmes. Adopted in 1998, the ILO Declaration on Fundamental Principles and Rights at Work is an expression of commitment by governments, employers and workers' organizations to uphold basic human values. It covers four fundamental principles and rights at work:

1. Freedom of association and the effective recognition of the right to collective bargaining
2. Elimination of all forms of forced or compulsory labour
3. Effective abolition of child labour
4. Elimination of discrimination in respect of employment and occupation

Principle Seven: Ensuring Good Working Conditions
The organization provides a safe and healthy working environment for employees and/or members. It complies, at a minimum, with national and local laws and ILO conventions on health and safety. Working hours and conditions for employees and/or members (and any homeworkers) comply with conditions established by national and local laws and ILO conventions.

Principle Eight: Providing Capacity Building
The organization seeks to increase positive developmental impacts for small, marginalized producers through Fair Trade. The organization develops the skills and capabilities of its own employees or members.

Principle Nine: Promoting Fair Trade
The organization raises awareness of the aim of Fair Trade and of the need for greater justice in world trade through Fair Trade. It advocates for the objectives and activities of Fair Trade according to the scope of the organization.

Principle Ten: Respect for the Environment
Organizations that produce Fair Trade products maximize the use of raw materials from sustainably managed sources in their ranges, buying locally when possible. They use production technologies that seek to reduce energy consumption and where possible use renewable energy technologies that minimize greenhouse gas emissions. They seek to minimize the impact of their waste stream on the environment.

Speed and distance

Ecology and waste

Sustainability and pleasure

Fashion business and manufacturing

Fashion cycles and clothing life cycles

New luxury

Fashion and environment

Pages 204–5: 'Adam and Eve' with clothing waste at the TRAID warehouse, London. Models' clothes by Jula Reindell; styling and photography by Gavin Fernandes.

Clothing waste and recycling

It is well recognized that globalization in the fashion industry has accelerated in recent decades due to major changes in international trade regulations and the relaxation of tariffs and quotas. As seen in Chapter 3, garment manufacturing for export is fostered in many developing countries as a key means of earning income. Clothes are now well-travelled commodities with very brief lives. The accelerated pace and varying rhythms of consumption and manufacturing are considered in essays by Kate Fletcher and Mathilda Tham on fashion life cycles, and in expert commentaries by Michael Flanagan and David Shah. Counter to this trend is the emerging concept of 'slow fashion', exemplified by the minä perhonen label, among others. In a similar vein, the feature 'Enduring Fashion' asks people to tell the stories of clothes that they have kept for a long time. The emergence of the concept of 'sustainable luxury' for the high-end fashion industry is outlined in Phyllida Jay's essay, with examples from brands Zegna and Noir.

The combination of speeded-up fashion cycles, increased rates of consumption and falling prices of clothing relative to income has created inevitable growth in fashion waste, as perceived value has declined and fashion has become a disposable commodity. The promotion of the new (and the rejection of the recently 'old') that is built into the fashion system is endemically wasteful. Expert commentaries discuss the issues that arise from the shorter fashion life cycle, such as reductions in quality and value. Several case studies highlight the innovative work being done to stem this tide and to re-examine the industry's relationship with waste at both pre-consumer and post-consumer stages, including in the often overlooked area of corporate clothing. There are clear signs that turning waste into new goods (known as 'upcycling') is set to move from niche areas to mainstream activity. Only when this takes place will the industry be able to regulate its waste and return useful materials to the system (or to external systems), saving virgin resources in a 'cradle to cradle' model.[1]

The fashion and textile industry currently consumes a vast amount of water and energy, from fibre growing and synthesis to textile dyeing and garment distribution. Reductions have to be achieved at macro level in order to have a significant impact on carbon reduction and energy consumption. Phil Patterson and Simon Bennett discuss these issues from a technical perspective, while artists such as Lucy and Jorge Orta and Gavin Fernandes find creative ways to reach hearts and minds in raising awareness of the ecological impact of current practices.

Sustainability, pleasure and fashion politics

KATE FLETCHER *is director of the design for sustainability consultancy Slow Fashion and a reader in sustainable fashion at London College of Fashion.*

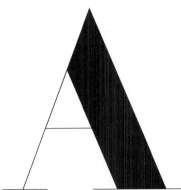few years ago I found out just how important fashion was to me. I had been working in fashion, textiles and sustainability for well over a decade. In those years I spent more time than most doing design projects, thinking and writing about the impact of fashion consumption on sustainability. But during that time my personal relationship with fashion consumption was probably pretty much as it had been since my teens: a strange blend of thoughtfulness, individualism and spontaneity. I bought clothes, in the main choosing carefully and mixing second-hand pieces with new items. I used my knowledge of materials and processes, brands and designers, to reduce the impact of this consumption where possible. I made and restyled pieces, embellishing them with my grandmother's hand-me-downs and treasures from my sewing basket. I tried to buy garments to which I felt a strong connection, items that were redolent with meaning, hoping that they would then take on an emotional durability that would ensure I wore them for many years. I bought other things too, impulsive fashion 'hits' that sometimes sat barely worn at the bottom of my wardrobe. Yet during this time, and notwithstanding the thoughtfulness with which I approached at least some of my purchases, I didn't fully appreciate my motivations or understand that my relationship with fashion was steeped in the buying of 'stuff'. For it's hard to see what you are – and I have been a consumer of fashion all my life.

Then came a change. I gave up my job, moved away from London and had a baby. Money was tight, and for a whole host of reasons I completely stopped buying clothes. My body rapidly changed shape and many of my clothes no longer fitted me quite as they had done before. My change of address meant that the people I met on a daily basis were hugely different from my London crowd. Fairly soon I began to detect that my relationship with fashion was on the move.

This was undoubtedly influenced, at least in part, by the relationship between fashion and identity. Clothes were a medium through which I was renegotiating my sense of belonging, where I fitted in and where I did not, the aspirations I had and those that were denied me. They were also a theatre in which the complex associations between fashion and consumption – in my case, the relationship between fashion and non-consumption – played out.

Almost forty years ago Georg Simmel described two social tendencies necessary in order for fashion to be established: the need for union and the need for isolation.[1] In my new situation the former – i.e. using fashion as part of building a collective experience – found much less expression than it had before. I began to use fashion to explore my new situation by using it as a tool for self-knowledge and self-determinism. What I chose to wear began to be an extension of my headspace, my values, and a reflection of my circumstances. My love of tending my vegetable patch left traces in most of what I chose to wear. When I did make it back to fashion capitals, I realized that my fashion expressions seemed dislocated. They felt clumsy, homespun and self-referential. The things I wore grated against the latest fashion backdrop as measured by glossy magazine spreads and window displays. I was no longer reading or performing the latest version of subtle media-driven, high-street fashion language. For when you stop consuming, the effect is to step out of one very particular fashion world, one in which we look (in vain) for a sense of community in clothing stores.

My journey into the world of forced simplicity and necessary non-purchasing of clothes brought into sharp focus two different though connected realizations. The first was about just how entwined fashion and consumption have become. So much so that when you're not buying clothes (for whatever reason), you can rapidly become distanced from the most ubiquitous and easy-to-access fashion experience that exists today: consumerist fashion. Indeed, within mass consumer culture, fashion that operates outside the shopping and magazine format is a largely alien concept. Yet people who engage with fashion don't do so solely in the guise of consumer. Fashion is not a phenomenon exclusive to the consumerist business model. Stitch 'n Bitch groups, for example, blend fashion creativity and craftwork with socializing, and user-generated websites such as citizenfashion.theqmode.com act as platforms for sharing fashion ideas and collaborating to develop new styles. In these instances fashion is not solely about consuming and having, but also about what it can enable us to be and become. We are moved away from fashion as a goal in itself to fashion as a means to an end for a more engaged life.

The second realization was tied to the potential of fashion as a tool to promote more connected, engaged lives (that is, to improve individual and collective wellbeing rather than just foster empty consumerism). My downshifting experience laid bare just how important fashion is to human culture and therefore sustainability: to our sense of connectedness and creative expression, to feeling in tune with the moment, to forming identity, to showing respect, to adorning ourselves and being part of the aesthetic of everyday life. I also realized how few fashion and sustainability discussions ever seem to recognize the primacy of this relationship. The popular view tends to dismiss fashion outright on environmental and ethical grounds because of its (serious) connections with short-termism, material excess and labour abuses, without seeing that the negative repercussions of this categorical stance would hit us hard in other parts of our culture. Yet fashion and sustainability are not two separate and antagonistic concepts and experiences; they are not opposite ends of a continuum. And it is not the case that when you have a bit more fashion, you have to have a bit less sustainability (or vice versa). The relationship between the two is dynamic and multi-dimensional. For just as fashion without sustainability is ignorant, sustainability without fashion is sad. Each has the potential to bring something vital and different to the other.

Perhaps above all, my two years of (in) voluntary simplicity reiterated the complexity of fashion's relationship with sustainability. It underscored the impossibility, to my mind, that an optimistic, desirable and beautiful future based on sustainability would not include fashion in some form. For without fashion opportunities for human flourishing and pleasure are diminished. Yet this is not a carte blanche for business as usual, chiefly because business as usual is an ongoing cause of unsustainability in the fashion sector. On the contrary, it is a challenge to envision a new type of fashion that actively and unremittingly fuses the best bits with an enlightened and re-imagined system of production and consumption. Or, to put it another way, to mingle sustainability and pleasure

When you stop consuming, the effect is to step out of one very particular fashion world, one in which we look (in vain) for a sense of community in clothing stores.

with fashion and politics. Until now pleasure through fashion has barely registered on the sustainability radar. By the same token, it can be argued that the development of a thoughtful, coherent politics of sustainability in fashion is long overdue.

Understanding the Problems of Business as Usual

Acknowledging the sustainability challenges of the current fashion business set-up and teasing apart their interconnections is essential for change. It is also an eye-wateringly complex process. For perhaps the most intractable issue within fashion and sustainability is not, as is sometimes claimed, the apparently contradictory nature of these two entities, but rather the wastefulness, irresponsibility, excess and exploitation endemic to most of the business models and production and consumption systems that have grown up around clothing, expression and identity. It is the prevailing business model of high-volume fashion production and consumption that is in most direct conflict with sustainability goals. For example, in the UK we are now buying one third more clothes than we did in 2001 (on average thirty-four items), and nearly 40 kg of clothing and textile waste are discarded per person per year.[2] In monetary terms £38 billion is spent on clothes annually, with £1 in every £4 being spent on bargain fashion. The sustainability implications of high-volume consumption include its effects on workers, resources, waste levels, air and water quality, and consumers' physical and psychological health; yet it is still a taboo subject for global brands and high-street retailers who depend on a high throughput of product for financial success. Indeed, high product throughput has come to characterize everyday living in the West, where shopping and spending are for many the leisure activities of choice. It should not be forgotten that fashion cycles and changing trends fan the flames of the consumerist lifestyle; we meet our desire for pleasure, new experiences, status and identity formation through the buying of things – many of them clothes.

There are no quick fixes in dealing with our addiction to consumption or the business models associated with consumerism. According to the eminent industrial ecologist John Ehrenfeld, 'Achieving positive results [with regards to consumption] requires drastic action. We need to shift from our reductionist, problem-solving mode to one that is driven by a vision of a sustainable future we all share. We need to reflect carefully on our current state of affairs and replace ineffective ways of thinking and acting.'[3] For sustainability advocates like Ehrenfeld, it is only when we grapple with issues at a fundamental level and rethink both *what* we do and *how* we do it that sustainability becomes a possibility. If we don't, we risk dealing in a piecemeal fashion with the symptoms of environmental and social crises while never tackling the underlying causes.

Bringing about change towards sustainability in the fashion sector requires root-and-branch reform. It necessitates both a new vision for what the sector can be and detail about how to make it happen. Yet we have precious little experience of working in such

We have to ask who benefits from the current set up, and who it actually should serve.

a way. This is for a host of reasons, including the sector's highly fragmented, secretive and globalized structure and the dominance of binary (either/or) and linear (not cyclical) ways of thinking that still monopolize our educational and business models. For the educationalist Stephen Sterling it is these non-holistic ways of thinking that blind us to the connective and dynamic reality of sustainability challenges. Our fundamental problem, he states, 'is one of inadequate perception'.[4]

Fashion Politics and Sustainability Pleasure
If we take up the joint challenges of Sterling and Ehrenfeld and attempt to change perceptions, and in so doing begin the process of reflecting on and replacing ineffective ways of thinking and acting in fashion, what begins to emerge? For me what surfaces is surprisingly closely informed by my experience of living and enjoying fashion without buying clothes. For, as Clive Hamilton has stated, '[U]ntil we individually and collectively stop to examine ourselves we do not know what is in our interests.'[5] It would seem that our interests are best served by a fusion of the pleasure fashion can promise with an active and effective political

restructuring of the entire sector in line with sustainability ideas. In effect this is a new model of individual, collective and societal action in which fashion production and consumption, properly valued, offer a route to becoming more fulfilled, engaged and connected with each other and with the world around us.

Perhaps the most obvious place to start fleshing out a coherent sustainability politics in fashion is to describe systems of production, consumption and aesthetics that are explicitly *based on sustainability values*. That is, to design a fashion system that is lively, creative, connected, democratic, participatory and inclusive. Such a system would contrast sharply with much of the fashion on offer today, which epitomizes value-free expression and equips us to appear in a world that has little or nothing to do with the earth, the health of its soil or its people. Such a world is abstract and remote, has a tenuous relationship with the reality of how fashion is made, used and discarded, and can be readily and pejoratively labelled as a 'world of ideas'.[6] Indeed in a world of absent connections between fashion and the social and ecological systems that support it, almost anything is possible – there are few limits. Yet our planet plainly does have limits. Many ecological systems are closed systems of finite capacity, and fashion is as subject to them as anything else. Thus, establishing boundaries for the fashion sector and anchoring practice within them are essential first steps for sustainability. Also essential is the notion that we must begin a dialogue about the rules and goals of the industry. We have to ask who benefits from the current set-up, and who it actually should serve.

The parallel part of this process of change, as hinted earlier in this piece, is to infuse the idea of sustainability with a sense of delight and pleasure as experienced through fashion. This may seem frivolous, but pleasure is far from incompatible with politics. It is a key part of wellbeing, of human culture, and is a great attractor, for people are drawn to that which is desirable. Sustainable pleasure will flow from strong, coherent fashion politics. It will emerge from different business models that disassociate profit from material throughput. It will be glimpsed in robust critiques of globalization. It will necessitate drastic reductions in consumption. It will reconceive the role of individuals as citizens and not just as consumers in the fashion process. It will add up to profound changes in power relations in the sector and revolutions in attitudes towards resource use, modes of production and ways of making. For sustainability gives us both the incentive and the opportunity to make the fashion sector meet our true needs.

TRAIDremade

TRAID (Textile Recycling for Aid and International Development) is an organization in London that collects unwanted clothing for reuse, recycling and upcycling.
By Sandy Black

Via a network of textile-recycling banks around the UK, TRAID collects unwanted clothing and diverts it from the waste stream into reuse and recycling. Of the 3,000 tonnes of clothing and shoes collected each year, 94% is repurposed. Although it is a relatively young charity, TRAID reports donations of £2.2 million, funding development projects throughout the world with partners such as Oxfam, War on Want, Africa Now, Solar Aid and the Fairtrade Foundation to tackle low wages, child labour, poor sanitation, health and education and emergency relief. The organization's website proclaims 'For every unwanted garment that TRAID collects for reuse and resale in the UK, there is a positive change in people's lives, somewhere in the world.'

Through its nine outlets in the London area and its education programme, TRAID has worked to change perceptions of charity shops among younger customers. A more fashionable second-hand retail experience was developed through the TRAIDremade initiative, established in 2003. At a workshop in Brighton, young designers are given free rein to customize, cut up, redesign and embellish handpicked items into fashionable outfits, appealing to on-trend consumers who are looking for something highly individual. TRAIDremade's 'Golightly' range of recycled textile footwear, made in the UK using selected textiles, donated zips and recycled leather from single boots, was introduced in 2010 to create a desirable new product from recycled materials.

Right: Lasting and soling of TRAIDremade 'Golightly' pumps is carried out in a factory in Norwich after stitching of the upper is done in London.

'For every unwanted garment that TRAID collects for reuse and resale in the UK, there is a positive change in people's lives, somewhere in the world.'

All images this page: One-off pieces designed and made from discarded clothes for TRAIDremade.

Can the clothing industry ever be sustainable?

MICHAEL FLANAGAN *is chief executive officer of Clothesource, which provides buyers and sellers with advice and information on sourcing and production.*

Is making a garment in a poor country, in a naturally ventilated factory manned by workers who walk, cycle or get a bus to work, then trundling it round the world, more or less sustainable than making it in a Western factory that's heated in winter, air-conditioned in summer and host to workers who drive to work? The honest truth is that we don't know yet. And there's no reason to imagine that sourcing and design strategies that make sense in terms of today's understanding will still make sense once we've learned more.

The world apparel market is dominated by clothes bought in rich countries but imported from poorer ones. Of the world's spending on clothes, 86% occurs in countries whose population accounts for 15% of the people on the planet. Ninety per cent of the clothes this wealthier group wear are made in poorer countries, and 80% of the world's spending on importing clothes comes from the EU, the US and Japan – a dominance that has never been seriously challenged. In 2009 a twenty-year emerging-market garment-making boom went into reverse. World garment imports had begun slowing in the second quarter of 2008; the fall reached its worst point a year later, when imports were about 9% below what they had been in 2007. By the end of 2009 they were back at about the 2007 level.

The market for clothes, measured in garments imported into rich countries from poorer ones, grew almost sixfold between 1990 and 2008, but fell by 4.3% in 2009 (the first decline since 2001). At the same time offshore relocation petered out because the sixfold growth in clothing imports over twenty years was mainly fuelled by increasingly liberalized world trade. However, at the end of 2008 restraints on trade finally dropped as the remaining American quotas on Chinese clothing imports were finally removed.

The unsustainability of the present-day clothing industry has little to do with the caprices of fashion. On average a European or American buys about 90 m² of clothing per year. The average Chinese citizen buys 8 m² – but China's clothing market has been growing at 20% a year for the past three years. The average Bangladeshi buys less than a single square metre. When – not if – the world's twenty most populous poor countries buy as many clothes each year as the rich world's most frugal country (New Zealand) does today, the world will need three times as much fabric as it does now, and it will use three times as much energy to make and transport those clothes. This will be the case even if today's rich-country markets remain static. The world just hasn't got the land or minerals to provide three times as much fabric.

Westerners don't buy so many clothes just because they are fashion addicts: they buy them because the richer people get, the more they want better fit (the longer you live, the more often your body changes), better protection, greater comfort, better performance enhancement (there really are swimsuits that help you go faster) and a hundred other real or perceived improvements that have nothing to do with pure fashion.

So the world needs to slay some false gods:

GM crops: Europe must scrap its superstitious and unfounded ban on genetically modified (GM) crops. GM technology can help us develop cotton that needs less water, less land and less use of pesticides. The sustainability movement must stop trying to recreate medieval subsistence farming and encourage practices that help higher yields. It must discourage practices such as organic cotton that encourage deforestation and water depletion.

Energy, water and carbon labelling and transportation:
Preferably voluntarily, but by law if necessary, clothes should carry labels stating how much energy and water have gone into their manufacture and distribution, how much carbon has been emitted, and how much energy and water will be used under different buyer habits of washing, drying and ironing. Doing so will reveal a truth that's profoundly uncomfortable. Freight the cotton for a typical T-shirt by land and sea from the USA to China, spin the cotton, knit it and make the T-shirt in China, then sea-freight it to Europe. The end consumer uses ten times as much energy washing, drying and ironing the shirt than gets used in the whole of its round-the-world transportation – as long as the intercontinental travel is all by sea. The garment's production uses up to three times as much energy as the intercontinental freight – but less than a third of what's used in care and maintenance. Moving production closer to where a garment gets made means *more* energy is used. Sea freight uses little energy – but making clothes in rich countries means more energy-intensive automation instead of job-creating manual work, and the few workers in a Western factory use more energy driving to work ever day than the average Bangladeshi uses in a week. The spectacular movement of production offshore from rich countries over the past twenty years has actually *reduced* the amount of energy used to make clothes.

Labelling will also reveal a truth that's uncomfortable for manufacturers and retailers. Air-freighting a kilogramme of clothing releases fifty times more carbon than sea-freighting it. So even though transport rarely affects a garment's sustainability, sending it by air in an emergency trebles the amount of carbon emitted across its entire life. Labelling a garment's carbon emissions is the easiest way to shame this bad practice out of existence. Labelling will also help switch attention to what really matters: developing garments that can be washed and dried with minimal energy and that don't need ironing, and discouraging the use of artificial drying methods.

Cotton subsidies: Governments must stop artificially depressing the price of clothing. America's cotton subsidies keep cotton too cheap. So do Europe's, although they do less damage since they're lower. China's restrictions on raw cotton imports don't help either.

Recycling used clothing: There's a great deal more to recycling clothes than a few choice vintage pieces bought at the local charity shop. Recycled garments from the West make up a substantial proportion of the apparel market in densely populated countries like Nigeria and the Philippines, thus providing the world's poor with decent clothes at near-zero ecological impact. Some governments – such as China – restrict the sale of recycled clothes to preserve local jobs. Sustainability activists need to promote large-scale recycling and campaign against protectionist bans.

For many environmentalists true sustainability means buying as few clothes as possible. Any clothes-buying causes more carbon emissions, so the answer is to buy less. Many retailers would conclude – as would many airlines – that hard-core sustainability customers simply aren't a priority. It's the next level that matters, and not all trends are ones you can make money out of.

> **The sustainability movement must stop trying to recreate medieval subsistence farming and encourage practices that help higher yields. It must discourage practices like organic cotton that encourage deforestation and water depletion.**

From eco-efficiency to the circular economy

NICK MORLEY *is director of sustainable innovation at Oakdene Hollins consultants, UK.*

Concerns for brand integrity and image, in tandem with scientific evidence of the substantial global environmental impact of the clothing industry, have accelerated efforts to improve the fashion industry's profile in social and environmental responsibility. It is an exciting time for those concerned with fashion and sustainability, perhaps not for what we know, but for what we can imagine and question.

Fundamental business models based on high volume and product turnover remain largely unchallenged, except at the margins of the industry. The popularity of approaches such as Cradle-to-Cradle[1] and closed-loop fibre-to-fibre recycling instead of downcycling fibres to industrial products indicates a desire in the industry for a more circular approach to materials. Yet these approaches are currently blocked by both technological barriers and the waste management system that we have inherited.

Designing and making a more sustainable item of clothing can be both conceptually simple and frustratingly complex in practice. Life-cycle thinking tells us that for reasonably durable products that do not consume energy (including clothes), extending the product lifetime will bring substantial environmental benefits. Hence there is a body of evidence that supports the sustainability credentials of vintage and second-hand clothing, be it sold in domestic markets or cascaded into secondary markets such as those in Africa and Eastern Europe. So longer-lasting clothes, and those with multiple lives, are definitely preferable.

Commonly accepted life-cycle thinking also indicates that the bulk of the environmental impacts of clothing occur in the use phase of the garment, which means that that improvements in laundering performance and behaviour matter more than the initial manufacture of the garment, or what happens at the end of its first life (although social concerns are still anchored in the manufacturing phase). However, this is where gaps start to appear in our evidence, and a wider range of options for improved sustainability emerge. The age of garments and their intensity of use and laundering are not really well known: most life-cycle assessments rely on assumptions not grounded in evidence or experience. Nor is the displacement function (avoiding use of virgin resources) of second-hand clothes known. The complex interplay between purchasing, caring and letting go of different sorts of clothes, with their different functions and values (monetary and non-monetary), and the consequent uncertainties around defining a single best product policy, presents opportunities for innovative designers and brands. Strategies have included single-fibre polyester garments designed to be collected and chemically recycled back to fibres, locally manufactured and sourced clothing, and clothing manufactured from recycled materials such as PET bottles. Future opportunities may be created by developing fibre-to-fibre recycling for cellulosics or for fibre mixes.

Despite these developments, it is likely that the conventional practices of design, use and discard, mainly to second users, will predominate for a considerable time to come. In the UK, charity shops and clothing banks form a reasonable collection network, although collection rates could be substantially improved by more kerbside collections from homes, or by in-store initiatives from retailers. Processing is likely to become more sophisticated, with greater attempts to increase value from the lower-quality recycling grades. With grades that are exported to developing countries, particularly those where imported used clothing has been implicated as a contributing factor in the decline of indigenous textile manufacture, we may see greater attempts to add value at a local level. Trade in used clothing has a long history, possibly almost as long as the trade in clothing itself, and the current system needs to be seen in the light of this continuity. The thirst of the middle classes in the developing world for our cast-offs seems likely to continue. Are we content with this business model or is there more that can be done? As we strive to collect higher percentages of discarded clothing, can we create markets and products that use lower-quality materials as feedstock?

Slow and fast fashion

MATHILDA THAM's *work is situated in the space between trend forecasting, sustainability and fashion. She is co-founder of the fashion company Curious Colour.*

This essay explores how strategies for more environmentally friendly fashion might go beyond mere material representation of fibres, processes and fabric and enter the realm of fashion's symbolic capital. It draws on empirical research conducted through two studies. The first, the Lifetimes project (with Kate Fletcher), explored the significance of rhythms in users' interaction with clothing and fashion.[1] In the second study, 'Lucky People Forecast', multiple stakeholder groups from the industry's mass-market sector enquired into the potential synergy between fashion and sustainability through the medium of future scenarios.[2]

Fashion and the Environment

The fashion product's life cycle is complex. Environmental degradation results from all of the life-cycle stages, from conceptualization and design to final disposal (incineration, landfill or, in the preferred case, reuse or recycling). The effects associated with processing and production are well known, particularly the tremendous amounts of water, energy and chemicals that are used. Less well known are the effects that occur during use, when up to 85% of a product's total energy cost might be expended through frequent washing at high temperatures and tumble-drying.[3]

Recently an important discussion has been taking place about the resource flows of fashion, a discussion that has achieved its form and kudos through legislation and policy globally, nationally and within fashion companies. Efforts to reduce the use of water, energy and chemicals have been direct results of this process of dialogue. While previous efforts have mainly targeted the so-called 'end of the pipe' – for example the engineering of better, cleaner waste management – measures are increasingly being put in place at earlier stages, such as eliminating harmful chemical substances from processing stages. Even more proactive efforts include the cultivation of organic cotton, in which the conventional and ample use of pesticides and herbicides is replaced by non-toxic farming methods.[4]

While these developments are highly positive, three key issues present significant barriers to substantial improvements: the complexity of fashion production and the appropriateness of targets; the industry's speed and scale; and the difference between fashion and clothing.

The Complexity of Fashion Production and the Appropriateness of Targets

Defining best practice in terms of environmental performance is a complex matter because of the range of variables in the fashion product's life cycle. The emphasis of environmental impact across the life cycle varies according to product type and the pattern of use and care. Whereas for a viscose blouse the relative impact may be highest in the production of the material, in the case of a standard T-shirt the user phase – including washing and drying – represents the largest environmental cost.[5] Yet to date the industry at mass-market level has targeted its efforts mainly at the production stage and has employed similar environmental strategies for all product types. The implication is that significant stages of impact, such as the user stage, remain largely ignored by industry.[6]

Speed and Scale

A trip to any shopping centre makes fashion's significant material throughput evident. For example, H&M alone handles over half a billion goods per year.[7] With the advent of fast fashion – short lead times, a profit-driven industry and high consumer demand – shops change ranges virtually every week, and many garments spend a limited active time in their wearers' lives.[8] Moderate environmental improvements at product level are therefore easily eaten up by the fashion cycle's astounding scale and speed. They do not constitute the systemic approach needed to reverse the alarming effects of a consumerist and producer-driven society.[9]

Clothing and Fashion

A distinction can be made between clothing and fashion: clothing can be described as answering to material or physiological needs, as in a coat offering warmth, whereas fashion operates primarily at a symbolic level. We purchase fashion not because we want protection against the elements, but to signify that we belong to a group or to manifest individuality. Therefore we do not disregard a fashion item because the garment is threadbare, but because it no longer communicates what we want it to communicate. It has lost its precious link to time and space.[10]

The distinction between clothes and fashion has not featured in predominant environmental strategies. Research into environmental issues associated with clothing production, use and maintenance tends to treat all items in the wardrobe as one unit when establishing a use profile (such as Sushouse 2000, a European research project concerned with developing and evaluating scenarios for transitions to sustainable households). Similarly the environmental strategies of fashion companies target a 'standard' garment, failing to differentiate between various types.[11] In contrast, an individual's wardrobe contains clothes of very different profiles, some washed frequently and worn for a long time, others worn only once and then discarded.[12] The literature also focuses almost exclusively on the material aspects of fashion. For example, durability is still a favoured strategy, although it is well known that many items are only used for a very short while. There is not much point in making a product last for decades if it is to be discarded in a month's time and end up in landfill. Yet another problem associated with durability is the specification of components within a garment. If, as often happens, the lining of a coat is of inferior quality to its outer fabric, the coat will be discarded prematurely. Repair culture is practically non-existent in the West, and the available services are expensive.[13]

Systemic Approaches to Fashion

The complexity of what fashion offers and uses, the speed and scale of the industry, and the difference between fashion and clothes all call for more diverse and systemic approaches to environmental improvement, particularly in the mass-market sector. The environmental challenge that we face demands a deeper questioning of the problem of unsustainability and more creative approaches to creating solutions, especially in the area of design, where '80% of a product, service or system's environmental cost is determined'.[14]

Earlier it was highlighted that hitherto environmental improvement has been targeted mainly at production and processing. This means that the huge potential of efforts involved at the conceptualization and design stages remains largely untapped. Yet this is where the creativity of design can be tremendously useful if harnessed.

The Lifetimes Project

In his book *The Clock of the Long Now*, Stewart Brand describes civilization as consisting of six layers of different paces. The slower layers, such as 'nature' and 'culture', serve to provide stability and continuity, whereas the faster layers, such as 'fashion', contribute with innovation. The layers need to respect each other's rhythms for a healthy 'learning with continuity'. Where one layer, for example fashion, overrides the paces of the others, there is unsustainability.[15]

The Lifetimes project took inspiration from these notions of rhythm in an exploration of how environmental strategies might respond to the complexities of fashion, in particular its speed, scale and intricate user patterns.[16] The project invited a range of users to document their interaction with fashion at both experiential and life-cycle data levels by means of verbal and visual diaries. It engaged with the whole system of fashion, questioning issues such as notions of ownership and hygiene. Perhaps most significantly, it acknowledged the difference between clothes and fashion. This led to an exploration of appropriate lifetimes and a diverse set of strategies for more sustainable fashion. The researchers came to the conclusion that the strategies for achieving more sustainable clothing and fashion must be as diverse as users' engagement with what they wear.

The findings were channelled into four future scenarios, from *slow* to *fast* fashion, for the mass-market sector. One of the slowest scenarios targeted a classic coat, the highest environmental impact of which concerned the production phase. Here the scenario suggested design involvement in the development of easily updatable styles in terms of both look and size; the availability of repair kits for the user thus inclined; and services provided by retailers. It was also recommended that materials of equal durability should be specified – i.e. lining, outer fabrics and other product components should be matched in terms of their expected lifetimes.

In contrast, the fastest scenario targeted a party top. It was found that most users had experienced a late Friday afternoon in the shops frantically looking for something to wear. A top was finally purchased, worn for one or two nights out and then, spent, sat as a bad conscience at the back of the wardrobe. The 'Rent-a-top' scenario proposed a subscription service through which the user, having signed up, would visit a shop, take a top, have fun wearing it for a night or two, return it unwashed and be given a new item. The environmental benefit of this scenario would be that all clothes could be bulk-washed, saving energy, and that there would be less material in circulation to fulfil the same needs. The company would make a profit on fewer garments as it was providing a service rather than a product. And the user could enjoy fast, changeable fashion with a clearer conscience.

Perhaps the most provocative case study addressed plain underwear, the most prominent environmental impact of which occurs at the user stage due to frequent washing and tumble-drying (after each wear). Here life-cycle data led to a scenario in which underwear produced from recycled natural fibres would be discarded after one use and composted.

Taken together, the scenarios from the Lifetimes project suggest a range of strategies that can coexist, responding to a variety of clothing archetypes, consumer needs, behavioural patterns and, most importantly, rhythms of interaction with clothing and fashion.[17]

'Lucky People Forecast'

The notion of varying rhythm in our relations with fashion and clothing, and its significance for environmental strategies for fashion, were further explored in the research for 'Lucky People Forecast'.[18] Here a series of creative workshops on the future of fashion within the context of sustainability generated scenarios around alternative modes of thinking and doing fashion, and being fashionable, in 2026. The participants consisted of thirty-two industry stakeholders: designers, buyers, environmental officers, project managers, educators, students, trade-union representatives, journalists, PR staff and users. The theme of a continuum between slow and fast rhythms featured in several of the scenarios. Interpretations often touched on other dimensions, including how experiences of fashion might be more meaningful and how fashion might be made more transparent to users in terms of its environmental effects. The reality behind the labour involved in making garments and where this labour occurs was also investigated.

Two scenarios are described here to illustrate the range from the more realistic to the fantastic.

In the 'Clear' scenario, transparency is drawn out to an extreme. In a shop, on big screens displaying imagery and maps, users can follow each garment's journey and life cycle. They can see how products have been made and by whom, and how clothes are transported to retailers. Customers have cards on which environmental points are registered. These increase with good environmental choices, such as handing back a garment for reuse

or recycling, and decrease with less sound choices, such as too-frequent washing. Each garment is supplied with a chip that enables customers to see exactly how much energy, for example, is being spent when doing laundry. The purpose of laying bare environmental and social issues in this way is to encourage more mindful user–object relationships. The visceral narratives of garments' origins are perceived to add value and quality to these relationships.

The 'All the Clothes in the World' scenario offers a comment on, and celebrates, extremely fast fashion by drawing inspiration from developments in the music industry. Just as we can download music files online, this scenario proposes that we will soon be downloading fashion. While the iPod or other MP3 player serves as an interface for tunes, the equivalent for fashion files downloaded from a website is a simple grey tracksuit or pyjamas. What users see in the mirror, and what other people see, is the fashion of choice, for example a style Martin Margiela designed in the early 1990s. The files can be locked or open for editing. Users set up daily fashion playlists, thus creating extremely fast fashion with limited material throughput. Fashion can be truly global without the negative impacts of transport, that is to say fashion miles.

This scenario, although fantastic, poses important questions. It addresses the exclusivity of high fashion – which in the scenario is as accessible as mass-market fashion – and the homogeneity of what is presently on offer. Perhaps most interestingly, it comments on fast fashion from a designer perspective. Designers can produce new fashions when they are ready and otherwise live on royalties instead of having to churn out new ideas in a twice-a-year (or more) cycle.

Together the 'Lucky People Forecast' scenarios constitute a rich series of imagery from the digital to the local. What unites them is the conviction that fashion is necessary and has something to contribute to a more sustainable future. The scenarios also show that designers can apply their creativity to the sustainability imperative – at both product and systems levels – and be sensitive to the intricate rhythms characterizing our interaction with fashion and clothing.

Slow and fast are commonly perceived as opposites and associated with positive and negative qualities, depending on whether the context is financial viability or the wellbeing of ecosystems and people. The projects addressed in this text instead invite us to engage with a continuum of rhythms and to seek *appropriateness* in our responses to the environmental challenge by attuning ourselves to users' real and diverse relationship with fashion.

Often perceived as anathema to fashion, sustainability, and in particular environmental improvement, have been constructed as a set of constraints, formalized through regulations in a series of noes and don'ts. Engaging with user–object rhythms, seen as a continuum from slow to fast fashion, offers up the potential for more creative approaches and for acting *with* fashion rather than against it.

Thoughts on sustainable fashion

DAVID SHAH *is an international textile and marketing consultant with a formidable track-record as a designer, publisher and serial entrepreneur.*

The very word 'fashion' conveys synonyms such as 'style', 'trend', 'in vogue' and 'transient'. So to ask if fashion could ever be sustainable seems to be a self-defeating question. Of course, on paper everything is possible. Indeed, some great companies and designers are working hard at making fashion sustainable. Brands such as Patagonia thrive on the principle, while high-street chains such as H&M have developed specific sustainable collections. In spite of all their sterling work, however, fashion can never be sustainable unless the public demands it, and not enough consumers are doing so. This is the fashion world, and whatever the public wants, the stores give. Unfortunately fashion retailing is not about education but about driving a bandwagon.

We have tried sustainability before, in similar circumstances. In 1987, following the Wall Street crash, the Western world became 'green'. The late 1980s and early 1990s were all about Gaia, Mother Earth, even the actual *colour* green. It was the time of Ecover washing powder, *khadi* hand-loomed cloth and vegetable dyes. Why didn't it work? It was seen as politically (left-wing) motivated; there was no single umbrella organization; there were no common standards or general legislation; there was no proper quality control and no experience or ability at the manufacturing level to deal with high-street retail's manufacturing requirements; there were too many middlemen jumping on the bandwagon; the clothes looked like sackcloth and veggie garb, and, worst of all, they were more expensive. Things are different today: the clothes

look much more fashionable, there are tighter rules on eco-labelling, and stores are working hard to contain prices. So why are more people not looking at sustainable clothing?

There is still too much confusion and not enough education about eco-production. Too many consumers, for example, think 'organic' and 'sustainable' are the same thing. Too many consumers also think that to be sustainable you can only use natural fibres (a notion strongly promoted by the natural-fibre producers themselves). This is simply not true. Try to explain the properties of non-compostable but definitely recyclable polyester, and the average person starts thinking about static and their father's or grandfather's Bri-Nylon shirt! It's ridiculous when you realize that there has been more innovation in synthetic and man-made fibres in the last twenty years than in the whole history of textiles!

Greenwashing

Then there are dubious labelling practices and greenwashing, the process of using spin to promote green practices. Too many stores offer 'organic' T-shirts that actually only contain 5% organic cotton and 95% normal cotton (there still is no more organic cotton grown in the world than would fill a couple of supertankers). Everybody from automobile companies to paint shops is green now – just show a few leaves and put some pretty handwriting on your recycled paper label. Consumers are suffering from eco-marketing fatigue. They do not believe it any more: for them it just means that a company is producing products that are not quite as environmentally damaging as before. The number of complaints to the Advertising

Standards Authority questioning claims made by companies has quadrupled. If companies want to make a convincing claim, they need to pick on a specific message of sustainability and be able to back it up with statistics and independently audited facts.

Cheap Fashion

After the financial meltdown in October 2008, I felt the world was going to adopt a genuine 'less is more' lifestyle. The consumer would buy less but better, with greater awareness of free trade and sustainability. Quite the opposite! The vast majority of consumers continued to buy as much as before. As the middle market collapsed and the celebrity brands went into temporary eclipse, budget retail boomed. When discounters were offering frocks for under £9, two pairs of jeans for less than £10 and maxi-coats for £29, who could say no? How was this done? For almost ten years Chinese manufacturing has enabled customers to buy at will and fill their wardrobes with cheap throwaway fashion. It has been estimated that trade with China has added $1,000 a year to the pockets of every American household thanks to cheaper goods in the country's stores, cheaper inputs for its businesses and stiffer competition in its markets.

But now things are changing. Not only are workers clamouring for higher salaries and a better standard of living, but the Chinese government has made it clear that it wants to move away from a one-sided economy that relies too much on cheap exports. On top of that, inflation is raging and the long-term effects of China's one-child policy are finally being felt, not only in an unbalanced population (it is estimated that 24 million men will not be able to find wives), but in the fact that the pool of inexpensive labour is drying up. Eventually the yuan will float much higher than current rates against the dollar. Above all, the cost of raw materials is rocketing. Cotton has doubled in price in the past few years, as has silk, and cashmere is not far behind.

Are we about to see the end of China as the primary source of cheap clothing? It very much looks like it. So are consumers going to change their ways? Certainly some companies are passing on the increase in costs; others, however, are clinging steadfastly to their policy of cheap outsourcing, moving production to Vietnam, Cambodia and Bangladesh to keep prices down. To counter the rising cost of fibres, they are turning to blends and cheaper accessories.

When it comes to sustainability, there is one word you cannot escape: 'money'. However great, however honourable the principles, it's the bottom line that matters in the fashion business. Take organic food. Everybody was busy buying organic food, supermarkets were building up ranges, and then the recession came. Sales fell by almost 70% because people could not afford it any more. We live in a service economy. Companies need to generate sales by selling marketing concepts that play on aspirations. If sustainability is really to work, companies need to see how they can turn it into a profit centre.

Luxury Brands

The luxury-brand business is adopting a careful stance on sustainability. Although there are big names that touch the area – such as Zegna and Dries Van Noten – the majority prefer to wear the figurative clothes of benefactors and dispense charity (i.e. donating a portion of profits on certain products to a given cause) rather than embrace sustainability wholeheartedly. They understand that their business is about status. Why else do people buy a Smythson diary when they have an iCalendar, or a $25,000 watch when they have a clock on their mobile phone? 'Craft', 'pedigree' and 'heritage' are the keywords of these status brands, not 'eco' or 'sustainability'. And although luxury is coming to be equated with experience and emotional factors in mature Western markets, it is still at level one ('Look at me') in the booming economies of China, India and Brazil, where all the new profits lie.

Too few people understand the full possibilities and potential of the word 'sustainable'; too many associate it with recycling. But it has other meanings too. Design has become a pollutant. Designers now need to think in new ways. How do we make iconic products that people will not

The push towards leanness, decluttering and no frills affluence is creating new aesthetics in products and packaging, for which 'extraordinary and ultra minimal' is the new design credo.

want to throw away? (It's interesting that the Anglepoise lamp and paper clips were invented in the middle of the 1930s Depression.) How do we make products that do not have a seasonal feel or a sell-by date? How do we design products that people will want to pass on to their friends, sisters, mothers? How do we develop the concept of swapping, renting and organic growth within a product – such as '125 things to do with a T-shirt'?

Not all is negative in the drive to marry sustainability with fashion. There is a core group of consumers and manufacturers who want to change the way the world works. They want to escape the rat race, to step back from the pressures that technology, consumerism and über-choice impose. It's back to first principles, a reappraisal of the basic and more manageable. Results of the recent move to thrift, austerity and make-do-and-mend have included the increased use of public libraries; higher sales of smaller, more environmentally friendly cars; a boost for traditional heritage brands; and new interest in home crafts and DIY. The push towards leanness, decluttering and no-frills affluence is creating new aesthetics in products and packaging, for which 'extraordinary and ultra-minimal' is the new design credo.

Alongside this are sustainable production systems. Brands, businesses and organizations now pay greater attention to operational efficiency, resulting in clarity of vision and higher trustworthiness. Retailers around the world are embracing more flexible, collaborative and 'Leanomic' working practices – practices that are Limber, Efficient, Alternative and Neutral – from carbon and waste perspectives.

The shift to more 'eco-nomic' agendas among businesses and consumers is also driving these changes. According to recent research by Future Poll for Oracle, 34% of large British businesses say sustainability is a topic of high concern at the moment – after business survival. Sustainability is currently more important than regulatory compliance, globalization, new product development and competition from emerging markets. The five reasons why businesses are adopting sustainable strategies appear to be: to gain customers' trust (68%), to make the businesses themselves more efficient (68%), to allow staff to make better operational decisions (62%), to meet new legislative standards (56%), and to better measure manufacturing processes (46%).[2]

Localism

Very much part of the recession environment is 'home-indulgence'. A feeling for 'homesteading' coupled with the desire for the home-grown has led to a gardening explosion. This involves not just the greening of urban wasteland but also a celebration of neighbourhood and community. The word 'local' has taken on new meaning, not just in terms of farmed produce but also in terms of manufacturing (clothes, beer, chocolate, even gin!) and retailing, with a revival of the corner shop and the local café. Textiles and fashion have been particularly cynical about these kinds of community movements, especially after seasons of lower and lower prices. Does it all sound too déjà vu and reminiscent of the hippie and Gaia eras? Well, one thing is certain: more and more people sense that being environmentally friendly will become the new status symbol. The younger generation wants to connect with people and causes, not hoard possessions. That's a very good thing.

Enduring fashion: favourite pieces

NILGIN YUSUF *and photographer* **EDWARD BARBER** *explore the personal stories behind favourite clothes.*

ashion is restless, always moving, never still. Fashion is change, and its new configurations transform themselves with ever-increasing speed. The desire to stay 'in' fashion is an ultimately fruitless and frustrating endeavour. No sooner have we consumed and displayed the latest version of what's 'in' than it's already 'out', already being redefined and reinterpreted so that we can be enticed by something more exciting and of the moment. Within the wardrobes of even the most fashion-conscious individuals, however, lurk a number of special garments. These are clothes that have endured and survived despite the onslaught of fashion. These jackets, coats, dresses or scarves loyally continue to adorn their wearers with style, elegance and efficiency, valiantly facing down the newest trends with a certain singularity and pride, or melding, chameleon-like, with changing aesthetic cycles, constantly recontextualized and reframed by the mores of fashion.

Over time these pieces cease to be anonymous products of the fashion industry, developing distinctive personalities and becoming almost talismanic to their wearers: highly narrative items bearing the individual marks, feelings and smells associated with certain memories and emotions. They have the power to tap into a reverie of personal experience for the wearer; they function like slide shows, recalling a sequence of events, moments, periods in time – snapshots of a life lived. Although these fabric garments are not living things, each has had its own life and represents a real relationship and ongoing dialogue with its wearer, with whom it is interwoven as one.

Fashion that lasts is essentially a contradiction in terms, a type of anti-fashion, but in the current climate of eco-awareness and desire for sustainability, these long-standing members of the collective wardrobe have renewed relevance. They offer an opportunity to question some fundamentals of fashion and reassess the values of consumerism. If clothes cannot physically withstand the test of time owing to diminished production values and design that lacks integrity; if the bond between wearer and garment is not able to form, then opportunities for clothes to have depth, poetry and magic are restricted. Ultimately, it is only clothing that means something to us that can endure.

Professor Christopher Breward
Principal of Edinburgh College of Art
Paisley Tootal scarf, acquired 1980 (made 1958)

My father bought this scarf in Bristol on the early 1960s. It's burgundy, deep blue, yellow and grey paisley by a brand called Tootal, which was promoted as British but was actually Dutch. Tootal pieces can fetch quite a lot in vintage shops now. My father was an engineering student at the University of Bath and quite a 'moddy' dresser, although he wouldn't have identified with the Mods, being more of the rock-and-roll generation. He would wear the scarf with white jeans, suede shoes and a corduroy jacket. I didn't ask for this scarf; I stole it, which in itself made it quite a subversive item. My father wasn't wearing the scarf himself by this stage, although he did wear it right up until the mid-1970s. People generally wore their clothes for longer then, and by the time we had moved into the Thatcherite 1980s there was a consumerist sensibility that saw us all starting to buy more, and buy more often.

Between 1978 and 1980, I would have been thirteen or fourteen, just starting to become aware of music and trends: new wave, Elvis Costello, early Ska. There was also a big Mod revival at that time. My peers were buying their clothes from charity shops or raiding their parents' wardrobes for corduroy or tweed jackets. I found this scarf in my dad's wardrobe alongside two others and thought 'I'll have that'. I was trying to put together a retro image and the scarf would have been worn much the way my father had worn it, quite relaxed and loosely knotted at the front.

These were the sorts of clothes that I would have worn to my first parties. There was a big paisley thing in the 1980s, which fitted in with the New Romantic

I found this scarf in my dad's wardrobe alongside two others and thought 'I'll have that'. I was trying to put together a retro image and the scarf would have been worn much the way my father had worn it, quite relaxed and loosely knotted at the front.

Left: Christopher Breward.

styling at that time, and also an ethnic, South West hippy Glastonbury vibe. The colours of this scarf, predominantly burgundy and grey, were also the same as my school uniform, which may have been another reason I was drawn to it. I've always liked a coordinated look. I used to put wash-in burgundy dye into my hair before I graduated to henna. I was still wearing this scarf when I moved to London in 1984, in the days of 'Coal Not Dole'. It has certainly adapted to fashion and bridged lots of the different movements of my youth.

The scarf has a real emotional resonance. Even though it's been washed many times, it still smells of home and my father. It is fifty years old but has no holes, even though it is a bit rubbed up in places. The colour is still rich, even though the scarf is older than me. I do possess older garments in my wardrobe, antique pieces, but generally I am very happy to get rid of clothes after a while. If I lost this scarf, it would be like losing part of myself, part of my personal and family history. The concept of sustainable fashion is fundamentally a contradiction, because fashion is ephemeral and about the moment. But when you factor in the emotions, psychology and the importance of memory, the notion of built-in obsolescence starts to look flawed. The theories of Walter Benjamin and Ulrich Lehmann that examine fashion's contradictions are pertinent to this. The memory and poetry of clothing can leave a space for people to think more imaginatively about fashion. In the past, fashion was used and reused until it fell apart. An engagement with fashion's intrinsic, historic character allows people to think about it in different ways.

Dai Rees
Course director, MA fashion artefact and MA footwear,
London College of Fashion
Wrangler denim jacket, 1981 (1975)
I originally bought this denim jacket from a second-hand shop in Bridgend, South Wales. It's a bizarre place, which originally started life as a small market town but in the early 1970s, when Sony and Ford moved in, it grew into a massive industrial place. Now it's known as Suicide Central because of the high number of suicides that have happened there. When I was a kid there was a thrift shop in Bridgend run by some old ladies. It was basically for poor people, a stigmatized place, not celebratory or aspirational. It had men's and women's clothes at the front: cardigans, pinafore dresses, slacks and shoes. I remember the smell – it stank. It's shut down since; I think it's a dole office now.

I was twenty and off to a Genesis concert. I'd been a fan for about two years and wanted a denim jacket. In the 1980s everything was baggy; I wanted something different. Baggy on a skinny guy like me is not a good look and I've always preferred tailored, nipped-in, tight clothes. At that time, Wrangler meant nothing to me as a brand – everything was about Levis. Denim jackets were a staple garment of the older generation, like my big brothers, who came out of the rockabilly era. I think it cost me about 50p and, although I bought it in 1981, it had probably been made around 1975. I wore it with beige peg trousers, a T-shirt and Chinese slippers. The collar was worn up and the buttons left undone.

I've now had this jacket for twenty-seven years. It has a small armhole and a high sleeve. It's such a lovely blue, which is a staple colour of mine. Nowadays I might wear it with Margiela or Prada. It's very tailored, so you have to have confidence when you wear it. The collar has started to go and the cuffs have started to fray and after the last Dai Rees collection in Spring/Summer 2002, which was neon-coloured, I used fluorescent-pink thread to stitch over the weaker points. On that occasion I actually wore it at the end of the runway show.

This denim jacket has my DNA in it. I could be cloned through it. It has a very specific patina. So much of the denim blue has run out that it's just about holding together. I wear my denim jacket to private views or functions. Sometimes I wear it just to wind people up, with the sleeves rolled up to show my tattoos. It still has a rebellious quality. In the summer, I might wear it with a nice white buttoned Helmut Lang shirt or jeans. And Ray-Bans. Very American.

There's no sense of longevity to clothing anymore. Clothes are made to be thrown away. I'd go mad if I lost this jacket because it would be like losing a friend. Certain pieces of clothing are like music to me: they're associated with specific memories. I can trace every rip and tear of this jacket. Clothes become part of your ongoing life, and denim is something that ages well. Modern denim is all about newness, having the latest. We don't celebrate aged denim in the way that we used to. Strong production values, classic shapes and quality are what make a garment last.

Sean Pilot de Chenecy
Trend forecaster, Captain Crikey
Crombie coat, 1992 (1950s)
Clash T-shirt, 1978
This Crombie, which originally belonged to my father, was from Simpsons of Piccadilly. He bought it during the 1950s when he was in the army. He was an officer in the infantry and a combat survival instructor for the SAS for a few years. He would have worn this Crombie with a dinner jacket for formal occasions (although in those days people dressed up to go to

the cinema) or he would wear it with his medals for Armistice Day. When he died in 1992, aged 62, I chose this coat from his wardrobe because it reminded me of him but also because it was usable. His other clothes were either massive, heavy greatcoats or just too obviously 1950s.

The Crombie has two different sides to its character. On the one side, it is serious and upmarket; on the other, it is the favoured topcoat of skinheads. No self-respecting suedehead of the 1970s would have been seen without a Crombie, so it means different things to different people. You could see it on old men at the Cenotaph war memorial or you could see it worn by The Specials as I did on the original 2 Tone tour at the University of Exeter. There is that thing about passed-down clothing being like a physical embrace. You don't have the actual physical connection with the person any more but you can still have it through their clothing. It's an incredibly personal, multi-layered thing; the touch, the smell. My father and I had similar physiques. I was in the army

for some time, too, so now I wear this Crombie to Armistice Day services and when I wear it I do so with pride and walk in a different way, with a straight back.

This black cotton Screen Stars Clash T-shirt was originally from their Out of Control Tour in 1977. I bought it in the Music Machine in Camden, which my sister took me to. She was ten years older than me, and had just left the Hornsey College of Art where she had been with Adam Ant. I was fourteen; she was twenty-four. It was one of my first gigs. The thing I always loved about the Clash was that they had so many references in their work, it wasn't just about anarchy and destruction. That is reflected in this T-shirt, which has a 1950s Bert Hardy Picture Post image on it, and a whole American Jive thing going on. There are lots of grey graphics all over it and the slogan 'It remains to be seen whether or not our ideals can survive.' I have worn this T-shirt constantly over many years. Back then I wore it with white Levis, old DMs [Dr Martens], a monkey jacket with safety pins through it, a Damned badge and spiky hair. I also

Why do we have to throw everything away after six months? If something's good, you build on it: a wardrobe is like a home.

wore it throughout my twenties and thirties and I last wore it two months ago when I went to see Carbon Silicon and the Buzzcocks. It's definitely been part of my formative years.

I hate throwaway fashion. In the current climate, everyone will soon be very poor and no-one will be throwing anything away. All of that throwaway fashion was so bland anyway, the uniform of the masses, but individuality is on its way back. A band like Glasvegas, who were photographed wearing Crombies for the cover of *NME*, are not trying to 'blend in'. Bands used to look so good because they bought their own clothes; this was before the tyranny of the stylist. Bands used to look like themselves, now they just look like each other.

Perhaps one day my son will inherit these clothes from me.

Susie Orbach
Psychologist and author
Black satin jacket, 1976

I bought this jacket with my best friend in 1976. We each bought one for £15, which at that time was half our weekly wage. So it felt like a huge investment. It's fitted satin and flared at the back. The label is Juliet Dunn and it was from Selfridges. I have a principle that you don't spend a lot of money on party clothes, but we saw this and thought it was really pretty. It is significant because it cost a lot of money. I certainly would not spend half my weekly wage on a single item now. It has always been in my wardrobe. I find it quite easy to wear with party dresses. It could go with lots of things. It's cute. It's sweet. I didn't imagine it would still be in my wardrobe thirty-two years later. When I was younger I used to think 'sling it out if you don't wear it'. Now I'm more likely to go shopping in my wardrobe and rediscover pieces.

This jacket still comes out for formal occasions. I was shocked to hear that my best friend has dispensed with hers. But I don't want to fetishize it. I have a similar relationship with lots of other clothes, too. It's not special but it is comfortable; it goes with any fabric; it has sweet little buttons; it fits in a snug way and is imbued with a sense of party. More than anything, I remember the pleasure of being with Louise and buying it. It felt a bit wicked, but not in a bad way. It looks as good as when I first bought it, but then how hard-wearing do party clothes need to be?

John Rocha
Fashion designer
Comme des Garçons coat, 2000

I bought this in Paris eight years ago in the Comme des Garçons shop for £800. It was a big investment at the time but it has paid dividends. I have worn clothes

by Comme des Garçons and Yohji Yamamoto since the 1980s. They are always comfortable, easy to wear and never seem to wear out. They are clothes that say something about you. It's fashion but not in-your-face. This jacket, which is made from boiled wool, feels as good today as it did eight years ago and I will probably wear it for at least the next eight years. My philosophy as a designer is that fashion should enhance individual personality. That's what this jacket does.

I have worn this piece constantly and it has not had a single loose stitch or lost button. It's quite roomy, so I can wear a jacket underneath it when it's cold without ruining the line. I dry-clean it and after it comes back from the cleaners I need to wear it a few times to make it look good again. I have a whole collection of coats from Margiela, Comme and Yohji, but six days out of seven days this is the one I choose. I don't really understand it myself but I know that I feel comfortable and confident in it. It's been with me to Beijing, Tokyo, Russia, all over Europe. This winter I bought a new Yohji coat and had two from my own collection, but I still come back to this one.

Why do we have to throw everything away after six months? If something's good, you build on it; a wardrobe is like a home. A good car like a Mercedes or a Volkswagen will last for many years and fashion should be the same. It shouldn't be here today, gone tomorrow. Beautiful design should be timeless, with proportion, detail and quality in harmony. It's easy to do something attention-grabbing, but creating something that both captures its time and lasts for a long time is the true test. Enduring design has more substance and integrity. We dress doctors and we dress pop stars. I love the fact that people will wear my clothes year after year. When I'm designing I look at the past and think of the future and try to find some common ground. Some of the past is worth preserving; we don't need to throw everything away.

Professor Elizabeth Wilson
Fashion author and novelist
Ocelot couture coat by Molyneux 1978 (mid-1950s)

This coat originally belonged to my great-aunt and I inherited it when she died in 1978. It is made from ocelot with beaver collar and cuffs. It is lined in brown silk and has velvet pockets, which feel lovely to put your hands in. She was a wealthy woman and married four times, each time to someone richer. She had a Chippendale bedroom suite that is even better than the one in the Victoria & Albert museum. This coat was made by the British couture designer, Molyneux. When I first inherited it in 1978, I used to wear it in quite a relaxed, hippy way as lots of people did then; now I would worry that I might be lynched if I wore it out.

Clockwise from top left:
Susie Orbach, John Rocha,
Caren Downie, Elizabeth Wilson.

Right: Hilary Alexander.

Of course endangered species shouldn't be slaughtered or animals treated cruelly, but I can't see a problem with fur from farms that treat animals humanely. Or why vegetarians can't wear fur. Some people are perhaps upset by the symbolism, the idea that you are wearing an animal, but I feel that this is a displacement of politics. Why isn't there such an emotive campaign against battery chickens or cashmere goats? Throwing out this coat is not going to bring back the cats that were killed fifty years ago.

This coat has resonance for me. I was always against my family, who were quite right-wing. My father was a colonial civil servant and we have been solidly middle class – professionals, merchants, landed gentry – for generations, hundreds of years. When I was young, I didn't want to be bourgeois – it seemed like the worst thing in the world. In a sense this coat is an acceptance of what I am, a kind of resolution. My grandfather did shoot big game. In his house there were lots of leopard skins lying around, bows

Buying fashion shouldn't be like buying a burger. We want to enjoy the experience.

and arrows and crocodile skulls. There was even an old elephant's foot that had been turned into a needlework box lined in pink satin. It was the most extraordinary, surreal object.

The last time I wore this coat was on a trip to Brussels and I felt quite good and powerful in it. There is a poignancy about young women in fur, but it's harder to wear fur coats as you get older because you just look like an old rich woman. I might consider wearing it if I was invited to a winter wedding. I've never actually had any negative responses in this coat, but there is a fear I might. A colleague of mine was attacked for wearing a fake fur coat. If anything, I feel slightly defiant that the anti-fur climate has turned it into such a subversive item.

As I've grown older I've become increasingly aware of how things last longer than people. This coat used to be a representation of my great-aunt and her colourful life with her four husbands, but now she's gone and the coat's still here. Clothes can be solid and worth something. I feel that fast fashion has destroyed the value of clothes.

Caren Downie
Fashion director, ASOS
Black wool coat dress by Nick Coleman, 1998 (c. 1988)
This cocoon coat dress is made from 100% Panama wool, which is very flat. It has a long row of small mother-of-pearl buttons, long sleeves and no cuffs. It used to be very wide on top, with large shoulder pads, but I took them out so that it's now more of a dolman style. Mind you, fashion being what it is, I might be reinserting them again soon! I bought this dress about ten years ago in a vintage store in London. I saw it and thought: Nick Coleman! I remember him; he was quite a talented designer. I wonder what Nick's doing now?

It's a bit of a fashion power dress; I'll wear it for important meetings, when I want to be taken seriously and not be seen as too fashion-fluffy. Because it's so fitted, it makes you stand up quite straight and walk properly. It's narrow at the hem and finishes just below the knee. It's stitched with folds of fabric into the pockets, which makes it mould over your body and look very curvy, even though it has no stretch. It's definitely quite a sexy dress that seems to get lots of responses from men, although it's much admired by fashion women, too. Perhaps its appeal lies that in the fact that everything is covered but easily accessible. It wasn't cheap, about £60 in 1998, by which time it was probably already about ten years old, but it was in very good condition when I bought it. I will keep wearing this dress for as long as it fits around my waist. It actually is very similar to some of the things we've been producing for ASOS recently: very figure-conscious designs, with shoulder pads.

As fashion consumers, we will always want the newest and next best thing. But I think we've passed beyond the whole throwaway culture. The quality of the fabric and finishing needs to be very good. I think fashionistas are becoming more conscious of this and will combine things: something new for a Saturday night with something they've had for ages. This Nick Coleman dress has endured because it has a unique handwriting that makes it special. It's not too of the moment. The armholes are the giveaway: if it was fashion now, it would have a narrower sleeve and be narrower at the cuff. I wear it quite a lot and will eventually wear it thin, but it has retained its colour, which is another sign of quality. In terms of money per wear it has been very good value for money.

Hilary Alexander
Fashion correspondent, Daily Telegraph
John Galliano jacket, 1990; dress by Whistles, 1994
This black crêpe jacket by John Galliano was a gift. It has matching trousers and I first wore it at a British Style Award event in 1990. The jacket has shoulder pads, which are now obviously back in fashion. The poppy print, bias-cut rayon Whistles dress just slips over your head. It has no zips, nothing. It works really well with my collection of tribal jewelry. I wear it for day with boots and combine it with high heels if I want to turn it into an evening dress. The jacket is just fabulous. It's single-breasted with narrow sleeves, small cuffs and covered buttons that have never fallen off.

They are both dry-clean only, which may have aided their longevity. In a sense they are pieces that have nothing to do with fashion. I always feel comfortable when I wear them and I like the fact that nobody can pinpoint their origin. They are not dateable to a particular season and they are not designer-ID-able. With this jacket, which was the first designer jacket I ever owned, people will think it's a Balenciaga, Balmain or Chalayan. Ironically I never have time to shop because of my job. I'm an impulse buyer who makes lots of mistakes. But when it works, as it has with these two pieces, it's right on the button.

We want our clothes to last longer. One wear–one wash–throw it out is so over! People feel cheated. Even if they have bought a T-shirt for a fiver and it loses its shape or colour or falls to pieces, that's still a fiver wasted. The novelty effect of pile 'em high, sell 'em cheap is out. When you're somewhere like Primark and see clothes being thrown on the floor, it's not a good feeling. Buying fashion shouldn't be like buying a burger. We want to enjoy the experience. These two pieces are my own personal bit of vintage. They have aged with me but they have aged gracefully. Even after all this time, when it's time to do the collections, these are the two things I will always pack.

'Precious things exist unnoticed'[1]

The Japanese label **MINÄ PERHONEN** *(meaning literally 'I, butterfly' in the original Finnish), designed by Akira Minagawa, exemplifies the values of slow fashion. The line, which is produced locally in Japan, is known for its high-quality fabrication and durable design values.*
By Sandy Black

Below: 'Fogland' textured jacquard-weave coat and appliqué leather bag, Autumn/Winter 2007/8.

Akira Minagawa's signature quirky hand-drawn printed and embroidered fabrics are applied to simply cut dresses, separates and accessories, and recently also to furniture. He works in close collaboration with artisan weavers, making use of both sophisticated technology and traditional Japanese methods of weaving, dyeing and printing originally used for kimonos, a legacy that goes back centuries. In this he follows in a long line of Japanese designers, such as Nuno, Makiko Minagawa for Issey Miyake and Jurgen Lehl, who have developed innovative fabrics with the benefit of the knowledge, experience and skills of individual weavers, dyers and embroiderers working in small production units, which are growing increasingly rare as a younger generation fails to preserve these textile skills.

Minagawa was born in 1967, and after graduating from the famous Bunka Fashion College in Tokyo, worked as a pattern-cutter and textile designer for a made-to-order clothing company before setting up his own business, now the company minä perhonen. What makes minä perhonen distinctive is not only the whimsical visual poetry of its prints, weaves and embroideries, but also the brand's corporate integrity and the values of sustainability that guide its production. Although its clothes are industrially produced, this is done so in a way that respects the time required to capture the nuances of Minagawa's hand-drawn imagery and the individual charm of each design, a refreshing approach in an age in which the need for speed and cheapness dictate most mass-manufacturing processes. Minagawa's exhibition for the relaunch of Japan Fashion Week in 2005 emphasized the value of time in fabric manufacturing by illustrating just how much (or how little) fabric could be woven or embroidered in one hour on industrial production machinery, although he insists that 'time does not determine the value of a product', i.e. its market price.

Minagawa's commitment to slow fashion is also apparent in the designs themselves. The

Right: Finely woven silk jacquard engineered designs: 'Hanako' (top two images) and 'Little Girl' (lower two images).

Far right, top: Knitted top and printed 'Flower Nest' skirt, Autumn/Winter 2007/8.

Far right, centre and bottom: 'Full Moon' woven fabric dress, Spring/Summer 2008.

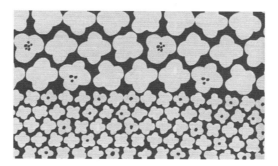

minä perhonen silhouette does not radically change each season, but evolves gradually with each new collection, sometimes with elements of fabrics reworked on a different scale. These collections are not presented in the conventional fashion catwalk format; instead Minagawa invites buyers and customers to touch and feel the clothes in his seasonal presentations, directly engaging with them.

Conceptually and visually charming, but technically challenging, minä perhonen fabric designs and clothing exhibit a synergy of three interwoven ideas: 'time', 'story' and 'life'. Minagawa views the production cycle – from concept through to fabric manufacture and finished garment – as incomplete until the customer brings her own personal story and develops a long-term relationship with the clothes. Durability and longevity are built into the concept: it is hoped that the wearer will grow older with her minä perhonen products, perhaps adapting a dress as her body size and shape change, and that the clothes will continue to have a life and meaning for many years to come.

In 2010 a retrospective of Minagawa's work was staged in Tilburg in the Netherlands, featuring over one hundred textile designs used in both fashions and furnishings. Minagawa has also produced a number of books and catalogues showcasing his drawings, manufacturing processes and timeless textile designs.

In the wake of the devastating earthquake and tsunami of March 2011, the minä perhonen brand, like many other Japanese fashion labels, has redoubled its efforts to be positive, optimistic and strong, and to make its clothes and products ever more relevant to its customers.

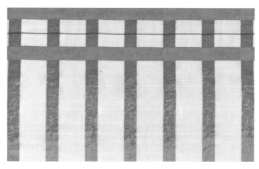

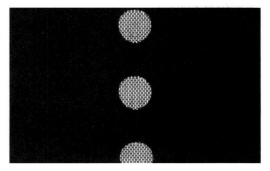

Sustainable luxury fashion: challenges and initiatives

PHYLLIDA JAY *is an anthropologist conducting research on the material culture of sustainable and ethical fashion, as well as in the field of sustainable luxury fashion.*

The term 'fashion paradox', coined by Sandy Black, captures the fundamental contradictions presented by a sustainable fashion agenda.[1] Between them the concepts 'sustainable' and 'fashion' imply different systems and rhythms of production and consumption. Luxury has a time-honoured association with values embedded in slow rhythms of production and consumption (which also serve in part to underpin the concepts of sustainable and ethical fashion). These values privilege durability, high artisanal skill, customization and the considered use of fine materials. Luxury brands have continued to trade on these traditional values, which are integral to their aura of desirability and exclusivity.

However, in the last two decades the democratization of luxury and the restructuring of many luxury brands from family-owned companies to incorporation by conglomerate groups have encroached more and more on the traditional ways in which luxury fashion is made. Luxury fashion's excess and creativity, alongside its increasing mass production, present as much of a paradox for environmental sustainability as does high-street fast fashion. The difference – theoretically – is that luxury brands, with their fine materials, high profit margins and influence on consumer aspirations, could lead the field in setting standards for ethical and sustainable fashion.

Deeper Luxury?

In a seminal World Wildlife Fund report on the luxury industry (2007), Jem Bendell and Anthony Kleanthous contend that luxury brands, '[w]ith booming sales and high margins, and an emphasis on consumer emotions…have the resources and mandate to develop a deeper, more authentic and sustainable luxury'.[2] Bendell and Kleanthous set out the business case for luxury brands to address issues of environmental responsibility and labour rights. The commercial logic for this is presented within the context of key challenges facing the luxury industry, such as the loss of brand cachet through mass production, the idea of 'affordable luxury' and the introduction of environmental legislation, as well as the potential for social backlash in societies where the newly rich indulge in extravagances a world away from the lives of the poor majority. In the wake of these challenges, investing luxury with the 'deeper' and more 'authentic' values of environmental and social responsibility is seen as expedient for restoring cachet and integrity and ensuring the long-term survival of luxury brands. Therefore although there are many examples of niche brands leading the way in sustainable luxury, this chapter focuses on the large companies whose brand recognition, scope of global sales and market segmentation most clearly highlight the aforementioned challenges.

Ethical Luxury: Artisans and Global Outsourcing

While philanthropy and charitable work continue to form the basis for many of the corporate social responsibility (CSR) agendas of large luxury brands, some are starting to address issues of supply-chain ethics and sustainability.

Global outsourcing is now a common practice. This represents a significant challenge in cases where brand value has largely depended on the cachet of, for example, French, Italian or British production. The heritage of European craft traditions is especially important to brand value in emergent Asian consumer markets. Large luxury brands must also contend with problems of traceability and supply-chain control presented by dispersed production networks. Two key challenges present themselves, that of supply-chain ethics and that of provenance.

The challenge of supply chains and ethics is demonstrated by the case of Italy, where cottage industries across different regions have traditionally served the luxury industry with high-quality artisanal products such as shoes or knitwear. The conglomerate restructuring of the luxury industry

The 'Zegna Oasis': a mountain area in the Piedmont region of Italy, reforested and landscaped by company founder Ermenegildo Zegna a century ago.

and mass production have put pressure on these cottage industries to compete with cheaper Asian suppliers. The Italian documentary *Schiavi del lusso* (Slaves of Luxury, 2007) revealed the use of illegal migrant labour in subcontracted supply chains for companies including Prada, Fendi, Versace and Dolce & Gabbana. Prada responded to the documentary-maker's questions regarding illegal workers this way: 'Regrettably, situations like the one described in the show, which we agree are unacceptable, may occasionally occur notwithstanding our controls…'[3] The documentary deliberated whether the problem of control lay solely with the subcontractor or also with Prada, given the company had paid the contractor $30 for nylon 'piattine' bags that retail at $440, putting undue pressure fell on the supplier to cut labour costs in order to deliver a luxury product at this price.[4] Prada has joined the ranks of high-street brands targeted by ethical labour campaign groups such as Labour Behind the Label and the Clean Clothes Campaign.

Regarding provenance, the issue of artisanal skill is foregrounded in the sense that crafts have developed within a trajectory of particular regions' economic, political, social and cultural history. Hermès is one of the few luxury companies that have retained traditional artisanal production in France.[5] While Mulberry, for example, has committed around 30% of production to its British factory, this is a rarity in British industry today.[6] On a different scale, Gucci has a commitment to 'Made in Italy', employing 45,000 people there.[7]

Given the economies of scale and profit margins of a large proportion of luxury and premium-brand fashion and accessories, the idea of being able to retain or return to the smaller scale and slower production times of traditional artisanal production is doubtful. This presents the challenge of investing in new production values in order to retain the exclusivity and authenticity so central to the cachet of luxury fashion. There is some evidence that resituating luxury fashion in sustainable and ethical terms may represent a way forward for certain brands.

The introduction of broad agendas for CSR has been the first wave of change within the industry, introduced by conglomerates such as PPR, parent company of the PPR Luxury Group, which owns Gucci, Balenciaga, Bottega Veneta, Yves Saint Laurent, Stella McCartney and Sergio Rossi. PPR, which set up its CSR department in 2007, responded to Bendell and Kleanthous's WWF report by saying they were willing to improve the way they did business.[8]

These industry-led initiatives have focused on 'continuous improvement' (a phrase popular in CSR discourse) as a way of ensuring workers' rights to free association, paid overtime and confidential methods to express grievances. How far a culture of CSR auditing can go in building ethical supply chains depends on a company's broader ethos. Jem Bendell, a professor of CSR who has advocated sustainable luxury, founded the Authentic Luxury Network to 'inspire social and environmental excellence in high-end brands'. He has noted: 'Some brands will look to philanthropy to support crafts and then connect their advertising to that instead. Good for the crafts, but not dealing with the issue of what makes something authentically high quality in terms of its manufacture…I don't think that claims about great factory conditions will ever be that enticing…Instead, I think excellence in supply chain ethics will simply be part of a new organisational values orientation that will flow through all its activities, including inspiring the designers and advertisers, to [form] great new holistic ideas.'[9]

The issue of what makes something 'high quality in terms of its manufacture' where there is a shift away from traditional craft processes is a key one for luxury companies to define and implement.

Sustainable Luxury

When *The Guardian*'s green pundits Leo & Lucy pose the question 'Should you buy the It-bag?' this reflects a general concern with the interpretation of sustainability the investment piece embodies: that something well made is durable and might be valued and used for a long time. They reflect: 'There is some logic in sustainable luxury. Luxury is supposedly reliant on superior, well-managed materials

Slow Luxury: Zegna

The concept of 'luxury' has evolved to include an expectation of authenticity: a luxurious object must possess substance as well as style. Consumers today increasingly want brands that emphasize craftsmanship, longevity and respect. Brands that demonstrate these principles with tangible actions, sustainable values and a social conscience elevate the appeal of their products in the new luxury arena.

The fashion industry has become progressively more concerned with environmental issues in order to meet this new consumer demand, which is also reflected in many other industries. I see this as a wholly positive development, which allows us to use our collective knowledge as an industry to bring specific issues of sustainability and environmental protection to the attention of consumers. At Zegna we have been conveying and representing these values throughout our 100-year history. My grandfather was a pioneer of social and environmental awareness and his principles have remained the cornerstone of our philosophy and business practices. My family set up Fondazione Zegna to ensure the continuity of the values and practices through which we keep our moral commitments to improve quality of life for individuals and communities, safeguard the environment, promote local culture, develop individual people's potential, and support medical and scientific research.

'Slow Luxury' is an important new concept that we are spearheading in partnership with supporters of the Slow Food movement. We have founded a network of Slow Natural Fibres Producers, with whom we have begun to raise awareness about the importance of using renewable natural fibres. The term 'Slow Luxury' can be extended to many other activities, such as our use of renewable hydroelectricity to power our woollen mill, or our stewardship of Oasi Zegna, a 100 km² protected environmental park. It is also reflected in the ethos that informs every product we create: what is beautiful must first be good.

'You must be the change that you want to see in the world', is what Gandhi said. Individuals, brands, societies and states can all make a difference by integrating this attitude into their mentality and processes. It is a cultural shift that needs to happen.

Anna Zegna, president of Fondazione Zegna

(so there should be a vested interest in the ecology of their habitats). It has that heritage of bespoke craftsmanship and attention to detail – in theory, offering the high-quality piece you can keep for ever. But the onus is on the conglomerates to prove they now mean it.'[10]

Zegna and Conservation

The hundred-year-old family-owned luxury company Ermenegildo Zegna aptly demonstrates the call to 'walk the talk' of sustainable luxury. Zegna provides the link between luxury and the preservation of ecological habitats as part of its mission to produce luxury wools and cashmeres.[11] The company recognizes that this mission depends on a positive and fair relationship with producers. Zegna became part of an effort to protect the near-extinct Peruvian vicuña (a relative of the llama) in the 1990s, building strong relationships with local communities and ensuring fair revenues derived from shearing to help protect the vicuña from poaching. Anna Zegna, image director at Ermenegildo Zegna, explains that Zegna provides project funding for irrigation vital to the survival of animals during the dry Andean winter months. Zegna funds the irrigation project to protect regional ecology and livelihoods and ensure the company's continued relationship with the farmers.[12]

In many ways Zegna embodies the concept of 'slow textiles' and the slow ethos of the bespoke suit. Within the luxury fashion industry more generally, the idea of the two-season cycle is increasingly obsolete, with resort collections and monthly product replenishment adding to the phenomenon that is 'fast

Opposite: Zegna 'Centennial' collection, featuring forty models wearing suits made from superfine wool, the first fabric made by the company, Autumn/ Winter 2010.

Below: Cashmere outfit using natural dyes, sourced locally, Zegna, Autumn/Winter 2010.

luxury'. This may imply that luxury brands generate carbon footprints and chemical inputs via fibre cultivation, fabric processing, finishing and dyeing that are comparable to those of the wider fashion industry. For example, cotton is a staple for many luxury brands, presenting the same problems of water use, toxic herbicides, pesticides and fabric processing. Luxury items such as Burberry trench coats, the canvas of Louis Vuitton monogrammed bags and designer denim may use cotton. Cotton also forms an element in a broader range of luxury clothing: it is frequently blended with other fibres such as wool, polyester, linen or viscose. In its 2009 CSR report Louis Vuitton Moët Hennessy (LVMH) flagged up its 49% investment in Edun (see pp. 34–37), the ethical fashion brand created to encourage trade in Africa, by profiling Edun's work on organic cotton.[13] Yet to date, although designers such as Stella McCartney have produced organic cotton collections, no large luxury conglomerate has integrated organic cotton across luxury product lines as a whole.

Indications of Change

Some large luxury brands are beginning to pay more consistent attention to sustainability; this may be as a direct response to legislation or as part of broad CSR

The idea of the two season cycle is increasingly obsolete, with resort collections and monthly product replenishment adding to the phenomenon that is 'fast luxury'.

programmes, with product specification guidelines created for designers across companies within conglomerate structures.

Legislation such as the European Union's Registration, Evaluation, Authorisation and Restriction of Chemical substances (REACH) has galvanized luxury conglomerates. The PPR Luxury Group (formerly known as the Gucci Group) has promised to 'review its supply chain' and Burberry to 'commit to adhere to' compliance with the list of chemicals banned under REACH legislation.[14] In response to REACH, LVMH, which owns brands such as Louis Vuitton, Celine, Kenzo, Givenchy, Fendi, Marc Jacobs, Donna Karan and Emilio Pucci, is working on possible substitutions for banned substances and notes that compliance with REACH now forms a core element in dealing with suppliers across its companies.[15]

Luxury conglomerates have made sustained efforts in reducing carbon emissions through measuring and cutting back on staff air travel, moving goods by boat rather than by air, and introducing energy efficiency measures into corporate offices as well as throughout stores. The Gucci brand, for example, has switched its packaging to Forest Stewardship Council-certified, 100% recyclable paper.[16] Yet the ongoing expansion of luxury brands is placing enormous pressures on the efficacy of carbon-impact reporting and reduction measures. LVMH, for example, has put a great deal of effort into reduction methods such as shipping alternatives, energy-efficient stores and office buildings. Nonetheless, its 2009 audits revealed a 24% increase in greenhouse gas emissions, a result of its expanding international retail networks.[17] For significant change to happen in the luxury industry, design needs fundamentally to transform the ways in which products are sourced, transported and consumed.

Left: Vicuña in Picotani, Peru, 2009.

For many designers and consumers animal fur is tantamount to a badge of cultural identity and the right to personal choice.

Design-led Change

There is nascent attention among luxury brands to product materials in supply chains, indicating that this could emerge as a significant arena for action. For example, Burberry agreed and signed an in-company contract to launch a Raw Materials Traceability project in 2010. As the company's director of CSR Sean Ansett explained, 'Issues related to biodiversity will be critical going forward, including the procurement of key raw materials related to luxury products, such as leather and exotic skins. So too will traceability of raw materials and the impact that cultivation has on water resources.'[18] The potential for design-led change is evident to some degree in LVMH's initiative to realize more sustainable product specifications through its annual 'environment trend book'. This introduces 'recycled and recyclable natural materials and processes for creative groups and designers working within the group'.[19] Louis Vuitton is committed to replacing solvent-based products with water-based ones: 'the substitution rate is currently at 50% for patent leathers and rose from 24% in 2007 to 45% in 2008 for glues'.[20]

In terms of traditional artisanal vegetable tanning processes, LVMH has taken a significant step with an 8 million investment in a joint venture with Belgium-based Tannerie Masure, which has provided LVMH with premium-quality leathers for many years. In 2010, along with Tannerie Masure, LVMH inaugurated Tanneries de la Comète, where hides will be tanned exclusively for Louis Vuitton using vegetable extracts, representing around 20% of the

company's leather products.[21] LVMH has described Tanneries de la Comète as 'the future centre for development and excellence for leather treated with vegetable extracts'.[22]

In general the issue of leather and the highly toxic impact of chromium-based tanning remains largely unaddressed by big luxury brands, which tend to pay attention to waste-water management but not to the actual chemicals used in tanning or dyeing. The problem of producing high-quality 'organic' or 'eco' leather at the speed necessary for the high volumes sold by luxury brands has yet to be addressed. Burberry joined the Leather Working Group of the BLC Leather Technology Centre 'in order to have a clearer understanding of the environmental impact of tanneries…'[23] Mulberry has also sought the services of the BLC Leather Technology Centre and does use vegetable tanning in a few of its product lines. However, the luxury leather industry's compliance-driven field of activity represents responsiveness to legislation rather than the more positive set of alternatives offered by the sustainable science of leather processing being pioneered by the BLC Leather Technology Centre among others.[24]

Fur

The use of fur in fashion has provoked some of the most fiercely fought battles for and against the use of a material, with Stella McCartney the most famous proponent of a fur- and leather-free approach. For some, fake fur is a moral imperative as an alternative to real fur, yet for many designers and consumers animal fur is a badge of cultural identity and the right to personal choice. In terms of sourcing practices, luxury companies such as Burberry[25] cite Finland-based Saga Furs, which launched the Origin Assured programme with the International Fur Trade Federation.[26] This programme claims to ensure that fox, mink or finn raccoon comes from a country enforcing all fur-animal welfare legislation. Yet certification, monitoring and interpretation of humane practices in the rearing of animals remain controversial. Furthermore the environmental impacts of the fur industry have not been addressed. Fur apologists claim that fur is a 'natural material', renewable, biodegradable and energy-efficient when compared to fake fur. But industrial-scale fur farms produce massive quantities of toxic substances such as phosphorous and ammonia, polluting local air and water.[27] Like the processing of leather, that of fur involves toxic chemicals such as chromium and formaldehyde.

Unlike much leather, most fur cannot, at least, claim to constitute a by-product of the food industry. However, the harvesting of certain non-native invasive species such as the Australian brushtail possum (also known as paihamu) and the bayou water rat (also known as nutria) as alternative sources of 'eco-luxury' fur actually helps to resolve problems relating to habitat and wetlands conservation.[28] Oscar de la Renta, for example, has used bayou water-rat fur in couture designs.[29]

Some alternatives to fur have themselves provoked controversy. While eliminating the need for animal skin, many fake furs and imitation leathers contain toxic substances that are harmful to humans and the environment, PVC being one example. The need for viable alternatives to fur – or even to 'fake fur' – underscores the imperative of new research. At present, however, most luxury companies comply with legislation on endangered species and do not go further in developing either fake fur alternatives or more environmentally sustainable sources of real fur.

Alternative Textiles

The PPR Luxury Group has sponsored a new PhD centred on 'Sustainable Technology for Future Luxury'.[30] Given the group's fashion and leather supply chain involves a wide diversity of luxury products, reordering materials procurement along sustainable lines is a huge challenge. A funded PhD scholarship is a step towards fostering innovation in research and design development for sustainability.

Ermenegildo Zegna is notable for its development of alternative textile technologies that have the potential to reduce reliance on virgin sources (including oil) and to provide alternatives to highly toxic forms of fabric finishing. Zegna is part of the Slow Textiles movement in Italy[31] and has also participated in the Italian Cittadellarte Fashion BEST (Bio-Ethical Sustainable Trend) project, 'a platform of yarn and textiles manufacturers, fashion designers, buyers and institutions for responsible social transformation in the world of fashion'.[32] Zegna's work with indigenous Andean farmers sits alongside textile innovations including nanotechnology-inspired fabric treatments for its wool suits, solar panels inserted into ski jackets, and its sportswear range using Ecotene 100% recycled polyester (see pp. 276–77). This balance that Zegna achieves between traditional and cutting-edge textile technologies is an approach that recognizes the key challenge of celebrating heritage while redefining luxury.

Initiatives such as the Authentic Luxury Network aim to build dialogue within the luxury industry about shared definitions of sustainable luxury and environmental and ethical excellence. Industry alliances such as the Conzorzio Pelle Conciata al Vegetale focus on the retention of skilled craftspeople and traditions such as vegetable

For many large brands, sustainable luxury is still a nascent field, demanding clear goals, and consistent organizational learning and transformation.

tanning.[33] Organizations such as Business for Social Responsibility and the Ethical Trading Initiative have luxury-brand members and could develop projects focusing exclusively on luxury-industry challenges. Multi-stakeholder initiatives will be vital in forming shared platforms for standard-setting and guidelines for practice.

The 2007 'Deeper Luxury' report helped to push many companies to begin to work towards addressing issues of ethics and sustainability; the recession that began in 2008 propelled much talk of humility and a return to core values, and seemed to fit well with ideas of sustainable and ethical practice. Yet many luxury brands experienced a return to booming sales figures in 2010, boosted by the growth of the Chinese market and returning consumer confidence at the premium end of the European and American markets. Luxury brands would appear to remain committed to ongoing programmes of CSR, yet the contradictions between environmental sustainability, large-scale production and expanding international retail networks remain ever-present.

Going forward, a key challenge will be for luxury companies to build upon their current initiatives, focusing on systems design, cutting-edge textile technology and materials procurement. Developing clear and credible ways in which to inform consumers of their ethical and environmental efforts is key. For many large brands, sustainable luxury is still a nascent field, demanding clear goals and consistent organizational learning and transformation. The contradictions between market segmentation and the challenges of sustainable materials procurement and ethical labour practices demand complex solutions. Yet this nascent field is also an exciting arena of innovation. In time it could become a beacon for how sustainable materials and ethical supply chains can express a politics of the finest and most durable materials.

'I had the idea of combining high-end fashion with ethics'

NOIR *is a luxury Danish label that aims to be both sexy and sustainable.*
By Stacy Anderson and Sandy Black

Below: Noir's Spring/Summer 2011 Collection
evokes a ghostly Victorian fragility.

Luxury Danish brand Noir is known for pairing dark with light, sheer with solid, and perhaps most prominently, sharp tailoring with soft and gentle silhouettes. Following his experience as brand manager for Levi's Red and Vintage labels, and as managing director at innovative Danish label Day, Birger et Mikkelsen, Peter Ingwersen masterminded the concept for Noir in 2004, delivering a brand that flirtatiously blends ideas of both sustainability and sexiness in fashion. Every detail was carefully considered, from the brand's ambigram logo, referencing notions of reflection, to its collection themes, such as 'Transparency', 'Nocturne' and 'Decadence'. Credited by the fashion press with breaking the mould by marrying provocative designs with sustainable ideals, Ingwersen describes Noir's mission as 'to bring sophistication and sexiness to corporate social responsibility.'[1]

Noir showed its first collection in Spring/ Summer 2006. After brief forays into lingerie and menswear, a brand extension collection was launched for Spring/Summer 2009: the diffusion range Bllack Noir. Building on Noir's sexy, bold styles, Bllack Noir maintains the brand's overall essence for a younger, more celebrity-inspired look at more affordable price points.

Although Noir is defined by its commitment to creating both sexy and sustainable attire, communicating such a proposition proves challenging, as Ingwersen explains: 'As a consumer who wants to buy sustainably, you do not necessarily know what sits behind brands or certifications'.[2] Company research showed that customers want to buy ethically produced and meaningful products 'but no matter what the credentials, when I am in the changing room – if it doesn't look good on me I'm never going to buy it'.[2] In other words, the product must first deliver a high standard of design. Consumer education therefore assumes an increasingly crucial role alongside supply chain transparency.

Noir therefore foregrounds corporate social responsibility (CSR) in all its communications, which is still an unusual practice for a high-fashion designer brand. As adherents to the UN Global Compact Agreement, Noir publishes a code of conduct rooted in the fundamental principles of the UN's Universal Declaration of Human Rights and International Labour Organization Conventions (see p. 203). There is a subtle difference in the practices and aims of the two labels: Noir complies with a 'Do No Harm' code of conduct, while Bllack Noir adheres to a 'Do Good' mandate. Noir is predominantly produced in Europe, whereas Bllack Noir is produced in India and China under SA8000 CSR guidelines (developed by Social Accountability International). Bllack Noir products require more certifications than those of Noir; more than 70% of all fabrics are certified by Oeko-Tex® Standard 100 or other certifications. When clothes are produced outside of Europe, factories are certified to ISO 14001 standard.

This insistence on high standards of environmental and social sustainability was a founding principle of the brand. As Ingwerson says, 'From the first collection I had the idea of combining high end fashion with ethics – the big brands such as those of the LVMH Group all have years of history behind them, and a tradition of craftsmanship. Noir had no heritage so I needed to invent a future. At the time I was writing the business plan Al Gore was introducing *An Inconvenient Truth* and the icebergs were melting. It all had a massive influence on me and I needed to find a deeper meaning after twenty years in fashion.' Ingwersen's early research in Italian weaving mills and European production factories found little awareness of fabric certification and traceability through the supply chain. EU legislation on working conditions and minimum wages ensured production units had high safety standards, but outside the EU there could be problems.

Finding high-quality sustainable fabrics proved difficult. For the first two seasons Ingwersen bought organic cotton on the world market, but it was hard to trace all the way through to ensure certification. Production manager Seyhan Melbye cites this as one of the key challenges faced by small and medium sized enterprises (SMEs) 'As an SME, we do not have the bargaining power that larger luxury companies have; and they may also not be demanding the same materials and fabrics we are looking for.' Although organic cotton fabrics are available, 'these materials may not be of a luxurious calibre, and many do not incorporate organic and fair-trade standards.'

Ingwersen's solution was fundamentally different from that of his competitors: to develop the highest possible quality certified-organic fair trade cotton fabric for Noir and make it available to others in the fashion industry. He planned to work in Africa, where the cotton grown by small farmers was by default organic, but could not easily compete in world markets due to its small-scale production.

Ingwerson therefore embarked on an ambitious programme under the name Illuminati II (evoking a second Enlightenment), aiming to produce quality

Above: Noir's 'Enchained' collection for Spring/Summer 2010 used decorative gold chains throughout, creating undertones of fetishism.

cotton fabrics from organic and fairly traded cotton grown in Uganda, directly supporting smallholder farmers, and with the long-term objective of keeping the entire production line in Uganda. He travelled there every three months.

Ingwerson says that progress has been gradual but consistent: 'Although it's not possible to be 100% ethical, you can set targets year on year that you can strive towards. For year 1, we wanted to ensure that at least 25% of our fabrics were certified,[3] and to produce within Europe...for year 3 we aimed for more than 50% certification and production outside Europe. Because of these targets we had to have our own production system and fabrics developed for us. We knew it would take time but didn't realize how hard it would be'.

Support came from the Danish government's foreign minister, who recognized that CSR could be a unique selling point for Danish brands, as could Noir's practice of manufacturing in

Africa rather than China; and from the Danish International Development Agency (DANIDA), which recommended a partnership business model for the fabric-development project. Accordingly Ingwersen forged a strategic partnership with Dutch organization Bo Weevil, which already employed 16,000 farmers in Uganda growing organic cotton under the Fairtrade label.

The development of Illuminati II cotton has not been without challenges, such as obtaining sufficient non-GM seed. Much time and investment have been required to ensure that the programme yields both high-quality cotton and long-term benefits to farmers (who receive a percentage of profits on sales), in the face of competition from major players in non-organic cotton production.

Following the first weaving trials (in Turkey) in spring 2009, Illuminati II cotton was finally introduced in both Noir and Bllack Noir for Spring/Summer 2010 collections, achieving Ingwersen's goal of producing high-quality sustainable cotton fabrics, and opening the opportunity to other luxury brands. Both fashion collections do, however, use other fabrics, including leather, silk and fur, which might be seen as contradictory to the organic ethos. In response, Ingwersen explains: 'Cotton is my focus, putting social ethics at the centre, but if I have the privilege to survive another fifteen years I would like to do the same with silk, wool and so on. With leather we predominantly use byproducts [of meat]. We work with Kopenhagen Fur, which maintains high ethical standards. I have deep respect for people not using fur, but I am from Scandinavia – fur is part of my culture'.

The success of the Noir brands continues despite Ingwersen's departure in 2011 to return to his roots as creative director at Day, Birger et Mikkelsen. Noir continues its attempts to break down the mutual exclusivity of sustainability and high fashion, and looks forward to a time when supply-chain transparency and corporate social responsibility are the norm, rather than unique selling points.

Questioning identity

LUCY ORTA *is professor of art, fashion and the environment at London College of Fashion, University of the Arts London.*

Clothes have always been primary signifiers of individual and social identity. They are shelter, an element fundamental to physical survival, and an interface between self and others, between what we are and what we wish to reveal of ourselves. So they can be mask, costume, vehicle of identity or element of recognition, distinguishing others from self but also a sign of belonging, even of extreme standardization. Clothes may reveal our way of life and our unconscious selves; they may communicate social position, aspirations and desires, needs and emerging aspects, visions of the world.

Throughout the 1990s I worked as an artist with the medium of clothing to express social and political issues. I developed series of works under the titles Refuge Wear, Nexus Architecture, Body Architecture, Connector and others. Each body of work explores themes such as liveability, recycling, the relationships and diversity among cultures, and the search for protection and safety. Since 2002 I have gradually moved away from the body to begin testing new materials (casting, welding, video, photography), new mediums of expression (installation, social networking) and new scales (architecture and public space). What remains constant is my attentiveness to changing social situations and the transformations underway within our environment at large. My more recent artistic enquiries consider aspects of society and the environment. The Amazonia series considers the natural environment and the threat of climate change to biodiversity; Antarctica deals with social sustainability, communities and migration; and 70 x 7 The Meal highlights intercultural communication.

The exhibition 'Aware: Art Fashion and Identity', which I co-curated at the Royal Academy of Arts, London (3 December 2009–31 January 2010) evolved out of a necessity to expand the definition of clothing within our society.[1] This exhibition brought together artists and designers who share the same dedication to questioning the definition of fashion and demonstrating that clothing is a powerful instrument for communication that we tend to choose, use and discard too arbitrarily. The questions I began posing just over two decades ago were generated by an uncomfortable doubt about my successful career as a young fashion designer and were linked directly to the economic decline of the early 1990s. The first Gulf War, followed swiftly by a stock-market crash and mass unemployment leading to social unrest, stood in stark contrast to the superfluous fashion we had been observing in extravagant catwalk shows. Along with a number of similarly disheartened designers, I began searching for alternative means by which to express the deep changes that were taking place in society. Our focus for redefining the role of clothing was directed towards basic needs such as protection, survival, shelter and cocooning. Kosuke Tsumura's parkas stuffed with newspaper for heat conservation, Vexed Generation's muffled jackets and C. P. Company's transformable shelters are examples that come to mind from the mid-1990s.[2]

I began spending less time in the Parisian couture houses fitting beautiful models with exquisite dresses and more time in my partner Jorge Orta's studio, sketching utopian responses to these fundamental needs. Among my early drawings are some of the Habitent, a dome tent that converts in a matter of seconds into a waterproof cape; the Ambulatory Survival Sac, a sleeping bag that divides into two parts: jacket and rucksack; and the Mobile Cocoon, reflecting on basic survival strategies such as staying mobile and warm, being protected from the elements and remaining reclusive in the face of an increasingly alien, hostile society. Not having much success with these proposals within the fashion world, I gravitated towards the Parisian contemporary art scene. The Refuge Wear 'prototype' sculptures were exhibited to much acclaim in a number of venues.

Around the same time a young avant-garde fashion scene was emerging in Holland and Belgium and diverting attention from elite Parisian couture. These designers, including Martin Margiela and Viktor & Rolf, presented their work in non-traditional catwalk venues in Paris. Within this truly exciting design context my practice as a contemporary visual artist developed out of

Antarctica Project

Antarctica is a territory at the 'end of the world', with the planet's most hostile climatic conditions. It is the coldest place on earth, with temperatures as low as -80° C. Its desert of ice is the largest in the world. No permanent human settlements exist there, and there is no native population. It is a nature reserve whose glaciers contain 80% of the fresh water of the planet, and it is the only region on earth not claimed by any country and therefore politically neutral.

The Antarctic Treaty of 1959, signed by twelve countries, has preserved Antarctica as an area for scientific research with pacific aims: to protect the environment and to encourage international cooperation. In this sense Antarctica is a symbol of the freedom of research, of sharing and collaboration, open to all who come in peace to work for the good of the whole planet. In spring 2007, Lucy and Jorge Orta were invited to participate at the first Bienal del Fin del Mundo, for which they created the project Antarctic Village – No Borders, developing a research project on the subject of refugees and human migration that began back in the 1990s. The project, organized in a series of different actions, is a metaphor for the condition of those who struggle to cross borders and to achieve the freedom of movement necessary to escape from social and political conflicts. For the artists, Antarctica becomes the symbol of a place that welcomes everyone, a place whose extreme climate imposes a situation of mutual aid and solidarity, a 'symbol of an earth looking toward the future, where the immaculate whiteness contains all the wishes of humanity to spread a message of hope for future generations'.

'Clothes may reveal our way of life and our unconscious selves; they may communicate social position, aspirations and desires, needs and emerging aspects, visions of the world.'

Opposite: Life Line, Lucy + Jorge Orta, 2008.

Above left and below: Antarctic Village – No Borders, Lucy + Jorge Orta, 2007, ephemeral installation in Antarctica.

Left: Urban Life Guard,
Lucy Orta, 2005,
installation in The Curve,
Barbican Art Gallery, London.

'I reflected on how we can harness the power that clothing exerts...in ways that can alter our daily actions or perhaps even change society.'

frustration with the established system. I staged an impromptu Refuge Wear Intervention (demonstration) outside the entrance to the Carré du Louvre Paris Fashion Week catwalk shows and, simultaneously, in abandoned squats around the city. My work became a longer and deeper enquiry into the communicative aspects of clothing, and the role fashion plays in the construction of individual and collective identities. I reflected on how we can harness the power that clothing exerts – through its extreme diversity and universality – in ways that can alter our daily actions or perhaps even change society.

You may wonder how clothes can make us think differently and how fashion can possibly transform lives. The 'Identity + Refuge' workshop I organized with residents of a Salvation Army hostel in 1995 demonstrated how fashion can play an important role in re-assuming an identity within society after circumstances that may have resulted in loss or deprivation. What began as a simple customization project, whereby we altered and arranged the second-hand garments distributed to each of the residents arriving at the shelter, evolved into a visionary couture project. Using basic transformation techniques, the residents designed and created an innovative collection of womenswear, developing creative skills, building confidence and reconstructing a psychology through the therapy of creating. On seeing the designs emerge from the makeshift cutting room in the Salvation Army's laundry area, more members of the hostel became involved. Together we were able to renovate all kinds of discarded items of furniture, lamps and other household objects, which then formed the backdrop to a catwalk show staged during Paris Fashion Week. These kinds of sustainable initiative are becoming more and more frequent, some with great long-term benefits. One example is the social enterprise Fine Cell Work, which helps to rehabilitate prisoners

by giving them the opportunity to earn and save money, and the chance to reflect on and rebuild their lives through craft and achievement.

Sustainability lies at the core of research carried out by many designers and artists as an expression of engagement with important social issues. I feel a deep need to explore these issues through a repertoire of mediums, of which clothing and the body are key components. Philosopher and urban theorist Paul Virilio has remarked on the 'prophetic dimension' of Refuge Wear and Nexus Architecture, going on to say:

'It is an acknowledged fact that our society has a packaging mentality that goes hand in hand with marketing and mobility. Packaging has a dual role; its prime role is to facilitate transport, and its secondary role is to facilitate the message. In Lucy Orta's work, clothes are no longer perceived as a mere covering close to the body, as a second skin, but also as a form of packaging, in other words, half-way between architecture and dress. We know that there are several skins: underwear, the clothes themselves, and the overcoat. We could continue this onion-layer approach by saying that after the overcoat there is the sleeping bag, that after the sleeping bag comes the tent, that after the tent comes the container... Clothes emancipate themselves, expand to try to become a house, a pneumatic raft...The garment becomes more than mere clothing; it is a vehicle, a survival vehicle certainly but also a vehicle which protects against anonymity.'[3]

It is true that the academic study of fashion is relatively young. We have a lot of terrain to cover if we are to convince the majority of consumers that fashion is more than a bulging wardrobe. I hope that the work of many artists is provoking us to look at and think about clothing differently.

Sustainability in the dyeing and finishing industry

PHIL PATTERSON *is managing director of textile consultancy Colour Connections and chairman of the RITE group, which aims to reduce the impact of textiles on the environment.*

The important thing to recognize is that the dyeing and finishing industry is not a homogenous entity: there are pockets of excellence, swathes of inefficiency and a significant minority who continue to pollute under the not-so-watchful eye of brands and governments. It is also wrong to assume that developed nations are 'good' and developing nations are 'bad'. It is true that most Western nations police pollution fairly well, but there are still a number of low-quality, inefficient factories in the West, just as there are many genuinely world-class dyehouses in India, China and Bangladesh.

There have been very few game-changing developments in dye and textile chemistry over the past few decades, although the general push to get a higher percentage of dyes to fix on the cloth (as opposed to washing down the drain) should be applauded. The obvious exception to this generalization is biotechnology, in which the use of enzymes to replace water, chemicals and energy is becoming more and more popular despite (some would say ill-founded) concerns over GM organisms being used in enzyme production.

Big changes have occurred in textile machinery, or, to be more precise, in machinery control and recycling systems. The ability to use lower levels of water while recycling water, heat and, in some cases, chemicals, means that dyers and finishers can make products with lower environmental impacts than ever before while still using mainstream methods.

Newer methods are emerging and 'waterless' technologies such as plasma finishing or super-critical carbon-dioxide dyeing are just becoming commercially available: one example is Dyecoo, a new waterless dyeing system using super-critical carbon dioxide that is being developed for commercial use in partnership with Nike. However, the biggest challenges to improvements in sustainability are not technological. They are behavioural.

New technology costs money, as does effluent treatment and the provision of a safe working environment for the people who labour in the factories, and the sad truth is that for clothing buyers it is often cheaper to buy from an inefficient, unsafe, polluting dyehouse than a world-class one.

New, improved machines are not cheap and, despite taking only a relatively short time to make back their initial costs, many mill owners report that loyalty from downstream customers is at an all-time low, so they are fearful that investment in new technology could in fact be a waste of money if buyers depart en masse to the next cheap production country.

To reduce environmental impacts new technology and efficiency drives have to be adopted, but, just as importantly, bad practice also has to be eliminated. The retail brands are vitally important in shaping a lower-impact future, but until more brands fully map their supply chains and eradicate polluters and inefficient factories, the effects of the bad parts of supply chains will outweigh those of the good, and progress will be slow, although it will still be made. Many brands' sourcing strategies (strategy being a rather grand word for 'finding something cheaper') continue to endorse pollution, suffering and inefficiency while hiding behind a cleverly constructed veneer of environmental responsibility created by high-profile pilot studies and small-scale initiatives.

The better end of the dyeing industry has made great strides in terms of reducing environmental impacts. We have to hope that legislation and brand-sourcing policy develops to the point that it becomes the norm for world-class textile-dyeing and finishing mills that exemplify best practice to be chosen in preference to those that do not.

Finally, it is important to focus on a balanced, holistic approach to reducing environmental impacts rather than getting side-tracked on one-dimensional anti-chemical campaigns. There are widely restricted harmful chemicals that are still legal in some countries, and these should be avoided at the input stage, but there also has to be zero tolerance of discharge of untreated effluent and a real push to minimize water and energy use in the dyeing process.

Synthetic fibres

SIMON BENNETT *is a visiting researcher at Imperial College London Centre for Environmental Policy.*

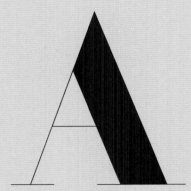

Artificial fibres have been with us since the end of the 19th century, when scientists first discovered that an artificial silk could be made by chemically treating cellulose derived from wood or cotton. In the century that followed, the chemical industry spawned many hundreds of new materials that would have astonished the early pioneers of rayon, acetate and Bakelite. The raw materials for these fibres slowly changed from cellulose to alcohol derivatives, and finally to oil and gas in the 1940s.

The refining of oil to fuel cars and planes generates vast quantities of byproducts that can be used for chemicals. This development, combined with the new technology for making nylon and polyester at the end of the Second World War, launched a new era for fabrics production. New fibres with specific properties could suddenly be produced at low cost in large volumes and could be completely disconnected from the complex and changeable supply chains of natural cotton and wool production.

Today over half of all fibres are synthetic. World production of synthetic fibres is approximately 35 million tonnes, and demand is predicted to rise further. This presents two intertwined sustainability challenges: climate change and raw material supply.

The manufacture of synthetic fibres generates greenhouse gases, such as carbon dioxide, which are responsible for climate change. These are mainly produced from the burning of fossil fuels to provide the energy for the chemical plants that make and process the fibres. Reducing the climate impacts of synthetic fibres could be achieved by greater efficiency in the production processes, use of renewable energy such as biomass, or application of technologies to capture and permanently store the carbon dioxide. The last is known as CCS (Carbon Capture and Storage) and the first major trials involving power plants are due to begin in the next few years. However, it will be difficult to cut carbon dioxide emissions drastically in the near future using these methods without increasing the costs of the fabrics. A much better option, therefore, is simply to use fewer synthetic fibres.

But with what can synthetic fibres be replaced to reduce environmental impact? This question is not as easy to answer as it might first appear. The carbon-dioxide emissions of nylon and polyester manufacture need to be balanced with the heavy use of fertilizers, pesticides and water in cotton production. Water use is a particular concern in some parts of the world where cotton is produced.

Another thing to look out for in relation to nylon is the emission of nitrous oxide, which is an air pollutant and a potent greenhouse gas – approximately 300 times more potent than carbon dioxide. Nitrous oxide is released in the making of adipic acid, a precursor to nylon. Adipic acid manufacture accounts for 5–8% of all nitrous oxide released worldwide. Efforts are being made to reduce this figure: hydrogen peroxide has been proposed as a so-called 'green chemistry' alternative to adipic acid in nylon manufacture. This is not yet widely used, but could be supported by the fashion industry to aid its development as a more mainstream technology.

The second concern is the raw-material source of synthetic fibres. Oil and gas are fossil fuels and our extensive use of them for energy and chemical production depletes their availability for future generations. Given the current rates of consumption, these unlucky 'future' generations' may in fact begin with the next generation. Geologists consider the probability of conventional oil resources 'peaking' before 2030 to be significant. This will push up the price of fossil fuels and could signal an end to cheap synthetic fibres unless alternatives are found.

World production of synthetic fibres is approximately 35 million tonnes, and demand is predicted to rise further. This presents two intertwined sustainability challenges: climate change and raw material supply.

The main alternative to oil is biomass. Biomass can be crops, trees, grass or biological waste – anything of biological origin that contains sugars that can be manipulated to make chemical products. Polylactic acid (PLA) is an example of a bio-based polyester that has become competitive with petrochemicals for some applications due to high oil prices. PLA in the US is produced from corn and can be biodegradeable – unlike fibres from fossil fuels, which never break down in the environment – but PLA currently retails at a premium price. If, as expected, oil prices rise again, we can expect to see a great deal of interest in these types of bio-based fibres. Producers such as NatureWorks, which makes a form of PLA called Ingeo, are looking at eco-friendly applications in the fashion world as initial markets in which the higher cost of PLA fabrics could be borne while research continues into mass-market performance aspects. For example, PLA does not currently tolerate the high temperatures required for ironing.

The twin concerns of climate change and oil depletion are set to bring about some major changes in textile production over the next few decades. Bio-based fibres such as Ingeo and DuPont's Serona have the potential to be sustainably sourced and generate lower emissions. But a transition will not happen overnight and progress may not be smooth. Bio-materials face many of the same challenges as biofuels, with which they might compete for raw material, and, depending on how they are made, similar issues surrounding genetic modification.

Real opportunities are now emerging for entrepreneurs who can produce more eco-friendly fabrics or develop methods of using fabrics more sustainably. The difficulties of comparing the different measures of environmental performance, as presented briefly here, mean that we will all have to read our labels very carefully in the future. Terms such as 'natural' and 'synthetic' are no longer enough to allow us to judge the environmental performance of our clothing.

Fossil fuel

GAVIN FERNANDES *presents a dystopian vision of the future. Styling by Stephanie Talbot and Gavin Fernandes.*

This collection of photographs was created at the end of the 20th century, when awareness of climate change, carbon emissions and fuel depletion was increasing rapidly. Inspired by these issues, Fernandes's series explores, in stark black-and-white imagery, the nature of survival, and our dependence on non-renewable fossil fuels as energy resources and as the basis of trade: 'Set in the near future, when fossil fuel has become an expensive commodity and the earth's reserves are nearing exhaustion, the visual story portrays a woman's desperate search for the last remnants of coal, gas and oil, employing primitive mining techniques, while dressed in protective clothing to guard against accelerated climatic change.'

Top: Makeshift Mine, 1998, portraying a woman's DIY attempts to find fuel.

Above: Oil, 1998, fetishizing the physicality of oil, with clothing by Jessica Ogden.

Above left: Coal, 1998, shows a woman collecting precious remnants of coal, while wearing protective clothing by Blaak and YMC.

Right: Sun Damage, 1998, evokes the theme of climate change with the image of a pieced-together dress by Jessica Ogden drying in the sun.

Zero-waste cutting

MARK LIU *experiments with a new form of eco-efficient fashion.*
By Sandy Black

Mark Liu adopted the principle of zero-waste pattern cutting to address the fact that in every garment approximately 15% of the fabric is wasted in the pattern-cutting process. His approach uses complex multiple pieces, some with intricately shaped edges, which create a striking 3-D textural 'feathered' effect when sewn together. Other pieces do not require sewing at all. 'We create garments in which waste is designed out at the beginning of the process. To do this all the rules of tailoring and textiles must be reinvented. Pattern-making is pushed to its very limits until waste is reduced to zero.'[1]

Liu explains the challenges of the process. 'The garment pieces are designed to fit together like a jigsaw puzzle so that nothing is wasted...It took a lot of trial and error to make the zero-waste patterns work. You have to be able to visualize the 2-D pieces in your mind to fit them together in 3-D, acting as both fashion designer and pattern maker at the same time.'

Liu views his approach as part of a wider trend towards improved sustainability in large and small companies across the fashion industry. '[To] sit back and be part of the system is not good enough. We have to try to invent new ideas and be continually researching.'

Above: 'Unicorn' by Mark Liu, demonstrating intricately shaped 'feather' edge-cutting, 2010.

'[To] sit back and be part of the system is not good enough. We have to try to invent new ideas and be continually researching.'

'I don't want to emulate what I'm born to antagonize: the fashion industry.'

FROM SOMEWHERE, *the name of Orsola de Castro's label, hints at the provenance of her fashions, which are made of pre-consumer surplus-fabric and cutting waste from garment factories in Italy and the UK.*
By Sandy Black

Launched in 1997, From Somewhere became a magpie within the hugely wasteful fashion industry, gathering its discarded treasures instead of using new textile products. In the brand's early days, de Castro travelled around Italian factories to collect waste fabric from the manufacturing floor; now this waste is collected by factory staff and sold or willingly donated to de Castro. Not all excess fabrics in factories are routinely thrown away: more valuable textiles such as jersey and silk are accumulated for the stockmen and sold on in bulk. From Somewhere diverts 3–4 tonnes of textile waste each season.

From Somewhere clothes are made in relatively small quantities: perhaps only 1,000–1,500 pieces annually. Production is situated in Italy and in the UK so that it is as close as possible to the source of the materials. Due to the eclectic mix of numerous different fabrics (everything from cashmere to tweed), each piece is unique; size is not always predictable; and dresses are sold by colourway rather than exact shade. The resulting designs are effortlessly beautiful and eye-catching due to their rainbow-like patchwork panels. However, there are sometimes issues with repeatability, and fashion buyers have had to be educated about the production process of the line and persuaded to accept variability as one of its distinctive selling points. Rather than selling through exclusive individual stores, as is the case at present, the company therefore wants to reach as many people as possible via an increased online presence.

In 2006 de Castro and her partner Filippo Ricci were instrumental in founding Estethica, the ethical fashion section of London Fashion Week that has become a fixture in the London fashion calendar and helped make London a global centre for ethical fashion. Estethica has influenced the wider industry by raising awareness of environmental and ethical issues in the fashion system, and promoting emerging sustainable fashion companies. After ten seasons of Estethica and fifteen years in the business, From Somewhere's collaborations with multinational companies have demonstrated the long-term influence smaller ethical business can have.

The first such collaboration was with British supermarket giant Tesco, which has committed to moving towards sustainability with its clothing label F&F, in accord with the British government's Sustainable Clothing Action Plan, launched in 2009. In this unique collaboration, entitled From Somewhere to F&F, de Castro developed a capsule collection of six pieces for Spring/Summer 2010, based on From Somewhere's best-selling styles, incorporating upcycled jersey fabrics from Tesco's previous production, including obsolete and damaged stock and 'end-of-roll' waste otherwise destined for landfill. A second range followed in the autumn; both ranges sold successfully online. The garments were produced in a pioneering 'green' factory in Sri Lanka as part of a wider long-term consultancy project. De Castro's direct engagement with the fast-fashion part of the industry represents a positive step for change with the capacity for genuine impact.

The second collaboration underway at From Somewhere has taken advantage of an opportunity to divert an unforeseen waste stream in a creative manner. The swimwear company Speedo, which was unexpectedly barred by changes in regulations from using some of its most technically advanced swimsuits for the 2012 Olympic Games, made these available to From Somewhere. De Castro and her team have developed an original range of signature upcycled dresses and tops that creatively reuse the fabrics, logos and trims from the disassembled swimsuits. The result is a range with a distinctive new aesthetic – and, de Castro hopes, with potential new uses. Given the synthetic swimsuit fabric's quick-drying properties, she envisages a new form of clubwear – the swimdress – that allows the wearer to go straight from swimming to an evening out without changing outfits. The impact of scale that can be achieved by working with large companies in collaborations such as these

Above: 'Viper' dress, part of a capsule upcycled collection by From Somewhere for Tesco, Spring/Summer 2010.

This page and opposite: From Somewhere, innovative range of upcycled Speedo swimwear remade into functional fashion garments, Autumn/Winter 2011.

'Fast fashion is unsustainable. but fashion can be sustainable. You have to work with nature. not against it.'

is enormous: for example, says de Castro, if Speedo were able to produce the new designs in volume, 50 million young people could be reached with this new concept in swimwear.

De Castro is also developing an upcycled line for high-street fashion chain Topshop, using its own manufacturing waste, under the label Reclaim to Wear, launched in Spring/Summer 2012.

The concept of upcycling is clearly taking hold, with mainstream retailers increasingly influenced by the movement's key pioneers. De Castro still has to tread carefully through the minefields of the fashion industry, however. 'I don't want to emulate what I'm born to antagonize – the fashion industry. Fast fashion is unsustainable, but fashion can be sustainable. You have to work with nature, not against it.'[1]

'Solving problems, not adding to them'

In the emerging fashion market of Estonia, Tallinn-based costume and fashion designer **REET AUS** *is testing the market for upcycled clothing via her label ReUse, founded in 2005.*

I graduated from the Estonian Academy of Arts as a fashion designer but I didn't want to go into the industry. I was lucky to have the opportunity to work with theatre directors and I started experimenting with recycled materials there. I developed a strong interest in alternative technologies and created the fashion brand ReUse in cooperation with the Estonian recycling centre. I have been working with them for several years and they are my main source of materials, which include uniforms from the army and the police and industrial waste from big companies. I have also been working with organic cotton, silk, hemp and bamboo – although it has been quite hard to source – trying to be sure about certifications and get good-quality materials.

My line is produced in Estonia. I have a studio where I make the samples and then I have three very good small companies located close by, who produce for me. To define the price point is quite tricky; producing recycled fashion is just so expensive. To make one piece can take two weeks: I have to collect the material, unstitch, wash it, sew it, design it. Working as costume designer has made me a good clothing designer. I have learned a lot by working with old costumes, redesigning and reusing them. I have taken apart so many pieces and seen so many technologies that my work as a designer has became much easier. In reaction to seeing lots of complicated things my own work also has become simpler.

Green fashion is currently a small niche-market. But good design is ageless. My aim has never been to produce as much as possible, but to come up with good solutions and try to influence the fashion industry from inside. Good design is the key to this and I hope that designers will take more responsibility and think about consequences. I would like my label to represent high quality and good design that is long-lasting and ethical in every sense; solving problems, not adding to them.

Right: Reet Aus, range made from discarded jeans and trousers mixed with velvet. Autumn/Winter 2009.

'Ethically intelligent and remade in England'

CHRISTOPHER RAEBURN, *named 'best emerging talent' for menswear at the British Fashion Awards in 2011, hopes to impart his sustainable design thinking to the wider fashion market.*
By Sandy Black

Following his graduation from the Royal College of Art, London, Christopher Raeburn showed his debut womenswear collection, 'Shadow', for Autumn/Winter 2009, making an impression with translucent fabric clothes (see p. 105) photographed on a lightbox to expose the 'skeleton' of each garment. It was this fashion aesthetic that first drew press attention; only later did it become apparent that the clothes were made from military-surplus silk parachutes that had been taken apart and remanufactured into fashionable yet functional outerwear. The Raeburn signature was established: reusing dead or faulty stock and dismantling and upcycling army uniforms and blankets into new stylish clothes with a practical bent and a quirky sense of humour. Once an end-of-line fabric has gone, new sources of fabric stock must be found. The parachute silk has been replaced by recycled nylon fabric to increase functionality and make the garments waterproof. Details such as pop-out linings, reversibility and adjustable elements set Raeburn's collections apart technically.

Until recently, everything was made either in the company's London studio – hence Raeburn's motto 'remade in England' – or in local garment factories, but the growing success of the brand inevitably presents the challenge of manufacturing larger quantities, a perennial dilemma for young designer fashion brands. Production in audited factories in Bulgaria was Raeburn's chosen solution, giving him access to expertise in manufacturing lightweight sportswear that was not easily available in the UK. As for the future, Raeburn simply wants to 'create good products – garments that have value and longevity.'[1] Via consultancies with large companies such as Victorinox and Moncler, Raeburn hopes to impart his sustainable design thinking to the wider fashion market.

Right: Christopher Raeburn, 'Freeze' collection, British wool jacket with recycled nylon skirt and shoes, Autumn/Winter 2012.

Right: Christopher Raeburn,
'Blast' collection, men's 'Parallel'
parka made from Hainsworth British
woollen fabric, Autumn/Winter 2011.

Right: Christopher Raeburn 'Blast' collection, women's wool duffle coat made from 1950s Swedish military uniforms, with overdyed snow-poncho lining, Autumn/Winter 2011.

'Taking old/worn/dated/shameful clothing and giving it a new life'

Based in London's thriving East End fashion district centred on Brick Lane, **JUNKY STYLING** *is one of London's pioneering design-led micro-companies that punch far above their weight, reaching a major audience through its internet presence and media profile. By Sandy Black*

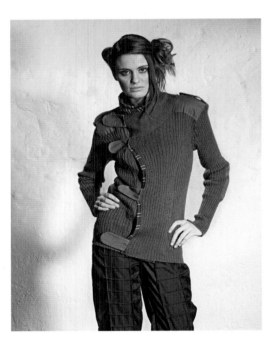

Above: Army wrap cardigan and ladder trousers.

Junky Styling's signature look involves deconstructing and reworking classic men's pinstripe suits, shirts and ties into surprisingly sexy and glamorous dresses, bustier tops, skirts and trousers. Other reworked fabrics include tweed suits, Welsh blankets, knitwear and silk scarves. This redundant garment stock is sourced through agents and charities in London and across the UK, and the resulting remade pieces are produced in the company's East End studio–shop. Each piece is individual: although patterns and styles are repeated, the ever-changing selection of recycled fabrics mean that no two garments are alike. As well as its evolving collection of pieces offered for sale in its studio–shop, Junky Styling also operates a 'Wardrobe Surgery' to which customers can bring fabrics or clothes that have been handed down or have fond memories attached, and have them remade into contemporary pieces. The largest single category of clothing brought in by customers is denim: a fabric often imbued with important aspects of a person's life-history, making its wearers loath to part with it.

Junky Styling partners Annika Sanders and Kerry Seager have been in business together for over fifteen years. In addition to selling pieces directly through their studio–shop, they have continued to develop their online wholesale business, with fashion retail stockists growing in the UK and Europe. Their latest venture has been a separate menswear line, promoted at the London and Paris fashion weeks.

A new Junky Styling venture launches in Seoul in 2012, in partnership with a major Korean company that holds licences for twenty clothing brands. Junky Styling plans to 'close the loop' on all the Korean company's textile waste by reworking dead stock and creating ranges for both men and women that the collaborating company will sell in the Korean market. This is a pioneering collaboration to upcycle on a much larger scale and divert a different waste stream.

In the context of the wider ethical and environmental fashion movement, the influence of companies such as Junky Styling is beginning to pervade the retail sector and affect charities and the textile-recycling industries on a much larger scale. They are creating a demand for used and waste clothing that increases its worth, and modelling how design and upcycling can be used to add value to surplus clothing and textiles.

The influence of companies such as Junky Styling is beginning to pervade the retail sector and affect charities and the textile recycling industries on a much larger scale… creating a demand for used and waste clothing that increases its worth.

Above and left: Two versions of Junky Styling's Chesterfield coat, using bold, contrasting recycled fabrics.

'Sustainability will be an inevitable issue for every company'

YOMODE *is an initiative proposed by entrepreneur Christine Tsui that aims to tackle the large volume of waste inventory currently languishing within China's retail supply chain.*
By Sandy Black

China is the largest producer of clothing in the world, and inevitably there is vast wastage from the system (generated by overproduction, cancelled orders, changed specifications, etc.), which results in large inventories of unused finished garments being stored in warehouses by Chinese companies. A new business-to-business initiative called Yomode is underway, instigated by entrepreneur and author Christine Tsui. Tsui hopes that her initiative will address this situation to improve sustainability in the industry.

Through the project, Tsui's first objective is to research the feasibility of developing this concept on a commercial scale. Initial experiments in redesigning unused clothing have been completed, and companies are now being approached for possible collaborations. Currently, as in other countries, some manufacturers in China donate or sell their unused clothes cheaply to NGOs for onward shipping to poverty-stricken areas; others incinerate the inventory to make way for new goods, but still this leaves a great deal of stock, which can end up being stored for some time. Tsui's initiative differs from current projects that promote the upcycling of used clothing, as it focuses on unworn surplus finished goods at the factory level. The aim is to demonstrate to companies the cost savings of upcycling over disposal and manufacturing new products, an ambitious goal, but certainly one worth striving for. As Tsui has observed, 'Very few people give attention to sustainability in the Chinese textile and clothing industry. However, the government committed to accomplish certain targets on climate change, so regardless of whether manufacturers agree or not, sustainability will be an inevitable issue for every company.'

Very few people give attention to sustainability in the Chinese textile and clothing industry.

Right: Prototype designs for Yomode's commercially oriented restyling of redundant stock.

Worn Again: corporate upcycling and remanufacturing textile waste

WORN AGAIN *is a company on a mission to 'transform textile waste and manufacturing patterns through upcycling and closed-loop systems'.*
By Sandy Black

Worn Again, founded in London in 2005, developed out of the sustainable lifestyles charity Anti-Apathy. The brand's first products were shoes, designed and made in collaboration with Terra Plana and famously worn by Prime Minister David Cameron. Its recent focus has been on upcyling and recycling textile waste from corporate clothing in the UK. The corporate clothing sector is responsible for generating some 10,000 tonnes of garments annually, of which only 5% is currently collected and reused or shredded, the rest most likely ending up in landfill. Founder Cyndi Rhoades decided to tap into this huge waste stream, developing partnerships that would both redesign the systems for collection and encourage initial design decisions to facilitate recycling and upcycling at the end of the uniform's first life. Worn Again's first corporate buyback business-to-business initiative, launched in 2010 with rail operator Eurostar, began with a project to develop a 100% remanufactured bag made from decommissioned company uniforms for Eurostar train managers to use. Other products made from Eurostar uniforms include wallets and phone accessories. In a similar vein, Worn Again also developed tote bags made from decommissioned Royal Mail uniforms.

The next phase is now underway, focusing on the introduction of closed-loop textiles into corporate clothing, including a project with designer Wayne Hemingway to produce 85,000 new uniforms for McDonald's. Eventually the uniforms will incorporate a type of recycled polyester that can be collected at the end of the uniform's life, repolymerized back to its original components and turned back into new polyester, without the degradation present in polyester made from PET/plastic bottles, which can only be recycled once. Rhoades hopes that if such initiatives succeed they will move upcycling and closed-loop innovations from the fringes of the fashion and clothing industry to centre stage.

Right: A Eurostar train manager with bag developed in collaboration with Worn Again, made entirely from upcycled Eurostar company uniforms.

Terra Plana footwear

TERRA PLANA's *ethically produced and environmentally friendly footwear has been as popular for its designs as for the values it represents.*
By Sandy Black; photographed by Maria Downarowicz.

The Terra Plana footwear company, which spawned VivoBarefoot (see pp. 82–83), was set up in 1989 with sustainable design at its core. It was built on artisan techniques, featuring vegetable-tanned leather and designs that considered the whole life cycle of the shoe; for example, reconstituted rubber soles that could be ground down into surfacing material for playgrounds at the end of the

shoe's useful life. Many styles incorporated recycled material uppers, such as e-leather, or reuse existing materials, such as old shirts or denim, for shoe linings. All the shoes are made with minimal toxins and water-based glues wherever possible.

Terra Plana's inspired use of vibrant Saami quilts incorporated into boots and shoes created a signature style for the company. The Saami are semi-nomadic people,

living in the desert of the Sindh province of Pakistan, and their distinctive quilts are made within family groups so no two are ever the same. Using recycled quilts sourced from a Pakistani women's cooperative, the shoes were handmade, so each pair was completely unique, and the range was only available in limited numbers. This is a good example of an environmentally and ethically

responsible product that sold primarily on the appeal of its design and the quality of its artisan manufacture, rather than on the basis of any overt claims about sustainability.

Above: Maria Downarowicz creates a 'flock' of shoes to illustrate the variety of colours and styles in Terra Plana's recycled 'Quilt' range.

Tamara Fogle upcycled bags

TAMARA FOGLE's *background in antiques and interiors has strongly influenced the design ethos of her accessories brand.*
By Sandy Black

Tamara Fogle reuses antique fabrics primarily for their aesthetic value, without deliberately setting out to be known as a 'sustainable designer', but her choice of materials has significantly reduced the environmental footprint of the business she established in 2007.

Fogle's bags are produced in family-run workshops in London. All her designs combine antique textiles with leather trims. The antique textiles include linen German flour sacks dating from the 1830s to the 1940's, sourced direct from country farms. The faded gothic-style lettering varies on each sack, usually stating the farmer's name, the location of the farm, and the date the sack was first used. Hand-stitched repairs visibly display the history of the fabric and its long use. Other handbags use Hungarian grain sacks dating from 1910 to 1930, which were hand-woven in linen for durability and strength and sometimes incorporate the weaver's initials. Each sack has a different central stripe in red or blue, unique to the farm on which it was originally used.

Representing an entirely different textile tradition, another range of Fogle's handbags is made from hand-stitched quilts from India and Pakistan, dating from the 1960s to the 1980s. The quilts themselves were made from old saris, so by the time they become Tamara Fogle bags, the fabrics have been reused three times, enduring as tangible bridges to other lives.

Left: Tamara Fogle weekender bag and handbag made from antique German flour sacks.

Maison Martin Margiela 'Artisanal' line

By Sandy Black

In its twentieth-anniversary exhibition at Somerset House, London, Paris-based avant-garde fashion brand Maison Martin Margiela described itself in a mock dictionary definition as making 'garments for women from ready-to-wear fashion to unique pieces (Artisanal collection)…Known for its taste for recovery and recycling of materials. May go as far as to reuse an existing garment (Replicas).'[1] Its founder, Belgian designer Martin Margiela, was an early exponent of recycling used clothing, which has remained a consistent theme throughout his work. Early 'Artisanal' pieces included a sweater made from old army socks (1991), and a vest made from discarded gloves (2001). More recent examples have utilized plastic garment tags to simulate the texture of a fur coat, and moulded old leather sandals or reptile-skin bags into jackets. The 'Artisanal' collection of one-off pieces produced each season is the Maison's answer to haute couture, replicating its labour-intensive nature, but using mundane waste materials rather than expensive high-quality fabrics. In this collection the notion of 'luxury' refers instead to the number of hours of labour invested in a specific garment; these figures were prominently displayed in the exhibition alongside the pieces.

Right: 'Shades of Denim', Spring/Summer 2009. Vintage jeans in various shades of denim are cut in strips and applied to an asymmetrical denim overall. Hours: 38; materials: denim jeans (7–8 pairs).

Opposite: 'Kite Tunic', Spring/Summer 2009. Hours: 35; materials: kite, 20 m of viscose fringes.

Textile recycling in the UK

ALAN WHEELER *is national liaison officer for the Textile Recycling Association (UK).*

A few years ago recycling of any waste stream was still viewed as something only environmentalists or eccentric people did. Now, with the UK's national recycling rate at around 35–40%, it is something that most people engage in. The public wants to know more about how and where it can recycle not just clothing but also other textiles. The collection of used clothing has increased sharply in recent years from about 300,000 tonnes in 2006 to over 500,000 tonnes today.

We are receiving increasing numbers of enquiries from businesses looking to recycle both their pre-consumer textile waste (usually offcuts resulting from a manufacturing product) and post-consumer waste (e.g. uniforms) as they attempt to improve their environmental credentials. As the Association only deals with post-consumer recycling, enquiries about pre-consumer waste are referred to fibre-reclamation merchants. About 60% of all clothing collected is suitable for reuse. The vast majority is exported and most of the remaining items are sent for

recycling, some of which takes place offshore. One of the barriers to higher-quality recycling is the lack of homogeneity in the fibres used in the manufacture of textile products. While it is technically possible to recycle mixed fibres into composite products that perform to a high standard, it is virtually impossible to source a homogeneous fibre for recycling that would allow you to manufacture that product on a commercial scale. Products made from mixed fibres therefore have to be used in lower-grade applications such as mattress filling or insulation.

Recycling in the UK and Europe

The UK performs reasonably well in textile recycling compared to other countries. Unlike many other countries in Western Europe, Britain has an established network of textile banks and charity shops, which have been part of the national psyche for years. So at least some people have always donated their clothing to 'charity' (or the commercial fundraising arm of a charity). In recent years the number of door-to-door collections has increased significantly.

If you compare the UK with France, which has a similar-sized population, estimates from FEDEREC (the French recycling federation) put the textile collection rate at less than half that of the UK. However, representatives from BVSE (formerly Fachverband), the equivalent German organization, estimate that around 85% of clothing and textiles is collected in Germany. At the same time they cite significant problems with the quality of the textiles they are collecting.[1]

The current textile-recycling system in the UK is adequate but could be improved. As the number of charity shops is probably near its maximum and all of the best sites for textile banks are probably occupied, the area where significant improvement can be made is through door-to-door collections. These are convenient and popular with the public, but there are significant issues, including bogus charity collectors, which have to be addressed. A revised code of practice for charitable door-to-door collections has now been developed and other initiatives are underway, but there is a need to review the licensing regulations

Right: Salvation Army badged clothing banks in the UK.

The public is not aware that the significant majority of used clothing donated to charity is not sold in charity shops.

surrounding them. If you collect clothing and textiles mixed in with other waste, there will be no market for the clothing and it will have to be dumped. But as long as textiles are kept separate and dry, there should be no problem in securing a market for them.

The Recycling Value Chain

There is a general perception that if you donate an item to a charity shop or put it in a textile bank, the charity will either sell it in that shop or somehow use it directly for a philanthropic cause in a developing country. The public is not aware that the significant majority of used clothing donated to charity is not sold in charity shops, yet what really happens to the rest is something that is very positive and should be celebrated. Much of the donated clothing is sold by charities to their textile collection partners, who then export the goods for resale in Africa or Eastern Europe. This promotes reuse over recycling, resulting in significant environmental benefits; it helps charities to generate substantial income; it creates employment both here and abroad; and it allows people in poorer countries to buy good quality, desirable garments.

Looking to the future, all the players in the clothing industry – including fibre manufacturers, garment producers, retailers and those involved in reuse and recycling – need to consider how to reduce their environmental impacts. While the export of used clothing should not be discouraged, we also need to encourage more clothing to be reused domestically and for potential new markets to be established for different recycling grades.

Above left: A typical selection of discarded clothing is emptied from a clothing bank.

Left: Sacks of waste clothing are bundled into bales at the Salvation Army Trading warehouse in Northamptonshire.

Everything Must Go

LUCY NORRIS, *an anthropologist, and* **TIM MITCHELL**, *a documentary photographer, travelled to India to research the journey of discarded clothing from the UK and the domestic recycling of saris in India. The resulting exhibition, 'Everything Must Go', was shown in London in 2012.*

Although we are encouraged to give our clothing to charities or put it into textile bins, we know little about what happens to it. About 60% is exported to growing markets in Eastern Europe, Africa and South Asia. Our used clothing is in demand – the UK export trade was officially worth $42.5 million in 2010.[1] Cotton clothing is torn up into industrial wipers, while winter clothing is shredded and used as

flocking or recycled into shoddy yarn. The world's largest textile recycling centre is in Panipat, north of Delhi.[2] Over 300 mills reclaim fibres from old clothing, spin them into shoddy yarn, and weave them into blankets, shawls and fabric. Most of these are low-quality items for the poorest Indian consumers, but the mills also manufacture 90% of the emergency relief blankets used by international aid agencies. However,

some of these recycled products contain unrefined waste oils and are often bulked out with salt and starch to increase their weight. The industry employs about 70,000 people, but workers are subcontracted, and pay and working conditions are poor, especially for women. Most clothing worn in India never ends up on the rubbish heaps, which are nonetheless scavenged by ragpickers.[3] It is used and reused until it

Most clothing worn in India never ends up on the rubbish heaps ... it is used and reused until it literally wears out.

literally wears out, handed down to younger siblings and domestic servants. However, as the consumption of new clothing grows, Waghri traders from Gujarat operate a thriving market in second-hand clothing across north India. Middle-class families barter their used clothes for new kitchen utensils, and the traders then sell them on to the poorer labouring classes. More valuable fabrics, such as used saris, are remade into Western fashions.

Opposite: Wastesavers, Oxfam's sorting warehouse in Huddersfield, UK, is unusual in that it is run by the charity itself. Other charities sell surplus clothing to commercial textile recyclers, or collect royalties for allowing recyclers to use their name on textile banks.

Above: Tonnes of imported clothing are sorted into general colour 'families' in a warehouse in north India. The quality of recycled shoddy yarn depends upon the extent to which the clothes are fine-sorted by fibre and colour.

Above: Recycled acrylic yarn can be woven into vibrant blankets on jacquard and dobby looms, with complex multicolour designs including vases of flowers, animals and abstract patterns.

Above: A wholesale market for used Indian clothing in a New Delhi suburb. Up to 2,000 dealers buy and sell old clothes every day, with traders who specialize in certain garments selling them on in weekly markets across Delhi and in surrounding towns.

'The need is for change now, but how can we moderate designers' thoughts and actions?'

GARTH WARD, *former head of business development at the Salvation Army Trading Company and owner of recycling consultancy Aestiva Ltd, discusses the changed textile-recycling landscape with Sandy Black.*

Q Charity shops and their role have changed significantly in the past decade – what do you think are the key factors in this? Do you consider the boom of cheap fashion retailers influential?

A Today there are more charities operating professionally managed shops in prime high-street locations than there were in the 1990s. This has increased competition, and, although turnover has also increased, profit generally appears to be steady. The 'value' retailers have affected the second-hand industry in two main ways. The first is in direct price competition: which would you prefer to buy and wear – a second-hand good-quality item for £1–5 or a new but lower-quality one at the same price? The second is that, due to the reduction in the quality of the clothing, the proportion of donated clothes suitable for sale in the charity shop has declined. This has meant that charity shops no longer rely on second-hand clothes but sell books, music, furniture and electrical goods as well.

When I started working with Salvation Army Trading in 1991, my knowledge of textile recycling was limited to childhood memories of the 'rag-and-bone' man. As I grew more involved with the day-to-day operation of the UK's largest collector of second-hand clothes, I became aware that innovation in this well-established industry was sadly lacking; indeed, the most recent documented radical innovation took place about 200 years ago when Benjamin Law introduced 'shoddy & mungoe' methodologies. Most current innovations in the industry are related to developing more efficient infrastructures.

You refer to the existing approach as 'cradle-to-grave'. Can you comment on this?

I am not a designer, just a relatively intelligent member of the public, but it seems to me that designers in all walks of life tend to be narrowly focused. Together with their marketing colleagues they have identified a need for Product X; they then, naturally, focus on satisfying that need in

the most fashionable, efficient and/or economic manner. Generally this means their product has a single use and usually it is not suitable for re-processing into something 'new'. In other words it is created, used and then discarded, generally into the rubbish bin. Today designers may also consider sustainability, but I'm not sure that this word is completely understood; indeed I'm not sure what it really means, as it is used in so many differing situations. In the textile field I have seen organic cotton referred to as 'sustainable', but is it? How much water does it use? Fair trade is often included, too, but in reality this refers to paying fair prices, not necessarily using sustainable practices. Sustainability really involves a series of trade-offs, but of what against what? The clothes that we wear naturally need to look good, to provide the wearer with that feel-good factor, but designers still need to think in more depth about this. They need to completely re-examine how they design and fabricate clothing by considering the first, second and even tertiary uses. They must understand fibre, its production and its many uses, not just in clothing. 'End of first life' also needs to be in the equation; for instance, single-fibre items are much easier to reprocess than those using multiple types of fibres.

Establishing a cradle-to-cradle system in fashion would be an incredibly complex process. Where do you think the starting point is?

This really is the nub! The need is for change now, but how can we moderate designers' thoughts and actions? This will have to start in the design colleges so that resource efficiency is part of the curriculum, which means ensuring that lecturers understand these needs and concepts so they can teach them. How well this is addressed will dictate the speed of change.

Do you see any new thinking present in the mainstream fashion industry?

My experiences in this field are limited, but from

my observations, the 'new' thinking does not appear to be there. New fibres such as bamboo, and Lyocell from eucalyptus trees, are of course being developed. But, again, it appears that they are often combined with other fibres, thus severely limiting any potential for reprocessing.

Some fashion retailers encourage recycling through schemes that involve incentives for a consumer to purchase more. What is your view on this?

From the standpoint of both a charity shop and a commercial retailer this makes sense, especially economically, with both parties receiving benefit. However, one of its major effects is to encourage a rise in the number of clothes in circulation, thus increasing the pressure on collection schemes, waste disposal and, therefore, the environment. Should resource efficiency, improved methods of disassembly and cradle-to-cradle thinking be taken up, it would moderate such schemes so that the used and discarded clothes, with certain provisos, could potentially become 'raw' material capable of being reprocessed into something new, i.e. representing a new potential profit.

Where do you see the future for charity shops?

It will be obvious that there has already been significant change in this retail sector. This is good news as it demonstrates that change can be incorporated and dealt with by charity shops. Change is coming to the commercial clothing retailer too, as concerns for the environment develop within the buying public. This will greatly assist the second-hand market, and could become a very powerful marketing tool if it is handled correctly! Charity-shop openings are still on the increase at an encouraging rate, although not as fast as before. This should continue for the foreseeable future. However, the sector will need to be continually aware of the necessity for change. Research into automated disassembly technologies and improvements in garment design could mean that cradle-to-cradle concepts become the norm. This may provide new opportunities to develop additional markets using recycled fibres. The future looks good but, as Albert Einstein said, 'The world we have created today…has problems which cannot be solved by thinking the way we thought when we created them.'

Could you comment on the impact of the export of second-hand clothes on developing countries?
Over the years several third-party reports have been published – from the US, Sweden and the UK. They all agree that exporting second-hand clothes to developing countries is beneficial to all; indeed, no significant adverse effects were noted. From my own knowledge the benefits are legion: it creates employment; it makes good-quality clothing available to that country's residents at affordable prices; it enables governments to collect duty from the importers of second-hand clothing and thus help their economy; it also makes a significant contribution to reducing the EU's carbon footprint.

Could we recover more fibres from reused clothing?
Fabric choice and garment design significantly influence our ability to reuse and reprocess clothing, as well as controlling their environmental impact on disposal. Nevertheless, processed recycled fibre can be a valuable secondary resource – research and development has already taken place to identify several potential industrial uses. However, for this to be economically viable, automated disassembly techniques need to become operational, and this in turn will mean that modifications to present fabrication methodologies need to be incorporated into mainstream garment construction. Happily, research into this area is well advanced.

Do you think that the general public perception of recycling is limited or out of date?
My thoughts do not coincide with some of the current mainstream concepts. 'Remember, Reduce, Reuse, Recycle' is a useful tool, because recycling is something we can all do and it helps to bring home to all of us the need to look after our world more

'Companies need to understand that approaching products from this standpoint will not necessarily increase their costs. but…may actually increase their profits'

effectively. Huge sums of money have been spent on these concepts and recycling rates continue to increase, but this approach only addresses symptoms, not the true source of the problem. Our natural resources are under pressure and require careful management; therefore when we design items consideration must be given to using the materials more than once. Naturally this brings with it producer responsibility and the need to understand all production steps, from the way the raw material is grown or obtained, to the effects of everyday use (such as washing, drying and ironing) and how the item can be disassembled and its component parts re-manufactured. Companies need to understand that approaching products from this standpoint will not necessarily increase their costs, but, handled correctly, may actually increase their profits: for instance, virgin cotton costs about £1,000 per tonne, but reclaimed fibre from second-hand clothes is estimated to cost only £640 per tonne.[1]

Techno
eco

New fashion
paradigms

Fashion and technology

Personalization and customization

Page 272: Manel Torres, 'Space Dress', 2009, using his Fabrican spray-on fabric technology to apply recycled white clothing fibres, appropriately recovered from used lab coats, directly to the wearer's body.

Page 273: Manel Torres, Fabrican fashion show of one-off designs created by spraying the fibres directly onto models wearing frames, London, September 2010.

Virtual fashion

Future textiles and fashion

Fashion and technology are becoming close bedfellows, from the way fashion is communicated and offered for sale via digital media and online platforms, to the way the garments themselves are manufactured and function for the wearer. Technological innovations increasingly allow textiles and clothing to be interactive – able to respond to both the wearer and the external environment.

Although fashion is still largely a skilled craft-based industry, fashion manufacturing is increasingly making use of the ongoing advances in digital, engineering and chemical technology. Research that has taken decades to mature is leaving the scientific laboratory and finding its way into both functional clothing and haute couture. The entertainment industry has been quick to take up the new opportunities for visual display and performance offered by clothing with embedded electronics, such as CuteCircuit's 'GalaxyDress' (see p. 315) and the similar illuminated outfit it produced for singer Katy Perry in 2010.

This chapter looks at how such emerging technologies can support the creation of more sustainable clothing and textiles, not only in manufacturing and design, but also in how we experience fashion as consumers, from shopping for clothes to how we actually wear them. This includes Sue Jenkyn Jones and Julia Gaimster's overviews of developments in virtual fashion and its interactions with the real world, and an essay by Agnes Rocamora and Djurdja Bartlett on the rise of the fashion blog. The case study of Fits.me and a commentary by Susan Ashdown show how digitized clothes can be fitted virtually to the wearer's body, giving real potential for waste to be reduced through better fitting clothes. The emergence of personalization and mass customization is outlined by Frank Piller and Frank Steiner, producing a form of 'digital bespoke' tailoring seen in action in the profile of Nutters of Savile Row. In addition to eliminating the waste of time, energy and textiles associated with ill-fitting clothes, such individually customized products may give the wearer greater satisfaction and a stronger emotional bond with the garment, meaning that it is likely to be used for many years, rather than discarded after a single season.

This chapter also examines a number of potentially paradigm-shifting innovations, such as direct digital 3-D manufacturing, which is predicted to offer designers and even consumers one-stop onsite manufacturing via devices similar to desktop printers, saving manufacturing and transport costs. New methods of creating fabrics, such as Manel Torres's spray-on Fabrican and Suzanne Lee's enzyme-grown BioCouture, offer more sustainably processed and flexible solutions to producing clothing, as does the use of biomimicry and nanotechnology in fabrics discussed by Veronika Kapsali and Richard Jones. The chapter concludes with four Future Scenarios for the fashion industry in 2025 and beyond as food for thought.

High-performance outdoor clothing

By Sandy Black

The quest to bring functional technologies to clothing began in the 1980s. Now, second- and third-generation products have been launched on the market, utilizing a range of technologies that include inbuilt heating elements and controls for mobile hand-held devices. Peratech's QTC (quantum tunneling composite) coatings give pressure-sensing and switching functions; solar panels collect renewable energy to power small batteries; micro- and nano-scale fibre engineering uses biomimicry to develop permeability and moisture-wicking qualities. These improvements in performance are beginning to be combined with attention to end-of-life issues such as design for disassembly. Luxury brand Zegna's (see pp. 234–35) solar-powered high-performance 'Ecotech' and 'Ecotene' jackets are made using recycled synthetic materials. Surfwear company Finisterre is another maker of high-performance clothing that aims to minimize environmental impact through technical research into materials and fibres; their efforts include breeding sheep to produce a British version of merino wool and developing recycled fibres for insulating fillings.

Above: Zegna Sport 'Ecotech' solar jacket, Autumn/Winter 2009–10. Entirely made from recycled materials (100% polyester), the jacket incorporates solar cell technology on each sleeve to power a heated collar or charge a mobile device.

Left: Tommy Hilfiger outdoor sportswear jacket with iPod controls on the outer sleeve and an inbuilt heating system, functionalized using Peratech QTC technology.

Opposite: Finisterre 'Stormtrack' jacket, 2009. Technical features for enhanced durability and waterproofing qualities include a lining with fibre-density gradients that mimic the hydrophobic plastron layers of natural fur, and an outer shell made from Teijin closed-loop polyester.

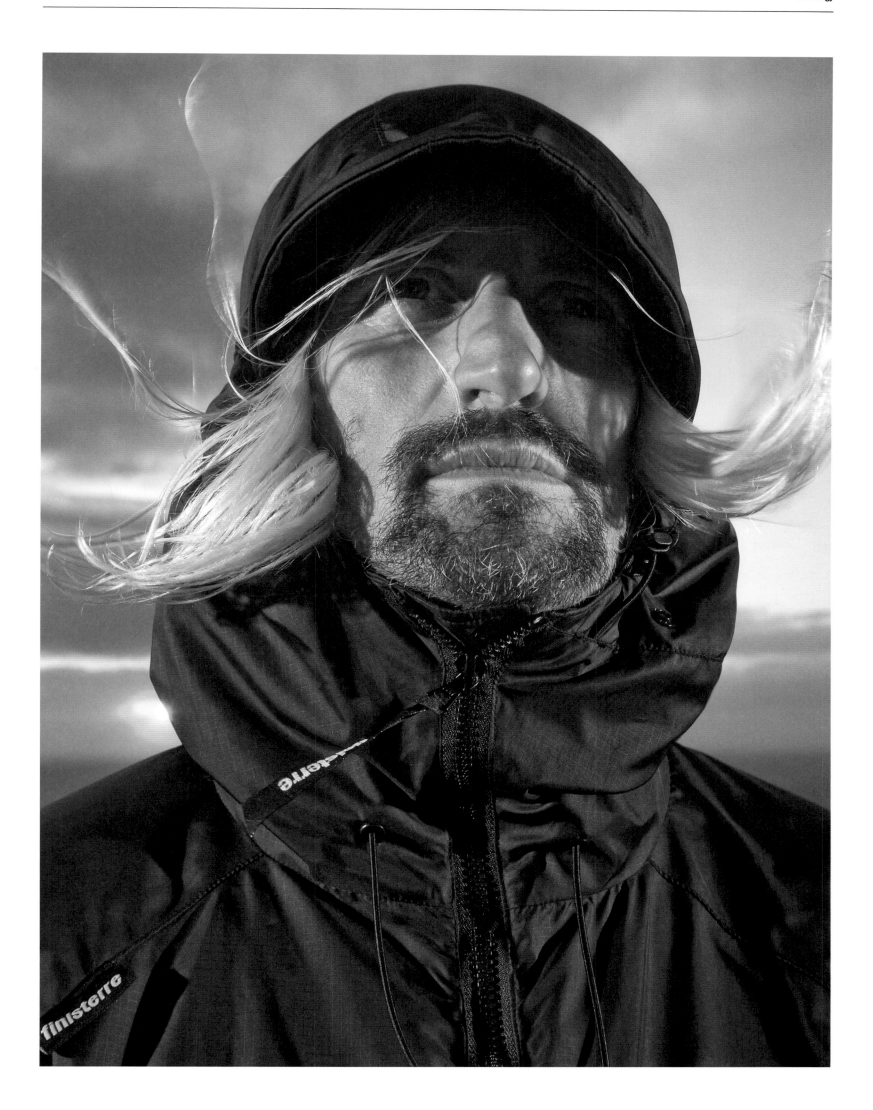

Nature as a paradigm for sustainability in the textile and apparel industry

VERONIKA KAPSALI *has studied both fashion and mechanical engineering, and is reader in biomimetics at Northumbria University.*

The functional profile of clothing and apparel is in the midst of reform. The boom in material science over the last twenty-five years has triggered a wave of new technologies that could have been extracted from science fiction. From composites that can alter their properties in response to stimuli to the manipulation of molecules on a nano-scale, many of these innovations have already been adopted by the textile industry and applied to other sectors, including defence, agriculture and medicine. Experimentation with clothing applications has begun to redefine the boundaries between garment and wearer and the role of clothing in users' lives.

Since 2000 there has been significant growth in this field. Innovations from a jacket that can couple with a mobile phone or MP3 player through to self-cleaning garments are accessible to consumers. With many more in prototype stage, the future promises a huge influx of new functionalities that will add to the repertoire of conventional clothing properties. The questions on many critics' lips are these: Do we need these new functionalities? Is there a consumer pull for this technology push?

Many factors are contributing to the purposeful integration of new technology into existing product groups. The key is that new technology must offer a solution or at least improve on a problem that cannot be solved using conventional methods. If we broaden our focus from the products on the shop floor to the key issues dominating the clothing sector, opportunities for innovation become apparent. The sustainability of existing practice within the industry is not a new issue; aspects have been surfacing and capturing media attention for decades. But there is far more public awareness of these issues now than there was even five years ago. Can new technology offer solutions? Are there any useful new paradigms?

'Biomimetics' is a term coined by the polymath Otto Schmitt in the 1930s to describe an electronic feedback circuit he designed to function similarly to neural networks as part of his doctoral thesis. Over the following decades synonyms such as 'bionic', 'biomimesis', 'biomimicry' and 'biognosis' cropped up to describe developments inspired by the functional aspects of biological structures. A compound word of Greek origin (*bio* meaning 'life', *mimesis* meaning 'to copy'), biomimetics describes the interpolation of natural mechanisms and structures into the man-made world.

The concept of biomimetics is not entirely novel to the textile industry; in fact it was attempts to recreate the properties of natural materials that resulted in the advent of the man-made fibre industry. The properties of silk have been the object of human obsession for centuries; efforts to synthesize a material imitating silk's strength, fineness and lustre date as far back as 3000 BC in China. It wasn't until the early 20th century that these efforts were successful, however; the first man-made silk-like fibre was mass-produced in the 1900s. Rayon imitated the lustre of silk but lacked its strength. During the 1930s the invention and consequent mass production of nylon by DuPont caused an unprecedented revolution in the clothing and textile industry as it provided a more successful alternative to silk that was both fine and incredibly strong.

The synthetic-fibres industry enjoyed a boom until the 1970s, when garments made from them began to fall out of favour and demand increased for clothing made from natural materials. The advantages of products made from the 'new' materials – such as ultra-fine, inexpensive stockings and quick-drying, no-iron clothing – were eclipsed by the technology's unforeseen shortcomings, including static, itchiness and a lack of breathability.

Biomimetic developments today are the product of collaborative work between the fields of biology and engineering. The conceptual link between the two disciplines is based on the use of available resources and energy. In nature, plants and animals live in competition with each other for access to limited

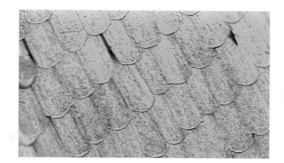
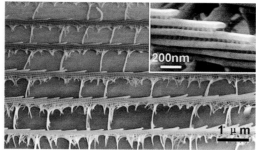

resources. Successful species evolve ways of living and reproducing using the fewest possible resources, which can only be enabled by clever design and optimal distribution of raw materials. This level of design optimization is what attracts engineers to search for paradigms in biology. Bearing in mind the greater cost to the environment in the construction of man-made products, nature can offer ideas for developing cleverly designed, low-energy materials and structures. If we look at the way materials and structures are formed, sustained and recycled in nature, we have a simple model that can offer ideas to improve practice in the clothing and apparel industry.

Often the most energy-intensive and wasteful processes occur before the garment reaches the consumer, the key area being fibre production and processing. Both natural and man-made fibres rely on high levels of resources such as energy (temperature, pressure) and water, as well as the use of toxic chemicals (such as fertilizers and insecticides in the case of natural fibres), to acquire grades of fibre suitable for use in textiles for clothing in terms of both quality and cost. Resource-heavy processes have replaced traditional low-energy methods to increase production and reduce cost, the processing of flax being just one example. Flax fibres have traditionally been separated from the stem and leaf by hand retting (i.e. the removal of seeds and leaves) in ditches, a low-energy process relying on the natural rotting of plant parts. In order to speed up this process to increase productivity, systems using chemicals and hot water have been introduced and are widely used.[1]

There are cases where low-energy alternatives have been developed to reduce the environmental cost of fibre processing. Colonies of enzymes, which thrive in damp yet mild conditions, are regularly used to clean and prime fibre surfaces for further processing such as dyeing and finishing. This process usually requires the use of hot water and harsh chemicals. Enzymes are also used in later stages of finishing to replace energy-intensive processes such as stone- and sand-washing.

Structural Colour

The use and production of surface coloration in natural materials can offer ideas for alternative methods to the highly toxic processes used today. One of the most polluting aspects of the textile industry is the hazardous chemicals used for printing and dyeing.[2] Pigment has been used to colour fibres and cloth for thousands of years. Morphotex™ by Japan's Teijin Fibers Ltd is a biomimetic innovation offering a non-toxic alternative in the form of a fibre that demonstrates structural colour. The design is based on the wings of South American morpho butterflies, which use the interference of reflected light to generate colour; this process is managed by the morphology of the biological surface.[3] Researchers at Teijin created a fibre composed of sixty-one alternating nylon and polyester layers capable of producing basic colours such as blue, green and red without the use of pigments.

Design versus Material

In nature materials are formed using minimal amounts of energy and rely on the resources found in their immediate environment. Plants, for instance, need nutrients from the soil, some sunlight and water. Imagine if we could 'grow' materials – it sounds like an idea from a science fiction narrative. Donna Franklin and Suzanne Lee share one such vision; both are investigating methods of growing garments using the cellulose-producing bacteria *Acetobacter xylinum*. This method is already being used on a commercial scale to produce biocellulose for the food, pharmaceutical and paper industries. Although both Lee's and Franklin's work is at a very early stage, it suggests possibilities for alternative methods of producing textiles and indeed garments (see pp. 310–11).

Cellulose, an abundant natural polymer, forms the basis of all plant structures. Cotton and flax fibres are both made from cellulose polymers, yet their properties are very different; generally, cotton fibres are weaker, more absorbent and more resistant to creasing than flax fibres.[4] Flax fibres come from the plant stem and need to be stiffer and stronger in order to support the structure, while cotton fibres come from

Above left and centre: Two microscopic images of the wings of the morpho butterfly, showing the overlapping scale structure (*left*) and the detailed surface morphology of the wing (*centre*), which refracts light in the blue spectrum.

Above right: Morphotex™ fabric made by Teijin, incorporating structural colour modelled on the morpho butterfly wing to produce a fabric that does not need to be dyed.

Above: Water-repellent wool fabric coated with the Nanosphere finish developed by Swiss company Schoeller.

the plant bud and do not need to be strong. These differences in mechanical properties are due to a range of factors involving the distribution of cellulose within the fibre cell, as well as the fibre's morphology. Similarly, while silk and wool are both made from proteins, one is long, fine and very strong, the other short, curly and a lot thicker. So they have very different properties.

The functional properties of biological materials are engineered through the design and distribution of their basic building blocks.[5] There are only two polymers in the natural world – protein and polysaccharide – whose structural variations offer a range of properties, such as stiffness, strength or elasticity, to larger formations such as natural cellulose (a type of polysaccharide) and protein fibres.[6] It is a completely different story in the man-made world. Conventional engineering relies on the properties of materials to deliver desired functions. Usually whenever a new property is required a new material is synthesized; as a result there are over 300 man-made polymers currently available. In terms of the clothing industry, the key problem arising from products made from a variety of raw materials is end of life.

The industry has for a long time recycled certain textile fibres and reintroduced them into clothing products. For example, recycled wool fibres are used in garments labelled 100% wool, whereas new non-recycled fibres are present if the composition states 'virgin wool'. In the Autumn/Winter 2007–8 season, Italian textile mill Figli di Michelangelo Calamai (founded in 1878) began to produce commercial volumes of fine single jersey from recycled cotton. Generally speaking, however, recycled fibres of mixed or unknown origin create fabrics that are bulkier and of low aesthetic value; quality fibres can only be reclaimed from 100% compositions. DuPont is attempting to create garments of 100% man-made fibre compositions in order to address this issue. Using their biodegradable polymer Apexa®, which can be melt-spun into fibres and also made into buttons, zips, tape and so on, it will be possible to produce synthetic-fibre garment systems from a single polymer.

Survival depends greatly on the structure's ability to adapt to the changing demands of the environment: some key properties are self-assembly, reproduction, self-repair and redistribution of vital resources.

Meanwhile researchers at the Centre for Biomimetics at the University of Reading have found that the insulating properties of down feathers are not due to the material composing the feathers but to its structure. A range of down feathers are being studied to understand the functional properties of this structural design in order to interpret the mechanism into a man-made equivalent. This could be made from any textile polymer and could effectively support the production of 100% single-polymer garments.

Materials and structures in nature need to be multifunctional without relying on a range of esoteric materials. Structural design features are a key tool for introducing additional properties. Surface texture, for instance, can evolve to provide water-resistant properties to a plant or animal. Functional surfaces often occur on the upper surface of a leaf, where they protect the plant from contamination; the lotus is well known for this property. The nano-scale proprietary finishing treatment Lotus Effect™ was inspired by the protective mechanism used by the lotus leaf and is by far the most popular biomimetic technology to have permeated the clothing sector. The technology was developed by German botanists W. Barthlott and C. Neinhuis, who discovered that the plants' self-cleaning properties were due to the surface morphology of their leaves.[7] This innovation, originally adopted by the paint industry to produce self-cleaning masonry paint, later found additional application in the clothing sector in the form of stain- and soil-resistant finishes.

Technologies such as Lotus Effect™ reduce the need for frequent washing, thus also reducing the resources necessary to maintain garments during use. The coating of fibres or textiles with compounds made from silicone or organofluorochemicals is one method that is currently being employed to protect garments from soiling and staining, but these substances are highly toxic.[8] Lotus Effect™ is an environmentally sound alternative. Enabled by nanotechnology, it offers a low-energy, low-pollution alternative to its silicone or organofluorochemical counterparts.

The Future

There is a fundamental difference between the nature of materials in biology and those of the man-made world. The biological organism creates the material or structure, which is defined partly by DNA and partly by the environment – 'nature and nurture'. Survival depends greatly on the structure's ability to adapt to the changing demands of the environment: some key properties are self-assembly, reproduction, self-repair and redistribution of vital resources. Man-made materials and structures are fabricated entirely by external efforts. Therefore the design brief is predetermined and aims to satisfy a specific set of requirements, which remain unaltered during a product's useful life. Once its original purpose is fulfilled, the object and its components become redundant unless it can be incorporated into some sort of recycling stream.

Just imagine if our textiles and clothing were able to adapt, change and self-repair. In today's throwaway society consumers are more likely to replace an item of clothing once it is damaged than to repair it. The additional resources necessary for repair such as cost, time, skill and availability of materials are generally not considered worthwhile to prolong the useful life of a particular item of clothing. In nature, plant and animals are able to self-repair or heal without the additional input of resources. Instead available resources are redistributed within the organism to address and resolve the damage. Although clothing able to repair internal structural damage may be reserved for the distant future, a self-healing membrane has been developed based on the structure of the vine *Aristolochia macrophylla*. It is possible that technology arising from this type of enquiry could be implemented into clothing structure in the future.

Adaptive or reactive shape change is an innovation that has been realized in conceptual and prototype garments. Several types of technology have enabled this to happen. In his Spring/Summer 2007 catwalk show, designer Hussein Chalayan explored mechanical methods using complex substructures and electronics to achieve clothing shape change. Chalayan's creations alter their length

The study of plants and animals is an ongoing process that offers a level of understanding of the world around us. from structure. function. growth and evolution to distribution. Biomimetics enables aspects of this knowledge to become technology.

and volume, suggesting garments that can modify their shape to suit different occasions, thus extending their usefulness.

Developments in shape-memory alloys and polymers allow a more seamless integration of technology and product. It is currently possible to spin smart alloys into fibres suitable for use in garments. In June 2001, Grade Zero Espace (a Corpo Nove spinoff company in Italy) successfully incorporated an alloy called Nitinol into a woven textile branded Oricalco. A prototype shirt manufactured using this textile is able to shorten its sleeves if the ambient temperature rises above a certain point. However, the cost of the Nitinol prohibited the commercial production of Oricalco; the production cost of the shirt prototype was estimated at $3,500. Other companies that experiment with shape-memory materials are Ebru Kurbak, Ricardo O'Nascimento and XS Labs at Concordia University in Montreal (led by Joey Berzowska).

SM polymers are considered to be a much cheaper alternative to Nitinol. Currently in development stage, they present another set of technical issues that need to be resolved before they can be applied to textiles and clothing. The key issues have to do with durability and processing that would allow the use of existing production methods.

Colour and pattern change is also an important area of research. Certain animals rely on these mechanisms for protection and communication. Chameleons are reptiles famous for their ability to take on the colours and patterns of their surroundings and become 'invisible'. Cephalopods (such as octopuses) use the surface of their skin to create complex visual displays, which can change within seconds. This is enabled by a sophisticated mechanism involving the use of both pigment and structural coloration.

It has been possible to create garments that can alter their colour in response to changing temperature since the 1990s, when T-shirts featuring thermochromic dyes flooded the market under the label 'Global Hypercolor'. Poor design and technology application relegated these products to the category of novelty items or gimmicks. Recently, sophisticated combinations of temperature-sensitive pigments with conductive yarns and LEDs have created textiles that deliver a series of changing visual displays. Designers exploring applications are Keri Wallace, International Fashion Machines, CuteCircuit, Philips Design and Suzi Webster.

In 2007 E. Thomas of the Massachusetts Institute of Technology led the team that invented a smart gel able to alter its colour in response to environmental stimuli such as moisture, temperature and pH. The mechanism is based on the way cephalopods alter areas of their skin structure to manipulate the light reflected off the surface and thus alter colour. Although this technology is in its infancy, several approaches are being explored that promise to deliver colour-changing clothing in the future. If a single garment could alter its appearance, it would be suitable for use in a range of

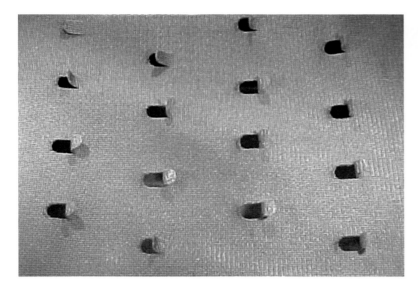 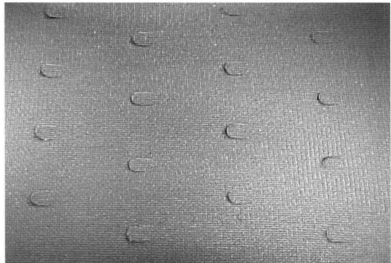

Above: Textile prototype based on the opening and closing mechanism of pinecones, showing the u-shaped vents open in dry conditions (*left*); in damp conditions the vents close and the textile becomes water-resistant (*right*).

circumstances. Effectively one could own as little as a single T-shirt that could appear different upon demand.

Imagine if a clothing system were able to adapt its insulation/ventilation properties in response to wearers' needs. In 1997 a team of biomimetic scientists at the University of Reading created a prototype textile system whose design was based on the opening and closing mechanism of a pinecone. A pinecone opens its structure in dry conditions and closes in damp ones. A composite textile was developed using a lightweight synthetic woven structure laminated onto a non-porous polyurethane membrane. Small U-shaped perforations were cut into the surface of the material (see illustration on p. 283). An increase in relative humidity causes the polyurethane film to swell. As a consequence the loose sections of fabric created by the incisions curl back, increasing the air permeability of the textile system.

Nike has developed a similar bilayer composite system that (instead of a textile/membrane system) uses two layers of knitted or woven cloth with different swelling properties (US patent application no. 2005208860). Maria Sharapova wore a tennis dress incorporating the active textile system during the 2006 US Open Championship. This composite textile can be a knitted or woven structure made from a hygroscopic yarn next to the skin. The top layer is made of a non-hygroscopic or non-swelling yarn; U-shaped perforations are created using either conventional slicing techniques or by laser cutting. As the wearer perspires, the base layer swells while the top layer remains unaltered. As a result the loose sections of textile curl back just like the structure developed at Reading. This mechanism has been further developed by a private UK-based research-and-development company called MMT Textiles Ltd, which is applying it to yarns and developing a range of commercial prototypes.

The study of plants and animals is an ongoing process that offers a level of understanding of the world around us, from structure, function, growth and evolution to distribution. Biomimetics

functions as a platform that enables aspects of this knowledge to become technology. Initial outcomes include design-based solutions such as Lotus Effect™, Morphotex™ and pinecone-inspired textiles. The future may hold paradigms for sustainable manufacture as suggested by the work of Suzanne Lee and Donna Franklin. Ideally this type of research will lead to innovations that require only slight modifications to existing technology.

There is a longstanding trend in fashion future-gazing towards multifunctional design. The benefits are obvious: one product, multiple applications. This area needs to be explored with caution if consumers are to experience benefits. Several companies have explored products that can transform into something else. In 2000–1, C. P. Company developed a collection branded 'transformables', in which clothing could become tents, cushions, armchairs and the like. Multifunctional design can also be realized through the concept of modular clothing, which dates back to the 1980s. The idea is to have a wardrobe of interconnecting pieces that can be added, subtracted and styled up or down to suit any occasion. However, none of these modular concepts has really caught on, perhaps because the design ambitions compromise the aesthetic outcome or because consumers are not convinced of the products' usefulness.

If new technology is going to be integrated into clothing and accepted by the consumer, fashion-conscious or not, the innovation must not interfere with the aesthetic outcome. In other words it needs to be invisible; otherwise it is in danger of becoming a gimmick. Is it possible to have multifunctional clothing that looks like ordinary clothing? When applied to textiles, the Lotus Effect™ can render any garment water-, soil- and/or stain-resistant, yet the difference between a treated and untreated sample is invisible. Functional surfaces are just one area of biomimetics that can offer additional properties to garments (mainly in care and maintenance). In the future, adaptive textiles will alter their properties to accommodate the needs of the wearer in a subtle, non-intrusive and useful manner.

Debating nanotechnologies

PROFESSOR RICHARD JONES *is pro-vice-chancellor for research and innovation at the University of Sheffield, with research interests that include the social and ethical implications of nanotechnology*

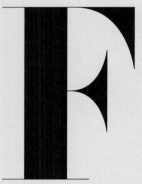

Few new technologies have been accompanied by such expansive promises of their potential to change the world as nanotechnology. Governments and multinationals around the world view nanotechnology as a future engine of economic growth, while campaigning groups foresee environmental degradation and a widening of the gap between the rich and poor. At the heart of these arguments lies a striking lack of consensus about what the technology is or will be, what it will make possible and what its dangers might be.

Nanotechnology is not a single technology in the way that nuclear technology, agricultural biotechnology, or semiconductor technology are. There is, as yet, no distinctive class of artefacts that can be unambiguously labelled as the product of nanotechnology. It is still, by and large, an activity carried out in laboratories rather than factories.

What unites the rather disparate group of applied sciences that are referred to as nanotechnologies is simply the length-scale on which they operate. Nanotechnology concerns the creation and manipulation of objects whose size lies somewhere between a nanometre and a few hundred nanometres. To put these numbers in context, it's worth remembering that as humans, the largest objects we can manipulate unaided are about a metre or so in size, while the smallest objects we can manipulate comfortably are about one millimetre. With the aid of light microscopes and tools for micromanipulation, we can also operate on another set of smaller lengthscales, which also span a factor of a thousand. The upper end of the microscale is thus defined by a millimetre, while the lower end is defined by objects about a micron in size. This is roughly the size of a red blood cell or a typical bacterium, and is about the smallest object that can be easily discerned in a light microscope.

The nanoscale is smaller yet. A micron is one thousand nanometres, and one nanometre (nm) is about the size of a medium size molecule. So we can think of the lower limit of the nanoscale as being defined by the size of individual atoms and molecules, while the upper limit is defined by the resolution limits of light microscopes (this limit is somewhat more vague, and one sometimes sees apparently more exact definitions, such as 100 nm, but in my view these are entirely arbitrary).

A number of special features make operating in the nanoscale distinctive. Firstly, there is the question of the tools one needs to see nanoscale structures and to characterize them. Conventional light microscopes cannot resolve structures this small. Electron microscopes can achieve atomic resolution, but they are expensive, difficult to use and prone to producing misleading images. A new class of techniques that has recently become available – scanning probe microscopies such as scanning tunnelling microscopy and atomic force microscopy – is better able to probe the nanoscale, and the uptake of these relatively cheap and accessible methods has been a big factor in creating the field of nanotechnology.

More fundamentally, the properties of matter themselves often change in interesting and unexpected ways when their dimensions are shrunk to the nanoscale. As a particle becomes smaller, it becomes proportionally more influenced by its surface, which often leads to increases in chemical reactivity. These changes may be highly desirable, yielding, for example, better catalysts for more efficiently effecting chemical transformations, or undesirable, in that they can lead to increased toxicity. Quantum mechanical effects can become important, particularly in the way electrons and light interact, and this can lead to striking and useful effects such as size-dependent colour changes. (One sometimes reads that 'the laws of physics don't apply at the nanoscale'. This of course is quite wrong: the laws apply just as they do on any other scale, but sometimes they have different consequences).

One further feature of the nanoscale is that it is the length scale on which the basic machinery of biology operates. Modern molecular biology and biophysics has revealed a great deal about the sub-cellular apparatus of life, revealing the structure and mode of operation of the astonishingly sophisticated molecular-scale machines that are the basis of all organisms. This is significant in a number of ways. Cell biology provides proof that it is possible to make sophisticated machines on the nanoscale and it provides a model for making such machines. It even offers a toolkit of components that can be isolated from living cells and reassembled in synthetic contexts – this is the enterprise of bionanotechnology. The correspondence of length scales also brings hope that nanotechnology will make it possible to make very specific and targeted interventions into biological systems, leading, it is hoped, to new and powerful methods for medical diagnostics and therapeutics.

Nanotechnology, then, is an eclectic mix of disciplines, including elements of chemistry, physics, materials science, electrical engineering, biology and biotechnology. The word 'nanotechnology' itself was coined by the Japanese scientist Norio Taniguchi in 1974 in the context of ultra-high-precision machining. However, the writer who unquestionably propelled the word and the idea into the mainstream was K. Eric Drexler. Drexler wrote a bestselling book entitled *Engines of Creation* (1986), which launched a futuristic and radical vision of a nanotechnology that transformed all aspects of society. In Drexler's vision tiny assemblers would be able to take apart and put together any type of matter atom by atom. It would be possible to make any kind of product or artefact from its component atoms at virtually no cost, leading to the end of scarcity, and possibly the end of the money economy. Medicine would be revolutionized; tiny robots would be able to repair the damage caused by illness or injury at the level of individual molecules and individual cells. This could lead to the effective abolition of ageing and death, while a seamless integration of physical and cognitive prostheses would lead to new kinds of enhanced humans. On the downside, free-living, self-replicating assemblers could escape into the wild, outcompete natural life-forms by virtue of their superior materials and design, and transform the earth's ecosphere into 'grey goo'. Thus, in the vision of Drexler, nanotechnology was introduced as a technology of such potential power that it could lead either to the transfiguration of humanity or to its extinction.

One source of early public excitement about nanotechnology was the idea, implicit in Drexler's worldview, that the nature of all matter can be reduced to a set of coordinates of its constituent atoms. Just as music can be coded in digital form on a CD or MP3 file, and moving images can be reduced to a string of bits, it is possible to imagine any object, whether an everyday tool, a priceless artwork, or even a natural product, being coded as a string of atomic coordinates. Nanotechnology, in this view, provides an interface between the software world and the physical world; an 'assembler' or 'nanofactory' could generate an object just as a digital printer reproduces an image from its digital, software representation. It is this analogy that seems to make the Drexlerian notion of nanotechnology so attractive to the information technology community. Drexler developed his ideas at a more detailed level, publishing a much more technical book called *Nanosystems* (1992), which develops a conception of nanotechnology as mechanical engineering shrunk to atomic dimensions. It is in this form that the idea of 'nanotechnology' has entered the popular consciousness through science fiction, films and video games.

Whether – or in what form – such radical nanotechnology does turn out to be possible, much of what is currently on the market described as 'nanotechnology' is very much more incremental in character. Products such as nano-enabled sunscreens, anti-stain fabric coatings, or 'anti-ageing' creams certainly do not have anything to do with sophisticated nanoscale machines; instead they feature materials, coatings and structures that have some dimensions controlled on the nanoscale. These are useful and even potentially lucrative products, but they certainly do not represent any discontinuity with previous technology. A prominent example are garments, particularly trousers, made from fabrics that use the textile treatments developed by the Nano-Tex corporation to improve their resistance to staining. To followers of the Drexlerian view, they are a symbol of how the word 'nanotechnology' has been debased to cover all kinds of mundane, incremental applications of technology, far removed from the original grand vision of the discipline. But to the nanobusiness community Nano-Tex is a splendid example of how nanotechnology can transform even traditional industries.

I looked up the Nano-Tex patents in an attempt to establish whether the 'nano' in these garments is real or simply marketing hype. There are eighteen of them, and it isn't obvious which technology is used in which product, but the general idea is clear enough. A typical product will be a copolymer: two or more chemically different polymer chains that are chemically attached to each other. One type of polymer will be hydrophilic, and this will tend to stick to a cotton or wool fibre. The other type is hydrophobic, and these hydrophobic bits of the chain will arrange themselves away from the textile surface, presenting a water- and stain-resistant surface to the outside world.

Two questions: is this novel, and is it nanotechnology? From the point of view of a scientist, rather than that of a patent lawyer, the technology clearly isn't that new. It is the same basic idea that underlies 3M's Scotchgard, invented in 1956, which is also based on a copolymer, in this case an acrylic backbone onto which water-repellent fluorocarbon side-chains are grafted. This works in the same way as Nano-Tex's molecules: the acrylic backbone sticks to the fibre surface, leaving the water-repellent side-chains to coat the surface with a non-stick layer. Nonetheless, I do think that it is nanotechnology, albeit of a rather rudimentary kind. A molecule has been defined with a specific architecture, which codes the information it needs to form a specific nanoscale structure (in this case, with sticky hydrophilic bits next to the textile surface, and non-stick hydrophobic bits on the outside). It exploits the principle of self-assembly, which, as I explain in Chapter 5 of my book *Soft Machines: Nanotechnology and life* (2004) is the principle by which the sophisticated nano-machines of cell biology are constructed, and which we will learn to use in ever more sophisticated ways to make synthetic nano-devices.

But if 'nanopants' really are nanotechnology, does that not imply that 3M has been developing nanotechnology since at least 1956, without using the label? Well, in this sense, yes. So the final lesson should probably be that the use of 'nano' as a label for incremental products such as Nano-Tex treatments does owe a lot to marketing, but that doesn't mean that they don't involve sophisticated technology – only that other products without the 'nano' label may in fact be just as nano-enabled.

Moving beyond these mundane current applications of incremental nanotechnology, it is realistic to hope for substantial impacts in the areas of energy, healthcare and information technology. It is clear that there will be a huge emphasis in the coming years on finding new, more sustainable ways to obtain and transmit energy. Nanotechnology could make significant contributions in designing better batteries and fuel cells, but its most important impact could be in making solar energy economically viable on a large scale. The problem with conventional solar cells is not efficiency, but cost and manufacturing scalability. At present the total area of conventional solar cells produced per year is many orders of magnitude too small to make a significant dent in the world's total energy budget. New types of solar cell using nanotechnology inspired by the natural process of photosynthesis are in principle compatible with large-area, low-cost processing techniques such as printing, and it is not unrealistic to imagine this kind of solar cell being produced in huge plastic sheets at very low cost. In medicine, even if the vision of cell-by-cell surgery using nanosubmarines is not realistic, the prospect of the effectiveness of drugs being increased and their side-effects greatly reduced through the use of nanoscale delivery devices is very probable, as is the prospect of faster and more accurate diagnosis of disease.

One area in which nanotechnology is already present in our everyday lives is information technology. The continuous miniaturization of computing devices has already reached the nanoscale, and this is reflected in the growing impact of information technology on all aspects of life for most people in the West. It is interesting that the economic driving force for the continued development of information technologies is no longer computing in its traditional sense, but largely entertainment, through digital music players and digital imaging and video. The continual shrinking of current technologies will probably continue for ten or fifteen years, allowing at least another hundred-fold increase in computing power. At the same time, developments in plastic electronics may make it possible to make computers that are not especially powerful, but very cheap or even disposable. These developments have the potential to facilitate 'ubiquitous computing' or 'the internet of things', in which it is envisaged that every artefact and product incorporates a computer able to sense its surroundings and to communicate wirelessly with its neighbours. One can see that as a natural, even inevitable, development of technologies such as the radio-frequency identification devices (RFID) already used as 'smart barcodes' by shops such as Walmart. These technologies have the potential to improve sustainability – for instance, allowing fashion companies to better monitor their supply chains – but it also is clear that some of the scenarios envisaged could lead to serious concerns about loss of privacy and, potentially, civil liberties.

Humankind depends on technology for its very existence at current population levels. As the world's population begins to stabilize, we have the challenge of developing new technologies that will allow everyone to enjoy decent standards of living on a sustainable basis. Nanotechnology could play an important role, but there will need to be real debates about how to set priorities so that the technology brings benefits to all.

Mass customization: a strategy for sustainability in the fashion industry

FRANK PILLER *is a professor of management and the director of the innovation management group at RWTH Aachen University.*
FRANK STEINER *is a research associate and PhD student at the same group. They share a passion for the topic of mass customization and customer co-creation and are involved in several research projects on that topic, including the EU-funded projects REMPLANET and SERVIVE.*

Since the early 1990s mass customization has been emerging as one leading idea for creating more customer-centric product assortments. In accordance with Joseph Pine we define mass customization as 'developing, producing, marketing, and delivering affordable goods and services with enough variety and customization that nearly everyone finds exactly what they want.'[1] In other words, the goal is to provide customers with what they want, when they want it. In this way customers have a much better chance of finding an ideal product that perfectly fits their needs, and the better a product fits the specific needs of a customer, the more valuable the customer will deem this offering.[2] However, the idea of mass customization has to be handled with care. Increasing product variety will most likely add value for the customers, but it will also increase complexity, and thus costs. Therefore mass customization will not become an attractive business paradigm unless resources can be utilized efficiently and without incurring excessive costs.[3]

The sportswear company Nike is often cited as an impressive example of a successful implementation of mass customization. The growth and success of NikeiD (www.nikeid.com) is based on the firm's ability to produce custom sneakers on demand, meeting precisely the needs of each individual customer and producing these items only after an order has been placed and paid for, thereby eliminating the risk of an unsold inventory of finished goods. But successful mass customization business models are not limited to large global companies such as Nike. There are also many other smaller companies and startups that have successfully employed mass customization in the fashion sector. Consider the following examples:

Selve, a London- and Munich-based manufacturer of women's custom shoes, is a fine example of a company that interacts well with its customers, both in the traditional store and online. Selve enables its customers to create their own shoes by selecting from a variety of materials and designs, in addition to offering truly custom-fit shoes, based on a 3-D scan of a customer's feet. Trained consultants provide advice in the company's stores and the online shop allows customers to re-order products if needed. Shoes are all made to order in a specialized factory in China and are delivered in about two weeks. Customers get this dedicated service for between 150 and 450, which is not cheap but still affordable compared to the price of traditional custom-made shoes (which can start at 1,000).

Zazzle has created a global marketplace for custom goods, particularly T-shirts, that allows designers to create unique products and offer them for sale in their own online shop. Zazzle is providing not just the design tool and a 'self service' webshop, but also all the fulfilment capability, enabling anyone to open their own fashion company in just a few minutes. Zazzle, and competitors such as CafePress and Spreadshirt, have now created a new market segment that is worth more than US $2 billion and growing quickly.

Belgian-based start-up Bivolino has created a successful custom-shirt business, not just by setting up its own supply chain for the efficient production of custom men's and women's shirts at very affordable prices, but also by enabling large retailers such as Marks & Spencer, Otto and WE to offer custom products under their own brand names with minimum effort. Bivolino has become one of the first dedicated integrated suppliers for custom fashion.

The traditional argument for mass customization has been its appeal as a differentiation strategy and as a way to build lasting relationships with consumers. We also see considerable opportunities for turning the fashion industry into a more sustainable business by moving towards mass customization. In addition to providing added value for the customer, mass customization also has the potential to reduce waste along the value chain and therefore not only provide economic benefits for industry, but also contribute to a more sustainable society. This is particularly important at a time when competition is no longer based only on price and quality, but also on the environmental footprint of a business. Interestingly, this potential benefit of mass customization has only recently begun to be discussed.[4]

Three aspects of mass customization demonstrate how this concept could provide environmental benefits in all phases of the product life cycle:

1. In the context of the manufacturing process, mass customization allows inventories to be considerably reduced or eliminated along the supply chain, as mass customization is usually based on a build-to-order production model. This means that the manufacturing of products does not start until a customer order has been received. No storage of finished products is needed and overproduction will not occur. Considering that in many consumer product branches, including the textile industry, about 40% of finished products are eventually destroyed as a result of overproduction, the build-to-order paradigm of mass customization offers great potential in terms of waste reduction.[5] At the same time, overall energy and resource consumption is reduced, as only those products that have already been purchased have to be manufactured and transported.

2. Mass customization could also provide environmental benefits during the use phase of the products. Customized products and services typically permit better fulfilment of customer needs than do standard products. Research has shown that customers perceive higher value in items that have been customized to fit their specific demands than in standardized products.[6] These findings support the notion that customers will probably handle their customized products with greater care than mass-produced standardized items, and even might develop a stronger emotional bond with products that they have co-created. In consequence, mass customized products tend to have a longer lifespan than standardized mass-produced goods.

3. As most mass customization offerings involve a high level of interactive engagement with the individual consumer, the customer–manufacturer relationship is often stronger and closer than usual. A strong customer–manufacturer relationship is necessary for establishing a closed-loop material flow (also known as the 'cradle-to-cradle' approach), as it enables efficient recycling and reuse of resources, so that product components can be used for multiple life-cycles.[7]

Despite all its potential benefits, a widespread adoption of mass customization has not yet taken place. This is because the shift from mass production to mass customization requires a profound paradigm shift along the entire knowledge and supply chain, particularly in the following areas:[8]

1. Designers have to adapt to a new way of thinking about product architectures.

2. The factory then has to be organized differently, with robust but adaptive processes in place.

3. The industrial technologies that are being employed must be highly flexible, reconfigurable and integrated.

4. Logistics operations have to focus on filling individual, rather than bulk, customer orders.

5. Customers have to change their purchasing habits.[9]

The evaluation of these points must move beyond the mere assessment of economic aspects, towards the integration of environmental and social considerations. We hope that more researchers and practitioners alike will recognize the opportunities that mass customization offers to create a more sustainable fashion industry, and that they will provide dedicated research and entrepreneurial action to overcome the barriers we have identified here.

Bodyscanning and fit: the impact of new technologies on sustainable fashion

SUSAN ASHDOWN *is a professor in the Department of Fiber Science and Apparel Design at Cornell University, researching fit and sizing using bodyscanning technology.*

Interactions among technology, design, culture and commerce have always had an impact on fashion production, and production technologies have had a part in forming the current conditions in our field and the development of many unsustainable practices. From the invention of the sewing needle (leading to shaped rather than wrapped clothing), to the industrial revolution (resulting in a shift from production of single crafted items to multiple manufactured items), the availability of the clothing that we purchase and wear has been dictated by technology. New technologies – including 3-D bodyscanning, software that optimizes the creation and use of avatars for fitting, a powerful and accessible internet, mass customization and automated custom-fitting systems, and production using modular manufacturing – now provide tools that have the potential to move at least some portion of clothing production away from the creation of ready-to-wear mass produced clones to individualized fashion.

Realistic projections of possible paradigms for clothing acquisition by consumers using these technologies include efficient distribution of well-fitted mass customized clothing utilizing online virtual fitting rooms in which customers are matched to garments styled and shaped for their body type, and/or the creation of individualized apparel designed and fitted to a specific person's body. Such innovations could lead to increased attachment to, and use of, the garments, as well as eliminating returns, unsold or discounted garments and the accumulation by consumers of purchase mistakes in closets or landfills. These approaches incur new costs for the industry and the consumer (in both time and money spent in the clothing purchase transaction). Only time will tell whether perceived benefits will offset these costs and how they will affect our overall relationship with our clothing.

Assuming that both technological and cultural barriers to these scenarios are overcome, what might the result be of these new ways of interacting with our clothing? If we can have well-fitted clothing suited to our body type and well-aligned with our personal tastes, will we purchase and use more or less? Will we forego the shopping mall and the fitting room for a virtual purchase experience that offers less instant gratification, but more choice and control? Will we invest in clothing that gives us greater enjoyment, and therefore want to wear it for more than one season, or will we find personalized clothing so appealing that we purchase more of it? If clothing purchases take more time and money, will we divert these resources from other activities in our lives to maintain our current volume of clothing, or will we purchase less and use it for a longer time?

We do not have answers to these questions, but some indications may lie in changes that are already affecting our relationships to other goods and services. One example is in the way that consumer demand has created access to more expensive locally produced food that is crafted on a small scale rather than factory farmed. This can provide us with a powerful model for clothing purchases that are specially crafted for us, possibly locally, using new technologies.

The assumption that as human beings we have an innate desire for new fashion that will result in clothing consumption patterns being limited only by available resources may be flawed. Perhaps these are learned impulses that can be unlearned and replaced with a preference for more individualized, valued and carefully conserved clothing that evolves with our changing bodies and needs, but not necessarily with the seasons.

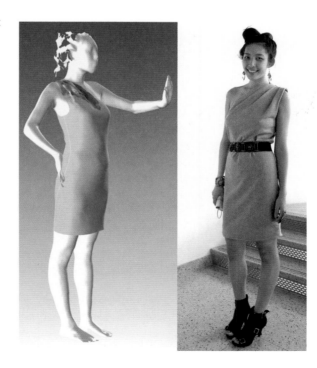

Left: A virtual dress, developed to fit a student's 3-D bodyscan (*far left*), is shown with the student wearing the resulting customized dress (*left*) in a study by Fatma Baytar, Cornell University, on the impact of technology on attachment to clothing, and the wearing of customized clothing over extended time.

'Tailoring was once a way to define yourself as an individual.'

DAVID MASON *of famed luxury tailoring firm Nutters of Savile Row uses 21st-century technologies to offer a new generation of high-end made-to-measure and bespoke services for its clients.*
By Sandy Black

Nutters of Savile Row, under the creative control of David Mason, builds on the legacy of well-known tailor Tommy Nutter, who revolutionized menswear in the 1960s by introducing fashion innovation to a highly conservative Savile Row, creating suits for the new pop aristocracy such as Mick Jagger and The Beatles. Mason, who started his career in the fashion industry making men's shirts in a Yorkshire factory, now caters for a different clientele with two service-based clothing companies (Nutters of

Savile Row and Anthony Sinclair), which not only celebrate traditional handcrafted production but also recognize a role for 21st-century technology to play in made-to-measure clothing.

'Tailoring was once a way to define yourself as an individual', says Mason of his craft, but despite a renaissance of interest in the late 1960s and 1970s, 'by the 1980s, Savile Row was out of fashion.' This was the decade of the designer brands, when men could buy a ready-made wardrobe from designers such as Armani in a one-stop package. The recent resurgence in quality tailoring as a sign of luxury has rekindled consumers' passion for personal and bespoke items handmade by master craftsmen (and women). This awareness has been spread by the rise of the internet and promoted in numerous sartorial blogs. However, such a personal and truly bespoke service requires both time and money, with four to six fittings being the norm.

Mason is constantly exploring new ways of doing business in the field. He was a major player in a project to trial new technology in the luxury retail market, and remains 'very excited' about the possibilities for digital technologies, such as bodyscanning, as long as they are service- and customer-oriented. There are subtle but important differences between being scanned by a computer and and being measured by a tailor. Despite the precision of scanned measurements, the stance a person takes when being scanned is not a natural one, whereas the tailor is able to observe the client, taking the measurements only when he is relaxed.

Furthermore, the client may have his or her own ideas about personal fit and comfort, which the tailor must negotiate, taking into account the actual fabric to be used and building the suit around the client's body shape. Until virtual fitting systems can be perfected, these differences will always be evident at the most expensive handcrafted end of the market. However, digital systems have proved ideal for use in fitting shirts cost effectively, in automated made-to measure systems and in creating new lasts in shoemaking via foot-scanning technology. Using the traditional carved wooden lasts, a pair of bespoke shoes can easily take a year to make, so technology can speed up this process.

Mason believes that tailoring will remain 'part science, part craft or artistry', but that technology can contribute in a number of ways. Importantly, scanner data can be used to define body shape, rather than simply to obtain measurements. This system has been adopted by the Bodymetrics company to offer customers in Selfridges in London the best-fitting jeans from a defined range.

Anthony Sinclair, Mason's second company, gathers together specialists in their fields, whether shirt-makers, shoemakers or tie-makers, using different production facilities and price points depending on the proportion of hand techniques versus technology involved. For example, there are three types of shirts available. The first and most expensive (at around £500) is hand-stitched in a family-run atelier in Naples, with fabric carefully pre-shrunk, and accompanied by a fitting service (in person or by transporting the shirt). A middle-priced shirt is available at about £250, produced in a workshop in Bergamo, Italy, where manual measurements are imported into a CAD (computer aided design) system to create the individual pattern for the client. Hand finishing is still evident in the hand-stitched buttonholes (a hallmark of bespoke quality) and hand-sewn buttons. The third and lowest price level, at £125, is produced in a factory unit making thousands of ready-to-wear shirts, but with the ability to create an individually customized pattern for each client with the help of CAD software and single-ply laser-cutting technology. In making this level of shirt, there are no hand processes at all – no 'needle and thimble' – other than the standard sewing machine operations, but a 'made-to-measure' service can still be offered thanks to technology. Each shirt production process therefore satisfies a defined market, is clearly differentiated by price and is transparent about its provenance.

Mason is proud of the success he has achieved in providing a customized service through technology with the manufacture of unique bespoke ties, which are woven in Suffolk by the company Vanners, first established in the 18th century. Advanced design and production technology now enables the weaving of only 3 m of fabric to be cost-effective, rather than the former 30 m minimum. Hundreds of designs and colourways are woven into sample 'blankets', from which the customer can select. The fabric (enough to make two ties) is woven to order and the tie – a virtually 'exclusive' product – is delivered within two weeks. A further venture in creating bespoke services through digital printing technology has been trialled by Mason in collaboration with London College of Fashion's Digital Studio, in which the linings for bespoke suits were custom-printed. Similar opportunities exist for shirts and ties to be decorated with 'engineered' prints individually designed around the specific garment, a facility made commercially feasible by digital technology, and which is currently being explored further in other research projects.

The democratization of luxury in clothing and the redefinition of personal service through technology are clearly evident, but its integration throughout the fashion industry is still in its infancy. Pioneers such as Mason who embrace both tradition and new technology show how, with a combination of craftsmanship, good customer service and keen commercial business sense, technology can produce sustainable clothing and new business models, exemplified by the new generation of bespoke and made-to-measure services.

Above: Tommy Nutter was known as 'the rebel of Savile Row' for his breaking of traditions. In this suit, for instance, the classic pinstripe fabric is used horizontally instead of vertically.

Opposite: David Mason poses with his dog.

'Better-fitting clothes sell better and create less waste.'

FITS.ME *is a virtual fitting room that uses robotic mannequins to ensure a perfect fit, reducing waste in online clothes shopping. By Sandy Black.*

Across the fashion industry, variations in sizing between brands are notorious, and returns (and therefore refunds) of unwanted clothing are a major issue for retailers, especially for fitted or tailored fashions. Returns are lowest for casual and sportswear (12–18%) but fitted fashions often have return rates of more than 35%. In Germany, the return rates for online clothing sales are even higher, as much as 40–60%, since 'open invoicing' policies encourage people to buy the same garment in multiple sizes and then return the ones that don't fit.

Recent collaborative research conducted in Estonia at the University of Tartu and Tallinn University of Technology, in collaboration with German body-scanner manufacturer Human Solutions, has developed a robotic mannequin that is able to mimic the shape and size of the human body. The mannequin (which is available in both male and female versions) can take the shape of either the statistical aggregate target market profile (for example, the average 30-year-old male in Italy), or that of a real individual who has either had his body scanned in 3-D (a webcam scanning method is proposed for the future) or provides the necessary numerical measurements online. After entering this data, the online customer is shown photos of the mannequin wearing different sizes of clothing in order to be confident of the fit. Self-measured entries are error-corrected by statistically comparing them to a database of about 40,000 human scans.

The robotic mannequin is articulated in many sections, and covered in a flexible but non-stretch material usually used for prostheses. It has far more sections than a standard tailoring dummy; each of them can be adjusted to a fraction of a millimetre and, most importantly, can take on asymmetric or unconventional body shapes. Special attention has been paid to shoulder and hip areas to make them look as natural as possible. This facility opens up possibilities for mass customization, made-to-measure fashion, remote fashion design, remote tailoring or any scenario in which the customer cannot physically visit the maker for fitting (this is especially important for layered and more complex clothing).

This virtual fitting-room technology has been tested and reported in the press,[1] and is expected shortly to be made available to retailers. Other benefit of the system will include creating a fitting-model for manufacturers that is statistically more representative of the target market, and facilitating remote fit–quality control for use when a product is being manufactured in a different country from the designer.

Heikki Haldre[2], the Fits.me company CEO, predicts the future growth of the system: 'Apparel retail growth will be 2–4% annually over the next eight years. At the same time the apparel e-commerce growth will be in double-digit numbers. It will have an additional short-lived accelerated growth as new technologies, such as the virtual fitting room, become mainstream…some analysts believe up to 35% of all apparel will be sold on internet by 2018. (The share is 9% today in the US; and some believe up to 14% in the UK).

'As total apparel sales will not grow significantly overall, e-commerce growth will reduce apparel sales in bricks-and-mortar stores. Up to one in four clothing shops will face closure, or be in dire need of changing their business models, as has already happened to bookshops and travel agencies. Yet three out of four clothing shops will stay open, especially those on the high street.

'While e-commerce is more environmentally friendly, apparel e-commerce today suffers from two obstacles. First, online retailers struggle to convince customers to buy clothes without first trying them on. The numbers illustrate this well: 9% of apparel is sold online versus 50% of computers and 40% of books. Although apparel e-commerce is one of the smallest in terms of share sold online, it is already the largest e-commerce category in terms of value (2010 US apparel e-commerce sales were US $31 billion, online computer sales were US $26 billion).

'As a virtual fitting room removes one of the main risks when buying online, sales will increase.

'The second obstacle is that apparel e-commerce is a category with one of the largest waste problems. Because of the lack of a fitting room, customers tend to buy more loosely fitting garments online than they do when shopping at

Below: The Fits.me adjustable mannequin can be programmed to the customer's size.

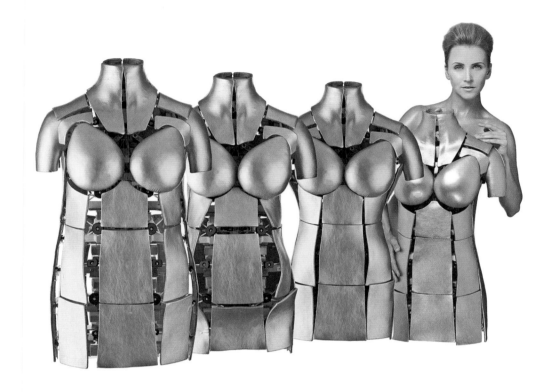

'As fashion is one of the most seasonal product categories, garments that fall out of the sales cycle – clothes that are purchased and then returned – represent a significant loss of revenue for retailers. On top of fixed reverse-logistics costs (such as return shipping, reverse warehousing and spillage), garments lose 20% of their value for every four weeks they spend out of the sales cycle.'

bricks-and-mortar stores. Research suggests that on top of the unwanted items actually returned to online retailers, up to a further 16% are not being returned because customers miss deadlines, or find alternative uses for these garments, such as giving them to charity. When we look at why customers return garments bought online, 5–7% of returns are due to computer screens rendering the colour slightly differently; 15% are due to the customer's inability to feel the fabrics; but a significant 60% are due to the garment being the wrong size. While Fits.me addresses only the fit issue, other technologies, such as haptics, seek to solve the problem of virtually 'feeling' the fabrics before purchase. In trials, the Fits.me Virtual Fitting Room increased sales between 57% and 300%; and reduced garment returns by 28% on average.

'As fashion is one of the most seasonal product categories, garments that fall out of the sales cycle – clothes that are purchased and then returned – represent a significant loss of revenue for retailers. On top of fixed reverse-logistics costs (such as return shipping, reverse warehousing and spillage), garments lose 20% of their value for every four weeks they spend out of the sales cycle. On average a returned garment is out of the sales cycle for 4–5 weeks in Europe; longer in the US where return policies are more lenient. Every 1% in reduced returns increases retailers' profits by 1.5–2%. As 10–15% of the value of a garment bought online (20–30% for a returned garment shipped both ways) is in transportation costs, reducing unnecessary transportation by reducing the number of returns decreases costs and helps to save the environment. Some returned garments are typically resold at discounted prices, but more often than not they are simply discarded to protect the brand's pricing policies.'

In addition to these potential improvements in efficiency and sustainability, the Virtual Fitting Room provides retailers with the body measurement data of their customers. This gives brands valuable information about which sizings should be changed and which fit styles should be added. As Haldre says: 'Better-fitting clothes sell better and create less waste.'

Fashion blogging: the new fashion journalism

AGNÈS ROCAMORA *is a senior research fellow and senior lecturer in cultural and historical studies at London College of Fashion.*
DJURDJA BARTLETT *is a research fellow at the same institution.*

The late 1990s saw the emergence in the global mediascape of a new type of interactive internet-based text: the blog.[1] A frequently updated chronological publication of personal thoughts and Web links, a blog is a platform for sharing reports on and snapshots of one's life, what is happening on the Web or in the world 'out there'.[2] The editors of blogs are known as bloggers. Their readers are able to respond to their entries, known as posts, and share their views on the topics discussed in a 'comments' section. Initially, blogs were created by people skilled in the building of websites.[3] However, the technique of automated templates, the rise in technological literacy and the appearance of blog providers such as blogger.com and blogspot. com have made it increasingly easy to create and maintain blogs. By the end of 2011 there were more than 176 million blogs.[4] Although blogs are similar in that they mainly convey the personal views and anecdotes of their editors in a format parallel to that of the diary, their topics differ widely. Some of them express adolescent anxieties while others communicate strong opinions on politics and various social and cultural issues.

The blog explosion has received a mixed reception from media analysts. Some have enthusiastically embraced the blog as a liberating, participatory medium that transfers power from established media to the citizen. David Kline and Dan Burstein, for instance, argue that '[b]logs help break through the anonymity and isolation of modern life. They give people a voice and a forum with which to speak truth to power or at least to reach out and touch someone …In other words, blogging's ultimate product is empowerment.'[5] Blogs, they contend, are 'one variant of citizen-controlled media'.[6] Other cultural analysts have shown cautiousness or even hostility towards the blogging phenomenon. Geert Lovink, for example,

notes that '[b]log entries are often hastily written personal musings, sculptured around a link or event. In most cases, bloggers simply do not have the time, skills, and the financial means to do proper research.'[7] In a similar vein Andrew Keen claims that blogging promotes the cult of the amateur, introducing 'a chaos of useless information'.[8]

Praised or despised, blogs have become influential sites of social, political and cultural mediation, in what sociologist John Tomlinson has identified as a context of transition from a culture of speed to one of immediacy.[9] Indeed, at the core of blogging lies immediacy, often hailed as an advantage over the printed media, for in the world of news and information flows time is an asset. A structuring principle of fashion in terms of both production and consumption, time also is of the essence. So before long a new genre emerged: the fashion blog.

A New Fashion Genre

Created in, respectively, May 2003 and the autumn of 2004, nogoodforme.com and myfashion life. com are early instances of the genre. Independent platforms for words and images about fashion situated outside of the publishing industry, they voiced the likes and dislikes of their editors. Such blogs have now proliferated, reporting on a variety of topics but all linked – metaphorically as well as literally, for links are intrinsic to the blogosphere – through their love for fashion.[10] Barneys Girl and Harrods Girl of iamfashion.blogspot.com put it this way:

We started blogging back in 2004, when we began college. We wanted a simple girly website where we can share our thoughts on fashion with other fashion lovers. We finally settled on blogspot, because we were both technically challenged and it was easy… We religiously stalked our blog and our heart would skip a beat whenever we get a comment. It gave us a warm and fuzzy feeling each time.[11]

Fashion blogs such as I am Fashion have introduced a new type of information rooted in the everyday experience and personal view of their authors, whether they are observing trends, reporting on street fashion, offering shopping advice or

At the core of blogging lies immediacy, often hailed as an advantage over the printed media, for in the world of news and information flows, time is an asset.

Below: London, May 2008, photographed by Scott Schuman (The Sartorialist).

commenting on the dress style of celebrities. With entries written in the first person, they are nearest to the diary format.

Although some well-known bloggers such as Diane Pernet (of ashadedviewonfashion.com) have had some experience in the field of fashion, bloggers are usually not professional journalists.[12] In contrast with fashion glossies, fashion blogs are less polished, written on the spur of the moment in what could be described as a spoken-written style, and often accompanied by amateurish images. Geert Lovink argues that 'blogs are primarily used as a tool to manage the self.'[13] This management includes 'the need to structure one's life, to clear up the mess, to master the immense flows of information', and to promote oneself in a culture that 'fabricates celebrity on every possible level'.[14] Online fashion diaries are an intricate part of this project of self-realization, sometimes leading to digital fame.

Indeed, within the quickly expanding phenomenon of citizen fashion reporters and their digital diaries, some, like Susie Lau (of stylebubble.co.uk), have acquired fame both inside and outside of the blogosphere. Lau started her blog in 2006 with the intention to 'write about stuff I like'.[15] She plays with technology to achieve an amateurish style, but insists that she is not very good at using Photoshop®.[16] Taking many images of herself and accompanying them with self-deprecating musings on dresses, shoes, colours, and emerging and established designers, as well as high-street finds, Lau has achieved her own eclectic and quirky aesthetic.

Another successful genre is the street-fashion blog. Privileging snapshots of ordinary people photographed on the street, and inspired by the conventions of 'the straight-up', street-fashion blogs document a variety of looks that can be seen in big cities worldwide.[17] Although fashion has been fascinated with youthful street looks since the 1960s, street-fashion blogs go further in their fetishizing of the relationship between fashion and the city. In the spirit of Walter Benjamin's *flâneur* and armed with their digital cameras, street-fashion bloggers cruise Stockholm, Moscow, Buenos Aires, Seoul (the cities of

Right: New York, September 2007, photographed by Scott Schuman (The Sartorialist).

the fashion blogosphere are numerous), offering to a huge audience of virtual *flâneurs* the real-life images of their cities and its stylish citizens.[18]

One of the most famous street-fashion blogs is Scott Schuman's The Sartorialist (thesartorialist.com), which, unlike the traditional fashion press, presents subjects of different ages, races, body shapes and dress styles, all distinguished by their sense of individuality.[19] Before starting his blog in 2004, Schuman was a New York-based sales and marketing entrepreneur for brands such as Valentino and Helmut Lang. For the blog, he started photographing people on the streets of New York, but soon brought his camera to the pavements of other cities. Schuman chooses ordinary people, but only those who are extraordinarily dressed. The ensemble is important, but the right detail – the colour of shoes, the length of a tie, a pair of socks or the lack of them, the shape of shirt collar or the shade of denim fabric – is even more significant. Thus street-fashion blogs such as Schuman's support a hierarchy of taste that is based not on the latest trends but on one's ability to display an idiosyncratic approach. They have also challenged the hierarchy of fashion geography by bringing new cities onto the map. In that respect street-fashion blogs have supported the decentralization of fashion away from consecrated metropolises such as London, Milan, New York and Paris.

Blogs that focus on particular types of goods, excelling in their fetishization, constitute another genre of popular fashion blogs. They include, for instance, bagsnob.com and purseblog.com, as well as the celebrated shoeblog.com by the now infamous Manolo. While online diaries and street-fashion blogs tend to contain few advertisements, object-centred blogs are more systematically commercialized. The Manolo, as he likes to call himself, attracts readers with his wit and knowledge about shoes, but this has also brought him many advertisers and collaborations with the industry, turning his blog into a lucrative business. Indeed, in an interview he referred to himself as a 'Six Figure Blogger'.[20]

The reservations many have about the consumption of fashion and its excesses have also found an echo in the blogosphere by way of blogs that suggest alternative ways of consuming fashion. Kathryn Finney, for example, recommends special offers and sales on her blog thebudgetfashionista.com. New Yorker Lauri Apple exclusively wears clothes found in the garbage that she carefully washes and repairs. Her now-defunct blog foundclothing.typepad.com was dedicated to items and accessories abandoned to waste, then saved by her and other salvagers.

Street fashion blogs such as Schuman's support a hierarchy of taste that is based not on the latest trends but on one's ability to display an idiosyncratic approach.

Below: New York, August 2006, photographed by Scott Schuman (The Sartorialist).

In the fashion blogosphere readers can find information that is not provided by the conventional media, whether their favourite blogger is quicker at providing it, more innovative in selecting what to present, or simply has the courage and independence to include it. Decentralization, eccentricity and the valuing of individuality may in some way be associated with the medium. Through highly personalized narratives, blogs offer a new way of spreading and cataloguing a vast amount of information and knowledge. These narratives are not only informative but very seductive too, a characteristic the established print media have praised, further legitimating the role of fashion blogs in the mediascape. In the British edition of *Vogue*, for instance, Linda Grant has defined blogs as 'the very best kind of girlie gossip: informative, frequently bitchy, but always focused and up to date'.[21] According to the *New York Times*, 'Garance Doré [of garancedore.fr] gives viewers the sense that they are in the urban splendor too, or could be, or should be – strolling or sauntering, rather than linking and clicking.'[22]

Shifting Boundaries

Fashion bloggers have emerged as increasingly valued players, with influential blogs followed by a vast constituency of readers. The years 2006–9 in particular saw the 'networked reputation' of various bloggers consolidate, with the most popular blogs read by tens of thousands of readers daily.[23] In 2006 popular bloggers started being invited to big events such as fashion shows and product launches.[24] Fashion bloggers are now regularly featured in newspapers' and magazines' 'most influential people' lists, their styles documented, and their tips and addresses shared with readers.[25]

Independent bloggers have thus carved out a space for themselves which has forced print-media titles to reconsider their own activities. Not only have most of the established magazines created their own blogs but they have also responded by recruiting esteemed bloggers to work on their websites or by hosting their blogs on their web pages.[26] Style.com, for instance, a digital publication of Condé Nast, hosts a blog edited by Scott Schuman; Géraldine Dormoy's blog CaféMode is hosted by the French news weekly *L'Express*; and between 2008 and 2010 Susie Lau acted as commissioning editor for dazeddigital.com at the same time as she was running her own blog. Lovink has noted the value of the blogosphere as a resource for traditional media: 'The cynical take on blogs is that their sole purpose has been to create a talent pool for the publishing industry. Signing up these talents is not only benefiting the media business, it is threatening the positions of those journalists who do not deliver. They will be fired. In the end, it is not

Through highly personalized narratives, blogs offer a new way of spreading and cataloguing a vast amount of information and knowledge.

Fashion journalism is often seen as little more than an extension of companies' PR.

Below: Susie Lau, aka Susie Bubble, in some of the daily outfits she shares via her blog Style Bubble.

Right: London July 2008,
photographed by Scott Schuman
(The Sartorialist).

the blog world but the media industry that will be strengthened.'[27]

Not only have bloggers emerged as possible competitors for professional journalists, as Lovink observes, but their absorption by established titles could arguably threaten blogs' position as an alternative space for discourse. Indeed, fashion magazines are often criticized for being driven by the agenda of the companies that advertise in their pages. As a result fashion journalism is often seen as little more than an extension of companies' PR. Similarly, the digital extensions of established print media are highly commercialized platforms. In contrast, independent fashion blogs have been seen as an alternative space for discourses on fashion preserved from the imperatives of commercialism, as a true voice on/of fashion. But with the growing popularity of blogs as a mean of mediating fashion and of bloggers as fashion intermediaries, many blogs have capitalized on their success through the selling of advertising space, the writing of sponsored posts and the use of affiliate marketing.[28] Moreover, with some bloggers attending promotional events organized by the industry and their names featuring in companies' PR contact lists, blogs have been incorporated into the marketing routine of businesses. Instead of outsiders with a critical eye, bloggers risk becoming insiders disciplined by the rules of commercialism, adding to the uncritical mass of commentators enthralled by the fashion commodity.

That bloggers have been courted by companies and advertisers, and that the blogosphere can be seen as a talent pool for the media, draws attention to the changing status of blogs and blogging: from an organic, independent and alternative means of communication to a tool for the promotion of business interests and a corporate genre of media text. However, the blogs that remain outside of the industry and the lure of advertising and PR while reaching large numbers of readers are still numerous, precisely because of their position as outsiders. Their authors may well be interested in attracting the attention of possible employers – in a 'risk society' in which employment is precarious and rarefied, individuals have to deploy creative ways of securing a position in the work sphere – and the media might well see blogs as a new form of publishing.[29] However, as social media analyst Nick Gall has noted, 'it's really a new form of conversation and a new form of community.'[30] However strategic some blogs may be, bloggers have managed to popularize new and diverse ways of communicating and mediating fashion, new modes of togetherness and connectivity on the planes of dress and appearance which draw attention to the importance of both fashion and the internet as meaningful sites of interaction and socialization.

Boom and bust in the betaverse

SUE JENKYN JONES *is a fashion designer, writer and futurist who has been fascinated for years by the gateways between mechanics, electronics and the tactile arts.*

In fashion some ideas catch fire merely by being glimpsed on a celebrity. But even in these fast-moving times it can take decades for a technological breakthrough to gain a cult following and ignite the social world. One such idea that is now smouldering brightly is the metaverse, a virtual and graphical meeting space initiated online in the 1980s by academics and computer scientists. The internet, as a low-cost communication space and the portal through which the metaverse can be reached, was quick to exploit the notion of bulletin boards and forums of geek interest. The first of these, Silicon Valley's The Well, was text-based, but was quickly followed by a meta-range of symbolic visualizations, 2-D graphic–sonic chatrooms such as The Palace, and massively multi-user online game worlds such as the 2.5-D isometric Cyworld. The boundary between work and play space was blurred by the lack of regulation and new adherents who created their own social agendas and game-like avatars to represent them. Perhaps the cold and inhospitable Nordic winters contributed to the success of the cosy Finnish Habbo Hotel (created by Sampo Karjalainen and Aapo Kyrölä), which by 2004 boasted 80 million members. As computing speed and graphics technology for military and medical simulations have advanced, the convergence of these social sandpits with games and Virtual Reality Modelling Language (VRML) has led to the expansion of three-dimensional virtual worlds.[1]

The Dutch historian Johan Huizinga, who explored the influence of play on European social life, described a game as a collective illusion that happens in a designated place or arena intended to host the suspension of normal interactions.[2] Huizinga would be surprised to find that today, with their fingers on touchpads, joysticks and keyboards, thousands are joining illusory spaces or virtual worlds. But to many it is much more than just a game. What distinguishes the customs of a metaverse from a game is that there is no single goal. There is only an ambiguous landscape; a large proportion of the content is the sum of the creative output, activities, misdeeds and rough justice of those who populate it. In game-play, rules are set rather than constantly fabricated. In software development, beta versions of new programs used to be released for evaluation and debugging by acolytes. Gradually developers have acknowledged that programs may be released and improved upon continuously. For example the internet browser Mozilla is updated daily. Thus it can be said that the metaverse, or betaverse, is in a continuous state of evolution. By aggregating computer power on server farms to simulate terrain, it became possible to create full 3-D simulated virtual worlds, or 'sims', with persistence (i.e. they are always on), as a shared and expanding space inhabited by an ever-present community of users who are adding to its features. In the case of Second Life, the inhabitants are given 3-D modelling tools and scripting language to produce homes, objects and clothing and to animate their avatars with gestures and dances. The technologically savvy can step it up a notch, using open-standards technologies and open-source protocols for more ambitious projects. The objective is to make the virtual world easy to maintain and open for development. By learning how to use the underlying source code and downloading freely available software kits, it is possible to extend and sell more ambitious environments than those offered in the world itself.

If the quality of simulation is crude to allow for fast processing in the betaverse, so too are the quickly wrought frontier-land laws and regulations. Rules and membership agreements vary from the tyrannical, God-like administrative edicts of the cyber-developers to the laissez-faire stance of Philip Rosedale, the entrepreneurial force behind Second Life. The betaverse allows the tolerance and tears of the sandbox without the pressures and physics of the real world. Rosedale, who formed Linden Labs to create Second Life in 1999, describes his world as a free and open metaverse. It is certainly free to join. Everyone starts naked, with nothing, and has to learn to walk, talk and then fly. Nobody waits for a rulebook. You – the avatar – write it yourself. There are no building regulations, health and safety inspectors, parking tickets, hospitals, bad weather or taxes – yet. But such utopias have a habit of imploding. Virtual spaces have come to be taken as seriously as real life (RL), not only by those who inhabit them but by external societies, which are beginning to draw up laws and gather taxes, marking lines of property ownership and values within and beyond the virtual realm. Activities within virtual worlds now have to comply broadly with sundry international commercial laws. And someone has to pay for the computing power.

As the avatars have gathered in the zero-gravity virtual hanging gardens of multicultural Beta-Babylon, the need for ground to stand on, furniture to sit on and clothing to wear demands ever more computing power to render it visible. Second Life covers approximately 1,300 km^2, with the population density of London. While other virtual worlds have disappeared or seem to have dipping membership

Left: Screen image from Second Life, with avatar.

posts, podcasts and RSS feeds, Web 3.0 is immediate, immersive and visually complex. For instance you can do things simultaneously from different locations, such as watching a video with others. This seemingly natural environment, tinged with the sense of 'otherworldly' or dream-like adventure, helps to create community. Moreover, Au proposes that as a generation comes to accept it, the metaverse will increasingly be used as a business tool and commercial environment. Companies, especially those that trade in music, youth and lifestyle products, are already using virtual worlds as spaces where executives can meet avatar-to-avatar in troubleshooting conferences, instead of wasting time, expense and fuel on travel.

The key to unlocking riches in the virtual world is through understanding the needs, desires and purchasing power of the avatar or avatar owner. What has become increasingly evident is that individuals feel a real emotional and responsible connection to their online avatar personas, and are prepared to lavish money, gifts and accoutrements on them, as in life. In 2007 the exponential propagation of virtual items and the appearance of a few Second Life millionaires saw a gold rush of corporations keen to participate in virtual worlds. Among these were a number of leading-brand fashion companies. Food and drink may be redundant in cyberspace, but clothing is symbolic of personality and necessary to create an avatar. Fashion has become the virtual worlds' most competitive and lucrative industry, indicative of a thriving social scene.

In Second Life, clothing has emerged as one of the hottest tradable commodities, attracting both amateur and professional cyber-capitalists. The clothing of avatars has been a critical issue for their owners. Early computer games offered little opportunity to customize what avatars wore, but appearance was soon seen as a compelling and differentiating attribute. Within the first few months of opening, the virtual American Apparel store sold over 4,000 T-shirts on its Lerappa island.[5] The brand also offered virtual buyers the incentive of 15% off the same item in a real store. American Apparel previewed its Fall collection in Second Life. Your avatar could try the jeans on before you could. Customer feedback was the buzzword. Second Life also attracted a sprinkling of luxury brands such as Armani and L'Oreal. Calvin Klein launched their ckIN2U perfume on Second Life. But the hard or gimmicky sell doesn't work in virtual worlds; many top brands have shown that they did not know how to translate their values in this offbeat world or attract the interest of avatars, and have subsequently withdrawn. Madison Avenue advertising is a throwback to the 20th century; Luxury with a capital 'L' is difficult to express in low resolution. And everyone can lead a luxury life in the betaverse. In the metaverse it is impossible to starve or freeze to death, although there is a real danger of addiction to the virtual life. You can try on the millionaire lifestyle for size; there is no upper limit. In contrast, real social kudos comes from more subtle connoisseurship of taste and demonstration of skills.

Undeterred or unimpressed by real-world rivals, and in the manner of any third-world economy, there is a myriad of shoestring fashion company start-ups.

statistics, the independent virtual life observer Metalife Statistics reported in 2012 that Second Life continues to see approximately 16,000 sign-ups per day, with even gender distribution and more than 1,200,000 avatars in the database, although many sign-ups last only two to three months.[3] Not only does Second Life occupy enormous virtual landmass; it runs on 2,579 servers, known as 'the Grid', using considerable space and at considerable cost. Online worlds are evolving into real economies and societies where profits can be made out of the vanity and greed that exist in any expanding economy. The revenue stream is driven by the rental of server space in the form of 'land', and objects bought with virtual money that has a real-world exchange value. Second Life inhabitants have created hundreds of millions of virtual objects that sell for Linden dollars. L$ can be traded with real cash or credit cards and have a stock-market value called the 'LindeX'. Sometimes virtual objects escape the metaverse and are auctioned on eBay. Virtual objects and clothing have been sold for more than the real items have realized. But in spite of the sense of ownership and control of the content you create or buy, the wealth and glory are largely illusory. Although there are a few well-publicized examples of 'avatarpreneurs', very few have managed to make a living from their commercial activities. The hands-down winners are the service providers, the wizards behind the scenes.

Wagner James Au, metaverse consultant and game developer, who was invited into the inner sanctum of the Second Life company in San Francisco to archive its evolution, describes how the paradigm of Second Life 'may be the fulcrum for a new generation of behaviours in how we work, shop, interact and spend our leisure hours'. In his book *The Making of Second Life: Notes from the new world* (2008) he suggests that beyond the text-based and flat worlds of the Web 1.0, one-way advertorial internet and the media-rich binary stream blogosphere of Web 2.0, Second Life represents the emergence of Web 3.0: a fully three-dimensional extra-terrestrial environment.[4] Where Web 2.0 generally implies a time lag between message and response, such as in MySpace and Facebook

Above: Screen images from Second Life, with avatars.

Twenty per cent of product is fashion-related, and almost everyone is self-employed. Bred-in-the-bone avatar designers who understand the value and methods of blogs and virtual-community building and who have different fashion-design skill sets (i.e. with software tools such as Photoshop and Poser) have had little trouble attracting interest in their wares. Shops were among the first buildings to spring up in the metaverse; avatars congregate in virtual malls just as teenagers hang out in real ones. As for the styles, items for sale include not only garments, gowns, shoes and accessories but also hair, skin and tattoos. Customizing your avatar is not only cheaper than plastic surgery but reversible. There is inevitably more flesh on display than in RL, and it is not always easy to guess the real gender of an avatar's owner. Second Life avatars are rarely shy, and a number of modelling competitions and virtual employment agencies are filling the growing demand for fashionable rent-a-crowds for events, parties, launches and shows. Appearances earn the avatars a few L$ and in-world celebrity stripes. Since the metaverse is not bounded by Newtonian physics, it is also possible to make extraordinary items to fit super-fit bodies. How about an evening gown of fire or dragonfly wings that flap? Megg Demina, who runs a millinery outlet, can customize the most outrageous Carmen Miranda bonnet for you. Nevertheless, there is, as in RL, a high demand for standard items. Some residents have owned up to hoarding up to 15,000 items in their virtual wardrobes and spending a small fortune of RL money. In contrast, according to virtual-world market research by Market Truths Ltd, others have managed to curtail their real-life shopaholic tendencies by staying indoors on the computer and buying and dressing online.[6]

Many real-world fashion brands and some of the less desirable industry practices are beginning to show up in Second Life. According to Janine Hawkins, known as Iris Ophelia (the fashion correspondent for *Second Style*, the in-world fashion glossy), rivalries among designers, knock-offs, theft and duplication are rife. Real-life sweatshops with underpaid workers busy churning out virtual objects and accessories for the parallel universe have been reported. Some designers have copyrighted their work to protect against counterfeiting. Alternatively, and more in keeping with the collaborative spirit of the betaverse, some designers see the infringers as allies, fans who can test, publicize and co-design with them. This may yet represent a new departure for test-marketing: timing and teasing the public's taste buds before product launches in the real-world marketplace.

The fascination with a nascent social world allows for an educative space not only for the armchair anthropologist but also for those who are bold enough to participate in experiments and collaborations that would be risky, impossible or too expensive in the real world. The virtual world can also be used as a training space, interviewing parlour or exhibition space. London College of Fashion and Buffalo State University are among a growing number of institutions that have an island in Second Life where students can display their designs and videos of fashion and artworks. Julia Gaimster, who set up the Second Life island site for LCF and worked with professional exhibitors On Off to create an alternative London Fashion Week show venue, says that the exhibition is visited frequently and leads to real enquiries for courses and information from around the world.

Metaverses are proliferating and more appear every month, jostling for supremacy. In South Korea the process has reached critical mass. There, supported by 90% broadband provision, over half the population have a presence in Cyworld, which is bursting with branded products like an out-of-town shopping mall. The Chinese government is building a cyber-park over 100 km² in size outside Beijing to host a server farm and training centre for future telecommunications and cyber-worlds. The government has confidence in the future benefits of virtual worlds and employment for the masses in making virtual cut-price objects. When the Swedish metaverse Entropia Universe saw a turnover in excess of $4 million, it was floated on the stock market. There is a rising number of branded pay-to-enter and corporate business virtual spaces. The Walt Disney Company operates Virtual Magic Kingdom, Club Penguin and Toontown. Mattel's Barbie Girls virtual world launched in April 2007 and signed up 3 million members in two months, adding 50,000 new members a day; membership stood at over 11 million within a year. But not everything is rosy in cyberspace. Stockholders like to see profits. The corporations, cowboys and *cosa nostra* are moving in, and squabbles are breaking out. Unable to account for any significant sales from their adventures in the metaverse, American Apparel has shut up shop in Second Life. If the metaverse holds up a mirror to the real world, rattled by a credit crunch and recession, perhaps we can predict that the risk-taking and shindigs will stop, that bubbles will burst and that bankruptcies will come in on the next virtual wave. Alternatively, perhaps we will be all the more encouraged to stop squandering our pennies and resources and step into the realms of virtuality to prototype a glowing and sustainable beta-world fit for future generations.

The future of virtual fashion

JULIA GAIMSTER, *head of e-learning at London College of Fashion, examines the growing importance of fashion in online virtual worlds, and the implications of virtualization for real-world fashion.*

The number of people participating in virtual worlds is growing year on year with almost 1.4 billion accounts registered in the second quarter of 2011.[1] Virtual worlds are used for education, business, social networking and gaming; they provide a cost-effective way of conducting meetings, training and enabling collaboration on creative projects.

In virtual worlds like Second Life (www. secondlife.com) virtual fashion products are one of the biggest selling items. Fashion in Second Life is a luxury purchase and the user can build an extensive wardrobe for his or her avatar (virtual model) at a fraction of the cost of buying the real thing. There are an increasing number of virtual worlds and games dedicated to fashion (www.girlsgamesy.com). The avatar can be an extension of the player's persona or, frequently, an alter ego with tastes and style that are radically different from those of their real-life owner. This kind of retail therapy generates income and provides real business opportunities for designers without the degree of waste that goes with real life consumption.

Maintaining an avatar and running a virtual world are not carbon-free activities. Equipment is needed to access the site; the site has to sit on a server and this is all powered by electricity and the carbon footprint of the internet increases by 10% each year. There is, however, an argument that the carbon footprint and the consumption of resources generated by creating a virtual garment represent a considerable reduction compared to creating a real one.

There is a far greater potential for the fashion industry to develop real-life products using virtual worlds. These are ideal environments for prototyping, product development, management training, visual merchandizing and customer service training. As systems are developed and refined, virtual technologies are increasingly having a direct impact upon how fashion is created, produced and sold. Virtual and 3-D technologies can work together to create and test realistic prototypes from which the consumer can order with growing confidence. Being able to cut out some of the wasteful processes in the current supply chain has many advantages for the environment, the manufacturer and the consumer.

Products for 3-D virtual prototyping and visualization such as OptiTex (www.optitex.com) and Modaris 3D Fit by Lectra (www.lectra.com) enable cloth simulation and 3D visualization of a real pattern on an avatar. These products have the potential to speed up the development process, reduce the need for sampling and therefore cut costs and promote sustainability. The take-up of 3-D virtual prototyping is on the increase and new workflows will develop to take advantage of the potential of this technology.

Dassault Systèmes, for instance, has developed Fashionlab (www.3ds. com/fashionlab/en/home) to bring together designers and engineers to create simpler, more sophisticated 3-D tools for fashion design. Tommy Hilfiger uses a virtual fitting room to cut down on corporate travel and the expense of creating and transporting multiple samples. Adidas also advocates a move to virtual sampling. Using Browzwear (www.browzwear.com) to create virtual samples of designs.

Virtualization will also have a major impact on retail. This is already evident in the increasing number of virtual mirrors for fashion and make-up being installed in stores, and online systems, such as Fits.me (http://fits.me/; see pp. 292–93), where you can create your own virtual model and have virtual fittings. Augmented reality technologies will close the gap between the virtual and the physical. In the future the Web will be three-dimensional and we will be able to browse through racks of virtual clothing and take them into the virtual fitting room to try on.

The internet itself is one huge virtual selling space and consumers are using it to meet and develop alternatives to mainstream shopping with sites such as Etsy (www.etsy.com), which enables users to buy and sell handmade and vintage clothing and gifts, or clothes-swapping sites such as www.bigwardrobe.com, where you can buy or exchange unwanted items of clothing and accessories. The internet is also becoming a channel for people to pass on their knowledge of how to create, customize and mend garments in a resurgence of the 'Make Do and Mend' mentality that last thrived in the Second World War, currently seeing a revival as a result of the recent recession.

One of the current downsides of virtual worlds is that they do not link together: you can't take your avatar from Second Life into World of Warcraft or Twinity. At present avatars are mostly locked into the world in which they were created, but this will change. OpenSim (http://opensimulator.org) already has the HyperGrid, which enables you to move from one OpenSim to another, opening up the possibility of interoperability between virtual worlds. Once this portability is fully established, the potential for a virtual web and a real 3-D shopping experience will become a reality. This will enable consumers to take personal avatars generated from their bodyscans on a 3D shopping tour of the web.

So can virtual technologies help the fashion industry to become more sustainable? The answer is yes and no. Virtual technologies can help to cut down on waste in the sampling and production process, and they can also help to ensure that manufacturers are not creating products that people do not want. On the negative side, they are powerful marketing tools that can be used to persuade consumers to buy goods that they do not need. Fundamentally the fashion industry thrives on peoples' desire for novelty, not sustainability. Although consumers are becoming more aware of these issues, there is still reluctance among many to ditch environmentally unfriendly disposable fashion. However, virtual technologies have the potential to enable the industry to be more sustainable while still meeting consumer demands.

Wonderland: disappearing dresses

HELEN STOREY AND TONY RYAN *This is the story of a collaboration between fashion design (Helen Storey) and polymer science (Tony Ryan). In a temporary studio, over twenty-six days from 3 February 2008, Storey made ten dresses that would disappear. The series was called Wonderland.*

Left: Wonderland printed polymer dress, 2008.

1. Tony is loud and likes rugby. Helen is quiet and likes Bikram yoga.

2. Tony was a teenage communist who wrote poetry and painted. Helen did ballet but hung about with skinheads who cut off her bun.

3. Tony is a scientist at the University of Sheffield. Helen is an artist and designer at London College of Fashion.

4. Tony used synchrotron radiation to look inside molecules. Like you do. Helen designed unusual dresses by looking inside the minds of women.

5. Tony worked very hard and was made a professor at the age of thirty-five. Helen worked very hard for Valentino and then began her own award-winning fashion business.

6. In 2002 Tony gave the Royal Institution Christmas Lectures on the science behind the stuff we take for granted. In 2004 he was awarded an OBE for 'services to science'.

7. In 1996 Helen was awarded a prize to design a twenty-seven-piece collection inspired by biology (the first 1,000 hours of human life) called Primitive Streak. This changed her life. Three more science/art projects later she got stuck...

8. Tony dragged science students into art galleries to see how the materials used influenced the work. A lifelong fan of The Clash, he knew not to confuse art with style.

9. In 2005 Helen heard Tony on the radio talking about materials chemistry. She rang him and provocatively asked, 'Can a bottle have consciousness? Can it know that it is empty and change its physical behavior to get rid of itself?' Tony did not laugh. Until he put the phone down.

10. Helen visited Tony and his colleagues in Sheffield. They all began to talk. Helen was questioning everything they knew and how they applied it.

11. Tony told Helen that in the course of a lifetime the average European throws away 20 tonnes of plastic. It's made from oil and is buried sunshine, and in three more generations it will all be gone.

12. Helen found that Tony was completely open to playing creatively, and, although each was fairly ignorant of the other's world, they began to consider things together, and discovered a mutual purpose for their new thinking.

13. Tony found that Helen's difficult questions challenged his assumptions and they realized that the power of their shared ideas could help others to understand difficult science.

Right: Disappearing dress installation *Say Goodbye*, 2010, for the exhibition 'Aware: Art Fashion Identity' at the Royal Academy, London.

Below: Printed polymer fabric dissolving in water, eventually leaving no trace.

14. They needed to create something that would be provocative, daring and bold.

15. At first the scientific world wasn't interested in disappearing bottles, so a Trojan horse was needed. Tony said 'What if you design some dresses that disappear?'

16. 'I don't design frocks any more!' said Helen, 'but if that's what's needed I'll do it.' And they were awarded a grant to start working with dissolvable fabrics and create new materials that could make consumer products less environmentally harmful.

17. But they could not do it alone. Textile designer Trish Belford (INTERFACE at the University of Ulster) started producing fabrics from polymers like the ones used in dissolvable washing detergents and then dropped them in big bowls of water.

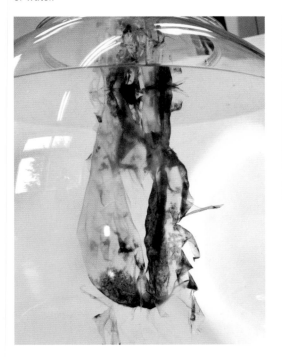

The meeting of fashion and science

We know that if we continue to live the way we are now, the earth will become uninhabitable. Yet we still struggle with the enormity of the thought and so, as often happens with war, it becomes something reported to us in our everyday lives, staining our hearts while frustrating our minds.

Experience shows that our enormous potential to think the unimaginable is increased most profoundly in collaboration. We deliberately collided our differently trained minds together to address some of the planet's greatest problems: lack of drinking water and the proliferation of non-recyclable plastics. This collision produced a new water-purification device and the disappearing plastic bottle, among other ideas.

We chose dresses to manifest our new approach because we wanted to create something beautifully familiar to stimulate

an emotional connection, particularly here at London College of Fashion (LCF). To watch a dress that has taken months to create disappear in a few days seemed to connect directly to that place of unfathomable loss. We hope this will serve as a metaphor for our disappearing world.

Through LCF's initiatives at its Centre for Sustainable Fashion and Centre for Fashion Science, and with the inspiration of Better Lives, this form of collided thinking can become powerfully embedded in our next generation of designers.

Wonderland is our call to creative arms. We all have a duty to use our talents, our imaginations and our rigour to create a healthier planet.

Helen Storey and Tony Ryan
Statement accompanying the 'Wonderland' exhibitions in London, Sheffield and Belfast.

Helen and Tony and others have come up with other ideas: a water purification pillow inspired by the crystals in nappies. an upper less shoe inspired by a barefoot summer. and a bottle that mostly vanishes under the tap. leaving only flowers.

18. Once in water the fabrics behaved like sea creatures. The dissolve was beautiful, the dance upsetting. Some chased each other around the bowl before disappearing altogether, a perfect metaphor for a vanishing world.

19. Helen and Tony and others have come up with other ideas: a water-purification pillow inspired by the crystals in nappies, an upper-less shoe inspired by a barefoot summer, and a bottle that mostly vanishes under the tap, leaving only flowers.

20. In January 2007 they showed the first dissolving dresses and shared their ideas with children, students and ordinary people in Sheffield. People were impressed.

21. The team decided to carry on with the journey. And here we are.

22. In this studio, over twenty-six days, Helen is making ten dresses that will disappear when shown in Sheffield and Belfast later this year. She made one earlier that is in the street window. It will be gone by 29 February.

23. Tony and Helen have taken a big bold risk in trying to do something different.

24. Wonderland could be seen as risky, but the pair are trying to suggest that we all need to share responsibility, use our creativity for a bigger purpose and open up a debate that can include everyone.

25. They do not have all the answers. But this is not about boring labs and test tubes. This is about turning ideas into reality.

Right: Field of Jeans installation, Euston Square, London, October 2011.

Catalytic Clothing: *Field of Jeans*

Following the success of the science and fashion collaboration Wonderland, Helen Storey and Tony Ryan developed a radical new project to explore how clothing and textiles can be used as a catalytic surface to purify air, employing existing technology in a new way. The concept of Catalytic Clothing was born, aiming to harness people power to tackle air pollution, a problem linked to increases in respiratory problems worldwide – just by wearing everyday clothing.

Catalytic Clothing utilizes a photocatalyst, activated by light, to break down airborne pollutants containing nanoparticles of titanium dioxide, a technology that is already used in commercial applications such as paint and cement.

The photocatalyst will be delivered to the surface of the clothing during the traditional laundry procedure, for example, as an additive in fabric conditioner. The active agent is packaged within a shell that binds to the surface of the clothing during the washing cycle. Although any garment that is treated with the product becomes active, a single garment is only able to remove a small proportion of the airborne pollutants. Therefore a large number of individuals, all acting together, is required to produce a noticeable reduction in the level of pollution.

A series of public presentations, such as the *Field of Jeans* installation, will create a dialogue about the project and serve as public experiments to test the activated clothing as the science is being developed.

Key directions for textiles and sustainability in the coming decade.

MARIE O'MAHONY *is a consultant, author, curator and academic specializing in advanced textiles for fashion design.*

ustainability is set to become one of the key issues influencing the direction of textiles over the coming decade. The move is towards a holistic view, with an acknowledgment that it is no longer enough to resolve one aspect – we must address everything from the source of the raw material through design, production, use and reuse of materials and products. Significant changes are likely to be seen in the following areas:

Sustainability and ethics: it is no longer enough for a material to be sustainable; it must also be produced ethically. Farmers, suppliers and workers will have to receive a proper wage and decent employment and working conditions. This means greater accountability and transparency in supply-chain management with developments in online and RFID (radio frequency identification) technologies, such as 'smart' tags capable of tracking the location of large numbers of individual items, facilitating this move.

Monomaterials: there are significant environmental benefits in producing fabric from a single type of fibre, such as polyester, as these fabrics are easier to recycle; there will therefore likely be a move towards using monomaterials. Advances in fibre and yarn engineering are set to make it easier to achieve the desired performance and to reduce the need for the addition of coating and finishing treatments.

Laundry and care: the labelling and care instructions for textiles will come under greater scrutiny, including recommended wash temperatures and 'dry-clean only' labels. This will not only have an impact on the textiles industry, but will also lead to changes in washing machines, tumble dryers and detergents.

Repair and mending: the next decade will see these practices become more widespread as consumers – motivated by both economic and environmental concerns – relearn the sewing skills that in previous generations were passed down in the home. The internet will play an important part in this educational process.

Carbon footprinting: concern about the carbon footprint of textiles will likely see a move towards bringing different stages in the manufacturing process closer together to reduce the miles travelled. The benefits of clustering related businesses in a single location (as, for example, in the grouping of surfing-related brands in the Torquay area of Australia) could increasingly apply to textiles and related chemical industries.

Waste as resource: industrial and post-consumer waste are set to be more widely acknowledged as important resources rather than simply as problems to be solved. The reuse of post-consumer textiles will likely move towards upcycling and the production of higher-value materials. There will also be an increase in the use of waste from previously untapped industries to manufacture novel fibres, such as yarn made from coconut husks that would otherwise become landfill.

'The method provides a new dimension for design.'

SIDDHARTHA UPADHYAYA, *while still a student at the National Institute of Fashion Technology in Delhi, developed an award-winning technology called DPOL (Direct Product on the Loom) to produce individually shaped and patterned garment pieces during the weaving of the fabric.*
By Sandy Black.

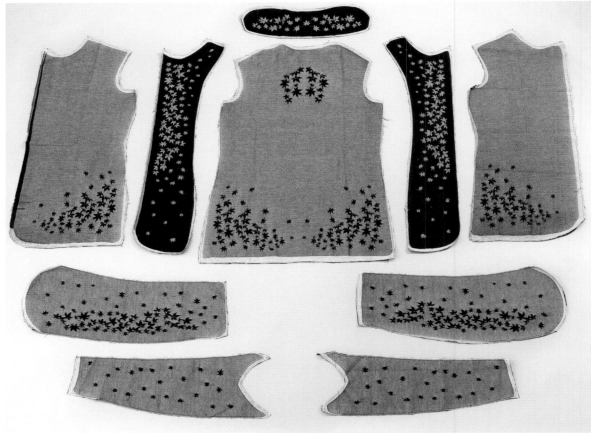

This page: The woven panels (*right*) and finished jacket (*above*): the designer first plans out the panel pieces and pattern imagery, which can be positioned precisely, and the pieces are then woven to shape, with an integral pattern.

Having registered a patent, Uphadhyaya set about promoting the concept. 'DPOL is a novel technology. It produces ready-to-stitch shaped woven garment components that are finished at the edges by a selvedge. This considerably reduces fabric loss by approximately 15% and lead time by approximately 50%. The DPOL technology can be used to manufacture high-quality fashion garments with mitering at various panels with respect to one another…and can support the creativity of the designer, offering design continuity and options for fabric surface ornamentation.'

Key features of the technology, which is designed on a computer linked directly to a loom, minimize the usual waste associated with cut and sewn woven garment manufacturing. The jacquard patterning is completely controlled by the designer, who can engineer every aspect of the individual garment, including continuity across darts and seams without loss of pattern, and multi-directional patterning around a garment such as a skirt. The entire process of design and production can be condensed down to only 4–6 hours using DPOL technology.

A collection of jackets, dresses and skirts produced using DPOL technology was shown at Lakmé Fashion Week 2009 in Mumbai under the label August, and the concept was also included in the exhibition 'Trash Fashion: Designing Out Waste' held in 2010–11 at the Science Museum in London.

'Instant fabric from a liquid spray'

MANEL TORRES *developed the radical spray-on fabric concept Fabrican while he was a graduate student at the Royal College of Art in London. Paul Luckam, a professor of particle technology at the same institution, has been a key advisor in developing Fabrican and is now Torres's business partner. By Sandy Black.*

The research unfolded in two stages. The first stage was to perfect the formulation, which would be applied using a simple spray technique (as in car paint spray). The second was to find a way to get the new liquid into an aerosol can. To create the formulation Torres and Luckam milled down old fabrics and mixed the fibres with a polymer to bind them together. They then added a solvent that evaporates instantly so that the spray turns into a solid on contact with a surface. The resulting non-woven fabric can easily be peeled off the surface of a mould or the wearer's body.

Torres completed his PhD research in 2000 and he and Luckam successfully produced a commercial aerosol version of Fabrican in 2008. Its potential uses range from single-use textiles for the medical sector to applications in the automotive industry. Additionally, Fabrican can be sprayed directly onto the body to create instant conceptual clothing, with applications in the film and theatre industry. Fabrican was used for costuming in the Belgian science fiction movie *Mr Nobody* (2009).

Torres comments on the sustainability benefits of Fabrican: 'Like many other businesses, we are conscious that there are aspects of the global textile industry that may be inherently unsustainable in the long term, resulting in a significant impact on the environment. The cotton industry alone is a major user of agrochemicals including synthetic fertilisers and pesticides...The textile manufacturing industry consumes large amounts of water and energy, contributing to the increasing pressure on the environment.'

Torres views his company as part of the solution to these problems, in part by offering a sustainable alternative to cheap 'fast-fashion' garments that are worn only once or twice before being thrown away. 'Fabrican believes that the textile and fashion industries have a responsibility for raising public awareness of these issues, and offer them the opportunity to choose alternative, greener products. We hope that we can contribute to changes in consumer behaviour through combining greener products with innovative, exciting fashion choices. Fabrican's patented spray-on fabric technology creates instant fabric...[and] part of our research is focused on reusing unwanted fabrics. For example, our lab test, entitled 'Space Dress', was created using our Fabrican formulation with fibres chopped and milled from our old white lab coats! The result was a startling fashion garment, created with minimal additional materials and energy resources.'

Torres emphasizes the fact that his product also has the potential to increase clothing recycling by providing a new market for unwanted textiles. 'Fabrican would like to encourage the greater use of collection banks for unwanted clothing, classified by the material and colour. We would then buy, ideally through a charitable trust, chop, and mill the material into flock fibres for use in creating garments.' He is currently refining the technology to improve the environmental impact of the aerosol delivery system itself. 'Fabrican is working closely with industry to commercialize technological applications using spray-jets with compressed air [as well as] environmentally friendly aerosols using greener gases and recyclable or refillable containers. Fabrican is working with an international aerosol supplier, Lindal Group, to create reusable aerosol containers for use with the spray-on fabric technology.'

Fabrican was selected as one of Best Inventions of 2010 by *Time* magazine. Clearly the future for this technology is bright.

Left: Mechanically milled fibres, here from recycled cotton clothing, are suspended in a solvent that evaporates when sprayed onto the body or any other surface.

Below: Fabrican is applied to a torso-shaped mould to make an instant garment.

BioCouture: growing fabrics for fashion

BIOCOUTURE *was developed by Suzanne Lee in 2004 in collaboration with biologist David Hepworth of CelluComp Ltd in Scotland. The project was named one of* Time *magazine's top fifty inventions of 2010. By Sandy Black.*

Lee and Hepworth's concept of growing fabric from organic matter is still in the early stages of development. It takes the age-old fermentation process used to produce kombucha, a type of green tea drunk in Asia, and harvests the cellulose mat that forms on the surface, which would normally be discarded. Once dried, it creates a skin-like material that can be cut and sewn like fabric.

The driving force behind BioCouture, the process of growing clothes from a bacteria–cellulose solution, is the search for alternative, sustainable materials for clothing. Lee is also looking at other potential uses for this new textile, such as home-interior and automotive applications. The cellulose material soaks up water like a sponge and is therefore very easy to dye, but it is also fairly unstable and further research is needed to engineer the microbial action to address this.

Recent experiments include investigating composite materials, in which the cellulose is combined with more traditional textile substrates such as cotton to create fabrics with new qualities. The resulting prototype garments were exhibited in the show 'Trash Fashion: Designing out Waste' (2010) at the Science Museum in London, and at the ModeMuseum Antwerp's 'Alter Nature: The Future That Never Was' (2011).

Right: Indigo-dyed BioCouture jacket constructed in the style of a classic denim jacket.

Opposite: Undyed BioCouture jacket with frill detailing.

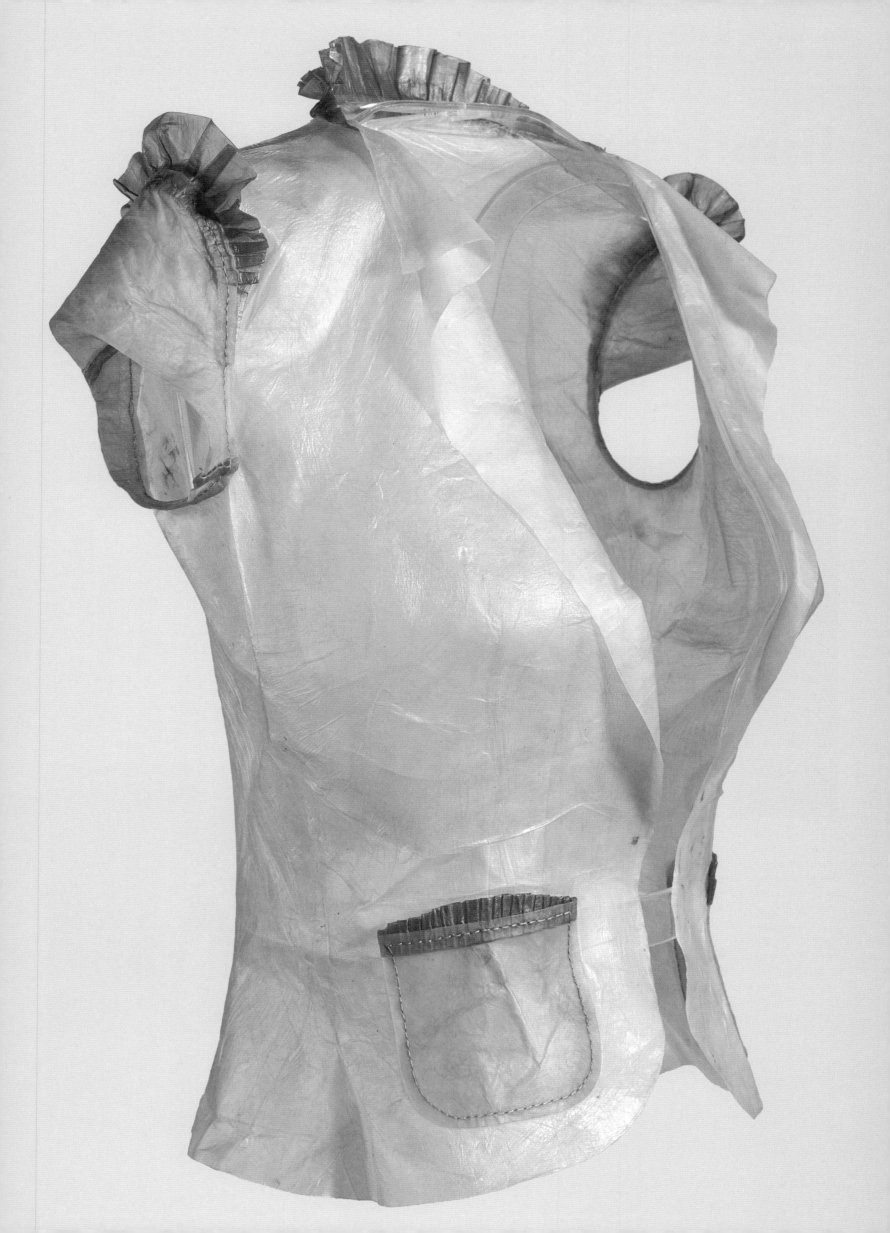

Boudicca: design in flux

BOUDICCA *is the innovative and experimental British design partnership of Zowie Broach and Brian Kirkby, who discuss the importance of emerging technologies in their work and the challenges of embracing sustainability as a smaller label. By Sandy Black*

'Avant-garde', 'non-conformist', 'experimental', 'edgy', 'conceptual' and 'politicized' have all been adjectives used by critics to describe the work of Broach and Kirkby. Since their debut in 1997 the experimental British duo have created powerful fashion statements for women that have more than passing reference to their muse, the British Iron Age warrior-queen Boudicca. Fiercely independent, despite being sponsored by American Express for two years, Broach and Kirkby have involved themselves in more political causes than most fashion designers, including the anti-capitalist demonstrations at the 2001 G8 Summit and campaigns to fight AIDS in Africa. Combining the best of both ready-to-wear and couture approaches to fashion, the pair conduct extensive research into new technologies to develop the concepts for each collection, which are then realized through intricate

tailoring. In recent years Broach and Kirkby's work has increasingly involved bodyscanning, multimedia platforms and software systems for generative design. They created their own 3-D scanner, using lasers generating structured light, and processed the resulting data through modified software to generate 3-D forms. Another exciting recent innovation – this time involving research into chemical technology – is their perfume WODE, which when first sprayed on has an indigo colour that disappears as it dries, leaving only the scent.

Q How do you describe Boudicca as a brand?

A Boudicca is both an exploration of design itself and an expressive biography of the times we live in. It represents the outcome of our ever-evolving process of questioning our methods of expression. One of the joys and rewards of Boudicca is the changeable nature of the label, which is in a constant state of flux. Even when we reread these [responses to the interview] questions we are already constructing other answers. The idea of a limited definition fills us with fear of being categorized. The duality of our perspective as both male and female designers contributes to what we see as the future of womenswear: an equality that is represented in dress. Boudicca has no wish to be a clothing factory making hundreds and thousands of the same garments, sold in stores that are uniform all over the world. We want to remain a niche and exclusive label, because that sense of discovery is part of the Boudicca experience. When you are wearing Boudicca you should feel powerful and safe in your own personal armour, yet capable of romance and emotionally attached to the garment itself. Boudicca is anti-mass-anything.

Does emerging technology play a part in your conceptual or practical development of collections? Do you have a wish list for future fashion?
New technology is without doubt pulling us all forward and this is definitely the most intriguing and

important aspect of our work. Rapid prototyping, online animation and laser and digital technology have all played a part in the story, but there is so much more that we would like to involve ourselves in as a company, to drive us and give us new frameworks to create within. Technology needs to be interwoven with our current skills and crafts, examined in a different mindset. Emerging technologies provide new tools with which to explore our methods and systems of work. We are currently interested in introducing a random generative design-producing code, which will further support our need for designing in a state of flux. New technology should not just be used for physical production but also to challenge the very nature of the process, using software developers and projection interwoven with animation to hack and merge all available 3-D technologies. Our ideal scenario would be to have

a small team of creative technical thinkers and the budget to trial the practical outcomes of their imaginative thought processes. We see a future in which people create their own software, which becomes an extension of themselves.

Do questions of sustainability have an impact on the way you design and produce your collections?

As a creative business we have usually been guided by our instincts and practical restrictions. So all the decisions we have to make – be they about the idea for the design, the quality of the make, the fabric or the ongoing knowledge of the team – are ultimately about a value. We approach these decisions instinctively, without too much questioning or discussion. Our responses are based upon our own core values of thinking, learning and living.

We try to create clothes that are outside the rapidly changing cycle of trends. This 'in-and-out-of-fashion' hype-mentality does not appeal to our sensibilities. We would rather make high-quality clothes that transcend the seasonal system of fashion. We see our clothes as part of a single ongoing narrative; they can be assembled together like a collage irrespective of which collection they are from. Our clients 'collect' Boudicca. Collecting rather than consuming seems a better way forward.

Do you think it is easier or more difficult for a smaller label to be ethically and environmentally sound in doing business?

Smaller businesses cannot make grand gestures, but they can hold core values together more easily, and should do so. These values do not have to be made obvious or used to sell your ideas – they can just be a natural part of how your company works. Limitations and obstacles will always be present for those who choose to put quality and ideas first, as Western culture and capitalism have not been structured to thrive on them. Until wider changes happen in society, you have to make your choices and stay true to them, learn to choose your battles and protect the space needed for the growth of ideas.

Everyone has a choice as to how they create and achieve the values of their business. This is what makes you – and your company – what you are. Budgets can always be shifted. Each decision is initially directed by your instincts, which then become your manifesto.

Boudicca has previously taken a more explicitly political stance than most other fashion designers. What are your proudest achievements and can you tell us about the direction you plan to take in the next five years?

Boudicca is proud to have been part of the Genoa Generation, a protest movement at the beginning of the 21st century. It was a steep learning curve, and at times depressing, but the experience demanded that we confront and understand more of the world we live in, and still does. Only this constant need to understand will make a difference. It is a long-term commitment, not a trend – to not accept the system just because it has always been there, and to realize that we all have the ability to make a world that is closer to the one we dream of living in.

Mass capitalism's main weapon is to keep us confused, not quite knowing what is happening, in constant fear and bombarded by fake cures. Look for clarity and hold fast to your own true self, because this self is being taken from us.

What is reasonable to expect of a fashion designer with regards to wider issues surrounding fashion?

Boudicca is part of an exchange culture…Being a role model is not the first consideration when you are led to a particular idea by instinct and emotion, but we absolutely have a responsibility to reflect the best possible values in our work.

Above: Boudicca 'Fragmented Dreams' collection, Spring/Summer 2011.

Opposite left: 'Private Scans 001', 2010. 3-D imagery is generated from a moving (rather than static) body within a 3-D bodyscanner, creating interference and distortion that is used to develop garment patterns.

Opposite right: Boudicca Couture 'Still' collection, 2002, shown in Paris.

Technology in fashion

In recent years a number of pioneering designers have experimented with clothing that is multifunctional, smart, responsive. It is possible that if clothes can give the consumer greater rewards, and maintain their novelty factor, this will counteract the current unsustainable popularity of short-life clothing.
By Sandy Black

The process of technology integration takes vision, investment of time and money, and skilled interdisciplinary teams. More than any other contemporary fashion designer, Hussein Chalayan has experimented with prototype concepts for transformation: remote-control moulded fiberglass 'aeroplane' dresses with moving panels ('Echoform', Autumn/Winter 1999; 'Before Minus Now', Spring/Summer 2000); 'motion' dresses that morph their structure and shape from the style of one era to another ('One Hundred and Eleven Dresses', Spring/Summer 2007); and a video dress projecting moving imagery through panels of LED lights ('Airborne', Autumn/ Winter, 2007).

CuteCircuit (Francesca Rosella and Ryan Genz) creates fun and innovative clothing with embedded electronic functionality, worn by celebrities such as Bono. One of its best-known ideas is its 'Hug Shirt', which transmits the sensation of a hug across mobile communication networks, and can also be disassembled at the end of its life for reuse and recycling of parts. CuteCircuit's 'GalaxyDress' (2009), commissioned by the Chicago Museum of Science and Industry, incorporates over 24,000 wafer-thin LEDs that create cascades of colour and movement

Above: Hussein Chalayan, video dress with LED display, sponsored by Swarovski, Autumn/Winter 2007.

Left: Hussein Chalayan, coat with mechanical moving hood that can be raised and lowered over the head, 'Airborne' Autumn/Winter 2007.

The process of technology integration takes vision, investment of time and money, and skilled interdisciplinary teams.

Below: Hussein Chalayan, 'Airborne', featuring remote-control dresses that could change their shape and form, Autumn/Winter 2007.

Above: CuteCircuit, 'Hug Shirt', which transmits signals via sensors and mobile technology to a loved one far away, 2006.

Left: CuteCircuit, 'GalaxyDress', commissioned by the Chicago Museum of Science and Industry's Innovation Gallery, 2009.

Above: Dai Fujiwara for Issey Miyake, Autumn/Winter 2011. For his final collection for Issey Miyake, Fujiwara presented origami fabrication, generating 3-D shapes from a single sheet of paper, then cloth, creating 3-D garments in a complex play of engineered forms, made with minimal seaming.

The Issey Miyake design studio and Reality Lab focuses not on electronics but on textile fabrication and innovative design systems.

on its surface. Despite its size, the dress has a low power consumption, requiring only the same rechargeable battery as an MP3 player.

The Issey Miyake design studio and Reality Lab focuses not on electronics but on textile fabrication and innovative design systems, including its groundbreaking A-POC concept (see pp. 80–81), a one-step manufacturing process utilizing complex knitting and weaving software systems. Miyake's Pleats Please heat-set pleated fabric, developed in 1993, is made from polyester, which is recyclable, highly durable and requires only low-energy washing and drying and no ironing. The latest Miyake project, '132 5', is an origami-style collection made from recycled polyester that is transformed from a flat sheet into a 3-D garment with the aid of a geometric-modelling program designed by computer scientist Jun Mitani, minimizing material and storage space.

Above right: Kate Goldsworthy, 'Mono Finished Garment', recycled polyester, 2010. Another technological innovator in textile design, Goldsworthy uses lasers as one-step decorative tools for synthetic textiles; the lasers also can be used to weld the seams as part of the same process.

Right: Issey Miyake, sculptural shape achieved with the Miyake signature pleated polyester fabrication process, Autumn/Winter 2011 pre-collection.

Direct product manufacturing

A new technology has the potential to revolutionize fashion production by eliminating traditional manufacturing, transportation and warehousing requirements. By Sandy Black

A paradigm shift in product manufacturing has been taking place over the last decade. Developed from the engineering process known as 'rapid prototyping', in which a 3-D physical model is 'printed' layer by layer from a tank of powdered nylon, direct manufacturing through deposition or laser sintering is now being harnessed to create finished products and components on demand. It is envisaged that in the future everyone will have a 3-D printer on their desk, and will be able to download files and 'print' objects, including clothing and accessories, in the same way we currently use 2-D printers to transfer documents. This will save on production costs, warehousing and transportation.

Freedom of Creation, a pioneering design and research consultancy in Amsterdam founded in 2002 by Janne Kyttanen and Jiri Evenhuis, is making the concept a reality, using 3-D software modelling to create lighting, furniture, and other products. The company has developed a unique chain-link 3-D structure that behaves remarkably like a textile, opening new possibilities for clothing and accessories. A one-piece chain-link bag and various prototype garments have been developed. For shoemaking, Kerrie Luft, a graduate from London College of Fashion's MA Fashion Footwear programme, has used the technology to replace traditional methods of casting and model-making to create contemporary heel designs digitally.

Right: Kerrie Luft, shoe with digitally manufactured heel, 3-D printed titanium, 2009.

Opposite left: Freedom of Creation, 'Palm' light digitally manufactured in one piece from nylon, 2006.

Opposite right: Freedom of Creation, chain-link textile made from 3-D printed nylon, 2004.

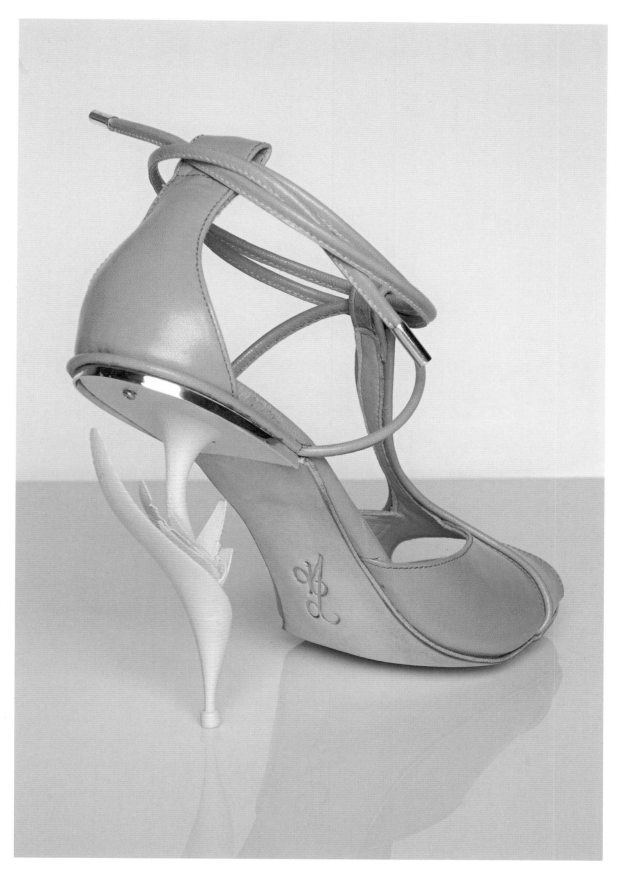

It is envisaged that in the future everyone will have a 3-D printer on their desk, and will be able to download files and 'print' objects, including clothing and accessories.

Future scenarios

FORUM FOR THE FUTURE, *an independent British think-tank, worked with students from London College of Fashion's MA Fashion and the Environment course to develop four possible global scenarios for 2025, focused on clothing, intended to stimulate discussion in businesses and educational settings about sustainability. The project was supported by Levi Strauss & Co.*

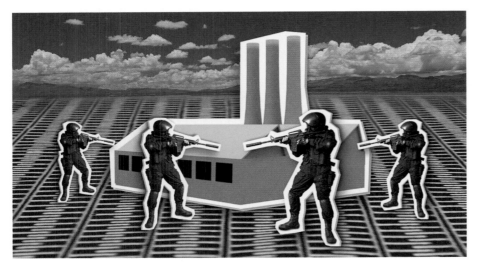

COMMUNITY COUTURE

It's 2025; there has been no effective agreement on climate change and the world is struggling to adapt to the new environmental reality. This means astronomically high prices for raw materials, water, oil and other forms of energy. Some communities have become self-sufficient, investing collectively in micro-generation. Clothes that can generate electricity also grow in popularity. Farmers are now given subsidies to grow food rather than cotton. In manufacturing, power shortages disrupt production everywhere. Factories that are able to get their hands on raw materials require armed protection; inside, escalating costs mean that conditions for workers deteriorate. China, long the manufacturing hub of the world, is facing a water crisis. New clothes are now very expensive to make; their high prices are out of reach for most and a culture of 'Make Do and Mend' predominates. In order to afford new items communities often purchase collectively to get better prices and some regions have introduced compulsory uniforms for all residents to save on raw materials. Unwanted and used clothing has become a valuable commodity. The old retail spaces now house huge thrift markets for clothes, and services such as on-the-spot tailoring. Clothing libraries have sprung up to satisfy demands for haute couture and vintage. Even the beautiful people use the community laundrette.

1. The world is: struggling to cope with the impacts of climate change and resource shortages, but community bonds are strong as many strive for self-sufficiency.

2. Fashion is: expensive new, or cheaper second-hand; very high costs of raw materials and disrupted supply chains have resulted in a dramatic fall in the production and sale of new clothing.

3. The fabrics we wear are: second-hand, or made from community-grown fibres such as hemp; only the rich can afford 'certified new' clothes made from expensive synthetics or virgin raw materials.

4. We get our clothes: at vibrant second-hand markets with tailors and stylists on hand, in retail stores with extra security, on the black market or from clothing libraries.

5. Clothes are made: at home or in community-run recycling centres linked to local hyper-efficient factories.

6. We care for clothes: using community laundries and washing machines that consume only one cup of water. 'Make Do and Mend' is taught in schools.

7. When we have finished with clothes: we sell them back for reuse to boost our incomes.

8. The industry is sustainable through: second-hand clothing becoming a valuable resource – nothing is disposed of.

9. Successful fashion businesses are: part of the local community, providing energy supply, education and even food to employees.

Statement from Peter Madden

A sustainable and profitable fashion industry is achievable if the businesses involved are willing to rethink how they do things in the face of issues like climate change, water scarcity and demographic change. This will be a stretch. It will need responsible sourcing, closed-loop manufacturing and genuine consumer engagement.

The industry also needs to work together better. There are some good joint initiatives – for example around cotton – but to meet the scale and urgency of the challenges we face, the key industry players need to come together quickly, and take action together across the entire fashion supply chain.

The fashion companies that take sustainability seriously now will be the ones that profit – from resilient supply chains, lower costs and more loyal customers – in the future.

Peter Madden is chief executive of Forum for the Future

PATCHWORK PLANET

In 2025 the balance of power has shifted. The Asian economies led by China are dominant, and the West is marginalized as other cultural and economic alliances achieve prominence. Companies and individual countries jealously guard their technologies. Fashions turn over quickly and an extremely localized celebrity culture develops. 'Sex, Drugs and Rock and Roll' is out; trends are now inspired by religious and cultural ideals. Some consumers express their individuality by personalizing their clothes. Those companies that assert their local connections do best. Textiles are made using native raw materials: Asians produce new materials from bamboo and Australians market their wool as an energy-saving material. Clothes are made close to where they are to be sold and big brands save resources by creating clothes that can be easily adapted. Cleaning clothes is easy for countries with sufficient renewable energy and water; for others, high-tech durable fabrics are being developed. In in this fragmented world bad environmental habits still persist, creating problems that can't be ignored forever.

1. The world is: broken into cultural 'blocs' with unequal economic performance; Asia is the economic and cultural powerhouse; there is conflict over scarce resources.

2. Fashion is: strongly influenced by regional trends and celebrities, and highly personalized.

3. The fabrics we wear are: made locally to supply local manufacturing – bamboo in Asia, wool in Australia, flax in India – and include smart materials that use nanotechnology. The choice of colours is limited to save water and energy in dyeing.

4. We get our clothes: online via mobile devices; consumers can personalize their clothes online.

5. Clothes are made: in regional factories; short supply chains mean clothes reach consumers quickly.

6. We care for clothes: according to wide regional differences; some companies have developed waterless washing machines; others use coatings to limit the need for washing.

7. When we have finished with clothes: they are (often illegally) dumped; one alternative to this is edible clothing, which is a popular trend in Europe.

8. The industry is sustainable through: a variety of locally appropriate strategies; sustainability know-how is guarded jealously so progress is slow and the world is struggling to cope with mounting social tensions and environmental constraints.

9. Successful fashion businesses are: national heroes; companies with strong local heritage do best.

'Luxury' now means something that is good for people and for the planet, and the fashion world embraces this new ethic. Conscientious consumers insist that businesses must be transparent.

SLOW IS BEAUTIFUL

In 2025 the world has slowed down, with communities and businesses using and emitting less. Lower-income countries that are less dependent on fossil fuels adapt quickly to low-carbon development, while China and the US go head-to-head in the race to develop sustainable technologies. Floods, resource shortages and ensuing conflicts mean that climate change remains at the top of the international agenda, but in most countries draconian legislation ensures that people don't exceed their new carbon allowances. 'Luxury' now means something that is good for people and for the planet, and the fashion world embraces this new ethic. Conscientious consumers insist that businesses must be transparent. Our clothes still come from all around the world but they arrive more slowly. Companies in most regions now pay a living wage. Africa does a roaring trade in organic cotton; synthetic fabrics are created from clean and renewable resources. New technology even allows some clothes to monitor people's health. To save carbon people buy clothing that lasts and needs less cleaning, but when things do get messy clothes are washed in cold water, without harmful chemicals. The high cost of transport means that shopping goes local again. For variety many turn to the vintage clothes they find online and elsewhere. Handcrafted clothes from around the world are also popular, but consumers generally buy fewer goods. As refugees flee climate change, they spread their fashions throughout the world.

1. The world is: moralistic, risk-averse, low-carbon, tightly regulated with sustainable lifestyles and mindsets.

2. Fashion is: über sustainable and über cool; most consumers are prepared to pay more for a smaller number of high-quality sustainable clothing items.

3. The fabrics we wear are: durable, organic natural fibres; man-made materials from renewable resources; handcrafted, vintage or second-hand; or even 'smart clothes' monitoring health.

4. We get our clothes: from small or virtual stores with hyper-efficient logistics, or we swap with friends.

5. Clothes are made: in different regions of the world according to the manufacturing processes they require; India and Nigeria have big 'refurbished clothing' industries; most workers are paid a 'living wage'.

6. We care for clothes: without harmful chemicals; clothes last longer and are washed less often, at lower temperatures.

7. When we have finished with clothes: we take them back to where we bought them to be shipped and remanufactured.

8. The industry is sustainable through: SustainGrade labelling and digital tagging, ensuring that consumers know exactly where their clothes have come from and what impact they've had, but a 'grey economy' with poor labour standards still exists to satisfy those who refuse to conform to the new slower world order.

9. Successful fashion businesses are: those that are radically transparent, most sustainable and offer best value.

TECHNO CHIC

Welcome to 2025, a healthier, wealthier world, in which fashion's influence is reaching further than ever before. Climate change has topped the global political agenda for over twenty years and low-carbon technologies such as wind and solar power have really taken off. Everything that goes into making a garment is designed for reuse and re-manufacture. Leading brands ask the public to vote online to decide which styles go into production, saving energy and waste, but in the factories unrelenting automation is leading to mass unemployment. Technology has also revolutionized textiles, producing advanced low-impact fibres – garments can literally be sprayed onto the body, which has kept clubbers smiling. High-tech 'chameleon' materials allow users to emulate the styles of any celebrity they see, but not everyone can keep up and many people experience burnout. High-tech shopping solutions keep pace with the demands of the speed-obsessed global consumer. Fads and fashions come and go, often within a few hours. 3-D bodyscanning brings the changing room to the bedroom and styles begin to look the same everywhere. Caring for clothes has gone low carbon, with fabrics that reduce sweating and door-to-door valet collection reducing the need to store and wash clothes at home. Some brands give up selling products and now lease clothes to consumers; tour operators do the same abroad. Living light is in; owning stuff is out.

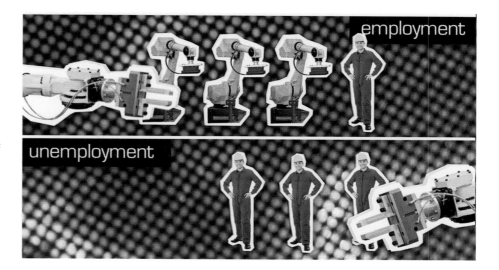

1. The world is: healthy, wealthy and ultra high-tech; materialism is out of favour and 'lightweight living' is the aim.

2. Fashion is: fast-paced, low-carbon and cheap.

3. The fabrics we wear are: made from new high-tech, low-impact fibres; we wear biodegradable, non-toxic spray-on clothing, nano-tech fabrics and programmable clothing.

4. We get our clothes: using 3-D bodyscanners that allow people to 'try on' clothes in virtual mirrors and on interactive screens.

5. Clothes are made: by machines, not people; sharp declines in the use of labour create pockets of crippling unemployment; modular clothing is manufactured in China and delivered to stores to be customized to consumer demand.

6. We care for clothes: using high-tech, personalized clothing valet services, nanotech coatings that reduce the need for washing, 'smart' solutions such as low-impact clothing care, and advanced recycling networks.

7. When we have finished with clothes: they are composted, disassembled, remanufactured or reused according to design.

8. The industry is sustainable through: financially viable low-carbon, low-impact production; technology delivers sustainable solutions but some people can't keep up with the fast pace.

9. Successful fashion businesses are: finding creative ways to keep their customers loyal and anticipating demand to avoid waste.

Notes

INTRODUCTION

Interrogating fashion
Sandy Black

1. 'The Fashion Paradox' was a theme of the cross-disciplinary research network Interrogating Fashion, begun in 2004 as part of the Designing for the 21st Century initiative, and funded by the UK Arts and Humanities Research Council and the UK Engineering and Physical Sciences Research Council from 2005 to 2009. 'The Fashion Paradox' examined the contradictions between the inherent transience and obsolescence of fashion cycles, and the global economic dependence on the industry by millions of workers throughout the complex textile and fashion supply chains. See also Sandy Black, *Eco Chic: The Fashion Paradox* (2008).
2. *A New World Map in Textiles and Clothing: Adjusting to change* (Organization for Economic Cooperation and Development, 2004).
3. Julian M. Allwood, Søren Ellebæk Laursen, Cecilia Malvido de Rodríguez and Nancy M. P. Bocken, *Well Dressed? The Present and Future Sustainability of Clothing and Textiles in the UK* (University of Cambridge Institute for Manufacturing, 2006), p. 12.
4. Portals such as <www.indicustom.com, www.makeyourownjeans.com>, or <www.tailorstore.com> typically require customers to select from multiple options and provide their own measurements.
5. Cited in Harry Wallop, 'M&S £30 made-to-measure shirt beats Savile Row rival', *Daily Telegraph*, 20 November 2008.
6. The Bodymetrics 'pod' installed in the Selfridges flagship store in London requires customers to be bodyscanned in 3-D, and then selects the best fit from a physical range of jeans, <www.bodymetrics.com>. The Brooks Brothers flagship store in New York offers 'digital tailoring' based on 3-D bodyscanning measurements, <www.brooksbrothers.com>.
7. N. Stern, *The Economics of Climate Change: The Stern Review* (2006).
8. *Sustainable Clothing Action Plan*, (Department for Environment, Food and Rural Affairs [DEFRA], 2008; updated 2010).
9. 'Green' publications included consumer guides such as Duncan Clark, *The Rough Guide to Ethical Living* (2006); Tamsin Blanchard, *Green is the New Black: How to change the world with style* (2007); Matilda Lee, *Eco Chic: The savvy shopper's guide to ethical fashion* (2007); and popular business titles such as Pietra Rivoli, *The Travels of a T-shirt in the Global Economy*, (2005) and Joe Bennett, *Where Underpants Come From* (2008). Influential films on these issues included Davis Guggenheim's *An Inconvenient Truth* (2006) and Leonardo DiCaprio's *The 11th Hour* (2007); along with televised documentaries such as the BBC's 'Blood, Sweat and T-Shirts' (2008).
10. See, for example: Victor Papanek, *Design for the Real World: Human ecology and social change* (1971) and *The Green Imperative: Ecology and ethics in design and architecture* (1995); Nigel Whitely, *Design for Society* (1993); Dorothy MacKenzie, *Green Design: Design for the environment*, 2nd edn (1997); and Graham Cavanagh-Downs, Helen Lewis, John Gertsakis and Tim Grant, *Design + Environment: A global guide to designing greener goods* (2001).
11. Jonathan Chapman, *Emotionally Durable Design: Objects, experiences and empathy* (2005); Stuart Walker, *Sustainable By Design: Explorations in theory and practice* (2006).
12. These include Kate Fletcher, *Sustainable Fashion and Textiles: Design journeys* (2008); Janet Hethorn and Connie Ulasewicz, *Sustainable Fashion: Why now?* (2008); and Black, *Eco Chic* (2008).
13. These Scandinavian initiatives include NICE (Nordic Initiative Clean and Ethical), and the Future Fashion project in Sweden funded by Mistra, the Foundation for Strategic Environmental Research.

14. The Sustainable Apparel Coalition was founded with thirty-three members to focus on the development of universal tools for measuring sustainability in apparel and footwear life cycles, and to drive best practice and innovation through collaboration.
15. The Interrogating Fashion network was funded under Phase 1 of the Designing for the 21st Century initiative, discussed in note 1, above. See also the project website at <http://www.design21.dundee.ac.uk/index.htm>.

CHAPTER 1

Self and beauty/Culture and consumption

Introduction
Sandy Black

1. 'Editorial: Global textile and apparel sourcing – the views of four brands', *Textile Outlook International*, 145 (June 2010), p. 4.

The game of fashion and LOOKBOOK.nu
Otto von Busch

1. Richard Dawkins, *The Selfish Gene* (1976).
2. Martin Gardner, 'Mathematical games: The fantastic combinations of John Conway's new solitaire game "life"', *Scientific American* 223 (October 1970), pp. 120–23.
3. John Holland, *Emergence: From chaos to order* (1998); Daniel Dennett, *Freedom evolves* (2003).
4. Gabriel Tarde, *Psychologie économique* (1902).
5. Gabriel Tarde, *The Laws of Imitation* (1903).
6. Pierre Bourdieu, 'Haute Couture and Haute Culture', in his *Sociology in Question* (1993), p. 135.

Sustainable fashion in the age of celebrity culture
Pamela Church Gibson

1. Thorstein Veblen, *The Theory of the Leisure Class* (1899; repr. 2000), pp. 49–70.
2. Jess Cartner-Morley, 'Eyes front', *The Guardian*, 13 March 2009.
3. See Pamela Church Gibson, *Fashion and Celebrity Culture* (2011), pp. 204–5.
4. Veblen, p. 60.
5. Quoted in Matthew Price, 'Weary of the leisure class?', *Boston Globe*, 12 December 2004.
6. See Jem Bendell and Anthony Kleanthous, *Deeper Luxury: Quality and style when the world matters* (World Wildlife Fund UK, 2007).
7. See Jackie Stacey, *Stargazing: Hollywood cinema and female spectatorship* (2004) and Rachel Moseley, *Growing Up with Audrey Hepburn* (2002).
8. Suzy Menkes, 'Sustainable luxury', *New York Times*, 26 March 2009.

The hidden persuaders and their dark screens of meaning
Emma Neuberg

1. Data from < http://www.sceniccolorado.org/articles/billboard-mythology> (accessed 05/ 11/08).
2. For YouTube link, go to <http://uk.youtube.com/watch?v=HkmNO9m7llg> (accessed 03/12/08).
3. For YouTube link, go to <http://uk.youtube.com/watch?v=gyruKxH5icg> (accessed 03/12/08).
4. For further explanation of Wilfred Bion's Basic Assumption Groups, see W. R. Bion, *Experiences in Groups and Other Papers* (1991).
5. These ideas were presented by Susie Orbach in a live debate at the Victoria & Albert Museum, London, on 17 October 2008.
6. The 'other' in psychoanalysis is an entity that represents a difficult, persecutory internal voice.
7. Sigmund Freud, The Interpretation of Dreams (1899; English translation 1913; repr. 1997), p. 4.
8. See <http://www.break.com/usercontent/2008/9/Diesel-SFW-XXX-577249.html> (accessed 3 December 2008).

9. See <http://shine.yahoo.com/channel/beauty/scariest-shopping-commercial-ever-450437/> (accessed 3 December 2008).
10. S. H. Foulkes is quoted by Farhad Dalal in T*aking the Group Seriously: Towards a post-Foulkesian group analytic theory* (1998), p. 58.
11. For further insights, see Adam Curtis's documentary *The Century of the Self* (2002).
12. Examples could be seen at <http://www.notcot.com>, <http://www.theviralfactory.com> and <http://www.setyourstyle.com> at the time of writing.
13. See Morris Nitsun, *The Anti-Group: Destructive forces in the group and their creative potential* (1996).
14. Ibid.
15. For a variety of figures, see <http://answers.google.com/answers/threadview?id=56750> (accessed 28 May 2009).
16. See Stephanie Nebehay 'Financial crisis may increase mental health woes', *Reuters*, 9 October 2008, available at <http://www.reuters.com/article/healthNews/idUSTRE49839M20081009> (accessed 12 December 2008); and Rebecca Smith, 'Financial crisis will hit mental health of the nation, warn government advisors' *The Telegraph*, 21 October 2008.
17. Ibid.
18. Vance Packard, *The Hidden Persuaders* (1957; repr. 1991).
19. 'Radicalization' is a psychological term suggesting the arousal of difficult feelings particularly associated with internal others – see note 20, below.
20. 'Internal others' is a psychological term that relates to the concept of cohabitation of internalized personae stemming from childhood trauma.
21. S. H. Foulkes and E. J. Anthony, *Group Psychotherapy: The psychoanalytic approach*, (1957), p. 54.
22. Dalal, p. 58.
23. S. H. Foulkes, *Therapeutic Group Analysis*, (1964), p. 42.
24. Dalal, p.58.
25. For original Spanish press coverage, see 'Dolce y Gabbana criticados en España', *Prensa*, 26 February 2007, available at <http://mensual.prensa.com/mensual/contenido/2007/02/26/hoy/vivir/900688.html> (accessed 3 December 2008).
26. See Herbert Rosenfeld, *Impasse and Interpretation: Therapeutic and anti-therapeutic factors in the psychoanalytic treatment of psychotic, borderline and neurotic patients* (1987).
27. For further information, see: <http://www.groupanalysis.org/site/cms/contentChapterView.asp?chapter=492> (accessed 26 May 2009).
28. For description see: <http://dvice.com/archives/2008/01/giant_light_up.php> (accessed 26 May 2009).
29. See: <http://www.jp.playstation.com/scej/title/dress/> (accessed 26 May 2009).
30. See: <http://mihara.puma.com/> (accessed 26 May 2009).
31. See: <http://www.adverblog.com/archives/003718.htm> (accessed 26 May 2009).
32. From 2007 onwards. See: <http://www.tokidoki.it/> (accessed 26 May 2009).
33. See: <http://www.adverblog.com/archives/003245.htm> (accessed 26 May 2009).
34. Mike Tait quotes from D. W. Winnicott's essay 'The Antisocial Tendency' in *Deprivation and Delinquency: D. W. Winnicott*, Madeleine Davis, Ray Shepherd and Clare Winnicott (eds) (1984).
35. Boff Whalley, 'In Defense of Anarchy', *The Independent*, 12 August 2011.

Stella McCartney
Sandy Black

1. *Evening Standard ES Magazine*, 18 May 2007.
2. *Le Monde*, 6 March 2011.
3. Interview by Charlotte Casiraghi, *Above*, July 2009.
4. Interview by Matilda Lee, *The Ecologist*, 1 May 2009.
5. Interview by Jess Cartner-Morley, *The Guardian*, 5 October 2009.

Edun
Sandy Black
1. Rogan Gregory interviewed in *Wallpaper**, 18 April 2007.
2. <http://www.edun.com/about-edun#our-mission> (accessed 26 May 2012).
3. Edun Autumn/Winter 2008 press release and promotional material.

EDUN's view on trade regulation in Africa (box)
1. Information and statistics provided by DATA (Debt AIDS Trade Africa). See also 'Stitched Up: How rich-country protectionism in textiles and clothing trade prevents poverty alleviation' Oxfam briefing paper 60 (April 2004); available at <http://www.oxfam.org/resources/issues/trade> (accessed 26 May 2012).

Vivienne Westwood
Sandy Black
1. Rod Stanley, 'A meeting with Vivienne Westwood' *Dazed and Confused* 63 (July 2008), p. 99 [special issue guest-edited by Vivienne Westwood].
2. 'Friday Night with Jonathan Ross', 10 July 2009 [BBC One television programme (UK)].
3. Eleanor Morgan, 'Vive la Resistance' *Dazed and Confused* 63 (July 2008), p. 137
4. 'Friday Night with Jonathan Ross, 10 July 2009.
5. Stanley, p. 98.
6. Hilary Alexander, *Daily Telegraph Online*, 3 March 2011.

Katharine Hamnett
Sandy Black
1. Katharine Hamnett Spring/Summer 2011 press release.
2. Author interview with Katharine Hamnett, 25 February 2011.
3. Katharine Hamnett Spring/Summer 2011 press release.
4. Author interview with Katharine Hamnett, 25 February 2011.
5. Ibid.

Eileen Fisher
Sandy Black
1. Eileen Fisher website <https://www.eileenfisher.com> (accessed 8 March 2011).
2. All other quotations from author interview with Shona Quinn, 20 December 2010.

Continental Clothing
Sandy Black
1. *Sustainable Clothing Action Plan*, (Department for Environment, Food and Rural Affairs [DEFRA], 2008; updated 2010).

ASOS
Sandy Black
1. All quotations from author (Sandy Black) interviews with Caren Downie, 21 November 2009 and 12 April 2012.

Muji and Uniqlo
Nick Cambridge
1. Kanai Masaaki, 'Muji's Product Strategy: Connecting with customers', *Axis* (July/August 2003), pp. 22–25.
2. Reported in *Drapers Record*, 28 February 1998, p. 7.
3. However, it was later suggested that some metal panelling had been custom-made and treated with acid to achieve the tarnished scrapyard effect, as reported by Janine Furness, 'The brand with no new name', *Interior Design*, 7/8 (September 1991), pp. 30–33.
4. This phrase features on the cover of the Fast Retailing Co. Ltd. annual report, 2005.
5. Reported by Marino Donati 'Understanding Uniqlo', *Drapers*, 24 September 2005, p. 39; and 10 June 2006, p. 7.

H&M
Amelia Williams
1. Clare Mathesen,'H&M heads back to basics', *BBC News Online*, 16 March 2007, available at < http://news.bbc.co.uk/2/hi/business/6451485.stm> (accessed 25 May 2012).
2. Johan Nylander, 'Swedish brands climb in global ranking', *Swedish Wire*, 16 September 2010, available at <http://www.swedishwire.com/business/6206-swedish-brands-climb-in-global-ranking> (accessed 25 May 2012).
3. Johan Nylander, 'H&M ranked 21st most valuable brand', *Swedish Wire*, 16 September 2010, available at <http://www.swedishwire.com/business/6207-ham-ranked-21st-most-valuable-brand > (accessed 25 May 2012).
4. *Style and Substance Sustainability Report* (H&M, 2009),

p. 31, available at <http://about.hm.com/content/hm/AboutSection/en/About/Sustainability/Reporting-and-Resources/Reports.html> (accessed 25 May 2012).

Consumer understanding of sustainability in clothing
1. All excerpts from T. Fisher, T. Cooper, S. Woodward, A. Hiller and H. Goworek, *Public Understanding of Sustainable Clothing: A report to the Department for Environment, Food and Rural Affairs* (Department for Environment, Food and Rural Affairs [DEFRA], 2008).

CHAPTER 2

Desire and fashion/Design and innovation

Dai Fujiwara
Sandy Black
1. Issey Miyake quoted in the introduction to Issey Miyake and Dai Fujiwara, *A-POC Making* (2001).

Galahad Clark
Sandy Black
1. All quotes are from author interviews, 24 November 2008, 15 November 2011 and 11 April 2012.

Designers are T-shaped
Clare Brass
1. Quoted in Tim Brown, 'Strategy by design', *Fast Company*, 1 June 2005, available at: <http://www.fastcompany.com/magazine/95/design-strategy> (accessed 1 June 2012).

Yohji Yamamoto
1. Ai Mitsuda, *Yohji Yamamoto – My Dear Bomb: A Biography* (2010), p. 57.
2. Ibid., pp. 29–30.

Considerate Design: Supporting sustainable fashion design
Sandy Black and Claudia Eckert
1. Interviews with Katharine Hamnett, July 2007 and February 2011.
2. Sandy Black, *Eco Chic: The Fashion Paradox* (2008).
3. Julian M. Allwood, Søren Ellebæk Laursen, Cecilia Malvido de Rodríguez and Nancy M. P. Bocken, *Well Dressed? The Present and Future Sustainability of Clothing and Textiles in the UK* (University of Cambridge Institute for Manufacturing, 2006), p. 12.
4. EU legislation in the mid-1990s banned the use of twenty-two azo dyes as potential carcinogens when broken down. REACH (Registration, Evaluation, Authorisation and Restriction of Chemicals) legislation is aimed at the protection of health and the environment. Implemented in 2007, it requires companies to register the manufacture and use of all chemicals above a threshold volume.
5. GfK Consultants, Organic Exchange Symposium, London College of Fashion, 13 June 2008.
6. T. E. Graedel and R. B. Allenby, *Industrial Ecology* (1995).
7. F. Kelday, cited in Kate Fletcher, *Sustainable Fashion and Textiles: Design journeys* (2008), p. 78.
8. Allwood, et al., p. 27.
9. Fletcher, *Sustainable Fashion*, pp. 175–83.
10. See, for instance, David C. Wynn, Seena M. T. Nair and P. John Clarkson, 'The P3 Platform: an approach and software system for developing diagrammatic model-based methods in design research', paper given at the International Conference on Engineering Design, Stanford University, 24–27 August 2009, available at <http://www-edc.eng.cam.ac.uk/p3/09-ICED09-Wynn-TheP3Platform.pdf> (accessed 25 May 2012).
11. See for example, N. Whitely, *Design and Society* (1993); V. Papanek, *The Green Imperative: Ecology and ethics in design and architecture* (1995); D. MacKenzie, *Green Design: Design for the environment*, 2nd edn (1997); E. Jones, D. Harrison and J. McLaren, 'Managing Creative Eco-innovation: Structuring outputs from eco-innovation projects', *Journal of Sustainable Product Design*, 1 (2001), pp. 27–39; H. Brezet and C. van Hemel, *Eco-Design: A promising approach to sustainable production and consumption* (1997); and S. Walker, *Sustainable by Design* (2006).
12. Brezet and van Hemel (1997). Adaptations of their eco-strategy wheel include the 'Ecodesign Web' tool developed by Vicky Lofthouse and Tracy Bhamra, available at <http://ecodesign.lboro.ac.uk/index.php?section=72> (accessed 25 May 2012); and one designed by L. Elvins and R. Bassett, *Financial + Social + Environmental + Personal = Sustainable: An introductory guide to sustainability for designers* (2005).

Designers fashioning the future industry
Dilys Williams
1. Lars Svendsen, F*ashion: A philosophy* (2006).
2. *Tactics for Change*, Centre for Sustainable Fashion Reports, 3 (2009).
3. Roland Barthes, *The Fashion System* (1983).
4. The first Shared Talent took place in South Africa over a three-week period in July 2007. It involved a group of fashion students from London College of Fashion and LISOF (a college based in Johannesburg), and members of Buotemelo, a South African women's cooperative.
5. The second Shared Talent took place in South Africa and Ghana over a four-week period in August 2008. It involved students and graduates from London College of Fashion and members of a number of women's cooperatives based across South Africa and Ghana.
6. Tabeisa supports organizations varying in size from sole traders producing accessories and gifts using recycled materials and local crafts, to small clothing-manufacturing units supporting up to twenty-five members of the local community.
7. Exclusive Roots <http://www.exclusiveroots.com> is the online store selling work created through the cooperatives in the Tabeisa network.
8. The third Shared Talent took place in Delhi, India, in July 2009, over a twelve-day period. It involved designers, textile makers, skilled artisans, members of NGOs and highly experienced buyers from the UK, the Netherlands and India. It evolved as part of a project carried out by London College of Fashion's Centre for Sustainable Fashion as part of the DEFRA Sustainable Clothing Action Plan initiative, and involved British retailer Monsoon. See the project website at <http://www.sharedtalentindia.com>.
9. Quote from a British participant's reflective diary.
10. Quote from a Dutch participant's reflective diary.
11. Ibid.
12. Miriam Rhida's work was subsequently selected by the Design Museum London as part of its exhibition 'Sustainable Futures' (2010).
13. London Style is an EU European Regional Development Fund project for which the Centre for Sustainable Fashion acts as a delivery partner, working with 100 London-based fashion-design businesses to support development through sustainable practice. For details about the project and designers, see <http://www.sustainable-fashion.com>.

Nike
Amelia Willams
1. For further details on this controversy, see 'Legal, cultural and ethical challenges that Nike faces in global business', *Phoenix Business*, undated article, available at <http://phoenixbusiness.hubpages.com/hub/Nike-Global-Business-and-Challenges> (accessed 25 May 2012).
2. Quoted in Marguerite Rigoglioso, 'Being socially responsible offers opportunities, says Nike's Hannah Jones', Stanford Graduate School of Business website, 1 April 2007, available at <http://www.gsb.stanford.edu/news/headlines/2007supplychainconf-jones.shtml> (accessed 25 May 2012).
3. A good summary of these activities is available at <http://www.mallenbaker.net/csr/CSRfiles/nike.html> (accessed 25 May 2012).
4. Quoted in Maxamillion Blick, 'Nike strategy for creating a more sustainable business', *Fashion Newspaper*, 22 January 2010, available at <http://www.fashionnewspaper.com/articles/2928/1/Nike-Strategy-for-Creating-a-More-Sustainable-Business--Footwear-News/Page1.htm> (accessed 25 May 2012).
5. Quoted in Rajesh Shhabara, 'Supply-chain briefing Part 5: Nike: Beyond tick-box auditing', *Ethical Corporation*, 5 July 2010, available at <http://www.ethicalcorp.com/supply-chains/supply-chain-briefing-part-5-nike-beyond-tick-box-auditing> (accessed 25 May 2012).
6. *Nike Corporate Responsibility Report* (2009) available at <http://www.nikebiz.com/crreport/> (accessed 15 May 2012).
7. Ibid.
8. Heather Clancy, 'Nike's latest substainability report reflects evolving link between being green and being innovative', SmartPlanet web blog, 25 January 2010, available at <http://www.smartplanet.com/business/blog/business-brains/nikes-latest-substainability-report-reflects-evolving-link-between-being-green-and-being-innovative/4613/> (accessed 25 May 2012).
9. Quoted in 'New NikeiD store opens at NikeTown London', Nike Inc. website, 1 November 2007, available at < http://nikeinc.com/news/new-nikeid-studio-opens-at-niketown-london http://www.nikebiz.com/media/pr/2007/11/01_nikeidlondon.html> (accessed 25 May 2012).

11. Rocco Penn, 'Nike+ shows why corporate social networking is important, MarketingHackz website, undated, available at <http://marketinghackz.com/nike-shows-why-corporate-social-networking-is-important/> (accessed 25 May 2012).

Bless
Sandy Black
1. All quotes from author interview, March 2009.

Peter Kallen (NAU)
Sandy Black
1. Quoted in Warren McLaren 'How Nau: Interview with eco activewear purveyor', TreeHugger website, 21 October 2008, available at <http://www.treehugger.com/sustainable-fashion/how-nau-interview-with-eco-activewear-purveyor-part-1> (accessed 4 March 2011).
2. All other quotes from author interview with Peter Kallen, 11 January 2011.

Catalysts for change: a political future for fashion education
Frances Corner
1. J. Laver, *Style in Costume* (1949).
2. J. Entwistle, The *Fashioned Body* (2000).
3. H. Blumer, 'Fashion: From class differentiation to collective selection', *Sociological Quarterly*, 10/3 (April 2005), pp. 275–91.
4. R. Martin, 'Beyond Appearance and Beyond Custom: The avant-garde sensibility of fashion and art since the 1960s', in *Fashion and Imagination: About clothes and art*, Jan Brand, Jose Teunissen and Catelijne de Muijnck (eds) (2009), pp. 26–43.
5. J. Schor, *The Overspent American* (1998).
6. *Consumer Goods: Global Industry Guide*, Datamonitor (2009). The apparel, accessories and luxury-goods market consists of men's, women's and children's clothing, jewelry, watches and leather goods.
7. 'Sustainable Clothing Roadmap: Meeting briefing note', (Department for Environment, Food and Rural Affairs [DEFRA], September 2007), available at <http://archive.defra.gov.uk/environment/business/products/roadmaps/clothing/documents/clothing-briefing-Sept07.pdf> (accessed 15 May 2012).
8. Julian M. Allwood, Søren Ellebæk Laursen, Cecilia Malvido de Rodríguez and Nancy M. P. Bocken, *Well Dressed? The Present and Future Sustainability of Clothing and Textiles in the UK* (University of Cambridge Institute for Manufacturing, 2006).
9. Helen Storey, MBE, cited on the Water Amnesty page of the Univerity of the Arts London website: <http://www.arts.ac.uk/water-amnesty-campaign.htm> (accessed 15 May 2012).
10. Interview with Keith Weed on Unilever website, available at <http://www.unilever.com/mediacentre/news/keith-weed-interview-transcript.aspx> (accessed 15 May 2012).
11. J. Bendell and A. Kleanthous, 'Deeper Luxury: Quality and style when the world matters' (World Wildlife Fund UK, 2007).
12. See: <http://www.ethicalfashionforum.com/the-issues/fashion-development> (accessed 15 May 2012).
13. P. Rivoli, 'Tanzania: A second-hand economy', *The Globalist*, 24 June 2005, available at <http://www.theglobalist.com/StoryId.aspx?StoryId=4621> (accessed 15 May 2012).
14. Allwood et al., p. 12.
15. 'Sustainable Clothing Roadmap'.
16. R. Wilkinson and K. Pickett, *The Spirit Level* (2009).
17. S. Spratt, A. Simms, E. Neitzert and J. Ryan-Collins, *The Great Transition: A tale of how it turned out right* (New Economics Foundation, 2009).
18. Quoted from <http://wwwtest.utexas.edu/architecture/testing//csd/about/> (accessed 15 May 2012).

Seven luxury myths
World Wildlife Fund
1. Text from J. Bendell and A. Kleanthous, 'Deeper Luxury: Quality and style when the world matters' (World Wildlife Fund UK, 2007), p. 23.

CHAPTER 3

Craft and industry/Transparency and livelihood

Hidden people: workers in the garment supply chain
Liz Parker and Sam Maher
1. 'Prospects for the textile and garment industry in Cambodia' *Textile Outlook International*, 133 (January/February 2008).
2. 'Garment industry in Sri Lanka', Trade Chakra website, 17 May 2010, available at < http://www.tradechakra.com/economy/sri-lanka/garment-industry-in-sri-lanka-352.php> (accessed 25 May 2012).
3. Zahid Hussain, 'Financing living wage in Bangladesh's garment industry', End Poverty in South Asia blog, 8 March 2010, available at <http://blogs.worldbank.org/endpovertyinsouthasia/financing-living-wage-bangladesh%E2%80%99s-garment-industry> (accessed 25 May 2012).
4. *Consumer Goods: Global Industry Guide*, Datamonitor (2009).
5. Text of the UN Universal Declaration of Human Rights is available at <http://www.un.org/en/documents/udhr/> (accessed 25 May 2012).
6. These are often referred to as the ILO Core Conventions, full text of which is available at <http://www.ilo.org/declaration/> (accessed 25 May 2012).
7. See for example, Anna McMullen, 'Press Release: Campaign group express shock but not surprise over British sweatshop exposé', Labour Behind the Label website, 8 November 2010, available at <http://www.labourbehindthelabel.org/news/item/902-press-release-campaign-group-express-shock-but-not-surprise-over-british-sweatshop-expos%C3%A9> (accessed 25 May 2012).
8. See for example S. Barrientos and S. Smith, *Summary of an independent assessment for the Ethical Trading Initiative* (Institute of Development Studies, University of Sussex, 2006), available at <http://www.ethicaltrade.org/sites/default/files/resources/Impact%20assessment%20summary.pdf > (accessed 25 May 2012).
9. 'Garib fire survivors call for justice and a safe industry', Clean Clothes Campaign website, 11 March 2010, available at <http://cleanclothes.org/urgent-actions/garib-fire-survivors-call-for-justice-and-a-safe-industry> (accessed 25 May 2012).
10. 'Harassment and Violence', Labour Behind the Label website, undated article, available at < http://www.labourbehindthelabel.org/issues/item/746-harassment-and-violence> (accessed 25 May 2012).
11. For example, Marks & Spencer stated in a press release (1 March 2010) that their commitments to sustainability will include 'Becoming the first major retailer to actively tackle and bring clarity to the living wage debate. M&S will do this by determining and agreeing a fair, living wage before implementing a process to ensure our clothing suppliers pay this wage to their workers in Bangladesh, Sri Lanka and India. Based on our successful pilot in Bangladesh, we will do this by working with our suppliers to improve productivity and management practices.' The full text of the press release is available at <http://corporate.marksandspencer.com/media/press_releases/plana> (accessed 25 May 2012).
12. See <http://www.asiafloorwage.org/> (accessed 25 May 2012).
13. See for example: 'Auditing working conditions' Ethical Trading Initiative website, undated article, available at <http://www.ethicaltrade.org/in-action/issues/auditing-working-conditions> (accessed 25 May 2012); D. Pruett, *Looking for a Quick Fix: How weak social auditing is keeping workers in sweatshops*, (Clean Clothes Campaign, 2005); *Getting Smarter at Auditing: Tackling the growing crisis in ethical trade auditing*, Ethical Trading Initiative members meeting report (2006). The limitations of the audit process have in some cases been noted by the brands themselves; see, for instance Nike's statement on its brand collaboration goals: <http://www.nikebiz.com/crreport/content/workers-and-factories/3-10-1-our-approach.php?cat=brand-collaboration> .
14. K. Raworth, *Trading Away Our Rights: Women working in global supply chains*, Oxfam International report, (2004).
15. F. Gooch, R. Hurst and L. Napier, *Material Concerns*, Impactt and Traidcraft joint report (2008).

Erin O'Connor meets garment workers in India
Text extracts adapted from Erin O'Connor, 'Weaving a Fairer Future', *Behind the Seams*, issue 2, 2009, pp. 4–5; available at <http://textiles.ribbweb.org/wp-content/uploads/2010/10/TRAID-Issue2.pdf> (accessed 25 May 2012). For more information on the programme see SEWA's website at www.sewabharat.org.

1. 'Weaving a Fairer Future', p. 4.
2. 'Weaving a Fairer Future', p. 5.

Tim Wilson: Historic Futures
Sandy Black
1. Quoted in <http://walmartstores.com/Video/?id=1378> (accessed 12 April 2012).
2. Mike Barry in his opening speech to RITE Conference, 2011.

Prosperity without growth
Tim Jackson
1. Text from Tim Jackson, *Prosperity without Growth: Economics for a finite planet* (Earthscan, London and Sterling, VA, 2009), p. 166.
2. Ibid., p. 169.
3. Ibid., pp. 152–53.
4. Ibid., pp. 194–96.

Allanna McAspurn (MADE-BY)
Sandy Black
1. All quotes from author interviews, 8 April 2010 and 11 April 2012.

Blueprint for sustainability: the evolution of traditional Indian textiles from local consumption to the global market
Eiluned Edwards with Ismail Khatri
Eiluned Edwards would like to thank Ismail Khatri and his brothers, Razzak and Jabbar, for their cooperation in the preparation of this essay. Thanks are also due to the three Mrs Khatri – Memuna, Sakina and Maryam – who have always made me welcome in their homes. Financial support for research in Kachchh has come from the Leverhulme Trust and the British Academy – my thanks to them.

1. Ismail Khatri has contributed to this essay an insider's view of the development of the family business over the past forty years.
2. Gujarat State Handicrafts Development Corporation, *Role of a State Handicraft Organization: An attempt at a definition*, GSHDC 2 (Gandhinagar, n.d.).
3. Personal communication, 18 December 2001.
4. In Kachchh *ajrakh* is a predominantly blue cotton textile with accents of red and white that is resist-dyed and block-printed using indigo and madder. It is printed on both sides of the fabric, features complex geometric and floral designs, and requires fourteen to sixteen different stages of printing and dyeing. It takes at least three weeks to complete the process. See Eiluned Edwards, 'Dyed, printed and painted textiles', in *Textiles and Dress of Gujarat* (2011), pp 140–46. The name for the fabric is said to be derived from *azrak*, the Arabic word for 'blue', although other interpretations have been offered (see E. M. Edwards and Ismail M. Khatri, 'The work of the Khatris of Kachchh', in *Traditional Arts of South Asia: Past practice, living traditions*, C. Branfoot (ed.) (forthcoming).
5. M. B. Khatri, personal communication, 7 December 2006.
6. Ismail Khatri, personal communication, 14 January 2002.
7. The ISO states the following: 'The ISO 14000 family addresses "environmental management". This means what the organization does to minimize harmful effects on the environment caused by its activities, and to achieve continual improvement of its environmental performance'. See: <http://www.iso.org/iso/iso_14000_essentials> (accessed 25 May 2012).
8. G. Fereday, *Natural Dyes* (2003), p. 22.
9. Ismail Khatri, personal communication, 9 August 2003.

Perpectives on manufacturing fashion and textiles
Sandy Black
1. Borås East was a joint project between the Swedish School of Textiles, Borås, Mid Sweden University, Sundsvall and Borås Art Museum, May 2007. Five teams of student designers, textile economists and photojournalists lived in 'Borås East' for two weeks.
2. Jan Carlsson and Pelle Kronestedt, project managers, quoted in their introduction to *Borås East: Textile production and people in Eastern Europe* (2007).
3. Pelle Kronestedt in correspondence with Sandy Black, 19 March 2012
4. Malin Palm in correspondence with Sandy Black, 25 January 2012.
5. Sandra Henningsson in correspondence with Sandy Black, 30 January 2012.
6. For example, following a campaign by Labour Behind the Label and the Clean Clothes Campaign, H&M

and others announced in 2011 that they would stop importing jeans that have been sandblasted, due to the toxicity of the process to workers.
7. *Dirty Laundry: Unravelling the corporate connections to toxic water pollution in China* (Greenpeace International, 2011), available at: <http://www.greenpeace.org/international/en/publications/reports/Dirty-Laundry/ > (accessed 25 May 2012). Further reports *Dirty Laundry 2: Hung Out to Dry* and *Dirty Laundry: Reloaded* were released in August 2011 and March 2012, respectively. Major brands, including Adidas, Nike and Puma, have committed to action on toxic effluents.
8. L. Greer, S. E. Keane and X. Lin, *NRDC's Ten Best Practices for Textile Mills to Save Money and Reduce Pollution: A practical guide for responsible sourcing*, (Natural Resources Defense Council, 2010), p.3, available at <http://www.nrdc.org/international/cleanbydesign/files/rsifullguide.pdf> (accessed 25 May 2012).
9. *Releases From the Use of Products*, Finnish Environment Institute report (2010), p. 4, available at <http://www.ymparisto.fi/download.asp?contentid=124343&lan=fi > (accessed 25 May 2012). Cited in *Dirty Laundry*, p. 26.
10. 'Expansion of textile industrial cluster in China', *China Textile Magazine*, 5 March 2010, available at <http://chinatextile.360fashion.net/2010/03/expansion-of-textile-industria> (accessed 25 May 2010). Cited in *Dirty Laundry*, p. 26.
11. *Dirty Laundry*, pp. 26 and 28.
12. Greenpeace Intimate Pollution in China campaign, available at <http://photo.greenpeace.org/C.aspx?VP3=ViewBox&STID=27MZIFIZ8T1S&CT=Story> (accessed 10 April 2012).

Risto Bimbiloski
Duska Zagorac
1. All quotations from interview conducted by Duska Zagorac, February 2009.

Monsoon
Sandy Black
1. Estethica Autumn/Winter 2011 brochure.
As outlined in the *Monsoon Ethical Trading Report 2010*, the ETI awarded Monsoon 'leader' status in commitment and transparency; the Ethical Consumer report for 2009 had rated Monsoon 'the most ethical on the UK high street'; Labour behind the Label's *Let's Clean up Fashion* 2011 report rated positively Monsoon's actions towards workers rights and a living wage.
2. Author interview with Shailina Parti, 3 April 2012.

People Tree
Sandy Black
1. Tracy Mulligan quoted in Safia Minney, *Naked Fashion* (2011), p. 146.
2. Interview with author, September 2009.
3. Safia Minney quoted in Anna Shepherd, 'From Rags to Righteous' *The Times*, 5 June 2006.

Annegret Affolderbach (Choolips)
Sandy Black
1. Tabeisa was a charity project funded to create and empower employment in Africa. Tabeisa approached the ETHICAL Fashion Forum to help set up the Design for Life Ghana competition, to promote the co-operative producers Global Mamas from Ghana.
2. Julia Smith also sold her dress designs to Topshop. She now has her own range, including Julia Smith Made in Africa: see www.juliasmithfashion.co.uk.

Manish Arora
Phyllida Jay
1. Quoted in Dolly Jones, 'Paco Rabanne show report', *Vogue Online*, 4 October 2011, available at <http://www.vogue.co.uk/fashion/spring-summer-2012/ready-to-wear/paco-rabanne> (accessed 12 April 2012).
2. Interview with Phyllida Jay, March 2012.

Gap
Amelia Williams
1. Dan McDougall, 'Child sweatshop shame threatens Gap's ethical image', *The Observer*, 28 October 2007.
2. 'Gap announces successful results from denim drive', Gap press release 22 April 2010, available at <http://bx.businessweek.com/gap-inc/view?url=http%3A%2F%2F3blmedia.com%2FtheCSRfeed%2FGap-Announces-Successful-Results-Recycled-Denim-Drive > (accessed 25 May 2012).
3. *Gap Inc. 2007/2008 Social Responsibility Report* , p. 82, available at <http://www.socialfunds.com/shared/reports/1249942124_GapInc0708SR.pdf> (accessed 25 May 2012).
4. Susie Rushton, 'Red carpet meets high street: Roland

Mouret brings star quality to Gap chain', *The Guardian*, 31 October 2006.
5. Quoted in Dolly Jones, 'Mouret for Gap', *Vogue Online*, 18 September 2006, available at <http://www.vogue.co.uk/news/daily/2006-09/060918-mouret-for-gap.aspx> (accessed 25 May 2012).

Walmart and Asda
Amelia Williams
1. Fran Daniel, 'Head of Wal-Mart tells WFU audience of plans for growth over next 20 years', *Winston-Salem Journal*, 29 September 2010.
2. 'Asda', undated article on Supermarket.co.uk website, available at <http://www.supermarket.co.uk/asda.html> (accessed 25 May 2012).
3. Daily Mail Reporter and Sean Poulter, 'Fast fashion at the supermarket', 12 July 2005, This Is Money website, available at <http://www.thisismoney.co.uk/bargains-and-rip-offs/article.html?in_article_id=402192&in_page_id=5> (accessed 25 May 2012).
4. These reports included *Fashion Victims: The true cost of cheap clothes at Primark, Asda and Tesco* (War on Want, 2006); *Let's Clean up Fashion: The state of pay behind the UK high street* (Labour Behind the Label, 2006–11); *Cashing In: Giant retailers, purchasing practices and working conditions in the garment industry* (Clean Clothes Campaign, 2009); and *Asda: Poverty guaranteed* (ActionAid, 2010).
5. *George: Doing the Right Thing 2011*, Asda company report, p. 7, available at <http://your.asda.com/system/dragonfly/production/2012/02/21/09_39_42_189_DTRT_updated_May_2011.pdf> (accessed 1/6/2012)
6. 'The real Asda price: poverty and abuse in George's showcase factories', ActionAid website, May 2011, p. 2, available at <http://www.actionaid.org.uk/doc_lib/the_real_asda_price.pdf> (accessed 1/6/2012).
7. *George: Doing the Right Thing 2011*, p. 9.
8. *Sustainable Clothing Roadmap Progress Report 2011*, (Department for Environment, Food and Rural Affairs [DEFRA], 2011), p. 15.
9. *Beyond 50 years: Building a sustainable future – Walmart 2012 global responsibility report*, p. 84, available at <http://www.walmartstores.com/Sustainability/7951.aspx> (accessed 1/6/2012)
10. *Building the Next Generation Walmart…Responsibly: Walmart 2011 global responsibility report*, p. 4, available at <http://www.walmartstores.com/Sustainability/7951.aspx> (accessed 1/6/2012).

New Look and Echotex
Liz Parker
Text adapted from: E. Parker, *Steps towards Sustainability in Fashion: Snapshot Bangladesh*, L. Hammond, H. Higginson and D. Williams (eds), (2011), pp. 12–15.

1. Kantar Worldpanel 24, 5 September 2010, cited in New Look's promotional brochure for the Deutche Bank 13th Annual Retail Store Tour, January 2011, p. 4.
2. *New Look Group's Commitment to Ethical Trading: Leaving a Legacy* [company report, undated]; available at <http://www.newlookgroup.com/newlook/dlibrary/documents/Leaving_a_Legacy_final_v8_low_res5.pdf> (accessed 3 May 2012).
3. *New Look Retailers Ltd: Our Ethical Aims* [company report, undated], available at http://www.newlookgroup.com/newlook/dlibrary/documents/NewLook_EthicalAims_July2011.pdf (accessed 3 May 2012)
4. *New Look Group's Commitment to Ethical Trading*, p. 28.
5. Ibid., p.14.
6. Ibid., p.14.

The GM cotton debate: science or ideology
Damien Sanfilippo
1. Andrew Malone, 'The GM genocide: Thousands of Indian farmers are committing suicide after using genetically modified crops', *Daily Mail*, 3 November 2008.
2. 'The Government's Response to the Foresight Report on Food and Farming,' talk given at the Oxford Farming Conference, January 2012, available at <http://www.ofc.org.uk/files/ofc/papers/bob-watson.pdf> (accessed 15 May 2012).

The GM cotton debate
Simon Ferrigno
1. This commentary is based on a presentation given at the RITE Conference in London in October 2010.
2. Dictionary definition from <http://wordnetweb.princeton.edu/perl/webwn?s=genetic%20engineering> (accessed March 2012).
3. M. Rafiq Chaudry and Andrei Guitchounts, *Cotton Facts* (International Cotton Advisory Committee, 2003).
4. Ibid.
5. See: <http://www.gmo-compass.org/eng/

agri_biotechnology/gmo_planting/257.global_gm_planting_2009.html and http://www.isaaa.org/> (accessed March 2012).
6. Terry P. Townsend, 'A Balanced Perspective on Cotton: Responding to valid problems, challenging irresponsible critics,' *Proceedings of the 69th Plenary of the International Cotton Advisory Committee*, available at <http://www.icac.org/meetings/plenary/69_lubbock/documents/english.html> (accessed December 2010).
7. Expert Panel on Social, Environmental and Economic Performance of Cotton Production (SEEP), 'An Interpretative Summary of the Study on: Pesticide use in cotton in Australia, Brazil, India, Turkey and the USA', *Proceedings of the the 69th Plenary of the International Cotton Advisory Committee*, available at <http://www.icac.org/meetings/plenary/69_lubbock/documents/english.html> (accessed December 2010).
8. Ibid.
9. Ibid.
10. Ian Sample, 'Scientists call for GM review after surge in pests around cotton farms in China', *The Guardian*, 13 May 2010; 'GM crops causing a rise in pesticide use', Ecologist website, 17 November 2009, available at <http://www.theecologist.org/News/news_round_up/364311/gm_crops_causing_a_rise_in_pesticide_use_in_us.html> (accessed March 2012).
11. Ahmet Yücer and Fatma Sarsu, 'Turkish Approach to Reducing Cotton Production Cost', *Proceedings of the 69th Plenary of the International Cotton Advisory Committee*, <http://www.icac.org/meetings/plenary/69_lubbock/documents/english.html> (accessed December 2010).
12. SEEP, 'An Interpretative Survey'.
13. 'Bt cotton: the facts beyond the hype', GRAIN website, 18 January 2007, available at <http://www.grain.org/seedling/?id=457> (accessed March 2012).
14. International Cotton Advisory Committee, 'Cotton yields: once again reached a plateau', *Technical Information Section ICAC Recorder* 28/3 (September 2010).
15. R. J. Hillocks, 'GM cotton for Africa' *OUTLOOK on Agriculture*, 38/4 (2009), pp. 1–316, available at <http://www.nri.org/publications/ahe/gm_cotton_for_africa-outlook_paper09.pdf> (accessed March 2012).
16. [Box] Text reproduced from GMO Compass website, <http://www.gmo-compass.org/eng/glossary/115.genetically_modified_organism_gmo.html> (accessed 16 October 2010).

The Asia Floor Wage campaign
1. Text from Jeroen Merk, 'Stitching a Decent Wage across Borders: The Asia Floor Wage Proposal', Clean Clothes Campaign website, October 2009. Full text available at <http://www.cleanclothes.org/resources/> (accessed 12 May 2012).

A few statistics relating to the international garment industry (box)
1. Julian M. Allwood, Søren Ellebæk Laursen, Cecilia Malvido de Rodríguez and Nancy M. P. Bocken, *Well Dressed? The Present and Future Sustainability of Clothing and Textiles in the UK* (University of Cambridge Institute for Manufacturing, 2006), p. 6.
2. *TNCs [Transnational corporations] and the Removal of Textile and Clothing Quotas* (UN, 2005), p. 4, available at <http://unctad.org/en/docs/iteiia20051_en.pdf> (accessed 6 June 2012).
3. Zahid Hussain, senior economist in South Asia Finance and Poverty group, cited in E. Parker, *Steps towards Sustainability in Fashion: Snapshot Bangladesh*, L. Hammond, H. Higginson and D. Williams (eds) (2011), p. 7.
4. 'End of the line for cheap clothing?', *Textile Outlook International*, 147 (October 2010).
5. <http://www.unido.org> (accessed March 2009).
6. 'Facts on child labour', *Accelerating Action Against Child Labour: Global report under the follow-up to the ILO Declaration on fundamental Principles and Rights at Work*, Report to the International Labour Conference, 99th Session (2010).

What Is Fair Trade?
1. Text from WTFO website, <http://www. wfto.com> (accessed 12 May 2012).

International Labour Organization declaration (box)
1. For full text see ILO website, <http://www.ilo.org/declaration> (accessed 12 May 2012).

CHAPTER 4

Speed and distance/Ecology and waste

Introduction
Sandy Black
1. W. McDonough and M. Braungart, *Cradle to Cradle: Remaking the way we make things* (2002).

Sustainability, pleasure and fashion politics
Kate Fletcher
1. G. Simmel, *On Individuality and Social Forms* (1971), p. 301.
2. Julian M. Allwood, Søren Ellebæk Laursen, Cecilia Malvido de Rodríguez and Nancy M. P. Bocken, *Well Dressed? The Present and Future Sustainability of Clothing and Textiles in the UK* (University of Cambridge Institute for Manufacturing, 2006), p. 4.
3. J. R. Ehrenfeld, 'Searching for sustainability: No quick fix', *Reflections* 5/8 (2004), p. 4.
4. S. Sterling, *Sustainable Education: Revisioning learning and change* (2001), p. 16.
5. C. Hamilton, *Growth Fetish* (2003), p. 130.
6. R. Farrell, 'Fashion and presence', *Nomenus Quarterly* 3 (2008), unpaginated.

From eco-efficiency to the circular economy
Nick Morley
1. W. McDonough and M. Braungart, *Cradle to Cradle: Remaking the way we make things* (2002). This book proposes that nothing should become waste, but new feedstock for either technical or biological processes.

Slow and fast fashion
Mathilda Tham
1. K. Fletcher and M. Tham, 'Clothing Rhythms', in E. van Hinte (ed.), *Eternally Yours: Time in Design* (2004).
2. M. Tham, 'Lucky People Forecast – A systemic futures perspective on fashion and sustainability', unpublished PhD dissertation, Goldsmiths, University of London (2008)
3. Franklin Associates, *Resource and Environmental Profile Analysis of a Manufactured Apparel Product: Woman's knit polyester blouse* (1993). For in-depth accounts of fashion's environmental impacts see, for example: S. Black, *Eco-Chic: The fashion paradox* (2008); M. Miraftab and A. R. Horrocks (eds), *Ecotextiles: The way forward for sustainable development in textiles*, Woodhead Textiles Series 60 (2007).
4. See for example, Julian M. Allwood, Søren Ellebæk Laursen, Cecilia Malvido de Rodríguez and Nancy M. P. Bocken, *Well Dressed? The Present and Future Sustainability of Clothing and Textiles in the UK* (University of Cambridge Institute for Manufacturing, 2006).
5. Allwood et al., pp. 28–9.
6. A key exception is the initiative by Marks & Spencer that encourages users to wash at lower temperatures. (Black, *Eco Chic*, p. 31).
7. *H&M 2004 Annual Report* (2005), p. 24. This figure is still current.
8. According to a Dutch study, a piece of clothing stays in the wardrobe for an average of three years and five months. During this time it is worn for 44 days and washed after 2.4–3.1 days of use. See: D. E. Uitdenbogerd, N. M. Brouwer and J. P. Groot-Marcus, *Domestic energy saving potentials for food and textiles: An empirical study* (1998). A 2006 British study calculated that approximately 55 kg of textiles and clothing were being consumed by each person in the UK per year, of which 12.5% was sent for reuse. The rest ended up as waste. At the same time, British consumers were spending an average of £780 on textiles and clothing per year (Allwood et al., p. 2).
9. See, for example, J. Lovelock, *The Revenge of Gaia: Why the earth is fighting back – how we can still save humanity* (2006); and N. Stern, *The Economics of Climate Change: The Stern Review* (2006).
10. See, for example, R. Barthes, *The Fashion System* (1983); Y. Kawamura, *Fashion-ology: An introduction to fashion studies* (2005); and E. Shove and A. Warde, 'Inconspicuous consumption: the sociology of consumption, lifestyles, and the environment', in *Sociological Theory and the Environment*, R. E. Dunlap, F. Buttel, P. Dickens and A. Gijswij (eds) (2002), pp. 230–51.
11. This can be compared to taking the measurements of a small child and a tall man and then constructing a chair based on the averages.
12. Fletcher and Tham, 'Clothing Rhythms'.
13. Ibid.
14. Design Council Annual Review (2002), p. 17.
15. S. Brand, *The Clock of the Long Now: Time and Responsibility* (1999), p. 37.
16. Fletcher and Tham, 'Clothing Rhythms'.
17. Ibid. See also: <http://www.lifetimes.info>.
18. Tham, 'Lucky People Forecast'.

minä perhonen
Sandy Black
1. Title quote from Akira Minagawa, *Particle of minä perhonen–Ryushi*, (2005), p. 41.

Sustainable luxury fashion: challenges and initiatives
Phyllida Jay
1. Sandy Black, *Eco Chic: The fashion paradox* (2008).
2. Jem Bendell and Anthony Kleanthous, 'Deeper Luxury: Quality and style when the world matters', World Wildlife Fund UK, November 2007; available at <http://www.psfk.com/2007/12/wwf-deeper-luxury-report> (accessed 5 July 2010).
3. Sabrina Giannini, 'Schiavi del lusso: in onda domenica 2 dicembre 2007', *RAI.it Report*, 12 December 2007, available at <http://www.report.rai.it/dl/Report/puntata/ContentItem-132f40c7-4377-4f83-a37f-78106ecb6dcc.html> (accessed 6 June 2012).
4. Quoted in Imran Amed, 'Made in Italy: time for accountability', Business of Fashion website, 4 December 2007, available at <http://www.businessoffashion.com/2007/12/made-in-italy-time-for-accountability.html> (accessed 6 June 2012).
5. Christian Blanckaert, *Luxe* (2007).
6. Corporate responsibility statement on Mulberry website: <http://www.mulberry.com/#/discovermulberry/aboutmulberry/csr/> (accessed 7 October 2010).
7. 'Made in Italy', Gucci website: <http://www.gucci.com/us/worldofgucci/articles/made-in-italy> (accessed 7 October 2010).
8. Joe Ayling, 'PPR Group commits to improving sustainability', Just-Style website, 5 July 2007; see: <http://www.just-style.com/news/ppr-group-commits-to-improving-sustainability_id99314.aspx> (accessed 7 June 2010).
9. Blog discussion between Phyllida Jay and Jem Bendell, 26 May 2010; see: 'Implications of inauthentic authenticity by Ogilvy & Mather for Louis Vuitton', available at <http://www.authenticluxury.net/profiles/blogs/implications-of inauthentic?xg_source=activity> (accessed 7 June 2010).
10. Lucy Siegle, 'Is luxury fashion good for the planet?, *The Guardian*, 31 May 2009.
11. Statement on Zegna website: <http://www.zegnacentennial.com/> (accessed 20 August 2010).
12. Interview with Anna Zegna, 24 March 2010.
13. *LVMH: Preserving the environment, 2009*, LVMH corporate responsibility report, p. 23, available at <http://www.lvmh.com/uploads/assets/Le-groupe/Documents/EN/Donnee_env_2009_gbr.pdf> (accessed 25 May 2012).
14. Personal communications from Burak Cakmak, 5 March, 2010, and from Sean Ansett, 16 April 2010.
15. Ibid.
16. Emma Grady, 'Gucci's Luxury Packaging Gets a Greener Makeover', treehugger website, 8 June 2010, available at <http://www.treehugger.com/files/2010/06/gucci-luxury-packaging-gets-a-greener-makeover.php> (accessed 7 July 2010).
17. *LVMH: Preserving the environment, 2009*, p. 12.
18. Personal communication from Sean Ansett.
19 *LVMH: Preserving the environment, 2008*, LVMH corporate responsibility report, p. 27, available at < http://www.lvmh.com/uploads/assets/Le-groupe/Documents/EN/Donnee_env_2008_gbr3.pdf > (accessed 25 May 2012).
20. Ibid.
21. 'LVMH: Translation of the French document de reference fiscal year ended 31 December 2008', 2008 financial report (2009), p. 16; available at <http://www.unglobalcompact.org/system/attachments/8479/original/LVMH_-_Reference_Document_2009.pdf?1290004413> (accessed July 2010).
22. Ibid.
23. Personal communication from Sean Ansett.
24. Research statement on BLC website: <http://www.blcleathertech.com/leather-technology/research-projects.htm> (accessed 8 October 2010).
25. *Product and Supply Chain Standards: Upstream, corporate social responsibility*, Burberry annual review (2009), <http://annualreview2009-10.<burberry.com/corp_responsibility/product_supply_chain.html> (accessed 8 October 2010).
26. Corporate responsibility statement on Saga Furs website: <<http://www.sagafurs.com/csr.html> (accessed 8 October 2010).
27. The Pew Charitable Trust and Johns Hopkins Bloomberg School of Public Health, 'Putting Meat on the Table: Industrial farm animal production in America', Pew Commission on Industrial Farm Animal Production (2008), p. 28. See: <http://www.ncifap.org/>.
28. See 'Paihamu wild-wool and eco-luxury fur', <http://thegreenconnoisseur.blogspot.com/2009/10/paihamu-wild-wool-and-eco-luxury-fur.html>.
29. Emily Cronin, 'Rat fur: The latest fashion accessory,' *The Guardian*, 6 June 2010.
30. The PhD is hosted by Central Saint Martins College of Art and Design and supported by the Textile Futures Research Group at the University of the Arts London.
31. 'Natural fibres at Terra Madre', Zegna press release, available at <http://www.zegna.com/media/press/EZ_NATURAL%20FIBRES%20PRESS%20RELEASE_ENG_FINAL.pdf> (accessed 20 August 2010).
32. Cittadellarte Fashion BEST Bio Ethical Sustainable Trend website, <http://www.cittadellarte.it/progetti.php?prog=52> (accessed 20 August 2010).
33. A. McMullen and S. Maher, 'The state of pay behind the UK high street', Labour Behind the Label website, <http://www.labourbehindthelabel.org/accessibility/item/593-lets-clean-up-fashion-2009> (accessed 20 August 2010).

Noir
Stacy Anderson and Sandy Black
1. Quote from Noir Spring/Summer 2008 and subsequent press releases.
2. All other quotes are from interviews conducted by Stacey Andersen, March 2008, and Sandy Black, September 2008.
3. These certifications included organic textile standards, Oeko-Tex® Standard 100 safety standards and EU Ecolabel certification.

Questioning identity
Lucy Orta
1. 'Aware: Art Fashion Identity', Royal Academy, London, 2 December 2010–30 January 2011; exhibition catalogue published by Damiani (2010).
2. Examples of work by these designers and of my own early work can be seen in A. Bolton, *The Supermodern Wardrobe* (2002).
3. P. Virilio, *Lucy Orta* (2003).

Zero-waste cutting
Sandy Black
1. All quotes from author interview, 2010.

From Somewhere
Sandy Black
1. All quotes from author interviews, February 2011 and April 2012.

Christopher Raeburn
Sandy Black
1. All quotes from author interview, 13 April 2012.

Maison Martin Margiela
Sandy Black
1. Quote from cover of *Maison Martin Margiela '20' The Exhibition*, exhibition catalogue, MoMu Fashion Museum, Antwerp (2008).

Textile recycling in the UK
Alan Wheeler
1. See press release, 'The European Conference on the future of the Textile and Clothing Reclamation Industry – Brussels – 13th October 2005: Textile Recycling Businesses: Are they an endangered species?', <http://www.textile-recycling.org.uk/press191005.htm> (accessed 25 May 2012).

Everything must go
Lucy Norris
Lucy Norris research in India has been principally supported by an ESRC PhD Studentship and a Research Fellowship with the Waste of the World project (RES-000-23-0007). Field photography was supported by a British Academy Small Research Grant (SRG 38685).

1. United Nations Commodity Trade Database (UNCTAD) 2010.
2. For more information, see L. Norris, 'Cloth That Lies: The Secrets of Recycling in India', in *Clothing as Material Culture*, S. Küchler and D. Miller (eds.) (2005); L. Norris, 'Shoddy rags and relief blankets: perceptions of textile recycling in north India', in *Global Recycling Economies*, C. Alexander and J. Reno (eds.)(2012); L. Norris, 'Economies of moral fibre: materializing the ambiguities of recycling charity clothing into aid blankets', *Journal of Material Culture*, 17/4(2012, forthcoming).
3. For more information, see L. Norris, *Recycling Indian Clothing: Global Contexts of Reuse and Value* (2010).

Garth Ward
Sandy Black
1. G. Villalba, M. Segarra, A. I. Fernández, J. M. Chimenos, F. Espiell, *A proposal for quantifying the recyclability of materials*, Resources, Conservation and Recycling. 2002, 37(1), pp. 39–53.

CHAPTER 5

Techno eco/New fashion paradigms

Nature as a paradigm for sustainability in the textile and apparel industry
Veronika Kapsali
1. K. Slater, *Environmental Impact of Textiles* (2003).
2. Ibid.
3. V. Rossbach, P. Patanathabutr and J. Wichitwechkarn, 'Copying and manipulating nature: innovation for textile materials' *Fibers and Polymers* 4 (2003) pp. 8–14.
4. G. J. Cook, *Handbook of Textile Fibres: Natural fibres* (1984).
5. J. M. Benyus, *Biomimicry: Innovation inspired by nature* (1997).
6. J. F. W. Vincent, O. A. Bogatyreva, N. R. Bogatyrev, A. Bowyer and A.-K. Pahl. 'Biomimetics: its practice and theory', *Journal of the Royal Society Interface*, 3 (2006), pp. 471–82.
7. W. Barthlott and C. Neinhuis, 'Characterization and distribution of water-repellent, self-cleaning plant surfaces', *Annals of Botany*, 79 (1997), pp. 667–77.
8. Slater (2003).

Mass customization: a strategy for sustainability in the fashion industry
Frank Piller and Frank Steiner
1. B. J. Pine and S. Davis, *Mass customization: The new business frontier*, (1993).
2. See N. Franke and F. Piller, 'Value creation by toolkits for user innovation and design: The case of the watch market', *Journal of Product Innovation Management* 21/6 (2004), pp. 401–15; and N. Franke, et al., 'The "I Designed It Myself" effect in mass customization' *Management Science* 56/1 (2010), pp. 125–40.
3. See P. Zipkin, 'The Limits of Mass Customization' *MIT Sloan Management Review* 42/3 (2001), pp. 81–87.
4. See R. Chin and D. Smithwick 'Environmental impacts of utilizing mass customization: Energy and material use of mass customization vs. mass production' *5th World Conference on Mass Customization and Personalization, Helsinki* (2009); and R. Kleer and F. Steiner, *Mass Customization: Bridging customer integration and sustainability?* (2011).
5. See M. Agrawal, et al., 'The false promise of mass customization', *McKinsey Quarterly* 3 (2001), pp. 62–71; and F.-H. Sanders, 'Financial rewards of mass customization' *2001 World Conference on Mass Customization & Personalization, Hong Kong* (2001).
6. See Franke and Piller (2004); and F. T. Piller, et al., 'Does mass customization pay? An economic approach to evaluate customer integration' *Production Planning and Control* 15/4 (2004), pp. 435–44.
7. F. Badurdeen, et al., 'Extending total life-cycle thinking to sustainable supply chain design', *International Journal of Product Lifecycle Management* 4/1 (2009), pp. 49–67.
8. C. Boer, 'Design and sustainability driven innovation for mass-customized products and services', *Proposal for a COST Action Project for the European Commission* (2011).
9. See Zipkin (2001); F. Salvador, et al. 'Cracking the code of mass customization', *MIT Sloan Management Review* 50/3 (2009), pp. 71–78; and Franke, et al. (2010).

Fits.me
Sandy Black
1. See, for instance, Enjoli Liston, 'Is it curtains for changing rooms?', *The Independent*, 3 February 2011; Lucie Green, 'Next big trend: Virtual fitting rooms?=', *Financial Times*, 14 January 2011.
2. Personal correspondence with Heikke Haldre, 21 February 2011.

Fashion blogging: the new fashion journalism
Agnès Rocamora and Djurdja Bartlett
1. A. Appadurai, *Modernity at Large* (1998).
2. Drawing on Rebecca Blood, 'Weblogs: History and Perspective', in *We've Got Blog* (2002), pp. 7–16, Mark Tremayne notes that 'the brief etymology of the term "blogs" goes back to the late 1990s and looks something like this web: web journal > web log > weblog > wee blogs > blogs'. See: 'Preface: Blog Terminology', in M. Tremayne (ed.), *Blogging, Citizenship, and the Future of the Media* (2007), p. vii.

3. For an overview of the history of blogs and blogging see: Blood, 'Weblogs'.
4. M. Deuze, *Media Work* (2007), p. 14; see also: <www.technocrati.com/>.
5. D. Kline and D. Burstein (eds), *Blog! How the newest media revolution is changing politics, business and culture* (2005), pp. 247–48.
6. Ibid., p. 276.
7. G. Lovink, *Zero Comments* (2008), p. 8.
8. Andrew Keen, *The Cult of the Amateur: How blogs, MySpace, YouTube and the rest of today's user-generated media are killing our culture and economy* (2008), p. 16.
9. J. Tomlinson, *Culture of Speed: the coming immediacy* (2007).
10. Tremayne ('Preface') notes that '[b]loggers often provide links to other web content and many have a blog roll: a list of links to favorite blogs as part of site navigation. Bloggers also use links within their posts.' The list of independent fashion blogs is vast, and includes sites such as <www.ashadedviewonfashion.com, www.stylebubble.co.uk>, <www.garancedore.fr>,< www.the sartorialist.com>, <www.shoeblog.com>, <www.iamfashion.blogspot.com>, <www.disneyrollergirl.net>, <www.fatgirlslikeniceclothestoo.wordpress.com>, <www.thecherryblossomgirl.com> and <www.stylesalvage.blogspot.com>.
11. <http://iamfashion.blogspot.com/>, 01/02/09 (accessed 30/03/09).
12. Before founding her blog in 2005, Pernet had worked as a fashion designer and as the editor of elle.com and vogueparis.com (now vogue.fr).
13. Lovink, Zero Comments, p. 28.
14. Ibid.
15. M. Uhlirova, 'In the Bubble', *City* 63 (April/May 2009), p. 60.
16. Susie Lau in conversation with Agnès Rocamora, London College of Fashion's series of conversations on fashion and the internet, 21 January 2009.
17. Rocamora and O'Neill define 'the straight-up' as 'the head-to-toe documentary portrait of a fashionable individual captured in the street', see A. Rocamora and A. O'Neill, 'Fashioning the street: Images of the street in the fashion media', in *Fashion as Photograph*, E. Shinkle (ed.) (2008). For some examples of street-fashion blogs see: <www.thecoolhunter.net>, <www.stilinberlin.blogspot.com>, <www.copenhagenstreetstyle.thepop.com>, <www.style-arena.jp>, <www.styleslicker.com>, <www.onthecornerstreetstyle.blogspot.com>, <www.missatlaplaya.blogspot.com>, <www.hel-looks.com>, <www.lookatme.ru> and <www.vivashanghai.com>.
18. See W. Benjamin, *The Arcades Project* (1999), pp. 448–54.
19. Massenet claims that she regularly reads The Sartorialist: 'We are huge fans of The Sartorialist at Net-a-Porter. The photography is sharp, the commentary astute, and we love that it celebrates individual style' (cited in J. Cartner-Morley, 'From catwalk to sidewalk', *The Guardian*, 8 December 2007).
20. D. Rowse, 'Six Figure Blogger', Problogger website, 23 September 2005, <http://problogger.net> accessed 23/03/09.
21. L. Grant, 'Trade Secrets', *Vogue* (UK) (January 2007), p. 59.
22. V. Heffernan, 'Pop Couture', *New York Times*, 19 December 2008.
23. In *Media Work* Deuze refers to the kudos that can be gained through online 'voluntary media work' such as blogging (p. 77). In 2007, for instance, 50,000 people a day visited The Sartorialist (Cartner-Morley, 'From catwalk').
24. In her article 'Bloggers Get under the Tent', *The Wall Street Journal*, 12 September 2006, Rachel Dodes claimed that forty American bloggers secured invitations for New York Fashion Week in autumn 2006. On the other hand Susie Lau was the only blogger invited to the exclusive Gucci charity gala event in New York in 2008 (*Evening Standard*, 8 October 2008).
25. See, for example: J. Davis 'Street Style', *Saturday Times Magazine*, 14 March 2009, pp. 52–57; D. Jones, 'Susie Bubble's Shopping Secrets', *Time Out*, 18–24 February, 2010, pp. 26–27; M. Holgate, 'Logged On', *Vogue* (US), March 2010, pp. 514–24. 26. While vogue.co.uk has introduced an online diary category, it is written by leading fashion designers such as Paul Smith or shoe designer Rupert Sanderson. Cathy Horyn's blog (<www.therunawaypoet.blogspot.com>) is attached to the online edition of the *New York Times*; she is also fashion reporter for the print edition.
27. Lovink, *Zero Comments*, p. xxiv.
28. See: U. Beck, *Risk Society: Towards a new modernity* (1992); idem, *The Brave New World of Work* (2000); and R. Sennett, *The Corrosion of Character* (1998).
29. N. Gall, 'Japanese Blogger Champions Internet

Democracy', in *Blog!*, D. Kline and D. Burstein (eds) (2005), pp. 143–50.

Boom and bust in the betaverse
Sue Jenkyn Jones
1. VRML is pronounced 'vermal'. VRML files are commonly called 'worlds' and have the *.wrl file extension.
2. Johan Huizinga, *Homo Ludens* (1938).
3. Up-to-date statistics for Second Life can be found at Linden Lab official live data feeds: <http://wiki.secondlife.com/wiki/Linden_Lab_Official:Live_Data_Feeds> (accessed 25 May 2012).
4. Wagner James Au, *The Making of Second Life: Notes from the New World* (2008); see also: <http://nwn.blogs.com>.
5. Lerappa is 'apparel' spelled backwards.
6. An overview of Market Truths's research is available at <http://sl.markettruths.com> (accessed 25 May 2012).

The future of virtual fashion
Julia Gaimster
1. L. Cremorne, 'Virtual Worlds Accounts: 1.4 billion and growing', Metaverse Journal website, 2 August 2011, available at <http://www.metaversejournal.com/2011/08/02/registered-virtual-worlds-accounts-1-4-billion-and-growing/> (Accessed 10 April 2012).

Future scenarios
Forum for the Future
Text adapted from *Fashion Futures 2025: Global scenarios for a sustainable fashion industry*, Forum for the Future report (2010), available at <http://www.forumforthefuture.org/sites/default/files/project/downloads/fashionfutures2025finalsml.pdf> (accessed 25 May 2012).

Bibliography

SUSTAINABILITY AND FASHION

Allwood, Julian M., Søren Ellebæk Laursen, Cecilia Malvido de Rodríguez and Nancy M. P. Bocken, *Well Dressed? The Present and Future Sustainability of Clothing and Textiles in the UK* (University of Cambridge Institute for Manufacturing, 2006)
Blanchard, Tamsin, *Green is the New Black* (2007)
Black, Sandy, *Eco Chic: The fashion paradox* (2008)
Black, Sandy, 'Interrogating fashion' in *Insights and Questions: Designing for the 21st Century*, Tom Inns (ed.) (2007)
Brown, Sass and Geoffrey B. Small, *Eco Fashion* (2010)
Fletcher, Kate, *Sustainable Fashion and Textiles: Design journeys* (2008)
Fletcher, Kate and Lynda Grose, *Fashion & Sustainability: Design for change*, (2012)
Gwilt, Alison and Timo Rissanen, *Shaping Sustainable Fashion: Changing the Way We Make and Use Clothes* (2011)
Hansen, Karen, *Salaula: the world of second hand clothing and Zambia* (2000)
Hethorn, Janet and Ulasewicz, Connie (eds), *Sustainable Fashion: Why Now?* (2008)
Lee, Matilda, *Eco chic : The savvy shopper's guide to ethical fashion* (2007).
Marchetti, Luca and Emanuele Quinz (eds), *Dysfashional* (2007)
Minney, Safia, *Naked Fashion* (2011)
Mulvey, Charlotte, *The Good Shopping Guide: Certifying the UK's Most Ethical Companies and Brands* (2011)
Norris, Lucy, *Recycling Indian Clothing: Global contexts of reuse and value* (2010)
Parker, Liz and Marsha Dickson (eds), *Sustainable Fashion: A Handbook for Educators* (2009)
Siegle, Lucy, *To Die For: Is Fashion Wearing Out the World?* (2011)
Worsley, Harriet, *100 Ideas that Changed Fashion* (2011)

DESIGN AND SUSTAINABILITY

Birkeland, Janis, *Design for Sustainability: A sourcebook of integrated ecological solutions* (2002)
Braungart, Michael and William McDonough *Cradle-to-Cradle: Remaking the way we make things* (2009)
Bell, Simon and Stephen Morse *Sustainability Indicators: Measuring the immeasurable?* (2008)
Brower, Cara and Rachel Mallory, *Experimental Eco-design: Architecture, fashion, product* (2005)
Chapman, Jonathan, *Emotionally Durable Design: Objects, experience and empathy* (2005)
Chapman, Jonathan and Nick Gant, *Designers, Visionaries and Other Stories: A collection of sustainable design essays* (2007)
Charter, Martin and Ursula Tischner, *Sustainable Solutions: Developing products and services for the future* (2001)
Chick, Anne and Paul Micklethwaite, *Design for Sustainable Change: How design and designers can drive the sustainability agenda* (2011)
Clayton, Tony and Radcliffe, Nicholas, *Sustainability: A systems approach* (1996)
Cooper, Tim (ed), *Longer Lasting Products: Alternatives to the throwaway society* (2010)
Corrigan, Nicola, Sarah Sayce and Ros Taylor (eds), *Sustainability in practice from local to global: Making a difference* (2009)
Edwards, Brian, *Rough Guide to Sustainability* (2005)
Datschefski, Edwin, *The Total Beauty of Sustainable Products* (2001)
Fry, Tony, *Design futuring: Sustainability, ethics and new practice* (2009)
Fuad-Luke, Alastair, *Design Activism: Beautiful strangeness for a sustainable world* (2009)

Fuad-Luke, Alastair, *The Eco Design Handbook* (2009)
Mackenzie, Dorothy, *Green Design: Design for the environment* (1997)
Manzini, Ezio, *The Material of Invention* (1989)
Manzini, Ezio, *Sustainable Everyday: Scenarios of urban life* (2003)
Orta, Lucy, *Food-Water-Life* (2011)
Papanek, Victor, *Design for the Real World: Human ecology and social change* (1971)
Papanek, Victor, *The Green Imperative: Ecology and ethics in design and architecture* (1995)
Petherick, Tom, *Sufficient: A modern guide to sustainable living* (2007)
Rheingold, H (ed.), *The Millennium Whole Earth Catalog* (1994)
Russ, Tom, *Sustainability and design ethics* (2010)
Thorpe, Ann, *The Designer's Atlas of Sustainability* (2007)
Walker, Stuart, *Sustainable by Design: explorations in theory and practice* (2006)

ECONOMICS AND FASHION INDUSTRY MANAGEMENT

Blackburn, William, *The Sustainability Handbook: The complete management guide to achieving social, economic and environmental responsibility* (2007)
Bruce, Margaret and Tony Hines, *Fashion Marketing: Contemporary issues* (2007)
Charlton, Andrew and Joseph Stiglitz, *Fair Trade For All: How Trade Can Promote Development* (2007)
Crane, Andrew, Abagail McWilliams, Dirk Matten, Jeremy Moon and Donald Siegel (eds), *The Oxford Handbook of Corporate Social Responsibility* (2009)
DeCarlo, Jacqueline, *Fair trade: a beginner's guide* (2007)
Ekins, Paul, Mayer Hillman and Robert Hutchison, *Wealth Beyond Measure: An atlas of new economies* (2001)
Ehrenfeld, John. R, *Sustainability by Design: A subversive strategy for transforming our consumer culture* (2008)
Epstein, Marc J., *Making Sustainability Work: Best practices in managing and measuring corporate social, environmental and economic impacts* (2008)
Hawken, Paul, *Ecology of Commerce: How business can save the planet* (1993)
Hawken, Paul, *Natural Capitalism: The next industrial revolution* (1999)
Jackson, Tim, *Prosperity without Growth: Economics for a Finite Planet* (2011)
Jackson, Tim and David Shaw, *The Fashion Handbook* (2006)
Hawkins, David E., *Corporate Social Responsibility: Balancing tomorrow's sustainability and today's profitability* (2006)
Klein, Naomi, *No Logo: No space, no choice, no jobs; taking aim at the brand bullies* (2000)
McCorquodale, Duncan (ed) and Siegle, Lucy (Intro), *Recycle: The Essential Guide* (2006)
Norris, Lucy, *'Shoddy rags and relief blankets: perceptions of textile recycling in north India'* in C. Alexander and J. Reno (eds), *Global Recycling Economies* (2012)
Porritt, Jonathon, *Capitalism: as if the World Matters* (2007)
Ransom, David, *The no-nonsense guide to fair trade* (2006)
Rivoli, Pietra, *The Travels of a T-Shirt in the Global Economy: An economist examines the markets, power, and politics of world trade* (2009)
Schumacher, Ernst Friedrich, *Small Is Beautiful: Economics as if people mattered* (1973)
Steffen, Alex (ed.), *Worldchanging: A user's guide for the 21st century* (2006)
Whitely, Nigel, *Design for Society* (1992)
Zaccai, Edwin, *Sustainable Consumption, Ecology and Fair Trade* (2008)

CULTURAL STUDIES

Bartlett, Djurdja, *FashionEast: The spectre that haunted socialism* (2010)
Banerjee, Mukulika and Daniel Miller, *The Sari* (2008)
Buckland, David and Chris Wainwright (eds), *UNFOLD: A cultural response to climate change* (2010)
Craik, Jennifer, *The Face of Fashion* (1994)
Crane, Diana, *Fashion and Its Social Agendas: Class, gender and identity in clothing* (2001)
Edwards, Eiluned, *Textiles and Dress of Gujarat* (2011)
Entwistle, Joanne, *The Fashioned Body: Fashion, dress and modern social theory* (2000)
Finkelstein, Joanne, *After A Fashion*, (1996)
Garcia Mira, Ricardo, José M. Sabucedo Cameselle and Romay Martinez (eds), *Culture, Environmental Action and Sustainability* (2003)
George, Susan, *Whose Crisis, Whose future?* (2010)
Gibson, Pamela Church, *Fashion and Celebrity Culture* (2012)
Kuchler, Susanne and Miller, Daniel (eds), *Clothing as Material Culture* (2005)
McRobbie, Angela, *British fashion design: Rag trade or image industry?* (1998)
Norris, Lucy, 'Creative entrepreneurs: the recycling of second-hand Indian clothing' in A. Palmer and H. Clark (eds), *Old Clothes, New Looks.* (2004)
Norris, Lucy 'Shedding skins: the materiality of divestment in India', *Journal of Material Culture*, 9/1 (2004), pp. 59–71,
Rocamora, Agnès, *Fashioning the City: Paris, fashion and the media* (2009)
Simmel, Georg, 'Fashion' in *On Individuality and Social Forms* (1973)
Schwarz, Michiel and Joost Elffers (eds), *Sustainism is the New Modernism: A cultural manifesto for the Sustainist era* (2010)

TEXTILES AND TECHNOLOGY

Balfour-Paul, Jenny, *Indigo* (2011)
Blackburn, Richard, *Biodegradable and Sustainable Fibres* (2005)
Blackburn, Richard (ed.), *Sustainable Textiles: Lifecycle and environmental impact* (2009)
Corbmann, Bernard, *Textiles: Fiber to fabric* (1985)
Elsasser, Virginia, *Textiles: Concepts and principles* (2010)
Fereday, Gwen, *Natural Dyes* (2003)
Ferrigno, Simon, *An Insider's Guide to Cotton and Sustainability* (2011)
Gale, Colin and Jasbir Kaur, *The Textile Book* (2002)
Gibson, Kenyon (ed.), *Hemp for Victory* (2006)
Handley, Susannah, *Nylon: The story of a fashion revolution* (1999)
Hatch, Kathryn, *Textile Science* (1993)
Hibbert, Ros, *Textile Innovation* (2004)
Jones, Richard, *Soft Machines: Nanotechnology and life* (2004)
McKibben, Bill, *Enough: Setting limits on human genetic technology* (2003)
Roulac, John, *Hemp Horizons* (1997)
Seymour, Sabine, *Fashionable Technology* (2008)
Seymour, Sabine, *Functional Aesthetics: Visions in fashionable technology* (2010)
Slater, Kieth, *Environmental Impact of Textiles* (2003)
Taylor, Marjorie Alice, *Technology of Textile Properties* (1991)

Resources

REPORTS AND CAMPAIGNS

An Overview of Working Conditions in Sportswear Factories in Indonesia, Sri Lanka and the Philippines (Labour Behind the Label, 2011)
Asda: Poverty Guaranteed (ActionAid, 2010)
Baden, Sally and Catherine Barber, *The Impact of the Second-hand Clothing Trade on Developing Countries* (Oxfam, 2005)
Cashing In: Giant retailers, purchasing practices and working conditions in the garment industry (Clean Clothes Campaign, 2009)
Co-op Bank Ethical Consumer Reports (National Economic Foundation, 2005–11)
Deeper Luxury (World Wildlife Fund, 2007)
Dirty Laundry: Unravelling the corporate connections to toxic water pollution in China (Greenpeace International, 2011)
Dirty Laundry 2: Hung out to dry (Greenpeace International, 2011)
Dirty Laundry: Reloaded (Greenpeace International, 2012)
Fashioning Sustainability: A review of the sustainability impacts of the clothing industry (Forum for the Future, 2007)
End of Life: Maximising reuse and recycling of UK clothing and textiles (DEFRA, 2009)
Fashion Victims: The true cost of cheap clothes at Primark, Asda and Tesco (War on Want, 2006)
Fisher, Tom, Tim Cooper, S. Woodward, A. Hiller and H. Goworek, *Public Understanding of Sustainable Clothing: A report to the Department for Environment, Food and Rural Affairs* (DEFRA, 2008).
Full Package Approach to Labour Codes of Conduct (Clean Clothes Campaign, 2008)
Killer Jeans (Labour behind the Label, 2011)
Let's Clean up Fashion, The state of pay behind the UK high street (Labour Behind the Label, 2006–11)
Looking for a Quick Fix: How weak social auditing is keeping workers in sweatshops (Clean Clothes Campaign, 2005)
Low Cost Clothing Waste (Salvation Army Trading Company, 2006)
Nanoscience and Nanotechnologies: Opportunities and uncertainties (The Royal Society, London, 2004)
Made by Women: Gender, the Global Garment Industry and the Movement for Women Workers? Rights (Clean Clothes Campaign, 2005)
Morley, Nick, C. Bartlett and Ian McGill, *Maximising the Reuse and Recycling of UK Clothing and Textiles: A report to the Department for Environment, Food and Rural Affairs.* (2009).
My Sustainable T-shirt (PAN 2007)
Organic Cotton: From field to final product (PAN, 1999)
Progress Report of Sustainable Products (Defra, 2008)
Shaw, Linda (ed.), *Co-operation, Social Responsibility and Fairtrade in Europe* (Co-operative College, 2006)
Stitched Up: How those imposing unfair competition in the textiles and clothing industries are the only winners in this race to the bottom (ICFTU, 2005)
Sustainable Clothing Roadmap – Progress Report (DEFRA, 2011)
Taking Liberties: the story behind the UK high street (Labour behind the Label, 2010)
The Deadly Chemicals in Cotton (PAN, 2007)
White Gold: The true cost of Cotton (Environmental Justice Foundation, 2007)

AGRICULTURE

ABM (AgriBioMediterraneo)
Germany
ABM was established as a regional initiative in Vignola, Italy, in 1990 and received recognition as an official IFOAM (see below) Regional Group in 1997. It includes affiliates from sixteen Mediterranean countries: Albania, Bosnia-Herzegovina, Croatia, Cyprus, Egypt, France, Greece, Israel, Italy, Palestine, Portugal, Serbia & Montenegro, Slovenia, Spain, Tunisia and Turkey.
+49 (0)22 8926 5010
http://www.ifoam.org

BETTER COTTON INITIATIVE
Switzerland
The Better Cotton Initiative (BCI) aims to improve the economic, environmental and social sustainability of cotton cultivation worldwide. Since 2005 the BCI has been working with stakeholders and organizations from across the cotton supply chain to develop a mainstream market for 'Better Cotton', which it hopes will bring long-term benefits for both the environment and people dependent on cotton for their livelihood. The first Better Cotton became available in 2011.
+41 2 2939 1250
http://www.bettercotton.org

BIOREGIONAL
UK
BioRegional is an entrepreneurial charity focused on creating practical sustainability solutions through a mixture of consultancy, education and informing policy.
+44 (0)20 8404 4880
http://www.bioregional.com

GALCI (El Grupo de America Latina y el Caribe)
Argentina
GALCI represent IFOAM (see below) members from Latin America and the Caribbean, including producers' associations, traders, certifiers, NGOS and individuals, with the aim of putting IFOAM directives into practice, supporting the expansion of organic agriculture.
+54 38 7401 2202
http://www.galci.net

HELVETAS
Switzerland
Helvetas, founded in 1955, is an independent trade association supported by approximately 38,000 members, more than 40,000 sponsors and fifteen regional volunteer groups. It aims to address not only material issues – such as improving food, living conditions, production, income and infrastructure – but also the social, cultural and spiritual needs of developing communities.
+41 44 368 6500
http://www.helvetas.ch

IFOAM (International Federation of Organic Agriculture Movements)
Germany
IFOAM is the worldwide umbrella organization for the organic movement, uniting more than 750 member organizations in 116 countries.
+49 22 8926 5010
http://www.ifoam.org

INCROPS PROJECT
UK
Based at the University of East Anglia, Norwich, the InCrops Enterprise Hub is a European funded, non-profit company whose research, public sector and corporate partners work collaboratively to develop the commercial potential of innovative crops.
+44 (0)16 0359 1765
http://www.incropsproject.co.uk

PAN INTERNATIONAL (Pesticide Action Network)
International
Pesticide Action Network (PAN) was launched in Malaysia in 1982 and is now an international network involving more than 600 non-governmental organizations, institutions and individuals to replace the use of hazardous pesticides with ecologically sound and socially just alternatives.
+32 2503 0837
http://www.pan-international.org
Contact information for local centres at http://www.pan-europe.info

PAN UK (Pesticide Action Network)
UK
PAN UK works closely with partners in developing countries to reduce the dependence on pesticides and encourage positive ecological, safe and sustainable alternatives. It has been instrumental in raising awareness of the serious health and environmental issues of growing cotton, particularly in developing countries and is founder of the Wear Organic campaign.
+44 (0)20 7065 0905
http://www.pan-uk.org and http://www.wearorganic.com

SCP (Sustainable Cotton Project)
USA
Since 1996 SCP has fostered information-sharing among farmers, manufacturers and consumers to develop a Cleaner Cotton™ industry. SCP provides growers with information about biological farming techniques and educates the public about the importance of supporting local farmers and reducing chemical use in fibre and food production.
+1 530 370 5325
http://www.sustainablecotton.org

SOIL ASSOCIATION
UK
The Soil Association was founded in 1946 and is now is the UK's leading campaigning and certification organization for organic food and farming. In 2003 it began offering accreditation to cover the processing and manufacture of organic textiles.
+44 (0)11 7314 5000
http://www.soilassociation.org

TEXTILE EXCHANGE (TE) [FORMERLY THE ORGANIC EXCHANGE]
USA
Textile Exchange provides tools for collaborative planning, problem solving, product development and sourcing and consumer education to advance the sustainable development of textiles.
+1 806 428 3411
http://www.textileexchange.orgg

COMMUNICATION AND NETWORKS

AMERICAN APPAREL AND FOOTWEAR ASSOCIATION (AAFA)
USA
AAFA is the national trade association representing American apparel, footwear and other sewn product companies and suppliers who compete in the global market.
+1 800 520 2262
http://www.wewear.org

BIONEERS
USA
Bioneers provides a forum and social hub for

education about cutting-edge environmental solutions inspired by nature. It runs a conference and education programs promoting 'a future environment of hope'
+1 505 986 0366 or +1 877 246 6337
http://www.bioneers.org / info@bioneers.org

DESIGNERS ACCORD
International
The Designers Accord is a coalition of designers, educators, and business leaders working together to create positive environmental and social change.
http://www.designersaccord.org
info@designersaccord.org

EDUCATORS FOR SOCIALLY RESPONSIBLE APPAREL BUSINESS
Denmark
Educators for Socially Responsible Apparel Business is a collaborative learning community whose members collectively share knowledge, build awareness and foster campus and community engagement to promote social responsibility and sustainability in the apparel industry.
+45 30 2831 8714
http://www.esrab.org
dickson@udel.edu

EDUFASHION
Italy/Netherlands
EDUfashion is a two-year project for the development of a collaborative platform for fashion creation and continuous education emphasizing skill-sharing and ethical branding.
http://www.edufashion.org
info@edufashion.org

EPEA (Environmental Protection Encouragement Agency)
Germany
EPEA works with organizations and their supply chain partners to develop industrial innovations that reduce environmental and human health impacts while improving quality, profitability and cost-effectiveness.
+49 40 431 3490
http://www.epea-hamburg.org/index.php
epea@epea.com

FASHIONING AN ETHICAL INDUSTRY
UK
Fashioning an Ethical Industry is a Labour Behind the Label project that works with students and tutors on fashion-related courses to give a global overview of the garment industry, raise awareness of current company practices and of initiatives to improve conditions, and inspires students to raise standards for workers in the fashion industry of the future.
+44 (0)11 7944 1700
http://www.fashioninganethicalindustry.org
info@fashioninganethicalindustry.org

FIBRE2FASHION
USA
Fibre2fashion is envisioned to be a market place for business in the entire value chain starting from fibre covering up to fashion.
http://www.fibre2fashion.com

FORUM FOR DESIGN & SUSTAINABLE ENTERPRISE (FDSE)
Netherlands
The Scandinavian based Forum for Design & Sustainable Enterprise (FDSE) supports a new generation of entrepreneurs, organizations and industry sectors in the development of innovative products and services that are environmentally viable, socially just and economically prosperous.
+46 73 330 9060
http://www.fdse.se
info@fdse.se

LOHAS
USA
LOHAS provides business-focused resources on the growing $290 billion market segment related to sustainable living, and serves as the central hub for education, updated news, and B2B gatherings of those cultivating the LOHAS movement.
+1 303 222 8209
http://www.lohas.com
info@lohas.com

NRDC
USA
The Natural Resources Defense Council is an environmental action group that combines the grassroots power of 1.3 million members and online

activists with the expertise of more than 350 lawyers, scientists and other professionals.
+1 212 727 2700
http://www.nrdc.org

RECYCLING INTERNATIONAL
Netherlands
Recycling International is an independent magazine written specifically for the global recycling industry, with ten issues published each year and a focus on textiles.
+31 26 312 0994
http://www.recyclinginternational.com

SUSTAINABLE APPAREL COALITION
Worldwide
Founded in 2011, the Sustainable Apparel Coalition is an international trade federation that aims to reduce the environmental and social impacts of apparel and footwear products around the world.
http://www.apparelcoalition.org

CERTIFICATION AND SUPPORT

ACOS
UK
Set up by DEFRA, The Advisory Committee on Organic Standards (ACOS) is a non-executive, non-departmental public body, which advises the government on organic standards, approval of organic certifying bodies and R&D. It was preceded by UKROFS.
+44 (0)84 5933 5577
http://www.defra.gov.uk

BLUE ANGEL
Germany
The Blue Angel is a German certification for environmentally friendly products and services. Introduced in 1978, it is the oldest ecolabel in the world and covers about 11,700 products and services in approximately 120 product categories.
+49 340 2103 3394
http://www.blauer-engel.de

BLUESIGN
Switzerland
The bluesign® is an independent textile industry standard and certification. The associated bluefinder™ is a growing online database specifically designed for textile manufacturers that contains bluesign® approved components such as auxiliaries, dyestuffs and finishing agents.
+41 (0)71 272 2990
http://www.bluesign.com

BSI (British Standards Institute)
UK
Since its foundation in 1901 as the Engineering Standards Committee, BSI Group has grown into a leading global independent business services. In 2006, the BSI developed an initiative to create a Community of Practices to support all types of stakeholders (individuals, retail, manufacturers, NGOs) in devising solutions to the ethical and social challenges faced throughout the fashion industry.
+44 (0)20 8996 9001
http://www.bsi-global.com

CHINA ENVIRONMENTAL LABELLING
China
In 2003, the China Environmental Labelling Program was launched by the Environmental Protection Administration Environmental Certification Centre (SEPA). Modelled on international labelling standards, it covers a wide range of product categories including textiles and footwear.
+86 10 5920 5856
http://www.sepacec.com/cecen

CONTROL UNION
Netherlands
Control Union (CU) is an international group of companies specializing in independent cargo surveying, superintending and certification. The CU offers two certification programmes for sustainable textiles: the EKO Sustainable Textile certification and Organic Exchange certification.
+31 (0)10 282 3333
http://www.controlunion.com

ECO MARK
Japan
The Eco Mark Program is operated by the Japan Environment Association (JEA), founded in 1989. Products must meet the necessary criteria in their categories order to be awarded by the Eco Mark Committee for Product Certification.
+81 3 5114 1255
http://www.ecomark.jp/english/

EPEA
(CRADLE TO CRADLE)
Germany
Founded in 1987, the Environmental Protection Encouragement Agency (EPEA) works with clients worldwide to apply the Cradle to Cradle recycling methodology to the design of new processes, products and services. +49 40 431 3490
http://www.epea-hamburg.org
epea@epea.com

ETKO
Turkey
ETKO is the national certification body in Turkey for the Global Organic Textile Standard (GOTS).
+90 023 2339 7606
http://www.etko.org

EU ECO LABEL
Belgium
Established in 1992, the EU Eco Label 'Flower' is a unique certification scheme aimed to help European consumers distinguish greener, more environmentally friendly products and services.
+32 2296 8075
http://www.eco-label.com

Fairtrade Foundation
UK
The Fairtrade Foundation is the independent non-profit organization that licenses use of the FAIRTRADE Mark on products in the UK in accordance with internationally agreed Fairtrade standards.
+44 (0)20 7405 5942
http://www.fairtrade.org.uk
mail@fairtrade.org.uk

FLO
Germany
Fairtrade Labelling Organizations International (FLO) is a group of twenty-four organizations working to secure a better deal for producers. FLO own the FAIRTRADE Mark – the product label that certifies international Fairtrade standards have been met.
+49 22 894 9230
http://www.fairtrade.net
info@flo-cert.net

GECA (Good Environmental Choice Australia)
Australia
Good Environmental Choice Australia (GECA) aims to reduce environmental harm by promoting the production and consumption of environmentally preferable products and services. The Environmental Choice Australia ecolabel provides the community and commercial markets with an environmental mark of recognition for a wide range of products and services.
+61 2 6287 3100
http://www.geca.org.au

GEN (Global Ecolabelling Network)
Japan
The Global Ecolabelling Network (GEN) is a non-profit association of third-party, environmental performance labelling organizations founded in 1994 to improve, promote, and develop the 'ecolabelling' of products and services.
+81 3 5114 1255
http://www.globalecolabelling.net

GOTS (Global Organic Textiles Standard)
Germany
GOTS is the worldwide leading textile processing standard for organic fibres, including ecological and social criteria, backed up by independent certification of the entire textile supply chain.
http://www.global-standard.org
mail@global-standard.org

THE GREEN COUNCIL
(HONG KONG GREEN LABEL)
Hong Kong
The Green Council (GC) is a non-profit, non-partisan environmental association formed in May 2000 with the aim of encouraging the industrial and commercial

sectors in Hong Kong to include environmental protection in their production and management processes.
+852 2810 1122
http://www.greencouncil.org/eng/index

ICEA (Institute for Ethical and Environmental Certification)
Italy
With twenty branches in Italy and ten abroad, CEA is one of the most prominent certification bodies in the field of sustainable development.
+39 05 127 2986
http://www.icea.info

IMO (Institute for Marketecology)
Switzerland
Active for over twenty years, The Institute for Marketecology (IMO) is one of the first and most renowned international agencies for the inspection, certification and quality assurance of eco-friendly products.
+41 71 626 0626
http://www.imo.ch

ISEAL
UK
The ISEAL Alliance is the global association for social and environmental standards. Working with established and emerging voluntary standard systems ISEAL develops guidance and helps strengthen the effectiveness and impact of these standards.
+44 (0)20 3246 0066
http://www.isealalliance.org

IVN (International Association Natural Textile Industry)
Germany
The International Verband der Naturtextilwirtschaft (IVN) aims to raise awareness of the benefits of eco-friendly textiles among consumers, press and the retail trade.
+49 673 7712 0802
http://www.naturtextil.com

JOCA (Japan Organic Cotton Association)
Japan
Japan Organic Cotton Association (JOCA) was founded in 2000 in order to promote and increase the production and consumption of organic cotton products. JOCA's activities are: the certification and labelling of organic cotton products and promotional projects.
+81 3 3341 7200
http://www.joca.gr.jp

KOECO
Korea
Established in April 1992, the Korea Eco-labelling Program is a non-profit organization certifying Eco Labels to qualifying eco-products for excellent quality and performance, as well as general environment-friendliness during the entire production process.
+82 2 2085 0012
http://www.eng.keiti.re.kr

MADE-BY
Netherlands
MADE-BY was launched in 2004 in direct response to rising consumer concern in Europe over social and environmental issues within the fashion industry. It supports fashion brands in implementing good environmental and social standards that can be developed and maintained within a commercial environment.
+31 20 523 0666
http://www.made-by.org
NOP (Natural Organic Program)
USA
The National Organic Program (NOP) develops, implements, and administers national production, handling, and labelling standards for organic agricultural products. The NOP also accredits the certifying agents (foreign and domestic) who inspect organic production and handling operations to certify that they meet USDA standards.
+1 1320 2720 3252
http://www.ams.usda.gov

NORDIC SWAN
Sweden
The Nordic Ecolabel, established in 1989, is one of the world's leading ecolabel with over 1,000 licenses just in Sweden alone, for a total of sixty-six product areas.
+46 8 5555 2400
http://www.svanen.se/en/

OEKO-TEX STANDARD
Switzerland
The International Oeko-Tex Association is a grouping of fourteen textile research institutes responsible for independent tests for harmful substances according to Oeko-Tex Standard 100. The Oeko-Tex Standard 100plus product label provides textile and clothing manufacturers with the opportunity to highlight the human-ecological optimisation of their products as well as their efforts in production ecology to consumers.
http://www.oeko-tex.com

ONECERT INC.
USA
Onecert is a certification body, which includes the following six international standards: USDA National Organic Program (NOP), European Organic Regulations (EU 2092/91), Japan Agricultural Standards (JAS), Organic Reference Standard (CAAQ), Bio Suisse Standards, and IFOAM Basic Standards.
+1 402 420 6080
http://www.onecert.net

SA8000 (run by Social Accountability International)
USA
Social Accountability International (SAI) is a global, multi-stakeholder, standards setting organization, whose is to advance the human rights of workers around the world. SAI established SA8000 a recognized benchmark among the voluntary codes and standards initiatives that employers use to measure their own performance and responsibly manage their supply chains.
+1 212 684 1414
http://www.sa-intl.org
info@sa-intl.org

WRAP (Worldwide Responsive Apparel Production)
USA
WRAP is an independent non-profit organization dedicated to the certification of lawful, humane and ethical manufacturing throughout the world.
It provides guidelines and forms for factories interested in becoming WRAP-certified and an application form for monitors seeking WRAP accreditation.
+1 703 243 0970
http://www.wrapapparel.org

ETHICAL TRADING

ASIA FLOOR WAGE
Worldwide
The Asian Floor Wage campaign acts as a platform for union leaders and labour activists to come together to explore a union-based Asian strategy for the global garment industry.
http://www.asiafloorwage.org
jeroen@cleanclothes.org

CAMPAIGN FOR LABOR RIGHTS
USA
The Campaign for Labor Rights (CLR) aims to end labour rights violations around the world and increase awareness of the underlying causes of the global sweatshop. Its campaign strategies are designed in collaboration with workers struggling to gain the right to organize, the right to earn a living wage in a clean, safe work environment, and the right to bargain collectively with their bosses.
+1 202 544 9355
http://www.clrlabor.org

CCC (Clean Clothes Campaign)
Netherlands
The Clean Clothes Campaign is an alliance of organizations in fifteen European companies that works to ensure the fundamental rights of workers are respected. Members include trade unions and NGOs covering a broad spectrum of perspectives and interests, such as women's rights, consumer advocacy and poverty reduction.
+31 20 412 2785
http://www.cleanclothes.org

CHANGE STAR
UK
Change Star is an agency and consultancy that focuses on finding the most effective ways for an organization to achieve its goals and positive change.
+44 (0)79 6822 7029
http://www.changestar.co.uk

EFTA (European Fair Trade Association)
Netherlands
EFTA is an association of eleven Fair Trade importers in nine European countries (Austria, Belgium, France, Germany, Italy, Netherlands, Spain, Switzerland and the UK).
+31 43 325 6917
http://www.european-fair-trade-association.org

EJF (Environmental Justice Foundation)
UK
Founded in 2000, EFJ makes a direct link between the need for environmental security and the defence of all basic human rights. EFJ works towards empowering people who suffer most from environmental abuses and to find peaceful ways of preventing them.
+44 (0)20 7239 3310
http://www.ejfoundation.org

ETHICAL COMPANY ORGANISATION ACCREDITATION
UK
The Ethical Company Organisation runs the Ethical Accreditation Scheme, which assesses the level of a company or brand's Corporate Social Responsibility record and awards Ethical Accreditation to top applications. The organization also publishes The Good Shopping Guide, the world's leading ethical shopping annual reference book.
+44 (0)84 5257 6818
http://www.ethical-company-organisation.org

ETHICAL CONSUMER RESEARCH ASSOCIATION (ECRA)
UK
ERCA is an alternative consumer organization produces research into the social and environmental records of companies in order to inform the development of ethical and sustainable consumerism. The organization publishes Ethical Consumer Magazine and runs http://www.ethiscore.org.
+44 (0)16 1226 2929
http://www.ethicalconsumer.org

ETHICAL FASHION FORUM (EFF)
UK
The Ethical Fashion Forum (EFF) is a large network of designers, businesses and organizations focusing on social and environmental sustainability within the fashion industry.
+44 (0)20 7739 7692
http://www.ethicalfashionforum.com

ETI (Ethical Trading Initiative)
UK
The Ethical Trading Initiative is an alliance of companies, NGOs, and trade union organizations. ETI was set up in 1998 to encourage UK companies to meet and exceed basic international labour standards by promoting and encouraging implementation or regimented corporate codes of practice. ETI encourages companies to adopt the ETI Base Code and implement it in their supply chains.
+44 (0)20 7841 4350
http://www.ethicaltrade.org

FAIR LABOR ASSOCIATION
Switzerland
The Fair Labor Association (FLA) brings together colleges, universities, civil society organizations and socially responsible companies in a unique multi-stakeholder initiative to end sweatshop labour and improve working conditions in factories worldwide. The FLA holds its participants – those involved in the manufacturing and marketing process – accountable to the FLA Workplace Code of Conduct.
+41 22 747 0088
http://www.fairlabor.org
info@fairlabor.org

FAIR TRADE CERTIFIED
USA
Fair Trade USA is the leading third-party certifier of Fair Trade products in the United States.
+1 510 663 5260
http://www.transfairusa.org

FAIR TRADE FOUNDATION
UK
Established in 1992, The Foundation is the UK member of Fairtrade Labelling Organizations International (FLO). Their key areas of activity are: providing an independent certification of the trade chain, licensing use of the FAIRTRADE Mark as a consumer guarantee on products; facilitating the

market to grow demand for Fairtrade and enable producers to sell to traders and retailers; and working with partners to support producer organizations and their networks.
+44 (0)20 7405 5942
http://www.fairtrade.org.uk

FAIR WEAR FOUNDATION
Netherlands
Fair Wear Foundation (FWF) is an international verification initiative dedicated to enhancing workers' lives all over the world. They work closely with a growing number of companies that produce clothing and other sewn products and that take responsibility for their supply chain.
+31 (0)20 408 4255
http://www.fairwear.org
info@fairwear.nl

FASHIONING AN ETHICAL INDUSTRY PROJECT
UK
Fashioning an Ethical Industry (FEI) is an education project of Labour Behind the Label. The project aims to raise standards for garment workers in the fashion industry of the future working with tutors and students to embed ethical issues into the curriculum of all fashion courses across the UK.
+44 (0)11 7944 1700
http://www.fashioninganethicalindustry.org

FLO-CERT
Germany
FLO-CERT GmbH is an independent International Certification Company offering Fairtrade Certification services. FLO-CERT certifies products with a retail value of about two billion euros per year, representing close to 2,000 clients in more than seventy countries around the globe.
+49 (0)22 824 930
http://www.flo-cert.net

HOMEWORKERS' WORLDWIDE
UK
The UK office of Homeworkers' Worldwide (HWW) was set up to provide a network for organizers in different countries; to produce information, newsletters and training materials useful to organizers and to advocate home-based work.
+44 (0)11 3217 4037
http://www.homeworkersww.org.uk
info@homeworkersww.org.uk

INTERNATIONAL LABOUR ORGANIZATION (ILO)
Switzerland
The ILO, founded in 1919, is the global body responsible for drawing up and overseeing international labour standards. Working with its Member States, the ILO seeks to ensure that labour standards are respected in practice as well as principle.
+41 (0)22 799 6111
http://www.ilo.org

INTERNATIONAL TEXTILE, GARMENT AND LEATHER WORKERS FEDERATION
Belgium
The International Textile, Garment and Leather Workers Federation (ITGLWF) is a global union federation bringing together 217 affiliated organizations in 110 countries. Its activities include drawing up policy guidelines for trade unions and coordinating the activities of affiliates around the world, undertaking solidarity action in support of unions in sectors whose trade union rights are being denied, and running a programme of education and development aid to assist unions in developing.
+32 (0)25 122 606
http://www.itglwf.org
office@itglwf.org

INTERNATIONAL TRADE CENTRE
Worldwide
The International Trade Centre (ITC) is a joint agency of the World Trade Organization and the United Nations. As the development partner for small business export success, ITC's goal is to help developing and transition countries achieve sustainable human development through exports.
http://www.intracen.org

LABOUR BEHIND THE LABEL CAMPAIGN
UK
UK Platform for the Clean Clothes Campaign, Labour Behind the Label supports garment workers' efforts

worldwide to defend their rights. Their mission is to educate consumers, lobby companies and government, raise awareness, and encourage international solidarity with workers.
+44 (0)11 7944 1700
http://www.labourbehindthelabel.org

MAQUILA SOLIDARITY NETWORK
Canada
Established in 1994, The Maquila Solidarity Network (MSN) works with women's and labour rights organizations in Mexico, Central and America to improve wages and working conditions in global supply chains. The organization's activities include corporate campaigning and engagement, networking and coalition building, and policy advocacy.
+1 416 532 8584
http://en.maquilasolidarity.org

NO SWEAT CAMPAIGN
UK
No Sweat campaigns against sweatshop exploitation, promoting unionization and international solidarity for sweatshop workers.
+44 (0)79 0443 1959
http://www.nosweat.org.uk

OXFAM
UK
Oxfam GB is a leading international NGO with a worldwide reputation for excellence in the delivery of aid and development work. Their purpose is to work with others to overcome poverty and suffering. Oxfam GB is a member of Oxfam International.
+44 (0)30 0200 1292
http://www.oxfam.org.uk

RESPONSIBLE PURCHASING NETWORK
USA
The Responsible Purchasing Network (RPN) is a national network of procurement-related professionals dedicated to socially responsible and environmentally sustainable purchasing.
+1 877 683 7326 or +1 301 891 3683
http://www.responsiblepurchasing.org

SEWA (Self Employed Women's Association)
India
SEWA is a trade union registered in 1972 working to organize women workers for regular salaried employment and its attendant welfare benefits. Low income, self-employed workers comprise 94% of the female labour force in India.
+ 91 79 2550 6444
http://www.sewa.org
mail@sewa.org

TRAIDCRAFT
UK
As one of the UK's fairtrade pioneers, Traidcraft is both a trading company and a development charity.
+44 (0)19 1491 0591
http://www.traidcraft.co.uk

USAS (United Students Against Sweatshops)
USA
Formed in 1997, United Students Against Sweatshops (USAS) is a grassroots organization of youth and students who believe that a powerful and dynamic labour movement will ensure greater justice for all people.
+1 202 549 5649
http://www.usas.org

WORKER RIGHTS CONSORTIUM
USA
The Worker Rights Consortium (WRC) is an independent labour rights monitoring organization, conducting investigations of working conditions in factories around the globe. Their purpose is to combat sweatshops and protect the rights of workers who sew apparel and make other products sold in the United States.
+1 202 387 4884
http://www.workersrights.org
theresa.haas@workersrights.org

WORLD FAIR TRADE ORGANIZATION (WFTO)
Netherlands
Membership of the WFTO is limited to organizations that demonstrate full commitment to Fair Trade and apply its Ten Principles of Fair Trade. WFTO members who are monitored against these Principles are listed in the Fair Trade 100 index of world-leading Fair Trade brands, businesses and organizations.
+31 (0)34 553 5914
http://www.wfto.com

AASBCI (The Association of Suppliers to the British Clothing Industry)
UK
The ASBCI is the only association to bring together the clothing industry from fibre manufacture through to garment manufacture, retail and aftercare. Since 1992, the ASBCI has grown from twenty members to over one hundred including some of the most prestigious names within the clothing and textile industry, forming a huge pool of expertise.
+44 (0)14 2235 4666
http://www.asbci.co.uk

AWI/WOOLMARK
Australia
Established in 2001, AWI's mission is to invest in research, development, marketing and promotion in order to enhance the profitability, international competitiveness and sustainability of the Australian wool industry; and increase demand and market access for Australian wool. It is the owner of the WOOLMARK label in Australia.
+44 (0)20 7845 5887
http://www.wool.com

BWBM (British Wool Marketing Board)
UK
A farmer run organization, the BWMB was established in 1950 to operate a central marketing system for UK fleece wool, with the aim of achieving the best possible net return for producers.
+44 (0)12 7468 8666
http://www.britishwool.org.uk

C.L.A.S.S. (Creative Lifestyle and Sustainable Strategies)
Italy
CLASS is an international organization working to promote commercially available eco-textiles, yarns, processes, finished products and services. The organization has three showrooms in Milan, London and New York, each featuring a comprehensive materials library available to businesses, designers and buyers.
+39 02 7601 8402
http://www.c-l-a-s-s.org

COTTON INCORPORATED
USA
From agricultural, fibre and textile research, market information and technical services, to advertising and public relations, fashion forecasts and retail promotions, the goal of Cotton Incorporated is to ensure that cotton remains the first choice among consumers in apparel and home products.
+1 919 678 2220
http://www.cottoninc.com

COTTON USA
USA
The National Cotton Council of America's mission is to ensure the ability of all US cotton industry segments to compete effectively in the raw cotton, oilseed and US-manufactured product markets at home and abroad.
+1 901 274 9030
http://www.cotton.org

DEFRA
UK
The Department for Environment, Food and Rural Affairs (DEFRA) is a legislative department in the UK, delivering environmental policies in areas and particularly investing in supporting the farming industry, protecting biodiversity and encouraging sustainable food production. It launched the Sustainable Clothing Action Plan in 2009 with 300 stakeholders
+44 (0)84 5933 5577
http://www.defra.gov.uk

EPEA
Germany
The Environmental Protection and Encouragement Agency (EPEA) Internationale Umweltforschung GmbH works with clients worldwide to apply the Cradle to Cradle methodology to the design of new processes, products and services. Materials are applied with respect for their intrinsic value and their use to create recycled or even 'upcycled' products, which have value and technological sophistication that may be higher than that of their original use.
+49 40 431 3490
http://www.epea.com

FORUM FOR THE FUTURE
UK
Founded in 1996, Forum for the Future is an independent, non-profit organization with a mission to promote sustainable development. They help businesses and public service providers to understand and manage the environmental risks that change will bring and to find new opportunities in tackling these global challenges.
+44 (0)20 7324 3630
http://www.forumforthefuture.org.uk

FRIENDS OF THE EARTH
Worldwide
Friends of the Earth campaigns for solutions to environmental problems. It is the most extensive environmental network in the world, with around two million supporters across five continents and more than seventy-five national organizations worldwide.
+44 (0)20 7490 1555
http://www.foe.co.uk

GREENBLUE
USA
GreenBlue is a non-profit institute that stimulates the creative redesign of industry by focusing the expertise of professional communities to create practical solutions, resources, and opportunities for implementing sustainability.
+1 434 817 1424
http://www.greenblue.org

INTERNATIONAL ALPACA ASSOCIATION
Peru
The International Alpaca Association (IAA) is a private-sector association with non-profit purposes. The IAA brings together companies and individual breeders involved in the production and commercialization of fibre from alpacas, llamas, and other South American camelidae and their hybrids.
http://www.aia.org.pe
aia@terra.com.pe

IWTO (International Wool Textile Organisation)
Belgium
The IWTO represents a highly international and global acting industry with an important impact on the world economy and the global textile industry. The IWTO's mission is to help their Wool Industry Members to understand the textile demands of the consumers, and to respond to them with products and promotional activities especially developed to meet their needs, with a fibre that is highly desirable for its social, technical, comfort and sustainable values.
+32 2505 4010
http://www.iwto.org

MASTERS OF LINEN
France
MASTERS OF LINEN is a subsidiary of the CELC (European Flax and Hemp Confederation), the only European agro-industrial body to bring together players working in all stages of the flax/linen supply chain. The organization provide information and handle promotion for European Quality Linen throughout the world.
+33 (0)1 4221 0683
http://www.mastersoflinen.com

MATERIAL CONNEXION
New York, Bangkok, Cologne, Daegu and Milan
Material ConneXion is made up of an international team of multidisciplinary experts that bridge the gap between science and design to create practical manufacturing solutions.
+1 212 842 2050
http://www.materialconnexion.com

MERINO INNOVATION
Australia
Merino Innovation produces environmentally assured Australian Merino wool and has an online sourcing page listing suppliers worldwide.
+61 2 8295 3100
http://www.merinoinnovation.com

TEXTILE EXCHANGE
[FORMALLY THE ORGANIC EXCHANGE]
USA
Textile Exchange is a charitable organization committed to expanding organic agriculture, with a specific focus on increasing the production and use of organically grown fibres such as cotton.
+1 806 428 3411
http://www.textileexchange.org

OTA (The Organic Trade Association)
USA
Since its inception in 1985, OTA has been a key player in shaping both the regulatory and market environment for organic products. The association runs four directories: The Organic Pages Online, Organic Export Directory, Organic Ingredients and Farm Supplies.
+1 413 774 7511
http://www.ota.com

RITE GROUP
UK
The RITE GROUP is a new industry association founded by Marks & Spencer, the University of Leeds and Ecotextile News. It aims to provide advice and information to minimize the negative environmental impact of the textile and apparel industries. The Group's ultimate goal is to drive forward the sustainable and ethical production of textiles and clothing throughout the global supply chain through a number of innovative initiatives.
http://www.ritegroup.org

SILK ASSOCIATION OF GREAT BRITAIN
UK
The Silk Association of Great Britain exists to further the aims of the UK silk industry. Membership currently includes raw material merchants, throwsters, dyers, weavers, printers, knitters, finishers, converters, garment manufacturers and retailers.
+44 (0)20 7843 9460
http://www.silk.org.uk

THE TEXTILE INSTITUTE
UK
The Textile Institute was incorporated in England by a Royal Charter granted in 1925 and is a registered charity with individual and corporate members in over ninety countries. Within the global textiles, clothing and footwear industries the aim of the Institute is to facilitate learning, to recognise achievement, to reward excellence and to disseminate information.
+44 (0)16 1237 1188
http://www.texi.org

RECYCLING

ALA RECYCLING
USA
About eight million pounds of textile waste is not recycled and is land filled each year. ALA Recycling Industries is experienced in the implementation, management, and marketing of all textile waste generated in today's textile recycling industry.
+1 617 332 3280
http://www.recycledfibers.com

BIR (Bureau of International Recycling)
Belgium
BIR represents the world's recycling industry, covering, in particular, ferrous and non-ferrous metals, paper and textiles. About 600 companies and national federations from over sixty countries are affiliated to BIR, who provide their expertise to other industrial sectors and political groups in order to promote recycling.
+32 2627 5770
http://www.bir.org

ECO CIRCLE
Japan
Eco Circle is a recycling system for polyester products developed by fibre producers Teijin.
http://www.ecocircle.jp/en/

LONDON REMADE
UK
London Remade is a non-profit group working to develop and improve waste management, recycling and green procurement in London. The group specializes in waste minimisation, recycling schemes and business support.
+44 (0)20 7061 6360
http://www.londonremade.com

OXFAM WASTESAVERS
UK
Oxfam Wastesavers is a national reclamation scheme for donated clothing and textiles with around 600 collection banks in supermarket and local council sites. Banks provide saleable stock for Oxfam shops; any items which do not sell are collected and used for other charities with special needs, sent overseas for emergency aid, or sold to recycling companies.
+44 (0)18 6547 3727
http://www.oxfam.org.uk

SALVATION ARMY TRADING CO LTD
UK
The Salvation Army operates a textile recycling scheme which offers local authorities the choice of clothing banks, kerbside collection, and jumble sale and charity shop clearances. The scheme provides regular monthly weight reports to all councils and funds the Salvation Army's projects.
+44 (0)19 3344 1086
http://www.satradingco.org

SMART (Secondary Materials and Recycled Textile Association)
USA
SMART strengthens the economic opportunities of their diverse membership by promoting the interdependence of their industry segments and providing a common forum for networking, education and trade.
+1 443 640 1050
http://www.smartasn.org

SORT IT
UK
Sort It is a national tool, developed as part of the Waste Aware Scotland campaign, that provides information on the various alternatives available to householders to minimize the amount of waste that is sent to landfill. It lists a wide range of local and national outlets, facilities and services to help do this.
+44 (0)80 8100 2040
http://www.sort-it.org.uk

TEXAID
Switzerland
TEXAID collects and recycles almost 20,000 tonnes of used textiles each year. It works with more than 450 grassroots groups and generates funding for six Swiss charities. It recycles the largest proportion of used textiles in Switzerland and creates jobs. TEXAID employs more than eighty people in Switzerland making a major contribution to the sensible recycling of raw materials.
+41 (0)41 874 5400
http://www.texaid.ch

TEXTIEL RECYCLING (VHT)
Netherlands
Founded in 1949, VHT has more than forty members. Nearly all major Dutch textile sorters and the large charitable and commercial collectors of used textiles are members. The VHT represents more than 90% of the businesses that are in the textile recycling industry.
+31 (0)70 312 3919
http://www.textielrecycling.nl

TRA (Textile Recycling Association)
UK
TRA comprises collectors, graders and reprocessors of second hand clothing, textiles and shoes. The association aims to represent the interest of its members internationally and locally, help create a favourable climate within which merchants can operate, and promote textile recycling and the second hand clothing/shoe recycling industry.
+44 (0)84 5600 8276
http://www.textile-recycling.org.uk

TRAID (Textile Recycling for Aid and International Development)
UK
TRAID is a charity committed to protecting the environment and reducing world poverty through recycling and delivering educational programmes within the UK. Funds raised by TRAID, through the collection and sale of reclaimed clothing and shoes, help to divert waste from landfill and fund sustainable development projects in some of the poorest regions of the world.
+44 (0)20 8733 2580
http://www.traid.org.uk

WORN AGAIN
UK
Worn Again creates new products from recycled materials that would otherwise end up in landfill. Worn Again aims to use their business as a platform for improving social, economic and environmental conditions in regions where they operate while building a profitable business.
http://www.wornagain.co.uk /
info@wornagain.co.uk

WRAP (UK Government Waste and Resources Action Programme)
UK
WRAP is a government organization with three key objectives: to reduce the waste stream by at least three million tonnes of materials; to increase the level of public participation in recycling; and to reduce the amount of food thrown away by consumers and ensure more of it is collected for composting and recycling.
+44 (0)12 9581 9900
http://www.wrap.org.uk

DYEING AND CHEMICALS

AATCC (American Association of Textile Chemists and Colourists)
USA
Founded in 1921, AATCC is the world's leading non-profit association for the textile design, materials, processing and testing industries.
+1 919 549 8141
http://www.aatcc.org

AURA
India
Aura's dream is to offer options to each and every user to choose a herbal-dyed textile over chemical dyed one, with no limitations to design, quantity, and quality.
+91 79 2571 1685
http://www.auraherbalwear.com

BASF
Germany
For over 100 years, BASF has been the partner of choice for the textile industry – offering textile chemicals and solutions in all essential textile-processing steps.
+49 (0)62 1600
http://www.basf.com

BEZEMA AG
Switzerland
Since 1980, BEZEMA AG has been developing, producing and distributing a complete line of textile dyestuffs for practically all textile materials and fibres. Efficient production processes, modern production facilities in Europe and overseas and a multiphase monitoring system guarantee the products' high quality.
+41 (0)71 763 8811
http://www.bezema.com

CIA (Chemical Industries Association)
UK
CIA is the organization that represents chemical and pharmaceutical businesses throughout the UK. Its activities are split between lobbying and the provision of advice and services. Its policy agenda encompasses the economy and competitiveness; products and the way they work; health, safety & environment and employment issues.
+44 (0)20 7834 3399
http://www.cia.org.uk

CLARIANT
Switzerland
The Special Dyes from Clariant offer a series of high quality products that are flexible in application, based on innovation and developed specially to be used in highly ecological conditions.
+41 61 469 7202
http://www.textiles.clariant.com

COLOURTEX
India
Colourtex is the largest textile dyestuff manufacturing facility in India and has been serving the textile industry world over for over three decades. Among the best environmentally managed industries in the country, Colourtex offers eco-friendly dyes.
+91 26 1289 7800
http://www.colourtex.co.in

COULEURS DE PLANTES
France
Couleurs de Plantes manufactures and sells plant extracts, natural dyes, dye-plant extracts, natural pigments, plant pigments, lake pigments, pigment pastes and natural inks. Its products cover a large range of colours for innovative natural coloured products.
+33 (0)5 4699 3249
http://www.couleurs-de-plantes.com

CSIRO
Australia
CSIRO, the Commonwealth Scientific and Industrial Research Organisation, is Australia's national science agency and one of the largest and most diverse research agencies in the world.
+61 3 9545 2176
http://www.csiro.au

DYES AND PIGMENTS
India
Dyes and Pigments is a virtual encyclopaedia offering comprehensive information about the various types of dyes, dyestuff, pigments and dyeing processes.
http://www.dyespigments.com

DYSTAR
Germany
DyStar and Color Solutions International are leading suppliers of products and services for the textile chain. They help reduce costs, shorten lead times and meet quality and eco specifications.
+49 (0) 69 2109 2734
http://www2.dystar.com

ECOTINTES
South America
ECOTINTES is a natural dye alternative for cotton, wool, alpaca and other fibres. It is environmentally friendly and is free of dangerous chemical agents.
+51 199 338 3190
http://www.ecotintes.com

ETAD (Ecological and Toxicological Association of Dyers)
Switzerland
ETAD was formed in 1974 to represent the interests of these industries on matters relating to health and environment. ETAD is an international organization and its forty-five member companies are based in sixteen countries worldwide.
+41 61 690 9966
http://www.etad.com

GENCOR (IndiStar™ ColorAdjust System)
USA
Genencor is a global leader in industrial biotechnology, currently extending its product portfolio for denim treatment to include an environmentally friendly solution for the replacement of harsh chemicals such as chlorine and permanganate.
+1 800 847 5311
http://www.genencor.com

HUNTSMAN
UK / International
Huntsman Textile Effects creates, markets and manufactures a range of chemical and dye products that enhance the performance properties and colours of finished textiles and materials.
+44 (0)12 2383 2121
http://www.huntsman.com

NATURAL DYES INTERNATIONAL (NDI)
USA
NDI is organized to facilitate international cooperation in sharing information on natural dyes. It supports and promotes regional and international natural dye events organized by others.
+1 800 665 9786
http://www.naturaldyes.org

PURE TINCTORIA
UK
Pure Tinctoria is a range of Eco-friendly natural dyes that are concentrated, inter-mixable that provide all the colour possibilities of natural dyes without the hazards of chemical dyes.
+44 (0)13 3537 0729
http://www.pure-tinctoria.co.uk/en

REACH READY
UK
REACHStart offers a strategic programme, run specifically for individual business, at their own place. It is intended for companies that have just started to think about REACH: what it means to their business and their supply chain.
+44 (0)20 7901 1444
http://www.reachready.co.uk

REACH (EU Programme Registration, Evaluation and Authorisation of Chemicals)
EU
The aim of REACH is to improve the protection of human health and the environment through the better and earlier identification of the intrinsic properties of chemical substances, while enhancing the innovative capability and competitiveness of the European chemicals industry.
+44 (0)800 6789 1011
http://www.ec.europa.eu/environment/chemicals/reach.htm

RUBIA PIGMENTA NATURALIA
Netherlands
Rubia Pigmenta Naturalia is a Dutch company that manufactures and sells vegetable dyes with the aim of eventually introducing vegetable dyes to cover the colour spectrum.
+31 (0)16 754 1113
http://www.rubiapigmentanaturalia.nl

SDC (Society of Dyers and Colourists)
UK
Established in 1884, SDC is the world's leading independent, educational charity dedicated to advancing the science and technology of colour worldwide. The Society provides tried and trusted practical support services focused on implementing best practice in textile colour management, resulting in improved efficiency and cost savings.
+44 (0)12 7472 5138
http://www.sdc.org.uk

THE COLOURS OF NATURE
India
The Colours of Nature is specialized in natural indigo fermentation. This process, which as existed for more than 7,000 years, is the most earth friendly process for indigo dyeing. It consumes less water than other indigo dyeing methods, does not require any fixing agents and does not use hydrosulphite.
+(91) 0 41 3262 2587
http://www.thecoloursofnature.com

SUPPLIERS

AGROCEL
India
Agrocel is one of the world's largest direct suppliers of organic, fairtrade and other speciality cotton grown to International Organic Standards. Agrocel Pure and Fair Indian Organic Cotton is a registered brand developed by Agrocel Industries Ltd in conjunction with Vericott Ltd and Traidcraft Exchange.
+91 28 3429 5158
http://www.agrocel-cotton.com

AVANTI
Japan
AVANTI's organic cotton business began in 1991, importing US-made organic cotton fabrics. It is now involved in all phases of the organic cotton business from raw cotton, yarn and fabric to garments.
http://www.avantijapan.co.jp/en/

BAMBRO TEX
China
China Bambro Textile Co., Ltd., the leading company of application, marketing and services of bamboo fibre, is a large-scale supplier focused on innovation and the manufacturing of natural, green and biodegradable bamboo fibre.
+86 10 6486 7890
http://www.bambrotex.com

BERGMAN/RIVERA
South America
Bergman/Rivera produces quality organic cotton, employing 435 farmers in more than six different valleys throughout Peru as part of its White Cotton and Wild Cotton (coloured cotton) projects.
+51 1242 3106 · http://www.bergmanrivera.com

CALAMAI ECO FABRICS
Italy
Calamai Eco Fabrics supplies recycled wools, cotton, polyester and polypropylene.
+39 05 746 1411
http://www.calamai.it

CLIMATEX LIFECYCLE BY ROHNER TEXTILE AG
Switzerland
Climatex® Lifecycle™ is a compostable upholstery fabric produced in Switzerland by Rohner Textil AG.
+41 44 789 8600
http://www.climatex.com

CLOVERBROOK FABRICS
UK
Cloverbrook Fabrics are fabric suppliers of the Ingeo™ Fibre, made entirely from annually renewable resources, such as corn.
+44 (0)12 827 1200 · http://www.cloverbrook.com

COCONA FABRICS
USA
Cocona, Inc. is a privately held Colorado company focused on developing innovative technologies from natural sources. Cocona® is the consumer brand name chosen for apparel applications of this natural, quick dry, odour and UV managing fabric technology.
+1 720 652 9726 · http://www.coconainc.com

CUPRO (Asahi Kasei)
Japan
Asahi Kasei Fibres is the core operating company for all fibres and textiles operations of the Asahi Kasei Group, offering a wide and expanding range of innovative materials for apparel and industrial applications.
http://www.ak-bemberg.com

CUPRO (Bemberg)
Italy
Cupro yarn is an extremely fine (up to 1 dtex) multi-filament of natural origin. The raw material is composed of very fine and very short cotton filaments known as linters.
+39 03 2291 4211
http://www.bembergitalia.com

ECO YARNS
Australia
Eco Yarns wholesale and retail Pakucho Organic cotton yarns, fibres and fabrics, sell eco friendly Soysilk and Bamboo yarns and fibre, organic wool yarn.
+61 (0)4 0306 8106
http://www.ecoyarns.com.au

ECOGEN (Design Ideas)
USA
EcoGenTM homewares, Design Ideas® offers durable and affordable household products made entirely from a biodegradable, injection moulded material developed from renewable resources.
+1 800 426 6394
http://www.ecogenlife.com

ECOLUTION
USA
ECOLUTION® has been an eco-focused hemp products manufacturer since 1990 in Transylvania, Romania.
+1 (800) 973 HEMP
http://www.ecolution.com

ELSE
Turkey
ELSE are producers of bamboo and organic cotton yarns and fabrics.
+90 21 2422 6670 · http://www.else.com.tr

ENVIRO FABRICS
USA
Many Enviro products are blended with a variety of other natural, sustainable fibres such as Tencel, bamboo, hemp, soybean, modal and organic Cotton.
+1 213 622 9904
http://www.envirofabrics.net

EVEREST TEXTILE
Taiwan
Founded in 1988, Everest Textile is an R&D-oriented and vertically integrated textile manufacturer that specializes in yarn spinning, twisting, weaving, dyeing, finishing, printing, coating, laminating and special finishing.
+886 65 782 5619
http://www.everest.com.tw

GETZNER TEXTIL AG
Germany
Getzner Textil AG is a Bluesign-approved supplier of fabric and organic cotton.
+43 5552 6010
http://www.getzner.at

GREEN TEXTILES
USA
Green Textile is a US manufacturer of circular knit, warp knit and woven fabrics, specializing in custom fabric production or premium-stocked fabrics.
+1 800 204 7628
http://www.greentextile.com

GREENFIBRES
UK
Greenfibres is an organic bedding and clothing company, launched in 1996 by Gabriela and William Lana and committed to ethical textile production.
+44 (0)18 0386 8001
http://www.greenfibres.com

HEMCORE
UK
From their decortication factory based in Essex, England, Hemcore produce Hemcore Hemp Fibre, pure bast fibre from the outside of the hemp plant stem.
+44 (0)19 8683 5678
http://www.hemcore.co.uk

HEMP TRADERS
USA
Hemp Traders are the world's largest supplier of hemp products.
+1 310 637 3333
http://www.hemptraders.com

HZDL FABRICS
China
HZDL Fabrics use natural material such as cotton, wood pulp, bamboo, soja and corn to weave fabric with properties such as biodegradability, bacteria repellence and moisture absorption.
+86 571 8691 2428
http://www.hzdl.com/English/index/asp

I-COTTON
Canada and Worldwide
Continuum Textiles offer a wide range of sustainable and organic fabrics made from natural fibres, as well as full garment production in 100% organic cotton. The factories and mills that they work with share in their strong commitment to having a positive impact on the world.
http://www.continuumtextiles.com

I-MERINO
Australia
I-merino is a performance activewear fabric that has all the high performance attributes of normal merino, but has been produced using leading environmental management practices. I-merino was the first merino production chain in the world to be awarded the European Union's Ecolabel.
+61 8 9380 6248
http://www.i-merino.com

INGEO
USA
Ingeo™ fibre delivers a natural fibre with the performance of a synthetic.
+1 989 633 1746
http://www.ingeofibers.com

INVISTA
Canada
INVISTA is one of the world's largest integrated fibres and polymers businesses. The company delivers exceptional value for customers through market insight, technology innovations, and a powerful portfolio of some of the most recognized global brands and trademarks in their respective industries.
+1 770 792 4221
http://www.invista.com

LENZING FIBRES
Austria
Seventy years of fibre production expertise make Lenzing Fibres the only producer worldwide of all three man-made cellulose fibre generations, from classic viscose to lyocell and modal.
office@lenzing.com
http://www.lenzing.com

LLYNFI TEXTILE COMPANY
UK
Llynfi Textile Company designs and makes environmentally friendly textiles using their own angora yarn and organic British wool. They are certified by the Soil Association for dyeing wool with natural dyes.
+44 (0)77 4719 4710 or
+44 (0)15 4558 0758
http://www.llynfitextiles.co.uk

NATURAL COLOUR COTTON COMPANY
UK
Natural Colour Cotton is a naturally pigmented fibre that grows in shades of green, brown and beige.
+44 (0)19 0886 6536
http://www.naturalcolourcotton.com

NATUREWORKS LLC
Worldwide
NatureWorks LLC, a joint venture between Cargill and Teijin Limited of Japan, offers a family of commercially available low carbon footprint polymers derived from 100% annually renewable resources with costs and performance that compete with petroleum-based packaging materials and fibres.
+1 800 664 6436 or +1 813 5224 5731
http://www.natureworksllc.com

PERU NATURTEX PARTNERS
South America
Peru Naturtex Partners is a contract manufacturing organization, vertically integrating organic fibre production – cotton and alpaca with sustainable processing for over 125 different eco textile products, including both carded and combed yarns, fabrics and apparel in a wide variety of weights and qualities.
+51 011 511 254 7469
http://www.perunaturtex.com

ROBERT KAUFMAN
USA
Robert Kaufman Co, Inc is a converter of quilting fabrics and textiles, and a fabric supplier to the apparel and other industries. The greenSTYLE line of fabrics uses environmentally-friendly materials and fabrication methods including low-impact dyes.
+1 310 538 3482
http://www.robertkaufman.com

SCHOELLER TEXTILES
Switzerland
Schoeller Textiles guarantee the lowest possible concentration of harmful substances in their products in compliance with the bluesign® standard.
+41 81 786 0800
http://www.schoeller-textiles.com

SEGANA TEXTILES
Turkey
Segana Textiles products include flax fibre, flax blend yarns and bloch wool.
+21 2528 2077
http://www.segana.com.tr

SMART FIBRE
Germany
The Smart Fibre AG develops, produces and distributes smartcelTM and SeaCell® Lyocell fibres with different functionalities and for different segments of industry.
http://www.smartfiber.de

TEIJIN
Japan
ECO CIRCLE® is a closed-loop recycling system for used polyester products that employs an innovative chemical recycling technology in which polyester is chemically decomposed and converted into new polyester raw materials of comparable purity to those derived from petroleum.
http://www.teijin.co.jp/english/

TENFOLD ORGANIC
USA
Tenfold Organic provides 100% naturally dyed organic fabrics to consumers, manufacturers, and retailers.
+1 206 930 6713
http://www.tenfoldorganic.com

UNIFI
USA
Unifi's commitment to the sustainability and preservation of natural resources is an enduring and global effort. Their facilities participate in environmentally-responsible practices and pursue Earth-friendly solutions, resulting in sustainable products such as their eco-friendly Repreve®.
+1 336 294 4410
http://www.unifi-inc.com

ADVISORY SPD

ACCOUNTABILITY
UK/USA
AccountAbility measure the social and ethical performance of organizations through professional auditing. They advise and mentor businesses, charities and governments in the development of their approach to accountability, learning and performance.
+44 (0)20 7549 0400 or +1 207 549 0400
http://www.accountability.org

ACTION FOR SUSTAINABLE LIVING (AfSL)
UK/USA
AfSL is a charity-based organization that works with schools, businesses and community groups to engage people with a wide range of sustainable living topics including recycling, waste management, organic gardening and fair trade.
+44 (0)16 1237 3357
http://www.afsl.org.uk

ANTI-APATHY (AA)
UK
Anti-Apathy promotes and supports people who take creative and innovative approaches to social and environmental issues and has incubated a number of initiatives in recent years, including The RE:Fashion Awards and Worn Again.
http://www.antiapathy.org
info@antiapathy.org

ASSOCIATION OF SUPPLIERS TO THE BRITISH CLOTHING INDUSTRY (ASBCI)
UK
The ASBCI is a centre of technical and commercial excellence where companies at the forefront of their specific sectors can discuss, share and develop practices, processes and initiatives that will benefit their organizations and the UK's clothing supply chain.
+44 (0)14 2235 4666
http://www.asbci.co.uk

BETTER THINKING CONSULTANCY
UK
Better Thinking Consultancy adds value to businesses through sustainable thinking.
+44 (0)17 7253 0375
http://www.betterthinking.co.uk

BIOTHINKING
UK
Biothinking is an educational resource for people wishing to understand how the world, both manmade and natural, operates alongside biological principles. Biothinking results in products, processes and business models that are adaptable, sustainable and well suited to their niche.
+44 (0)18 8365 0238
http://www.biothinking.com

BUSINESS IN THE COMMUNITY
UK
Business in the Community is a charity working to inspire, engage, support and challenge companies to continually improve the impacts they have on society and the environment through the charity's responsible business programme, often referred to as Corporate Social Responsibility (CSR).
+44 (0)20 7566 8650
http://www.bitc.org.uk

BUSINESS LINK
UK
Business Link are an organization offering practical advice for businesses in a wide range of areas including start-up and finance, health and safety, environmental efficiency and trading practices.
+44 (0)84 5600 9006
http://www.businesslink.gov.uk

CARBON TRUST
UK
The Carbon Trust accelerates the move to a low-carbon economy by offering businesses advice on energy saving, renewable energy and reduction of carbon emissions.
+44 (0)80 0085 2005
http://www.CarbonTrust.co.uk

CENTRE FOR ALTERNATIVE TECHNOLOGY (CAT)
UK
The Centre for Alternative Technology (CAT) exists to promote sustainable living by teaching people how to reduce the negative environmental effects of their day-to-day actions. The organization integrates ideas and practice relating to a range of topics including land use, shelter, energy conservation, diet and health, waste management and recycling.
+44 (0)16 5470 5950
http://www.cat.org.uk

CENTRE FOR DESIGN
Australia
Centre for Design are recognized internationally for their innovative design methods and tools to support sustainable design of products and services – everything from packaging and consumer products to buildings, suburbs and cities.
+61 3 9925 2000
http://www.rmit.edu.au/cfd

CENTRE FOR SUSTAINABLE FASHION
UK
The Centre for Sustainable Fashion at London College of Fashion connects research, education and business in order to nurture innovative and sustainable approaches to fashion. Through collaboration they design transforming solutions that balance ecology, society and culture.+44 (0)20 7514 7497
http://www.sustainable-fashion.com
sustainability@fashion.arts.ac.uk

COMMUNITY RECYCLING NETWORK UK (CRN)
UK
The CRN promote and offer help and advice on community-based sustainable waste management as a practical and effective way of tackling the UK's growing waste problem.
+44 (0)20 7324 4708
http://www.crn.org.uk

COUNCIL FOR RESPONSIBLE JEWELLERY PRACTICES
UK
The Council for Responsible Jewellery Practices is an international non-profit organization representing over eighty member companies across the gold and diamond supply chain. Council members are committed to promoting responsible business practices in a transparent and accountable manner throughout the industry from mine to retail.
+44 (0)20 7836 6376
http://www.responsiblejewellery.com

CREATE
UK
CREATE is a non-profit organization working with communities and businesses through training and support programmes to advise on methods of energy efficiency and waste minimization at work.
+44 (0)12 5742 2800
http://www.create.org.uk

DEEDS (Design Education and Sustainability)
UK
DEEDS aims to demonstrate the actual and potential added-value of a sustainable design approach to design educators, students and professionals, as well as the wider design industry and policy-makers.
+44 (0)18 0388 3683
http://www.deedsproject.org and http://artsresearch.brighton.ac.uk/research/projects/deeds-1

DEMI
UK
Demi is a web-resource bringing together wide-ranging information on design for sustainability. It was developed in response to the growing realization that design activities have a major negative impact on society and the environment.
http://www.demi.org.uk
info@demi.org.uk

ECOBALANCE
France
Ecobilan, also called Ecobalance, advises industry and government on the environmental performance of products and services. Supported by a number of cutting edge environmental analysis and management software tools, Ecobilan provides services, methodologies and tools that promote the integration of environmental performance across the varying functions of an organization.+33 1 5657 5859
http://www.ecobalance.com

ECO DESIGN NETWORK
UK
Eco Design Network (EDN) is a membership-based organization supporting fashion, jewelry and gift designers and the businesses within their supply chains.
+44 (0)20 8522 5700
http://www.ecodesignnetwork.org

Eden Project
UK
The Eden Project in Cornwall is wholly owned by the Eden Trust, an educational charity. They use exhibits, events, workshops and educational programmes to remind people what nature gives to us and to help people to learn how to look after it in return.
+44 (0)17 2681 1911
http://www.edenproject.com

ENTIRELY SUSTAINABLE PRODUCT DESIGN (ESP Design)
International
ESP Design is an online resource for design professionals and students seeking practical advice and guidelines on sustainable product design.
http://www.espdesign.org
tom@espdesign.org

ENVIROWISE
UK
Envirowise provides a government-funded business advice service focused on enabling companies to increase profitability and reduce negative environmental impacts. Practical guidance is available through a free advice line, an informative website and various events and seminars throughout the year.
+44 (0)80 058 5794
http://www.envirowise.gov.uk

ENVOCARE
UK
Envocare is a small organization that aims to encourage the preservation and improvement of the environment by offering practical advice and information on a wide range of environment topics.
http://www.envocare.co.uk

ETHICAL FASHION FORUM
UK
The Ethical Fashion Forum (EFF) is the industry body dedicated to a sustainable future for fashion, representing thousands of industry members in over one hundred countries. A non-profit organization, EFF aims to facilitate sustainable industry practice and recognize businesses which excel in ethical practices.
+44 (0)20 7739 7692
http://www.ethicalfashionforum.com
info@ethicalfashionforum.com

FORUM FOR THE FUTURE (TNS Framework)
UK
The Natural Step (TNS) is an international sustainable development charity, which Forum for the Future holds the license for in the UK. Using the internationally endorsed TNS Framework, businesses, government agencies, policy-makers, individuals and communities are engaged in training and partnerships, research and development, and community involvement to lead the transition to an ecologically, socially and economically sustainable future.
+44 (0)20 7324 3630
http://www.forumforthefuture.org/projects/TNS-framework
t.chambers@forumforthefuture.org

FUTERRA SUSTAINABILITY COMMUNICATIONS
UK and USA
The Futerra group is a communications agency that offers expert advice, workshops and masterclasses in the areas of business ethics, sustainable communication and corporate responsibility.
+44 (0)20 7549 4700 or +1 646 536 3417
http://www.futerra.co.uk

GLOBAL ACTION PLAN
UK
Global Action Plan work with schools and small businesses to provide programmes of tailored advice and support over a wide range of environmental issues, from minimizing negative environmental impact through increased resource efficiency, to becoming a carbon neutral business.
+44 (0)20 7420 4444
http://www.globalactionplan.org.uk

GREEN DESIGN INSTITUTE
USA
The Green Design Institute is a major interdisciplinary education and research effort to improve environmental quality through green design. The institute works in patnership with companies, government agencies and foundations to develop pioneering design, management, manufacturing and regulatory processes that can improve both environmental and product quality while enhancing economic development.
+1 412 268 2299
http://www.ce.cmu.edu/GreenDesign

GREEN MAP
USA
Green Map aims to engage communities worldwide in creating a sustainable future. Green Map System empowers a diverse global movement mapping green living, nature, social and cultural resources in cities, villages and neighbourhoods in over fifty countries.
+1 212 674 1631
http://www.greenmap.org

GREEN PAGES
Switzerland
The Green Pages is a practical and comprehensive guide to green products, services, publications, organizations and events.
+41 44 272 3479
http://www.eco-web.com

IMPACTT
UK
Impactt is a business that helps companies to improve labour standards in their supply chains. Their work includes advising on strategy development and review, developing and delivering training courses for internal teams and suppliers, supporting the management of ethical trading programmes, production site assessments and consultancy, research and report writing and coordinating collaborative projects to tackle labour standards issues on the ground.
+44 (0)20 7242 6777
http://www.impacttlimited.com
info@impacttlimited.com

INTERTEK
Worldwide
Intertek is a leading provider of quality and safety solutions serving a wide range of industries around the world. From auditing and inspection, to testing, quality assurance and certification, Intertek are dedicated to adding value to customers' products and processes, supporting their success in the global marketplace.
+44 (0)20 7396 3400
http://www.intertek.com

ISLAMIC FOUNDATION FOR ECOLOGY AND ENVIRONMENTAL SCIENCES (IFEES)
UK
The Islamic Foundation for Ecology and Environmental Sciences (IFEES) provides teaching materials and training to raise awareness, particularly amongst the UK's Islamic communities, of the negative effects of pollution on the local and global environment.
+44 (0)12 1440 3500
http://www.ifees.org.uk

KATE FLETCHER CONSULTANCY
UK
KateFletcher.com is a sustainable fashion and textiles filter which emphasises diversity, creativity and ecological awareness.
http://www.katefletcher.com
kate@katefletcher.com

LIFEWORTH
UK & Switzerland
Lifeworth is a boutique professional services firm committed to helping people contribute to and benefit from systemic social change. Their current advisory work focuses on the luxury industry, sustainable investing, and cross-sectoral partnering and networks.
+44 (0)20 812 3894 or +41 (0)22 548 1911
http://www.lifeworth.com

LONDON SUSTAINABILITY EXCHANGE (LSX)
UK
The London Sustainability Exchange (LSX) run a number of work programmes and events to motivate and teach both individuals and businesses across London how to take steps in reducing their environmental impacts.
+44 (0)20 7234 9400
http://www.lsx.org.uk

NATIONAL INDUSTRIAL SYMBIOSIS PROGRAMME (NISP)
UK
NISP works to generate sustainable resource management solutions with businesses of all sizes and from all sectors. The organization aims to be at the forefront of industrial and ecological thinking and practice worldwide and hold talks and workshops.
+44 (0)84 5094 9501
http://www.nisp.org.uk

NATURAL LOGIC
USA
Natural Logic delivers strategic sustainability consulting to companies and communities with integrated, results-focused programmes that build profit and competitive advantage while reducing an organization's environmental footprint, waste and risk.
+1 510 248 4940
http://www.natlogic.com

1% PERCENT FOR THE PLANET
USA
Since 2002, 1% For The Planet has inspired members of the business community to contribute 1% of sales to environmental groups around the world. In return, this growing alliance of companies is given the opportunity not only to see their self-worth rise, but their net worth climb as well.
+1 802 496 5408
http://www.onepercentfortheplanet.org/en/

PRÉ CONSULTANTS
Netherlands
PRé Consultants support companies and governments in developing and managing sustainable products and services. In cooperation with their global partner network they offer a wide range of products and services.
+31 33 450 4010
http://www.pre.nl

[RE]DESIGN
UK
[re]design is a social enterprise that propagates sustainable actions through design. They seek out and promote products and projects that are friendly to people, planet and partner with a wide range of organizations to pioneer sustainable innovation.
+44 (0)20 8406 4160
http://www.redesigndesign.org

RESOURCE RENEWAL INSTITUTE
USA
Since 1985, Resource Renewal Institute has facilitated the creation, development and implementation of practical strategies to solve environmental problems in a comprehensive framework.
+1 415 928 3774
http://www.rri.org

SCAMPER
UK
Using a combination of research, analysis and creativity, Scamper provides world-class brand development services to ethically responsible organizations.
+44 (0)84 5862 4442
http://www.scamperbranding.com

SD3
UK & Korea
Sd3 are a consultancy group that run training courses, help businesses to improve performance and create value through adopting sustainability practices that integrate economic, environmental and social management.
+44 (0)20 7937 7228 or +82 (0) 2732 2638
http://www.sd3-global.com

THE SLOW DESIGN GROUP
UK
SLOW is a cultural space to stimulate debate around the concept of 'slow design'. It is an ongoing dialogue; an open-ended project.
+44 (0)18 0388 3683
http://www.slowdesign.org

SPROUT DESIGN
UK
Sprout Design is an industrial design consultancy that aims to integrate the disciplines of sustainable and inclusive design into mainstream design practice.
+44 (0)20 7645 3790
http://www.sproutdesign.co.uk

SUSTAINABILITY
UK, USA and Switzerland
SustainAbility is a values-driven consultancy and think-tank, advising clients on the risks and opportunities associated with corporate responsibility and sustainable development, as well as helping them to develop greener business strategies.
+44 (0)20 7269 6900 (UK); +1 202 315 4150 (USA) or +41 (0) 44 265 1228 (Switzerland)
http://www.sustainability.com

SUSTAINABLE DESIGN NETWORK, LOUGHBOROUGH UNIVERSITY
UK
The aim of the Sustainable Design Network is to establish multi-disciplinary research network for industries and universities, which will focus on the issues of sustainable design (particularly the methods, tools and techniques to aid its implementation).
+44 (0)15 0926 3171
http://www.sustainabledesignnet.org.uk

TED, CHELSEA COLLEGE OF ART & DESIGN, UNIVERSITY OF THE ARTS LONDON
UK
The Textiles Environment Design (TED) project at Chelsea was established in 1996 and comprises of a unique collective of practicing designers/educators. TED has always sought to consider what role the textile designer can play in the field of eco-design.
+44 (0)20 7514 7811
http://www.tedresearch.net

WBCSD (World Business Council for Sustainable Development)
Switzerland and USA
WBCSD is a CEO-led global association of some 200 companies dealing exclusively with business and sustainable development.
+41 22 839 3100
http://www.wbcsd.org

NEWS, INFO AND EVENTS

BIOFACH
Germany
BioFach is the world's largest trade fair for organic food and agriculture. It is held every February, in Nuremberg, Germany. It brings together nearly 3,000 exhibitors and approximately 50,000 trade visitors from around 130 countries.
+49 (0)911 8606 4909
http://www.biofach.de/en/

ECOCENTRIC
UK
EcoCentric offers a selection of sustainably designed products for work and living spaces.
+44 (0)80 0019 7855
http://www.ecocentric.co.uk
info@ecocentric.co.uk

ECOTEXTILE NEWS
UK
Ecotextile News is a business-to-business magazine dedicated to the production of sustainable and ethical textiles and apparel.
+44 (0)19 7770 8488
http://www.ecotextile.com

ECOUTERRE
USA
Ecouterre is a website dedicated to the future of sustainable fashion design, showcasing and supporting designers who consider a garment's social and environmental impact, from the cultivation of its fibres to its use and disposal.
http://www.ecouterre.com
info@ecouterre.com

FUTURE LABORATORY
UK
Established in 2001, the Future Laboratory is recognized internationally for its innovative approach to trend forecasting, consumer insight and brand strategy.
+44 (0)20 7791 2020
http://www.thefuturelaboratory.com

IFAT ENTSORGA
Germany
Following its amalgamation with ENTSORGA, IFAT has celebrated a successful premiere and established itself firmly as the world's leading trade fair for environmental technology.
+49 89 9491 1358
http://www.ifat.de/en/Home

INHABITAT
USA
Inhabitat.com is a web blog devoted to the future of design, tracking the innovations in technology, practices and materials that are pushing architecture and home design towards a smarter and more sustainable future.
http://www.inhabitat.com
info@inhabitat.com

JUST-STYLE.COM
UK
Founded in 1999, just-style.com is an online resource for the apparel and textile industries, delivering independent, authoritative and timely business information.
+44 (0)15 2757 3600
http://www.just-style.com

NUTEC
Germany
NUTEC combines an international trend-setting congress and a trade exhibition for the use of materials, products, and services for companies that produce products using the Cradle-to-Cradle approach.
+49 69 7575 5430
http://www.nutec.de
katrin.ordnung@messefrankfurt.com

SOCIAL ALTERATIONS
USA
Social Alterations is a resource-based website that aims to bridge the gap between theory and practice within existing perceptions of socially responsible fashion design education.
http://www.socialalterations.com
maryhanlon@socialalterations.com

TREEHUGGER
USA
TreeHugger is a social media outlet dedicated to driving sustainability mainstream by providing green news, solutions, and product information.
http://www.treehugger.com
marketing@treehugger.com

SUBLIME
UK
Sublime is a bi-monthly international lifestyle magazine promoting ethical values.
+44 (0)20 8374 7695
http://www.sublimemagazine.com

THE ENDS REPORT
UK
The ENDS Report is a leading source of environmental intelligence for professionals, delivering news, analysis and reference across the carbon, environmental and sustainability agenda.
+44 (0)20 8267 8100
http://www.endsreport.com

TRACEABILITY AND TRACKING

HISTORIC FUTURES
UK
Historic Futures provides experts in supply-chain traceability, enabling brands and retailers to visualize their entire supply-chain, from finished product to primary production, and to communicate good practice to their customers.
+44 (0)19 9388 6420
http://www.historicfutures.com
info@historicfutures.com

MADE-BY
UK
MADE-BY is an independent consumer label for fashion companies that are transparent about the social, economic and ecological conditions throughout the whole supply chain of their collections and constantly seek improvement in these areas. The mission of MADE-BY is to make sustainable fashion common practice.
+44 (0)20 7636 3910
http://www.made-by.org
infouk@made-by.org

SEDEX
UK
The Supplier Ethical Data Exchange (SEDEX), is a membership organization for businesses committed to continuous improvement of the ethical performance of their supply chains.
+44 (0)20 7022 1955
http://www.sedexglobal.com
helpdesk@sedex.org.uk

FOOTPRINTING

BEST FOOT FORWARD
UK
Best Foot Forward offers footprint assessments. They help organizations to measure, manage, communicate and reduce their environmental impact.
+44 (0)18 6525 0818
http://www.bestfootforward.com
mail@bestfootforward.com

CARBON TRUST
UK
Carbon Trust provide specialist support to business and the public sector to help cut carbon emissions, save energy and commercialize low carbon technologies.
+44 (0)80 0085 2005
http://www.carbontrust.co.uk
customercentre@carbontrust.co.uk

CLIMATE CARE
UK
Climate Care offer carbon offset credits. They help lower business emissions and individual carbon footprints through credible, verified carbon reduction projects.
+44 (0)18 6520 7000
http://www.jpmorganclimatecare.com
jpmcc.mail@jpmorganclimatecare.com

GLOBAL FOOTPRINT NETWORK (USA)
USA
Global Footprint Network is an international think-tank working to advance sustainability through use of the Ecological Footprint, a resource accounting tool.
+1 510 839 8879
http://www.footprintnetwork.org
info@footprintnetwork.org.

WATER FOOTPRINT NETWORK
Netherlands
The mission of the Water Footprint Network is to promote the transition towards sustainable, fair and efficient use of fresh-water resources worldwide by advancing the concept of the 'water footprint'.
+31 53 489 4320
http://www.waterfootprint.org
derk.kuiper@waterfootprint.org

ZERO FOOTPRINT
Canada
Zerofootprint Software develops software-based enterprise carbon management solutions for corporations and multinational organizations. Clients use software developed by Zerofootprint to measure and manage carbon across their balance sheet and supply chain.
+1 416 365 7557
http://www.zerofootprint.net
info@zerofootprint.net

Select contributor biographies

SUSAN ASHDOWN

Ashdown is the Helen G. Canoyer professor in the Department of Fiber Science and Apparel Design at Cornell University, where she has taught and conducted research since 1991. Her research is on interactions between apparel design and technology, and changes in design, production and distribution, with a focus on apparel sizing and fit.

EDWARD BARBER

A photographer specializing in portraiture, Barber has an enduring interest in uniforms, work and individuality. His subject matter is often hidden, overlooked, personal or difficult to access. He has exhibited at the National Portrait Gallery, Flowers East, the Royal Hibernian Academy, the Horse Hospital, the Photographers' Gallery, the Museum of London and Tate Britain. He is director of programmes for fashion photography in the School of Media and Communication, London College of Fashion.

MIKE BARRY

Head of sustainable business at Marks & Spencer, Barry has led the retailer's high-profile Plan A since its inception in 2007 and oversees 180 environmental and ethical commitments, ranging from cutting carbon and waste to reducing natural resource use and supporting communities, with the aim of making the company the world's most sustainable major retailer by 2015.

DJURDJA BARTLETT

Bartlett is a senior research fellow at London College of Fashion, University of the Arts London. She has contributed to many journals in the field of fashion and the media and is the author of *FashionEast: the Spectre That Haunted Socialism* (2010).

SIMON BENNETT

Visiting researcher at the Centre for Energy Policy and Technology at Imperial College London, Bennett's research interests are in the area of sustainable energy technologies, including CCS and alternative chemical feedstocks. He is currently working in the following subject areas: transitions to more sustainable technologies, industrial dynamics, energy policy, renewable raw materials, biorefineries, CO2 capture and storage, and socio-technical and co-evolutionary approaches to technological change.

SANDY BLACK

Professor of fashion and textile design and technology at London College of Fashion, Black is a designer, author and researcher with extensive experience in both the fashion industry and academia. After studying mathematics at university, she created the Sandy Black fashion knitwear designer label, selling in prestigious fashion stores internationally. She began lecturing at University of Brighton in 1985 and moved to London College of Fashion in 1997 to set up its MA fashion studies programme. She now focuses on interdisciplinary design-led research in the context of sustainability. She developed the Interrogating Fashion research network in 2005 (a Designing for the 21st Century EPSRC/AHRC funded project), and leads the Considerate Design project, which aims to assist designers in developing

sustainable fashion products. She is founder and co-editor of the journal *Fashion Practice: Design, creative process and the fashion industry*. Her publications include *Eco Chic: The fashion paradox* (2008), *Knitwear in Fashion* (2002), and *Knitting: Fashion, industry, craft* (2012).

CLARE BRASS

Brass moved to London in 2004 to become campaign leader for manufacturing at the Design Council, developing a business support system at the core of the Designing Demand programme to help small and medium enterprises use design more profitably. She became leader of sustainability in 2006, before leaving the Design Council in 2007 to set up SEED (Social Environmental Enterprise and Design), which explores new avenues of cross-collaborative entrepreneurship for designers.

OTTO VON BUSCH

Von Busch is a haute couture heretic, DIY-demagogue, designer and researcher in socially engaged fashion design at Parsons the New School for Design. More of his work can be found at www.selfpassage.org.

BURAK CAKMAK

Cakmak is sustainability professional with over thirteen years business experience. Most recently, he worked as the director of corporate sustainability for the Gucci Group, where he was responsible for the implementation of a sustainability framework with a mission to help the Group and its brands develop tailored initiatives and stay committed to business ethics, human rights and environmental stewardship. He previously worked in the social responsibility department of Gap Inc. in San Francisco and London, where he developed CSR management experience related to sustainable design, environmental and community initiatives.

NICOLAS CAMBRIDGE

Cambridge trained as a designer in London before relocating to Japan in order to study the martial art of *kendo*. He worked in a number of positions in the Japanese fashion industry, and was awarded his PhD by London College of Fashion, University of the Arts London in 2009.

SIMONETTA CARBONARO

Carbonaro is an expert in consumer psychology, strategic marketing and design management. She carries out research in the area of consumer ethos and behaviour. Since 2002 she has been a professor in design management and humanistic marketing at the Swedish School of Textiles, University of Borås, where she directs the Design of Prosperity, an action-oriented cross-disciplinary centre focused on socio-cultural forces influencing consumer behaviour, driving societal changes and fostering new lifestyles. She sits on the research committee of the postgraduate design school Domus Academy in Milan, and is a member of the advisory board of the Swiss Gottlieb Duttweiler Institute for marketing and social sciences. For the last fifteen years, Carbonaro has been working as senior strategic advisor for major retail companies. She is a partner at REALISE, a business consulting firm based in Germany, where she is actively involved in values branding, strategic design and innovation management.

MARTIN CHARTER

Charter is the director of the Centre for Sustainable Design at University of the Creative Arts in Farnham, Surrey, and organizer of the 'Sustainable Innovation' international conference series, now its seventeenth year. He was formerly launch director of Greenleaf Publishing, marketing director at the Earth Centre and founding editor of the publications *Journal of Sustainable Product Design*, *The Green Management Letter* and *Greener Management International (GMI)*. He is presently a member of the editorial boards of *GMI*, *International Journals of Sustainable Engineering* and *Sustainable Design*, and sits on the expert boards of the EC Eco-Innovation Observatory and the World Resources Forum. He is also convenor of the international standard for eco-design management systems ISO 14006 and previously advised on the eco-design standard ISO TR 14062.

PAMELA CHURCH GIBSON

Reader in cultural and historical studies at London College of Fashion, Church Gibson has written extensively on the subjects of film, fashion, fandom, history and heritage. Her publications include two edited anthologies, *The Oxford Guide to Film Studies* (1998) and *More Dirty Looks: Gender, Power, Pornography* (2004), and *her recent monograph Fashion and Celebrity Culture* (2011). Her next project will examine media targeted at young adult women, the schisms this has generated within contemporary feminism and the extraordinarily lucrative nature of the franchise films aimed at this particular demographic.

JUDITH CONDOR-VIDAL

Condor-Vidal originates from Bolivia and is currently based in Oxford. Her educational and professional background is in economics. She is an associate of the World Fair Trade Organization, and in 2004 founded the NGO Trading for Development. She is also a founder member of the Ethical Fashion Forum, an association that develops educational initiatives around social justice in the fashion supply chain.

FRANCES CORNER

Professor Frances Corner, OBE, has been head of college at London College of Fashion since 2006. She has over twenty years experience within the higher education sector on both a national and international level and advises stakeholders on the future of the fashion industry and the role that higher education can play in the development and support of the creative industries. She has championed the use of fashion as an agent for innovation and change, especially in the areas of sustainability, health and wellbeing. This emphasis has seen the creation of the Centre for Sustainable Fashion at London College of Fashion. Professor Corner was a London Leader for Sustainability and regularly speaks on this subject both nationally and internationally. She has also been the Chair of CHEAD (Council for Higher Education in Art and Design) and currently sits on the British Fashion Council Advisory Committee and is an executive committee member for IFFTI (International Foundation of Fashion Technology Institutes).

REBECCA EARLEY

Earley is a reader in Textiles Environment Design (TED) at Chelsea College of Art, and director of the University of the Arts London's Textile Futures Research Centre (TFRC). She is a textile designer and academic whose research work and creative practice seeks to develop strategies for designers in reducing the environmental impact of textile production, consumption and disposal. She is currently working with the Mistra Future Fashion project funded by the Swedish government.

CLAUDIA ECKERT

Eckert is senior lecturer at the department of design, development, environment and materials of the Open University. She is interested in understanding different design domains and the different phases of the design process, and in developing techniques and computer tools for facilitating design activities. Most of her research is based on empirical studies in industry, but she is also interested in bringing theories and methods from different disciplines into design research. Eckert is currently working to apply insights from philosophy and sociology of science to design process modelling and from complexity theory to change prediction.

EILUNED EDWARDS

Edwards is currently a senior lecturer in design and visual culture at Nottingham Trent University and a visiting lecturer for the Victoria & Albert museum and the Royal College of Arts. She trained as a textile designer and completed her master's degree at Manchester Metropolitan University, before working as a designer and lecturing in textiles and design history. Her interest in craft and handmade textiles led to a number of research trips to Central and South America and Cuba. Since 1991, the focus of her research has been South Asia, in particular the crafts, textiles and dress of India. A Leverhulme fellowship in 1993 enabled her to spend over two years living in Gujarat, western India, during which time she started working within the Khatri Mohammad Siddik and his family in the village of Dhamadka, and other craftspeople in Kachchh district, which eventually formed the basis of her PhD, awarded by the University of Manchester in 2000. Her book *The Textiles and Dress of Gujarat* was published in 2011. She currently holds a two-year Leverhulme Research Fellowship and is writing a book on Indian block-printed textiles.

GAVIN FERNANDES

Fernandes was born in Kenya and educated at Middlesex University, Royal College of Art, London College of Communication and London College of Fashion. He is an art director, photographer, fashion stylist, curator and university lecturer, whose work encompasses themes such as cultural identity, religion, feminine empowerment and gender. Fernandes has exhibited in London at the Victoria & Albert Museum, the Photographers' Gallery, the Whitechapel Gallery, the Institute of Contemporary Arts and the Museum of London, and in galleries in France. He has contributed to many publications including *i-D*, *Dazed & Confused*, *Tank*, *The Observer*, *The Guardian* and *British Asian Style* (2010).

SIMON FERRIGNO

Ferrigno has been working on cotton and sustainability since 2000, with a focus on alternatives such as organic cotton and integrated pest management. He has also conducted research on related issues such as the impacts of pesticide and insecticide use on human health and the environment in Africa. Ferrigno is currently a freelance researcher and writer advising both public and private clients on sustainable cotton, assisting them in developing supply chain partnerships, educating staff and supply chain partners as well as donors and investors. He writes regularly for Ecotextiles News and is the author of *An Insider's Guide to Cotton and Sustainability*, published by MCL Global in 2012.

MIKE FLANAGAN

Flanagan is the CEO of Clothesource Ltd, the world's largest collection of information on clothing price comparisons, supplier capabilities and national resources, which provides both buyers and sellers with advice and training on improving sourcing and selling skills. He began his career in the advertising industry in the UK and Italy, and later moved into retail. Before setting up Clothesource, he held a number of senior international buying, marketing and operations posts in the retail divisions of groups such as Associated British Foods, British Petroleum and US Shoe.

KATE FLETCHER

Fletcher, one of the originators of the 'slow fashion' movement, views her work as simultaneously rooted in natural principles and engaged with the cultural and creative forces of fashion and design. Fletcher has established a number of directional sustainability projects, including Local Wisdom, involving hundreds of people worldwide. She is also the founder of the design for sustainability consultancy Slow Fashion, and the author of over fifty scholarly and popular publications in the field, including *Sustainable Fashion and Textiles: Design journeys* (2008) and *Fashion and Sustainability: Design for change* (2012, co-authored with Lynda Grose). Fletcher is currently reader in sustainable fashion at the Centre for Sustainable Fashion, London College of Fashion. Over the last fifteen years she has brought design principles to the fields of fashion, textiles and sustainability, with a progressive outlook that has come to define the discipline.

SHELLEY FOX

London-based designer Fox trained both in textiles and in fashion design, which has inspired her distinctive forms and textile treatments, such as blow-torching sequinned fabric, or singeing textiles. She created a series of experimental collections throughout the 1990s together with fashion-led installations that were widely exhibited. She is a senior research fellow at Central Saint Martins College in London and became the inaugural Donna Karan professor of fashion at Parsons The New School of Design in 2010.

JULIA GAIMSTER

Gaimster became associate dean (academic) in the Graduate School at London College of Fashion University of the Arts London in 2012. She has a doctorate in education studies and is the former head of e-learning at LCF. She coordinated the Textiles Online Resource Guide at UAL, and is the author of *Visual Research Methods in Fashion* (2011). She has contributed as an international expert in information technology and CAD to UNIDO-sponsored projects in Bangladesh and Syria.

LEE HOLDSTOCK

Since joining the Soil Association in 1999, Holdstock has been heavily involved in the development of textile standards and certification systems. He represented the Soil Association at the 2002 Intercot conference where the Global Organic Textile Standards were initially conceived and has been closely involved in their development ever since. Holdstock is currently part of the Soil Association's Trade Support function, which works to support, advise and encourage UK organic food and textiles businesses, and is a member of the RITE Group Steering committee.

TIM JACKSON

Jackson is professor of sustainable development at the University of Surrey and director of the ESRC Research Group on Lifestyles, Values and Environment (RESOLVE). He also directs the recently funded DEFRA/ESRC Sustainable Lifestyles Research Group. For over twenty years he has been at the forefront of research and teaching in sustainability, working closely with the New Economics Foundation and others on measures of sustainable wellbeing at the national and regional level. He has served in an advisory capacity for numerous government departments. In 2004 he was appointed economics commissioner on the Sustainable Development Commission, leading the Redefining Prosperity programme and authoring its controversial report, which was later published as *Prosperity Without Growth* (2010).

CHRISTIAN JARDINE

Jardine is a senior researcher at the University of Oxford and a member of its Environmental Change Institute. He is a research analyst in the Lower Carbon Futures team and studies technologies for greenhouse gas emission reductions, with a focus on renewables, especially the use of solar photovoltaics within the household and on commercial buildings.

PHYLLIDA JAY

Jay is an anthropologist conducting research for a PhD on the material culture of sustainable fashion and design within India and the UK. Her research explores concepts of craft, sustainable business models and the aesthetics and practices of design in fashion. She also works as a journalist, focusing on business and luxury.

SUE JENKYN JONES

A fashion designer and writer, interested in the connections between mechanics, electronics and the tactile arts, Jones has owned and managed fashion businesses and sold her designs internationally to prestige stores and celebrity clients. Recently she has worked as a key research consultant for two major EU Information Society Technology projects for advancing the representation of fabrics and fashion online and improving e-commerce website interfaces. As a university lecturer she has pioneered the development of digital fashion and CAD/CAM technologies in the curriculum at Central Saint Martins and London College of Fashion, where she was the course director of the digital fashion MA programme. Ongoing interests include immersive and animated environments, games, mobile and shopping technologies, and the development of high-tech materials for wearable computing, sportswear and dance. Her publications include *Fashion Design*, 3rd edition (2011), and *Digital Fashion* (forthcoming).

RICHARD JONES

Jones is an experimental physicist, professor of physics and the pro-vice chancellor for research and innovation at the University of Sheffield. His research interests include experimental studies of macromolecules at interfaces, soft and polymer nanotechnology and the social and ethical implications of nanotechnology. Between 2007 and 2009 he was the senior strategic advisor for nanotechnology for the UK's Engineering and Physical Sciences Research Council.

VERONIKA KAPSALI

Kapsali is an expert in the field of clothing comfort and biomimetic textiles and the co-founder and research and design director of MMT Textiles Limited. She studied fashion and textile design at London College of Fashion before working as a freelance designer, consultant and lecturer while conducting research into biomimetics and smart materials. In 2009 she was awarded a PhD in mechanical engineering from Bath University's Centre for Biomimetic and Natural Technology and has since set up several research projects exploring the application of biological principles and mechanisms in the textile sector.

ISMAIL KHATRI

Khatri belongs to a hereditary caste of dyers and block-printers from the village of Dhamadka in east Kachchh. Like his father, Mohammad Siddik, he has specialized in working with natural dyes and has been instrumental in reviving their use in India. His family is famous for making resist- and mordant-dyed textiles that are printed with hand-carved wooden blocks; their signature cloth is known as *ajrakh*, a cotton textile dyed with indigo and madder. Khatri and his brothers, Razzak and Jabbar, have translated *ajrakh* and other block-print designs into contemporary fabrics for fashion and furnishings, printed on cotton, silk and wool. His work is sold worldwide and examples of *ajrakh* are held in the collections at the Ashmolean Museum, Oxford and the Victoria & Albert Museum, London. Khatri has received numerous awards for his work, including a National Merit Award from the government of India and a Hon. D.Art from De Montfort University, Leicester, in 2003.

SAM MAHER

Maher has worked for UK-based campaign group Labour Behind the Label (LBL) since 2002. LBL coordinates the UK platform of the Europe-wide Clean Clothes Campaign, which supports the efforts of garment workers worldwide to improve their working conditions. He works closely with trade unions and workers rights organizations, is responsible for the development of the policy and demands for LBL campaigns and provides policy input to other non-corporate initiatives. He is the author of two reports on conditions in the industry: *False Promises* (2009) and *Taking Liberties* (2010).

NICK MORLEY

Morley is a director of Oakdene Hollins Ltd, a sustainable technology and waste consultancy based in Aylesbury, UK. His personal research interests include a number of specific new sustainable technologies, including remanufacturing, which the company hopes to develop to commercialization. He is increasingly interested in consumption issues, including the aesthetics of sustainable development.

JOHN MOWBRAY

Founder and editor of *Ecotextile News*, Mowbray is an environmental biologist and textile journalist who also founded the not-for-profit RITE Group, which is dedicated to reducing the impact of textiles on the environment.

EMMA NEUBERG

Neuberg is the founder of the Slow Textiles Group, a non-profit organization that promotes ethical and sustainable practices in the fashion industry. She is a key member of the textiles environment design group at the Chelsea College of Art and Design where she pursues her research in textiles practice, discourses on slow textiles and consumerism. She is also lecturer in fashion and textiles critical theory at the Chelsea College of Art.

LUCY NORRIS

Norris is an anthropologist with a PhD from University College London and an expert on textiles in India, with particular reference to recycling practices. Her knowledge of the Indian subcontinent and its textile and craft practices has been gained by extensive research in the field, including a research fellowship with the EPSRC Waste of the World project. She has published numerous papers and a book entitled *Recycling Indian Clothing: Global contexts of reuse and value* (2010).

MARIE O'MAHONY

O'Mahony is professor of advanced textiles for fashion design at Ontario College of Art and Design University and visiting professor at University of the Arts, London. From 2009 to 2011 she served on the Australian government's Textile, Clothing and Footwear Innovation Council. She was previously based in London and worked worldwide for fifteen years as a textile and technology consultant. Her books include *TechnoTextiles 2*, *Cyborg: The Man Machine* and *Sportstech*.

LUCY ORTA

Orta studied fashion-knitwear design at Nottingham Trent University and began practising as a visual artist in Paris, where she and her husband, Argentian artist Jorge Orta founded Studio Orta in 1991. Her artwork investigates the boundaries between the body and architecture, using sculpture, public intervention, video, and photography. Lucy + Jorge Orta's collaborative practice focuses on a number of sustainability issues, employing a wide range of media and in workshops, ephemeral interventions and performances. Orta is professor of art, fashion and the environment at London College of Fashion, University of the Arts London. From 2002 to 2005 she was the head of Man and Humanity, a pioneering masters' programme at the Design Academy Eindhoven.

LIZ PARKER

Between 2006 and 2010 Parker was joint project coordinator of Fashioning an Ethical Industry, a project of Labour Behind the Label, which supports the integration of workers' rights issues into fashion education. A commitment to social and environmental justice underpins her work as a freelance researcher, consultant, facilitator and educator. Her work focuses on corporate practices, supply chains, labour and environmental standards and international trade policy in the garment and agriculture sectors.

PHIL PATTERSON

Managing director of Colour Connections, Patterson has wide-ranging expertise in the textile industry from a career that has spanned research, manufacturing and retail; fibres, fabrics and garments; legislation, environmental compliance, standardization and innovation, and is recognized as an expert solutions provider to those trying to meet the most demanding technical and compliance standards. Patterson was a founder member of the multi-brand Afirm group, is chairman of the newly formed RITE group, which aims to reduce the impact of textiles on the environment, and sits on the Soil Association Textile Committee and the British Retail Consortium REACH implementation committee.

FRANK PILLER

Piller is a leading expert on mass customization, personalization and open innovation. A scientific adviser, frequent corporate speaker and keynote presenter at conferences, he holds the chair of management at the Technology and Innovation Management Group of RWTH Aachen University, Germany, and is a founding faculty member of the MIT Smart Customization Group at the Massachusetts Institute of Technology. He is also chair of the World Congress on Mass Customization and Personalization (MCPC) and founding director of the International Institute of Mass Customization and Personalization. He has published numerous books on mass customization, edited over 50 other books and numerous journal papers and is also founder of *The International Journal on Mass Customization*.

AGNÈS ROCAMORA

Senior research fellow and senior lecturer in cultural and historical studies at London College of Fashion, Rocamora has contributed to many journals and books in the fields of fashion and the media and is the author of *Fashioning the City: Paris, fashion and the media* (2009).

TONY RYAN

Ryan is a polymer chemist and pro vice chancellor at the Faculty of Science at Sheffield University. He was awarded an OBE in 2005 for services to science. As a media fellow for public understanding of science, he is a regular broadcaster on science subjects and since 2007 has collaborated with artist and designer Helen Storey at London College of Fashion on a number of hybrid science–art projects addressing environmental issues, such as clean water for Africa, through new patented processes and open source applications.

DAMIEN SANFILIPPO

Sanfilippo is product manager for cotton at the Fairtrade Labelling Organization (FLO). Until 2010 he was the international project officer responsible for PAN UK's Cotton Project, where his work involved facilitating and coordinating with PAN's African partners on ongoing organic cotton and cotton and health projects, and developing a programme of work to raise public and business awareness of cotton and organic cotton issues in the UK.

DAVID SHAH

Shah founded the international fashion media group View Publications in 1988. He is one of the world's leading experts on colour and textiles, as well as a designer, consultant, publisher and serial entrepreneur.

LUCY SIEGLE

Siegle is the author of *Green Living in the Urban Jungle* and a journalist specializing in ecological and ethical lifestyle matters. As well as writing her weekly Observer column, she is an environmental columnist for Marie Claire and a regular contributor to Grazia, The Guardian, New Statesman, Elle and New Consumer magazine, and a frequent commentator on television and radio, regularly appearing on BBC One's The One Show. Her most recent book is *To Die For: Is Fashion Wearing Out the World?*

HELEN STOREY

Storey is a designer and artist whose work spans the arts, sciences and new technology fields. She is currently professor of fashion and science at the Centre for Sustainable Fashion, London College of Fashion. After graduating in fashion from Kingston Polytechnic in 1981, she worked for designers in Rome and London before running her own awarding-winning label from 1983 to 1995. She has since worked on a number of cross-disciplinary projects, including Primitive Streak, on which she collaborated with her sister Kate, a developmental biologist at the University of Oxford. She was awarded an MBE for services to fashion in 2009.

MATHILDA THAM

Tham's work encompasses fashion design, futures studies and sustainability. She is a visiting professor of fashion at Beckmans College of Design, Stockholm, and a lecturer in design and sustainability at Goldsmiths, University of London. She is a member of the board of Mistra (The Foundation for Strategic Environmental Research, Sweden) and an associate of the Sustainable Fashion Academy, which provides education for the Scandinavian fashion industry.

PETER WAEBER

CEO of Bluesign Technologies AG, Waeber is a chemist and textile engineer who has also studied economics. He began his career as a researcher in the chemical industry and has been CEO of a printing mill in Switzerland and technical director and member of the board at Schoeller Textil AG, Switzerland. He had also served as president of SVTC (the Swiss Association of Textile and Chemistry) and as a member and council delegate of IFATCC (International Federation of Associations of Textile Chemists and Colourists). He holds several patents in nanotechnology for textiles.

GARTH WARD

Ward set up Aestiva Ltd, a consultancy company, to promote cradle-to-cradle precepts for clothing and fashion. He contributes to DEFRA's Clothing Road Map, is a member of the Resource Recovery Forum (RRF), attends meetings of the Associate Parliamentary Sustainable Resource Group (APSRG) and is a member of the Chartered Institute of Waste Management (CIWM). He also organizes and guides the Salvation Army's European Network on Recycling (ENoR).

ALAN WHEELER

Wheeler has been senior manager of the Textile Recycling Association and currently sits on the steering group of WRAP's Sustainable Clothing Roadmap. After dabbling in retail banking he completed a master's degree in environmental issues and management at King's College London and subsequently took on management roles for two community-based recycling organizations in the West Midlands, followed by a post in waste management for a local authority in Kent. He represents the TRA on the Textiles Division of the Bureau of International Recycling and has sat on many important government-led and industry-run stakeholder groups. He regularly appears in the media as a representative of the UK's used clothing and textile reclamation industry.

AMELIA WILLIAMS

Williams is a fashion and lifestyle journalist who has written for a range of publications online and in print. She studied culture, media and communication at the University of Surrey and fashion and lifestyle journalism at the London College of Fashion. Williams has worked in PR and on consumer magazines. She is currently an e-commerce content writer and editor and contributes to noted eco fashion websites.

DILYS WILLIAMS

Williams is a designer and innovator, and director for sustainable fashion at London College of Fashion, where she developed an MA degree in Fashion and the Environment. She established the Centre for Sustainable Fashion, a University of the Arts research centre, industry network and catalyst for change, promoting sustainability and innovation across the entire supply chain of the fashion sector. Previously she worked with Katharine Hamnett on collections using organically produced materials and promoting awareness of issues surrounding ethical and environmental design and production methods.

TIM WILSON

Wilson co-founded Historic Futures with partner Simon Warrick in 2003. Wilson, with ten years experience in the software industry, had previously written software especially for farmers, and was motivated to work on traceability after the 'mad cow' disease BSE devastated the British beef industry. The result was the Supply Chain Traceability and Transparency Service (String), designed to assist companies to track and trace their products through all levels of the supply chain.

DAVID WOLFE

Wolfe is one of the fashion industry's most quoted authorities, known for his work as a fashion, color and trend forecaster. He spent ten years at The Fashion Service, a trend-forecasting service he founded and managed, and was formerly creative director with I.M. International, one of the world's first fashion forecasting and consulting firms.

NILGIN YUSUF

Yusuf is director of programmes in media at the School of Graduate Studies, London College of Fashion, where she teaches journalism to postgraduate students. Former fashion editor of the *Sunday Times* and fashion writer at *Elle* and the *Daily Telegraph*, she recently completed an MA in Fashion History and Culture and is currently working on a book that explores the styles and sub-cultures of the criminal world.

Picture credits

Key: a=above; b=below; c=centre; l=left; r=right; t=top

CHAPTER 1

2, 3 Photography Matjaz Tancic 7 Styling and photography Gavin Fernandes; accessories by Shared Talent students from the London College of Fashion, LISOF and Boitumelo Project, Johannesburg 12, 13 Styling and Photography Gavin Fernandes; make-up and hair Jun Sato, Yvonne Sou, Satsuki Yamashita and Kenny Leung; model Jon Hosking; used clothing by TRAID 16 Screenshot from Lookbook.nu, courtesy Otto von Busch 17 tl Photo Leopard Z (Zhang Jing) 17 tr Photo Andy T (Andre Torres Rodriguez) 18, 19 Images courtesy Otto von Busch 21 Photography Fred Duval, FilmMagic/Getty Images 22 Photography Chris Jackson, Getty Images 23 Photography Mel Bouzad, FilmMagic/Getty Images 24, 25, 26, 27, 28, 29, 30, 31 Images by Emma Neuberg 32 Photo Mary McCartney, courtesy Stella McCartney Ltd. 33 Photo Jody Rogac for *Nylon* Dec/Jan 2010/11, pp. 106–13 34 Photo Kevin Ito, courtesy Edun 35 t Photo Annie Leibovitz, courtesy Louis Vuitton UK 35 b Photo Kevin Ito, courtesy Edun 36, 37 Photo courtesy Edun 39 Photo Mary McCartney courtesy Vivienne Westwood Ltd 40, 41 Photo Benjamin Alexander Huseby for Dazed and Confused, July 2008 42, 43 Courtesy Vivienne Westwood Ltd 44, 45 All photos Alex Sturrock, courtesy Katharine Hamnett 46, 47 Courtesy Eileen Fisher 50, 51, 52, 53 Photography Edward Barber 54 bl Courtesy Continental Clothing 54 tr Courtesy Mariusz Stochaj, Continental Clothing 55 Images courtesy ASOS 56 a Image courtesy Uniqlo 56 b Image courtesy Muji 57 Image courtesy Uniqlo 58 Image courtesy H&M 59 Image courtesy Environmental Justice Foundation 62 Graphic based on original by Bio Intelligence Service, France; photo courtesy Levi's 66, 67, 68, 69 Photography by Gavin Fernandes.

CHAPTER 2

72, 73 Styling and Photography Gavin Fernandes 76, 77 Photos Catwalking 78, 79 Photos courtesy Puma 80 Photo Catwalking 81 Animation by Pascal Roulin, courtesy Issey Miyake Inc. 82, 83 Photography by Maria Downarowicz 84, 85 Courtesy Timberland 86 Courtesy Emma Rigby 88 Courtesy Shuan Samson 89 Courtesy Emma Rigby 90, 91 Photos Catwalking 93 Diagram Sandy Black 94 Diagram Sandy Black and Claudia Eckert 95 Diagram Sandy Black, Fatemeh Eskandarypur, Claudia Eckert 96, 97 Styling and photography by Gavin Fernandes; accessories created by Shared Talent students from the London College of Fashion, LISOF and the Boitumelo Project, Johannesburg 98 Photo Sean Michael 100 All photos Centre for Sustainable Fashion, London College of Fashion 101 Photo Kerry Dean 102 Photo courtesy Lu Flux 103 Image courtesy Borders and Frontiers 105 Photo courtesy Christopher Raeburn 106, 107 Photos courtesy Michelle Lowe-Holder 112, 113 Photos courtesy Nike 114, 115 Photos courtesy Nike 116, 117, 118, 119 Photos courtesy Bless 120, 121, 122, 123 Photos courtesy Eley Kishimoto 124, 125 Photos courtesy Nau 132, 133 Photos courtesy Laura Queening 134, 135 Photography Gavin Fernandes.

CHAPTER 3

136, 137 Styling and photography Gavin Fernandes; make-up and hair Jun Sato, Yvonne Sou, Satsuki Yamashita and Kenny Leung; model Seung Mo Hong; model wears clothes and sun visor by Bless, synthetic slacks with belts by Primark, industrial accessories by C. W. Tyzack 141, 142, 143, 144, 145 Images courtesy Clean Clothes Campaign 146, 147 Photos Rufus Exton/TRAID 151 Diagram based on original by Tim Jackson 153 Photo courtesy Ted Baker 154, 155,

156, 157 Photos Eiluned Edwards 158 Photo Sandra Henningsson 159 tl Photo Malin Palm 159 tr Photo Sandra Henningsson 159 cl, cr Photos Pelle Kronestedt 159 b Photo Malin Palm 160, 161 Photos Lu Guang/Greenpeace 162, 163, 164, 165 Photos courtesy Dries Van Noten 167 Photo courtesy Risto Bimbiloski 168, 169 Photos courtesy Monsoon 170 Photo courtesy People Tree 171 Photos Miki Alcalde, courtesy People Tree 172, 173, 174, 175 Photos courtesy Choolips 176, 177 Photos courtesy Andrew More O'Connor 178, 179 Photography Matjaz Tancic 182, 183 Photos courtesy Whistles 184 Photos courtesy Gap Inc. 186, 187 Photos courtesy New Look 188, 189 Photos Catwalking 190 Photo courtesy Marks and Spencer 193 Photo courtesy Muji.

CHAPTER 4

204, 205 Styling and Photography Gavin Fernandes; make-up and hair by Pace Chen; models Robyn Kotze and Jamie Litster; models' clothes by Jula Reindell; photographed at TRAID warehouse, London 211 Photo TRAID/Leigh McAlea 212 al, bl Photos TRAID/Mike Blackett 212 r Photo TRAID/ Domenico Sansone 223, 225, 227, 228 Photography Edward Barber 230, 231 Photos courtesy Minä Perhonen 233, 234, 235 Photos courtesy Zegna 238, 239 Photos courtesy Noir 240, 241, 242 Photos courtesy Lucy Orta 246 l Photography Gavin Fernandes; styling Stephanie Talbot and Gavin Fernandes; clothing Blaak and YMC 246 tr Photography Gavin Fernandes; styling Stephanie Talbot and Gavin Fernandes 246 br, 247 Photography Gavin Fernandes; styling Stephanie Talbot and Gavin Fernandes; clothing Jessica Ogden 248 Photo courtesy Mark Liu 249, 250, 251 Photos courtesy From Somewhere 252 Photo courtesy Reet Aus 253 Photo courtesy Christopher Raeburn 254, 255 Photos Sam Scott-Hunter, courtesy Christopher Raeburn 256, 257 Photos courtesy Junky Styling 258 Photos courtesy Christine Tsui 259 Photo courtesy Eurostar 260 Photography Maria Downarowicz 261 Photo courtesy Tamara Fogle 262, 263 Photos Giovanni Giannoni, courtesy Maison Martin Margiela 264, 265 Photos courtesy Salvation Army Trading Company Ltd. 266, 267, 268, 269 Photography Tim Mitchell.

CHAPTER 5

272 Photo Miguel Sobreira, courtesy Manel Torres 273 Photo Ian Cole, courtesy Manel Torres 276 bl Photo Marte Lundby Rekaa, courtesy Materials Knowledge Transfer Network, UK 276 tr Photo courtesy of Zegna Sport 277 Photo courtesy Finisterre UK 279 Images courtesy of Teijin 280 tl Image courtesy Schoeller 283 tl, tr Photos courtesy Veronika Kapsali 289 Images courtesy Susan Ashdown 290, 291 Photos courtesy David Mason 293 Image courtesy FitsMe 295, 296, 297, 299 Photos by Scott Schuman from THE SARTORIALIST (2009), used by permission of Penguin, a division of Penguin Group (USA) Inc. 288 Images courtesy Susanna Lau www.stylebubble.com 301, 302 Images courtesy Sue Jenkyn Jones 304 Photo Nick Knight; model Alice Dellal at Select 305 bl Photo Trish Belford 305 tr Photo Andy Stagg 306 br Photo Caroline Coates 308 Images courtesy Siddhartha Upadhyaya 309 Images courtesy Manel Torres 310 br Photo Gary Wallis for BioCouture 2010, courtesy Suzanne Lee 311 Photo Santiago Arribas for BioCouture 2010, courtesy Suzanne Lee 312 tl, br Photos Catwalking 313 Image courtesy of Boudicca 314, 315 tr Photos Catwalking 315 l, br Images courtesy CuteCircuit 316 Photo Catwalking 317 tr Photo courtesy Kate Goldsworthy and Science Museum, London 317 br Photo Catwalking 318 Images courtesy Freedom of Creation 319 Image courtesy Kerrie Luft 322, 323, 324, 325 Animations by Dom del Torto, courtesy Forum for the Future in collaboration with Levi Strauss & Co.

Acknowledgments

A great many people have contributed to the creation of this broadly scoped book. I thank them all: the authors from academia and industry who have drawn on their expertise to create this rich tapestry of perspectives and opinions on the complex cross-disciplinary landscape of sustainable fashion; the photographers, designers, companies and researchers who have provided both information and images to create the visual narrative; and the many designers and company representatives who made time for interviews, providing voices from the front line of the fashion industry. Thanks are due to Jamie Camplin of Thames & Hudson for sowing the seeds for the book, and to the head of London College of Fashion, Frances Corner, for her support from the outset. This enabled new photography to be commissioned from Gavin Fernandes, Edward Barber, Matjaz Tancic and Maria Downarowicz, and the engagement of Duska Zagorac, whose untiring work as project manager in the early stages helped to shape the content and provided vital organization for the growing number of contributions. A number of people assisted with picture and information research, including Phyllida Jay, Stacy Anderson, Veronika Kapsali, Claire Smith, Emma Rigby, Maria Lamle and Sarah Ditty. I am especially grateful to Zoe Norton and Sharn Sandor for their help in coordination of content, interviews and picture research. I would like to thank Bianca Wendt for designing the book, and the team at Thames & Hudson for their meticulous attention to detail, which is greatly appreciated. Final thanks go to my family and friends, especially to Morris, for unfailing encouragement, support and patience.

Sandy Black

Index